RUSSIA'S ROAD FROM PEACE TO WAR

Books by Louis Fischer

Russia's Road from Peace to War
The Life of Lenin
The Essential Gandhi (*Editor*)
Russia, America, and the World
The Story of Indonesia
Russia Revisited
This Is Our World
The Life and Death of Stalin
The Life of Mahatma Gandhi
The God That Failed (*Co-author*)
Thirteen Who Fled (*Editor*)
Gandhi and Stalin
The Great Challenge
Empire
A Week with Gandhi
Dawn of Victory
Men and Politics (*An Autobiography*)
Stalin and Hitler
The War in Spain
Soviet Journey
Machines and Men in Russia
Why Recognize Russia?
The Soviets in World Affairs (2 *volumes*)
Oil Imperialism

RUSSIA'S ROAD FROM PEACE TO WAR

Soviet Foreign Relations 1917–1941

By LOUIS FISCHER

HARPER & ROW, PUBLISHERS

NEW YORK, EVANSTON, AND LONDON

1817

 For information address Harper & Row, Publishers, Incorporated, 49 East 33rd Street, New York, N.Y. 10016. Published simultaneously in Canada by Fitzhenry & Whiteside Limited, Toronto.

FIRST EDITION

LIBRARY OF CONGRESS CATALOG CARD NUMBER: 69-15306

CONTENTS

Part Two: Hitler and Stalin

Part Three: Origins of the Soviet-German War

A NOTE TO THE READER

When I began writing this book I thought it would be a history of Soviet foreign affairs from the birth of the Bolshevik revolution to the present. But there is so much new material, there are so many new insights, that to have compressed the entire period into one volume would have made it a superficial and two-dimensional chronicle. I accordingly decided to stop at June 22, 1941, the day of the Nazi invasion of the Soviet Union. By that time the future course of Soviet foreign policy had been set.

I was given access to hitherto unpublished documents in the German Ministry of Foreign Affairs in Bonn, in the British Foreign Office, and in the Quai d'Orsay. A library of western memoirs and data now available in Soviet publications likewise called for a complete rewriting of my *Soviets in World Affairs*, which ends with the autumn of 1929.

The foreign policy of any country remains elusive without an understanding of its internal affairs and of the men and forces that rule it. This principle guided me as I worked on the present volume. At times I was afraid I was writing a history of the Soviet Union from 1917 to June, 1941. But having determined on the broad approach I could no longer limit myself to the record of Soviet foreign relations. I had to paint on a large canvas. I found a new joy in doing so. This may communicate itself to the reader. One writes to have and give pleasure.

LOUIS FISCHER

Part One

Forging a Foreign Policy

I PEACE OR WORLD REVOLUTION?

Millions of lives and limbs would have been saved and Russia might have been spared decades of totalitarian tyranny if the first world war had ended in 1917 instead of 1918. Peace at the earlier date, Winston Churchill and Eric Ludendorff wrote in their memoirs, was possible, desirable, and desired. But war with its mountains of maimed and dead fixed the national mind on complete victory.

President Woodrow Wilson told the United States Senate on January 22, 1917, he preferred "peace without victory." The French government, fearing "a dangerous dependence on England" if it did not gain territory from the defeated, thought Wilson would use the Allies' need of American military power and Germany's dread of it to achieve a non-punitive peace. But after the United States became a belligerent on April 6, 1917, Wilson never reverted to the idea.[1] His mind was now geared to triumph on the battlefield. In time of war it is unusual to prepare for peace.

Intent on triumph, Russia's western partners had no eye for her exhaustion. Unaware that she teetered on the brink of Bolshevism, Paris, London, and Washington urged her to continue the fight. The March-to-November, 1917, republican regime, heir to the last Tsar, was itself apprehensive lest withdrawal from the conflict invite a German invasion and kill the democratic benefits of the Tsar's overthrow.

Russia's reluctance to quit the war and Allied insistence that she stay were the biggest single factor in the downfall of the Provisional (Kerensky) government. Thus Bolshevism came to a prostrate Russia.

[1] Princeton University's professor Arthur S. Link is the authority for this statement. Dr. Link, Wilson's multi-volume biographer, copied and translated many documents in the secret files of the French Foreign Office.

While still in exile in Switzerland Lenin had proposed converting "the predatory imperialist war" into civil wars against capitalism. This moved Ludendorff, bogged down in a two-front war, to provide the Bolshevik leader and his comrades with a privileged passage in an unsealed railway carriage through Germany en route to Petrograd. Berlin wanted peace with Russia-in-civil-war-chaos. The Bolsheviks, however, hesitated to sign a separate peace with Germany and so lend credence to reports that Lenin was a Kaiser puppet. The Soviet government's first act, accordingly, was to broadcast a manifesto urging all nations to stop fighting.

Armies were being bled white as mass murder continued amid the lice, rats, and mud of the trenches. Economies reeled. Peoples hungered. Governments faltered. The prolongation of the war into 1919 or 1920 might have turned all Europe Red. Yet the Bolsheviks called for a general peace because peace, they felt, would enable them to stay in power. This was the first case, the first of many, in which the requirements of the Soviet state clashed with the cause of world revolution. Nationalist interest transcended internationalist ideology.

Nevertheless, world revolution remained the heart of communist credo. "When the armistice was signed on November 11, 1918," Maxim M. Litvinov, Soviet Foreign Commissar, said to me in the 1930's, "I knew the prospect of world revolution was nil." Litvinov had resided long in England, married an Englishwoman, and understood the inner strength of western society. Lenin, on the contrary, spent many years in western and central Europe without ever leaving Russia. His Russocentric brain lived in Russia while his body occupied tight little apartments in Zurich, Geneva, Paris, and London. The western social system remained an enigma to him. He predicted its imminent doom, as Karl Marx had in 1848, and was blind to its potential of survival.

In the autumn of 1902 Leon Trotsky escaped from Siberian exile, traveled by train westward through Russia reading the *Iliad*, and, practically penniless, crossed Europe to London where he called on Lenin, who took him for a stroll. "He showed me Westminster Abbey (from outside)," Trotsky recalled,[2] "and some other famous buildings. I no longer know how he expressed himself, but the meaning was: that is *their* Westminster. The *their* meant, naturally, not the English but the enemy. . . . This meaning was obvious when he spoke of any kind of cultural value or new conquests." An outsider in the enemy camp, Lenin feared that Trotsky, age twenty-three, avid for culture, might fall in love with the West, the bourgeois West marked by Marx for destruction.

In 1918, however, Soviet Russia was weak, "a military zero," Lenin

[2] Leon Trotsky, *Lenin*, pp. 7-8.

said. An economic zero, too. The Bolsheviks, therefore, could only sit by the sea and, reversing Canute, bid the waves advance and engulf their foe. Hence their focus on propaganda; the big mouth rather than the strong arm would bring world revolution. This was the lamentable Bolshevik situation when communist commissars met Kaiser counselors in Brest-Litovsk from December, 1917, to March, 1918. Russia's western allies, foreseeing the loss of a partner, absented themselves. Germany and her allies—Austria-Hungary, Bulgaria, and Turkey—seeking to eliminate an adversary, attended gleefully.

From Brest Trotsky wrote Lenin a private letter on January 13, 1918. "The German press," he reported, "has commenced to make loud noises that we do not want peace at all and only are concerned with the extension of the revolution to other countries. These jackasses cannot understand that, just from the point of view of the development of the European revolution, a very early peace is of tremendous significance for us. Yours, Trotsky."[3]

This was Trotsky's cardinal error, the key to his tragic end. Faith can move mountains and dull the most brilliant brain. War, not peace, is the crucible of communism. The first extension of Soviet power resulted from the second world war, and then by armed invasion, not by revolution.

Lenin never came near the Brest-Litovsk conference. But as leader of the Russian Communist Party (Bolsheviks), and prime minister (Chairman of the Council of People's Commissars), he guided the Soviet delegation and the heated domestic arguments on policy. Foreign Commissar Leon Trotsky was in direct charge of the negotiations. Occasionally during the protracted, oft-postponed sessions, Lenin and Trotsky disagreed. Key communists disagreed with both of them. But in that early phase of the Soviet dictatorship, opposition, however vehement, and criticism, however extreme, remained unpunished. The life of the Soviet revolution hung by the hair of the Brest-Litovsk conference (no peace treaty posed the possibility of a German invasion), yet Lenin permitted himself to be outvoted in party conclaves and yielded to Trotsky on basic diplomatic strategy.

Although Lenin considered world revolution "inevitable" and anticapitalist insurrections in Germany and France imminent, he refused to imperil the Russian revolution for Red birds in the European bush: "Germany," he declared, "is only pregnant with revolution and here a perfectly healthy baby has been born . . . we already have a newly born, lustily screaming infant, and if we, at this moment, do not clearly say that we accept peace, we shall perish." Germany, to be sure, had an-

[3] From the Trotsky Archive in the Houghton Library of Harvard University. Document T 7. Copy supplied.

nexed vast Russian territories with a population of 55 million and wanted more. But Lenin was prepared to exchange space for time, time for foreign revolutions to ripen. His slogan read "Survival." Ultimately survival depended on revolution in Europe. "There is no doubt," Lenin insisted, "that the socialist revolution in Europe must and will come. All our hopes on the *final* victory of socialism rest on this certainty and on this scientific prophecy." This "scientific" prophecy, however, would be disproved if the Russian revolution succumbed to Ludendorff's legions. Hence Lenin's passionate pleas for peace at Brest no matter how humiliating the terms.

Russian communists had been bred to the doctrine of world revolution. Lenin exploited this faith to justify the one-party dictatorship which was never Marxist dogma. (Dictatorship of the proletariat was.) "We took the whole situation into the hands of the Bolshevik Party alone," Lenin asserted, "we took it for ourselves, in the conviction that the revolution is ripening in all countries." But "if no revolution erupted in other countries, our position would be hopeless." Communist critics charged that Lenin made it hopeless by excluding the other socialist parties—the Mensheviks and Right and Left Social Revolutionaries (SR's) and the trade unions they dominated—from the central Soviet government though they belonged to the local soviets or councils. Several critics in topmost party and Cabinet posts resigned in protest against the one-party system and warned it would have to rely on terror. They declared further—November 17, 1917—that the exclusion of "mass proletarian organizations from political life" must conduce to "an irresponsible regime." This prophetic opposition broke on the steel wall of Lenin's will.

Significant communist party segments rejected Lenin's policy of extending the life of the Soviet state at the price of its deformation. The Moscow Bureau of the party, for example, resolved unanimously on February 24, 1918, not to obey the party's Central Committee (the highest authority in the land) in implementing the peace with Germany, and added, "In the interest of the world revolution we consider it advisable to risk the destruction of the Soviet government which has now become a pure formality."

One hundred and nine days after the establishment in Russia of the world's first communist government, it had, in the opinion of the most important unit of the Soviet Communist Party, become "a pure formality" without content, its form not worth saving, worth sacrificing on the altar of world revolution. The Left Communists and Left SR's concurred; they preached "revolutionary war" without specifying how it was to be waged; presumably through fraternization of troops at all fronts, general strikes, guerrilla warfare, and propaganda.

Trotsky, to no one's surprise, took an intermediate position between revolutionary war and Lenin's sign-the-peace-immediately program. He would sign because Lenin threatened to resign if the party rebuffed him on this life-and-death issue, but he would delay the signing. He refused to join the pessimists who thought the Russian revolution of so little value that they would sacrifice it for a dream. Here he stood shoulder to shoulder with Lenin. But he believed that war is a poor incubator of healthy revolution; it might produce "an historic miscarriage" instead of Lenin's "perfectly healthy baby." He was afraid that Russia was too underdeveloped to be the first country to reach for socialism. That role belonged to a western industrialized country. Hence his stress on propaganda beamed to Germany.

Trotsky was on good Marxist ground; a socialist revolution, according to Marx and Engels, must stem from organic growth: the expansion of industry, mechanization of agriculture, and an enlarged working class in advanced countries. Trotsky's trouble was that Marx and Engels erred; history shows that advanced countries do not make socialist revolutions. Lenin was right in insisting on his revolution in Russia, where the feeble capitalist class could be overthrown, in wartime, because capitalism was underdeveloped. If Bolshevism had waited for the "organic growth of inner forces" in Russia it would now be a two-line footnote in academic tomes.

In 1917 and 1918 Trotsky was acutely afraid that the premature Russian revolution, unaccompanied by socialist revolutions in the West, would succumb to its own infirmities. (Perhaps his subconscious warned him of the personal fate that awaited him should Russian "socialism," disfigured by cultural and technological backwardness, remain an isolated phenomenon.) Trotsky, accordingly, wished to drag out the negotiations at Brest and, over Lenin's quick body, won the approval of key communist committees. He used the time gained to call from the Petrograd and Brest-Litovsk radio towers for proletarian insurrections throughout Europe.

Trotsky was an artist whose words became fiery darts that seared the thick skins of the Kaiser's generals and ripped the nerves of the German, Austro-Hungarian, Bulgarian, and Turkish diplomats assembled at Brest in the last good hope that Russia's capitulation would save their hides and countries. He prolonged the discussions by every known debating stratagem. His mind nursed the misconception that verbal emissions sired revolutions.

Lenin squirmed. He expected a German invasion if Russia delayed signing a peace treaty with the German-led Quadruple Alliance. Prominent communists accused him of being Russia-oriented. Moisey S. Uritsky, for instance, said: "Comrade Lenin's mistake is . . . that he looks at the matter from the point of view of Russia, and not from the international point of view."

Trotsky was more sensitive than Lenin to the widespread revulsion, reflected in the votes of communist party organizations and in official soundings among Soviet supporters, against signing a heavily punitive peace with predatory Prussian militarists. And he dreaded a Kaiser victory that would kill the chances of a communist revolution in Germany and condemn Europe to reaction. Lenin was less concerned with the character of bourgeois regimes abroad. He was an either-or man; "no third path," he declared. Trotsky preferred the neither-nor way. So at 5:58 P.M. on February 10, 1918, seconds after German State Secretary Baron Richard von Kuehlmann opened the session in bleak Brest-Litovsk, Trotsky rose, faced the military in sparkling uniforms and medals and the diplomats in striped pants and high collars and, after a scorching indictment, said, "We are leaving the war but are compelled to refuse to sign the peace treaty." It was a magic formula that met practical problems and fed revolutionary sentiments.

Trotsky returned to a hero's welcome. But within a week the Germans denounced the armistice and crouched to spring at the throat of the revolution. Lenin said sign. Trotsky said wait. Wait till the invasion actually begins. That would at least convince the proletariat everywhere that German militarism and Soviet Bolshevism were mortal foes. The Germans marched. The Soviets signed on March 3, 1918, and after lengthy, acrimonious debates, with Trotsky now seconding Lenin, they ratified.

The Kremlin, forced to choose between peace and annihilation, chose peace and relegated world revolution to second place. Yet it pinned world revolution on its banner. Trotsky was the passionate internationalist who, on becoming the first Soviet Commissar for Foreign Affairs, announced that he would take over the old Tsarist-Kerensky foreign office and then close down the shop; his business would be world revolution. Lenin was an international in himself: Russian and Kalmuck on his father's side; German, Swedish, and probably Jewish on his mother's. But the Bolsheviks, even Lenin, had little confidence in the stability of their state. Most of them foresaw endless difficulties or early defeat if they tried to convert retarded Russia into a lone socialist dominion. They regarded world revolution as a Soviet Russian necessity and the Bolshevik revolution as the first in a chain of similar social explosions which would guarantee the survival and safety of the new regime in Russia.

Lenin's subjective internationalism thus merged with what was, objectively, a still-unrecognized nationalism. In addition, Russia needed peace to save the nation from collapse and further slaughter.

By making peace with Germany the Bolsheviks served the cause of the nation while assuming they served a world cause. Conceived in internationalism, the Soviet revolution was nevertheless a national act with a national purpose. This brought the Bolsheviks appreciable popular support.

II BARREN ADVENTURES AGAINST SOVIET RUSSIA

The November 7, 1917, Bolshevik coup d'état, using minimum violence, inaugurated a revolution of maximum violence. The coup was successful because, in a war-exhausted country whose underdevelopment had left multitudes unhappy in peacetime, few raised a finger to save the Kerensky government. Lenin, hiding in a hut outside Petrograd, insisted with utmost nervous impetuosity on a swift lunge for power: "We must not wait. We may lose everything." Trotsky too knew, as he wrote in his *Lenin,* that "if there had been any vacillation on our part . . . then in the course of two or three months they—'the masses'—would have drifted away from us . . . the bourgeoisie would have had a breathing spell to conclude peace . . . It was this that made Lenin decide to act."

In two or three months the anti-Bolsheviks did indeed recover from the shock that shook the world and launched a civil war. Monarchists who would restore the Tsar, republicans who opposed dictatorship, landlords who had lost their estates, industrialists and merchants who feared for their properties, socialists who abhorred the Bolshevik brand of socialism, generals deprived of status and power—all rallied armies to oust the Lenin-Trotsky regime.

In the circumstances foreign intervention was inevitable.

The Soviet government, born to struggle, created much trouble for itself. It proposed to remake the world through violence; the world resisted. Never was peaceful coexistence less likely, never was protracted hostility more probable.

The ostensible reason for foreign intervention was Lenin's wish to take his country out of the world war.

It is in the nature of a nation facing a clear and grave danger to think first and only of itself and to regard the future of enemies and friends as irrelevant to today's business. Russia's western allies accordingly looked upon her intended exit from the war as a betrayal, a betrayal of the September 5, 1914, agreement of the anti-German coalition not to sign a separate peace. Lord Robert Cecil, Under Secretary of State for Foreign Affairs, therefore declared on the British government's behalf that should the "extremists in Petrograd" withdraw from the war it would be "a direct breach" of the no-separate-peace pact and "if adopted by the Russian nation would put them outside the pale of the ordinary council of Europe. . . . There is no intention of recognizing such a government."

Cecil spoke on November 23, 1917, sixteen days after the Bolshevik coup d'état and months before they signed and ratified the Brest-Litovsk peace. His words indicate how little the British government understood Russia.

The British soon turned words into deeds. Desperate in the fourth year of a man-eating war, they grasped at broken reeds. The problem was to re-create an eastern front and thereby prevent Germany from shifting all her forces to the west and gambling for victory in a great ordeal by blood. Throughout 1917 the transfer of German troops from east to west had assumed considerable proportions. They were not needed in the east. By January, 1917, writes Alexander F. Kerensky, "more than a million [Russian] deserters were roaming around in the rear of the army." Their number increased during the year. The soldiers, most of them peasants—for Russia was then a peasant country—were leaving trenches and barracks to join in the spontaneous seizure and parceling of estates. With the assumption of power by Russia's communists the eastern front froze literally and militarily.

The western powers wondered: Germany might tap Russian food, raw mineral resources, and manpower to win the war. Surveying the scrambled scene, Winston Churchill, Secretary of State for War, submitted a memorandum to the War Cabinet: "There are two perfectly simple things to do . . . (1) Above all things reconstitute the fighting front in the East; (2) Make a plan for an offensive battle in France in 1919. . . . If we cannot reconstitute the fighting front against Germany in the East, no end can then be discerned of the war. Vain will be all our sacrifices of the peoples and the armies."

Such unwarranted pessimism—but how was Churchill or anyone to know that Germany would surrender on November 11, 1918?—fathered the British decision to convert Cecil's betrayal-and-no-recognition statement into military intervention with a view, ostensibly, to re-establishing the eastern front by rallying anti-Bolshevik armed forces.

Major General Alfred W. F. Knox, the senior British officer in Soviet Russia, demurred: "I did not believe in the power . . . of any . . . organization in Russia to force its soldiers to continue the war against the Central Powers." This was the heart of the Russian matter in a sentence. Sir George Buchanan, the British Ambassador in Petrograd, likewise telegraphed his dissent to London. But London put its trust in the fabled Cossacks and in General Alexei Kaledin, elected ataman of the Don Cossacks, in June, 1917. With him when the Bolsheviks seized power were General Lavr G. Kornilov, who failed to unseat the Kerensky government in the autumn of 1917; General Mikhail V. Alexeyev, former Tsarist chief of staff; and General of the Infantry Anton I. Denikin, subsequently the author of five fat volumes of memoirs on his efforts to take Moscow and topple Bolshevism. One cannot blame British authorities remote from the scene for being impressed by this accumulation of old brass. One can only chide them for ignoring the sober views of their own high representatives in Petrograd.

Nor did the British government pay heed to the opinion of its senior military officer in London. At a meeting of the War Cabinet on September 17, 1917, General Sir W. R. Robertson, Chief of the Imperial General Staff, said "it was quite clear that the Russian soldier does not want to fight any more."[1] For this and political reasons Buchanan urged his government "to set Russia free from her agreement with the Allies, so that she will act as she chose, and decide to purchase peace on Germany's terms or fight on with the Allies." This "would make it impossible for the Bolsheviks to reproach the Allies with driving Russian soldiers to slaughter for their Imperial aims."[2]

Cecil, however, believed in Kaledin. He proposed sending "General Ballard to Kaledin, and if he found Kaledin genuinely in favour of the Allies, General Ballard should be authorized to take what steps he deemed wise, and to incur expenditures up to 10,000,000 pounds sterling."[3] The War Cabinet could not decide between Buchanan and Cecil, between acquiescing in Russia's wish to quit the war and using Kaledin to push her back into it. Cecil was accordingly asked to inform Prime Minister David Lloyd George, Foreign Secretary Arthur J. Balfour, and Lord Milner, then in conference in Paris with French leaders, that "the members of the War Cabinet in London were divided in opinion as to the immediate steps to be taken."[4]

The Anglo-French conference in Paris had been the subject of deliberations at the War Cabinet meeting on September 17, 1917, where it was decided that "Owing to the uncertainty at present prevailing in Russia it was thought to be undesirable that any definite communication should be made in writing, especially one which might be construed by

[1] *Minutes of a Meeting of the War Cabinet held at 10 Downing Street, S.W., on Monday, September 17, 1917, at noon.* Crown-copyright records in the Public Record Office, London.

[2] War Cabinet, Nov. 19, 1917.

[3] *Ibid.*

[4] *Ibid.*

one or other party in Russia as interference in Russia's internal affairs."[5] The reason for secrecy is not far to seek. Ideas were germinating in the minds of Cecil and friends that had best not see the light of day. On December 12, 1917, Cecil received a memorandum from Commander Josiah C. Wedgwood to which Cecil attached a handwritten instruction reading, "Print and circulate to Cabinet with following note. Commander Wedgwood left me this note. It seems to raise a question of policy of high importance." Cecil's judgment was right. Commander Wedgwood assumed that "Russia will in effect become a German Colony or Dependency, much as India is dependent on us." Wedgwood therefore felt it to be in the interest of Britain "that Russia should be as small as possible. Any bits which can be induced to clip off should be encouraged to do so,—Trans-Caucasus, Ukraine, Don Cossacks, Finland, Turkestan, and above all Siberia." Siberia, Wedgwood explained, "is the country of the future, the extension of the American Far West." He suggested that any governments that may have been formed in Siberia should be persuaded to separate from Russia. "Americans would be the best material to use,—they are less suspect. . . . When Independence has been recognized the steps towards 'guaranteeing that Independence' are easy. They could be induced to apply for help to keep themselves in power, to protect themselves from invasion." Detaching from Russia such "bits" as Siberia would be of much "importance to the future supremacy of English or German throughout the world."[6]

Importance attached not to the English or German language but to British or German power. Wedgwood, who later rose to be a broad-minded Labour Member of Parliament, was not alone in foreseeing the desirability of making Russia "as small as possible." Winston Churchill added a statesman's cynical touch to the proposal. Writing of the situation at the end of 1917 and early in 1918, he said, "The immense conquests which Germany had made in Russia, and the hatred and scorn with which Bolsheviks were regarded by the Allies, might well have made it possible for Germany to make important territorial concessions to France, and to offer Britain the complete restoration of Belgium. The desertion by Soviet Russia of the Allied cause, and the consequent elimination of Russian claims, created a similar easement of negotiations for both Austria and Turkey. Such were the elements of this great opportunity. It was the last."

The implications are plain. Peace would come as a result of a deal at Russia's expense; Germany would renounce her conquests in the West and take compensation by clipping off bits of Russia; Austria and Turkey would join in cutting Soviet Russia down to manageable size. "But

[5] *Ibid.*, Sept. 17, 1917.
[6] Foreign Office Document No. 234843.

Ludendorff," Churchill commented, "cared for none of these things."[7] Ludendorff still hoped for total victory over the West and annexations in Russia.

Britain's antagonism to Russia stemmed from centuries of recurrent lunges by Russians southward into the Black Sea region, the Caucasus, and Central Asia ever nearer the Khyber Pass, the historic invasion gateway to India. Russia's unfortunate geography gives her an almost useless northern frontier with the Arctic and a southern frontier stretching many thousands of miles from the Pacific Ocean to the heart of Europe. Throughout history she has probed along this southern frontier for soft spots where she might expand. Checked on one segment of that long line—as she was in the 1904-1905 war with Japan—she tried to recuperate and push elsewhere. Sensing the new pressure in Central Asia and wishing to make the Tsar a secure ally against Germany, London came to an agreement with St. Petersburg on August 31, 1907. Russia got the northern zone of Persia, Britain the southern (the center remained unassigned); Afghanistan would be a British sphere of influence; Tibet was neither man's land. In a subsequent secret treaty Great Britain took cognizance of Russia's claim to Constantinople. These irksome concessions to Russian imperialism fed anger beneath the surface alliance, and when the Bolsheviks broke the alliance by quitting the war British hostility burst into full flower.

British sensitivity to Russian power in the South was particularly marked in Lord Curzon of Kedleston. A former Viceroy of India, he had lived long in Central Asia and written two books on the region: *Russia in Central Asia* and *Persia and the Persian Question.* In the latter he called Russia "the mammon of unrighteousness,"[8] a description amply deserved. Equally Curzon deserved the title of rhapsodic imperialist. Central Asia obsessed him. "Turkestan, Afghanistan, Transcaspia, Persia," he exclaimed in *Persia and the Persian Question,* "to me . . . they are the pieces of a chessboard upon which is being played out the game for the dominion of the world. . . . The future of Great Britain . . . will be decided not in Europe . . . but in the continent whence our emigrant stock first came, and to which as conquerors their descendants have returned."

As a member of the War Cabinet and later Foreign Secretary after Bolshevism came to power in Russia, Curzon could not help acting out these passionate imperialist beliefs. He, as well as Churchill and Cecil, forgot that it takes strength to play in the game of world dominion. The strain and drain of the first world war started Britain's descent as a contender for world supremacy. The second world war finished it.

[7] Winston S. Churchill, *The World Crisis, 1917-1918,* Vol. II, pp. 123-124.
[8] Vol. I, p. 211.

World dominion now eludes every contender. The lava-like flow of nationalism across all continents has spelled the end of empire. But in 1917, 1918, and 1919 the future remained veiled, and British as well as French imperialists saw the uncertain crawl of infant Bolshevism as an opportunity to augment their power by robbing Russia of territory.

Curzon, Cecil, Churchill, and some of their colleagues were undoubtedly and understandably bitter over Russia's exit from the war just when Germany prepared to make one last drive to the English Channel and victory. They hated everything they then thought communism stood for. But the essence of international politics is the balance of power. Anti-Russianism antedated the anti-Bolshevism of the British champions of intervention in Soviet Russia. Foreign military action against the Bolsheviks rose to new fury after the West had defeated Germany and when Russia's defection from the alliance had become history. Clearly the central aim of British, and French, intervention was to make Russia "as small as possible."

This is the background of the December 23, 1917, Paris conference where Premier Georges Clemenceau, Foreign Minister Stephen Pichon, General Ferdinand Foch, and Paul Cambon, the French Ambassador in London, met Lord Milner, Lord Robert Cecil, Major General Sir G. M. W. MacDonogh, and Sir George Clerk. The British leaders were mindful of the War Cabinet's view that consideration of war aims, a synonym for annexations, should be "debarred," and that any definite communication in writing was "undesirable." The French did not have to be told the virtues of devious diplomacy.

Lord Milner opened the proceedings by stating the purpose of his and Cecil's mission to Paris: "to discuss with the French Government the situation in Russia, and the question of providing help to the various Provisional Governments that showed signs of opposing the Bolsheviki." Cecil then asked the French for information. "The main thing to know was, what was the real position in the Ukraine. This was most important. The Ukraine was rich, with a population of 30 million and the source of the bulk of Russia's food supplies." Supplies from the Ukraine could reach Germany. Moreover, the Allies might succeed in making the Ukraine a barrier. "But if it were true that the Ukraine as a fighting force was useless, that no organization could make them fight, then it might, perhaps, be urged that the better policy was to try to bring about friendly relations with the Bolsheviki, and give them support in the difficulties of their negotiations with Germany, and in this way possibly prevent all Russian supplies from going to Germany. There were some who said that the Ukrainians were merely a mob, and that it would be foolish to trust them; to do so would merely antagonize the rest of

Russia." Cecil therefore asked the French for information about the Ukraine.

Clemenceau said Cecil "had stated the position very clearly. He, however, was going to confuse it." He had no "decided opinion on either the Ukraine or Petrograd. We are playing a game of which we did not know the elements that composed it." Information from the Ukraine and from neighboring Rumania was conflicting. "M. Clemenceau's conclusion," the War Cabinet's report of the Conference continues, "was that it was not easy to draw one. . . . we should not take decisions on questions on which we do not know the facts." He favored continued relations with the Bolsheviks, but "On the other hand, we must support the Ukraine. It may not prove feasible, but we must do all we can to make it so."

Cecil and Milner agreed with Clemenceau, but, said Milner, "the point was to have a clear idea as to whether we were prepared, in the ultimate resort, to quarrel with the Bolsheviki or not.

"M. Clemenceau replied that he would lengthen the spoon to the uttermost limit, but he would not let the Ukraine go." (The spoon was the one they were using to sup with the Bolshevik devil.)

Here Milner stated "as a general opinion of the Conference" that in a crisis "we would keep in with the Ukraine and let the Bolsheviki join up with Germany, and with this M. Clemenceau emphatically agreed."

The British now announced that they proposed sending Sir George Buchanan on leave "for reasons of health" and read a prepared declaration stating "that any idea that we favour a counter-revolution is a profound mistake . . . but we feel it necessary to keep in touch as far as we can with the Ukraine, the Cossacks, Finland, Siberia, the Caucasus, etc. . . . we should carefully refrain from any word or act condoning the treachery of the Russians in opening peace negotiations with our enemies. But we should continually repeat our readiness to accept the principles of self-determination." "Self-determination" implied that various "bits" of Russia could self-determine themselves out of the country. And in fact Foreign Minister Pichon read to the Conference the draft of a telegram which he proposed sending to the Central Rada, or anti-Bolshevik, government of the Ukraine promising in the name "of the right of self-determination" to give powerful aid to the nationalist movement of the Ukraine.

Therewith the morning session of the Conference was concluded. During the session differences had emerged on the exact demarcations of the French and British areas. The French were already financing Cossack units around Novocherkassk near Rostov-on-Don, a territory claimed by the British. Generals Foch and MacDonogh were therefore asked to fix the boundaries of the two "zones of influences." The afternoon session heard and adopted their compromise "Convention Between France and England on the Subject of Activity in Southern Russia." France was to remain, at least temporarily, in Novocherkassk, and with this exception the Convention reads, the "zones of influences" were as follows: "The English zone: the Cossack territories, the territory of the Caucasus, Armenia, Georgia, Kurdistan.

"The French zone: Bessarabia, the Ukraine, the Crimea."[9]

In communicating the decisions of the Conference to Sir George Buchanan on December 30, 1917, the British Foreign Office admitted that "it is highly anomalous" to maintain relations with the Soviet government while "British Agents are also in relations with the Ukraine and the Cossacks who are engaged in a form of civil war" against the Soviets. However, this was exactly what the British government intended to do. "I would extend this principle to Finland and Siberia as well as the Caucasus."[10]

This telegram was unsigned, but the "I" in it certainly refers to Lord Robert Cecil, for in the handwritten draft of a telegram above his initials and sent to Buchanan "in most Secret cypher," Cecil told the ambassador on December 3, 1917, that the War Cabinet had decided that very morning to bend "all our efforts . . . on trying to prevent Russia from making a separate peace with Germany. They believe that the only hope of doing this is to strengthen by every means in our power those elements who are genuinely friendly to the Entente of whom the chief are Kaledin, Allexeieff and their group." He rejected the notion of a coalition between Bolsheviks, Social Revolutionaries, and Mensheviks. "Such a combination would be under Bolshevik influence and would besides consist of talkers and theorists. If on the other hand a southern block could be formed consisting of the Caucasus, the Cossacks, the Ukraine, and the Roumanians it would probably be able to set up a reasonably stable government and would in any case through its command of oil, coal and corn control the whole of Russia. You are therefore authorized to take whatever steps you regard as possible with a view to carrying out this policy either directly or through such agents as you select."[11]

Cecil's superior, Foreign Secretary Arthur J. Balfour, did not agree. In "Notes on the Present Russian Situation," dated December 9, 1917, and addressed to his colleagues in the government, he took deep exception to the Cabinet's Russian policy: "It was suggested at Cabinet on Friday that, after their recent proclamations, the Bolsheviks could only be regarded as avowed enemies. . . . I entirely dissent from this view and believe it to be founded on a misconception." The Bolsheviks' "appeal is

[9] *Printed for the War Cabinet, December, 1917*, Secret. *I.C.* 37.
[10] F.O. No. 2567. Draft telegram to Sir G. Buchanan.
[11] F.O. Document No. 2407.

to every revolutionary force, economic, social, racial, or religious, which can be used to upset the existing political organizations of mankind. If they summon the Mohammedians of India to revolt, they are still more desirous of engineering a revolution in Germany. They are dangerous dreamers . . . who would genuinely like to put into practice the wild theories which have so long been germinating in the shadow of the Russian autocracy.

"Now, contrary to the opinion of some of my colleagues, I am clearly of opinion that it is to our advantage to avoid, as long as possible, an open breach with this crazy system. If this be drifting, then I am a drifter by deliberate policy."

Whereas Cecil on December 3 had "authorized" Buchanan to send agents to anti-Soviet groups, Balfour in his next paragraph, written December 9, said, "I have already instructed Sir George Buchanan to abstain completely from any action which can be interpreted as an undue interference with the internal affairs of the country to which he is accredited."[12] After such do-and-don't confusion Buchanan perhaps did need sick leave.

The policy of Cecil prevailed, for he enjoyed the powerful support of Milner and Churchill, and of Curzon, who replaced Balfour as Foreign Secretary in October, 1919.

Meanwhile the military were busy building chaos. An inventive British officer, who as a boy probably pushed toy soldiers about, conjured up whole armies out of his imagination. On November 20, 1917, he presented a handwritten memorandum to the Chief of the Imperial General Staff in which he created an East European anti-Bolshevik fighting force of "500,000 Poles, 400,000 Cossacks, 80,000 Czechs and Slovaks, 300,000 Rumanians, 15,000 Serbs, 105,000 Armenians, and 25,000 Georgians, etcetera." To these he added 575,000 Knights of St. George, storm battalions, volunteers, loyal elements. Total: a round two million. The military genius who authored this document preserved in the Foreign Office archives then writes, "Kaledin is reported by the consul in Odessa to have declared himself dictator of the Donetz Basin and to be moving on Moscow. In the former capacity he may well become dictator of Russia as he controls the coal supplies of the Empire." After this piece of deterministic nonsense the officer reveals that "The Russian government is at present nonexistent," therefore the United States could send troops without interfering in the internal affairs of another state. (Stalin offered the same flimsy excuse for seizing half of Poland in 1939.) And if the United States sent an army to Russia, "it seems not unlikely" that Japan would do the same.

[12] *War Cabinet Minutes,* Appendix, G.T.-2932.

From Petrograd Buchanan poured ice water on the officer's arithmetic fantasies. On December 5, 1917, he forwarded, with approval, his military attaché's estimate of the situation: "Alexieff and Kaledin have nothing except two companies with the promise of two more. . . . There are no Ukraine troops except a few mutinous regiments at Kieff. . . . No Russian, Cossack or otherwise, will fight unless compelled to by foreign force. To ask us to intrigue with Cossacks while we are here in the power of the Rebel government is merely to get our throats cut to no purpose."[13]

The French had similar information about Cossack morale. Eric Labonne, a French diplomat in Moscow, telegraphed Paris on January 3, 1918, that "The tired Cossacks wanted nothing more than to settle down at home in peace, and they refuse to enter again into combat for an idea and for the benefit of a regime which have not been explained to them with clarity, and above all they fear being made the instruments of a monarchist restoration."[14]

Facts, however, were easy targets for wishes. Foreign Minister Pichon dreamed big dreams. "It is indeed the creation of a new Russia to oppose Germany," he wrote the French ambassador in Rome on January 17, 1918, "which is the aim of our action in South Russia."[15] The nucleus of the "new Russia" would be the Rada government of the Ukraine. At the Anglo-French Conference on December 23, 1917, both delegations had agreed that it was too early to recognize the ramshackle Rada regime. But on January 10, 1918, Clemenceau telegraphed the chief of the French Mission in Petrograd: "The independence of the Ukraine having been recognized by the French government, General Tabouis is for practical purposes the chief of the French Military Mission in that country. His position is therefore regular from the point of view of international law."[16]

An "independent" Ukraine under French hegemony—that is how Premier Clemenceau understood the December 23, 1917, Convention between England and France.

The interventionists' White hope was the Ukraine. But the Bolsheviks also needed the Ukraine's grain and coal. The Rada had declared the Ukraine independent of Russia, and the Bolsheviks of course proclaimed a belief in self-determination. But, as Lenin said on January 21, 1918, "no Marxist who has not abandoned the basic ideas of Marxism or in general of socialism can deny that the interests of socialism stand higher

[13] F.O. Document No. 232002.

[14] Documents seen in the Ministry of Foreign Affairs in Paris in the summer of 1968: Volume XIII, Carton IX, Serie A, Carton 369. Clos le 31 Mai 1918.

[15] *Ibid.*

[16] *Ibid.*

than the interests of the right of nations to self-determination."[17] The Soviets acted on this principle in subsequent decades. In January, 1918, Lenin and Trotsky ordered an army into the Ukraine. On the 15th of the month the British consul in Odessa wired home that the Ukrainian army was melting away. Soldiers were selling cavalry and artillery horses and deserting. "The front is abandoned." The Bolshevik forces were making progress and the population was thinking of peace at any price.[18] Trotsky therefore was able on January 30 to tell the Brest-Litovsk peace conference that "the power of the Central Rada has vanished and the only area over which its representatives had a right to dispose was their rooms in Brest-Litovsk."[19]

Once again powermen availed themselves of fiction. The Rada was dead but on February 8, 1918, the German Quadruple Alliance signed a treaty with the keepers of the corpse, and advancing behind this scrap of paper the German army drove out the Bolsheviks, took over all of the Ukraine, and spread out from there into the North Caucasus and the Caucasus.

Since Turkey, Germany's ally, held Baku on the Caspian Sea and the Dardanelles, only two entrances to Russia were left open to the anti-German coalition: the far north Murmansk-Archangel region and the Far East. The western allies and Japan used both.

Britain led the intervention. Long after the first world war had ended Prime Minister Lloyd George, a far less fervid interventionist than Cecil, Curzon, Churchill, and Milner, still harbored the idea of dismembering Russia. In the Guildhall speech on November 10, 1919, he mentioned Bolshevik military victories over foreign-supported Russian White armies, but warned, "You must not imagine that I am reading from the present situation any prediction that the Bolshevists are going to conquer the whole of Russia. I do not believe it. The free peasantry of the South have in their hearts a detestation of Bolshevism and I do not believe that the Bolshevists will conquer that aversion." The "South" included the Ukraine, Crimea, North Caucasus, the Caucasus, and Turkestan.

That is how the British government understood the December 23, 1917, Convention between England and France.

An official Blue Book states that shortly after the end of World War I, on January 2, 1919, the British had a rifle strength in North Russia of 3,905 and a ration strength of 6,832.[20] On June 11, 1918, 150 American Marines had disembarked at Murmansk; on September 4, 1918, between

[17] Cited in Louis Fischer, *The Life of Lenin*, p. 193.
[18] Documents seen in Paris in the summer of 1968.
[19] Fischer, p. 198.
[20] British Blue Book, Army, *The Evacuation of Russia, 1919*. Cmd. 818.

4,000 and 5,000 U.S. infantrymen and engineers joined the motley military assemblage at Archangel. Frenchmen, Serbs, and Italians were present in negligible numbers.

These figures indicate how minuscule was the Allied military attack on European Russia in 1918 and how incapable it was of re-establishing an eastern front or of overthrowing the Soviet government even in collaboration with eager anti-Bolshevik Russian collaborators who staged short-lived insurrections in July and August, 1918, and who on August 30 assassinated Uritsky, a prominent Petrograd communist, and made an attempt on Lenin's life in Moscow.[21] Allied forces attempting to penetrate inland from Murmansk and Archangel never won significant terrain.

* * *

Remained the Far Eastern door. The Soviet leaders feared Japanese intervention more than any other. During the Soviet debates early in 1918 on the Brest-Litovsk peace treaty Trotsky declared, "I, of course, object to both armies, but if there is no alternative, I say, better the German army than the Japanese. . . . If Japan sends an armed force she will not withdraw it."[22]

Lenin concurred. He asked Colonel Raymond Robins, the unofficial American intermediary, "Should Japan . . . attempt to seize Vladivostok and the Eastern Siberian Railway . . . what steps would be taken by the other Allies, particularly by the United States, to prevent a Japanese landing in the Far East?"[23]

One can almost see the mischievous twinkle in Lenin's narrow eyes; he had conceived a clever chess gambit—move the white queen to immobilize Japan's black bishop. But it was not Lenin's queen, it was President Wilson's.

In an address to the U.S. Senate on January 11, 1917, Woodrow Wilson had asked, "Is this war a struggle for a just and secure peace or only for a new balance of power?" He put little faith in any balance of power not "guaranteed" by a "community of power"—a league of nations. Yet even the President of the United States could not make his own world or his own rules. Though he opposed balance-of-power politics he championed that aspect of it which concerned America most: the containment of Japan. Aware of Japan's interest in expanding into China and Siberia, a development that would tip the balance in the Pacific against the United States, Wilson did not wish to see Russia, even

[21] Details in Fischer, *The Soviets in World Affairs*, Chap. II.

[22] Leon Trotsky, *Collected Works*, Vol. XVII, Part I: *The Soviet Republic and the Capitalist World* (in Russian).

[23] William Hard, *Raymond Robins' Own Story*, pp. 134-139.

Soviet Russia, weakened. He therefore made a sharp distinction between U.S. participation in the Murmansk-Archangel expedition for the ostensible reason of saving the mountain of military supplies sent there by the Allies for Russian use and, on the other hand, participating in or approving of Japanese intervention in the Soviet Far East.

There now began a political battle between Great Britain, France, and Japan, who favored Japanese intervention in Russia, and the United States, determined to prevent it. All were engaged in a colossal war against a common enemy—the German alliance—and all were preparing for their postwar rivalries.

More than balance-of-power considerations motivated President Wilson. He told the Supreme Council on January 12, 1919, that communism was indeed a "social and political danger," but "there was great doubt in his mind whether Bolshevism could be checked by arms."[24] (He had had personal experience with U.S. intervention in Latin America and knew it could defeat itself.) Wilson, moreover, did not understand the Russian situation. He wrote Colonel Edward House, his foreign affairs adviser, on July 28, 1918, "I have been sweating blood over what is right and feasible (*possible*) to do in Russia. It goes to pieces like quicksilver under my touch." All of Wilson's studies and experience had centered on the process of democracy. He did not understand the disorderly process of revolution. His speeches, including the one in which he announced the famous Fourteen Points, suggest that he at first thought the communists were a new if strange species of democrats who should be courted. Disappointed at their rebuffs, he desisted. His professorial mind told him that when you do not understand you do not act. He consequently turned a deaf ear to repeated appeals for intervention in Russia that reached him from Lloyd George, British Foreign Secretary Arthur J. Balfour, Premier Clemenceau, and Marshal Foch. Wilson admitted he had a one-track mind. That mind was focused on crushing the main enemy, Germany; nobody had convinced him that this objective could be advanced by the use of American, Anglo-French, or Japanese troops against the Soviets in the Far East.

Japan, however, would not be denied.

Japanese intervention had its roots, like every international affair, in domestic politics, and Japanese politics was notoriously elusive. "Perhaps the single most powerful force in the Japanese government in 1918 was the Chōshū clique, which included a broad range of civilian and military officials . . . all of whom were loyal to the senior Genro, Prince Yama-

[24] From the official minutes quoted in Ray Stannard Baker, *Woodrow Wilson and World Settlement, Written from his Unpublished and Personal Material,* Vol. I, p. 166.

gata. It is perhaps true to say that no one, including the emperor, exercised more real authority."[25]

The Prince chieftain of the Chōshū clique and his mighty following wished to avoid an American veto on Japan's territorial gains in China. Hence their reluctance to antagonize Washington by engaging in an adventure in Siberia while America disapproved.[26] The politicians behind the Japanese navy, however, found enfeebled Russia an irresistible magnet drawing them to Siberia. They could not wait. They were inclined to listen to British and French encouragement rather than to America's eternal negations. But the Japanese army was a restraining influence, and the army and the Chōshū clique were hand in glove. The divisions in Japan and the differences among the Allies explain Japanese hesitation.

The central issue between the rival factions in Japan was not so much whether to intervene but whether to intervene in western Siberia and European Russia as the British and French governments urged. The Chōshū resolutely opposed an adventure toward Europe. The Army General Staff accordingly prepared a report entitled "Analysis of a European Expedition" and submitted it to the Cabinet. It concluded that transportation facilities through the vast roadless wastes of Siberia served by one railway, much of it single-tracked and all of it in disrepair due to wartime abuse, ruled out a costly Japanese expedition into European Russia. "The question is," said the army, "would it be worth the sacrifice?" The report answered with an emphatic negative. The government, the army recommended, should devote itself to "solving the China Problem" and "leave European Russia alone."[27]

But not Asiatic Russia, not eastern Siberia or Sakhalin. The Bolshevik revolution whetted Japan's appetite for these. Her cliques, generals, admirals, and ministers agreed that with eastern Siberia in their hands they could force China into an alliance while stripping her of valuable provinces. Yet many Japanese made their support of intervention contingent on America's approval.

The very month the Bolsheviks came to power in Petrograd Japan's navy prepared to move on Vladivostok, the terminal of the Trans-Siberian Railroad and an important port and base. The army, backed by the Chōshū clique, subsequently took the same stand as the navy, and

[25] James William Morley, *The Japanese Thrust into Siberia, 1918*, p. 19. Professor Morley of the East Asian Institute of Columbia University, a master of the Japanese language, had access after the second world war to the secret archives of the Japanese War, Navy, and Foreign Ministries, as well as to other classified Japanese material. In my account of Japanese intervention in Russia I lean heavily on Mr. Morley's book, the standard work on the subject.

[26] *Ibid.*, p. 15.

[27] *Ibid.*, pp. 29-31.

army headquarters drew up a "Plan to Send Troops to the Russian Far East to Protect Foreign Residents."

Foreign Minister Motono Ichiro wished to implant Japan's "natural influence in northern Manchuria" to acquire the northern—Russian—half of the island of Sakhalin and to help anti-Bolshevik elements in the Russian Far East "set up an autonomous regime."[28] This had the virtue of honesty and therefore remained secret. The protection of foreign residents, however, enjoyed the legitimacy of frequent use.

To achieve its purpose in Russia the Japanese government inaugurated a many-sided military-diplomatic enterprise: the army strengthened its grip on China, the navy sent warships to Vladivostok; agents bought Semenov, an adventurous, shrewd manipulator who commanded a detachment of Siberian Cossacks; ambassadors maneuvered to obtain a free hand for Tokyo in Chinese Manchuria, traversed by the Russian-owned and Russian-operated Chinese Eastern Railway, as well as in the Russian valleys of the Amur and Ussuri rivers. (The two rivers formed the boundary between Russia and China.)

The British also dispatched naval units to Vladivostok and scattered money among Cossack leaders, notably Semenov and Ivan Kalmykov, a pretender to authority among the Ussuri Cossacks. The French backed Semenov. The United States had introduced a large mission of experts and engineers under John F. Stevens and Colonel George H. Emerson to rehabilitate the Russian-owned railroads in Manchuria and Siberia.

China was a problem. Russia had not only owned and managed the Chinese Eastern Railway which runs through Chinese Manchuria; she also policed a wide zone on either side of that railway. With Russia eliminated from Manchuria, the Chinese government expected to take over the zone and the railway. Encouraged by the presence of the Stevens-Emerson mission, it began dispatching troops into the zone. Japan resented these moves. Any hint of American special interests in the Far East disturbed Tokyo.

The British ambassador in Tokyo handed Japanese Foreign Minister Viscount Motono a note dated March 11, 1918, reiterating London's desire for a Japanese expedition to Cheliabinsk, a city near the Ural Mountains, or "at least as far as Omsk." The next day Jean Jules Jusserand, French Ambassador in Washington, told U.S. Secretary of State Robert Lansing that Japan would intervene in Siberia "in defense of her present position and of her future. If she does so without our assent, she will do it against us and there is some likelihood of her later arriving at an understanding with Germany." Japan's army could support the anti-Bolshevik forces of Siberia; that would assist similar forces in southern

[28] *Ibid.*, p. 55.

Russia. Morley comments: "It seems safe to assume that France's eyes were really on the Ukraine"—her zone of influence—"and the western front, and not on what Japan might do in Asia."[29]

No such arguments, not even the bogey of a Japanese-German alliance to rule the world, could double-track Wilson's one-track mind. He remained opposed to Japanese intervention. His eye was on the western front where the war would indeed be won by the Allies.

Nor was Japan moved by British insistence on an expedition as far as Cheliabinsk. The Tokyo Cabinet resolved on March 18, 1918, that "even with American support Japan could not consider operating beyond the Amur basin." This was "an indispensable condition" of any Japanese intervention in Russia.

When diplomacy failed to bring Japan the sanction she wanted for intervention, her navy fell back on the "humanitarian" alibi—"the protection of foreign residents." Robbers allegedly entered a Japanese shop in Vladivostok on the morning of April 4 and attacked three Japanese, killing one. To this day nobody knows who the robbers were or what their motives were. Their purpose might have been the same as that of robbers anywhere at any time—to rob. But Rear Admiral Kato Kanji, aboard his flagship *Iwami* in Vladivostok harbor, ordered two companies of marines into the city one hour after the reported killing took place. The next day four more companies went ashore and Kato asked Tokyo for reinforcements.

The future of Japanese intervention in Russia now depended on Woodrow Wilson. All interventionists, British, French, and Nipponese, knew that if the United States acquiesced in Japan's intervention the Japanese moderates could no longer oppose it. The British played the central role in the campaign to erode the President's will. Though London was aware as early as March 19, 1918, that Tokyo had decided not to move into western Siberia[30] and that it would not, therefore, contribute toward rebuilding the eastern front, British diplomacy assiduously promoted Japanese intervention. England seemed reconciled to Japanese domination of eastern Siberia and, by inference, to the dismemberment of Soviet Russia. This did not accord with the American policy of maintaining Russia's territorial integrity.

The person best placed to conduct the assault on Wilson's will was Lord Reading, the new British envoy in Washington. Governments do well to designate ambassadors whose appointment is a compliment to the country to which they are accredited and whose qualities of character and mind give promise of close contacts with the chief executive and

[29] *Ibid.*, pp. 128-134.

[30] Richard H. Ullman, *Anglo-Soviet Relations, 1917-1921, Vol. I: Intervention and The War*, p. 143.

other powermen in the foreign nation where they are to function. The first Marquis of Reading was such a man. Son of a Jewish fruit merchant and at one time a seaman on a coal freighter, he became a Liberal member of the House of Commons and rose to the exalted office of Lord Chief Justice. His high intellectual and forensic skills, his democratic lineage and leanings, and his promotion on merit to the aristocracy were likely to appeal to Woodrow Wilson, the Virginian and university president who descended into the political pit only to be lifted to the political peak. In 1918 Reading was fifty-eight years old, Wilson sixty-two.

One of the great attorneys of England, Reading presented his brief with grace and sagacity. He did not prevail. He argued the case for Japanese intervention in Siberia on March 6, 1918, with Colonel House, Wilson's confidential adviser, who wrote to the President that same day, "I think I talked Reading out of his position into ours. He tried to argue but could not maintain his position, and agreed to send a cable to his government this afternoon advising them to conform with your ideas in the matter."[31]

Even discounting part of House's letter as boasting to the boss—a temptation which even the most prominent rarely resist—the least one can deduce is that Reading had failed to convince House.

A few days later London took a new tack and Reading offered it to House: the restoration of the eastern front would improve Allied morale. House agreed that this would be so but wondered whether the gain was worth the gamble. Wilson, when the British proposition was placed before him, wrote on March 14, "They still do not answer the question I have put to Lord Reading and to all the others who argue in favor of intervention by Japan, namely, What is it to effect and how will it be efficacious in effecting it?"[32]

On May 11 Secretary of State Lansing told Reading that the United States was as opposed as ever to Japanese intervention.[33]

The British government, now beginning to doubt the efficacy of words, searched for some action that would compel Wilson to retreat from his stubborn negative attitude. Deeds did indeed succeed where diplomacy failed.

What breached the walls of Wilson's resistance was a whiff of "sentiment" for the Czechoslovaks. The British, writes Ullman, "consistently probed for a solution; the one they chose—forcing President Wilson's hand by seeing to it that the Czechs became embroiled in Siberia—had

[31] *Ibid.*, p. 107. H. Montgomery Hyde's 1967 *Lord Reading, the Life of Rufus Isaacs, First Marquess of Reading,* adds some new documents on this subject but no new facts or analysis.

[32] *Ibid.*, pp. 143-144.

[33] *Ibid.*, p. 193.

the defect of being devious, but at least it was a means of securing the end that both they and the French desired."[34]

The saga of the Czechoslovaks is a most bizarre episode of the first world war.[35] Czechs, Slovaks, and other Slavs (as well as Hungarians), mobilized by the multi-national mottled Austro-Hungarian Empire at the beginning of that war, eagerly deserted in thousands on reaching the Russian front. The Tsar rejected a proposal to enlist them in his army to fight their native land. They were antimonarchist secessionists and, for the most part, Roman Catholics. Nicholas II, reluctant to set an example for his own disgruntled minorities—approximately half of Russia's population—and hesitating to close the door to the possibility of a separate peace with the Austro-Hungarian Empire, kept the Czechoslovaks in prison camps.

The republican successors to the Tsar released the prisoners. Thomas G. Masaryk, the father of independent Czechoslovakia and its first president, came to an agreement with the Provisional (Kerensky) government and with the French military mission in Russia "to send thirty thousand prisoners to France. . . . We were promised . . . that transports would be sent via Archangel as soon as possible." The French mission, headed by General Maurice C. T. Pierre Janin, who later described his experiences with the Legion in *Ma Mission en Siberie, 1918-1920*, undertook in May, 1917, to retrain the former prisoners. France, bleeding from every pore, needed manpower. Masaryk, eager to raise a free Czechoslovakia out of the ruins of defeated Austria-Hungary, hoped the Legion would fight in France before the eyes of the world, and there earn its country's visa to freedom.

The Czechoslovak corps, stationed in the Ukraine, consisted of some 30,000 to 40,000 men and officers; it gathered additional recruits from Czechs and Slovaks long resident in South Russia. In February, 1918, however, the German army began moving into the Ukraine and the Legion hastened to move out toward central Russia. On March 14 the Bolshevik Sovnarkom, or Cabinet, sitting for the first time in Moscow's Kremlin (the government, fearing a German advance, had moved the capital from Petrograd), voted to allow the Czechoslovaks to proceed through Siberia to Vladivostok. The Legion, which would be re-equipped in France, agreed to leave its arms, except a minimum for guard purposes, to the Soviets. Masaryk approved. He stipulated that "our army

[34] *Ibid.*, p. 171. Ullman enjoyed the enviable advantage of access to the papers of Lord Milner, prominent member of the British War Cabinet, of Sir William Wiseman, chief British Intelligence agent in the United States, and to many other revealing unpublished documents.

[35] The best account of the Czechoslovak Legion's anabasis in Russia is in George F. Kennan's *Soviet-American Relations, 1917-1920. The Decision to Intervene.* Some quotations in the pages that follow are from Fischer, *The Life of Lenin.*

would be used only against the foreign enemy"—not in Russian internal conflicts.

The British had other ideas. As early as April 1, 1918, the British War Office communicated with the Czechoslovak National Council in London and expressed "doubt that the Czech corps could actually get to Europe via Siberia and voicing the view that it ought, therefore, to be used in Russia or Siberia." Eduard Beneš of the National Council reported this to Premier Clemenceau; both rejected the plan. The British persevered and won over the French. When the Permanent Military Representatives of the Supreme War Council met in Versailles on April 27 they drafted a joint note which took cognizance of Anglo-French deliberation regarding "the transportation of Czech contingents from Russia" and urged that their departure occur "at the earliest possible date." But the corps was to be divided. The legionnaires who had gone no farther east in Siberia than Omsk would turn around and proceed to Murmansk and Archangel where they could "be profitably employed in defending Archangel and Murmansk and in guarding and protecting the Murmansk railway." Those troops who had passed beyond Omsk on the way to Vladivostok might cooperate with the Allies in Siberia.

This decision, the key to the fate of the Czechoslovak Legion, led to American approval of Japanese intervention and to American intervention in Siberia. Kennan, citing the joint note, comments: "The wording of the note, together with the fact that as much as six weeks later no serious move had been made by either government"—British or French —"to provide shipping at Vladivostok or at the northern ports, makes it very difficult to believe that the idea of dividing the Corps was anything other, in the minds of its authors, than a disingenuous one, designed to give perfunctory recognition to the principle of the eventual removal of the Czech units to France but actually to assure their availability for service in Russia in the event of Allied intervention."[36]

It was disingenuous and worse: it was a coldly cynical scheme to maneuver the Czech Legion into a position to trigger the intervention. Lord Robert Cecil made the British purpose clear in a long letter to Clemenceau dated May 18, 1918. The problem, he wrote, was simply that the Americans, for reasons such as "tenderness towards Revolutionary Russia" and suspicion of Japan, would not approve of Japanese intervention. In this dilemma Cecil said, "I ask myself . . . Is there no way of creating a diversion in the East if the Japanese and Americans combine to delay matters?" He could think of only "one possible plan"—to utilize the Czechs now reaching Vladivostok; "they could be used to start operations in Siberia . . . there could be little doubt that the

[36] Kennan, pp. 146-147.

Japanese would move and the Americans would find it impossible to hold back."[37]

To judge by this letter Cecil could have written the scenario of coming events.

Sniffing the air with their highly sensitive olfactory nerve, the Bolsheviks moved to disarm the Czechoslovaks. The legionnaires, officered in some cases by anti-Soviet Russians, resisted. Incident followed incident and on May 26 armed hostilities commenced between the Legion and the Kremlin. The legionnaires began fighting their way along the Trans-Siberian Railroad to Vladivostok. By mid-June the 14,000 to 15,000 Czech troops reached Vladivostok. The Czech Legion was the most formidable military force in the strange world of anarchy called Soviet Russia.

The Legion troops in Vladivostok were under the command of a Russian major general named M. K. Dietrichs. On the evening of June 28, 1918, Dietrichs informed the Allied consuls in Vladivostok that at 10 o'clock the next morning he would face the city's soviet with a thirty-minute ultimatum to disarm and, in effect, to disband. He did so. Czechs then seized the city. "Although the Czechs had been the chief agents, the overthrow of soviet authority in Vladivostok was obviously a combined British-French-Japanese-Czech affair. The local naval and diplomatic officials of the three powers had given the Czechs their fullest cooperation in carrying out the seizure."[38]

With the terminus of the line thus firmly in their hands the Czechs faced about and sent detachments westward, back over the Trans-Siberian, to reinforce their comrades in the numerous cities and stations between Vladivostok and the Volga. By a strange twist of fate which they neither desired nor foresaw—their target was always the Germans on the French front—the Czechoslovaks were manipulated into going to war against Soviet Russia.

The developments in remote Siberia produced precisely the repercussions Cecil envisaged. For months the British and French ambassadors had been nudging Lansing toward intervention, and while he resisted their nudges they left a mark and he began to vacillate as early as March, 1918.[39] When, therefore, the Czechoslovaks seized Vladivostok and commenced moving westward into Siberia, Lansing abandoned his former no-yes stand and, as Cecil had anticipated, adopted the firm stand of the British and French. The Secretary of State now apparently felt that Wilson too was ripe for conversion.

[37] Ullman, pp. 169-170. A copy of Cecil's letter was found by Mr. Ullman among Lord Milner's papers.

[38] Morley, p. 248.

[39] *United States Foreign Relations. Lansing Papers, 1940,* Vol. II, pp. 354-355.

The President had received Dr. Thomas G. Masaryk on June 19. Wilson favored self-determination for small nationalities and Masaryk was the leader of a small nation seeking self-determination. Their minds met. Wilson conceived a special sympathy for the Czech cause. News of the Czech seizure of Vladivostok reached Lansing on July 2; the next morning he telephoned the glad tidings to the President. Earlier that morning Lord Reading had come to see Wilson and bring him the latest appeal drafted by Lloyd George from the Supreme War Council in Paris for action in Siberia before it was too late: "The necessity of American support and encouragement for the military expedition was stressed. It was stated as the unanimous opinion of Foch and the military advisers that the immediate dispatch of such an expedition was essential for the victory of the Allied army."[40] Aid to the Czech Legion also was mentioned.

The following day, July 4, 1918—142nd anniversary of the Declaration of Independence, mankind's first anticolonial manifesto—Wilson, Lansing, and a large number of guests sailed to Mount Vernon in the presidential yacht, the *Mayflower*. During the trip Lansing wrote a memorandum for Wilson on the Siberian problem. The Czechs' occupation of Vladivostok and their success in Western Siberia "had materially changed the situation," wrote Lansing, "by introducing a sentimental element into the question of duty."[41]

Lansing calculated shrewdly that "sentiment and duty" was a combination Wilson could not resist. He knew Wilson had developed a sentimental attachment for the Czechs. And he knew that the Presbyterian Professor-President would rise to the call of duty. But why would he answer that call now and not during the preceding months when British and French leaders battered in vain at the closed doors of Wilson's mind? Throughout the spring of 1918 the war on the western front raged in a climax of fury. The Germans were making their last bid to attain the English Channel and victory. The Anglo-French, depleted by four years of murderous trench warfare amid mounting horrors of gas, tanks, shells, bullets, and bayonet charges, were bleeding profusely, taking the offensive in places, and hoping the Americans would soon enter the battle in considerable numbers. When, in such circumstances, Foch and the British military pleaded with Wilson to arrive at a decision on Siberia which they professed would win the war, he had to lift his veto. The rules of alliances, especially wartime alliances, are intolerant of permanent obstruction by a minority of one. Wilson perceived this; he was worn down by persistent pressure in a crucial hour. Sentiment for the Czechoslovaks sweetened the bitter potion. Yet the inner turmoil re-

[40] Kennan, p. 394.
[41] *Ibid.*, p. 395.

mained and came to the surface in the announcement of American sanction of a joint U.S.-Japanese expedition to Siberia.

The announcement followed discussion within the administration which could only have been painful to the President. Thus on July 6 Wilson invited Lansing, Secretary of War Newton D. Baker, Secretary of the Navy Josephus Daniels, General Peyton C. March, Chief of Staff, and Admiral W. S. Benson, Chief of Naval Operations, to meet him in the White House. He outlined his views: it would be impossible by the program envisaged to re-establish an eastern front, but the Czechoslovaks needed help; the U.S.A. could not quickly supply the necessary armed units, therefore Japan would furnish the munitions and equipment for which the U.S.A. would share the expense; 7,000 American and 7,000 Japanese troops were to be assembled at Vladivostok to guard the lines of communication of the Czech Legion moving westward in Siberia toward Irkutsk. Seeing General March shake his head vigorously in opposition, Wilson said with some asperity, "Why are you shaking your head, General? You are opposed to this because you do not think that Japan will limit herself to 7,000 men and that this decision will further her schemes for territorial aggrandizement?"

March: "Just that, and for other military reasons which I have already told you."

Wilson: "Well, we will have to take that chance."[42]

The statement of America's readiness to participate in a Siberian expedition with Japan was finally published on August 4, 1918. Wilson did not sign it. Nor did Lansing. It carried the signature of Acting Secretary of State Frank L. Polk. Did Wilson wish to escape the verdict of history? He had actually typed the original on his Hammond typewriter and made corrections in his own hand in ink.[43]

"In the judgment of the Government of the United States," the statement read, "a judgment arrived at after repeated and searching considerations of the whole situation, military intervention in Russia would be more likely to add to the present sad confusion there than to cure it, and would injure Russia rather then help her out of her distress.

"We are bending all our energies now," the statement continued, "to the purpose, the resolute and confident purpose, of winning on the western front, and it would in the judgment of the Government of the United States be most unwise to divide or dissipate our forces."

Why, then, did Wilson adopt the "most unwise" policy? To protect

[42] Peyton C. March, *The Nation at War*, p. 126.

[43] I had suspected for years that Wilson wrote it, it sounded so much like him. While working on my book, *The Life of Lenin*, I asked Professor Arthur S. Link, director of the Woodrow Wilson Papers at Princeton University, whether he had the document. He gave me a Xerox copy of the original.

and help the Czechoslovaks, the announcement replied, "against the armed Austrian and German prisoners who are attacking them . . ." —there were some 50,000 armed Czechoslovaks in the Legion; there were by official British and American count fewer than 1,000 armed enemy prisoners in Siberia—"and to steady any efforts at self-government or self-defense in which the Russians themselves may be willing to accept assistance," Wilson added in justification of the move he had consistently condemned.

Accordingly the United States and Japan agreed to send 7,000 troops each to Vladivostok and Siberia.

Years later, on May 11, 1924, U.S. Supreme Court Justice Louis D. Brandeis, a friend and admirer of Wilson, wrote in a letter, "Mr. Wilson . . . should be judged by what he was and did prior to August 4, 1918, the date of the paper justifying the attack on Russia. That was the first of his acts which was unlike him, and I am sure the beginning of the sad end."[44]

The United States sent 9,000 men, Tokyo sent 12,000, and before the end of 1918 Japan had 70,000 soldiers in the Russian Far East and prepared for a long stay.

Foreign intervention in Soviet Russia, seen in the perspective of many decades, was a total waste and complete loss. It cost innumerable lives, ruined innumerable families, and destroyed material that could have fed, clothed, and housed hundreds of thousands, perhaps millions. It left in Russia a sea of distrust and ignorance. Truth, the first casualty of wars, was the first and last victim of this one. On the Soviet side it gave birth to a library of lies enjoying record-breaking longevity. There is still no honest Russian history of the civil war and intervention of 1918-1920. The facts are a football; the realism used to depict it is socialist, which means it is cut to suit the Soviet foreign policy of the day. In 1938 Stalin, in need of good relations with the United States, played down American intervention, making it less than it was; in 1959 Khrushchev, conducting an anti-American symphony, played it up, making it much more than it was. It was nothing of which Great Britain, France, Japan, Italy, or America can be proud.

Foreign powers intervening in Soviet Russia in what they conceived or misconceived as their national interests supported anticommunist governments and groups which lost. They lost for various reasons: the peasants believed they backed landlords who wanted their estates returned; the national minorities were convinced that a White victory would mean more Russification and oppression; the workingman expected new freedoms from the Reds; finally, many Russians with no

[44] Kennan, p. 405.

sympathy for Bolshevism found it difficult to join a general propped up by Japan or England, the traditional enemies of their country. It is not certain that the Soviets would have been defeated by internal enemies acting without foreign support. It is certain that foreign intervention helped the Lenin-Trotsky regime by placing it in the role of defending the nation against invaders.

* * *

If foreign military intervention in Soviet Russia had been conceived only as a means of establishing an eastern front against Germany it would have stopped on November 11, 1918, when Germany surrendered. But intervention found welcome friends in those Russians who opposed the Bolsheviks on social, economic, political, and personal grounds. This bond remained after the first world war. Intervention continued. Interventionists always find new excuses for old.

After the war ended Lenin said to Georgi V. Chicherin, who succeeded Trotsky as Commissar for Foreign Affairs, "Na nas idyot das Weltkapital"[45] ("World capitalism is advancing against us"). He saw armies and armadas, freed from the struggle with Germany, Austria-Hungary, Bulgaria, and Turkey, moving into Soviet Russia to crush her. And, in fact, plans to do just that did exist.

To fashion the peace after World War I the Allied and Associated Powers created the Council of Ten: two representatives each of Great Britain, the United States, France, Italy, and Japan. It discussed military intervention in Russia. On February 18, 1919, Churchill substituted for Lloyd George, who had been called to London by grave labor troubles. "The first thing Winston Churchill did was to demand instant action against Russia, and he practically supported Foch's Napoleonic scheme which was now resurrected with new determination, for applying military force against Soviet Russia."[46]

Lenin, with the usual communist catastrophe-mindedness, exaggerated Russia's peril. Foch and Churchill, blinded by imperial ambitions, exaggerated their countries' capacities. The end of World War I found the European victors lying on a bed of nails instead of in a bower of roses. Their armies were crumbling. On February 3, 1919, Marshal Foch told Sir Henry Wilson, the new British Chief of the Imperial General Staff, "that his men won't stand it any longer, and will demobilize themselves as the Belgians are doing."[47] Foch could not forget the mutiny in General Robert G. Neville's army which began on April 29, 1917, and

[45] Repeated to me by Chicherin.
[46] Baker, p. 297.
[47] Major General Sir C. E. Callwell, *Field-Marshal Sir Henry Wilson, His Life and Diaries*, Vol. II, p. 169.

lasted with varying intensity through May and June. Fifty-four divisions of the French army were involved. Masses of men refused to fight. Some were executed.[48] To restore discipline Marshal Pétain relieved Neville.

The cause of the mutiny was the many tens of thousands of dead and gravely wounded in week-long battles which did not seem to bring victory one hour nearer. Finally, however, after France had lost over a million dead, victory did come. By that time the soldiers had had enough and wanted to go home and stay home, not go off to Russia to fight for an unknown reason in an unknown land.

The situation in the British army was similar. At a Cabinet meeting on January 22, 1919, according to Sir Henry Wilson's diary, General Douglas Haig, British field commander in France, reported "that even now we dare not give an unpopular order to the troops, and discipline is a thing of the past. . . . By February we would have no more army in France."[49] The British Tommies were eager to return to the "homes for heroes" which Lloyd George had promised them—and never built.

To make matters much worse, the British Empire roared with unrest. Administrators and generals in Ireland, India, and Egypt were bombarding Whitehall with urgent requests for additional troops.

But the military everywhere have contingency plans, and the Anglo-French plan prepared before war's end called for the dispatch of armed forces to Russia. As early as November 22, 1918, only eleven days after Germany's surrender, British and French warships accordingly streamed through the Dardanelles and into the Black Sea with aid in materials and men for General Denikin, whose headquarters were in the North Caucasus. On December 17 French units landed at Odessa. Gradually the entire coast of the Ukraine and the Crimea and a belt reaching in places as far back as one hundred miles inland were occupied by some 12,000 French soldiers (including Algerians, Senegalese, Poles, and Greeks). They were equipped with tanks, artillery, and airplanes, and could rely for support and supplies from the Anglo-French fleet of three dreadnoughts, eight cruisers, twelve torpedo boats, and a changing number of transports anchored in the Black Sea.

The French were prepared to occupy the Ukraine and Crimea after the defeated Germans withdrew. But they were in no mood to fight; when they encountered resistance from the Red army and from detachments of fiercely nationalistic anti-Bolshevik Ukrainians under Hetman Petlura and lost 414 dead in a battle for the city of Kherson, they abandoned Kherson and Nicolaiev and took refuge in Odessa. Bolshevik forces closed in on Odessa. General d'Anselme, the French commander, telegraphed Paris about "the excellent condition" of the enemy and hun-

[48] John Williams, *Mutiny 1917*.
[49] Callwell, p. 169.

ger in the port city. A mutiny in one or two ships of the French fleet added to d'Anselme's troubles. At home the parliamentary opposition demanded that the troops and squadron be brought home. On April 2, 1918, the commander received instructions to leave south Russia in forty-eight hours. He and his men joyously complied. This lowered the curtain on Foch's grandiose scheme for intervention in Russia by French forces. The French government, however, continued to send supplies and officer-advisers to anti-Soviet armies fighting in Russia.

The British government, the father and mentor of anti-Soviet intervention, was more reluctant to desist. Sir Henry Wilson told the War Cabinet on January 10, 1919, that "there had been signs of unrest in the Army at home, and it was notorious that the prospect of being sent to Russia was immensely unpopular." The result was, he said, according to the official minutes, "that it was impossible for us to reinforce our troops in North Russia and Siberia."

In this desperate dilemma Winston Churchill, the Secretary of State for War, offered the same session of the War Cabinet a remarkable idea: "He suggested to the Cabinet that it might be advisable to let Germany know that if she were prepared to organize her Eastern Front against the ingress of Bolshevism, the Allied governments would raise no objection." The late enemy would be harnessed to the chariot of the victors. German troops did in fact fight the Bolsheviks in the Baltic region.

On January 26, 1919, Sir Henry Wilson wrote Prime Minister Lloyd George that he "was in favor of pulling out of Omsk now, if France would agree"—Omsk was the headquarters of Admiral Alexander V. Kolchak, the British choice as leader of all the White Russians—"and getting ready to clear out of Murmansk and Archangel next summer, but on the other hand, I would want to strengthen our position on the line Batum-Baku-Krasnovodsk-Merv."[50]

Russia's biggest oil field was at Baku. Her only oil pipeline ran from Baku on the Caspian Sea to Batum on the Black Sea. Across the Caspian from Baku sat Krasnovodsk in Turkestan. Merv was the nerve center of Russian Central Asia. A British protectorate over these centers would keep Russia away from Persia, Afghanistan, and India. The oil of Baku was a supplementary attraction.

This was the region of greatest interest to Lord Curzon, and he insisted on holding it. Churchill's horizon, however, embraced the whole of Russia. But things were going badly for the interventionists. In the south and north of Russia and in Siberia "Our enterprises there are crumbling," he told the War Cabinet on February 12, 1919. "The Bolsheviks were getting stronger every day," the minutes record Churchill

[50] *Ibid.*, p. 169.

as saying. ". . . If we were going to withdraw our troops, it should be done at once. If we were going to intervene, we should send larger forces there. He believed that we ought to intervene."

Here Lloyd George injected an ostensibly innocent item of information designed to ridicule the Churchill proposal: "The Prime Minister said he understood the military view to be that, if we were going to do any good, we should need a million men, and these should be dispatched in the spring." An obvious impossibility.

Churchill replied that he "did not suggest intervention on that scale." If England could not intervene effectively, the sooner the anti-Bolsheviks knew it the better. "On the other hand," he warned, "if the Allies would not help Russia, Japan and Germany would certainly do so, and in a few years' time we should see the German Republic united with the Bolsheviks in Russia and the Japanese in the Far East forming one of the most powerful combinations the world had ever seen."

It is not recorded how many British ministers were frightened by this unlikely horror. The Cabinet merely decided to ask Churchill for a memorandum on what could be done and what it would cost.

At a War Cabinet meeting on February 26, 1919, the Chancellor of the Exchequer spoke on the question of costs. He had seen Admiralty reports, he stated, which made it "very doubtful if, from the point of view of oil and supplies, our occupation of Baku was very likely to lead to any useful results, and he suggested that it ought to be terminated as soon as possible." Moreover, General Denikin was "attacking Georgia. The proposal made by the C.I.G.S."—Chief of the Imperial General Staff—"was to send men to the number of one or two thousand." The Chancellor would have preferred to limit British intervention in the Caucasus to "help with military equipment and stores and a few experts."

Next "Lord Curzon said that one of the conditions which we have made with Denikin was that he was to fight against Bolshevism and not against Georgia and Armenia."

Churchill asked for "a definite policy . . . in each locality."

Denikin's behavior continued to trouble the British government. Churchill argued at a War Cabinet session on March 6, 1919, that "the supply of arms" to Denikin served as a lever "on the one hand, to enable him to fight the Bolsheviks, and on the other, to prevent him from maltreating the Southern States." By furnishing supplies to Denikin, he said, Britain would be in a position to remove "our troops as quickly as possible. He proposed," the minutes read, "to spread the supply over the next few months, doling it out to General Denikin. . . . It was necessary to retain the power to control him."

Lord Curzon "concurred with Mr. Churchill's observations" and also clarified British policy. "We were relying," Curzon declared, "on General Denikin to fight and beat the Bolsheviks. He had shown a tendency, however, to turn southward and attack the states on the other side of the Caucasus as an easier target. He was a type of an old-fashioned monarchical Russian who regarded it as his natural role to bring back the Caucasus states under Russian rule."

Curzon preferred the Caucasus not to be under Russian rule. That would have given Britain a free hand there.

Presently the sky grew brighter. Admiral Kolchak's army was advancing rapidly westward toward the Volga. Churchill, Secretary of State for War, told a War Cabinet meeting on May 6, 1919, "Five new Russian divisions were being formed in Siberia, and were now being brought into action. The victories of these troops are being won with British weapons and uniforms. . . . It was quite possible that the Bolshevik regime would crumple up, and we should get a civilized Russia friendly to us above all other Powers if events continued to proceed on satisfactory lines." Kolchak, Churchill continued, would soon be in Archangel, and this would permit the British troops in the Murmansk-Archangel district to be brought home. However, Churchill said, Kolchak needed Russian officers and many of these were available in the West. "The War Cabinet decided," according to the minutes, "that . . . The Treasury should provide the necessary funds to transport, feed, and equip the 1,200 Russian officers whom the Secretary of State for War proposed to recruit and send to North Russia."

The military have their own illogic. To withdraw from Murmansk-Archangel it was decided that the British army there first had to be reinforced, and it was in fact reinforced from a strength of 6,832 to 18,400. Now the generals, instead of evacuating the expedition, launched an offensive in the hope of joining up with Kolchak's forces. In May, 1919, however, Kolchak, battling Red Army divisions in front of him and rebellious peasants in his rear, withdrew precipitately toward his base in Omsk. The British then did, in fact, "clear out of Murmansk and Archangel," in Sir Henry Wilson's words, and pull out of Omsk. Pressed by Bolshevik armies, Kolchak fled from Omsk to Irkutsk, where he was executed on February 7, 1920.

A similar fate overtook General Denikin. Using cavalry to great advantage and helped by British tanks and artillery and by British officer-advisers ("The whole burden of fighting the Bolshevists in Russia," the Chancellor of the Exchequer complained at a War Cabinet meeting on May 29, 1919, "was now being borne by Great Britain alone and the situation was becoming intolerable"), General Denikin advanced rapidly in the direction of Moscow. On September 20, 1919, he captured Kursk, 330 miles from the capital, and on October 14 he took Orel, about

240 miles from the capital. Then the Kolchak story was repeated. Bled by the Red Army at the front, his rear chewed up by the anarchist-guerrilla bands of Nestor I. Makhno, Denikin retreated rapidly southward and soon departed for the Balkans with many thousands of officers and men, leaving Baron General Peter von Wrangel to command the remnants.

In October, 1919, General Nikolai N. Yudenich, commanding a small army of White Russians and Estonians, threatened Petrograd, cradle of the Bolshevik revolution. Lenin, alarmed by Denikin's progress toward Moscow, counseled abandoning Petrograd in order to shorten the Soviet line. Trotsky took charge and Yudenich was repulsed, in part because the Estonians deserted him when he announced "There is no Estonia."

Yudenich had enjoyed British support. The British wanted a Russia "as small as possible." Their military puppets in Russia, particularly Yudenich and Denikin, hoped to restore "united and indivisible" Holy Russia. If the Russian Whites had won, British imperial policy would have been defeated. Because Yudenich lost, because the Bolsheviks were weak, because Germans fought the Bolsheviks in the Baltic, the British did extricate Estonia, Latvia, and Lithuania from Soviet rule, thus slicing a slab off Russia's western flank.

The eclipse of Yudenich and Denikin cast its shadows before, and on September 2, 1919, the War Cabinet discussed withdrawal from the Caucasus. But "Curzon favored leaving a brigade there," Sir Henry Wilson recorded in his diary. "So did Milner, but Bonar Law, Montagu, Austen [Chamberlain] and I opposed this."[51]

The Supreme Council of the victorious Allies met in Paris on January 11, 1920, and voted to recognize Georgia and Azerbaijan and "to arm, equip, and feed the Georgian, Azerbaijanese, and Armenians." Sir Henry noted that "Curzon now wants to hold Batum-Baku and Montagu backs him." Curzon had become Secretary of State for Foreign Affairs, Sir Edward Montagu had taken Curzon's place as Secretary of State for India, and both were interested in the Caucasus as a buffer against Russia in Central Asia.

In the end, conditions in Britain forced Curzon, Montagu, Churchill, Milner, and other interventionists to retreat from their costly and fruitless adventures in Russia. The U.S. troops in Siberia, who never fought a serious engagement against Russians and who were in Siberia to impede the Japanese, left Soviet soil in the spring of 1920. When hope of victory over the Bolsheviks grew dim, all other foreign forces likewise withdrew —except the Japanese. They remained in Eastern Siberia until the autumn of 1922, and in Russian Sakhalin until 1925. In both these re-

[51] *Ibid.*, p. 216.

gions the Japanese units were harassed by the Red Army, but the supplementary and weighty reason for their ultimate exit from Russian soil was the pressure of the very anti-Soviet Charles Evans Hughes, Secretary of State of the United States. He wanted to weaken Japan's position on the Asiatic mainland.

Foreign intervention in the Soviet civil war demonstrates the folly of governments. This is no novelty. Much of history is the record of the mistakes of governments whose hopes are longer than their reach and their self-confidence greater than their understanding.

III PLANNING PEACE IN PARIS

In Paris in 1919 the Big Four—Premier Georges Clemenceau, President Woodrow Wilson, Prime Minister Lloyd George, and Prime Minister Vittorio Orlando of Italy—proposed to make the peace by remaking the map of Europe. They also dealt with Soviet Russia. Their immediate problem on March 25, 1919, was to prop up Rumania with food and arms. They decided to do so. France was evolving a more ambitious scheme. The British government placed its fondest hopes on Denikin and Admiral Kolchak. But Marshal Ferdinand Foch, summoned for consultation, told the Big Four that "whatever is sent to Denikin is lost. I do not attach any great importance to the army of Denikin." He preferred to create a barrier against Bolshevism by strengthening Poland and Rumania. He called it a "cordon sanitaire." Wilson objected. Orlando favored the occupation of Red Budapest by Allied troops provided they did not include Czechs, Rumanians, or Poles. He said Vienna feared Bolshevism and was inviting Italian troops to come and save it.

At their session on April 30, 1919, Lloyd George expected an early juncture between the forces of Kolchak moving out of Siberia toward northern Russia with the Allied and anti-Bolshevik units in Archangel. Nevertheless, he said, "the government of Lenin is still strong."

Clemenceau: "Our information tends to show that the power of the Bolsheviks is declining."

Lloyd George: "Here our information differs."

By May 7, 1919, Lloyd George was jubilant. The situation in Russia had undergone a remarkable transformation. "We are witnessing the veritable collapse of Bolshevism . . . according to our information Kolchak is about to join his forces with those at Archangel; it is also possible that he will arrive in Moscow soon and establish a new government." However, the situation was not all roses. The Poles were afraid of Kolchak's politics and even more so of Denikin's, whom they accused of being Germanophile. President Ignace Paderewski (the pianist-President of Poland), Lloyd George declared, "feared the triumph of Russian militarism which would then ally itself with Germany."

Clemenceau put no trust in Polish judgments about Russia. They are, he said, "distorted by hate."[1]

The British were still optimistic at the Big Four meeting on May 9, 1919. Kolchak was still advancing. President Wilson wished to withdraw the American expedition from Siberia. Lloyd George begged him to delay that decision. Wilson objected that "he had always been of opinion that the proper policy of the Allied and Associated Powers was to clear out of Russia and leave it to the Russians to fight it out among themselves."[2]

But on June 25 Lloyd George reported to his colleagues that Kolchak had been driven back 300 kilometers. On the other hand, Denikin had defeated the Bolsheviks and captured 50,000 Red army soldiers and 300 cannon.

Foch did not believe in the fortunes of the White Russian military. He saw them as armies without governments. He preferred governments which could be supplied with arms and army advisers. His scheme remained unaltered whether Kolchak advanced or retreated, whether Denikin advanced or retreated. They were British puppets. He was dominated by one idea: organize Poland and Rumania for a crusade into the Ukraine and tear that large and rich territory from the power of the Bolsheviks.

[1] Paul Mantoux, *Les Délibérations du Conseil de Quatre* (*24 mars-28 juin 1919*). *Notes de l'Officier Interprête*, Vol. I: *Jusqu'à la Remise a la Délégation Allemande des Conditions de Paix*, pp. 19, 56, 430, 505, Vol. II: *Depuis la Remise à la Délégation Allemande des Conditions de Paix jusqu'à la Signature du Traité de Versailles*, pp. 16, 515. All quotations translated from the French.

[2] U.S. Department of State, *Papers Relating to the Foreign Relations of the United States. The Paris Peace Conference*, 1919, Vol. V, p. 529.

IV BOLSHEVISM'S BIGGEST GAMBLE

A communist is a person whose abhorrence of gradualism makes him see politics in terms of catastrophe. The capitalist system, he knows for certain, cannot improve itself and will therefore be smashed by violent revolution. Although noncommunist nations have for decades surmounted one crisis after another by remedial measures and climbed to new heights of prosperity and power, their ultimate demise and a harried life of hard struggle in the meantime continue to be communist doctrine.

The same calamity mentality shaped the communists' view of their own fate for years after the advent of Bolshevism to Russia. Its leaders exaggerated the strength of the forces arrayed against them. They discerned crafty foes constantly conspiring to destroy them and predicted that the Soviet government would die unless European nations, having gone communist, came to its rescue. The men in the Kremlin were nervous, devoid of a sense of humor, a sense of proportion, an air of relaxation, and a spirit of live and let live. They were racked by fear, rocked by suspicion, and worried by dangers spawned in their own fantasies. Despite a puerile insistence on the superiority of the Soviet system and its inevitable global triumph, they suffered from the historic Russian inferiority complex intensified by the frailty born of revolution.

So it was that Lenin, herald of communist salvation and prophet of capitalist death, saw Soviet Russia's doom too. When the first world war ended he saw black and said to Foreign Commissar Georgi V. Chicherin, "Na nas idyot das Weltkapital" (World capitalism is marching against us).[1]

Lenin's dream of disaster came paired in his anxious mind with a vision of sudden deliverance. The closing days of the war brought revolution to Germany; soviets sprouted in German cities. Lenin sent Karl Radek, his, and later Stalin's, adviser on German and world affairs, to Berlin. Before Radek left, Lenin talked with him. Lenin anticipated massed armies of the victorious western Entente invading the Ukraine from bases in Hungary and Rumania. Allied fleets would steam through the Dardanelles.

[1] Repeated to me by Chicherin on several occasions.

Radek said the troops would not fight.

"They will dispatch colored troops," Lenin argued. "How will you make propaganda among them?"

Radek: "We will agitate among them with cartoons. Besides, colored troops would not stand our climate. If revolution does not come soon in Entente countries and they are able to send troops to the land of the revolution their troops will become disaffected here."

Lenin: "We shall see." He then stressed the urgency of fomenting revolution in Germany. "Remember," Lenin admonished, "that you will be in action in the enemy's rear. Intervention is inescapable, and much depends on the situation in Germany."

Lenin regarded revolt in Germany, behind the Entente's interventionist lines in Russia, as a decisive factor in Russia's safety. Radek, born in the East Galician province of the Austro-Hungarian Empire, took a world view. "German revolution," he said to Lenin, "is much too great a development to be regarded as a diversion in the rear of the enemy."[2] Radek thought of it as a major leap toward world revolution; he was impractically internationalist. Lenin was functionally Russocentric.

History knows that Lenin magnified the menace to Soviet Russia. The Allied countries, their energy and will sapped by the long world war, did intervene, but with one finger of their left hand. In most cases the willing spirit found the flesh weak. France spent money and sent some battleships and several thousand troops to Odessa and other Ukrainian cities. After a few small, sanguinary battles with the Red army the troops were withdrawn, and after a mutiny on one man-of-war the fleet was withdrawn. The French people had had enough fighting. Britain did more. The United States participated with 5,000 men in north Russia and 7,000 in Siberia. Italy, Germany, and Serbia contributed their mites to postwar intervention. The Japanese were the worst culprits. But the sum of all this bore no resemblance to Lenin's mirage of "world capitalism" assaulting the fragile walls of the first communist-ruled state. World capitalism was licking its war wounds. Soviet Russia, child of the first world war, was saved by that war's ravages among the child's enemies.

History also knows that Radek was wrong: the 1918 German revolution fizzled. The "great event" did not eventuate. Moscow's explanation stressed the weakness of the communist party and the strength of the large moderate, reformist, therefore anticommunist, Social Democratic Party. Primarily, however, the 1918 communist coup and subsequent efforts failed because Germany was a developed, industrialized nation. Such countries do not make communist revolutions. It is underdeveloped

[2] Karl Radek, "Noyabr. Stranichka iz Vospominanii" (November. A Little Page of Reminiscences), *Krasyana Nov*, Moscow, November, 1926, pp. 139-175.

lands like Russia and China that are subject to seizure by communists if prolonged foreign war or civil strife causes the administration of law and order to break down.

Radek dimly realized this and returned to the Kremlin with his internationalism deflated. He learned another lesson: Soviet Russia would gain more by an alliance with German nationalists than with German communists. Jailed in Berlin on February 12, 1919, for subversive activities, his cell became a salon where he received important Germans, among them some most reactionary, conservative, and militaristic Germans. They engineered his release and gave him living quarters in the apartment of Baron Georg von Reibnitz whom Radek christened a "national Bolshevik." To the apartment came other "national Bolsheviks," including Colonel Walter Bauer, Ludendorff's right-hand man during the war, and Admiral Paul von Hintze, Foreign Secretary under the monarchy. Hintze, Radek wrote in his reminiscences, "stood for a deal with Soviet Russia." Thereafter Radek lobbied in the Kremlin for a deal with the German army which hoped to rearm illegally in secret agreement with the Muscovite state.

But Lenin decided to make one more throw of the dice of history to win Europe for communism. The conscious gamble—the first and last in the long record of Soviet foreign relations—became a possibility when, in 1920, Poland launched a military attack on the Bolshevik regime.

Throughout 1919 Poland, having achieved national independence thanks to Germany's defeat and Russia's inability to regain possession, seized considerable Soviet territory. On August 8 Polish troops were able to take Minsk, largely because the Russian Red army was locked in combat with Denikin's forces which, of all White armies, came closest to capturing Moscow. On September 20, 1919, Denikin entered the city of Kursk; on October 14 he was in Orel. Lenin feared for the capital so much that he proposed shortening the Soviet defense line by abandoning Petrograd, cradle of the revolution, to the Whites. "The military power of the Entente *can* crush (but still in fact has not crushed) us," he wrote on October 10, 1919.

In this crisis a major military effort by Poland might have put Denikin in Moscow. The Poles held their hand. Count Alexander Skrzyński, Polish Foreign Minister in 1922-1923 and 1924-1926, explains why: "Undoubtedly, Denikin would have received with great gratitude the help of the Poles, but only on the understanding, scarcely concealed, that such help was forthcoming from the Poles as faithful subjects of Russia. With Denikin reasoning in this way the Poles could have no interest in giving him help."[3]

[3] *Poland and Peace* by Count Alexander Skrzyński, p. 39.

Marshal Joseph Pilsudski and his associates in the Warsaw leadership knew that if Denikin ousted the Bolsheviks he would establish a nationalistic regime under the Tsarist motto of "Russia, one and indivisible," and aim to reabsorb Poland into the empire. This point was emphasized by an agent of Lenin who had been in Poland during most of 1919 negotiating secretly with persons in Pilsudski's entourage.[4] Whether or not Pulsudski needed such prompting, the fact is he delayed major aggressive action against Russia until 1920 when the only White Russian commander left in the field was Baron Peter von Wrangel at the head of the hopelessly outnumbered remnants of Denikin's army whom the Bolsheviks soon bottled up in the Crimean peninsula.

"Polish Eastern Policy" was federalism. "Federalism (its most eminent exponent was Pilsudski) was an audacious, romantic scheme for the solution of the eastern borderlands question by the creation, at the expense of Russia, of a series of independent states—Lithuania, [ethnically] White Russia [just east of Poland], Ukraine—federated with, and under the hegemony of, Poland."[5] It harked back to the Polish kingdom's hoary days of glory. Now opportunity knocked, Warsaw believed. Having waited until the Red Army exhausted itself in combat with the Whites, Poland would pounce on Russia and rip vast domains from her bulky body. On April 26, 1920, Marshal Pilsudski announced that "the army of the Polish Republic has moved forward and penetrated deep into the Ukraine." Kiev, the ancient capital, fell on May 8.

The Red Army struck back; it recaptured Kiev on June 13. The Poles retreated toward their homeland with Russian regiments in hot pursuit. The Kremlin faced a fateful decision: should the Red Army invade Poland and push to Warsaw? Lenin answered yes; Trotsky said no; Radek warned Lenin against it. Lenin won. The Red Army, under General (later Marshal) Mikhail N. Tukhachevsky, age twenty-seven, advanced so rapidly on Warsaw that, as Pilsudski wrote, the Polish "government trembled"; Tukhachevsky's march was a "terrible kaleidoscope."[6] Meanwhile General Simeon M. Budenny's Red Cavalry army slashed southwest into Galicia. Poland seemed destined to become a Soviet satellite. In Moscow the Third (Communist) International or Comintern, meeting in its second congress—the first was the founder assembly in March, 1919—paid less attention to its proceedings than to the movement of the flags on a huge war map in the hall. The delegates thought they were seeing the dawn of world revolution. Large numbers

[4] Details in Fischer, *The Soviets in World Affairs,* Chap. VI.

[5] H. H. Fisher, *America and the New Poland,* p. 249.

[6] Joseph Pilsudski, *L'Année 1920, Edition complète avec le Texte de l'Ouvrage de M. Toukhatchevski "La Marche Au-de là Vistule" et les Notes Critiques du Bureau historique Militaire de Varsovie,* Traduit du Polonais, pp. 112-114.

of Soviet communists, who shared the enthusiasm of the foreign communists, yielded to the important added sentiment of nationalism. Communism is no vaccination against nationalism. A military confrontation with Poland was sure to release an upsurge of nationalist passions in Great Russians and Ukrainians irrespective of politics. Alexei A. Brusilov, an anti-Bolshevik general of the Tsar, volunteered his service to the Red Army and was accepted. He summoned White officers to join him; many did. In the Ukraine, and especially among the Cossacks, angry memories of epic battles with Poland, reflected in Russian literature, stirred in broad segments of the population when Pilsudski's divisions cut through to the heart of their country. Probably for the first time since November 7, 1917, Lenin sensed widespread popular support, something every supreme ruler appreciates.

Lenin's immediate goal was a communist Poland, in effect a return to Tsarist Russia's prewar frontiers. His ultimate goal was Germany, perhaps Europe.

Neither Germany nor the rest of the continent nor Britain had recuperated from the world war. War's devastation, ubiquitous cripples, mass unemployment among war heroes, and the failure of the statesmen at Versailles to devise a peace that looked stable created an atmosphere of hostility toward governments and ruling classes. Hopeless people suspected past politicians and distrusted present leaders. Despair fed rebellion. The vanquished were disgruntled. The victors, counting casualties in millions, were disappointed with the disproportionate gains. For Moscow this looked like an opportunity not to be missed.

Analyzing his Polish campaign in two lectures before the Military Academy in Moscow on February 7 and 10, 1923, Tukhachevsky said, "There can be no doubt that if we had been victorious on the Vistula the revolutionary fires would have reached the entire continent."[7]

Poland was weak, undernourished, underdeveloped, and ravaged by the first world war. In January, 1920, 34,000 cases of typhus were registered in the country. Herbert Hoover's American Relief Administration and other foreign agencies fed millions of hungry children and adults. Polish leaders dreamed of empire.

Pilsudski, knowing he could not win without massive non-Polish assistance, sent his Prime Minister, Vladislav Grabski, and Foreign Minister Patek to see Lloyd George. Grabski saw the British Prime Minister on July 10, 1920, and made his plea. Lloyd George noted that the Polish army was 125 miles east of its own frontier, on Ukrainian soil. Grabski could not deny this, but he added that the army was beginning a hasty

[7] *Ibid.*, pp. 230-232.

retreat in a state of thorough demoralization and the Russians would soon be in Poland.

Lloyd George realized that if Poland fell and the Bolsheviks became Germany's neighbors, the flimsy scaffolding of postwar Europe, so painfully constructed at Versailles, might collapse. He promised aid should Poland be invaded. The next day this British stand was communicated to Moscow by radio. On July 25 a special official British mission, led by Lord D'Abernon, Ambassador in Berlin, and including Sir Maurice Hankey, Secretary of the British Cabinet, and General Sir Percy Radcliffe of the British Imperial Staff arrived in Warsaw. The same day a French commission headed by Ambassador J. J. Jusserand and including General Weygand, Marshal Foch's chief of staff, reached Warsaw. The French and British were supplying the Polish army with munitions.

Earlier, French diplomacy had engaged in a subtle maneuver to bring Hungary into the war on Poland's side; it failed. Rumania likewise refused offers from Paris to join the fray; she feared the loss of Bessarabia, a province taken from Russia in January, 1918. She also suspected that the French scheme assumed the transfer of Rumanian territory to Hungary as a reward for doing battle for Polish imperialism.[8] To enable her Polish satellite to annex the Ukraine, France was ready to unscramble the old and paste together a new map of eastern Europe.

Meanwhile Tukhachevsky pressed on with "kaleidoscopic" speed. On July 20 British Foreign Secretary Lord Curzon warned Moscow not to allow its forces to cross the Curzon Line drawn by the Supreme Council in Paris on December 8, 1919; it ran from Grodno to Byalostok to Brest-Litovsk and then south along the Bug River. Deaf to restraint while triumph beckoned, Moscow paid no heed. Tukhachevsky crossed the line on July 27. On August 16 he stood at the Vistula. Across the river lay Warsaw. Three top-rank Soviet communists of Polish origin were already in the environs of the capital preparing to form the Soviet government of Poland.

So hopeless and chaotic did the Polish situation appear that the entire diplomatic corps, with the exception of the papal nuncio, Cardinal Ratti, later Pope Pius XI, left Warsaw for Posen. The D'Abernon and Jusserand missions fled too.

Tukhachevsky breathed on Warsaw. General Alexander I. Yegorov, with Stalin as his political commissar and Budenny's cavalry as his roughriding pathfinders, was thrashing through East Galicia toward Germany. Lenin had seized fate by the forelock.

Suddenly everything changed with the dramatic suddenness that

[8] Fischer, Chap. VI.

characterized the entire Polish-Russian war. Pilsudski struck at Tukhachevsky's flank. The Red Army, panting from its headlong drive to apparent victory, cracked. Some units avoided capture by choosing internment in East Prussia. Others fought their way back to Soviet territory at a heavy price in lives and equipment.

In his 1923 dissection of the debacle Tukhachevsky blamed Yegorov's army for not obeying repeated orders from staff headquarters to abandon its objective in East Galicia and turn north to succor the Red force outside Warsaw. Trotsky in exile published the text of these orders and charged Stalin with deliberately disobeying them.[9] (The Stalin-Trotsky feud, fruit of mutual revulsion, had commenced in 1918.)

Lenin knew that the military reverse was the result of his own political blunder. He confessed it to Clara Zetkin, a leader of the German Communist Party, when she visited Moscow in 1920.[10] She told him of the excitement among her party comrades when Soviet soldiers "in impossible old scraps of uniform and civilian clothes, in bast shoes or torn boots, spurred their small, brisk horses right up to the German frontier," and how the German bourgeoisie and petty bourgeoisie "with their reformist followers from the working class," observed these events "half pleased" because Poland, the "hereditary enemy," was being beaten, and "half afraid" because of the approach of the Red Army.

Lenin "sat silently for a few minutes" sunk in gloomy reflections. "Yes," he said at last, "so it has happened in Poland, as perhaps it had to happen. You know, of course, all the circumstances which were at work; that our recklessly brave, confident vanguard had no reserves of troops or munitions, and never once got even enough dry bread to eat. They had to requisition bread and other essentials from the Polish peasants and middle classes. And in the Red Army the Poles saw enemies, not brothers and liberators. They felt, thought, and acted not in a social, revolutionary way, but as nationalists, imperialists. The revolution in Poland on which we counted did not take place. The workers and peasants, deceived by the adherents of Pilsudski and [Ignatius] Daszynsky [Vice-Premier of Poland], defended their class enemy, let our brave Red soldiers starve, ambushed them and beat them to death."

"Radek," Lenin continued, "predicted how it would turn out. He warned us. I was very angry with him and accused him of 'defeatism.' But he was right in his main contentions. He knows affairs outside Russia, and particularly in the West, better than we do, and he is talented. He is very useful to us. We were reconciled a short while ago by a long political conversation over the telephone in the middle of the

[9] Trotsky, *My Life. An Attempt at an Autobiography,* p. 458.

[10] Klara Zetkin, *Reminiscences of Lenin,* pp. 18-23. The book was published in the Soviet Union as well as in Germany and other countries.

night, or rather towards morning."

Lenin had also been warned by Paul Levi, one of the two or three leaders of the German Communist Party. Brought together with Levi by Angelica Balabanoff in her Moscow apartment, Lenin was hardly seated when he put the question that obsessed him: "After the victorious entry of the Russian troops in Warsaw, how long will it take before the revolution breaks out in Germany?"

Paul Levi: "Three months, or three weeks; perhaps the revolution won't break out at all."[11]

Lenin shook his head, rose, and left.

Lenin had little or no personal vanity, but he was supremely self-confident, at times arrogant. In October and the first week of November, 1917, he had insisted that now was the time to make the revolution, now or never. He proved right. Later would have been never, Trotsky wrote.[12]

Having achieved this historic success in the face of skeptics, Lenin in 1920 scoffed at doubters; Radek was a "defeatist," Paul Levi irked him. He knew best because he believed in the invincibility of revolution and in its capacity, by drastic action, to convert men and alter allegiances. He therefore resolved to export revolution on the tips of sabers and bayonets.

The Poles' failure to welcome his army surprised Lenin. But the red cloak did not transform the Russian invader into a brother or the Cossack into a liberator any more than it concealed the tatters and rags of the eastern aggressor. Lenin might have remembered his own words. In a lecture delivered in Petrograd on May 27, 1917, first published in Moscow *Pravda* of April 23, 1929, he said, "Together those three crowned brigands [the monarchs of Russia, Prussia, and Austria-Hungary] partitioned Courland and Poland. They partitioned them for a century, they tore the living flesh, and the Russian brigand tore away more because at that time he was stronger." Lenin, furthermore, had declared in 1916 that "the proletariat does not become wholly insured against mistakes or weaknesses only because it has carried out a revolution." A victorious socialist proletarian revolution might be motivated by "selfish interest." It might try to "ride on somebody else's back."[13]

The same thoughts occurred to the Poles in 1920.

During the debate on the ratification of the Brest-Litovsk separate peace with Germany Lenin addressed a conference on January 21, 1918,

[11] Angelica Balabanoff, *Impressions of Lenin*, p. 111. Angelica Balabanoff had been a friend of Lenin in European exile and secretary of the Third International or Comintern.

[12] Leon Trotsky, *Lenin*, p. 87.

[13] Louis Fischer, *The Life of Lenin*, p. 93.

and asserted that if the Soviet government preferred revolutionary war to peace "we would be fighting, objectively, for the liberation of Poland, Lithuania, and Courland." Then he added, "but no Marxist who has not abandoned the basic ideas of Marxism and in general of socialism can deny that the interests of socialism stand higher than the interest of the rights of nations to self-determination."[14] Lenin was saying that the right to self-determination, of national independence, can be suppressed in the name of Marxism or socialism as embodied in the Soviet state. This Lenin legacy would justify Soviet imperialism and Soviet aggression. In another time and in other places it was "the white man's burden." Now it was the Red mission.

Lenin's "miscalculations" about a communist revolution in Poland stemmed from a failure to understand nationalism—including his own. He had reacted gleefully to Russia's defeat by Japan in 1905 and hoped for the defeat of Russia after 1914. Her setbacks would hasten the revolution. Lenin expected the Polish workers and peasants to feel as he did. Socialism, Marxism, or communism, however, is no emotional substitute for love of country. A nation is a nation and behaves like a nation no matter what adjective it prefixes to its name. The conduct of a nation in world affairs is shaped by geography; by economic development; by its culture and spiritual heritage; by armed strength and the readiness or reluctance of what President Dwight D. Eisenhower, in his White House valedictory, called "the military-industrial complex" to apply that strength to the aggrandizement of territory, power, or influence; by the fervor, real or manipulated, of its nationalism and the real or imagined feeling of national humiliation; by leadership and the extent of its response to the popular wishes, pressures, and needs; by correct, full, unhampered public access to information; by relations with foreign allies; by sensitivity to foreign opinion; and finally by the opportunities for good or evil beyond its borders. In 1920 Soviet Russia, feeble and friendless, its people yearning for peace after six years of war and its deluded leaders pursuing the mirage of proletarian revolutions abroad, gambled big and lost.

Though Lenin's gamble was not repeated, the Marxist reasoning that caused him to blunder survived; communists dissect situations by the criteria of class—they "class-angle" everything. A workingman must see and react to events in one way, a millionaire in a very different way. This is often true; class cleavages do exist. But during the Nazi blitz on London in the second world war, lord and plumber joined to fire-watch together "for Britain." The assassination of a President unites a people in an abiding emotion. Patriotism, religion, and sentimental attachment to

[14] *Ibid.*, p. 193.

a person may paper over or cement together that which class might divide. The Kremlin fully understood this in the 1930's and yielded to no government in the exploitation of nationalism and even racism (Pan-Slavism). Yet Marxist dogma continued to obstruct correct analysis of international politics.

* * *

Baron Wrangel took advantage of Bolshevik preoccupation with Poland to leave his Crimean bottle and advance into the Ukraine. Early in June, 1920, he captured the Ukrainian city of Melitopol on the main railway line to Kharkov. Instead of encouraging Wrangel to divide the Soviet forces by continuing his progress northward, the British government used his offensive action as an excuse to wash its hands of him. "Cabinet consider that Wrangel's action in taking offensive releases us from our responsibilities towards him," the Admiralty telegraphed to the Commander in Chief, Mediterranean, on June 11. "British naval forces are therefore to be strictly neutral and are to afford no repeat no support to Wrangel in offence or defence."[15] The same day the British Mission in Constantinople reported: "Admiral de Robeck is informed that the British Military Mission is to be withdrawn from the Crimea without delay, and also British ships from the Crimean waters."[16]

Wrangel pleaded for a continuation of aid; the situation at the front was favorable. "We can do nothing to assist Wrangel," the War Office replied on July 30. Lord Curzon concurred.[17]

This was the last illogical act in the illogical western crusade against Bolshevism.

V THE SCHIZOID KREMLIN

The Russian retreat from Poland and the defeat of Baron Wrangel, the last of the Whites, in November, 1920, inaugurated an eighteen-year period of peace for the Soviet regime. Japan still held territory in the Russian Far East and a few bands of anti-Bolshevik guerrillas operated here and there. But fighting soon ceased altogether. The Kremlin could

[15] British Foreign Office Documents 371/3982. Admiralty Telegram No. 21Z.

[16] *Ibid.*, G.M. 273.

[17] *Ibid.*, 371/3984. War Office. Copies supplied by the Public Record Office, London.

now attempt to implement the peacetime foreign policy that had been maturing in Lenin's brain for some time. His word was not law (he had to persuade), but nobody in the country compared with him in power and authority.

Lenin once said—April 3, 1919—"If I am pursuing an adversary who moves not in a straight line but in zigzags, I must also, in order to overtake that adversary, move in zigzags." Moving in zigzags in response to many adversaries executing conflicting zigzags can hardly be conducive to a fruitful foreign policy, especially when it is based on mistaken ideas about world affairs. Speaking in Moscow on March 1, 1920, for instance, Lenin declared, with habitual communist exaggeration, "Japan and America are on the eve of war, and there is no possibility of preventing such a war in which more tens of millions will die and twenty million will be mutilated."[1]

Nine months later Lenin used the same sensational prediction as the centerpiece of a larger portrait of the international scene.[2] He saw three "basic contradictions in the contemporary capitalist world." The first, "the nearest to us, is the relation between Japan and America. A war between them is being prepared . . . It is inescapable, that is indubitable."

The second "contradiction which we must make use of" is "the contradiction between America and the rest of the capitalist world." America was hated everywhere, he found, and, consequently, there was a mounting demand in the United States for an agreement with the Soviets. "America cannot make peace with the rest of Europe—that is a fact demonstrated by history." Ergo, America would link her fortunes to Soviet Russia, and not in the remote future but soon. When the Soviets conclude their trade treaty with Great Britain, Lenin wrote to Chicherin on November 19, 1920, "America will immediately join." The treaty was signed on March 16, 1921. America did not join immediately or ever.

"And the third contradiction is between the Entente and Germany." In this projection Lenin hit the bull's-eye. Unable to live under the terms imposed by the Versailles peace, Lenin elaborated, "Germany must seek an ally against world imperialism." He named the ally on October 2, 1920, in a post-mortem analysis of his egregious blunder in Poland: "If Poland had become a soviet country . . . the Versailles Peace would have been destroyed, and the entire international system achieved by victories over Germany would have collapsed. France would then not have had a buffer [Poland] separating Germany from Soviet Russia. . . . The situation was that, given several more days of victorious progress by the Red Army, not only would Warsaw have been taken (that would not have

[1] Louis Fischer, *The Life of Lenin*, p. 386.
[2] *Ibid.*, pp. 424-428.

been so important) but the Versailles Peace would have been ruined." This would have indicated to the Germans, he said, "that in its struggle for survival, the Soviet Republic was the only force in the world that was combating imperialism—and imperialism now means the alliance of France, England, and America."[3]

To make the French and British look less formidable and a German alliance with Russia more alluring, Lenin added that France was "on the way to bankruptcy" and—equally untrue—even the old leaders of the British workers "who formerly opposed the dictatorship of the working class have now come over to our side."

Lenin directed his offer of an alliance at Germans nursing the wounds of defeat, some of whom Radek had christened "national Bolsheviks." Their opposition to imperialism as embodied in the Versailles peace treaty differed little in intent from communist anti-imperialism. The extremes touch; right meets left.

Communism, like capitalism, was ensnared in a contradiction; while ready to aid German militarists and militant nationalists, Moscow encouraged German communism. The Kremlin shuttled between black and red. For a time Radek contemplated marrying the two color strains to produce a hybrid progeny. His superiors preferred the strange dichotomy. But the large German Communist Party, dancing puppet-like to a Russian tune, did help bring the National Socialists (Nazis) to power, and then the vestiges of Versailles tumbled into the abyss of Hitler's anti-imperialist imperialism.

Lenin's December 6, 1920, speech on the three contradictions was a defense of his policy of granting economic concessions to big foreign capitalists and specifically a concession for mining rights in the Kamchatka peninsula (in the Russian Far East north of Japan) to Washington Baker Vanderlip, Jr., an American representing, so he said, great U.S. business interests. "At the present time," Lenin had announced on October 2, 1920, "an American billionaire (Washington B. Vanderlip) is in Moscow negotiating with us for concessions on Kamchatka. By granting this concession, we aggravate the relations between Japan and America."

In the war that Lenin saw coming soon, "we communists," he asserted on December 6, 1920, "must use one country against the other. Are we committing a crime against communism? No, for we are doing this as a socialist state conducting communist propaganda and compelled to use every hour given it by circumstances to grow strong with maximum speed. . . . We must use the situation that has been created. That is the essence of the Kamchatka concession."

[3]*Ibid.*, pp. 400-401.

The Soviet state could do anything, even aggravate the relations between two major powers on the eve of a war in which tens of millions would die. It salved its conscience by engaging in communist propaganda and found comfort in the assurance that Russia would benefit. Perhaps the capitalist nations did not deserve better at the hands of the Bolsheviks. Perhaps Lenin was playing the game of power politics as other governments had played it. Nations must be selfish (though sometimes the best selfishness is unselfishness). But there are degrees of selfishness, and surely the highest degree is reached when a state deliberately undertakes to hasten the coming of an Armageddon with millions of casualties.

The wave of the future arrogates to itself the right to drown the present. Proof is written large in Soviet history.

* * *

Lenin's goal in the proposed Vanderlip concession was largely political, for Kamchatka was then under Japanese occupation and Vanderlip had promised that, as Lenin reported it, "If you sell us Kamchatka, I give you a guarantee that the enthusiasm of the American people will be so great that we will grant you diplomatic recognition." Despite the wild claim of the would-be concessionaire, Lenin took it seriously; "We must grab this with both hands," he told his audience.

He likewise proposed pooling the world's raw materials. "For us it is important," he said, "that there be no famine anywhere. You capitalists cannot eliminate it. We can. . . . We undertake to restore the international economy—here is our plan." Soviet Russia, further would tell the capitalists of the world, "you are no good . . . isn't it time, gentlemen, for you to reach an understanding with us?" And the world capitalists (Lenin thought of them as either invading Russia or negotiating with Russia as a collective) would reply, "Why, indeed, it is time, let us sign a trade agreement."

Here was the schizoid Kremlin saving capitalism while plotting to destroy it. Here was Lenin, normally shrewd and preaching "practicality," desperately concocting naïve schemes. Russia lay in ruins. World war, civil war, intervention, revolution, Soviet mismanagement, and communist policy had brought the country to the brink of economic collapse and inflicted unimaginable suffering on its people. Russia lost 1.7 million soldiers in the first world war and a corresponding number of wounded. The civil war took fewer casualties—there is no exact count—but it did more damage to the nation's economy and morale. Some cities and their hinterland in the Ukraine changed hands seventeen times; each new army introduced its own paper currency which peasants, workers, and merchants were forced to accept in return for their labor and produce. When the next conqueror took over, that currency became so much trash and the process was repeated—again and again. The retreating army, moreover, conscripted the young men of the area and took them away. Advancing and retiring armies also confiscated grain, leaving tillers neither food nor seed. Urban dwellers carried gramophones, chinaware, samovars, cooking utensils, carpets, icons, used clothing, and shoes to villagers and exchanged them for scarce food. Trains carrying these "bagmen" back to town were often pillaged by hungry people turned bandits. Workingmen, who had no possessions to exchange, organized armed squads and, with encouragement from Lenin, descended on the peasantry and seized their reserves. Tired of state and squad requisitions, the peasantry sowed less and invited famine to lay its bony hand on them and the entire country. Russians thought and talked food. The February, 1921, Moscow Expanded Conference of Metal Workers discussed not wages, not hours, not the function of their organization, but food, and demanded that Lenin come talk to them about it. He said, "The root question for the Soviet government is that after our victory we still do not have victories in other countries . . . there is not one European who has visited our country who says that they could have managed without ragged people and 'queues' or that England, after six years of war, did not suffer from similar conditions." (The communist refrain to this day runs, It's as bad or worse under capitalism.) "This winter," Lenin admitted, "the peasants are in a desperate situation." The peasant must "sow all the land, otherwise we perish—inescapably." He promised nothing; he had nothing.

The workers' plight was just as sad. With matches in short supply, factory hands spent much working time making simple cigarette lighters for sale on the black market. This became so widespread a phenomenon that the party and government tried—unsuccessfully—to deal with it. Industry lacked raw materials, electric current, and fuel. Industrial output fell. Pig iron production dropped to less than 4 percent of the 1914 figure. Unemployment rose. Strikes multiplied.

To make extremely bad matters worse, the railroads were crippled. Lenin said, "The railway transport position is catastrophic. Bread transport to Moscow has ceased." He decreed a ration cut for nontransport workers and an increase for transport workers. "Let thousands perish," he said, "but the country must be saved."

Trotsky studied the situation and in February, 1920, told the communist party's Central Committee that Bolshevik policy had to be altered drastically. He proposed a tax in place of grain requisitioning, and the restoration of a free market where peasants could trade legally. Lenin attacked the proposals and they were voted down 4 to 11.[4]

A year of suffering followed. Peasant revolts swept the country. One

[4] Leon Trotsky, *My Life. An Attempt at an Autobiography,* p. 464.

which began in the province of Tambov in October, 1920, gained so many recruits that Lenin sent cavalry to reinforce the infantry in suppressing it. For months shipments of grain from Siberia to European Russia were blocked by other peasant insurrections. "Somebody," Lenin asserted on February 28, 1921, "spoke of taxes. This makes a lot of sense." Taxes instead of arbitrary requisitions. Just what Trotsky had urged in February, 1920.

Taxes in place of grain requisitions and a free market were the essence of the New Economic Policy. The NEP was adopted before the Kronstadt rebellion, which commenced on February 28, 1921, and lasted until the island fortress fell after sanguinary battles on March 18. The Central Committee had sanctioned the reform on February 24, 1921, but Lenin delayed the announcement until the eve of the sowing season, "that is, right after the party Congress" due to meet the next month.

Russia's Bolsheviks had hoped for salvation through foreign revolution. They were encouraged when the Hungarian communists, led by Bela Kun, established a Red regime in Budapest on March 21, 1919. Bavaria followed suit a fortnight later—April 5. The Bavarian soviets, however, fell within weeks and Bela Kun's government succumbed to inner weaknesses and outside pressures on August 1, 1919. Moscow planned to rescue it by dispatching troops across Rumania, but it lacked the reserve strength. Disappointed, Lenin decided to give Poland a revolutionary push with the butt of the Russian soldier's rifle. This too failed. Russia would now have to avert disaster by the limited restoration of domestic capitalism or NEP.

The Soviet communists were ready to salvage world capitalism in order to save their state. They were ready to destroy world capitalism to save their state. They were ready to restore a considerable measure of Russian capitalism to save their state.

With the exception of some idealistic Russian communists who thought Lenin was selling them down the river into the dead sea of capitalism, the Soviet population welcomed the NEP: the peasantry because it freed them from the confiscation of their crops and permitted them to sell; the workers because they were, for a time, paid part of their wages in kind, say textiles, which they could barter for farm produce and, too, because it contained the promise of more food; the merchants or Nepmen who hoped to make money; the bureaucrats and party members because they expected the new dispensations to ease their task of governing a near-paralyzed nation.

In contrast, the granting of mining, lumbering, and manufacturing concessions to foreign capitalists aroused frenetic opposition. During the Eighth Congress of Soviets in December, 1920, Lenin assembled a caucus of communist delegates to discuss the question. "Wouldn't concessions amount to a recognition that world capitalism still had a long lease on life and that hopes for an early world revolution were unjustified?" one delegate asked.

". . . Our existence," Lenin replied, "and the hastening of our escape from a critical situation and from hunger is a gigantic force and a revolutionary factor much greater . . . than the few pennies they will earn from us."

"If American unemployment is accelerating revolution, don't we, by granting concessions, enable America to get through the crisis, that is, we retard the revolution?"

Lenin: ". . . The crisis of capitalism grows month by month, disintegration in the whole world proceeds further and further and only in Russia has an upward trend commenced toward a stable and serious improvement."[5]

Wishful thinking, delusion, fear, xenophobia, and nationalistic megalomania dominated Soviet foreign policy. Unreality permeated even the highest ranks of the party leadership. The Cabinet sanctioned negotiations for concessions in Baku and Grozny, then the only two large Russian oil fields, on February 1, 1921. That month the party's Central Committee debated the issue. Members sent scribbled notes up to Lenin, who presided. Alexei I. Rykov, chairman of the Supreme Council of National Economy, Lenin's successor as a prime minister, and usually regarded as a "rightist," wrote, "We are in a position to teach Europe. . . . We can do everything ourselves." Next, a note from Stalin was passed up to Lenin: "they will pump water, not oil . . . The proposal is frivolous, not thought out . . . The workers cannot be convinced." Mikhail P. Tomsky, head of the Soviet trade unions, contradicted Stalin in his note: "The workers will succumb . . . It's better next door," they would say, better under capitalism. Trotsky backed Lenin. At a subsequent meeting on March 28, Lenin tossed a letter to Trotsky with a note: "Look at this, (interesting), and return it to me." The letter was from Kharkov and protested the idea of opening the Donets Coal Basin to foreign concessionaires. "Isn't it interesting about concessions," the Lenin memo continued, "Baku and Donets-Basin (plus Krivoi Rig)"—iron deposits—"to concessionaires is most desirable. Your opinion?"

Trotsky wrote on the back of Lenin's note: "There is no reason to exclude the Donets Basin from concessions."[6]

[5] The text of this question-and-answer quiz was first published in the Moscow monthly *Kommunist* for April, 1963, on the authority of the Institute of Marxism-Leninism which said in an introduction, "V. I. Lenin accepted concessions as permissible in principle as one of the forms of state capitalism."

[6] These notes have been preserved and are published in *Leninskii Sbornik* (Lenin Miscellany), Vol. XX, p. 147. Quoted in Fischer, p. 475.

Washington Baker Vanderlip was still on the scene. Lenin wrote Chicherin in April, 1921, "Has it been explained to Vanderlip that we could grant Americans a concession to *tremendous* oil fields (Baku, Grozny, Emba, Ukhta) and that Americans would thereby beat England? Telephone as soon as you have read this."[7]

Thus Lenin's concept of the Vanderlip concessions envisaged Russian aid to America to beat Japan and Russian aid to America to beat England—a misreading of the world scene.

Lenin struck back at Rykov. Was the Bolshevik economic strategy to be "we can do it ourselves? or is this leftist infantilism, or foolish doctrinairism?" Concessions to one fourth of the Soviet oil fields, he continued, would be "ideal for training" and would permit the communists to overtake capitalist techniques. In fifteen years, he added, the Kremlin could buy out the concessionaires and "in thirty years . . . world victory" —for the revolution—"is guaranteed."[8] Thirty years would have been 1951.

Presently Lenin faced the reality of famine. On July 13 Maxim Gorky, the popular Russian author, appealed to "all honest people" for prompt aid to the Russian nation; "Give bread and medicine," he cried. This evoked an immediate favorable response from Herbert Hoover's American Relief Administration (ARA) which had been feeding the hungry in Belgium, Hungary, Poland, and elsewhere. Its operations from September, 1921, to July, 1923, saved millions of lives in the Ukraine and in the Volga Valley.

On March 21, 1921, shortly after he became Secretary of Commerce, in the administration of President Warren G. Harding, and shortly after the NEP was introduced, Hoover had said, "The question of trade with Russia is far more a political question than an economic one so long as Russia is under the control of the Bolsheviks. Under their economic system, no matter how much they moderate in name, there can be no real production in Russia, and, therefore, Russia will have no considerable quantities to export, and, consequently, no great ability to obtain imports." Maxim Gorky's appeal for famine relief seemed to reinforce Hoover's prejudiced prophecy and both tended to discourage American businessmen and potential concessionaires but not the Soviet government. Through the Far Eastern (Chita) Republic, which everybody knew to be a Kremlin puppet—yet the puppetry made a difference, and Chita's representative (Boris Skvirsky) was permitted to function openly in Washington for many years—the Soviet government signed an agreement with the Sinclair Exploration Company for the exploitation of the oil resources of northern Sakhalin, then under Japanese occupation,

[7] *Ibid.*, Vol. XXXVI, p. 215. Fischer, p. 510.
[8] *Ibid.*, pp. 194-197. Fischer, p. 510.

and the right to build two ports on the island's east coast facing Japan. Meanwhile, the offer of mining rights in Kamchatka, with a base for the U.S. navy opposite Japan thrown into the bargain, still stood. The communist credo says a capitalist state is controlled by capitalists and since Harry F. Sinclair, and allegedly Vanderlip, had friends in the Harding Cabinet, Moscow hoped views other than Hoover's would prevail. They did not. The Sinclair company never worked its concessions and Vanderlip never got his.

The most serious attempt to win a large concession from the Kremlin was made by Leslie Urquhart, chairman of the Russo-Asiatic Corporation which, before the Bolshevik revolution, had mined gold, silver, copper, lead, and zinc in a vast area in the Ural and Altai regions. In 1921 Urquhart came to Moscow and asked to have his properties back in the form of a concession. Urquhart carried considerable economic and political weight in Great Britain; he was a member of the British government delegation to the international Genoa Conference in April, 1922. The concession was actually signed on September 9, 1922, in Berlin by Urquhart and Leonid B. Krassin, former Soviet trade treaty negotiator in London. But in the end Urquhart never received the concession.

Three times Lenin changed his mind about Urquhart. In June, 1922, Lenin wrote Krassin in London, "We agree to grant a concession to all our enterprises" in Siberia. For the rest, Lenin's instructions to the envoy were expressed in one word: "Bargain." Bargain about the size of the concession and its duration; bargain about the percentage of the mined products to go to the Soviet government. (Krassin had suggested 25 percent.) Lenin consented to clothe Urquhart's foreign personnel with "immunity" from arrest and harassment but expected Urquhart to help the Soviets acquire British machinery for their own mines.

But when Lenin saw the contract Krassin had signed with Urquhart in Berlin he exploded. "It is slavery and robbery," he wrote Stalin. "While promising us income in two or three years, Urquhart takes money from us immediately." The supreme Political Bureau (Politburo) of the party considered the issue at three sessions: September 14, 21, and 28. Lenin's proposal to reject encountered vehement opposition from members of the small body. On October 5, 1922, the larger Central Committee of the party accordingly considered the matter and, yielding to Lenin, voted to reject.[9] Uppermost in Lenin's mind was his fear of a tacit alliance between resurgent Russian NEP capitalism and foreign capitalism.

In 1922 the NEP was reviving the national economy. Peasants, taking heart, began to sow more. Nepmen were growing rich. Lenin wondered

[9] Fischer, pp. 605-614.

how this would affect even his closest associates in the communist party leadership. A hot controversy over the monopoly of foreign trade revealed what troubled him.

The monopoly, introduced in 1918 and functioning to this day as a main prop of the Soviet system, makes the Soviet government the sole importer and exporter; no Soviet individual and no foreign person, company, or state can participate in Soviet foreign trade except through an official Moscow agency.

However, the wish to expand foreign trade led Stalin, supported by Finance Commissar Gregory Y. Sokolnikov, but opposed by Foreign Trade Commissar Krassin, to urge a relaxation of the monopoly. The very session of the Central Committee which, on Lenin's forceful insistence, turned down the Urquhart concession, approved a measure the next day—October 6—providing for free entry ports at Petrograd and at Novorossisk on the Black Sea. Lenin had absented himself on account of "this damned tooth." (He was just back at work after his first stroke.) A week later he sent Stalin an angry protest. He pictured the concrete situation that would arise: "Purchasing offices are opened [by foreigners] for import and export. Where then is the control? Where are the means of control? The price of flax in Russia is four and a half rubles, in England fourteen rubles . . . what force will restrain the peasants and [NEP] merchants from profitable transactions? . . . On such a matter, 'legality' in peasant Russia is absolutely impossible."[10] The muzhik would find a path to the foreign exporter's door.

Communism's first commandment reads, Thou shalt have no other power but mine. The Soviet monopoly of foreign trade is a facet of the communist monopoly of political power. Lenin, knowing Trotsky agreed, asked him to defend their views at the next plenary session of the Central Committee. What occurred is reflected in a letter dated December 21, 1922, Lenin dictated to his wife: "Comrade Trotsky, it seems we succeeded in taking the position without a single shot by a simple maneuver. I propose we do not stop and continue the attack. . . . N. Lenin.[11] The "simple maneuver" was Trotsky's appearance as Lenin's spokesman. Lenin proposed they continue the attack against Stalin on other burning issues.

The NEP, which lived until the end of 1928, confronted the schizoid Kremlin with pointed dilemmas. It wanted the peasants to grow more but not to grow richer. It wanted Nepmen to produce on a small scale and foreign concessionaires to produce on a larger scale lest citizens in misery threaten the regime's power, yet it did not want private capital-

[10] V. I. Lenin, *Sochinenia* (Collected Works), Vol. 22: *December 1915-July 1916*, pp. 338-341. Fischer, p. 635.

[11] From the Trotsky Archive in the Houghton Library of Harvard University, T.770. Copy supplied.

ism to get big enough to become a rival power. It wanted to import and export but it put foreign trade in a monopoly straitjacket so as to protect the party dictatorship. It wanted to trade with Great Britain, the greatest western nation that would trade with Russia, but it irritated England by a foreign policy in Asia which reduced the trade.

The United States was not interested in Soviet commerce and hostile despite Moscow's dangling of concessions and strategic plums near Japan. France was even more hostile, and bitter about the loss of her large investments by small investors and big capitalists in Tsarist Russia. Germany, Sweden, and Italy among others were doing business with the Soviets but the scope was limited. Real help to rehabilitate Soviet industry could come quickest from the British Isles. Here, however, Soviet foreign policy stepped on the toes of the Soviet economy. The Soviet system is thought to be monolithic. Nothing human is.

* * *

Two decades after the 1920's the world became conscious of the "Cold War" between the Soviet Union and the West, specifically between the Soviet Union and the United States, and historians debated whether the Cold War commenced in 1945, during President Franklin D. Roosevelt's lifetime, or in 1947. An earlier cold war between the Soviets and their opponents followed the hot war of foreign intervention from 1918 to 1920. That intervention had its roots in nineteenth-century antagonisms between England and Russia over Central Asia and between the Tsarist empire and the expanding Japanese empire. When the shooting ceased, the antagonism remained. The Soviet Union, underdeveloped economically and militarily, had little power. It accordingly availed itself of a new-age weapon: revolution. In the early post-1917 years it fomented revolution. Subsequently it merely preached revolution though all the signs were unfavorable.

In November, 1922, during the Fourth Congress of the Third International (Comintern), when noncommunist journalists were still admitted to the public deliberations, I was leaving a session in the throne room of the Tsar's palace in the Kremlin—just behind Gregory Zinoviev, the Comintern chief, and saw him put his arm around the waist of a man and heard him say in German, "Na, wann kommt die soziale Revolution in der Schweiz?" ("when is the socialist revolution coming in Switzerland?"). I could not observe whether Zinoviev or the Swiss communist or both laughed. Switzerland was, and probably is, the least congenial place for the eruption of a communist revolution. Yet there and elsewhere Moscow, in its impotence, answered the cold war of its enemies with the only arms in its arsenal: the pale specter of a proletarian uprising and, in the East, encouragement to awakening nations.

VI EAST IS TRUMP IN MOSCOW

The Soviet Commissariat of Foreign Affairs included westerners and easterners. The westerners did not ignore the East, they merely did not wish to obstruct fruitful relations with the great capitalist nations of the West by crudely courting the peoples of Asia. Nor did the easterners turn their backs on all of Europe.

The leading Westerner was Deputy Commissar Maxim M. Litvinov—tough, gruff, sometimes obscene in his language, and always firm, forthright, courageous. He would challenge the views of his superior, Foreign Commissar Georgi V. Chicherin, and on one occasion banged the table while talking back to Stalin. In a land where the big and little lie was both policy and shield, Litvinov told the truth oftener than most, and at times it was sensational. Subordinates entered his office with trepidation, never knowing whether he would upbraid or praise. But he staunchly defended them against the secret police and saved the lives of several during the period of the "cult of personality," Kremlin euphemism for Stalin's awesome terror. He could be friendly to foreigners and was extremely tender to his two children, Misha and Tanya, who frequently sat on the broad arms of his chair as he talked to me at home about the international scene. Mrs. Litvinov—Ivy—regularly embarrassed him by making loud, biting comments on Soviet leaders and decrees in the presence of diplomats and foreign journalists. He never succeeded in curbing her; she was as irrepressibly ebullient as he. Litvinov belonged to an older generation of Bolsheviks who protected their prerevolutionary ideals against the cynicism that luxuriated in Red soil. But he refused to defect to the West. A second emigration, this time not from the ghetto of Tsarist Russia but from a high post in the country he had expected to fulfill his dreams, lacked attraction.

Chicherin was of different stuff. He belonged to a family, originally Italian (Cicerone), which had close ties through marriage to Russian royalty. His mother was a Narishkin; Natalya Narishkin, of Tartar descent, was Peter the Great's mother. A native of Tambov province, Chicherin mingled Tartar, Polish and Russian blood. His voice was thin and high, his manner gentle. Yet he had bulldog persistence, and when he held an opinion he would not relinquish it; he pressed it on others, on

Lenin, on foreign governments, until they accepted it or totally rejected it. He was a shrewd, highly intelligent intellectual who read and spoke French, English, German, and Italian. He engaged in hardly any physical activity, he never walked (his figure showed it), and gave no evidence of interest in women or men. Next to foreign politics, his passion was music. He played the piano like a professional and reveled in Mozart, the subject of his only book. The Kremlin blocked its publication: a Bolshevik leader writing about a composer!

To Chicherin England was the enemy. She had been the enemy in Tsarist times and again during the 1918-1920 period of foreign intervention. Japan ranked as coenemy number one. Commissar Chicherin accordingly cultivated Turkey, Iran, and Afghanistan, which he regarded as objects of British imperial ambitions, and China. A strong China might act as a counterweight to Japan and England. In Europe Chicherin wanted good relations with Germany and Lithuania; Lithuania because Poland, another enemy, coveted some of her territory, and Germany for several reasons: Marx and Engels, the fathers of "scientific" socialism, were Germans, and most Bolshevik leaders knew German and Germany and admired German technical proficiency and military prowess. Moreover, post-1918 Germany was a pariah among the nations, so too Soviet Russia; Germany needed Russian raw materials and trade, Russia needed German skills, credits, markets. Both countries harbored a resentment against France and England. In foreign politics the pattern is: the enemy of my enemy is my friend.

Great Britain, however, had skills to offer and credits as well. Litvinov contended that it did not serve communism's purposes to antagonize England by courting minor powers like Turkey, Iran, and Afghanistan, which wanted Russia as a balance against the West. Moscow, however, desired successes. Chicherin produced them in the East. Litvinov would have liked to tip the scales toward the West by opening commercial and political doors to the United States. Early in Soviet history he wrote Lenin from London asking for authority to go to Washington as a special envoy, and Lenin sent him a credential dated June 21, 1918; the U.S.A. refused him a visa. The trip was delayed until 1933.

The gates to the East, on the other hand, and to Germany, were wide open. The period, therefore, from 1918 to 1929 might be called the Chicherin Era of Soviet foreign relations.

* * *

No sooner had the Bolsheviks seized power and appealed to the belligerent governments of the West to end the war than they appealed to the peoples of the East to overthrow those governments. The Council of People's Commissars (Cabinet), sitting in Petrograd, issued a proclamation on December 3, 1917, to the "Laboring Moslems of Russia and the East," signed by Lenin as Chairman of the Council and by Stalin as Commissar of Nationalities; it called on the faithful to rise up against their "oppressors" and end foreign domination in all colonies. It announced that "Constantinople must remain in the hands of the Moslems," that the treaty of August 31, 1907, between the Tsar's regime and Great Britain dividing Persia "is torn up and annulled," and that the agreement to partition Turkey and seize Armenia "is torn up and annulled."[1]

On September 1, 1920, Gregory Zinoviev, addressing the "First Congress of the Peoples of the East," at Baku exclaimed, "The Communist International turns to you today and says, 'Brothers, we summon you to a holy war first of all against British Imperialism.' " The 1,891 delegates —Hindus, Turks, Turkomans, Bokharans, Uzbeks, Ingushi, Persians, Chechentsi, Tadjiks, Armenians, Jews, Russians, Georgians, and others —sprang to their feet, lifted aloft studded daggers and naked swords and shouted, "Jehad, Jehad. We swear, we swear." Lenin called them "The infantry of the East" who, joining the "Cavalry of the West"—the working class—would demolish capitalism and imperialism.

The "First Congress of the Peoples of the East" was the last. In 1920 and throughout the 1920's and 1930's India looked to Gandhi, not to Lenin, to nonviolent civil disobedience, not violent revolution. There and elsewhere nationalism rode high. Communism had no chance. The communists tried. Stalin tried in Persia, a neighbor of his native Georgia.

In a resolution dated November 7, 1920, and written by Lenin, the Politburo ordered "an extremely conciliatory policy toward Georgia, Armenia, Turkey, and Persia, directed above all, that is, to the avoidance of war."[2] Georgia was then still ruled by the anti-Bolshevik socialist Mensheviks. After the Bolsheviks occupied Georgia, Lenin wrote a letter on March 2, 1921, to Sergo Orjonekidze, the Georgian leader, urging a "coalition government with Mensheviks."[3] Though Lenin hated all Mensheviks, he wished to smooth the task of governing. The Mensheviks represented Georgian nationalism. Lenin put practicality above ideology.

Even before the Soviet annexation of Georgia, Stalin and Orjonekidze, who scorned a bloc with the Mensheviks, had, in contravention of Lenin's specific command, sent Red troops into the north Persian province of Ghilan in 1920 and sovietized it. Lenin reprimanded Stalin at a

[1] U.S.S.R. Ministry of Foreign Affairs, *Dokumenty Vneshnei Politiki SSSR* (Documents on the Foreign Policy of the U.S.S.R.). Vol. I: *November 7, 1917-December 31, 1918*, pp. 34-35.

[2] *Leninskii Sbornik* (Lenin Miscellany), Vol. XXXVI, p. 144.

[3] Lenin, *Polnoye Sobranye Sochinenii* (Complete Works), Fifth ed., Vol. 42, p. 367.

session of the Politburo, and the troops were withdrawn in May-June, 1921, in accordance with the Soviet-Persian treaty of February 26, 1921. (As a result, the British abandoned their plan to establish a "South Persian Federation.") By the terms of the treaty the Soviet government nevertheless retained the right to return its armed forces to North Persia if Britain established a military base in the South.[4]

Had Soviet troops remained in Persia, the British would have remained too, and the effect would have been to partition the country and exacerbate Bolshevism's relations with England at a time when the Kremlin possessed little reserve strength to resume the historic rivalry with Britain in Central Asia. The Kremlin, in addition, was eager to expand trade with the West. A trade treaty had been signed with Britain on March 16, 1921, and the Soviets expected British credits to renovate their industries. Irritation in Persia might have closed purses in London.

A basic Leninist proposition motivated Moscow's Persian policy: a communist revolution must be staged by the proletariat, and Persia was an underdeveloped country with only a handful of factory-employed, class-conscious proletarians. The sovietization of northern Persia meant its annexation, and though Stalin was ready in 1920 to start Soviet Russia on her career of imperialism, Lenin, after his painful Polish experience, was not.

Stalin also differed with Lenin and the entire Bolshevik leadership on Soviet policy toward Turkey. The Turks had, in pursuance of the Brest-Litovsk peace treaty, occupied Baku and Batum. The latter belonged to Stalin's native Georgia, and his nature was not forgiving. He lacked the power, however, to interfere with the knitting of intimate Turko-Soviet relations in the early years of Soviet history.

There are few rules in international politics; its essence is instability. Governments are fickle. Nevertheless, one rule has the sanction of history: when Russia, whether monarchist or communist, is strong and expansionist, Turkey is afraid and hostile; when Russia is feeble and recessive, or sated and turned inward, she and the Turks can be friends. A powerful Russia wants the Turkish Straits open. A weak Russia wants them closed.

In 1920 Russia and Turkey were weak. The Turkish Empire had commenced to decline before the nineteenth century; it died in the first world war. Turkey lost all her Arab colonies—everything except Turkish Anatolia in Asia and Constantinople, renamed Istanbul, and a narrow hinterland in Europe. Nothing better could have happened to Turkey. Something else happened that was just as good: Mustapha Kemal Pasha (Ataturk). The loss of empire and Kemal cured the "sick man of

[4] Louis Fischer, *The Soviets in World Affairs,* Chap. XIII.

Europe," as Tsar Nicholas I called Turkey in 1853 when he, ruler of a powerful Russia, coveted the patient's possessions.

Ataturk, professional soldier, political physician, was Paris and the wild Anatolian plateau, gentleman and Tamerlane. Though head of state and dictator, he would vanish for days into a limbo of sex-drink-and-card-playing orgies only to reappear in an explosion of creative turbulence and a prophet's reforming zeal. Intemperate and tempestuous, he rode his horse into the hearts of a people close enough to the primitive to admire his daring and masculine stamina and the unconventionality with which he swept away the effete sultanate with its eunuchs and bureaucrats and the ossified caliphate with its backward-looking servitors. Kemal was a rebel. He broke precedents and heads with equal abandon. Cast in a hero's mold, he gave the nation the feeling of living an epic.

Ataturk prohibited the veil, the harem, and polygamy, replaced the cursive Arab script so conducive to illiteracy with an adapted Latin alphabet, substituted Sunday for Friday as the Moslem Sabbath, ordered the muezzin called in Turkish rather than Arabic, proscribed the fez, and fostered European dress. His most popular photograph, displayed in public places and engraved on the national currency, shows him in white tie and tails, the furthest remove from the traditional caricature of Turkey in baggy trousers, fez, and moccasins with curled-up toes. He shifted the capital from the Asiatic city of Constantinople on the lip of Europe to Ankara high on the brow of Asia, where he built a European city. Since private-enterprise money was scarce in the wreck of war, he created a system of state capitalism with state-subsidized industries and government monopolies for matches, tobacco, salt, alcohol, and other products.

All this and more was revolution enough, and, what with the imprisonment of anybody called a communist, Turkey remained immune to communism. Moscow showed no displeasure. Even before the Soviet-Turkish Treaty of March 16, 1921, and certainly after, the relations between the two countries, until Stalin thought he saw an opportunity in 1939 for imperial expansion, were as close as relations between two nations are likely to be. When, in disregard of their leaders' promises to leave a Turkish Turkey intact, the victorious Allies—England, France, Italy—made war on Turkish Turkey, and a Greek army landed in Smyrna (Izmir) on May 15, 1919, an alarmed Moscow sent munitions and advisers to Kemal. Twice Ismet Pasha defeated the Greeks at Inonu (he later assumed that place name as his surname) but the war dragged on for more than three years until Kemal himself, in the field from July-September, 1922, compelled the Greeks to go home.

Had the western powers smashed Turkey and controlled the Dardanelles, Russia would have been bottled up in the Black Sea and its access to the Mediterranean subject to the whim of unfriendly countries. That disaster was averted by Kemal, and the Kremlin felt relieved. Turkey was Soviet Russia's buckler. When, therefore, the powers large and small—Great Britain, France, Italy, Japan, Rumania, Greece, Yugoslavia, Turkey, Soviet Georgia, the Soviet Ukraine, and Soviet Russia—met at Lausanne on November 20, 1922, to hammer out a new regime for the Dardanelles, the Sea of Marmora, and the Bosporus (the Straits), Chicherin, more Turk than the Turks, defended Turkey's position and Russia's; the famous jousts of the conference occurred between Lord Curzon and Comrade Chicherin, with Ismet Pasha applauding the latter. The *Manchester Guardian* declared that "In M. Chicherin," Curzon "for the first time met a foeman whose rapier was sharper and quicker than his own." Quick wit and justice, however, are nought in politics compared to power, and Britain with her allies had more strength than exhausted Russia and shorn Turkey. Chicherin contended that "the Dardanelles and the Bosporus must be permanently closed both in peace and in war to warships, armed vessels and military aircraft of all countries except Turkey."[5] He stressed too Soviet Russia's readiness to undertake of her own free will not to send her Black Sea fleet into the Mediterranean. (That frail fleet would scarcely have ventured from home waters on a hostile mission.) Unmoved, the western nations insisted on open, demilitarized straits. Turkey, at the end of her tether, acquiesced.

Soviet diplomats grudgingly signed the Lausanne treaty on August 14, 1923, and the Foreign Commissariat explained in print why it had signed and why it had agreed to participate in the International Commission which would exercise jurisdiction over the Straits. The Soviet government, however, had second thoughts, and Moscow refused to ratify the treaty or join the Commission. The document and the body represented western power over eastern and the Kremlin wanted no part of them. Chicherin had thought it might help Turkey to have a friend in the Commission. But Moscow was no counterweight to the West and would merely demonstrate impotence by being present.

The Soviet state, in principle, abstained from noncommunist international organizations. Chicherin accordingly opposed Soviet membership in the League of Nations (born January, 1920), which the Kremlin regarded as a capitalist conspiracy against Red Russia. (Individuals are subject to megalomaniacal paranoia, and governments, after all, are groups of individuals.) The Soviet Union remained aloof from the League for many years and Chicherin attempted to keep friendly na-

[5] British Blue Book, *Lausanne Conference on Near Eastern Affairs, 1922-23*, Cmd. 1814, p. 129.

tions out. He succeeded in keeping Turkey out. On December 27, 1925, Russia and Turkey signed a new treaty regulating minor differences, and in November, 1926, Chicherin and Turkish Foreign Minister Rushdi Bey met in Odessa where, Chicherin later told me, they again agreed to boycott the League. Chicherin also assured Rushdi that Moscow would not harm Turkey's interests in the Balkans. Subsequently, Turkey announced its condition for participation in the League: a permanent seat on the League's Council. This effectively excluded her from it.

Strong bonds of mutual need and common mistrust of the Western powers connected Soviet Russia and Turkey. Such indeed was Kemal's dependence on Moscow that he did not scruple to flirt with communism, while jailing communists, and to use communist terminology. Although the Soviet regime called itself communist and Turkey wrote nationalism on its banner, the course of both was shaped by revolutionary populism. Both were secular, indeed antireligious. Both were poor and largely peasant. Russia was far more advanced than Turkey, but neither was a developed country.

Persia, poor, peasant, and pastoral, was even more backward than Turkey, and Afghanistan stood still lower on the ladder of modernization. The thirteen million or more Afghans occupy a mountainous country that is in the unfortunate position of being landlocked. Its approaches to the outside world were through British India or Russia. It is in the nature of nations to take advantage of a country in this predicament. For a time England exercised a protectorate over Afghanistan. Though the Tsar, in 1907, acquiesced in this arrangement, he ordered his agents to maneuver secretly for influence among the tribes and khans. The Soviets, who denounced the treaty, felt free to court Kabul. The Afghan King now had a counterweight to the British raj and was delighted. Today, the British raj is gone. Pakistan and Afghanistan have occasionally engaged in serious quarrels over territory. In those circumstances, Afghanistan's opening to Russia, as an alternative to the road through Pakistan's deserts to the sea, fosters Kremlin-Kabul cooperation. Moscow, to boot, has built an all-weather highway for the Afghans through the Hindu Kush to the neighboring Tadjik Soviet Republic and sprinkled it with gold. All this makes a mighty magnet for a small, have-not nation. Geography tips Afghanistan's scales toward Moscow. Afghan nationalism brings them back to neutral.

In Afghanistan, Persia, and Turkey, Moscow, from the very inception of the Soviet regime, fostered nationalism, not communism. Chicherin, in conversations with me, ridiculed Stalin's efforts to communize Persia as a poorly disguised form of annexation. Under Lenin and under Stalin —until 1939—the Kremlin's Middle East policy was aimed at building a defensive buffer against Great Britain which, weak from the great war and having failed during the period of intervention to strip Russia of some of her non-Russian eastern territories, lacked offensive power. Moscow did not notice the change. Its slender political hold on the peoples of Soviet Central Asia made it apprehensive.

VII CHICHERIN AND CHINA

China was the new Bolshevik regime's most important neighbor on the Eurasian continents; the advent of communism to China would make her more so.

The imperialisms of Europe and Japan had tortured China throughout modern times. They were all capitalistic. The rise of anticapitalist Bolshevism gave many Chinese nationalists the conviction that they had acquired a firm friend. Moscow's relations with China began with this enormous advantage. The Kremlin, mindful of the dangers lurking behind the 5,000-mile Sino-Russian boundary, did not wish to see China dominated by Japan and England, the two most active interventionists in the Soviet civil war. Lenin and his aides and heirs were therefore interested in developing an independent China with strong ties to Moscow. The dispute over how this was to be achieved, by a bourgeois-capitalist revolution or a soviet-communist revolution, exacerbated the Stalin-Trotsky feud and illumines the subsequent Sino-Russian conflict.

Lenin, true to Marx, had advocated capitalism for China and Russia. "In countries like Russia," he wrote in 1905, "the working class suffers not so much from capitalism as from the insufficient development of capitalism. The working class is therefore certainly interested in the broadest, freest, and quickest *development of capitalism*."[1] This pro-capitalism of the anticapitalist is what some call dialectics. For Marx and Friedrich Engels had declared in the *Communist Manifesto* of February, 1848, that as capitalism develops "What the bourgeoisie . . . produces, above all, are its own gravediggers." The more capitalism the more workers and hence the more gravediggers who would, in their inevitable—so Marx believed—pauperism, want to bury capitalism.

Lenin applied this theoretical reasoning to China. Dr. Sun Yat-sen had

[1] V. I. Lenin, *Polnoye Sobranye Sochinenii* (Complete Works), Fifth ed., Vol. 11, p. 37.

published an article in the Brussels socialist paper, *Le Peuple;* and Lenin commented on July 15, 1912.

Dr. Sun, born in 1866, educated in Hawaii and Hong Kong, began in 1905 to formulate plans for the revolutionary transformation of his country. He was well-meaning, high-minded, and inexperienced in politics, but he evolved a program which was simple, novel, and necessary, and his assiduity in advocating it made him, despite organizational ineptitude, the father of the new China and the Provisional President of the Chinese Republic when the Manchu or Ch'ing dynasty fell in 1911.

Sun's program, "The Three Principles of the People," proposed "People's nationalism," or the unification of China and the expulsion of foreign imperialists; "People's democracy," or government by popular elections and popular recall, initiative and referendum (ideas acquired in America); and "People's livelihood," or land reform, and a measure of state capitalism in heavy industry and railways.

In 1912 Provisional President Sun exercised no power. Power, where it existed at all in the anarchy of cracked China, belonged to regional or provincial military cliques. Lenin nevertheless regarded Sun as "the European-educated representative of the militant and victorious Chinese democracy." And though Sun is not acquainted with Russian history or literature, "This progressive Chinese democrat literally thinks like a Russian."

Lenin called Dr. Sun "a Chinese populist," and "populist" in his mouth was an ugly word, for the Russian populists or social revolutionaries were Bolshevism's rivals. Like the Russian populists, Lenin said in his commentary on Sun's article, the Chinese leader combined "socialist dreams with the hope of avoiding the capitalist way in China" and with "radical agrarian reform. Such populism," Lenin asserted, is the theory of "a petty bourgeois 'socialist' reactionary." The notion that China could avoid capitalism and vault from feudalism to socialism was, to Lenin, "completely reactionary"; so was the thought that "a social revolution would be easier in China because of her backwardness."

Nevertheless, Lenin argued, Dr. Sun, writing with "maidenly naïveté," smashes his own reactionary populist theories into smithereens by affirming that "China is on the eve of a gigantic industrial (that is, capitalist) 'development,' " trade is expanding, and "in fifty years we shall have many Shanghais"; in other words, Lenin added, million-headed centers of "capitalist wealth and proletarian privations and poverty."

This grim prospect inspired roseate hopes in Lenin and reconciled him to Dr. Sun. For "in the end, inasmuch as the number of Shanghais will grow in China so also will the Chinese proletariat." Then, "probably," a socialist party would arise to criticize Dr. Sun Yat-sen's "bourgeois utopias and reactionary views" while expanding "the revolutionary-democratic nucleus of his political and agrarian program."[2]

When, accordingly, the infant Soviet regime moved to establish diplomatic and other relations with China it had a ready-made blueprint: support Sun Yat-sen's program; denounce foreign imperialisms; renounce Tsarist imperialism's privileges and territorial grabs; and, while encouraging the Chinese to carry out agrarian reform and capitalist industrialization, look to the distant day when a communist party would go beyond reform and capitalism to revolution and socialism.

At times in the years that followed, however, it was difficult to determine whether Lenin's (and Stalin's) new communism or the Tsar's old Russia shaped Kremlin relations to China. For the map is a tyrant. Geography holds international politics in thrall. Foreign policy often results from a tug of war between static factors like the map and fluctuations in national power. Personal and national jealousies and claims on lost territory add their pulls. Moscow's relation to China consequently followed a zigzagging course: now it was Russian, now Red, now both.

The Soviet government's first note to China stated that the former Russian minister to Peking as well as General Dmitry Leonidovich Horvath, manager of the Chinese Eastern Railway, had been dismissed by the Commissariat of Foreign Affairs.[3]

The Chinese Eastern Railway runs straight through the heart of Manchuria from west to east and straight through the heart of Russo-Chinese relations from 1895 to the 1950's. The history of the line mirrors the fate of China. Its prehistory begins with Japan's aggression in Korea in 1894. China objected. War erupted. China suffered complete defeat. The "treaty of peace" signed at Shimonoseki on April 18, 1895, precipitated China's partition. China recognized the "independence" of Korea—tantamount to Japanese sovereignty; China also gave Japan Formosa, the Pescadores Islands, and a large part of the highly strategic Liaotung Peninsula, which juts out from the southern tip of Manchuria into the Yellow Sea about halfway between Korea and Peking and Tientsin. Two ports, Dairen and Port Arthur, enhance the peninsula's value.

The treaty of Shimonoseki awarded Japan what Russia craved. Hiding envy under the guise of outrage and cupidity under the cloak of friendship, Nicholas II, newly enthroned and ill-advised, undertook to rally the powers against Japan's depredations. Great Britain refused to be rallied; some British politicians had set their long sights on an Anglo-Japanese alliance (signed January 20, 1902) aimed at Russia. But

[2] Lenin, Vol. XXI, pp. 400-406.

[3] U.S.S.R. Ministry of Foreign Affairs, *Dokumenty Vneshnei Politiki SSSR* (Documents on the Foreign Policy of the U.S.S.R.), Vol. I, pp. 46-47.

France, Russia's ally, promised cooperation, and Kaiser Wilhelm II egged on his Romanov cousin to expand into the Pacific arena. Thus encouraged, St. Petersburg "advised" Tokyo to return the Liaotung Peninsula to China and, for facial salvation, accept an enlarged financial indemnity from the defeated clay colossus. Simultaneously, Russian, German, and French men-of-war moved into the northern Pacific to prove that the advice was sound. Japan acquiesced—less than three weeks after the signing at Shimonoseki. For their services to China, Germany and France annexed Chinese territory.

China now needed money. Once again Russia acted the generous neighbor. The Russo-Chinese Bank chartered in 1895 by its owner, the Tsarist government (capital supplied by the French), proposed to aid China and became, as intended, a means to Russian domination of Manchuria, China's key region. The chief instrument of domination was the Chinese Eastern Railway.

The Trans-Siberian Railroad, begun in 1891, would soon be completed to Chita, and the question arose whether its last segment to Vladivostok might not be laid across Manchuria, rich in industrial potential, instead of adding four to five hundred miles to its great length by rounding the northern curve of Manchuria through sparsely inhabited, underdeveloped Russian terrain that presented serious engineering difficulties. St. Petersburg naturally preferred the shorter, cheaper route. That needed China's assent and the Tsar meant to get it.

The setting was right. Nicholas had succeeded his father in 1894 but was not crowned until 1896. Princes of the blood, foreign statesmen, Russian nobility gathered for the tremendous and tragic coronation. Nicholas, tutored by Konstantin P. Pobedonostev, arch-reactionary Procurator of the Holy Synod, believed in the unity of church and state in the person of the supreme autocrat. He believed too in Russia's eastern destiny, a euphemism for imperialism. The new Tsar accordingly sent a personal message to the Dowager Empress asking that Li Hung-Chan, outstanding statesman, represent China at the ceremonies. Li, smarting under the China defeat by Japan while he was Peking's premier politician, felt grateful. To show him ingratiating favoritism and to isolate him from European blandishments, Li was met at the Suez Canal by Prince Ukhtomsky, the Tsar's deputy, and carried on a Russian battleship to Odessa. In St. Petersburg the Tsar and his ministers conferred with Li before and after the May, 1896, festivities.

Nothing so vulgar as a railroad was the focus of the talks. Instead China, vanquished by Japan, needed a protector; Russia volunteered for the role. The two nations would sign a defensive alliance. To defend China, Russia might have to transport troops into China, and a railroad (the Chinese Eastern) through Manchuria would serve this purpose. So would a Russian lease on Port Arthur and Dairen and a branch line from the Chinese Eastern to those ports. Li signed the secret treaty of defense after receiving a bribe, it is said, of $1,500,000.[4] Gold has often lubricated the wheels of diplomacy.

This brilliant diplomatic success led directly to Russia's dismal military defeat in the 1904-1905 war with Japan; Tokyo resented the lunges of the Slav mammoth into the Far East. The total debacle on land and sea, demonstrating tsarist ineptitude and indifference to the national welfare, aroused popular bitterness and sparked the 1905 revolution, petite rehearsal for 1917, when Nicholas II abdicated.

By the terms of the Russo-Japanese treaty of peace signed on August 9, 1905, at, of all places, Portsmouth, New Hampshire (President Theodore Roosevelt chose it after intervening to stop hostilities and give the United States a foot in the open door of Manchuria), the Tsar of defeat "leased" Port Arthur and Dairen to Japan and surrendered to her the South Manchurian branches of the Chinese Eastern Railway and the lower half of the island of Sakhalin; Korea became an undisguised Nipponese colony.

Thus ended the tsarist dream of greater glory at China's cost. Yet such is the compulsion of geography and the pull of history to repeat itself that the Russian communists, though bred on Lenin's anti-imperialist bible, *Imperialism, the Highest State of Capitalism,* refurbished the old tsarist imperialist goals in Manchuria, Mongolia, and Korea, and again and again retook the Chinese Eastern Railway, Port Arthur, and Dairen —until the China of Mao Tse-tung, no longer feeble, said a final no to Moscow.

* * *

China had known a brief period of national unity after the fall of the Manchu dynasty in 1911. But divisive tendencies, accentuated by Japanese encroachments during the first world war, broke up the vast country into feuding warlord fiefs. The Kuomintang (National People's Party) thereupon thought it wiser to flee Peking for Canton, where, however, it and its leader, Sun Yat-sen, were kept powerless by local generals. But to Moscow Dr. Sun remained the symbol of China's revolution, and to him, therefore, Chicherin, on behalf of the Soviet government, sent a piquant letter dated August 1, 1918. It answered Sun's greeting "several months ago" to the Soviet state. "You, Esteemed Teacher," Chicherin wrote, ". . . asserted that the Russian and Chinese revolutions have the same goals," that both aimed to liberate "the

[4] Harry Schwartz, *Tsars, Mandarins, and Commissars. A History of Chinese-Russian Relations,* p. 66.

workers" and establish a secure peace based on "recognition of the common interests of the two great proletariats, the Russian and the Chinese."

Whether or not Chicherin, who knew the Oriental mind, took at face value the words of Dr. Sun, whom he had never met, he used the opportunity to spread the Bolshevik viewpoint. "We too, like you," his letter continued. "are encountering unexampled difficulties in our path. Encircled by a steel ring of the bayonets of the imperialist governments, hirelings of the bourgeoisie,—of the Czechoslovak hordes and the Russian bourgeoisie, striving to restore the monarchy in Russia—we have been cut off from our friends, the South-China proletariat." For two months Moscow could not communicate with Canton. False rumors, circulated "by our common enemies" through the press, "which is corrupted by the bankers and capitalists," tried to hide from the Chinese people that "the workers and peasants government [of Soviet Russia] lives and wages a mighty and uninterrupted struggle, now as before carrying the banner of the victory of the proletariat over the world bourgeoisie and the European thieves and robbers."

The Peking government, "created by foreign bankers," Chicherin noted, supported Moscow's foes. The Russian toilers therefore appealed to their "Chinese brothers" to help them. "For our success is your success, and our destruction is your destruction."[5]

Chicherin and Sun's heavy emphasis on the Russian and Chinese proletariats contrasts sharply with the Joint Manifesto signed in Peking on January 26, 1923, by Sun Yat-sen and Soviet Ambassador Adolf A. Yoffe, in which the Chinese leader objected to "communism or even the Soviet system" in China "because the conditions do not exist for the successful establishment of Communism or Socialism. Mr. Yoffe absolutely agrees with this view."[6] The statement reflected Lenin's 1912 proposition that a successful Chinese socialist revolution would spring from a developed capitalism and its by-product: a proletariat large enough to make and maintain the revolution.

But decades are needed to create a capitalist economy. Nor is an industrial proletariat born in a day. Yet Moscow was impatient to gain influence over China. It chose the Kuomintang as its partner for penetra-

[5] *Dokumenty Vneshnei Politiki SSSR,* pp. 415-416.

[6] Translated from the fortnightly bulletin of the Soviet political representative in Peking, dated Feb. 1-15, 1923, which I saw in the archives of the Commissariat of Foreign Affairs in Moscow while writing *The Soviets in World Affairs.* The document, however, does not appear in *Dokumenty Vneshnei Politiki SSSR, Vol. VI, November 20, 1922-December 31, 1923.* On the other hand, *Istoria Diplomatii* (The History of Diplomacy), Vol. III, p. 436, mentions the Sun-Yoffe meeting, places it in Peking, and quotes excerpts from their decisions but not the text of their rejection of communism and the Soviet system. The past succumbs to its future in Soviet historiography.

tion and sealed the partnership with a gift of Bolshevism's most precious secret: the role of the party.

Lenin's major achievement did not lie in the realm of ideology or philosophy or economics or even polemics, but rather in fathering the idea of a compact party of professional organizers and propagandists that would reshape society. He based his entire career on the application of this principle and added two elements of his own personality: stern discipline and puritanism.

Chicherin offered the Lenin method free of obvious charge to Sun Yat-sen.

On September 17, 1923, Dr. Sun had written a letter in Canton to Leo M. Karakhan, Soviet Deputy Commissar of Foreign Affairs (for Asia). "What follows," he warned, "is *rigidly confidential.* Some weeks ago I sent identical letters addressed to Comrades Lenin, Tchitcherin and Trotsky introducing General Chiang Kai-shek who is my Chief of Staff and confidential agent. . . . In particular, General Chiang is to take up with your government and military experts a proposal for military action by my forces in and about the regions lying North-west of Peking and beyond."

Moscow apparently feared that militaristic tendencies, always strong in China, would gain the upper hand in the Kuomintang. Chicherin therefore penned a letter on December 4, 1923, to Dr. Sun which, after alluding to Chiang Kai-shek's stay in Moscow, stated, "We think that the fundamental aim of the Kuomintang party is to build up a great powerful movement of the Chinese people and that therefore progaganda and organization on the biggest scale are its first necessities. Our example was significant; our military activities were successful because a long series of years had elapsed during which we organized and organized and instructed our followers, building up in this way a great organized party throughout the whole land, a party capable of vanquishing all its adversaries."

Sun agreed. For on January 7, 1924, Karakhan wrote the Chinese leader, "Now that you have said that it is not in the army but in the party that force lies, there can be no defeat. The army may be defeated, but not the party. Standing on right, healthy social historical paths, the party will never be defeated . . . we always told ourselves," Karakhan stressed in conclusion, "let there be fewer of us, but we shall be as one will. In that lies our strength."

This was the essence of Leninism. The Bolsheviks were exporting to China, for use by a noncommunist, nonproletarian, nationalistic party, a system of political organization to which they attributed their power over Russia. At the same time, November 28, 1923, the Executive Committee of the Comintern, sitting in Moscow, adopted a resolution marked "confidential" and signed "Kolarov," instructing the Chinese Communist Party to collaborate with the Kuomintang for the nationalization of land, which Lenin had considered a measure to strengthen capitalism, the reduction of land taxes, and the nationalization of foreign (but not Chinese) industries and banks.[7]

Thus early in life the Soviet government recognized that an underdeveloped country like China would, whatever its name—soviet or socialist or people's democracy—have to pass through a period, undetermined in length, of nationalism and capitalism before arriving at the goal, never described by Marx, Engels, Lenin, or any Marxist, of socialism. But though the Kremlin knew this to be true for China, it skillfully hid the reality of underdeveloped Russia under elaborate camouflage and refused to admit that there too the social system officially called socialist and internationalist was in fact monopoly-state-capitalist and nationalist. Yet Lenin had declared that the thought of leaping from feudalism to socialism or of skipping capitalism was "completely reactionary." It was wrong as well. State capitalism is capitalism with many differences from, and more similarities with, private capitalism. The biggest difference—ownership—has less significance than was once attached to it.

VIII OPEN DIPLOMACY, SECRET DESIGNS

Now that the Soviet government's prestige had been enhanced by diplomatic recognition from Great Britain, Sun Yat-sen wrote Leo Karakhan on February 2, 1924, it did not need relations with "nonrepresentative, antinational and proforeign capitalist" Peking. Ties with Canton were preferable.

[7] The text of this resolution and copies of the Chicherin, Karakhan, and Sun letters were in a file which Karakhan handed to me during one of the many sessions I had with him while writing *The Soviets in World Affairs*. "What shall I do with these?" I asked. "Take them home and copy them," he replied. Afraid that they might be lost or burned by accident, I sat down in one of Karakhan's tiny anterooms in the former building of the Commissariat of Foreign Affairs on Kuznetsky Must, made copies, and returned the file to him. I did not publish the documents in *The Soviets in World Affairs* because I thought Karakhan's generosity would get him into trouble. He was executed without trial during Stalin's "cult of personality," and rehabilitated as innocent in the Khrushchev era.

But the Kremlin had business in Peking. It would also negotiate with Marshal Chang Tso-lin, warlord of the autonomous fief of Manchuria, traditional focus of Russia's national interests. Peking, like Mukden, was the political present, Canton a political potential. Moscow planned to have its cake and eat it, eat from the China plate and break it. At home the Soviet government followed an either-or policy, you were either for it or against it. Abroad the Bolsheviks would, when necessary, sup with the devil. Playing the diplomatic game with Peking did not preclude stabbing it in the back in Canton.

The Soviet regime addressed Peking with undisguised brusqueness. "The not-unknown robber band" of Gregory Semenov, said a Chicherin note telegraphed "Urgent, Special" in May, 1918, had invaded Soviet territory from bases in China and received food, recruits, and sanctuary in Manchuria. Though this "criminal element" had been "liquidated" by the Red Army, it might try again to attack in Siberia. "In case the Peking government considers itself powerless to end the criminal actions of robber bands in Manchuria, the People's Commissariat [of Foreign Affairs] request the Peking government's agreement to liquidate that element by the use of Soviet troops on Chinese territory in conjunction with regular Chinese soldiers or without their cooperation."[1]

There is no record of a Chinese reply. Peking was not master in its own house; Japan was, and Japan refused to readmit Russia to Manchuria. To the Chinese, Chicherin's proposal must have been ominously reminiscent of the Tsarist past.

A big event, however, deflected Chinese wrath from Russia to the West: the Versailles peace conference had not ousted Japan from the important Chinese province of Shantung. Students, intellectuals, nationalists, blamed western imperialism. A high wave of protest roared across China, and Moscow, ever eager to capitalize on capitalist transgressions, rode in on its crest. The Soviets, in a July 25, 1919, appeal to the "Chinese people and the Governments of South and North China," announced that the Red Army, having defeated "Kolchak, the counterrevolutionary despot," was moving east across Siberia carrying "help not only to our toiling classes but also to the Chinese people." Leo Karakhan, who signed the appeal, reminded China that the Bolshevik regime had, early in 1918, offered to confer with the Chinese government on the cancellation of pre-1917 unequal treaties and to return to China everything taken from her by the Tsar. Negotiations, he stated, continued until March, 1918, when "The Allies unexpectedly grabbed the Peking government by the throat, heaped gold on the Peking mandarins and

[1] U.S.S.R. Ministry of Foreign Affairs, *Dokumenty Vneshnei Politiki SSSR*, (Documents on the Foreign Policy of the U.S.S.R.), Vol. I: *November 7, 1918-December 31, 1918*, pp. 339-341.

the Chinese press," and forced the Chinese government to reject relations with the new Russia. "Without awaiting the return of the Manchurian railroad"—the Chinese Eastern—"Japan and the Allies seized it, invaded Siberia themselves, and even forced Chinese troops to aid them in this criminal and unprecedented brigandage." Now the Soviets had restored to China all the Tsar's plunder, including "Manchuria and other provinces. Let the peoples who inhabit those provinces decide for themselves in what country they wish to live and what form of government they wish to establish on their territories."

This could be read as anti-imperialism or a recommendation that Manchuria and Outer Mongolia opt out of China and into Soviet Russia. In fact, the appeal went on to suggest that if China wished to avoid becoming "a second Korea or a second India," she must understand "that her only ally and brother in the struggle for freedom is the Russian worker and peasant and his Red Army." Finally, Karakhan asked "the Chinese government" to establish relations with Moscow and "to send its representatives to welcome our army."

Here, once again, the Soviet government was not one thing but at least two. With the left hand it returned what the Tsar had taken, with the right hand it took it back by self-determination in the presence of a foreign army. Apparently the Lenin leadership believed that China was ready, in whole or in part, for submergence in Russia.

The first part submerged was Outer Mongolia. The last Tsar had converted that huge realm into a Russian satellite. The world war shortened Petrograd's arm and enabled China to reassert her sovereignty. But Chinese rule was alien rule; Chinese merchants, moreover, exploited Mongol herdsmen. When, therefore, the Soviet civil war spilled over into Outer Mongolia, Red Army units pursued White military remnants into that country and, under the guise of liberating it from China (and from anti-Bolsheviks who dreamed of resurrecting the empire of Genghis Khan), helped set up "the Provisional Revolutionary Government of Mongolia" which they smothered with powerful embraces. Given a choice, the Mongols might have preferred the unknown Red face emitting slogans of national independence to the heavy foot of Chinese domination. The choice was denied them.

Soviet encroachment into what China had long considered her province chilled Peking's feelings for Moscow and blocked the establishment of normal diplomatic relations. The European powers and Japan added their obstructions. Presently Karakhan himself appeared on the scene.

Leo M. Karakhan was suave, mild as Bolsheviks go, handsome, and meticulously groomed. Karl Radek, an exceptionally ugly man, used to call Karakhan "the beautiful jackass." His good features, however, did not exclude good sense and skill. Karakhan was an Asian, an Armenian, a patient bargainer yet not personally devious, and no fanatic. He liked fine food, pretty women, and gracious living. His easy manner, his warmth, created a pleasant impression on official Peking and more so on the capital's population. The diplomatic colony remained frigid.

Chicherin, fastidious and finical, undoubtedly tugged at Karakhan's well-tailored coattails with a long wire and directed his efforts toward a peace treaty. Karakhan obeyed instructions, served the Kremlin's objectives, and preached anti-imperialism. But his task was so complex, Moscow had so many irons in the Chinese fire, that a foolish diplomat would have faltered.

En route to Peking in the summer of 1923 Karakhan stopped at Harbin on the Chinese Eastern Railway, where Russians long employed by the line greeted him as a representative of the Russia which had induced Japan to leave eastern Siberia. They probably thought their jobs would be in jeopardy if China took over the C.E.R., and hoped that a show of enthusiasm for Russia's return would be a guarantee against wholesale dismissals.

Karakhan next stopped in Mukden to negotiate with Marshal Chang Tso-lin. But he concluded no agreement because Manchuria nominally belonged to Peking's China. On the other hand, the Kremlin diplomat's friendly talks in Mukden intimated that Moscow had an alternative should Peking prove recalcitrant. They also served Chang Tso-lin by indicating that he too had an alternative in the event Peking aspired to operate the railroad.

Arrived in Peking on September 2, 1923, Karakhan pursued the same tactic of sitting on several baskets of eggs. He paid his respects to Wu Pei-fu, the master, at the moment, of Peking. He made contact with Feng Yu-hsiang, the "Christian general," a subordinate of Wu's who aimed to achieve independent warlord status on territory near Peking. Karakhan, in addition, wrote Dr. Sun Yat-sen down south.

Karakhan's talks in Peking were conducted with Dr. C. T. Wang of the Chinese Foreign Office. The Muscovite's first demand was complete *de jure* diplomatic recognition, a logical demand, for how could China negotiate with a government whose rightful existence it did not accept? Logic, however, is not characteristic of international affairs. If Soviet Russia desired full recognition, the Chinese intended to make her pay for it.

The obstacle to a settlement was Moscow's attitude to Outer Mongolia and the Chinese Eastern Railway. On both issues Peking remained adamant, and the Wang-Karakhan talks started, broke down, resumed, and continued inconclusively during many months.

The art of the diplomat is to paint with gray. The Soviet government had detached Outer Mongolia from China and made it an independent state in name, a satellite in fact. When Dr. Wang vehemently objected, Karakhan agreed that Outer Mongolia was, as the Sino-Soviet Treaty of March 14, 1924, stipulated, "an integral part of the Republic of China." This changed nothing; Outer Mongolia remained Russia's satellite.

Similar hedging produced a solution of the Chinese Eastern problem. Karakhan's resounding manifestoes of 1919 and 1920 relinquished to China all the Tsar's imperialistic spoils. Those declarations dated back to an early period when Kolchak, Japan, Semenov, and Soviet weakness barred Soviet Russia from contact with China. But on August 3, 1923, Karakhan, packing for his trip to Peking, told *Izvestia* that the Chinese Eastern "belongs to the workers of Russia." In Peking, Karakhan argued that the C.E.R. was necessary to Russia's prosperity and development; if Moscow surrendered the 1,320-mile railway, it would have to build another, much longer, through wild Siberian terrain; it lacked the means.

In the end China agreed to a compromise. Moscow abandoned the rights acquired by the Tsar to police and administer a broad zone on both sides of the railway. China's sovereignty was restored—a political victory for Peking. Moreover, the treaty affirmed that "The Chinese Eastern Railway is a purely commercial enterprise." China, said the treaty, could buy it from Russia with Chinese capital—an unlikely prospect for a country in permanent penury. Russia retained possession of the railroad and ran it behind a veil of fictitious Chinese participation in management.

Morality is usually foreign to foreign affairs. The degree of immorality differs from government to government, from time to time, from issue to issue. The communists followed a guiding principle enunciated by Lenin: "We say," he told a congress of the League of Communist Youth (Komsomol) in Moscow on October 2, 1920, "morality is that which serves the destruction of the old exploiting society and the unification of all working people around the proletariat engaged in creating a new communist society. . . . We do not believe in eternal morality." This the-end-justifies-the-means doctrine might lead to total immorality and lay the basis for refusing to relinquish a satellite or a railroad. Why, communists would ask, give up the C.E.R. to the reactionary governments of Manchuria and China who might sell or lease it to an imperialist power capable of using it to menace the Soviet Republic? The fact is that when Moscow gave up the Russian territorial enclaves in Hankow and Tientsin, the French moved into the former. France also claimed the Chinese Eastern because she had furnished the money with which Nicholas II built it.

So strenuous was the objection of the powers to the Sino-Soviet Treaty of March 14, 1924, that the Peking Foreign Office disavowed Dr. Wang's signature and declared the treaty null. France, the Kremlin's intractable enemy, and Japan, its most ambitious foe, joined forces in this successful démarche. They reckoned without Karakhan. No sooner had Peking canceled the treaty than he published it. A storm raged. On paper the accord looked good: the return of the concessions; the acceptance of Chinese sovereignty in Outer Mongolia; Russia's position of the C.E.R. no longer an alienation of territory, merely a contractual arrangement for business purposes. And Moscow refused further Chinese payments of Boxer Rebellion reparations. Above all, the Wang-Karakhan document gave the appearance of an equal treaty freely concluded in contrast with so many international agreements imposed on China.

When public-opinion makers and demonstration organizers read the canceled treaty they rose in nationalistic wrath and forced their government to return to the negotiating table; this time Foreign Minister Dr. Wellington Koo spoke for Peking. After a decent interval to save face, the interred treaty was resurrected and approved. Full diplomatic recognition of each signatory by the other was the concomitant.[2]

Leo Karakhan was by nature frank and open. His open diplomacy in Peking achieved its purpose: a treaty with Wu Pei-fu's government, but did not deflect Moscow from a secret design to subvert Wu and mold another China more resistant to the imperialist powers, more pliant in Moscow's hands.

To achieve its purpose the Kremlin sent Michael M. Borodin to China. Borodin has been regarded as an agent of the Comintern or Third International. He actually represented the Soviet government. Among the documents Karakhan gave me in Moscow was a copy of a letter he wrote to Dr. Sun in Canton on September 23, 1923, saying, "Please regard Comrade Borodin not only as a representative of the government, but as my personal representative." Karakhan recommended him as "one of the oldest members of the party, having worked for a great many years in the revolutionary movement of Russia."

When Borodin arrived in Canton it resembled a cauldron churning with military cliques and mercenary camps which poured in and out of the city in no discernible pattern. Generals were bought and armies sold. Borodin, however, saw his mission as something much larger than the creation of yet another center of military power. He could not, given his Marxist-Leninist cast of mind, think of an army as a rootless collection of rifle-toting men who considered soldiering the means of earning a livelihood in an impoverished country. He was a revolutionist and regarded himself as the midwife of China's revolution. But what kind of revolution—communist or nationalist?

[2] *Dokumenty Vneshnei Politiki SSSR*, Vol. VII: *January 1-December 31, 1924*, pp. 331-346, for full text of treaty and its accompanying declarations.

IX REICHSWEHR OR REVOLUTION?

Like a supercolossus the Soviet Union sprawls over Eurasia with one foot on the heart of Europe and the second in the waters of the Pacific. What happens to the right foot is communicated, through the brain in Moscow, to the left foot in China, Japan, or Korea. Borodin's actions in China between 1924 and 1927 reflected German events between 1919 and 1923.

The Lenin Kremlin regarded Germany as a shield against invasion and political and economic pressures by England and France. It hoped China would divert the Japanese and British menace from the Soviets in Asia. The alliance Lenin offered Germany against Anglo-French imperialism on December 6, 1920,[1] was intended to appeal to most Germans for nationalist reasons and some Germans for Marxist reasons. But instead of giving all Germans one unifying goal Lenin gave Russia two conflicting goals: collaboration with the German army and promotion of a German communist revolution.

The genesis of Reichswehr-Russian intimacy is hidden in the mists of history. Radek apparently broached the possibility to visitors who came to his political salon in Moabit jail, Berlin, where he was confined after his failure in December, 1918-January, 1919, to help German Spartacists or communists seize power. The Kaiser's defeated army, impelled into unaccustomed republicanism by the Red threat, acted swiftly in support of the infant postwar regime and smashed the workers' councils in Berlin, Munich, and other cities. Impressed by German military strength, sobered by German communist weakness, Radek began to court German extreme reactionaries, stalwarts of the deposed monarchy and closely linked to the old Prussian establishment.

The first contact between Radek and General Hans von Seeckt, future chief of the Reichswehr, was made indirectly during the autumn of 1919 by Enver Pasha.[2] War Minister Enver, with Djemal Pasha and Taalat Pasha, constituted the triumvirate of Young Turks which ruled Turkey before and throughout the world war; he worked with Seeckt when

[1] See Chapt. V, pp. 50-51.

[2] Francis L. Carsten, *Reichswehr und Politik, 1918-1933*, p. 80.

Germans trained and in part directed the Turkish armed forces. After Turkey's collapse and war's end Enver, a short man with tall ambitions, sought new worlds to conquer or, at least, a new ego-satisfying role.

In the course of the war Enver and Kemal Pasha (Ataturk), the hero of Gallipoli, quarreled. Early in 1919, with Kemal in power, Enver, sentenced to death for his part in the country's defeat, escaped and tried to reach Odessa in a small sailboat. A Black Sea storm broke the mast and he was forced to return to Turkey and hide. Soon he arrived in Germany. His goal was Soviet Russia. He dreamed of building a Pan-Turanian empire in Central Asia; he hoped too to overthrow Kemal.[3] Aware that neither objective would charm the Kremlin, he planned to make himself acceptable in Russia by serving as Seeckt's intermediary with the Soviet government. Some time late in 1919, Enver, in disguise, boarded his own airplane for a flight to Moscow. The plane crashed and he was incarcerated in Kovno, Lithuania; later the same fate overtook him in Riga, Latvia. On finally reaching Moscow in midsummer, 1920, he was given a room in the Sugar King's Palace, a government guest house across the Moskva River from the Kremlin. There he wrote a letter to Seeckt in August saying Ephraim M. Sklyansky, Trotsky's deputy in the Revolutionary War Council (War Office), had told him that the Russian Communist Party saw only one way out of "this world chaos": Soviet "collaboration with Germany and Turkey." Being a no-nonsense politician, Enver proposed a first practical step: "the sale and smuggling of arms" as well as "intelligence information about the Polish army."[4] He sent the letter by messenger.

Count Ulrich von Brockdorff-Rantzau, Berlin's Ambassador in Moscow in the 1920's, noted in 1922 that "already in 1920 the [German] military had conducted direct negotiations with Trotsky."[5] During the Russo-Polish war, which ended in August, 1920, Germany held her breath; if the Red Army swallowed Poland, Soviet Russia and Germany would have a common frontier. Germans of all hues, from black to red, including many Reichswehr leaders, ardently desired the proximity. As Lenin put it in an address to the Russian Communist Party Conference on September 22, 1920, "When our troops approached Warsaw all Germany began to boil. . . . And we saw in Germany an unnatural bloc of Black Hundreds and Bolsheviks."[6] The "unnatural" naturally happened again.

[3] Louis Fischer, *The Soviets in World Affairs,* Chap. VII.

[4] Enver's original German, with all its bad grammar and misspellings, is cited in Carsten, pp. 80-81.

[5] *Ibid.,* p. 81. Carsten had access to Brockdorff-Rantzau's archives.

[6] V. I. Lenin, *Polnoye Sobranye Sochinenii* (Complete Collected Works), Fifth ed., Vol. 41, p. 282. (Hereafter this edition will be cited as *Polnoye Sobranye.*)

The Versailles treaty sought to bind the German military hand and foot. They were therefore eager to rearm secretly and in contravention of the treaty by working within the closed society of Soviet Russia ruled by a party addicted to conspiracy. Moreover, the destruction of Poland was in itself a primary German nationalist goal; Poland held territory Germans called their own. On January 31, 1920, Seeckt, the father of Soviet-German military collaboration, had written General von Massow that Russia "should not be prevented from regaining her former Imperial frontiers." He rejected German "support of Poland against Bolshevism," and favored "a political and economic agreement with 'Great Russia.'"[7] Prophetically, he told the German Chancellor in writing in September, 1922, "Poland's existence is intolerable, incompatible with the existence of Germany. It must disappear and it will disappear through its own internal weakness and through Russia—with our assistance. For Russia Poland is even more intolerable than for us; no Russia can reach agreement with Poland. . . . Russia and Germany within the frontiers of 1914!"[8]

Seeckt and his uniformed colleagues, as well as the Berlin government, lived in fear of a two-arm pincer by France in the West and Poland in the East. To make Soviet Russia powerful enough to paralyze or annihilate Poland and to enhance German power by evading the disarmament provisions of Versailles were the twin pillars of Seeckt's policy.

Part V, Articles 159 to 213 of the Versailles treaty stipulated that by March 31, 1920, the German army was to be reduced to and remain permanently at a maximum strength of 100,000 men and 4,000 officers using 102,000 rifles and carbines, 1,134 light and 792 heavy machine guns, and a limited amount of light artillery. The personnel of the German fleet was restricted to 15,000 sailors and 1,500 officers. Germany was prohibited from having military airplanes, tanks, submarines, poison gas, and, except in several specified forts, heavy artillery, and from manufacturing or importing such munitions. Noncommissioned officers and privates were to serve for at least twelve years and officers twenty-five years. The treaty proscribed war academies and a general staff. (Most soldiers trained for twelve years acquired the qualifications of officers; the 100,000-man Reichswehr accordingly became the cadres of Hitler's expanded many-million-man Wehrmacht.)

Before the German delegates put pen to paper at Versailles on June 28, 1919, it was clear that Seeckt and his comrades intended to circumvent these disarmament clauses. Some generals actually proposed a con-

[7] Carsten, "The Reichswehr and the Red Army," *Survey*, London, October, 1962, p. 115. Carsten had access to Seeckt's secret papers.

[8] *Ibid.*, p. 116.

tinuation of the war in the East to wrest from Poland the German territories—Silesia, Posen, and East Prussia—the victors gave her. After turbulent scenes within the German Cabinet, political sobriety prevailed. Germany now entered a period of reluctant fulfillment and clandestine evasion. In Soviet-German relations it was the Era of Seeckt and Brockdorff-Rantzau, two conservatives who wanted communist Russia to help save the fatherland.

Hans von Seeckt, son of a general of noble rank, joined the Imperial army at nineteen, rose quickly to general, and fought with distinction on the western and eastern fronts in the first world war. His face says authority, power, and culture. The high, hard forehead with a diagonal line from temple to right eyebrow, the troubled look in the right eye, the monocle over the left, and the strong nose reflect great intelligence, great shrewdness, the weight of responsibility, and a determination to reveal his mind to no one. The long upper lip covered by a triangular mustache, the full lower lip, and the dip in the middle of his chin spell sensitivity. Meticulous Prussian staff officer whose glance would command instant obedience, Seeckt, however, was no wooden Hindenburg or cast-iron Ludendorff. He had imagination, political subtlety, and a love of the delicate things of life which was almost French. Lord D'Abernon, the British ambassador in Berlin, wrote that Seeckt had "a broader mind than is expected in so tight a uniform, a wider outlook than seems appropriate in so precise, so correct, so neat an exterior . . ."[9]

As Commander in Chief of the Reichswehr, from 1920 to 1926, General von Seeckt rescued the new German Republic from assaults on its life by monarchists, militarists, and rightists though by birth and experience he belonged in their camp. On the other hand, he regarded his army as "a state within a state." With haughty arrogance he wrote Chancellor Gustav Stresemann on September 7, 1923, "The Reichswehr will stand behind you if the German Chancellor goes the German way."[10] The Reichswehr gave the Republic stability and demanded and received independence in compensation. President Friedrich Ebert, a Social Democrat, remained ignorant for years of the Reichswehr's secret arrangements with the Kremlin, and Seeckt felt no obligation to keep even chancellors and foreign ministers fully informed.

The second steel support of Soviet-German friendship in the 1920's was Brockdorff-Rantzau. Rantzau—he once said to me, "I hope history will know me as 'Rantzau' "—came of a rich, landed, aristocratic Holstein family whose forebears served the kings of France and Denmark. "One of his ancestors, Count Josias Rantzau, Marshal of France, was

[9] Viscount D'Abernon, *Portraits and Appreciations,* pp. 158-159.
[10] Carsten, *Reichswehr und Politik.* Title page of Part Two. Carsten also had access to Stresemann's papers.

indeed alleged to have been the father of Louis XIV, and, when questioned about this legend by one of the French officers attached to the German Peace Delegation at Versailles, Brockdorff-Rantzau replied coldly: 'O yes, in my family the Bourbons have been considered bastard Rantzaus for the past three hundred years.' "[11] The Count, as Foreign Minister and leader of the German delegation, remained seated when Premier Clemenceau, after a brief address, handed him the peace treaty. He replied without rising. He refused to sign and resigned. This gave him enormous prestige among his countrymen. He used it to enhance his authority. On returning to office to become ambassador in Moscow in 1922 it was agreed that he could go over the head of the Chancellor or Foreign Minister and appeal directly to the President of the Republic. In several crises his policy won when he threatened to resign.

Rantzau established an especially warm personal relationship with Georgi V. Chicherin, the Soviet Foreign Commissar. Though Chicherin spoke a fluent German, they usually conversed in French. They shared a common passion for politics and literature, a common disinterest in women, and a common dislike of England. Chicherin lived like a recluse in the Foreign Commissariat building, normally worked at night, and spent leisure hours reading belles-lettres in European languages or playing classical music, preferably Mozart, on the piano. Few were allowed to hear his virtuoso performances. Sometimes, at midnight or early in the morning, Rantzau would visit him to sip wine and talk. The Count valued this oasis in what, to him, was the Moscow cultural desert for its own sake and for its political importance. Chicherin too enjoyed the civilized contact and appreciated the direct channel it gave him to Germany's powermen. This was an extraordinary friendship between two aristocrats who ignored ideological barriers.

Seeckt in his way and Rantzau in his—they often disagreed—were not engaged in a one-sided courtship of the Soviet government. "Our existence," Lenin told the Eighth All-Russian Congress of Soviets on December 21, 1920, "depends, on the one hand, on the circumstance that there is a basic cleavage between the imperialist powers and, on the other hand, that the victory of the Entente and the Versailles peace have driven the overwhelming majority of the German nation into a situation in which they cannot survive." Germany's "only means of saving herself," Lenin continued, "is by an alliance with Soviet Russia. . . . The German bourgeois government furiously hates Bolsheviks, but its foreign affairs interests propel it, against its own desires, toward peace with Soviet Russia . . . there is no salvation without the Soviet Republic."[12]

[11] John W. Wheeler-Bennett, *The Nemesis of Power; The German Army in Politics, 1918-1945*, Footnote p. 49.

[12] Lenin, Vol. 42, p. 105.

At the request of the German government the Kremlin sent Victor Kopp to Berlin in November, 1919, to negotiate the exchange of prisoners of war and the restoration of diplomatic relations.[13] Kopp had other business too. On April 7, 1921, he addressed a letter to Trotsky on his months of conferences with German companies and officials. The letter, marked "Secret," and forwarded personally to Trotsky's deputy, E. M. Sklyansky, asked him to send copies to Lenin and Chicherin. It also went to Vyacheslav R. Menzhinsky, Djerzhinsky's deputy in the Cheka, or Security Police. Kopp wrote: "The negotiations with the German group known to you on the basis which we discussed in Moscow has led to the following results. This group believes, first of all, that it is indispensable to cooperate with us in restoring our munitions industry, in specifically these three directions: the building of an air force, of a submarine fleet, and the manufacture of weapons. The group has, on condition of strictest secrecy, brought into the matter the firm of Blohm and Voss (submarines), the Albatross works (air force), and Krupp (arms)." Detailed plans would be available soon. On the 20th, "Neumann, whom you know, leaves for Moscow to arrange to coopt several technicians (five or six) from here"—from Germany—"for the further discussion of the matter" in Moscow. "After receipt of this communication please reply immediately by radio in the secret code of Comrade Chicherin whether you regard the arrival of Neumann desirable at this moment and the fulfillment of these plans altogether in our interest."

On the copy sent him Lenin wrote by hand, "Comrade Sklyansky, Drop me a line, have you replied and how, I think, Yes. *Return* this. Lenin." Menzhinsky commented: "Agree to admit" into the country.[14] The "Neumann" whose trip to Moscow Kopp announced was Major Oskar von Niedermayer, a Reichswehr officer who spoke fluent Russian. The "group" mentioned by Kopp was the Reichswehr. The Reichswehr drew on German industry.

Negotiations with the Soviet government at any time and on any issue are plagued by mutual suspicion. It is an ancient Muscovite proclivity, intensified by Bolshevism, to doubt foreign motives and declarations. Foreign firms and governments have likewise looked for hidden, sinister meaning in everything the Kremlin says and does. If this is true of ordinary commercial transactions, how much more so in negotiations on military affairs and the admission of Germans into the Soviet defense establishment? Reichswehr-Russian collaboration, moreover, was complicated by the desire of some leading Germans to improve Berlin's ties with the West at the expense of Soviet-German relations. In

[13] Gerald Freund, *Unholy Alliance. Russian-German Relations from the Treaty of Brest-Litovsk to the Treaty of Berlin*, p. 51.

[14] Trotsky Archive, Harvard University, T.666. Copy supplied.

addition, German companies asked by the Reichswehr to invest in Soviet munitions works wondered about the permanence and stability of the Lenin-Trotsky regime, its ability to pay, and the feasibility of building up a potential competitor. Influential German, and French, industrial magnates inclined to the view, after Moscow launched the New Economic Policy (NEP) in March, 1921, that it would soon be compelled to invite western capital to take over Russia's collapsing economy.

But the biggest obstacle to smooth Reichswehr-Russian and, in general, German-Russian relations was the Kremlin's faith in the imminence of revolution in Germany. There were myriad reasons for unhappiness in that defeated country. The entire nation was unhappy. What distinguished the communists was a mixture of fury, adventure, and idealism which translated itself into violent uprisings doomed to fail. Yet Russian revolutionary tradition taught—and German communist leaders, with notable exceptions, believed—that each repulse was a rehearsal for "inevitable" victory according to the prophecy of Marx. If the November 7, 1917, coup d'état triumphed in backward Russia, why should not a similar coup succeed in the Germany of advanced capitalism and a massive, well-organized proletariat?

The bulk of the German working class, however, voted for the reformist, antirevolutionary Social Democratic Party (SPD) whose detestation of tsarist despotism was no small factor in its decision to support the Kaiser's entry into the first world war. The overthrow of the Romanovs might have altered the party's attitude toward Russia, but before the democratic Kerensky interregnum could make a deep impression the SPD's abhorrence of Russia was confirmed by the terror of the Bolshevik dictatorship. Karl Kautsky, the ideological heir of Marx and Engels, attacked the new absolutism. So did Rosa Luxemburg, the SPD's best theoretical brain. She had expected her god, revolution, to descend upon earth clad in the immaculate white of freedom.

The German Communist Party consequently began life as a small minority of the working class and a smaller minority of the nation. But the communists scoffed at the religion of numbers called democracy. Their credo was violence. "Objectively," they said, Germany was ready for revolution. They were riding the coattails of history as agents of a dawning future. This, and Moscow's approbation, weighed more than big battalions.

From 1919 to 1923, accordingly, the German communists launched several poorly planned, poorly armed attempts to seize political control of the country.

Communism's only chance to win in Germany vanished with the signing of the armistice on November 11, 1918. Eleven days earlier sailors at

Kiel had mutinied. Soviets of workers and soldiers sprang up in Berlin and other cities. Their purpose was peace and the death of the monarchy; when the war came to an end so did the soviets. Where they did not disintegrate the Reichswehr dispersed them. The communists, however, could not read this handwriting on the wall. With persistence worthy of a better prospect they jumped to the barricades in every national crisis, real or imagined. In January, 1919, a few days after the formation of the Communist Party of Germany (KPD), adventurous elements of the Independent Social Democratic Party, a radical offshoot of the SPD, and the Revolutionary Shop Stewards took to the streets dreaming they could overthrow the new republican government. The KPD blithely joined. Result: a waste of human blood, the brutal assassination by embryo Nazis of KPD leaders Rosa Luxemburg and Karl Liebknecht, and revulsion among German workers against communist irresponsibility.

Communism was synonymous with discipline, yet in the country famous for discipline it galloped into battle like a frisky colt ignorant of where it was going. Uncoordinated, sporadic fighting between disgruntled workers and the army occurred throughout Germany. In Bavaria, land of monarchism and separatism, the Independent Social Democrats (USPD) had formed a government under Kurt Eisner. When he was assassinated by an officer, a group of radicals distinguished by the membership of Ernst Toller, a moody poet who committed suicide in New York in the 1930's, and Gustav Landauer, a literary critic, and led by Russian-born Eugene Leviné, set up a Bavarian Soviet government in Munich on April 13, 1919. It was an amateurishly welded coalition of Independents, communists, and Bohemians. A fortnight later the Independents bolted,[15] thus robbing the government of much of its grassroots strength. That very day—April 27—Lenin, who could hardly have had adequate information on the Bavarian chaos, wrote a telegram: "Thanks for your greetings and on our part we greet the Bavarian Soviet Republic with all our heart. . . . Have you formed soviets of workers and maids in all wards of the city, have you armed the workers, disarmed the bourgeoisie, used the warehouses of clothing and other goods for immediate and general aid to workers and especially to farm laborers and poor peasants, have you expropriated the factories and the wealth of the capitalists in Munich as well as the capitalistic farms in its environs, have you canceled the mortgages and rents of poor peasants, doubled or tripled the wages of farm laborers and unskilled workers, confiscated all the paper and all print shops in order to issue popular circulars and newspapers for the masses, introduced the six-hour day and two- or

[15] Lenin, Vol. 38, Editorial note, pp. 477-478.

three-hour courses on how to run a government, squeezed the Munich bourgeoisie into one or two rooms of their apartments so as to move workers into the rich homes, have you taken over all banks, have you taken hostages from the bourgeoisie, introduced bigger food rations for the workers than for the bourgeoisie, conscripted every single worker for defense and for ideological propaganda in nearby villages? . . ."[16] Alas, poor soviets, they lacked the power to do any one of these things. In fact, the central soviet, drugged by Ernst Toller's oratory, overthrew the communist government and substituted "a dictatorship of natives."[17] But the days of the soviet were numbered. On May 1, the proletarian holiday, troops entered Munich against negligible resistance and restored Bavarian reaction. Leviné was executed.

The first (and last) years of the Weimar Republic saw the so-called Right and the so-called Left eating at the vitals of the weak postwar democratic system with the declared purpose of killing it. The western victors made no contribution to its stability. In fact, one might have suspected them of colluding with the reactionaries or Reds in undermining it. On February 7, 1920, the Allies ordered the German government to surrender more than eight hundred military and civilian leaders as war criminals. No Cabinet could have lasted one day after complying. They were never surrendered. The Allies likewise demanded reparations beyond, as subsequent events demonstrated, Germany's ability to pay. The uncertain future of the nation convinced adventurers they could shape it.

From the middle of 1919 a militarist-monarchist cabal, led by Dr. Wolfgang Kapp, a rabid Pan-German imperialist, and General Walther von Luettwitz, high-ranking Reichswehr commander, had been planning to overthrow the government of the republic; it struck early on the morning of March 13, 1920, when the Erhardt and Baltic Brigades, known for reactionary sympathies, marched into Berlin and were welcomed at the Brandenburger Tor by Ludendorff and Luettwitz in uniform and Kapp and civilians of his staff in cutaways, top hats, and spats.[18] The government fled to Stuttgart.

The Kapp Putsch succeeded—for four days. On March 17 Kapp escaped to Sweden, his escapade over for two main reasons: Seeckt said the Reichswehr would not shoot at Kapp's troops, neither would it support Kapp; secondly, the Social Democratic trade unions called a general strike which paralyzed the country. Kapp proved deficient in ruthlessness and political sense.

16 *Ibid.*, pp. 321-322.

17 F. Borkenau, *World Communism. A History of the Communist International*, New Introduction by Raymond Aron, p. 150.

18 Wheeler-Bennett, p. 77.

The German Communist Party made no move against the Kapp coup. On the contrary, when the SPD proclaimed the general strike the party told workers "not to lift a finger for the democratic republic." The Berlin communist daily, *Rote Fahne,* of March 14 declared that the "Republic, the bourgeois democracy, can no longer be saved; it is merely an empty pretense, merely a cracked mask for the capitalist dictatorship. . . . All revolutionary workers must rally around the red flag of the proletarian dictatorship."[19] Not for the last time the communists acted under the illusion that victory for one form of dictatorship would pave a short highway to their own. Some communists and Independent Socialists actually thought the Kapp Putsch a proper prelude to a Red Putsch and took up arms in the Ruhr and Chemnitz. They fought the Reichswehr bravely. The army subdued them.

Lenin, addressing the Russian Communist Party Congress on March 29, 1920, found encouragement in the Kapp Putsch. "And internationally," he said, "our situation has never been as favorable as now, and what especially fills us with joy and courage is the news which reaches us from Germany and which shows that, however difficult and hard may be the birth of the socialist revolution, proletarian soviet power in Germany is growing irresistibly." After the Kapp Putsch, he added, "the tide began to turn toward proletarian power not only among the mass of city workers but also in the village proletariat of Germany, and this development is of global historical significance . . . it gives us confidence that the day is not remote when we shall walk hand in hand with a German Soviet government."[20]

How close to fantasy Lenin's hopes were is indicated by the results of the first national elections of the Reichstag on June 6, 1920: the Social Democrats won 6, 104,000 votes and 102 seats, the Independent Social Democrats 5,046,800 votes and 84 seats, the communists 589,000 votes and two seats.

Undaunted by this electoral fiasco, undeterred by the Red Army's failure to carry communism to Germany after the invasion of Poland in midsummer, 1920, the Kremlin tried a novel gambit: it sent Zinoviev to Germany. Zinoviev was the president of the Third International which proposed to make the world safe for communism and Soviet Russia safe from disaster. He had faltered on the eve of the Bolshevik revolution by opposing Lenin's plans for a coup d'état. Forgiven, Lenin, who sometimes displayed a sense of humor, put him in charge of the export-of-communism business. In this capacity Zinoviev arrived on October 12, 1920, in the German city of Halle where the Independent Social Demo-

[19] Werner T. Angress, *Stillborn Revolution. The Communist Bid for Power, 1921-1923,* p. 45.

[20] Lenin, Vol. 40, pp. 225-226.

cratic Party met in convention. A month and a day later, back in Petrograd, he had finished an 88-page pamphlet on his twelve-day stay in Germany.[21]

The Independents were revolution-minded, hence their secession from the gradualist SPD. They had sent observers to the Second Congress of the Third International (Comintern) held in July-August, 1920, in Petrograd and Moscow, who accepted eighteen of the "Twenty-one Conditions" adopted by that congress for the admission of new parties. These provided, for instance, that every communist party must conduct illegal propaganda in the armed forces of its country; oppose "the hypocrisy of social pacifism"; insist that "without the revolutionary overthrow of capitalism" no League of Nations, or arms reduction, or international arbitration can "prevent new imperialist wars"; formally call itself "communist" and a branch of the Comintern; and undertake to publish all important documents emanating from the headquarters of the Comintern. But they denounced the last three conditions because, as Zinoviev phrased it for them in his pamphlet, "we reject the dictatorship of Moscow." Why they strained at the three, which merely dotted the "i," and swallowed the eighteen, which gave the Kremlin intimate control of every foreign communist party, is not clear. They probably anticipated that their party would be torn asunder by the question of joining the Comintern and used the last three conditions, which made the subjugation explicit, as a possible escape hatch.[22]

It was to convince the Independents to accept all twenty-one conditions that Zinoviev went to Halle. He addressed small groups of delegates; he addressed the entire congress in his high, feminine voice for four hours. He reports that in the end "nearly two thirds" of the delegates voted to approve the Twenty-one Conditions. In consequence, the Independent Social Democratic Party (USPD) split. By December, 1920, some 300,000 of the USPD's 890,000 members entered the German Communist Party which, before that windfall, counted, officially, 78,715 members.[23] Thus reinforced, the communists proposed to conduct subversive propaganda within the Reichswehr while the Soviet government negotiated with it and to prepare for the always-"inevitable" German communist state.

However, the Stalin era of the monolithic Soviet state and submissive world communist movement had not yet arrived. Incontrovertible evi-

[21] G. Sinowjew, *Zwoelf Tage in Deutschland* (G. Zinoviev, Twelve Days in Germany).

[22] Complete German text of the twenty-one conditions in Hermann Weber, *Die Kommunistische Internationale, Eine Dokumentation*, pp. 55-62. Unabridged English text in Jane Degras (Ed.), *The Communist International, 1919-1943, Documents*, Vol. I, pp. 166-172.

[23] Angress, pp. 72-73.

dence points to sharp divisions inside foreign communist parties and, more important, to actions by some Moscow leaders which clashed with the views of other leaders, including Lenin, on the correct strategy the parties should pursue. But it is unfair to blame those who took an anti-Lenin direction; they did not always know what direction he was taking. For at the very time—March 29, 1920—he told the party congress that "the day is not remote when we shall walk hand in hand with a German Soviet government" he was writing a book, *The Infantile Disease of 'Leftism' in Communism,* completed on April 6, 1920, which excoriated German communist-leftists for their revolutionary impatience.[24] "Decades ago," he wrote, "it was possible, with complete justice, to proclaim that capitalism was 'historically obsolete,' but this does not in the least remove the necessity of a very long stubborn struggle *within the framework* of capitalism." Therefore the German leftists were wrong, Lenin contended, in scorning work in trade unions and parliament. "It is obvious that parliamentarianism *is not yet* politically obsolete. It is obvious that the 'leftists' in Germany have taken their *wishes* . . . for objective fact." "Revolutionary parties," Lenin emphasized, "must continue their studies. They had studied how to advance. Now they should understand that this science has to be supplemented by the science of how better to retreat." During the present revolutionary trough communists "must certainly learn to work legally in the most reactionary parliaments, in the most reactionary trade unions, cooperatives . . . and similar organizations."

Within three months Lenin nevertheless decided to bring communism to Poland and Germany on the tips of Red army bayonets, and when Paul Levi, leader of the German Communist Party, expressed skepticism about the prospects of revolution in Germany, Lenin bristled. Thereafter Moscow turned its back on Levi. Yet Paul Levi's policy for the KPD was identical with Lenin's. He advocated "an alliance with Soviet Russia." This meant either a German government alliance or a KPD alliance with Russia. If the former, he was not out of line with Moscow. If the latter, he was anticipating and voluntarily accepting the role imposed by Moscow a few years later on all foreign communist parties. He abhorred premature revolutionary uprisings, resented the heavy hand of the Kremlin on the KPD, and stood on the Leninist platform of slow uphill work in trade unions, parliament, and elections. The KPD leadership voted against him, as much for his political independence as for his political strategy. He accordingly resigned as party chairman. Clara Zetkin, Lenin's friend, resigned from the leadership; others too. The new leadership thereupon launched an uprising in March, 1921.

[24] Lenin, Vol. 41, pp. 3-104.

"The various steps which led to the March uprising are even today a matter of controversy."[25] Everything about the uprising remains controversial because the party leadership operated in secret, some of the party's branches operated in secret from the leadership, Moscow acted secretly, and the police which coped with the uprising concealed its plans. The general German background of the abortive coup, however, was clearly discernible: inside: hunger, inflation, unemployment, strong reactionary trends, political instability; abroad: Allied pressure for excessive indemnities and procedures threatening to rob Germany of more territory. Those whom Lenin had branded "infantile leftists" decided to snatch power from the feeble hands of the anemic republic.

During the first week of March, 1921, three foreign communists, representatives of the Comintern, arrived in Germany. They were Bela Kun, who had presided over the short-lived communist regime in Hungary; Joseph Pepper, also known as Joseph Pogany, formerly president of the Hungarian Soldiers' soviet, subsequently Comintern agent in the United States; and a Pole named August Goralsky. March, 1921, was a crisis month in Soviet Russia marked by the Kronstadt revolt and the official legalization of petty capitalism to forestall even graver peasant revolts. Large-scale strikes had closed Petrograd factories in February. For Zinoviev, political boss of Petrograd, president of the Comintern, victory in Germany would offset defeats at home. Bukharin, foremost champion of revolutionary war against Germany in 1918 as an alternative to signing the Brest-Litovsk treaty, had not yet shed his youthful leftism; he wished to implement abroad the radicalism the New Economic Policy (NEP) now precluded within Soviet Russia. Only the third member of the Comintern's managing triumvirate, Karl Radek, cynic, skeptic, and expert on German affairs who had sided with Paul Levi against the "leftists," opposed drastic measures in Germany. But Lenin was absorbed by the problems of the NEP, Trotsky directed the attack against the mutinous Kronstadt fortress, and Zinoviev, Bukharin, and Bela Kun consequently felt free to encourage irresponsible elements of the KPD who yearned for violent action and had already started what Clara Zetkin called "revolutionary calisthenics."

The turmoil raged from March 19 to March 31, when the well-built, highly trained men of the Prussian security police (Schupo) restored calm. A few weeks later the KPD admitted that its membership had fallen to 200,000. Just as many had left the unseaworthy ship sailing under two flags and a committee of captains.

This was not the end.

[25] Angress, p. 110.

X RAPALLO

Mountainous obstacles met General Hans von Seeckt, commander of the Reichswehr, in advancing toward his goal of Russo-German military collaboration. He had to dispel the army's angry mood after the German Communist Party's attempts at revolution. The uninterrupted and precipitous fall in the value of the mark reduced the usefulness of German currency in the kind of investment he contemplated in Soviet armament industries. He encountered hard-necked resistance among officials who warned that Moscow would betray Germany and sell itself to France by revealing his secret projects, illegal under the Versailles peace treaty; Paris might then penalize the Reichswehr and the national exchequer. Nothing deterred Seeckt. He considered his pro-Soviet strategy vital to the fate of the army and Germany. Brockdorff-Rantzau condemned Seeckt's eagerness; the Russians, he prophesied, would give less than they took. Seeckt called him a "Querkopf."[1] Scanning the horizon he saw no ally but Russia. A bridge between Germany and Russia would be a barrier between France and Russia.

The informal initiative of Enver Pasha, Seeckt's emissary in Moscow, was soon followed by direct negotiations between the German military and War Commissar Leon Trotsky. When Rantzau mentioned this pathfinding event to Chancellor Joseph Wirth in 1922, Wirth said "the steps taken by General von Seeckt are known to me by and large but not in detail."[2] The Chancellor apparently wished to intimate that civilians would escape responsibility and Seeckt's ire by remaining interested yet remote. It transpired that neither Wirth nor Rantzau left the field to the general. In Moscow, under the Lenin principle of party paramountcy, the military sat in the second row during decision making.

In the summer of 1921 Seeckt established Special Group R. Nobody was to guess that the "R" stood for "Russland" (Russia). Shortly thereafter Major Oskar von Niedermayer (Neumann for concealment), again appeared in Moscow. With Deputy Foreign Commissar Leo Karakhan, Victor Kopp, Soviet representative in Berlin, and Gustav Hilger, a German born in Moscow who later became Rantzau's counselor of embassy,

[1] An untranslatable word. It might be rendered: cranky, queer, obstructionist.

[2] Francis L. Carsten, *Reichswehr und Politik*, p. 81, from Rantzau's archives.

Neumann-Niedermayer traveled to Petrograd to inspect large munitions plants the Kremlin wanted restored. But the plants had been so overworked during the world war and the civil war that the Germans despaired.[3] The future thus emerged: Special Group R would have to build new factories in Soviet Russia.

Moscow persistently expressed a desire to have the German firm of Junkers construct airplanes on Soviet territory. In December, 1921, Junkers representatives and Reichswehr officers, notably Colonel Otto Hasse, Seeckt's right-hand man in these matters, interviewed Trotsky and Chief of Staff General P. Lebedev. On March 15, 1922, an agreement was signed by Junkers and a Reichswehr commission for the erection of an airplane factory at Fili, eight miles from Moscow.[4] The commission supplied the capital.

The road to Rapallo was now open. Rapallo is the name of a place and the symbol of the policy embodied in the Rapallo treaty of close cooperation between the Soviet and German governments. Neither side called the treaty an alliance, the Soviets because they still shrank from such a tie with a bourgeois state, the Germans because they feared the repercussions at home among anticommunists, abroad among the victors. The Rapallo treaty was signed during a pause for intrigue in the Genoa Conference.

Politicians convene diplomatic conferences for a variety of purposes, not the least being an all-consuming desire to prolong their tenure in office. The Genoa Conference was cofathered on the Cannes golf course in January, 1922, by British Prime Minister David Lloyd George and French Premier and Foreign Minister Aristide Briand. France was divided between advocates of Briand's political-financial solution, without ultimatums, of the German reparations problem and the supporters of a drastic, even military, solution sponsored by former President and former Premier Raymond Poincaré intent on unhorsing Briand. To stay the lance Poincaré had pointed at his career, Briand concocted the idea of a conference at Genoa to deal with German reparations and Russia's debts. Before the conference met, Poincaré drove the weapon into Briand's back. The Premier fell. Poincaré succeeded him. The question of German reparations was removed from the Genoa agenda. Remained Russia only.

Lloyd George's political future was likewise threatened. He had led Britain to victory in 1918 and governed ever since. His fiery Welsh temperament and Welsh eloquence made him Britain's finest political orator of the century and her most effective House of Commons man. In

[3] Gustav Hilger and Alfred G. Meyer, *The Incompatible Allies, A Memoir-History of German-Russian Relations 1918-1941*, p. 195.

[4] Carsten, p. 144.

office or out, the House filled whenever he rose to speak. With his sparkling eyes, ruddy face, ready smile, and long mane, silvery white when I saw him on his farm in Churt in the late thirties and in 1941, he was a charismatic figure. He had not scrupled to manipulate men and money for his own greater glory and that of his Liberal Party. A populist craving popularity and power, he hated church, army, and landlords (the English establishment) and fathered the country's first long-range welfare legislation. Now, in 1922, he had ruled too long and accumulated enemies determined to oust him from the premiership. Success at Genoa would extend his lease on No. 10 Downing Street.

Lloyd George wanted Genoa to be a spectacle where "big men met big men" and he voiced the hope that Lenin would attend. When the invitation came, Lenin sent a note to fellow members of the Politburo opposing his or Trotsky's or Zinoviev's trip to Italy or any foreign country.[5]

Lenin named the possibility of assassination by Russian Whites "as one reason among others" for his refusal to go abroad. Severe headaches, storm warnings of an impending stroke, gave him insomnia; bad health was an additional major reason. Moreover, he was reluctant to contribute to a spectacle he wanted to fail. On January 23, 1922, Lenin telephoned a message to all Politburo members saying, "I consider it absolutely necessary to accept the Krupp proposal, right now, before the Genoa Conference. For us it would be endlessly important to conclude at least one, and preferably several, concession contracts with German firms in particular."[6]

Lenin considered an agreement with Krupp to manufacture arms in Soviet Russia a means of blocking Lloyd George's grandiose scheme for a European settlement that might menace Russia's economic independence. The scheme, adumbrated at Cannes for presentation to the Soviet diplomats at Genoa, envisaged the formation of an "International Corporation . . . for the purpose of the economic reconstruction of Europe" with government financing. In Cannes German Foreign Minister Walther Rathenau, a pro-western industrialist and sensitive writer on philosophical matters, dwelt on his nation's right to join. "Germany," he submitted, ". . . is acquainted with the technical and economic conditions and with the customs of the East."[7]

Lenin's eye penetrated the design: the British, with or without France, would link Germany to themselves and together take over the floundering Soviet economy. International action was what the Kremlin

[5] Trotsky Archive, Harvard University, T. 722. Copy supplied.

[6] *Ibid.*, T. 726.

[7] Walther Rathenau, *Cannes und Genoa. Vier Reden Zum Reparationsproblem. Mit Einem Anhang*, p. 18.

feared most. Lenin preferred granting business concessions to Krupp and similar German trusts in order to draw Germany away from the West to Russia. The ideologues of socialist collectivism repulsed capitalist collectivism. And not without cause, for the "Europa Consortium," so named after the United States refused to join, went so far as to propose what Foreign Commissar Chicherin judged to be "economic domination over Russia." On January 27, 1922, he told the All-Russian Central Executive Committee (VTSIK), Russia's nearest approach to a parliament, that the Soviet government would never accept foreign aid on those terms. To confirm his blackest fears, the French Cabinet published a note, dated February 15, 1922, urging the introduction of "an actual system of capitulations" for Russia, a system prevailing in China and Turkey before the war. Capitulations were spelled out in the London Memorandum drafted in March, 1922, by government experts from England, France, Italy, Belgium, and Japan under the attentive eye of French Finance Minister Louis Loucheur: A foreigner could be arrested in Soviet Russia only in the presence of and with the consent of his consul; no searches were to be undertaken in the homes or industrial installations of foreigners; sentences on foreigners passed by Soviet courts required consular approval; Soviet labor laws would not be maintained in foreign plants; etc.[8] This would have denied the Soviet secret police one of its greatest pleasures. The London Memorandum also envisaged the creation of free entry zones in two or three Russian ports and thus a partial dismantling of the Bolshevik monopoly of export-import trade which Lenin would resist to the death.[9]

Small wonder Lenin preferred an agreement with Germany before Genoa to anything the conference might produce. In fact Lenin and Chicherin contemplated the desirability of torpedoing the Genoa Conference before it convened or, at worst, during its sessions. For this purpose the Kremlin had a choice of missiles, small and large. Twice, on January 29 and February 10, Trotsky wrote Lenin, copies to other Soviet leaders, expressing alarm over news that the British Labour Party had urged Lloyd George to invite to Genoa representatives of the Menshevik government of Georgia deposed by the Soviets when the Red Army occupied that Caucasian state. Trotsky also feared the western powers might ask agents of Denikin and similar White Guard groups to Genoa. This "would certainly make it impossible for us to participate in such conferences." He suggested that the Soviet press and trade unions protest admitting delegations from Georgia, nationalist Armenia,

[8] Complete text in British Blue Book, *Papers Relating to the International Economic Conference, Genoa, April-May, 1922*, Cmd. 1677.

[9] Louis Fischer, *The Life of Lenin*, Chap. L.

Wrangel, and so forth to Genoa.[10] Lenin disagreed mischievously: "I don't agree with you about [Arthur] Henderson [British Labour leader] concerning Georgia (at Genoa). In my opinion, Henderson, like Kerensky, *helps us* (out of folly). . . . Just let Henderson put *them* (Lloyd George and Poincaré) to shame. The Soviet Trade Union Council and the trade unions are to keep quiet. *Izvestia* is to praise Henderson for 'the happy thought' of enlarging the scope of the conference, enlarging it, of course, not only by including Georgia but all nations and colonies . . . Lenin."[11]

The Soviet diplomats would have walked out had the Genoa Conference seated spokesmen of the Georgian Menshevik government in exile. The Kremlin disposed of more potent ammunition too. Karl Radek saw General von Seeckt on February 10. In October, 1921, the western victors, ignoring the unequivocal results of a plebiscite in Upper Silesia, had assigned the greater part of that territory, rich in coal and heavy industry, to Poland. Radek understood the thoughts and emotions this development aroused in Seeckt and knew how to play on them. Cynically Radek declared Soviet Russia planned to attack Poland in the spring and required reinforcements for its air force. En route to Genoa in April, Chicherin too stopped in Berlin and conferred with Chancellor Wirth. The Chancellor was by this time convinced that "Poland must be finished off."[12]

Chicherin, as he told me some years later, had by now despaired of any positive outcome of the Genoa Conference, and, knowing that Krupp, Hugo Stinnes, the mighty industrial wizard of German heavy industry, and Gustav Stresemann, leader of the Volkspartei, favored bilateral Russo-German negotiations without waiting for Genoa, the Foreign Commissar, in his squeaky voice and with relentless persistence, asked that a treaty between the two countries be signed forthwith, in Berlin. Litvinov, Commissar of Foreign Trade Leonid B. Krassin, Ambassador Adolf A. Yoffe, Christian G. Rakovsky, and Foreign Commissariat legal advisers and experts, in the German capital on their way to the Italian seaport, added their weight to Chicherin's demand. The document was therefore drafted and prepared for signature. Foreign Minister Rathenau objected; he still hoped Genoa would provide international economic collaboration with Russia through the Europa Consortium and an amicable settlement of the German reparations issue. The President of Germany, Friedrich Ebert, and his Social Democratic Party upheld Rathenau's hand. Rathenau realized that a Russo-German

[10] Trotsky Archive, T. 727 and T. 731.
[11] *Ibid.*, T. 732.
[12] Carsten, pp. 144-145.

treaty would torpedo the Genoa Conference before it opened. The Soviet diplomats did not care. Nor did Seeckt. Rathenau prevailed, and the Soviet and German delegations proceeded south separately. To strengthen its own position at Genoa by creating the impression of Russo-German friendship the German government gave the Soviets the building of the Tsarist Embassy at No. 7 Unter den Linden.

From Berlin Litvinov had reported to Moscow that "according to preliminary information, France has decided, come what may, to blow up the conference. . . . Lloyd George remains in power through the kindness of his Conservative colleagues in the Cabinet . . . on the Russian question he meets serious opposition from the Conservative members of his Cabinet and his friend Churchill. In London our uncompromising attitude on the question of debts is already known and the Conference is considered doomed."[13]

When Soviet diplomacy has nothing to lose it revels in propaganda, tail-twisting, and general mischief.

This set the stage for the Soviet actors at Genoa. They appeared in costume: striped pants and cutaways, black top hats and white silk gloves; Chicherin clinked glasses with an archbishop and bowed to the King of Italy. Italian communists, members of a party recently formed by the Comintern's emissary Matthias Rakosi out of a rib taken without anesthetic from the body of the Italian Socialist Party, watched goggle-eyed. They had expected to see the proletarian leaders of their new world. The real spectacle came inside during the first act, with Chicherin in the stellar role. He had rehearsed the role in Moscow with Lenin.

The official designation of the Genoa conference was European Economic Conference, and Lenin specifically stated on March 6, 1922. ". . . *we greet Genoa and will go there* . . . we are going there as merchants." But he was no merchant, nor was Chicherin, and when they realized that the chances of achieving a settlement of Russia's financial debts to the West (and of obtaining credits) were dismal, they reverted to type.

Chicherin, in Moscow, drafted his speech for the Genoa Conference opening session and sent it to Lenin, who commented on March 10: "It seems to me you yourself have made an excellent presentation of the pacifist program." Chicherin was no pacifist. Lenin was no pacifist. Communists believe in civil wars as well as in "just" international wars. (To belligerents all wars are "just.") "The whole art consists in stating it"—the "pacifist" program—"and our merchants' program," Lenin's letter to Chicherin continued, "clearly and loudly *before* the dispersal (if 'they' bring about an early dispersal). . . . If they don't allow you to read it, we will *publish* it with a protest."

[13] U.S.S.R. Ministry of Foreign Affairs, *Dokumenty Vneshnei Politiki SSSR* (Documents on the Foreign Policy of the U.S.S.R.), Vol. V, pp. 184-185.

"They" allowed Chicherin to read it on April 10. He spoke in French and translated his speech into English. "The Russian delegation," he asserted, "has not come here to propagate its own theoretical ideology but to establish business relations with the governments and the commercial-industrial circles of all countries on the basis of mutuality, equality of rights, and complete and unconditional recognition." Russia, "the largest nation in Europe," had endless natural wealth in Europe and Siberia and was ready to offer it to foreign concessionaires. The Soviet government would also "open its frontiers for international transit." In this connection Chicherin referred to Russia's debts: "However, the economic restoration of Russia and, with it, the effort to end economic chaos in Europe would take a false and disastrous road if the economically stronger nations, instead of creating the necessary conditions for the economic restoration of Russia and facilitating her future development, burdened her with excessive demands left over from her hated past." The legislation accompanying the introduction of the New Economic Policy (NEP) "offered the necessary guarantees for economic collaboration with Soviet Russia by states based on private property."

There followed the "pacifist" caveat which Chicherin had discussed with Lenin: ". . . all efforts directed to the restoration of world economy would be vain as long as the threat of new wars hovers over the earth." Therefore, "the Russian delegation intends, during the further labors of this conference, to put forward for consideration the universal limitation of armaments" and the "total prohibition" of poison gas, air bombardments, and especially attacks on civilians." Watching with pleasure as the hackles rose on some delegates, Chicherin urged that future conferences—Lloyd George had proposed convening them—be attended by "the representatives of all peoples"—colonial peoples too—and by "workers' organizations." He also suggested "the amendment of the charter of the League of Nations" to convert it into "a true union of nations without the domination of some by others."[14]

The moment Chicherin resumed his seat, Jean Louis Barthou, Poincaré's newly appointed Foreign Minister to succeed Briand, sprang to his feet. He strenuously objected, he said, to the kind of permanent institute envisaged by the Commissar, with world conference following world conference. Moreover, there was nothing in the Genoa agenda about disarmament and for him this question was sternly excluded from the deliberations.

Chicherin rose to reply. The agenda was open, nevertheless he would not insist on expanding it. He alluded to disarmament merely because at the 1921-22 Washington Arms Limitation Conference Briand stated that

[14] *Ibid.*, pp. 191-195.

France could not disarm while Russia was armed and not participating. Russia was prepared to disarm yet would not press the matter here. Lloyd George, foreseeing a perpetual duel between the Soviet and French delegates which threatened death to his political-lifesaving conference, poured wit on the stormy waters. The conference laughed and retired to the safety of commissions working behind closed doors on concrete issues: Russia's debts, Russia's counterclaims, Russia's need of credits, and Russia's readiness to trade.

On March 6, 1922, Lenin addressed the communist fraction of the All-Russian Congress of Metal Workers, and, discussing the impending Genoa Conference, said, "If the capitalist gentlemen think that they can delay matters and the later it gets the more concessions we will make to them, I repeat, we must say to them, *Enough, tomorrow you will get nothing.*"[15]

This is the whole story. The foreign governments and foreign individuals and companies delayed matters at Genoa and at subsequent conferences. They delayed matters for years of endless meetings, angry denunciations, and threats. In the end they got nothing. The Soviet government never paid.

It is uncertain whether Moscow would have admitted a large measure of foreign capital. Chicherin said at Genoa it would, and at the moment he may have been speaking the truth. But his superiors could have changed their minds when they saw the beginning of the flood. Where, as in the case of Reichswehr-Russia relations, both sides needed one another and quickly saw the first beneficial results, satisfactory arrangements were made and maintained. But the West was suspicious of the Bolsheviks, expected them to fail without foreign aid and then accept China-like capitulations. Many capitalists thought it would be foolish to prop up a government committed to destroying them. In the end that government prospered and grew mighty without them but at inhuman cost to the people of Russia.

One further mistake remained for the victorious allies to make at Genoa and they made it; they excluded Germany from the top-level private discussions in the First (Political) Commission consisting of representatives of twenty-seven European countries, Japan, three British dominions, and Russia. Its first session created a subcommission of delegates from France, Britain, Italy, Japan, Belgium, Soviet Russia, Germany, Poland, Rumania, Sweden, and Switzerland. For the record, the Russians protested the presence of Rumania which had occupied Bessarabia and of Japan which held Russian territory in the Far East. But even a subcommission of eleven was unwieldy and untrustworthy; some-

[15] V. I. Lenin, *Polnoye Sobranye,* Vol. 45, p. 13.

body would reveal the inside story. Soon, therefore, the Soviet delegates were closeted alone with Lloyd George and his assistants in the Villa d'Albertis. The French were kept informed. The German delegation was isolated in the cold.

This presented the Soviet delegation with an opportunity for blackmail. Diplomatic blackmail is a lethal weapon wrapped in beautiful paper and tied with a red silk ribbon—like a Christmas gift. The weapon this time was Article 116 of the Versailles peace treaty by which "The Allied and Associated Powers reserve the rights of Russia to obtain from Germany restitution and reparation based on the principles of the Present Treaty." Rumors began to spread that Article 116 was a subject of discussion between the Russians and Lloyd George. Russia would get German reparations; with these she could pay part of her debt to the West; Germany would be burdened with additional reparations. The rumors made the Germans squirm. The conference might produce an arrangement between West and East for which Germany would have to pay.

The British and the Soviets were trading astronomical figures.

The Soviet delegation came to Genoa armed with a most detailed memorandum—it filled sixty-one pages, in fine print, of an average-size book[16]—giving the official Kremlin account of Russia's foreign debts and her counterclaims on foreign governments. The killed and dead from wounds and illness, the men lost without trace, and the crippled in all countries that fought the German coalition in World War I, the memorandum said, numbered 17 million persons of whom 7.5 million were Russian citizens. That entitled Russia to 35 billion gold marks (approximately $8.6 billion) in German reparations. Further: the first world war had cost the Russian budget 35.5 billion gold rubles (approximately $17.75 billion). The Soviet government regarded this as an Allied debt to Russia, for whereas the several peace treaties after the war had brought the Allied belligerents compensation in the form of colonies and enemy territories, Russia received nothing. There followed a minutely itemized statement of Russia's losses in agriculture, industry, mining, transportation, and so forth from Allied blockade, intervention, and civil war totaling 39,044,970,000 gold rubles (approximately $19, 522,485,000). In that remote age these were dizzying sums.

Against Russian claims on foreign governments, the Soviet memorandum gave Russia's debt to the West as, more or less, 9.5 billion gold rubles (approximately $4.75 billion). Chicherin, reporting to Moscow from Genoa on April 15, 1922, intimated that, while the western powers might refuse to recognize Russia's counterclaims, they would, in effect,

[16] *Dokumenty Vneshnei Politiki SSSR,* Vol. V, pp. 298-359.

"write off our war debts and our interest payments with our counterclaims."[17]

This left prewar debts the biggest sticking point: compensation to individual foreigners and foreign firms who had suffered from Soviet nationalization of alien properties. Lloyd George spoke to Chicherin, Litvinov, and Krassin about the restitution of those properties, or concessions in lieu of restoration, or compensation. For the Bolsheviks, however, this was a matter of principle; a sovereign government has the right, they argued, to nationalize foreign installations within its boundaries.

The claims and counterclaims, the arguments pro and contra had scarcely been presented, much less exhaustively studied, and no quarrel or crisis had yet arisen between the two sides. But the Soviet delegation, knowing Moscow's preference for an agreement with Germany, maneuvered to conclude the treaty which had been drafted but not signed in Berlin. Chicherin and his coworkers played skillfully on the psychology of the Germans. The Foreign Commissar and his deputy, Maxim M. Litvinov, saw German Chancellor Wirth during the days after the opening Genoa session on April 10, and kept him informed on the proceedings in the Villa d'Albertis; things were going well, they stated on April 14. The German leaders tried to make an appointment with Lloyd George in order to hear his version of the talks with the Russians but failed to reach him. Meanwhile, Baron Ago von Maltzan, of the Russian division of the Berlin Foreign Office, told E. Frank Wise, one of Lloyd George's secretaries, about the draft Russo-German treaty, thus intimating that if it looked as though the Allies were prepared to assign German reparations to Russia, Germany would conclude the treaty with Moscow to prevent this. But no word came from Lloyd George and deep depression settled over the Hotel Eden where the German delegation lived.

The German delegation was divided between easterners and westerners. Maltzan, an easterner, had wanted to conclude the treaty in Berlin. Foreign Minister Rathenau, a westerner, hesitated even now. Out of the encircling gloom he still hoped to pluck a reduction in reparations. Maltzan took the initiative; he invited Soviet diplomats Rakovsky and Yoffe to meet him in a Genoa café at 10 A.M., April 15. Over the café table he inquired whether the Russians were ready to resume the treaty negotiations interrupted since Berlin. He hinted that if Russia came to an understanding with the Allies Germany would withhold industrial and military assistance from the Soviets. Yoffe and Rakovsky replied that

[17] *Ibid.*, p. 220.

they were not averse to putting the finishing touches on the treaty.

The Germans immediately carried this information to the British.

Saturday evening, April 15, the atmosphere in the Eden Hotel was bleaker than before, for rumor had it that the talks in Lloyd George's villa were moving toward success. This meant German reparations to Russia. In a black mood the Germans went to bed. At one in the morning, Easter Sunday, Yoffe awakened Maltzan with a telephone call. Would the German delegation come to the Hotel St. Margherite, the Soviet headquarters in nearby Rapallo, at eleven that morning? What about the discussions in the Villa d'Albertis? Maltzan asked. Those, Yoffe explained, were proceeding well; a recess had been called over Easter Sunday and Monday.

Maltzan awakened the entire German delegation for the famous "pajama party." They talked until three in the morning. Rathenau's opposition remained, but he was yielding ground. In the end the Germans decided to motor to Rapallo, and at 7 A.M. they telephoned Chicherin and told him so. Half an hour later a German diplomat tried to reach Frank Wise to pass the news on to Lloyd George; Rathenau probably hoped the British Prime Minister would pull Germany out of Russia's embrace. Wise was not attainable. At noon that Easter Sunday, accordingly, the Germans drove to the Russians' hotel, negotiated, edited the Berlin text, lunched late, and, at 6:30 P.M., Chicherin and Rathenau signed the document known as the Rapallo treaty.

The concept, text, and effect of the Rapallo treaty signed on April 16, 1922, are simplicity itself: it wiped the slate clean of all government and private claims and counterclaims of each party upon the other. No more debts, no more accounts. Secondly, the two governments would cooperate in the economic sphere, and, "The German government announces its readiness to give every possible support" to private German firms undertaking operations in Soviet Russia. In other words, Berlin would finance, and facilitate the construction by Germans, of military and nonmilitary installations on Russian territory. No need of a secret clause about military collaboration; if one had existed it would, now that the German archives are open, have come to light. Rapallo did not provide for mutual *de jure* recognition; that, the legal experts found, was the result of the Brest-Litovsk treaty of 1918. Rapallo merely said "diplomatic and consular relations between the RSFSR and the German Government would be resumed immediately."[18] Chicherin and Rathenau, however, exchanged similar, secret letters: in case the Soviets compensated any non-German private owners of enterprises nationalized in

[18] *Ibid.*, pp. 223-224. (English text, *League of Nations Treaty Series*, Vol. 19, pp. 250-252.)

Russia, Germans who had owned similar enterprises could claim their compensation.[19] This constituted a large obstacle to a Soviet settlement with the West.

After Rapallo—it created a great stir throughout the world; "German alliance with Bolshevism," many westerners cried—the Soviets lost interest in the Genoa Conference, which dragged on for almost six weeks of fruitless world diplomacy, until May 19. To conceal its useless life and unmourned death the Conference voted to resurrect itself in June at The Hague where, with fewer great names and less fanfare, the delegates again applied themselves to the knotty problems of debts, nationalized properties, credits, and industrial concessions; and, again, after millions of wasted words and tens of thousands of wasted diplomat man-hours, adjourned in failure and frustration. The non-Russians overestimated ruined Russia's capacity to pay. They underestimated Russia's fear of foreigners and her horror of foreign governments and trusts acting in unison. Finally, the outside world underestimated the Kremlin's ability to remain in power despite widespread discontent. After eight years of war, civil war, and famine, the Russian people, softened by centuries of docility and hardened by centuries of privation, were unlikely to rise up against a totalitarianism at once ruthless and flexible. The NEP nourished hopes of better times. Rapallo breached the solid capitalist front against Soviet Russia and strengthened the Bolsheviks' faith in their survival.

XI THE AGE OF STALIN

One year to the day after the opening of the Genoa Conference Brockdorff-Rantzau wrote a long letter in code marked "Personal for the Reich Chancellor." Foreign Commissar Chicherin had asked him, Rantzau reported, to express to the Chancellor "his most sincere thanks" for today's news. "These decisions, the People's Commissar stressed, were all the more valuable" in view of the impression created in February, 1923, that "an understanding between Germany and France was imminent" and that therefore Germany no longer attached any importance to business

[19] *Ibid.*, pp. 224-225.

with Russia. "Chicherin," Rantzau's letter concluded, "further requested me to pass on to you his cordial thanks for the settlement of the horse-hair matter."[1]

Horsehair ("Rosshaar" in German) in the military files! The aristocratic Soviet Commissar and the Chancellor of Germany dealing in horsehair? The term can only refer to some form of munitions. On April 10, 1923, when Rantzau wrote his letter, military collaboration between the two countries had considerably improved due to several tragic and crucial events. A little more than a month after Genoa German Foreign Minister Walther Rathenau, riding in a car to his office, was shot dead by two young men who, after a 23-day, nationwide manhunt, were tracked to a mountain lair; one was killed by police, the other then committed suicide. Years later the Hitler regime erected a monument to them. They assassinated Rathenau because he was a Jew, a westerner, because he had sought reconciliation with the West as a means of scaling down reparations. In 1921 and 1922 political rowdies of the same ilk assassinated 354 leading German republicans. The day Rathenau died Chancellor Wirth, standing on the Reichstag podium, turned to one side and exclaimed, "Gentlemen of the Right, things cannot continue as they have till now. There must be a thoroughgoing change. This growing terror, this nihilism which often hides under the cloak of patriotic sentiment, must no longer be treated with consideration. We shall act quickly." Early in November, 1922, the Wirth Cabinet fell; Wilhelm Cuno, director of the Hamburg-Amerika Line, replaced Wirth. Seeckt trusted him as he had not trusted Wirth and briefed him fully on the Reichswehr's deals with Moscow.

The passing of Rathenau and Wirth may have reinforced Premier Poincaré in his firmly held determination to collect reparations with bayonets. On January 11, 1923, the French army occupied the Ruhr, heartland of German industry. Belgium also sent troops; Britain abstained. The occupation of the Ruhr was a national calamity. The mark fell so fast that wages in Germany were paid out every evening and workingmen and employees rushed to the shops immediately after work hours lest the value of their money be cut a fifth by morning. In the Ruhr workers and protofascists, subsidized by the Cuno Government, battled foreign soldiers.

Leon Trotsky had made an unusual gesture to Germany on December

[1] *Politisches Archiv.* Auswaertiges Amt. *Akten betreffend: Militaerische Angelegenheiten m. Russland, vom Maerz 1923, bis August 1924. Bd 1, s.Bd* 2. During July, 1966, in Bonn, I was given access to the German Foreign Office archives for 1919 to 1941 and obtained permission to make photostats of more than 200 secret documents relating to German-Soviet affairs.

22, 1922: he visited Rantzau to tell him that if, as rumored abroad, France invaded the Ruhr, the Soviet government would stand by Germany and prevent Poland from making hostile military moves. Moscow realized that supreme antagonism between Germany and France might turn into its opposite, might persuade Germany to cooperate with France or face national disintegration, economic collapse, and starvation. To cope with the possibility of losing German friendship and thus nullifying Rapallo, Karl Radek appeared in Berlin in November, 1922, saw General von Seeckt, and re-emphasized Moscow's eagerness for military collaboration. He also discussed with the Reichswehr Commander in Chief his old idea of a united front between German communists and extreme-nationalist Germans. The idea was not as fantastic as it sounded; if the Soviet government could cooperate clandestinely with the rightist Reichswehr, why not collaboration between the German Communist Party (KPD) and the kind of embryo Nazis who killed Rathenau? This Radek strategy—it became known as the "Schlageter Line"—was frankly enunciated by him after the Ruhr occupation.

Albert Leo Schlageter, a German nationalist in his twenties, arrested by the French in the Ruhr for attempting to blow up railway tracks, was court-martialed and shot on May 26, 1923. Radek wrote an article for the Soviet press lauding the exploit of the young man as a patriotic act. When, on June 23, 1923, the Executive Committee of the Comintern (ECCI) met in Moscow to deliberate on the spread of fascism in Italy and Germany, Radek, speaking after Clara Zetkin, the German communist leader, said, "I could not follow Clara Zetkin's speech all through because all the time I had before my eyes the corpse of the German fascist, our class enemy, condemned and shot by French imperialism. . . . The fate of this German nationalist martyr should not be passed over in silence, or with a contemptuous phrase. . . . Schlageter, the courageous soldier of the counterrevolution, deserves honest and manly esteem from us, soldiers of the revolution. . . . Against whom do the German nationalists want to fight? Against Entente capital or the Russian people? With whom do they wish to ally themselves? With the Russian workers and peasants, together to shake off the yoke of Entente capital, or with the Entente to enslave the German and Russian peoples? Schlageter is dead and cannot answer this question. . . . If German patriotic circles do not decide to establish a front against Entente and German capital, then Schlageter's road was a road into a void, and Germany, faced by foreign invasion and by constant danger with the victors, will become the field of bloody internal battles, and it will be easy for the enemy to dismember and destroy it."[2] Subsequently, Radek revealed that this speech

[2] Jane Degras (Ed.), *The Communist International, 1919-1943.* Vol. II: *1923-1928,* pp. 39-40.

had been approved by the ECCI and specifically by Zinoviev, the leader of the Comintern, and that his Schlageter Declaration, published in the *Rote Fahne,* had been signed by Ernst Thaelmann, Ruth Fischer, and Arkad Maslow,[3] leaders of the KPD (Fischer and Maslow were known as "leftists").

The Schlageter Line, however, was not well baited, and the Right did not bite. The German Right was essentially the petty bourgeois middle class driven by despair into fervent patriotism. In many cases they had been impoverished by the fall of the mark, yet they disdained to work with communist workingmen, members of a "lower" class. The two extremes merely joined in undermining the Republic separately. Both regarded themselves as victims of monopoly capitalism and considered the government its tool. Both therefore attacked the government, but found the capitalists inaccessible. In the Ruhr the Schlageters and communist and noncommunist workers engaged in similar sabotage and guerrilla actions against the French intrusion.

It is not difficult to see why the Schlageter Line as well as the thought of Reichswehr-Russian collaboration germinated in the fertile and cynical brain of Karl Radek, and why he objected when Lenin sent the Russian Red Army into Poland with a view to winning that country and Germany for communism. In his 101-page pamphlet, *The Infantile Disease of 'Leftism' in Communism,* published in May, 1920 Lenin told German leftist communists and leftist Independent Socialists that they would have to struggle for a very long time inside the framework of capitalism. Yet he also told those "infantile" extremists that "the communists of Germany must not tie their hands and commit themselves absolutely to the renunciation of the Versailles peace in case of the victory of Communism. That is stupid." A "Soviet Germany (if a Soviet German Republic arose in the near future)" would be wrong in refusing "to recognize the Versailles peace for a certain time and submit to it."[4]

It was just as stupid to think that the French army, or even the British army, would wait until a German Soviet Republic deigned to recognize the Versailles peace. They would move forces into Poland to prevent the union of a Soviet Germany with Soviet Russia and then deal Red Germany a short crushing blow. Radek understood this, hence his efforts from 1920 to 1923 to discourage communist and Independent Socialist Party attempts at revolution; they were too weak, the enemy too strong. The Allied "policy of strangling Germany, of destroying her as an international factor," Radek told the Fourth Congress of the Comintern on October 28, 1922, "implied the destruction of Russia as a great power." ". . . irrespective of who governs Russia," Reds or Whites, he explained,

[3] *Ibid.,* p. 40.
[4] V. I. Lenin, *Polnoye Sobranye,* Vol. 41, p. 60.

"her interests require at least the existence of Germany."[5] Radek did not wish to make it easier for the western victors to eliminate Germany as an international factor serving Russia's defense. Seeckt, Schlageter, Reds, Russia—that was Radek's prescription to prevent French militarism and Poland from crippling Germany. His mixture did not include revolution.

Trotsky too blew cold on the idea of a revolution arising out of the Ruhr invasion. "Certainly we are interested in the victory of the working class," the *Manchester Guardian* of March 1, 1923, quoted him as replying to its Moscow correspondent, "but it is not in our interest that the revolution should take place in a Europe exhausted and drained of blood, and that the proletariat should receive from the bourgeoisie nothing but ruins as we received them after tsarism and the Russian bourgeoisie." Trotsky felt that revolution would bring another European war and with it "the postponement of revolutionary perspectives. That is why we from a revolutionary point of view are vitally interested in the preservation of peace." War in 1923 might have wiped out Germany as a viable nation, hurt Russia, and introduced, as Trotsky put it, "the economic beggary of Europe."

This was not "peace" propaganda to mislead the outside world. Trotsky joined Lenin with alacrity in 1917 to launch the Bolshevik revolution, born of the first world war, because he agreed that the party could seize power. Yet, though his theory of the "Permanent Revolution" envisaged revolution in the West which would enable backward Russia to build the socialism she could not build in one country, he recoiled in 1923 from premature revolution that sprang by miscarriage from the turbulence of civil war. His position was ambivalent. He was an ambivalent person; he appeared on the stage of revolution as a writer for Lenin's magazine *Iskra,* broke with Lenin and worked with the Mensheviks, broke with the Mensheviks and edited his own paper in Vienna, and finally joined the Bolsheviks. In 1914 Trotsky wrote that the Russo-Japanese War of 1904-5 "hastened the outbreak of the [1905] revolution [in Russia]; but for that very reason it also weakened it." Now, in 1914, "If we presuppose a catastrophic defeat, the war may bring a quicker outbreak of the revolution, but only at the cost of its inner weakness."[6] This prophecy proved true; the Soviet revolution suffered for decades from congenital weakness. Prophecy and practice, however, may be unrelated. When Lenin and history beckoned in November, 1917, Trotsky, a man of action, could not resist any more than he resisted the opportunity to lead the premature revolution of 1905. In 1923, however,

[5] Xenia Joukoff Eudin and Harold H. Fisher in collaboration with Rosemary Brown Jones, *Soviet Russia and the West, 1920-1927. A Documentary Survey,* p. 157.

[6] Louis Fischer, *The Life of Lenin,* p. 184.

he again counted the cost to Germany, Russia, and Europe of a premature revolution prepared in the pressure cooker of civil war and found it excessive.

But in 1923 Trotsky's star was sinking. Lenin, felled by a second stroke on December 13, 1922, commenced writing his famous last will and testament as well as several articles of astonishing brilliance. He finished the last of these articles on March 2, 1923, and on March 9 suffered a third stroke which destroyed his ability to speak, think, and coordinate. By this time the intriguing triumvirate—Stalin, Zinoviev, and Kamenev—who took power after Lenin's death on January 21, 1924, were already squeezing Trotsky out of the leadership. The result was a menacing chaos at the Kremlin summit equaled only by the confusion in the German Communist Party. The issue for the German party and the Kremlin triumvirs, chiefly Stalin, was: To make or not to make a revolution in Germany?

Stalin—age forty-four in 1923, the same age as Trotsky—had had a career different from those of almost all other Bolshevik chiefs. They had lived in exile for many years in Europe and some, like Trotsky and Bukharin, in America too. They mastered several foreign languages, were immersed in western culture and versed in Marxist classics. Most of them, particularly Trotsky, Bukharin, Lenin, and Zinoviev, were sparkling speakers. Stalin possessed none of these talents. He had spent only a few weeks of his life abroad, much of the time at party congresses, was neither well-educated nor well-read, spoke a plebeian Russian with a thick Georgian accent, and his withered left arm, pockmarked face, low brow, blackened teeth, grim visage, and short stature made him a mockery of the handsome men of his native Georgian race. Envy and vindictiveness therefore came naturally to Stalin. Since he lacked the equipment for popular appeal, he joined not the large Menshevik or reformist-socialist party in Georgia, which represented a Georgian-nationalist protest against Great Russian oppression, but rather the small conspiratorial Bolshevik group which did not shrink, especially under his inspiration, from armed robberies to fill the party treasury and, it is surmised, from occasional service as police informers to trap Menshevik opponents. Slowly, prosaically, Stalin climbed to the top rung of the short Bolshevik ladder. After the Soviet revolution, he remained behind the scenes less from modesty than from a conviction that there, his deficiencies concealed, he could find power. In public he kowtowed to Lenin. Stalin's father had been a drunkard who left home. Enrolled by his mother in the Tiflis theological seminary, the young Joseph rejected Christ and dropped out. In Lenin he at last found the father he had missed throughout life. But the towering Trotsky stood next to Lenin. To replace Trotsky there became Stalin's supreme goal.

When, after Lenin's death, he reached the pinnacle of the Soviet power pyramid, the sense of inferiority the environment of giants had given him turned into an insatiable appetite for lavish, tasteless, endless orgies of personal glorification and a brutal resolve to annihilate not only those giants but everybody except fawning, self-effacing courtiers.

Stalin had one god: Power. His cringing adulation of Lenin was a stratagem in his ascent to the peak. (Lenin did not notice until too late.) He thrived and reached his goal thanks to the dictatorship. In a democracy he might have been a local machine politician, or a corrupt trade union leader, or a capitalist robber baron. Totalitarianism was made to order for him. It put a premium on ruthlessness, intrigue, hate, envy, and readiness to shoot without reason, restraint, or regret. Those he could not shoot he silenced and humiliated. Stalin called himself "an Asiatic." Bukharin called him a "Genghis Khan."

Such a man could be neither a revolutionist nor a rebel. He was a communist in name only; he killed more communists than anybody before or since. His dislike of foreign communists was notorious; those who took refuge in the Soviet Union from their repressive governments were not safe from his executioner's bullet.

Stalin abhorred the West; he did not understand it. He had nothing but contempt for the western (and eastern) communists who came to Moscow to kneel at the Red shrine and beg for money and instructions. Their weakness aroused his primitive urge to exterminate. He respected only the strong, Hitler and the United States, for instance. From March, 1923, to his death in March, 1953, this brutal cynic shaped the foreign policy of the Soviet government and of the Comintern.

In the summer of 1923, with the political and economic situation of Germany nearing catastrophe, Stalin said in a letter to Zinoviev and Bukharin, "If today in Germany the government, so to speak, falls, and the Communists seize hold of it, they will fall with a crash. That in the best case. And at the worst, they will be smashed to pieces and thrown back. . . . In my opinion, the Germans"—the German communists—"must be curbed and not spurred on."[7]

Zinoviev and Bukharin, who with Radek constituted the Big Three of the Comintern, had been spurring on the German communists. Radek wished to curb them and had persuaded Stalin, who needed little persuading. Radek told the KPD to broaden its support, court the Social Democrats and the petty bourgeoisie by "the deliberate acceptance of such compromises" as would achieve an extension of its power. This was his way of saying: Don't play with revolution.

Before many years Stalin would cast Zinoviev and Kamenev over-

[7] Eudin and Fisher, pp. 178-179. Also Leon Trotsky, *Stalin,* pp. 368-369.

board and form a new coalition of Kremlin leaders whom he in turn would discard to become the autocrat until he died. But in 1923 his two colleagues in the triumvirate enjoyed considerable freedom of action while he built his impregnable citadel of power. This applied especially to Zinoviev, whom Lenin had appointed the keeper of the revolutionary fire. Zinoviev felt sanguine about the prospects of a German communist revolution, and, indeed, given his life's function, his ebullient nature, and events in Germany, his view could hardly have been different.

The dollar stood at 20,000 marks in February, 1923. In May a dollar bought 48,000 marks; in July, 350,000 marks. As the value of German money dropped, people with fixed incomes or pensions were wiped out. The rise in paper wages never kept pace with the rise in prices which went up hourly. While millions descended into dire poverty, thousands of speculators grew rich and flaunted their easy wealth, which might vanish overnight if they did not spend it in night clubs, fancy restaurants, and spas. The unhappiness of individuals and the helplessness of the government were matched by the arrogance of the great industrial barons who thought this the time to abolish the eight-hour day, strikes, and overtime pay.

The proto-Nazi groups and reactionary monarchist organizations were arming their members against French imperialism, they said, but also against domestic enemies if the opportunity presented itself. Under communist urgings, "Red Hundreds" were formed to fight for political power when the signal came from the Kremlin. No signal came. A communist conference, convened in Frankfurt am Main on March 17, 1923, was addressed by Vasil P. Kolarov, a Comintern representative of Bulgarian origin, and Solomon A. Lozovsky, head of the Soviet-managed Red Profintern or Trade Union International, who gave only stale, flaccid advice: organize, get strong, fight French imperialism. All Germans were opposed to French imperialism; the Cuno Cabinet was financing much of the anti-French resistance, communist and noncommunist, in the Ruhr. Should the KPD or the Kremlin aim to overthrow that government? The Radek-Stalin strategy, accepted by Heinrich Brandler and August Thalheimer, foremost leaders of the KPD, still dominated its councils: No revolution yet. The Kremlin saw little reason to plan the destruction of an anti-French German government with which its military were in intimate collaboration. Chancellor Cuno and General von Seeckt were closely associated in this secret enterprise, and Seeckt was making progress in forging additional ties with the Red Army.

Nevertheless, an unseen Red hand had been dispatching Russian army officers and military experts to Germany since the beginning of 1923 to train proletarian fighting hundreds for "the last struggle" with the bourgeoisie. Germany's crisis was so grave that no Bolshevik, taught to think of foreign situations in terms of Russia's past, could exclude the possibility of her capitalist system succumbing to communism. The most prominent of the Russian military sent into the German communist underground was General Peter A. Skoblevsky (alias Goryev), who was arrested by the German police, tried in the so-called "Cheka Trial" in Leipzig in February, 1925, and sentenced to death.

Meanwhile other Russian military were conferring with the Reichswehr. The Junkers contract had been signed early in 1923 to build airplanes at Fili, near Moscow. "In the same months a German-Soviet joint-stock company, 'Bersol,' was founded for the purpose of manufacturing poison gas at Trotsk, in Samara Province, under the management of a German named Dr. Hugo Stolzenberg. Contracts were also concluded for technical assistance from Germany in the manufacture of ammunition in Zlatoust, Tula, and Petrograd."[8]

Ambassador Rantzau was not satisfied. In a "Top Secret" report to Cuno dated July 29, 1923, he complained that "our military have made excessive concessions [to Russia]." He had warned, he recalled, that the Russians might not deliver to Germany the munitions provided for in the contracts. "The negotiating procedures of the past have created the impression that we had come to Moscow as petitioners." Actually, Russia needed the reconstruction of her armaments industry more than Germany. In conversations with Chicherin and Arkady P. Rosengoltz, member of the Revolutionary War Council and chief of the Central Board of the Soviet Air Force, Rantzau had therefore urged that a prominent Soviet military personality go to Berlin. "I made the suggestion to bring a Russian delegate to Berlin," Rantzau wrote Cuno, "not only to correct as far as possible the disadvantageous results of the mistakes of our military, but also, in case the negotiations become known, to prevent the responsibility from being loaded off on Germany alone."

In accordance with this suggestion, Rosengoltz himself proceeded to Berlin. Rantzau likewise left for the German capital and handed his July 29 report to Cuno in person. The report included a concrete proposal: No foreigners, except Germans, were to be employed in munitions factories set up by Germany on Soviet territory, "in any case, not without the prior agreement of Germany." There followed a political proposition: "There is no question and can be no question of a political or military alliance. But we should attempt to obtain security in the event of, in the very dangerous event of, a Polish attack on us."[9]

[8] Hilger and Alfred G. Meyer, *The Incompatible Allies*, pp. 193-194. Gustav Hilger was counselor of the German Embassy in Moscow.

[9] From the German Foreign Ministry archives in Bonn, *Akten betreffend "Fischer Telegramme" vom April 1927 vis Dezember 1928*, Bd. 2 app. 30 sec. E162539 to E 162549.

Rantzau's report briefed Chancellor Cuno for the conference the next day between Rosengoltz, who traveled under the pseudonym of Raschin, Soviet Ambassador in Berlin Nikolai N. Krestinsky, and Embassy Secretary Ustinov, on the one hand, and Cuno and Rantzau, on the other. For concealment, the meeting took place in the home of Rantzau's twin brother, and lasted from 9:45 P.M. on July 30 until midnight.

Offstage, outside Rantzau's home, Germany rocked with emotion. It seemed the country might crack. France fostered separatism in the Rhineland and Bavaria, two regions vital to the nation. Nationalism flared in protest. Strikes multiplied because wages had fallen to starvation level. The German Communist Party supported the strikes out of necessity, it could not now ignore the proletariat's insistence on life-sustaining pay, but the KPD's gaze had been directed to a higher star: a Red revolution of defense, for it appeared that the fascists were planning their revolution, a middle-class and upper-class revolution of defense against angry workers. The KPD leadership accordingly announced July 29 as "Antifascist Day." Huge demonstrations scheduled in cities conjured up the specter of civil war. Heinrich Brandler, cautious leader of the KPD, drew back. The communist forces, he knew, were too weak to defeat the Reichswehr-supported government. Moscow too knew this. Radek, seconded by Stalin, opposed a KPD challenge to the German state. The July 29 "Antifascist Day" was canceled. The meeting in Count Rantzau's home on the evening of July 30 consequently convened without what could have become deafening noises offstage of bloody battle in which the Reichswehr shot down Moscow-oriented workingmen while a Muscovite was conferring with the Reichswehr in a Berlin villa.

Brockdorff-Rantzau kept the minutes of the discussions in his brother's home. The Chancellor opened with a long statement: he proposed to continue and expand the economic and military collaboration between the two countries. But Germany "must protect herself against being squeezed out later by competitors with more capital, France or Belgium, for instance. . . . Regarding the financing of the Russian armaments industry" the Chancellor would "like to suggest that Russia come to an understanding with us before admitting [other] foreign countries."

Arkady Rosengoltz's reply enabled Rantzau to say in the minutes that it would give him the possibility of "a further exchange of view with Mr. Chicherin in Moscow." Soviet negotiators rarely give direct replies on major issues.

Cuno thereupon touched on the problem of Poland, "next to France, the most dangerous menace to peace not only in Europe but in the entire world. The German-Russian agreement about the reconstruction of the armaments industry in particular pursues the sole purpose of guaranteeing the peaceful development of both countries and to see to it that, in the event of a threat to this peaceful labor, Germany and Russia shall not be helplessly exposed to avaricious enemies."

Rosengoltz's answers, "more or less verbatim": "Of course, but we must also see to it that we are in no circumstances defeated. Therefore we must wait."

Cuno: "I agree with you completely, but unfortunately it does not lie in our power to choose the moment for this confrontation which is favorable to us."

Rosengoltz: "I share this view. That is exactly the reason why we should work intensively together. Quite frankly, without wishing to criticize, we, and especially our General Staff, have the impression that a military confrontation, which must remain unavoidable in the long run, is not kept in mind sufficiently and that adequate countermeasures are not being taken in Germany. Above all, the expansion of air strength is not receiving enough attention. The danger remains that the Entente might first attempt to crush Germany and then destroy Russia."

"We must definitely avoid the impression," Cuno commented, "that we want to prepare for a war of revenge. The less obvious the preparations the greater the advantage. . . . Moreover, more is being done to repel a hostile attack than is known in even well-informed circles."

Rosengoltz: "This information is of the greatest value to me."

Cuno declared that the existence of different social regimes in Germany and Russia was no obstacle to close collaboration. Rosengoltz suggested, in conclusion, that a representative of the Reichswehr be sent to Moscow for negotiations. Rantzau objected. He, the ambassador, must conduct all negotiations. Cuno agreed and authorized Rantzau to enter into discussions "in Russia with the authorized political and military officials." Rosengoltz welcomed the Chancellor's decision.

The offstage noises rose in a mighty crescendo. German currency dropped so precipitately that the dollar, which bought 350,000 marks in July, bought 4.6 million marks in August. Life for most Germans was becoming unlivable. Strikes were ubiquitous. In Saxony and Thuringia workers clamored for political power. Bavaria wished to secede from the Reich. Hitler made his appearance in Munich; Ludendorff, the great warlord, stood by the side of the corporal with the ridiculous mustache whose frenzied oratory hypnotized multitudes of misguided patriots unsure whether they wanted to rule Germany or leave Germany.

The noises of discontent beat against the mud walls of Jericho until they collapsed; Cuno's government fell on August 13, eleven days after he countersigned Rantzau's minutes. Gustav Stresemann, leader of the People's Party, the party of big industry and stout nationalism, succeeded Cuno as Chancellor; he was also Foreign Minister.

Stresemann formed a "Grand Coalition" of all parties except the extreme reactionary monarchists (though he himself had monarchist sympathies) and the communists. He soon canceled passive and active resistance to the French in the Ruhr which was emptying the federal exchequer and bankrupting the German economy. Steps were taken in western capitals to improve relations.

On September 26 Stresemann declared a State of Emergency. "In effect, for half a year—for the emergency powers were not rescinded until February 1924—von Seeckt and the Reichswehr governed Germany."[10] Seeckt might have become dictator. He preferred the less conspicuous role of behind-the-throne savior of the state; he supported Stresemann. Moscow's leaders, absorbed though they were in the life-and-death battle of the succession to Lenin, noted Germany's disturbing twist, backed by Seeckt, toward the West.

Germany's problems were not curable by domestic political manipulations; her future depended on western decisions about reparations. Hence the Stresemann-Seeckt policy. But the West had not yet acted—it would, definitely, in September, 1924, with the inauguration of the Dawes Plan for reparations payments. Meanwhile the mark continued to drop, unemployment rose, and extremism flourished. Some Kremlinmen heard the call to action. Heinrich Brandler, moderate leader of the KPD, was summoned to Moscow. "Brandler, who came to Moscow early in September for guidance and help, could not even get an interview with the leaders of the world revolution. After being shunted from office to office day after day and week after week, he finally secured an opportunity to air his knowledge and his views of the German situation in the presence of Stalin and Zinoviev."[11]

"Being shunted" from office to office is normal procedure in the Soviet Union. That Brandler dallied in Moscow for a month while his country sizzled was apparently due to indecision at the highest Kremlin level. But things were moving fast in Germany and, in diplomacy, Stresemann and Seeckt seemed to have moved west. Both circumstances influenced the Kremlinmen. Trotsky was more sanguine now about German revolutionary prospects than he had been earlier in the year. So was Zinoviev. Stalin, who could not afford to be outdone by Trotsky in revolutionary zeal, accordingly threw skepticism to the winds and contrived a cautious, dry-run experiment in revolution. Leftist social democrats had won control of the provincial government of Saxony in March, 1923, and in Thuringia in September. Brandler was therefore instructed to return home, try to persuade the Saxon and Thuringian cabinets to coopt com-

[10] John W. Wheeler-Bennett, *The Nemesis of Power; The German Army in Politics, 1918-1945,* p. 110.
[11] Trotsky, *Stalin,* p. 369.

munists, and, this success achieved, the comrades were to use their official positions to arm the workers, call a general strike, and launch a nationwide revolution. Brandler, who knew his party and country better than the Muscovites, accepted the orders reluctantly. How could he oppose the experts in revolution, the victors of November 7, 1917, ready to help with military men, money, and their prestige?

To stiffen Brandler's spine, Stalin gave him a handwritten letter in Russian. Brandler returned to Berlin on October 8. Two days later the *Rote Fahne* printed the letter in facsimile and German translation; it was addressed to the editor, Number Two KPD leader, and read, "Dear Comrade Thalheimer, The approaching revolution in Germany is the most important event of our time. The victory of the revolution in Germany will have a greater importance for the proletariat of Europe and America than the victory of the Russian revolution six years ago. The victory of the German proletariat will undoubtedly shift the center of world revolution from Moscow to Berlin. . . . From the bottom of my heart I wish the *Rote Fahne* new, decisive successes in the struggle ahead, for the conquest of power by the proletariat, for the unity and independence of a Germany about to be born."[12]

Moscow began to see visions. A German workers' government, *Pravda* predicted on October 14, 1923, would join hands with Soviet Russia "and unite in Europe a tremendous power of 200 million people . . . no one would be able to face such a force." "The German steel hammer and Soviet bread will conquer the world," *Izvestia* of October 25, thundered.

The Kremlin dichotomy remained. *Izvestia* of October 20 published two articles, one by Trotsky, the other by V. D. Vilensky (Sibiryakov). Trotsky wrote, "According to all information, the working class of Germany, which is struggling against fascism, is sufficiently strong to be the victor in the present conflict." Was he attempting to reassure doubters who feared that, no matter what happened in Germany, Russia would have to fight? Vilensky was one of the doubters: "If the German revolution is victorious, capitalist Europe will probably launch a violent struggle against the victorious German revolution." And if the revolution is defeated, "we have no guarantee that triumphant reaction will not turn its bayonets against the first republic of soviets. Who knows whether or not this will be a starting point for the advance of world reaction against our country of peaceful labor?" Vilensky was arguing against a German revolution, Trotsky for. Win or lose, Vilensky was saying, the German revolution might damage Russia's national interests.

Trotsky wanted to believe in a German revolution. It would save Germany, save him from political eclipse, and save Russia from the

[12] Werner T. Angress, *Stillborn Revolution. The Communist Bid for Power in Germany, 1921-1923*, p. 428.

nationalism Stalin intended soon to proclaim. Stalin's thoughts were revealed, perhaps inadvertently, in his letter to Thalheimer: "The victory of the German proletariat will undoubtedly shift the center of world revolution from Moscow to Berlin." Stalin would have rejoiced. He wasted no love on the Comintern, no hope on the world revolution. Ethnically a Georgian he was politically a Great Russian. His role in history was to make Russia a strong nation. The inherited duty to foment global Red revolt irked the shrewd provincial conservative from the border of Asia. Objectively, Stalin was right; Comintern headquarters belonged in the heart of Europe, not in the capital of remote, retarded Eurasian Russia.

Without faith, Brandler went through the motions of obeying Stalin's orders. Dutifully he negotiated the entry of communists into the left social democratic government of Saxony on October 12 and of Thuringia on October 16. The communist ministers thereupon began arming communist workers. Seeckt and Stresemann acted with dispatch. On October 20 Seeckt ordered General Alfred Mueller to march his Reichswehr troops into the two provinces. The next day Brandler addressed a congress of social democratic organizations in Chemnitz. The Reichswehr's invasion, he urged, was to be met by a proletarian general strike. No tongue or hand moved; Brandler's proposal was greeted with "icy silence." He knew this doomed the planned revolution. He had said of himself he was "no Lenin." He thought Germany unripe for revolution. On November 7, 1917, Kerensky found no army ready to fight anybody. In October, 1923, Seeckt commanded a Reichswehr eager to fight communists and other enemies of the state. Germany was not Russia. Moscow had ignored the difference.

Brandler had sent messages to all German communist units to begin the revolution on October 23. After the ice of Chemnitz he sent messages countermanding the order. Hermann Remmele, communist member of the Reichstag, brought Brandler's first message to Hamburg in the night of October 21 to 22. He then proceeded to Kiel, where Brandler's second order reached him canceling the insurrection; he passed this on to the Kiel communists. "Only in the night of October 22 to 23 did Remmele inform Ernst Thaelmann," the Hamburg communist leader, "that Brandler had given orders to Hamburg to refrain from beginning the rising."[13]

But October 23 had already begun; in the early morning hours workers stormed precinct police stations and barracks in the suburbs of the great seaport with a view to capturing weapons. Here and there they succeeded. Anticipating the arrival of the Reichswehr and police rein-

[13] Heinz Habedank, *Zur Geschichte des Hamburger Aufstandes, 1923* (On the 1923 Hamburg Uprising), pp. 10-11.

forcements from other cities, communists attempted to cut highways by felling trees and blowing up railway tracks. The workers, outnumbered and poorly armed, fought on bravely until October 26. "When it became clear several hours before the planned nationwide beginning of the uprising," writes Heinz Habedank, the East German Soviet Zone author, "that messengers from Brandler headquarters had broadcast orders in all of North Germany not to start the attack, the [communist] Supreme Command [in Hamburg] did not call off the uprising but consistently continued it in order to win over the German working class through a revolutionary example and to prevent complete demoralization."[14] Lives did not matter.

The fiasco of October, 1923, in Germany wrote "Finish" to the Moscow policy of foreign revolution. Never after that date did the Kremlin or Comintern order another communist uprising in Europe. The Age of Lenin was ended. The Age of Stalin had begun. Foreign Communist parties now ceased to be "the locomotive of revolution" and became the fifth wheel of the chariot of Soviet foreign policy.

XII EXPORTING A REVOLUTION

If Germany with a large, highly disciplined working class failed to establish a communist regime, how could Moscow expect overwhelmingly peasant China to become a communist country? Dr. Sun Yat-sen had, despite his sympathy for Russia, declared he opposed anything resembling the Soviet system for his country. It apparently never occurred to Dr. Sun, or to the Soviet leaders who saw the world through Russian lenses, that the Chinese peasantry might supply the force to make China Red. Marx, Engels, Lenin, and their ideological heirs regarded the peasant as an actual or potential capitalist and therefore antisocialist. The Kremlin accordingly decided that China first needed a "bourgeois-democratic" revolution which would unite the country, destroy feudal vestiges, strengthen native capitalism, and oust European and Japanese imperialists. Huge benefits would accrue to the Soviet Union from a China no longer dominated by foreigners and friendly to the Soviet

[14] *Ibid.*, p. 203.

Union. The imperialists' endeavors to retain their hold on China would occupy them for years and relieve Russia of British and Japanese pressures on her long Asian frontier.

These were the instructions Moscow gave Michael M. Borodin, the Soviet government's emissary to the Chinese nationalist revolution.

Borodin was a big man, tall and broad-shouldered, with a large shaggy head and a bushy walrus mustache. From his long chest came roars like a lion's—even in private conversation. That was the result of years as a revolutionary propagandist. Secret communist activities also taught him to whisper; he had worked underground for the movement in Mexico, Scandinavia, Great Britain, and Turkey. Then life's greatest opportunity beckoned: he went to China as Dr. Sun Yat-sen's chief adviser. Here he proved himself a big man politically. Dropped into an Oriental maelstrom where loyalty was a hazard, because masters rose and fell, and elusiveness an instinctive reaction to uncertainty, Borodin held many Chinese leaders firmly in tow and became, for four turbulent years, the central figure in China's swirling politics. His problem was not only the easy adjustment Chinese made to lures and pressures, Moscow was a problem too, for ideologically he stood with one foot in Trotsky's camp, yet his assignment required obedience to Stalin's anti-Trotskyist orders. The resulting debacle thrust him out of China in 1927. He was forty-three. The next twenty-four years were an anticlimactic descent to a tragic death.

Back in his Moscow apartment on Sheremetyevsky Pereulok, Borodin waited. Normally he would have been summoned to the Central Committee of the party to report on China. No summons came. Months went by; he waited with mounting tension, never knowing what might befall. It was not yet the time of official murder; Stalin did not begin executing party members until 1934. It was the time of cutting big men down to a size suitable for facile destruction.

Borodin fell victim to this process because he had failed in China to perform the impossible task Stalin set for him, and failure was punished lest blame attach to the infallible dictator. Borodin was Stalin's failure personified and therefore had to be kept out of the political limelight. First, accordingly, the party appointed him director of the Soviet Union's paper manufacturing trust, a job for which he was unfitted by temperament and experience. Next he became director of a paper factory. In each of these he earned a reprimand written into his party membership book. In 1932 Borodin was made editor of the Moscow *Daily News*, an unimportant English-language publication, where two petty party bureaucrats were placed at his side to veto, humiliate, and diminish him. At the height of Stalin's anti-Semitic purge, in February,

1949, the secret police carried Borodin off to a concentration camp, or, as Lieutenant General A. Cherepanov (Retired), who served under Borodin in China, wrote in *Pravda* of June 20, 1964, "In the period of Stalin's cult of personality, M. M. Borodin was repressed without cause"; he died in the camp in 1951. Now, the general continued, "the party had restored his good name." This typical delayed obituary is Kremlinese for "rehabilitation." The title of Cherepanov's article read, "A Revolutionary-Leninist." It washed away Borodin's "sins."

Soviet Marshal Vasili K. Bluecher, known to the Chinese as General Galen, operated in China as Borodin's military counterpart. Borodin, Bluecher, and their Soviet aides played a decisive role in the 1923-1927 Chinese upheaval. Without them Chinese cliques, parties, and warlords mustered just enough determination to weaken one another. The Soviet agents never eradicated endemic internecine strife. But the magic of personality, the myth of the Russian revolution, and Moscow's money and munitions started China on her long march to national cohesion.

When Borodin returned to Moscow in 1927, I telephoned for an appointment. He never said no, never said yes; it would have been embarrassing, in his political condition, to receive a foreigner. I persisted, and he finally invited me to his apartment on February 26, 1929. From that day until June 26, 1929, I had ten interviews with him for a total of thirty hours. Several times he fixed the rendezvous at 9 or 9:30 A.M., and since I always arrived punctually I would find him not quite awake, lying on the floor on a blanket which was his bed. He immediately dressed in my presence while continuing the recitation of his life's great adventure. Nor did breakfast—a glass of amber-colored tea and a lump of sugar brought by a maid—interrupt the telling. My detailed notes lie before me.

Borodin's dilemma in China is illustrated by the situation at the Whampoa military academy opened in May, 1924, in the harbor of Canton, as soon as the Russian army advisers arrived to train Chinese officers. The Soviet government, Leo M. Karakhan told me, paid the first three million gold rubles ($1.5 million) to launch the school. Borodin named General Chiang Kai-shek its commandant and Chou En-lai, a communist, the future foreign minister and prime minister of Red China, as its political commissar—to watch over Chiang.

Chiang Kai-shek was anything but a communist. In Moscow in 1923 he interviewed Trotsky, Chicherin, Zinoviev, Bukharin, Radek, and others, and received promises of arms and dollars. But he wrote in his diary that when, on November 28, 1923, he was shown the secret Comintern resolution of that day on China he was so anguished "he had to force himself to say his farewells at the headquarters of the Comintern and of the Russian Foreign Office."[1] This revealing resolution not only ordered Chinese communists to join the Kuomintang and press for the nationalization of land (a bourgeois-democratic reform, according to Lenin) and of foreign firms, foreign railways, foreign banks and waterways, it also stressed the need of "forming a general front with the Soviet Union of Workers and Peasants against imperialism and imperialist influences in China as well as of coordinating the movement for the emancipation of China with the revolutionary movement and peasants of Japan and the movement for national emancipation in Korea."

Small wonder Chiang Kai-shek raged. He went to Moscow for munitions, not for a revolutionary program. Merging his efforts in China with the workers' and peasants' movements in Japan and Korea looked like madness to him. He aimed to conquer and rule China.

This was Borodin's problem. Chiang's goal was military, Borodin's political. Chiang wanted power without revolution, some Chinese wanted a bourgeois-democratic revolution, some a communist revolution.

In his last public statement, in *Pravda* of March 2, 1923, Lenin declared that the outcome of the struggle between socialism and capitalist imperialism "will be determined by the fact that Russia, China, India, etc. constitute the overwhelming majority of the population" of the planet, and "there cannot be the slightest shadow of a doubt" which side will win: "the final victory of socialism is fully and absolutely assured."[2] A billion Asians, Lenin calculated, would undermine western capitalism and make the world socialist. Marx believed he had prepared a program for advanced western countries. Lenin discerned a revolutionary potential in retarded colonial or semicolonial eastern countries.

Russia has, throughout her millenary history, envied, copied, and feared the West, feared conquest by the idea of freedom which, imperfectly practiced in the West, might yet erode Slav-communist autocracy. Stalin distrusted the West. Less than three months before the Bolshevik revolution, he wrote in a legal Petrograd daily, "Once upon a time it was said in Russia that the light of socialism came from the West. And that was true. For there, in the West, we studied revolution and socialism." But in 1906, after Russia's defeat by Japan, France bolstered the Tsar with a 2-billion-ruble loan, and, in 1917, Stalin added, "the West exported to Russia not so much socialism and liberation as slavery and counterrevolution."[3] In the next three years the West gave him

[1] C. Martin Wilbur, *Sun Yat-sen and Soviet Russia, 1922-1924*. Preliminary Report on Columbia University Seminar on Modern East Asia: China, March 10, 1965. Mimeographed.

[2] V. I. Lenin, *Polnoye Sobranye*, Vol. 45, pp. 389-406.

[3] J. V. Stalin, *Sochinenia* (Collected Works), Vol. 3, p. 234.

better ground for complaint. Germany's retreat from revolution in 1923 confirmed Stalin's resentment. He and Trotsky, indeed all communists, accordingly pinned high hopes on China. They would get at the West through the back door, thereby fulfilling Lenin's prophecy—false, as events proved—that an advanced capitalist society would die from loss of empire.

It did not follow that Moscow intended to implant communism in underdeveloped China. Lenin's anti-imperialism appealed to Chinese nationalists. His advocacy of a ruling party of professional revolutionists sounded a familiar note to intellectuals bred in the tradition of a mandarin elite trained to govern. Moscow's messianic mission to transform the world acted as a magnet to professors, students, writers, artists eager to lift China out of centuries of stagnation and humiliation by foreigners. In 1918 Chinese at Peking University formed several Marxist study groups. But only after the arrival from Soviet Russia, in June, 1920, of Gregory Voitinsky, a Comintern agent, did the Chinese Communist Party come into being.

Soon the Kremlin clipped the fledgling party's wings by directing it to cooperate with the bourgeoisie in the Kuomintang. The special plenary session of the Chinese Communist Central Committee, meeting in Hangchow in August, 1922, ordered party members to strengthen the Kuomintang by joining it. At the Fourth Congress of the Comintern (Moscow, November-December, 1922) Radek advocated a Chinese communist alliance with the Kuomintang.[4] And the secret resolution of the Comintern of November 28, 1923,[5] which so infuriated Chiang Kai-shek, instructed the Chinese Communist Party to work with the Kuomintang for a "bourgeois-democratic" revolution. Thus did the long lash of Red Mecca reduce the inspired messiahs to grubbing in coalition politics. It smelled of compromise, expediency, and low purpose. Again the voice of the alien was heard in the land. The seed had been sown of the Sino-Soviet dispute decades later.

In commanding the Chinese communists to work with the Kuomintang for bourgeois democracy, Moscow hewed to the straight and narrow path paved by the *Communist Manifesto* and interpreted by Lenin, who believed no backward country could vault from tribalism, feudalism, or despotism to socialism; it must first experience a capitalist, bourgeois-democratic interval in which it achieved adult franchise, fair treatment of nationalities (self-determination), equality of women, trade unionism. The bourgeoisie, he declared, would obstruct these and similar

[4] Conrad Brandt, Benjamin Schwartz, and John K. Fairbank, *A Documentary History of Chinese Communism*, pp. 29-31.

[5] The text of this resolution was among the papers lent me by Karakhan. It has never before been published.

reforms. Therefore, the proletariat, led by communists, must compel the ruling capitalists to act. In the process the workers would acquire the power to dethrone capitalism. This is what had happened in Russia after the Bolshevik revolution, Lenin held. In a few weeks the Soviet regime, he claimed, liberated women, nationalized land, freed the national minorities from Great Russian domination; then the Kremlin moved into the second phase: socialism. In a notable letter to Lenin in 1919, Foreign Commissar Chicherin, dissenting, argued that "We do not yet have communism"—then synonymous with socialism—"but state capitalism." Lenin sternly demurred.[6] Yet Chicherin's description of the Soviet social system: ". . . unequal pay even to the extent of piecework, and forms of compulsion which sometimes recall the old [Tsarist] regime and the centralization even of management which restricts self-management," remained valid for decades after he put it in his letter to Lenin. This truth did not elude Lenin's heirs. In 1924 Soviet Russia, far more advanced economically than China, had not achieved socialism, had, indeed, taken a long step back to private farming, private trade, and concessions to foreign capitalists. How, then, could the Chinese communists, few and alone, convert China to socialism in the face of tremendous opposition from foreign imperialists and capitalists linked with domestic militarists who had fragmented the country?

A Soviet revolution in China (or in Germany) could have come only with further deterioration in Europe. This did not happen. Europe, to be sure, never recovered from the first world war as it did after the second. The loss of blood, treasure, and confidence was too great, the hostility between the several parts of Europe too deep to permit restoration. But by autumn, 1924, the headlong descent to social catastrophe ended with the introduction of the Dawes Plan for collecting German reparations; Trotsky characterized the change as "the policy of American capitalism . . . to put Europe on rations." At first, according to Trotsky, "the resurrection of European life which began with American aid was flatly denied" by Stalin. He remained "under the spiritual hegemony of Zinoviev," who continued to pursue the disappearing phantom of revolution. "Stalin," Trotsky continues, began to liberate himself from Zinoviev when it became "impossible to ignore the process of stabilization." Trotsky's next sentence is crucial for the personal histories of Stalin and Trotsky, and for Soviet policies in China. "It may be said," Trotsky asserted, "that Stalin was strengthened by the strengthening of European capitalism."[7]

[6] Louis Fischer, *The Life of Lenin*, pp. 345-346.

[7] From the unpublished manuscript, in Trotsky's hand, of a continuation of his biography of Stalin, now deposited in the Trotsky Archive at Harvard University, Chap. XXIV, p. 15.

Had Europe's social structure continued to crumble as it did in the early postwar years, had a socialist revolution loomed there, Trotsky might have been right in urging socialism for China. Europe could not have prevented it. But the invigoration of Europe capitalism through injections of American dollars reinforced European imperialism in China and the Chinese forces who cooperated with it.

Stalin drew two crude deductions from these circumstances. Since Europe would not, by adopting socialism, help Russia create a socialist economy, the Soviet Union would undertake the task alone. The Fourteenth Communist Party Congress in December, 1925, ratified the program of socialism in one country. Internationalism flew out the Kremlin window. Since Europe could prevent a Chinese socialist revolution, Stalin proposed a Chinese nationalist revolution to oust the Europeans.

Trotsky, on the contrary, believed "every success of Americanism . . . will prepare the ground for the growth of Bolshevism . . . on a gigantically large scale."[8] European radicalism was not dead, he contended. Witness the British coal strike and the general strike of May, 1926. The cooperation between England and America was incomplete, their antagonisms incurable. He even foresaw an Anglo-American war. Germany's troubles with France would likewise increase. European stability, therefore, was neither secure nor permanent. This, and the intensification of the class struggle in China due to the prolonged civil war—it began in 1911—augured well, Trotsky held, for a Chinese socialist revolution.

Stalin possessed little talent or training for theory. When he sloughed off Zinoviev in 1925 he needed a substitute and took the young, charming, artistic Nikolai Bukharin whom Lenin had adored. In the early post-1917 years Bukharin staunchly held a "leftist" position. He opposed the signing of the Brest-Litovsk peace treaty, advocated revolutionary war in Europe, fostered German communist insurrections. He told the Fourth Congress of the Comintern, Moscow, October-November, 1922, "*The Communist Manifesto* says that the proletariat must conquer the world. But this cannot be done simply by snapping one's fingers. For this we need bayonets and guns. Yes, the expansion of the Red Army is also the expansion of socialism, of proletarian authority, of the revolution. It is on this ground that the right of Red intervention is justified, when it technically simplifies the realization of socialism."[9]

". . . can a proletarian state sign military alliances with bourgeois states?" Bukharin asked the same audience. "Here there is no difference in principle between a loan and a military alliance; and I affirm that we

[8] *Izvestia,* Aug. 5, 1924.

[9] Xenia Joukoff Eudin and Harold H. Fisher, *Soviet Russia and the West, 1919-1927. A Documentary Survey,* p. 159.

have already grown up enough to conclude a military alliance with the bourgeoisie of one country, so as to be able, with its help, to crush the bourgeoisie of another country." Lest this be frankness enough Bukharin outdid himself by adding in the next breath, "If, in the future, the bourgeoisie of an allied country is defeated, then new tasks will arise."[10] The laughter of the delegates showed they understood what those tasks were: to make a revolution. In 1922 Bukharin was dialectically rightist and leftist, for Reichswehr and revolution.

But when the German revolution of October, 1923, fizzled, when Europe achieved relative stability, when the abhorred NEP opened the bud of prosperity in Russia, when, as a result Stalin rose to the Soviet summit and invited Bukharin to join him there, Bukharin, affected by the same major changes, entered his "rightist phase." Echoing Guizot, he told the Russian peasants in 1925 to "Enrich Yourselves." And in the endless controversy among Soviet leaders on China he upheld Stalin against Trotsky and against Radek who had opposed a communist revolution in advanced Germany and opposed it, in the beginning—1922—in China as well, but, having joined the Trotsky opposition at home, favored socialism in retarded China.

As the political struggle on the Kremlin summit raged from autumn, 1923, to its climax in November, 1927, with the expulsion of Trotsky from the Soviet Communist Party, Borodin in Canton tried to understand what the Moscow debate meant for China. He also had to accommodate himself to the men and politics around him.

Surveying the Canton situation, Borodin found the workers divided, the peasants asleep, the Kuomintang inactive, Sun Yat-sen a sick and broken man (he died on March 12, 1925), the militarists fickle, corrupt, self-seeking. Borodin, old Bolshevik and ex-American pedagogue, knew he had to give the people something to fight for. He accordingly cajoled the Kuomintang executive committee into issuing a manifesto to peasant communities to confiscate landlords' holdings with or without compensation, distribute them among the peasants for rent, and use the rent for the common welfare. The workers were promised an eight-hour day and a minimum wage. The land reform aroused towering opposition in the Kuomintang leadership and was watered down beyond recognition. Borodin immediately saw the problem destined to wreck the Kuomintang: it was too landlord-ridden to win the support of the peasants in a predominantly peasant country.

Instead of social change, Kuomintang officials were intent on a military expedition north to the Yangtze River and then Peking "to punish Wu Pei-fu," as Dr. Sun urged. Borodin resisted; he wanted first to build

[10] *Ibid.*, pp. 209-210.

a solid popular base in Canton and the surrounding Kwangtung Province. He wanted to strengthen the Kuomintang army technically and politically.

Events which were unplanned yet not accidental, for they sprang from distress and discontent, now intervened to raise Borodin's hopes. On May 30, 1925, Chinese students and other demonstrators in the International Settlement of Shanghai were fired on by European police. Borodin called it "a bloody baptism" for the forces of revolution. A general strike erupted in Shanghai; British and Japanese goods were boycotted. Canton proclaimed a three-day sympathy strike. It and the accompanying demonstrations provoked clashes between workers and French and British police. Chinese were killed. Now the workingmen of the British Crown Colony of Hong Kong struck and withdrew, a hundred thousand strong, to nearby Canton. The strike lasted sixteen months, caused heavy economic losses in the colony but also in Canton, and showed Borodin that, though human resources could be rallied against imperialism, "it had become necessary to terminate the battle in this corner"—Canton-Hong Kong—"in order to start out with greater vigor to fight imperialism throughout China—on the wider base." He threw his support to the Northern Expedition. Borodin did not take this decision without an eye on the Soviet intraparty struggle. In March, 1926, he said, the Trotsky opposition in Moscow demanded "a more revolutionary and purely communist policy in Canton." One of its secret circulars proposed "An open struggle with the Chinese bourgeoisie, not an alliance with it." The Stalin majority vetoed any such move. According to Borodin, however, the Trotsky opposition "was not without friends in the Chinese Communist Party, especially in its Shanghai headquarters. I felt that the Northern Expedition would prevent precipitate action" of Kuomintang leftists, aided by communists, against the conservative Kuomintang majority. This was a pregnant error.

To win an ally for the Northern Expedition, Borodin traveled to the camp of Feng Yu-hsiang, "the Christian general," northeast of Peking. Borodin had visited Feng on two previous occasions to convert Feng to nationalism; Feng accepted Borodin-trained propagandists into his army. Now Borodin sought Feng's participation in the Northern Expedition. Feng gave a typically Chinese-warlord evasive reply; in fact, his troops had been pushed back toward Mongolia and he soon left for Moscow to request aid.

While Borodin lost time with Feng, Chiang Kai-shek executed a coup d'état in Canton on March 20, 1926. Irked by the mounting power of the Left Kuomintang-Communist bloc who enjoyed Soviet encouragement, Chiang surrounded the quarters occupied by the Kuomintang's Russian military advisers and the offices of the Hong Kong strike committee, arrested Chinese and Soviet communists, and seized control of the Canton administration. He then moved to end the Hong Kong strike.

Fearing Borodin's reaction, for Borodin was the Kremlin, and Chiang's future still depended on Russian arms and good will, Chiang Kai-shek sent his secretary to Peking with a letter begging the Muscovite to return south at once. Borodin returned by ship. The entire small Kuomintang navy, with Chiang on board, met him as his vessel approached Hong Kong. Chiang, all apparent contrition, explained the coup: he was as pro-Soviet as ever but disliked the Left-Kuomintang-Communist coalition which planned to dominate him. Borodin charged that he was becoming a militarist like all the other provincial warlords. Chiang, feigning humility, asked advice. Should he retire to Moscow to absorb the proper spirit? "Prepare for the Northern Expedition" came the Russian's answer. Borodin realized that Chiang had tasted power and could no longer be tamed. For the coming struggle all parties needed a larger battlefield.

To please Borodin, Chiang made a coup against reactionaries in the Canton Kuomintang. Borodin summarized the situation as follows: The Left-Kuomintang-Communist bloc was far too weak to eliminate Chiang and Chiang hesitated to challenge the pro-Soviet Chinese grouping. The enemies therefore cooperated behind friendly masks. Karakhan in Peking counseled Borodin against a break with Chiang. "Wait till you reach Peking," he wrote. All elements favored moving north in search of political reinforcements. Ostensibly, the Northern Expedition aimed to unite China. Actually it split the alignment which might, against enormous odds, have performed that task. This left the epic opportunity to Mao Tse-tung.

For some time the life of China had resembled a wild game of checkers (draughts seems a more appropriate name) whose rules allowed kings to move diagonally, vertically, and horizontally from one end of the board to the other. Thus:

January 29, 1925. Marshal Chang Tso-lin's troops, coming down from the far north, capture Shanghai.

September. Chen Chiung-ming's "Anti-Red Army" occupies Swatow.

October 15. Sun Chuan-fang's army drives Chang Tso-lin's army from Shanghai.

October 20. Sun Chuan-fang takes Nanking.

November 6. Chiang Kai-shek captures Swatow.

November 26. Feng Yu-hsiang occupies Peking after Wu Pei-fu's departure.

December 6. Kuo Sung-ling, former Chang Tso-lin ally, defeats Chang Tso-lin.

December 24. Chang Tso-lin defeats Kuo Sung-ling.

December 27. Kuo Sung-ling executed by Chang Tso-lin.
January 21, 1926. Wu Pei-fu, Chang Tso-lin, and Sun Chuan-fang, who had driven Chang Tso-lin out of Shanghai in October, agree to move on Peking.
March 22. Feng Yu-hsiang retreats from Tientsin, remains in Peking.
April 25. Feng retreats from Peking.
July 13. Northern Expedition, coming from Canton and commanded by Chiang Kai-shek, seizes Changsha in Hunan Province.
September, early. Hanyang and Hankow captured by Northern Expedition.
September 17-October 15. Sun Chuan-fang resists Northern Expedition in area of Nanchang.
November 5. Sun Chuan-fang in retreat.
December 2. Wuchang entirely in hands of Northern Expedition. Wuchang, Hankow, and Hanyang united into one city to be called Wuhan.
February 10, 1927. Chang Tso-lin announces he will march on Wuhan.
February 18. Sun Chuan-fang retreats toward Shanghai; announces he does not resent the presence of British in that city.
February 28. Sun Chuan-fang defeated at Shanghai.
March 6. Chiang Kai-shek offers an alliance to Sun Chuan-fang.

This incomplete calendar of Chinese chaos omits the hardships inflicted on tens of millions of poor people by marauding, foraging armies crisscrossing the country in endless, senseless campaigns; monster political strikes in most major cities; countermeasures, often fatal, by foreign and native police forces; and the landing of Japanese army units.

The Northern Expedition was smoothly successful. "We paid as much attention to posters as to rifles," Borodin said. The army's political department numbering thousands made propaganda among the peasants. Towns and villages willingly submitted to the presence of muffled force and the sound of nationalistic argument. By November 5, 1926, the triangular coalition forged by Borodin (the Left Kuomintang, the Communist Party, and Chiang Kai-shek,) had, in the Russian's words, "asserted itself throughout South China."

Victory spelled trouble. It had been agreed in Canton, Borodin recalled, that the new Kuomintang capital would be Hankow. There, however, Chiang Kai-shek would have been the shortest leg of the triangle. He therefore remained at Nanchang, southeast of Hankow, while Borodin, Foreign Minister Eugene Chen, Finance Minister T. V. Soong, Mrs. Sun Yat-sen, and others proceeded to Hankow.

Foreign armored cruisers lay at anchor in the Yangtze 200 meters from Borodin and Eugene Chen's office windows. Factory owners closed their plants in the new capital because foreign gunboats blocked ships bringing raw materials and because workers, sensing the advent of a new day, struck for higher wages. Banks suspended business. The bourgeoisie was hostile. Borodin had chosen Hankow in expectation of proletarian support. The proletariat melted away to the villages to escape urban famine and unemployment. "Hankow," Borodin said, "was an illusion."

Stalin, addressing the Chinese Commission of the Comintern on November 30, 1926, nevertheless defended communist collaboration with the Kuomintang: "It would be the greatest mistake for the Chinese communists to leave the Kuomintang at the present time." Trotsky considered it the greatest wisdom. He advocated the immediate organization of peasant soviets in China. "I believe that this is a mistake," Stalin replied. City soviets should come first, but "the question of organizing soviets in the Chinese industrial centers is not on the agenda at the moment . . . to speak of soviets at the present time means to run too far ahead." Nine-tenths of the Chinese population were peasants, Stalin asserted, and "to assume that a few tens of thousands of Chinese revolutionaries can permeate this ocean of peasantry is a mistake." The Trotskyists cried, "Counterrevolution."

Bukharin explained Stalin's position before the Seventh Enlarged Plenum of the Executive Committee of the Comintern (ECCI) in December, 1926: ". . . our next task in China is to break the power of the imperialist enemy. That is the chief aim at the present moment." This could be achieved because "in my opinion, a war among the European nations is possible in the nearest future." Later "a war could explode between Europe and America." Therefore the central purpose of Comintern policy in China ought to be "a united front of all national-revolutionary forces including the anti-imperialist stratum of the bourgeoisie" and at the same time to draw the peasantry into a league with the workers and "prepare the proletariat of China for its role as leader of the Chinese revolution." The goal of that revolution would be "the noncapitalist development of China."[11]

"Noncapitalist" was a craven word; Bukharin dared not say capitalist because that would invite Trotskyist criticism and he could not say socialist because the Trotskyists were advocating a socialist China. No date was set for even the timid "noncapitalist" revolution. The workers were merely to "prepare" for it. The thrust of Soviet policy was against imperialism. Moscow dreaded foreign attack. Hence the wishful thinking about a war in Europe and a Euro-American conflict which would divert western hostility from Russia. Fear is a bad counselor, nor did Marxism improve the quality of Red prophecy.

[11] N. I. Bukharin, *Kapitalisticheskaya Stabilizatsia i Proletarskaya Revolutsia* (Capitalist Stabilization and the Proletarian Revolution), p. 5-343.

The Stalin-Bukharin statements, calculated to mollify the Chinese bourgeoisie, disheartened the peasants, workers, and communists. Borodin remembered with a thrill the enthusiasm of village communities traversed by the Northern Expedition. Now Moscow ordered a curb on the revolutionary spirit of the masses. They were to collaborate with the masters who had starved them and their ancestors, who paid children and women a pittance to work eighteen hours a day, seven days a week at machines by the side of which they slept for want of a home.

"Hankow was an illusion," Borodin had said. Yet on January 3, 1927, the workers who remained in Hankow occupied the British Concession in the city, and on January 7 Chinese seized the British Concession in Kiukiang on the Yangtze. "Nobody foresaw the events of January 3," reported three Comintern officials in their letter from Shanghai. "The occupation of the Concession by the Hankow workers took place spontaneously, without any leadership, either from the [Nationalist] government, from the Kuomintang, or from our party."[12]

General Chiang Kai-shek, still at Nanchang, had failed to subdue radical Hankow, but he did not intend to submit to the radicals. He felt the attraction of the great city of Shanghai, bastion of foreign imperialism, capital of Chinese capitalism, where he boasted friends in the impenetrable underworld and among the compradores, those sharp-witted, ubiquitous intermediaries between world business and China. Shanghai spelled money and power and freedom from irksome ideological ties with communists and Left Kuomintangists whom he had never more than tolerated. Chiang in Nanchang began issuing anticommunist pronouncements, prologue to his role of military dictator. The closer his troops came to the shelter of Shanghai the more belligerent became his tones. On February 17, 1927, Chiang's men took Hangchow and on February 18 Kashing, less than fifty miles from Shanghai. On March 7, he attacked Borodin and his staff of advisers. Russia did not wish "to tyrannize over us" but her representatives in China had been "insulting our every movement."[13] Three days later the Central Committee of the Kuomintang, in Hankow, condemned Chiang's conduct. The gulf between the general and Hankow seemed unbridgeable even though the political geography of China was never stable, and gulfs often closed, making very strange neighbors.

Communists build social castles on a hope. Being by nature sanguine, optimistic, assiduous organizers, and busy borers from within, they assume that when they infiltrate a party or an institution they can capture or at least wreck it. In China in the 1920's these calculations proved erroneous. Chiang Kai-shek was not only the leader of a segment of the

[12] Harold R. Isaacs, *The Tragedy of the Chinese Revolution*, p. 124.
[13] *Ibid.*, p. 127.

Kuomintang, he commanded an army, and he zealously guarded both against Reds. In Hankow too the Left Kuomintang's position depended in considerable measure on the support, or tolerance, of the local warlord. (This had been true even in Canton in 1924 and 1925.) And every warlord, large or small, lived off the peasantry whom he despoiled and conscripted. The Hankow warlord objected as strenuously as did Chiang Kai-shek to communist "mischief" in the villages, to the formation of peasant unions which sought to reduce rent, sometimes to seize estates. It is not, therefore, that rural China was unripe for revolution. The weakness of the communists was that they had no army. They had to recruit, bribe, or persuade marauding army chiefs to march with them against another army chief. Given sufficient reward, the local warlord succumbed to the lure of a march and a fight. But he never accepted the communists' peasant policy which, though not socialist, threatened to rob the militarists of the main source of their existence.

This is why Moscow's China policy of communists joining the Kuomintang failed to produce the results Stalin expected. Workers' strikes and peasant protests suited none of the warlords, and even when these phenomena of mass discontent were spontaneous, the communists were blamed. Stalin's program envisaged a nationalist, anti-imperialist Chinese revolution backed by everybody from bourgeois to coolie. But the imperialists were capitalists and the Chinese bourgeoisie was capitalist in league with the foreign imperialists, and the nationalist revolution so stirred the tens of millions that it overflowed its shores and became, in part, an antibourgeois social revolution with economic goals and political-power aspirations. Moscow saw danger in this mass movement and instructed the Chinese communists to check it. Some obeyed, some balked, all felt uncomfortable.

At that juncture—the end of 1926—the Kremlin sent M. N. Roy to China. Manabendra Nath Roy, an Indian from Bengal, came to the United States in 1916 as "an emissary of 'revolutionary nationalism.'" His purpose was an "alliance with Germany against British imperialism."[14] America was halfway house to Berlin.

When Roy left India in 1915 at the age of twenty-six, the Indian Congress Party, embodying Indian nationalism, consisted largely of lawyers and other rich, upper-class professionals and businessmen who asked no more of the empire than greater representation in its Indian legislature of limited authority. Mohandas K. Gandhi had just come home from two decades in South Africa and England, and the mass movement for independence was not yet born. The tepid nationalism of his countrymen repelled Roy. He yearned for a victory by imperial

[14] *M. N. Roy's Memoirs*, p. 22.

Germany that would quickly liberate India. Before long, however, his anti-imperialism extricated him from such unprincipled nationalism and catapulted the young firebrand into what he regarded as antinationalist, internationalist communism.

In 1920 Roy appeared on the world communist stage to challenge Lenin. At the Second Congress of the Comintern, Roy took issue with Lenin's proposals for backward countries. Lenin, impressed, invited the Indian for several private talks. Roy considered India's nationalists mild, antirevolutionary collaborationists with imperialism. But Lenin, in his "First Draft of Theses on National and Colonial Questions," wrote that "all events in world politics are concentrated, inescapably, around one central point, namely, the struggle of the world bourgeoisie against the Soviet Russian Republic." The Republic had "inevitably" attracted "the oppressed nationalities which have become convinced by bitter experience that there is no salvation for them except through the triumph of the Soviet government over world imperialism." This wildly exaggerated piece of Russocentricity was followed by Thesis Six: "Therefore . . . it is necessary to carry out a policy of achieving the closest alliance of all national-liberation and colonial-liberation movements with Soviet Russia."[15]

Roy bristled. Given his Indian background, he translated this into "the closest union" of Soviet Russia with the bourgeois, collaborationist Indian Congress Party. Moreover, Lenin went so far—in Thesis Eleven—as to say that workers and communists in retarded countries had "an obligation to render the most active aid" to "the bourgeois-democratic liberation movement." The Soviet leader, however, added an important caveat: the alliance of communists with bourgeois-democratic nationalists was to be "temporary," and communists were "not to merge" with such parties but "definitely safeguard the independence of the proletarian movement even if it is in its most embryonic form." Finally, and piquantly pertinent to subsequent events in China, Lenin wanted "soviets of toilers" organized in the East among peasants whose dissent must acquire "the strongest revolutionary character."

Roy's objections to Lenin's theses were discussed by a commission of twenty members appointed by the Second Congress and in private conversations. "In our first discussion," Roy writes, "he [Lenin] frankly admitted his ignorance of the facts, but took his stand on theoretical grounds. . . . I pointed out that . . . in India . . . the nationalist movement was ideologically reactionary. . . . The role of Gandhi was the crucial point of difference. Lenin believed that, as the inspirer and leader of a mass movement, he was a revolutionary. I maintained that, as a

[15] V. I. Lenin, Vol. 41, pp. 163-164.

religious and cultural revivalist, he was bound to be a reactionary socially, however revolutionary he might appear politically."[16]

The Commission's work began on July 25, 1920. The Lenin-Roy talks took place during and before and after that day. On July 25 the Red Army was dashing headlong toward Warsaw. Two days later General Tukhachevsky's troops crossed the Curzon Line. A communist Poland seemed within the Kremlin's grasp. Germany would be next. Lenin, preoccupied and exhilarated by these major events and prospects, blithely requested Roy to draft supplementary theses on the colonial question and present them to the Second Congress of the Comintern whose delegates were watching the progress of red pins on the map of Poland. The Congress adopted Lenin and Roy's theses unanimously.

"I maintained," Roy explains in his memoirs, "that, afraid of revolution, the nationalist bourgeoisie would compromise with Imperialism in return for some economic and political concessions to their class. The working class should be prepared to take over at that crisis the leadership of the struggle for national liberation and transform it into a revolutionary mass movement." Lenin agreed.

More than four years passed. The last three of these—from the fourth quarter of 1923 to the fourth quarter of 1926—were marked by violent social convulsions in China which Stalin sought to restrain by remote control while ignoring Roy's prophecies and Lenin's injunctions. It finally dawned on the dictator that something was wrong. The great danger for Stalin lay not in the possibility of a revolutionary recession in China but in the likelihood that his guidance of the revolution would be proved faulty and the stand of the Trotsky-Radek opposition correct. Roy was accordingly sent to China as a Comintern delegate.

Lenin had pleaded for soviets in backward countries experiencing revolutions. Soviets for China and arming of the workers were on Trotsky's flag. Stalin, through Borodin, had discouraged the Chinese communists and peasants and workers from organizing soviets lest the bourgeoisie and the warlords be antagonized. The Chinese Communist Party had not, to be sure, "merged" with the Kuomintang; it maintained its own apparatus, yet it collaborated so intimately with the Left Kuomintang (two of its members entered the Hankow Left Kuomintang Cabinet) and identified itself so closely with nonrevolutionary or antirevolutionary policies that the party's separateness almost vanished. Now, early in 1927, it seemed that the Chinese bourgeoisie, in the person of Chiang Kai-shek, was about to compromise with the imperialists while the workers and peasants had not been prepared by the communists to seize the leadership of the national revolution from the re-

[16] Roy, p. 379.

actionaries. Roy went to China to make it easier for Stalin, as the deadly feud with Trotskyism approached its climax, to meet the opposition's challenge by altering his interpretation of Chinese developments.

The shift was not long in coming. It involved the painful surgery of disengaging the Kremlin from Chiang Kai-shek. Troops of the Generalissimo—his new, self-conferred title—had taken Shanghai and he made an entry into the great city on March 26. His soldiers and police continued to behead communists, radicals, workingmen, and innocents at street corners. Foreign Commissar Chicherin told me of a Politburo meeting where Chiang was discussed. The Politburo—it consisted, in 1927, of Joseph V. Stalin, Nikolai I. Bukharin, Alexei I. Rykov, Mikhail P. Tomsky, Vyacheslav M. Molotov, Klimenti E. Voroshilov, Mikhail I. Kalinin, Valerian V. Kuibyshev, and Jan E. Rudzutak—met once a week and invited nonmembers to report and comment. Karl Radek, the communist gadfly and chameleon, and by this time an expert on China and Rector of Moscow's Sun Yat-sen University, predicted that Chiang Kai-shek "will betray the revolution." Stalin, Chicherin said, "vehemently disagreed. The next day news came from China that Chiang was executing communists and Left Kuomintangists. That is why Stalin then took the Trotskyist line in China." Chicherin asked me not to publish this until he died. He died in 1936.

Deprived of his rectorship for being right, Radek argued angrily against Stalin's China policy. "The Chinese workers and middle-class people," he said to me in Moscow, "should have occupied the International Settlement in Shanghai. With two million Chinese in the Settlement, no Sikhs or gunboats could have prevented it." Today, Radek declared, the Trotsky Opposition advocates a frankly communist program carried out by communists only. "If there can be a purely capitalist state in Manchuria," he asserted, "there is no reason why you cannot have a Soviet state in the south" of China. "Anti-imperialism alone," Radek added, "is not revolution." He put his trust in the Chinese peasantry. "The cause of the hundreds of millions may take months and years to succeed but succeed it must," Radek concluded.[17]

In saying "Anti-imperialism alone is not revolution" Radek implied that Stalin's China policy, directed against foreign imperialism, was Soviet nationalism, not revolution. But when he proposed a Soviet state in south China, Bukharin wondered how Radek, like Trotsky, could deny Russia the possibility of building socialism in one country and grant the possibility of building socialism in one part of one country.

Stalin never hesitated to adopt an opponent's policy. But Stalin did not go as far as Trotsky or Radek. After a preliminary barrage of articles

[17] This interview was reported in my article in the New York *Nation* of Nov. 30, 1927.

by lesser men, Stalin, and his theoretical armor-bearer Bukharin, entered the fray to execute a retreat while seeming to advance. Stalin urged that "the proletariat clear away the national bourgeoisie and draw to it the mass millions of toilers in city and village in order to overcome the resistance of the national bourgeoisie, carry the bourgeois-democratic revolution to complete victory, and gradually transfer it to the tracks of the socialist revolution."

This seemed like a long lunge toward the Trotsky-Radek program as well as a disavowal of the alliance with the Generalissimo and his Kuomintang. "The crisis of world capitalism and the existence of a proletarian dictatorship in the Soviet Union," Stalin maintained, would help in shunting the revolution from its bourgeois-democratic to its socialist phase. "On the other hand," reads the next paragraph, "the fact that, by and large, imperialism is advancing against the Chinese revolution on a united front, that there is no division and no war among the imperialists like those which existed, for instance, before the Bolshevik revolution and which weakened imperialism—that fact indicates that the Chinese revolution will encounter many more difficulties on the road to victory than did the revolution in Russia."

To justify his past support of Chiang Kai-shek, Stalin added that the recent upsurge of the revolution, the rising of the Shanghai workers had "thrown the Chinese national bourgeoisie back into the camp of counterrevolution" and united the imperialists with a view to "smothering the revolution." Chiang Kai-shek was now ready for "a deal with the imperialists and the national bourgeoisie against the workers and peasants of China." It followed, Stalin announced, that human material should be prepared "for soviets in the future" and that "the basic guarantee of the victory of the revolution is . . . the arming of the workers and peasants."

Nevertheless, Stalin would not admit that he had erred or that Trotsky's judgment had been superior. Instead, the following section of his article (in *Pravda* of April 21, 1927) is subtitled "The Opposition's Mistakes." Here Stalin employed a common communist gambit: past policy suited past conditions; the opposition's program then was premature; conditions had changed, therefore policy must change; the opposition's proposals were still wrong. Since Chiang was in the camp of the national bourgeoisie and the imperialists, cooperation with him would end. Prepare for organizing soviets. And the only road to success is by arming the workers. These were planks in the Trotsky platform.

"But what is the meaning of forming soviets *now*?" Stalin asked in his article. "First, you cannot launch soviets at any moment—they are formed only in a period of an extraordinary rise in revolutionary will. Second, Soviets are not formed for chatter—they are formed above all as organs of government against the existing government." If soviets emerged in the region governed by the Wuhan authorities, this would mean "to fight the government of the revolutionary Kuomintang . . . to replace the government of the revolutionary Kuomintang." Foreign enemies would say that "in China not a national revolution was in progress but an artificially transplanted 'sovietization.' " The opposition demanded the exodus of communists from the Kuomintang. But "the entire imperialist pack" was insisting that communists be driven from the Kuomintang. Why give "joy" to the enemy? Why "hand over the banner of the Kuomintang, the most popular of all Chinese banners, to the rightist Kuomintang?" Conclusion? The opposition, by asking for the exit of the communists from the Kuomintang *"at the present moment* is doing the work of the enemies of the Chinese revolution."[18]

Thus Stalin stole the thunder of the Trotsky opposition—soviets and arming the workers—but refused to use it; too early. By waving a wand of words Stalin removed the crown of revolution from the head of Chiang Kai-shek and placed it on the brow of the "revolutionary" Left Kuomintang in Wuhan where Borodin was having trouble: economic hardships due to the blockade of the Yangtze by foreign gunboats, internal party bickering, and friction between the Left Kuomintang party and the local generals who shared power with the party and regarded it, with abhorrence, as communist.

Borodin weighed the alternatives. He might stage a coup against General Tang Shen-chi and other "reactionary Hankow generals." Tang held the Hanyang arsenal, the second largest in China—output 6,000 rifles a month—with a force of three army corps. But Borodin feared that "the Left Kuomintang, faced with a communist coup, would have listed sharply toward the generals." This gave the lie to Stalin's designation of the Left Kuomintang as "revolutionary."

At this juncture—the first week of April, 1927—M. N. Roy arrived in Hankow. He was Borodin's subordinate, but the temperamental Indian and the deliberate Russian soon clashed. Roy, claiming to reflect the latest changes in Moscow's mood, pressed Borodin to adopt a more radical policy; he wished to see the revolution deepened by mobilizing the peasants against their landlords. Borodin, knowing this would incense the generals and the Left Kuomintang moderates, knowing, too, that Chang Tso-lin was advancing toward the Yangtze, decided this was no time for land reform. The spontaneous seizure of estates by insurgent peasants should be stopped and preparations made to save Wuhan from enemy assault.

[18] The article is reprinted in Stalin, Vol. 9, pp. 221-230.

A victory over the Manchurian marshal's forces, Borodin reasoned, might bring an extra dividend: Feng Yu-hsiang would become a Wuhan ally. At Chumatien, 125 miles northwest of Hankow, the Wuhan and Manchurian armies fought a sanguinary battle lasting three days. Wuhan won, but it also lost, it lost 14,000 dead, many of them ardent communists. The Wuhan military thereupon withdrew to Hankow, and Feng began to treat with Chiang Kai-shek.

Meanwhile Roy preached his radical, "noncapitalist" program. Addressing the Fifth Congress of the Chinese Communist Party on May 4, 1927, he said the Chinese revolution "has become the direct instrument of the struggle for socialism in the whole world. . . . For this reason, imperialism is concentrating all its forces on crushing the Chinese revolution." Imperialism must be defeated. The Chinese bourgeoisie, weak, underdeveloped, and allied with imperialism, could not be entrusted with this task. Communists, Roy asserted, preferred a revolution by three classes: the working class, the peasantry, and the small bourgeoisie (merchants, intellectuals, artisans, and so forth) "under the hegemony of the proletariat." The "democratic dictatorship" established by these three classes would destroy the roots of capitalism by nationalizing "land, the large-scale industry, the railroads, the waterways." That would still not be socialism, merely an advance toward socialism.[19]

This was Moscow's new message to China modified in the mouth of M. N. Roy.

Roy went beyond making speeches, he inspired the communists to organize peasant uprisings against landlords. Especially in the province of Hunan, where Mao Tse-tung, a minor communist official, busied himself mobilizing farmers for revolution, and in Hupeh Province land confiscation had proceeded apace. When the Wuhan military heard of this, they demanded to know who organized these "excesses." According to Wang Ching-wei, the foremost leader of the Left Kuomintang, "Borodin denied that he was responsible for the movement, but mentioned his colleague M. N. Roy, an Indian communist, as the instigator of all the trouble, stating that Roy had the complete confidence of Stalin, even more so than himself." In view of the military's hostility, the Chinese Communist Party ordered land seizures rescinded, and Mao Tse-tung, an obedient party member, annulled his own revolutionary achievements,[20] which scarcely increased his fondness for Moscow.

Borodin resented Roy's activities. As a fervent, veteran Bolshevik he would have been happy to put Trotsky's proposals and the less extreme

[19] Robert C. North and Xenia Joukoff Eudin, *M. N. Roy's Mission to China. The Communist-Kuomintang Split of 1927*, pp. 216-230.

[20] *Ibid.*, pp. 102-103.

Roy proposals to the test and try to foment communism in China. But as a practical statesman he knew this to be beyond the power of the men and means at his disposal.

The dilemma of the Chinese revolution consisted in the simultaneity of civil war and revolution. This became a boon when the communists mastered the China mainland in 1949, for unlike the Russian Bolsheviks who seized power in 1917 and were almost immediately immersed in a costly three-year civil war, the Chinese civil war ended before the communist entry into Peking, and Mao accordingly ruled a country rid of warlords. But in 1927 the Chinese civil war raged furiously and the commanders of independent provincial armies were needed by all revolutionists. Roy argued that a peasant revolution—a land reform—would impel the peasants, the backbone of all warlord armies, to desert, therewith abolishing those armies and ending the civil war. But even the communists doubted this analysis, and the communist party congress he addressed exempted small landlords and army officers who were big or small landlords from the confiscation of their estates. During a debate in the Eighth Plenary Session of the Central Executive of the Comintern in Moscow on May 27, 1927, "Stalin produced telegrams from Borodin which asserted that the Kuomintang Left was determined to fight against the agrarian revolution even if it meant a break with the Comintern. The Left bourgeoisie, Stalin insisted, was still too powerful. 'Its armies will not disband in the twinkle of an eye, and we will then be defeated in a civil war before the insurgent agrarians are able to connect with the proletarian insurrection.' "[21]

That was the issue. After all his declarations about organizing soviets and arming workers in the vague future, Stalin counseled winning the civil war and postponing the revolution. Yet there was Roy, delegated by Stalin, apparently acting contrary to Stalin's (and Borodin's) expressed opinions. Borodin sensed a Moscow maneuver: Stalin was preparing a defense against the Trotskyists: If they accused him of inhibiting the Chinese revolutionaries, he could point to Roy who pursued a radical line; if the Roy program failed, Borodin could be made the scapegoat. Borodin expected it to fail.

The transcendent fact is that by June-July, 1927, Borodin realized the Left Kuomintang was too weak to win civil war battles or to effect an agrarian revolution. The warlords linked with the Wuhan Left Kuomintang-Communist coalition had enough strength to emasculate the Chinese revolution but not to win the civil war against Chiang Kai-shek and other warlords. On June 30 Chiang and Feng Yu-hsiang urged the ex-

[21] *Ibid.*, pp. 90-91.

pulsion from Wuhan of all Russian advisers and Chinese communists. Borodin told me he could have ignored these repeated summonses. "I felt disavowed by Moscow, not by Hankow." He was irritated by Roy and frustrated by the impasse at Wuhan which permitted neither military success nor revolutionary progress. He could do nothing. On July 20 Borodin consequently announced his retirement from politics in China and moved into the home of T. V. Soong, Chiang Kai-shek's brother-in-law and Wuhan Finance Minister. Thither came a stream of Left Kuomintang leaders and generals begging the Russian to reconsider. After a week of these ceremonial Chinese obeisances, Borodin and his staff left for the long trek via the Gobi Desert to Moscow.

Thus ended the Russian phase of the Chinese revolution.

It is impossible to prove a case about something that has not happened. It is impossible to prove that a Trotskyist policy in China could have succeeded. Soviet and Chinese communist participation in the 1923-1927 Chinese revolutionary era aroused the sleeping millions of China against their masters. Those masters, foreign and Chinese, recognized the threat and used their power to suppress the popular revolutionary trends. Not until the Japanese were defeated and Britain and France gravely debilitated in the second world war did the Mao-led Chinese communists, who meanwhile assembled their own effective army, cope with Chiang Kai-shek and drive him off the mainland. The Generalissimo had ignored the crying needs of the peasantry, the people of China. No amount of American aid sufficed to overcome that handicap.

* * *

The Soviet Communist Party Congress is, at least in theory, the highest authority of the country. The Fifteenth Party Congress, scheduled for December 2-17, 1927, would mark Stalin's triumph over Leon Trotsky. There was no doubt about the triumph; Trotsky was in exile in Alma-Ata, in Soviet Central Asia. But Stalin suffered from an inner need, never to be satisfied, to demonstrate his own omnicompetence—in linguistics as in biology, in music as in agriculture, in Greek mythology as in Russian literature—and his devotion to revolution. Trotsky's charge that he had sown confusion, not revolution, in China riled the megalomaniacal dictator. Stalin proposed to prove Trotsky wrong. Soviet Party congresses are occasions for special display of the administration's prowess. Stalin would demonstrate his revolutionary ardor to the Fifteenth Congress. He commanded the Chinese Communist Party to launch insurrections timed for the congress.

The departure of Borodin from Wuhan and the eclipse of the Left Kuomintang-Communist bloc had unleashed a terror of mass proportions. Roy estimates that a quarter of a million communists were executed from March, 1927, until the early months of 1928.[22]

This mountain of communist dead, added to high totals during previous years, was no contribution to the party's morale. Decimated, dispersed, and discouraged, it needed a respite, not a revolution, especially since the adversaries had tasted blood and were well placed to exact more. Nevertheless, Moscow's words was law, and the Chinese Communist Party launched several hopeless, expensive coups in southern China. The largest of these and the most costly began on December 10, 1927. Years later, after the communists ruled the mainland, an East European communist ambassador, traveling with Liu Shao-chi, the President of Red China, arrived in Canton. "This is where Stalin staged his slaughter of our comrades," Liu remarked to the diplomat.[23]

Besso Lominadze, a Soviet Georgian communist, served Stalin in 1927 as the Comintern's agent in China. He was joined somewhere on the mainland by a twenty-five-year-old German communist, Heinz Neumann, carrying a false passport which named him Gruber, an Austrian businessman. (Neumann was executed by Stalin's secret police in the late 1930's.) His widow, the writer Margarete Buber-Neumann, who communicates these facts, adds that Neumann and Lominadze kept a rendezvous in China where they received a big suitcase heavy with bundles of United States dollars in large denominations. Thus armed, they proceeded to Canton. Neither had had previous experience in China.

Harold Isaacs quotes a Chinese source who states that the Neumann-Lominadze leadership corralled 4,200 Chinese for their adventure; Neumann himself left a record giving the number as 3,200. The Canton military authorities "had 5,000 well-armed soldiers in the city, in addition to 1,000 policemen and 1,000 armed gangsters." In the environs of Canton, warlord armies "totaling about 50,000 men" lay at their stations. Yet the communist rebels captured "most of the city" by dawn, December 11. Immediately, a "Soviet of Workers', Peasants', and Soldiers' Deputies" sprang into being. It released one thousand political prisoners from jail and decreed the confiscation of banks and the properties of the rich.

On the morrow troops from the suburbs invaded the city and "Chinese, British, and Japanese gunboats . . . joined in the battle of repression." By December 13 the Canton Commune was crushed. "Soldiers," writes Isaacs, "seized any woman they found with bobbed hair, which was regarded as infallible evidence of radicalism. Hundred of girls were

[22] *Revolution and Counter-Revolution in China*, p. 528.

[23] Repeated to me by the ambassador. By far the best-documented, and most dramatic, account of the Canton communist uprising is in Isaacs, Chap. 17.

shot and otherwise killed after being subjected to indescribable indignities." The Soviet Consulate was raided and five Russians assassinated. "The final toll of the counted dead was 5,700." Heinz Neumann escaped. Lominadze likewise, only to become one of the first Soviet leaders executed on Stalin's orders.

Deprived of the possibility of announcing a spectacular Moscow victory in China, Bukharin told the Fifteenth Congress that the Chinese Communist Party had between 20,000 and 25,000 members. "The Chinese revolution is far from dead," he said consolingly.

* * *

Exporting a revolution is monumental arrogance.

In the age of lava-like locomotion on foot, donkey, camel, and sailboat, cultural influences and technological change traversed deserts, continents, and seas. In recent centuries the interchange of knowledge and experience has been swift and constant. Regions, nations are necessarily borrowers and lenders.

But a nation is a nation and behaves like a nation no matter what flattering adjective it prefixes to its name. Though the nation be genuinely generous without precedent, yet is the profit motive rarely absent even if the profit is nothing more substantial than friendship and much-desired love.

In fomenting revolution in China between 1923 and 1927 (and in Germany in October, 1923), the Kremlin engaged in national defense. National defense is regarded universally as a legitimate undertaking. Governments wage war, threaten war, institute blockades, form alliances, grant loans, and make propaganda to weaken a real or imaginary enemy. To this arsenal the Soviet government added revolution.

Stalin was less of a socialist or internationalist than Lenin. Yet Lenin considered peace and revolution a means of saving the Soviet regime and protecting Russia from attack. Trotsky may have wanted to plant socialism abroad—he offered to go to Germany to lead the October, 1923, revolution—as a desirable end in itself but also to stop the Soviet Union's descent into the black hole of Stalinist totalitarianism. And when the worst had occurred at home and after the Soviet-Nazi Pact of August, 1939, Trotsky still championed the cause of Soviet national defense—against Finland! No statesman, in office or in exile, Marxist, fascist, or democrat, can avoid being a nationalist as long as nations have not merged a considerable fraction of their egos in an internationalism.

On the pretext of national defense, enormous empires have been acquired either absent-mindedly or deliberately. Who can say that China would not have become a Russian satellite had Borodin been successful?

Moscow assumed he would succeed. The Kremlin powermen called themselves communists and intended to establish socialism in the Soviet Union but were, in fact, tolerating an increasing measure of private capitalism. The economic and social content of their revolution had never been planned. Yet they presumed to plan a revolution in an ancient, complex society and to implement the plan through their own representatives who would tell the Chinese, in Russian or English, what to do. In articles before and after his fall and exile, Trotsky stressed the need in China of a "dictatorship of the proletariat" though the proletariat was a negligible percentage in the population. Stalin entered an alliance with the Chinese bourgeoisie and thus, in effect, with the foreign imperialists whom he wanted to expel. The peasantry, the decisive factor in the country, the people who enabled Mao Tse-tung to conquer two decades later, were treated as politically expendable rifle fodder. Moscow did not know China. It believed it could superimpose the Russian revolutionary pattern on China; it talked of the bourgeois-democratic revolution, soviets, arming the workers. The Chinese communists, when they rid themselves of Russian supervision, organized an army, chiefly of villagers.

Lenin was able to seize power because his predecessors could not rally a regiment to defend them. In China the situation was totally different: Mao won because he had large armies which fought Chiang Kai-shek and the Japanese for many years. In the interests of communism in China it would have been better for Moscow to help the Chinese communists carry out their own policy. Stalin acted in the interest of the Soviet nation, and acted badly partly because of the inherent anomaly of exporting a Russian-type revolution to a country very different from Russia, partly because of the Trotsky-Stalin feud.

The war between Trotsky and Stalin which shook the world commenced in 1918 when the issues of China, industrialization, and collectivization were absent even in the germ. The two men automatically repelled one another. Trotsky haughty and highly endowed, Stalin crafty and envious. But there were objective elements even then. Trotsky was the cosmopolitan, the European, Stalin the provincial from the tiny town in the narrow Caucasus valley. Trotsky had studied world culture and Marxism, Stalin had been taught by life to compete in the dark. In 1923 and 1924 China became a major problem in Soviet foreign and domestic affairs. Trotsky wished to export socialism to China, Stalin hoped to defeat Europe in Asia. Given the initial arrogance of the exportation of a revolution, Stalin was the more practical politician of the two. But Trotsky had a vast Soviet audience, and he could not easily be defeated in a country where communists, disappointed by the setbacks of socialism at home, sought solace by carrying it to neighboring China. Though the

Soviet revolutionary flame still burned, the revolutionists knew it needed fresh oil. Perhaps from China. Perhaps the Chinese revolution would restore the flagging spirit of the Russian revolution.

Stalin was too clever a tactician to ignore Trotsky's arguments. He adopted the words, rejected their substance. Having wrenched Trotsky from power he applied the substance disastrously in Canton in order to rehabilitate himself as a revolutionary.

China was a pawn in the Moscow power struggle. China was the victim of the Kremlin leadership which arrogated to itself the right to redirect the life of a great people. In theory such action ought to be acceptable, for it might redound to the welfare of the host nation. In practice it is likely to become a selfish enterprise. This is the era of passionate nationalism when foreign intervention, however motivated, antagonizes.

Moscow's attempt to carry revolution to China (and to Germany) proved to be an exercise in futility. The Kremlin saw its failure and retired from the export business.

XIII THE "LOGIC" OF LOCARNO

When the communists captured Peking on October 1, 1949, and became the rulers of mainland China, they showed little interest in recognition by other countries. Even after diplomatic relations were established with some powers, the Mao Tse-tung regime never cultivated them, in fact kept them at the lowest temperature commensurate with life. China was the "Middle Kingdom," the center of the world, and the "barbarians" would not be courted. Soviet Moscow, on the contrary, eagerly sought recognition by great and small foreign lands. Recognition facilitated trade, opened channels of information, and conferred status. The Soviets wanted status. "By thy untiring labors and by thy sole leadership," Chancellor Count Golovin said as he crowned Tsar Peter the Great Emperor on October 22, 1721, "we have stepped forth from the darkness of insignificance and ignorance on to the road of glory and have joined in equality with the civilized states of Europe." The need to be equal survived the eighteenth century and lives to this day when the sense of inferiority produces loud assertions of superiority.

The Kremlin garnered many recognitions in 1924 and 1925, and finally the most reluctant United States granted Moscow *de jure* recognition at the end of 1933. But none of these bore rich fruit until Stalin negotiated the pact with Hitler in August, 1939, and began annexing territory. Then the U.S.S.R. became a great power.

The Soviet relationship with China until 1927 was important because of the Chinese revolution; with Germany until 1933 because of military collaboration and commercial transactions; and with Turkey, Persia, and Afghanistan because it was their counterweight to Great Britain. The only other countries which had recognized the Soviet Union by the end of 1923—six years after the revolution—were Finland, Estonia, Latvia, Lithuania, Poland, and Outer Mongolia. In the many remaining nations, political, religious, and ideological opposition to recognition was so strong, the expectation of benefits so minimal, that they refrained from establishing diplomatic ties. A change of attitude usually followed a change of government. Thus the British Labour Party took office on January 23, 1924, and on February 2, Prime Minister Ramsay MacDonald granted Moscow *de jure* recognition. In France Edouard Herroit, of the Radical Socialist Party and leader of a so-called Left Bloc, became Premier on June 14, 1924, Poincaré was defeated, and the new government recognized the Soviet Union on October 28, 1924. Franklin Delano Roosevelt, inaugurated President on March 4, 1933, recognized the Soviet government on November 16, 1933. In all three instances several factors conduced to recognition. But none was as decisive as the election of an administration less conservative than its predecessor. Until the signing of the Soviet-Nazi pact domestic politics in foreign countries, and in the Soviet Union, played the major role in Soviet foreign affairs.

(Great Britain's example was quickly followed by a number of other states. Norway recognized the Soviet Union on February 13, 1924, eleven days after England did; Greece on March 8; Sweden on March 15; Canada on March 24; Denmark on June 18; Albania on July 6; Mexico on August 1; Iceland on June 22, 1925.) Mussolini's Italy recognized the Soviet government on February 7, 1924, Japan on January 20, 1925.

For years British diplomatic relations with Moscow led an uncertain existence. Labour rule in Britain was as new as recognition of the Bolshevik regime; the Conservatives were reconciled to neither. In 1924 MacDonald's Cabinet enjoyed only minority support in the House of Commons. The conservatives accordingly set their hearts on ousting him from office and cutting the tie with the Soviets.

Conservatives had long opposed the lesser contacts with the U.S.S.R. resulting from the Anglo-Soviet commercial treaty of March 16, 1921. Indeed, Lord Curzon of Kedleston, Foreign Secretary in the Cabinet which preceded MacDonald's, clearly intended to inflict maximum injury on the Soviets—a resumption of intervention this time through diplomacy rather than with arms. Curzon, a proud, hypersensitive person of noble lineage, a former Viceroy to India still hoping to become Prime Minister of Great Britain, precipitated a crisis in May, 1923, which plagued the 1924-1929 period of Anglo-Soviet relations.

The episode opened with the trial in Moscow in March, 1923, of Cardinal Cieplak, Monsignor Butkevich, and several other priests of the Roman Catholic Church in Russia charged with espionage and treasonable activities during the civil war and the Russo-Polish war. There could have been no doubt that the accused were hostile to communism or that the trial formed part of the campaign against all churches then reaching its most virulent form. The Cardinal was sentenced to ten years' imprisonment, the Monsignor to death.

Protests poured in on Moscow from numerous foreign religious and lay institutions and individuals. R. M. Hodgson, chief of the British mission in Moscow, acting on Curzon's instructions, presented the official British protest on March 30. With calculated offense, the Soviet reply was signed not by Foreign Commissar Chicherin or Deputy Commissar Litvinov or some other high official but by Gregory Weinstein, head of the Foreign Commissariat's Anglo-American section. The Weinstein note rejected Britain's protest on the normal grounds of interference in the domestic affairs of a sovereign state and then gratuitously condemned "the hypocritical intervention of the British Government which is responsible for the assassination in cold blood of political prisoners in Ireland, where 14,000 men, women, and young girls are treated in a barbarous and inhuman fashion."[1]

Moscow apparently felt this action was a model of restraint, for M. Tanin, the pen name of Maxim M. Litvinov, subsequently wrote that "but for diplomatic conventions, which Comrade Weinstein did to a certain extent nevertheless observe, one might have pointed to the massacre in Amritsar (India), to the bombing by airplanes of peaceful Arab and Egyptian villages, etc."[2]

London rejected Weinstein's note, whereupon he signed another, reiterating the Kremlin stand. Downing Street held its fire and gathered ammunition from new and dusty files. Hodgson finally, on May 8, 1923, handed the Foreign Commissariat not a note, not a protest, but a document known as the Curzon Ultimatum. If, in ten days, Moscow gave no satisfactory answer, the British government would examine whether "it

[1] British White Book, *Correspondence between His Majesty's Government and the Soviet Government respecting relations between the Two Governments*, Cmd. 1869.

[2] M. Tanin, *Mezhdunarodnaya Politika SSSR 1917-1924* (Foreign Policy of the U.S.S.R. 1917-1924), p. 16.

is desirable, or indeed possible, that the relations between the two Governments should remain any longer on so anomalous and indeed unprecedented a footing." This suggested the abrogation of the 1921 trade treaty and narrowing the slight chance of *de jure* recognition.

The ultimatum concentrated on the Soviet government's alleged revolutionary activities in India via Afghanistan and Persia. It quoted from messages, said to have been intercepted by British authorities, giving chapter and verse regarding money, munitions, and men sent by Moscow for anti-British purposes to the mutinous tribes on India's northwest frontier. Evidence of these "pernicious activities" had come to the British government "upon unimpeachable authority." It would fill many pages. "Such a narrative would doubtless provoke, as it did before, an indignant denial from the Soviet Government with allegation as to false information and spurious documents." Lord Curzon had "no intention of embarking on such controversy." He demanded the recall from Tehran of Soviet Minister Shumyatsky and from Kabul of Soviet Minister Raskolnikov whom he held responsible for the anti-British acts.

The ultimatum also discussed "a series of outrages inflicted upon British subjects in the last few years," the most conspicuous being the murder of C. F. Davison in January, 1920, and the arrest and imprisonment of Mrs. Sten Harding on the charge of espionage. "His Majesty's Government are unable to allow the matter to trifle with any longer." It asked "equitable compensation" on these and other unnamed personal claims.

The Soviet government had extended the three-mile limit on its Arctic seaboard to twelve miles. Accordingly, the Red Navy interfered with the fishing by British trawlers within the new zone. One trawler was sunk, two arrested. Curzon insisted on release, compensation, and noninterference with British shipping outside the three-mile limit.

Lastly, Lord Curzon wanted the two Weinstein notes withdrawn.

The ultimatum depressed Moscow. The French had invaded the Ruhr in January. On March 9 Lenin suffered his third stroke, which completely incapacitated him. Germany appeared on the brink of collapse; Poland might take advantage of the situation to seize German territory. A rupture of the tenuous Anglo-Soviet relations could place danger on Russia's doorstep. This was no occasion to temporize. The Politburo, joined by top men of the Foreign Commissariat, quickly decided to return a soft answer that turneth away wrath. Trotsky wrote the final text. Tanin-Litvinov, in his book, hailed "the cautious and conciliatory policy" adopted by the Soviet government.

The Weinstein notes, read Russia's reply, "can . . . be considered as nonexisting." The Kremlin agreed to pay damages to the family of Mr. Davison although he had operated in Russia, during British intervention, with the espionage organization of "the well-known Paul Dukes"; Mrs. Sten Harding had been branded a spy by Mrs. Margaret Harrison, an American journalist whom Chicherin, in a public address in those tense days, called "an American spy"; nevertheless, the Soviets would pay her the 13,000 pounds stipulated in Curzon's ultimatum. British trawlers could fish outside the Soviet three-mile limit until the question was settled in negotiations.

Although the Soviet government thus yielded ground, the tone of its reply was not abject. It argued: "The path of ultimata and threats is not the road to the resolution of particular and secondary misunderstandings between governments; in any case, the establishment of proper relations with the Soviet Republics cannot be achieved in this manner."

On the main issue Soviet subversion in Central Asia and the approaches to India so near to Curzon's heart, the Kremlin's answer first took a tu quoque line: The Soviet government "has not a few reports and documents indicating very energetic activities by agents of the government of Great Britian in the Caucasus and especially in areas contiguous to the Central Asiatic parts of the Soviet Union." It also mentioned British support of Basmachi banditry in Soviet Turkestan and in eastern Bokhara and the aid given by British consuls "in relatively recent times" to White Guard generals. All governments have material of this nature, and if they used it not for orientation but to create conflicts, peaceful relations between any two governments could hardly exist. The authenticity of intercepted letters and messages "always remains under some doubt." The author of the Soviet reply was obviously trying to convince not Curzon but British public opinion in this You-too-and-everybody-else gambit.

The Soviet government then denounced as "absolutely fictitious" Curzon's quoted excerpt regarding alleged Soviet deeds in Persia. As for the telegram transmitted by Raskolnikov, about 3,000 gold rubles and ten boxes of ammunition sent to Waziristan, this was a deliberate distortion, such assistance was rendered not by Raskolnikov but by "somebody else unrelated to the Russian government whose name the generally accepted rules of international decency do not permit the Soviet government to reveal."

Nevertheless, Moscow agreed to recall Raskolnikov but not Shumyatsky.

Running through the Russian note[3] are pleas for more trade, reminders of the adverse effects a break would have on peace, and indica-

[3] Excerpts used here were translated from the original in U.S.S.R. Ministry of Foreign Affairs, *Dokumenty Vneshnei Politiki SSSR* (Documents on the Foreign Policy of the U.S.S.R.), Vol. VI; *November 20, 1922-December 31, 1923*, pp. 288-296.

tions that Moscow would contribute to better over-all relations.

Curzon congratulated himself on the result of his ultimatum. "I think," he wrote Lord Crewe, "I may claim to have won a considerable victory over the Soviet government, and I expect them to behave with more circumspection for some time to come." The "circumspection" was not perceptible in China, where, from 1923 to 1927, Stalin's target was British, and Japanese, commercial and imperial power. Litvinov, who signed the May 11 Moscow reply, also congratulated himself: "Our diplomacy maneuvered beautifully in that decisive moment. And in the final end the plans of Curzon, who hoped to force us to capitulate on the entire line of our Eastern policy and to tear up the Anglo-Soviet [trade] treaty, were smashed."[4]

A large element in the softness of Moscow's reply was its length—approximately three thousand words. Brevity is the soul of wit but diplomatic retreats and the cutting edge of sharp rejoinders are best concealed in the cotton wool of much verbiage. Both governments and many factions in England found something to please them in the long Soviet note, and that was its purpose.

One omission marked Curzon's ultimatum; he made no reference to Russia's debts. Would the Kremlin, "in that decisive moment," have departed from its conditional refusal to pay foreign creditors? Possibly, perhaps probably. But Curzon stood above crass questions of money, he concentrated on power in Central Asia where, he believed, the future of mankind would be determined. British creditors and bondholders, however, took umbrage at his neglect of their interests, and immediately after Prime Minister Ramsay MacDonald recognized the Soviet government in 1924 they knocked at the door of Christian G. Rakovsky.

Rakovsky, born in Bulgaria in 1873, lived long in Rumania, in Vienna, and in France where he studied and practiced medicine. He was a European. Most of the early Bolshevik leaders, and none since Stalin's purges, were Europeans by experience and culture. Shortly after the November 7 revolution Rakovsky became Chairman of the Soviet Ukraine, and in 1919 he was elected a member of the Central Committee of the Soviet Communist Party when that body consisted of nineteen members and, unlike the Central Committees of the Stalin reign, which numbered more than a hundred and which Nikita S. Khrushchev sometimes converted into mass meetings of nonmembers, the nineteen exercised real power. In the Trotsky-Stalin controversy Rakovsky joined Trotsky as much from cultural affinity as political agreement. But as Trotsky's influence waned in 1924 and Stalin's waxed, Rakovsky was sent "into exile" to London. And since MacDonald's rec-

[4] Tanin, p. 16.

ognition was grudging (he had to consider Conservative sentiment in the House of Commons), Rakovsky was chargé d'affaires, not ambassador. Moscow accorded the same mistreatment to Hodgson, who had been the British diplomat in the camp of Admiral Kolchak.

Rakovsky's first business was to deal with Russian debts to Britain. He made more progress than the Soviet delegation at the Genoa Conference. A treaty was signed, but nothing came of it; British domestic politics intervened.

The problem and the arguments pro and contra were the same as at Genoa and The Hague, but with the French not present to obstruct, and given the essential advantage of bilateral negotiations, greater progress was registered. Rakovsky urged, as Chicherin had at Genoa, that Russia's war debt to Britain which amounted to $2,766,000,000, according to one authority,[5] be canceled by Soviet claims for British damages inflicted on Russia during the 1918-1921 period of intervention. But if London wiped out Russia's war debts, France and Italy would ask the same dispensation. Arthur Ponsonby, MacDonald's Under Secretary of State for Foreign Affairs, accordingly proposed on May 15 that war debts and counterclaims "be reserved for discussion at a later date," and he subsequently announced in Parliament that both had been placed in "cold storage," a circumlocution for cancellation.

There remained prewar debts and the bondholders. Russia, wrote Leo Pasvolsky and Harold G. Moulton, "was an old country with a large existing debt resulting from past wars and bad financial administration." "The Russian bureaucrats," the same authors asserted, "were quite content with the feudal economic system of the country; they were not interested in internal development."[6]

The Tsarist government was corrupt, inept, slothful, aloof from the people, and unpopular. The bulk of the Soviet nation felt no loyalty to the monarchy and no obligation to embitter their lives by paying its debts. Every Soviet negotiator was bound to express this sentiment in negotiations with foreign governments.

The Soviet government had confiscated and nationalized the factories, mines, and other enterprises of British subjects. They asked compensation. One Englishwoman wanted to call on Rakovsky to collect rent for the three years he lived in her house in Kharkov when he was Ukrainian Chairman. "Nationalization as a result of the revolution is legal," Rakovsky declared publicly, "and . . . we must refuse to pay for its consequences."

Yet the Soviet government did not refuse to compensate claimants. It would pay if it obtained a loan in the London money market. "The

[5] Harvey E. Fisk, *The Inter-Ally Debts.*

[6] *Russian Debts and Russian Reconstruction,* p. 38.

central issue is the loan," Rakovsky told the Moscow *Izvestia* of July 30, 1924. "Everybody knows," Zinoviev declared at the Thirteenth Soviet Communist Party Congress in May, 1924, "that we have no possibility of paying debts" out of Russia's own financial resources. The Kremlin would have to borrow in order to pay.

But the Soviets knew that their credit in the London City was bad. They therefore asked the MacDonald government to guarantee the loan from private banks. At the May 20 session of the Anglo-Soviet financial conference, Arthur Ponsonby stated emphatically that "the British government can in no way guarantee such a loan." When Rakovsky went to the City and spoke with England's foremost bankers, all rebuffed him. He told them the Soviet government would pay a higher than normal rate of interest on the loan and use it for productive purposes: industrialization, building railroads, and so forth; the difference between the normal rate of interest and what Moscow paid would go to reimburse Russia's debtors. The bankers offered Rakovsky a simpler procedure: if the Kremlin wished to rebuild Russia, British industrialists would do it provided their companies and foreign employees operated on Soviet territory under agreements which exempted them from Soviet laws.

Therewith the talks in the City reached an impasse.

Again the question of the guarantee. Throughout June and July, 1924, the Labour Party's leadership debated the matter and disagreed. In a Cabinet meeting late in July, however, MacDonald, Foreign Secretary Arthur Henderson, Ponsonby, and their supporters prevailed over the followers of Chancellor of the Exchequer Philip Snowden, trade union leader J. H. Thomas, and Lord Oliver, Secretary of State for India. The August 4 session of the Anglo-Soviet Conference heard Ponsonby declare, "At the earlier meetings, I repeated more than once that the Government could not undertake to guarantee a loan. That decision has been reversed."[7]

The leaders of the British Labour Party and of the Soviet Communist Party were with few exceptions middle-class or upper-class intellectuals committed to a better life for the workingman. Yet the distance between them was as great as that between pacifism and violent revolution, between Christianity and atheism, between seven British centuries of evolution toward democracy and Russia's ten stagnant centuries of autocracy. When MacDonald became Prime Minister Leon Trotsky called him a "Christian Menshevik," neither of the words carried praise.

[7] In the exposition thus far and in what follows regarding the Anglo-Soviet negotiations of 1924 I have followed the unpublished protocols of the Conference which Rakovsky allowed me to see and copy when I visited him in exile in Saratov in 1928. He also gave me access to letters from many British politicians and editors. A more detailed account will be found in *The Soviets in World Affairs*, Chap. XVII.

Nor did Trotsky expect MacDonald to "seize a broom and sweep the cockroaches from his monarchy." Yet the Labour Party reflected considerable working-class and intellectual sympathy for the Bolshevik revolution. This and the reluctance of the trade unions to see Britain intervene again against the Soviet regime prompted a widespread refusal of British dockers to load munitions for Poland in 1920. Something of the same sentiment favored a positive conclusion of the Labour government's financial negotiations with Rakovsky. If the long negotiations came to nothing, moreover, the Conservatives would charge Labour with failure and denounce diplomatic recognition as an error. Political strategy required MacDonald to breach the logjam to a loan and thereby to a debt settlement. After many a slip, therefore, the loan was guaranteed and on August 10, 1924, the Anglo-Soviet General Treaty and a Commercial Treaty were signed by MacDonald and Ponsonby and by Rakovsky and four Soviet colleagues.

The two treaties would lie on the table for twenty-one days before they could be ratified by the British Parliament. Their fate depended on the Liberal vote in the House of Commons. David Lloyd George, the Liberal Party leader, favored a financial settlement with Russia, he had striven for it in Genoa, but he hoped to bring down the MacDonald government and return to power as a result of the ensuing elections. While discussion raged in the press and Parliament a former associate of Lloyd George wrote Rakovsky that "a considerable proportion of the Liberals will definitely vote against ratification of the treaty and, of the balance, a considerable number will not vote at all." The treaty, and with it MacDonald, were thus doomed. Labour's *Daily Herald* of October 2, in a prominent headline, called on its readers to "Prepare for a General Election."

During the debate on the treaty the MacDonald Cabinet withdrew proceedings against John Ross Campbell, editor of the Communist Party's *Workers' Weekly,* for inciting the King's armed forces to mutiny. On October 8, Conservatives and Liberals in Parliament voted against the government and defeated it for releasing Campbell from the charge. Nobody doubted but that the Campbell case was a pretext and that the real cause was the Anglo-Soviet settlement and the opportunity it gave the two opposition parties to try for office. National elections were scheduled for October 29.

The usual short election campaign has gone into history for an unprecedented episode which reflects no credit on British democracy. The facts are beyond dispute. Russian anti-Bolshevik émigrés in Berlin forged a letter, the so-called "Zinoviev Letter," in which Gregory Zinoviev, the head of the Third International (Comintern), allegedly instructed the British Communist Party to "paralyze all the military preparations of the bourgeoisie" through subversion in the British navy and army. The letter reached the Foreign Office in London and was published by the *Daily Mail,* a mass circulation Tory newspaper, under lurid headlines: "Moscow Orders to Our Reds. Great Plot Disclosed Yesterday. 'Paralyze the Army and Navy.' And Mr. MacDonald Would Lend Money to Russia!"

The Conservative Party was swept into power by a huge majority: 415 Conservatives were elected to the House of Commons, 151 Labourites, 44 Liberals, and 5 Independents. Perhaps the Conservative Party would have won without the "Zinoviev Letter." But it did not think so. It paid a large sum for the "letter" and made the fullest, most sensational use of it until the polls closed.

The proofs of forgery are multiple. The Communist International is described in the communication as "The Third Communist International." This was a clumsy trick designed by the forgers to help the ignorant recognize the organization; some people knew it as the Third International and some as the Communist International, so both descriptions were introduced. In the "letter," Zinoviev signed "President of the Presidium of the Executive Committee of Communist International," whereas any number of published letters he signed designate him as "President of the Executive Committee of the Communist International."[8]

Thomas Marlowe, editor of the *Daily Mail* which first published the forgery in 1924, explained in a letter to the editor of the London *Observer* of March 6, 1928, that he had, at the time, received two copies of the "Zinoviev Letter." "The important difference was that in one copy the name of McManus, to whom the letter was written, appeared immediately under the name of Zinoviev, as if McManus were the cosignatory." In the official British Blue Book[9] McManus is the cosignatory. In a second copy which came to Marlowe, McManus was the recipient. The forgers, in haste, erred. The day after Marlowe's letter appeared in the *Observer,* the *Times* urged the government of Prime Minister Stanley Baldwin, who owed his majority at least in part to the "Zinoviev Letter," to open an investigation. "No reason seems to exist why the demand should not be granted," the *Times* thundered. ". . . The refusal might conceivably confirm some lingering suspicion that the present Government . . . has something sinister to hide." "We fear," said the Conservative weekly *Spectator* of March 10, "an inquiry is necessary." Stanley Baldwin permitted no inquiry.

[8] For instance, see the cover of *"L'Oeil de Moscou" à Paris* by Jules Humbert Droz, which prints the facsimile of an authentic Zinoviev letter.

[9] *A Selection of Papers Dealing with the Relations between His Majesty's Government and the Soviet Government, 1921-7,* Cmd. 2895, pp. 30-32.

Lenin and Trotsky reviewing Soviet troops. *The Bettmann Archive*

Molotov, Stalin and Litvinov walking inside the Kremlin. *Sovfoto*

Sun Yat-sen.
United Press International Photo

General and Mme. Chiang Kai-shek outside their residence in Nanking in 1930. *United Press International Photo*

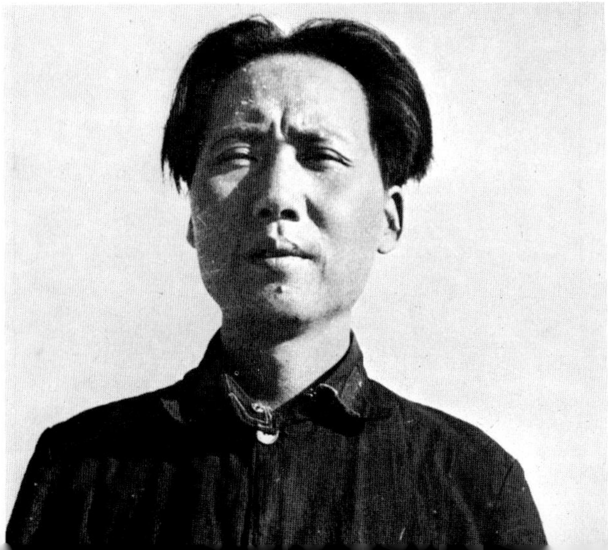

Mao Tse-tung.
United Press International Photo

General Hans von Seeckt.
United Press International Photo

esident von Hindenburg eets Marshal Tukha-evsky (third from left), neral Y. E. Yakir (with nom he is shaking nds) and other Red my observers at the 32 summer maneuvers the Reichswehr. *Oscar llgmann*

Maxim M. Litvinov, Louis Fischer and J. Alvarez del Vayo at Geneva in September, 1938.

On September 24, 1938, von Ribbentrop, Chamberlain, Hitler, an interpreter and Sir Nevile Henderson (then British Ambassador to Germany) met at Berchtesgaden. This "Talk over Tea Cups," as it was subsequently called, was a prelude to the Munich Conference. *United Press International Photo*

September 30, 1938. Chamberlain, Daladier, Hitler, Mussolini and Ciano after signing the Munich Agreement. *United Press International Photo*

Von Ribbentrop, Gaus, Stalin and Molotov having signed the German-Soviet Pact of 1939. *United Press International Photo*

Molotov in Berlin. To his left are von Ribbentrop and Field Marshal Keitel. *Ullstein*

Molotov and Goering. *Ullstein*

Molotov in conference with Hitler. *Wide World Photos*

Rudolf Hess inspecting Channel fortifications in February of 1941. Five months later he flew to England. *United Press International Photo*

Stalin and Japanese Foreign Minister Yosuke Matsuoka after signing the Russo-Japanese Neutrality Pact of 1941. *Wide World Photos*

German troops move eastward through a burning Soviet city shortly after their invasion of June 22,

Marlowe's revelation and the editorial demands for an investigation led to a debate in the House of Commons on March 19, 1928, in the course of which James Maxton, Independent Labour M.P., charged that the permanent officials of the Foreign Office, who had the "letter" on October 10, 1924, hid it from Ponsonby. Ponsonby, sitting nearby, nodded agreement. They also hid it from Prime Minister MacDonald. He was in London until October 13, and the so-called letter could not be published without his consent. Only on the 14th, when he was far off in the country and could not see the paper, was he informed of its existence. He permitted it to be published. In the 1928 debate he expressed regret at that decision and described the "letter" as "a deliberately planned and devised concoction of deceit, fitted artfully for the purpose of deceiving the public and to influence the Election. That it played a major part in the verdict, no one will deny. That it was a fraudulent one, few will dare to deny." The truth came slowly to Ramsay MacDonald.

The editorial comments and the parliamentary debate apparently cost the Conservative Party a considerable sum: two weeks after the debate —on April 2, 1928—C. Donald im Thurn, a former British army officer and uncle of Lady Nabarro, wife of Sir Gerald Nabarro, a Conservative M.P., wrote a letter to the Conservative and Unionist Central Office in London, saying, "I beg to acknowledge the sum of five thousand pounds (£ 5,000) on behalf of X. For a period of ten years I will additionally receive two hundred and fifty pounds (£ 250) a year, paid on the 1st June to him by our agent in the Argentine. At the end of ten years this payment will cease and he will be paid the sum of two thousand five hundred pounds (£ 2,500)." In all, 10,000 pounds. At the top of this letter, on the same line with "Dear Sirs," are two underlined words, "*Zinovieff Letter.*" Almost four years after the appearance of the "Zinoviev Letter" the Conservative Party headquarters began to pay "X" for his imperfect yet valuable services. Nobody pays a man 10,000 pounds for a letter unless he has worked very hard manufacturing it. Can one assume that after the parliamentary debate the forger threatened to reveal the truth unless he was paid?

C. Donald im Thurn's letter was printed in facsimile on the front page of the Weekly Review of the London *Sunday Times,* a Conservative paper, of December 18, 1966, as part of an exposé of the "Zinoviev Letter." "Zinoviev letter was a forgery," reads its headline. The exposé, covering nearly two large pages of the Sunday newspaper, gives the names of the Russian émigré forgers in Berlin and the manner in which the letter reached the Foreign Office and the press.

Two last facts revealed by the *Sunday Times:* One of the three forgers, Alexis Bellegrade, says the newspaper, died in London in 1945 "after surviving four years in Berlin as a second world war British spy."

The "X" of the 10,000 pounds, according to C. Donald im Thurn's 1928 letter, would "be given Argentine papers . . . he will sail as a deck hand and on arrival will present himself to our agent who will only know him under his new name and will know nothing further about him, except that he will pay these yearly sums over to him for the said period of ten years."

Why all this secrecy if the "Zinoviev Letter" was not a forgery? Why did Conservative Party headquarters want "X" far out of the way in the Argentine and make sure, by annual payments, that he would remain there?

Born under the evil star of the "Zinoviev Letter," the Cabinet of Prime Minister Stanley Baldwin and Foreign Secretary Austen Chamberlain considered that it had a mandate to congeal Anglo-Soviet relations and, at the opportune moment, disrupt them. Just as British recognition of the U.S.S.R. spread like the circular ripples caused by a stone thrown into a lake, so the freeze in London tended, for years, to stop movement in the world's relations with Russia. England ranked above all others as the leader in international politics; the United States, increasingly influential, nevertheless remained isolationist and off-stage, and to the extent that it showed its hand the effect was anti-Soviet. London had no rival as diplomatic style center.

In December, 1924, soon after taking office, Chamberlain visited Premier Herriot in Paris. "With respect to Soviet Russia," read the official communiqué, "it was agreed that both governments practise a common policy." They decided to combat Bolshevik propaganda in Europe and their colonies.[10] Although these words would seem to indicate coordinated or at least parallel policies, Chamberlain's direct purpose, as his acts soon proved, was to draw Germany away from Russia and nearer to England by protecting the Reich against France.

With the introduction on September 1, 1924, of the Dawes Plan for German reparations the mark and, contrary to Moscow's predictions, the German economy were stabilized and Germany became an important figure on the European chessboard. President Friedrich Ebert of Germany, a former leather worker, and leader of the Social Democrats, died February 28, 1925. On April 26 Field Marshal Paul von Hindenburg, responsible, with Ludendorff, for Germany's defeat in the first world war yet a national hero, was elected President of the Republic at the age of seventy-nine. Neither the wreckage of war nor the collapse of the Kaiser Reich diluted the "wooden Titan's" loyalty to militarism and monarchy. He died, as President, in 1934 after having inducted Adolf Hitler into the Chancellorship the year before. Hindenburg's unusually

[10] *Quotidien,* Dec. 6, 1924.

tall, unbent figure, broad, square shoulders, block head, and immobile face lent the post-Kaiser state a new dimension of strength within and enhanced the outward impression of national stability. The West and the Soviets courted Berlin with greater vigor. Austen Chamberlain in particular distinguished himself by his efforts to tighten the British bond with Germany. This labor came to fruition in the Locarno treaties.

Chamberlain aimed to give France an increased sense of security and thereby wean her from the "intransigent attitude towards Germany" that had led to the occupation of the Ruhr and, in turn, "tended to encourage the extremists in the Reich itself, and to bring Berlin and Moscow closer together—an approximation which boded ill for the peace of Europe."[11]

The preliminaries of the Locarno treaties lasted almost a year. The initiative, in the form of an offer to guarantee the eastern frontiers of France and Belgium, and, in accordance with Articles 42 and 43 of the Versailles peace treaty, demilitarize the Rhineland, came from Berlin to London on January 20, 1925. The architect of the pacts was Austen Chamberlain. He proposed to win Germany without alienating France. Changed circumstances helped. Poincaré's scheme for collecting reparations by bayonet had failed—the task now lay in the lap of S. Parker Gilbert, the American in Berlin charged with fulfilling the Dawes Plan. ". . . due entirely to Austen's representations in Paris and Brussels,"[12] French and Belgian troops evacuated the Ruhr and Duesseldorf, Duisburg, and Ruhrort in August, 1925, thus taking from France, caught in the undertow of inflation, her chief means of exercising pressure on Germany. To correct the balance, Britain would join Germany in guaranteeing France's and Belgium's frontiers with Germany.

But Paris demanded an additional prop for her security: German membership in the League of Nations. Under Article 16 of the League Covenant, however, member states undertook to grant passage through their territories to foreign armies marching to aid the victim of aggression. Berlin balked. Chicherin fought fiercely to dissuade Germany from entering the League which he and all Bolshevik leaders regarded as a capitalist conspiracy against the Soviets. Moreover, Germany refused to give to Poland and Czechoslovakia the guarantee she volunteered to give France and Belgium. Foreign Minister Gustav Stresemann yearned to regain the free city of Danzig and the Polish Corridor "for which," Austen Chamberlain wrote in a letter on February 16, 1925, "no British Government ever will or ever can risk the bones of a British grenadier."[13] Yet if Poland and Czechoslovakia, allies of France, were attacked by

[11] Sir Charles Petrie, *The Life and Letters of the Right Hon. Sir Austen Chamberlain, K.G., P.C., M.P.*, Vol. II, p. 249.

[12] *Ibid.*, p. 283.

[13] *Ibid.*, p. 259.

Germany or Russia, France wanted to be able to help them by sending an army through Germany. Germany had her own reasons for not resigning herself to this ominous eventuality, and Moscow threatened to end Soviet-German military collaboration if Germany joined the League of Nations and accepted the obligation under Article 16.

To mollify France, Chamberlain brought in Italy as another guarantor, with England, of the French and Belgian borders. Sir Austen—his Locarno success earned him a knighthood—was "attracted" by Italy's "redoubtable dictator." "It is not part of my business as Foreign Secretary to appreciate his action in the domestic politics of Italy, but if ever I had to choose in my own country between anarchy and dictatorship I expect I should be on the side of the dictator. In any case," Chamberlain continued, "I thought Mussolini a strong man of singular charm and I suspected of not a little tenderness and loneliness of heart. . . . I believe him to be accused of crimes in which he had no share . . . I am confident that he is a patriot and a sincere man."[14]

Wooed by a British statesman harboring such sentiments, Mussolini gladly traveled up the peninsula and into Swiss Locarno to initial the Locarno mutual security treaties with the representatives of Britain, France, Germany, and Belgium. Date: October 16, 1925. The treaties were signed in London on December 1. France acquiesced faute de mieux; the pacts granted her the maximum possible. She had sought a guarantee at Versailles from Britain and America of her eastern marches, and when Washington demurred so did London. Locarno was a guarantee without the United States but with a Germany that had begun to recover economically and was rearming thanks, in part, to Soviet assistance.

Much was made of Locarno. "English diplomacy," Lord D'Abernon wrote in his *Diary*, "never achieved a more striking success than the Treaty of Locarno." A new spirit, "The Spirit of Locarno," hovered, politicians said, over a tired Europe clutching peace to her bosom. Less than eleven years later Hitler reduced the Locarno treaty to worthless scraps of paper. "If, for instance," Chamberlain wrote Lord D'Abernon, British Ambassador in Berlin, on August 11, 1925, "German armies are on the march or troops are being assembled in the demilitarized area, Germany cannot expect those who are threatened to do nothing till they are on French or Belgian soil. . . . In such a case it is we, the guarantor, who would have to be satisfied that the flagrant act had taken place."[15] The flagrant act took place for all the world to see on March 7, 1936, and Britain and France did nothing. Hitler was permitted with impunity, and in violation of Locarno, to militarize the demilitarized zone

[14] *Ibid.*, pp. 295-296.
[15] *Ibid.*, p. 283.

on the left bank of the Rhine. But, as Austen Chamberlain remarked, "I profoundly distrust logic when applied to politics, and all English history justifies me."[16] Truly, Locarno lacked logic. The Locarno treaties were as unsubstantial as the "spirit of Locarno," a house of paper perilously poised on a balance of power which the dictators blew over with the first huff. Throughout history the road to war has been strewn with the loose leaves of treaties ignored. In that era of rampant nationalist rivalries the preservation of peace depended not on promises but, unfortunately, on an organized superior force ready for use and put to use at the first sign of aggression and at the first foreign interference in civil wars. Instead, the democracies in the 1930's allowed themselves to be lulled into complacency and disarmament by trust in treaties and in an impotent League of Nations and by the hope that the tiger dictatorships would grow tame if fed enough live nations.

The Kremlin had opposed the Locarno pacts. Count Ulrich von Brockdorff-Rantzau protested with extreme vehemence to President Hindenburg against Germany's entry into the League of Nations. Both received some consolation from the government of Chancellor Hans Luther and Foreign Minister Stresemann in the form of the Soviet-German Economic Treaty signed in Berlin on October 12, 1925, almost simultaneously with the agreement in Locarno. It promised continued friendly relations and granted extraterritoriality to most of the offices of the Soviet trade delegation in Berlin. At the same time a consular convention was concluded, and the German government provided short-term credit for Soviet purchases in Germany to the extent of 106 million stablized marks (approximately $25 million). In April, 1926, a long-term credit of 300 million marks was added. Chicherin regarded these arrangements as a victory for Soviet diplomacy.

The Dawes Plan and Locarno closed the postwar period. Therewith the prewar period began and, simultaneously, a new balance-of-power struggle that ended on September 1, 1939, bringing tragedy to many millions of human beings.

[16] *Ibid.*, p. 269.

XIV THE BALANCE OF POWER

Balance of power is the absence of principle; it merely conforms to the physical laws of balance. When one country is pulled in one direction attempts are made to pull it back. When two countries weigh down one end of the international seesaw, two or more other countries try to weigh the up side down. Moscow participated in this costly game.

The Kremlin powermen regarded the negotiations that led to Locarno as a British anti-Soviet success in building bridges to Berlin. They accordingly undertook to correct the German tilt toward London. Foreign Commissar Chicherin harbored no love for Britain, indeed in private conversation he often expressed the wishful thought that England would soon lose the Dominions and become a second-class power; he now hoped to show London and Berlin that the Soviets had alternatives, they could side with France and France's ally, Poland, thereby creating a new European balance of power. To herald this possibility, Christian G. Rakovsky, Moscow's foremost diplomat abroad, was shifted from London and appointed ambassador to Paris in November, 1925.

French policy was unmistakably anti-German. The Versailles treaty stipulated that the Cologne zone of Germany be evacuated on January 10, 1925. The French stayed. In March, 1925, Germany applied for admission to the League of Nations. France blocked her entry. The election of Field Marshal von Hindenburg as President of Germany on April 26, 1925, reinforced anti-German sentiment in France.

Noting these developments, Chicherin, with Stalin's consent, played the French card. The political road to Paris, he knew, lay through Warsaw. Chicherin visited Warsaw in September, 1925. This was no ordinary visit. Traditionally anti-Russian as a result of centuries of resented Russian rule, Poland's hostility flared anew after the 1920 Red Army invasion. Chicherin brought an olive branch.

From Warsaw Chicherin traveled to Berlin. There, with quiet but characteristically merciless persistence, he harassed Stresemann until an hour before the Foreign Minister left for Locarno. Chicherin objected to Germany's joining the League of Nations and, if she did join, to her acceptance of Article 16 of the League Covenant. Chicherin won the battle, for at Locarno, at Stresemann's suggestion, all participants in the treaty signed a note which said, "Each state member of the League is bound to cooperate loyally and effectively in support of the Covenant and in resistance to aggression"—so far a strong, binding commitment; then the undermining amendment: "to the extent which is compatible with its military situation and takes its geographic position into account." The amendment would permit Germany to opt out of League sanctions and foreign troop transit rights. When I asked Chicherin whether this satisfied him, he replied, "Article 16 was really emasculated." Officially disarmed, Germany could not, without inciting her population to dangerous nationalistic fury, grant passage to a Polish army going to the aid of France or a French army going to the aid of Poland which had annexed the Polish Corridor and parts of German Upper Silesia.

From Berlin Chicherin moved on to Paris where he met Aristide Briand just as the French Foreign Minister returned from Locarno in no glow of victory; it had been Austen Chamberlain's victory. But the Locarno treaties did not become effective until Germany entered the League, and in March, 1926, with the German delegates already in Geneva, the League Council again rejected Germany's application for membership. That was Briand's inning.

Various obstacles barred the way to a Soviet rapprochement with France. Chicherin had gone to Warsaw and Paris in order to strengthen his hand in Berlin. The Soviet government's goal was a treaty that reaffirmed the Rapallo agreement of April, 1922. Chicherin got it. German banks, German industrialists wanted Bolshevik business, and the Reichswehr still needed Russia's great spaces for illegal rearmament. Moreover, the League's rebuff to Germany in March, 1926, required a response, a Stresemann victory; on April 24, accordingly, he and Soviet Ambassador Nikolai N. Krestinsky signed the Berlin Treaty of Nonaggression and Neutrality.[1]

The new treaty reaffirmed Rapallo as "the basis of the mutual relationship between the U.S.S.R. and Germany" and committed the two parties to continue friendly contact with a view to achieving agreement on all political and economic questions of common concern. If one of the two countries was attacked, the other would remain neutral. Each government undertook not to participate in a financial or economic boycott of the other. In his note to Krestinsky, Stresemann asserted that Germany's adherence to the League of Nations would not alter her friendship for the Soviet Union and that the question of German sanctions

[1] Russian text in U.S.S.R. Ministry of Foreign Affairs, *Dokumenty Vneshnei Politiki SSSR* (Documents on the Foreign Policy of the U.S.S.R.), Vol. IX, pp. 252-253. Exchange of notes between Stresemann and Krestinsky, pp. 252-253. English text, London *Times*, April 27, 1926.

against Russia under Article 16 could only arise if the Soviets were the aggressor; the determination on the existence of aggression would lie exclusively with the German government.

Logically the treaty and the note should have kept Germany out of the League of Nations. But at the September, 1926, session of the League Germany was admitted and became a member of the Council. It was the wish of France—a complete reversal of her previous position. During the session, on September 17, Briand and Stresemann, unaccompanied by advisers or secretaries, slipped away from Geneva to lunch across the border in France at a charming gourmet restaurant in Thoiry. They talked for five hours and smoked endless cigarettes (Briand) and endless cigars (Stresemann). The ex-enemies were smoking the pipe of peace.

In balance-of-power physics every action induces an equal, or sometimes unequal but always opposite, reaction. After the duet at Thoiry, Sir Austen Chamberlain went from Geneva to Italy to see Mussolini at sea. They discussed the weather, the Balkans, and the future of Ethiopia.

Mussolini had been the editor in chief of *Avanti,* the official daily newspaper of the Italian Socialist Party. When the first world war commenced he adopted the Lenin line: "We mean to remain scrupulously faithful to our Socialist and Internationalistic doctrine," he wrote on August 16, 1914; "It is our right and duty to urge the revolt of the working classes against today's events," he wrote on September 4. For Italy the only course was neutrality. But "In October, 1914, Mussolini began to advocate Italy's intervention in the war on the side of the Entente and against Germany" and he branded as "irresponsible traitors, deserters," all socialists who took a contrary stand. In November, 1914, he left *Avanti* and, "with subsidies from the French government, launched a new daily, *Il Popolo d'Italia* ('The People of Italy') to promote 'the war of Liberation' and the emancipation of oppressed peoples."[2]

Italy had been an ally of Germany before the war, but she remained neutral when the guns began to thunder. Soon, however, Italian and Entente diplomats established unpublicized contacts and on April 26, 1915, Rome signed the secret Treaty of London which made Italy a belligerent. In return, the Entente promised Italy the Italian-speaking Trentino; Gorizia and Trieste, two cities heavily Italian in population, and western Istria, largely inhabited by South Slavs; German-speaking South Tirol; the Slav-speaking Dalmatian coast and the islands off the coast; a protectorate over Albania; and a share of the colonial empires in

[2] Gaetano Salvemini, *Prelude to World War II,* pp. 29-30. A refugee from Mussolini's fascism, Salvemini taught for many years at Harvard University.

Africa and the Middle East which the German coalition would lose after their defeat. Later the Entente awarded Italy the Turkish city of Smyrna.

This Anglo-French generosity with other people's territory sowed the seeds of Italian fascism, for the victorious Entente failed to deliver in 1919 the booty it had promised in 1915. A disgruntled Italy, which paid for the war with 650,000 dead, became the easy prey of supernationalists, notably Mussolini, the former internationalist. He joined the fascists in 1919. In December, 1921, one of the country's largest banks closed its doors. Unemployment mounted. Socialist and fascist deputies hurled inkwells and chairs at one another in provincial legislatures. Eventually Mussolini "marched" on Rome all night in a sleeping car and was handed power peacefully on October 28, 1922, by the diminutive King and the pusillanimous Prime Minister Facta.

In their search for diplomatic recognition in 1924 the Soviet government offered a prize to the important country which recognized it first. Mussolini was first in announcing his readiness to recognize, but Prime Minister Ramsay MacDonald was the first to recognize formally. Being second riled the Duce, but he quickly negotiated a favorable commercial treaty with Moscow which granted extraterritoriality to the Soviet official trade mission. When several of his advisers raised their eyebrows he reprimanded them saying, "You were never socialists, you don't understand." Moscow felt grateful.

On June 10, 1924, Italy was shaken and Europe shocked by the news that some weeks earlier Giacomo Matteotti, a leading Italian socialist, had been mysteriously kidnapped and murdered by never-apprehended assassins. Many fingers pointed to Mussolini as the instigator of the atrocity. His power-throne rocked, for he was not yet entrenched. The entire Rome diplomatic corps boycotted him for months. But on July 11 Soviet Ambassador Konstantin K. Yurenyev, certainly not without consulting Moscow (Soviet ambassadors would even request the Kremlin for permission to hold a cocktail party), gave a dinner in the Duce's honor which was "marked," wrote the fascist *Giornale d'Italia* of July 12, 1924, "by a singular tone of cordiality." Mussolini had received his reward.

The Italian Communist Party writhed and wriggled. Its national daily organ, *L'Unità* of July 13 carried an unsigned article entitled "Frank Words to Comrade Yurenyev." It called the dinner an "inappropriate gesture" and declared, "we cannot allow the opposition press to attribute to the Russian workers' and farmers' government diplomatic methods for which Comrade Yurenyev personally is alone responsible." It apologized. "Soviet diplomacy," *L'Unità* wrote, "is very young. . . . It is natural that some of its men are not equal to the tasks entrusted to them

. . . they are not able to protect the working class's dignity . . . Yurenyev's act resulted in injury to the Soviet Union's prestige among Italian workers. Therefore Yurenyev made a mistake. It was necessary to say all this so that the tale of a nonexistent and impossible sympathy on the part of the Russian workers for Mr. Mussolini did not spread throughout the world."

The Italian Communist Party was still living in the innocence of infancy. In the years to come foreign communists and noncommunists would learn that the Russian workers were not considered in the formulation of Soviet diplomacy and that in its dealings with Mussolini or Hitler or any other government the Kremlin acted in Russia's national interest, leaving it to the communist press abroad to find brittle excuses.

Outside Italy the Matteotti murder was soon blurred by the onrush of events. Statesmen, moreover, must ignore statesmen's crimes. Mussolini was a welcome guest in Locarno, and in the fall of 1926 Sir Austen, cruising on the Mediterranean, came to Leghorn where Mussolini met him. "On his way home he [Chamberlain] saw M. Briand in Paris so as to kill the rumors that his meeting with Signor Mussolini had some sinister significance."[3]

Mussolini had launched an anti-French campaign "with the idea of frightening the French, and then, when they were sufficiently cowed, presenting them with the Ethiopian agreement for signature."[4] Mussolini explained the content of this agreement in an interview with the Paris *Petit Parisien* of September 29, 1935. "After all," he said, "England only recently regarded Abyssinian independence as an absurdity. In 1925, Sir Ronald Graham [British Ambassador in Rome] and I signed an agreement that practically cut Abyssinia in pieces."[5] This, presumably, was in conformity with the Treaty of London of April 26, 1915, which brought Italy into war on the Entente side. But Italy never received Smyrna; at the Versailles peace conference Lloyd George gave it to the Greeks and later instigated Greece to go and get it. The result was a Greek disaster inflicted by Ataturk.

Britain added further injury to Turkey. Two months after "peace" had been waged at Locarno, the League of Nations, obedient to great power pressure, assigned Mosul and its oil fields, which Turkey claimed, to Iraq, then under British rule. In Paris two days later—December 17, 1925—Chicherin and Tewfik Rushdi Bey, the Turkish Foreign Minister, signed a treaty of friendship and neutrality designed to keep Turkey out of the League. British diplomacy counterattacked. Thereupon, a Turkish

[3] Sir Charles Petrie, *The Life and Letters of Sir Austen Chamberlain*, p. 306.
[4] Salvemini, p. 77.
[5] *Ibid.*, p. 76.

squadron accompanied Rushdi Bey to Odessa late in 1926, where he met Chicherin. "Odessa," Chicherin said to me on December 4, 1926, in Berlin, "was a demonstration." It reaffirmed the Paris treaty of December, 1925. The most important question discussed, according to Chicherin, was Italy. The Foreign Commissar gave Rushdi Bey a memorandum for assuring Ataturk that Moscow would do nothing to damage Turkish interests in the Balkans. Mussolini's eyes, eyes which Mahatma Gandhi, when he visited the Duce in Rome in December, 1931, described as "the eyes of a cat, they moved in every direction as though in constant rotation," were focused on the Balkans.

Before the first world war the Balkans were a cockpit in which all the great European powers fought for supremacy. Soviet Russia was eliminated from the balance-of-power competition because the revolution sapped her strength; Austria-Hungary, another key contender, was destroyed by self-determination; Germany lacked offensive ability; Turkey, shorn of all her colonies, lived on the Anatolian plateau and on the easternmost lip of Europe. These historic changes left the Balkans and part of Central Europe open to France and England. They whetted Mussolini's appetite. Moscow had no power to return to the cockpit but sought to buttress the position in the region of her ally, Turkey.

The postwar Balkan-Central European alignment favored France; the Little Entente—Czechoslovakia, Yugoslavia, and Rumania—formed in 1920 leaned heavily on France. Poland, the neighbor of Rumania and of the Soviet Union, also cleaved to France. Mussolini hoped to correct this imbalance. He flirted with Austrian fascists and monarchists. He tried to win Bulgaria and tear Rumania from the Little Entente by recognizing Bessarabia, which Moscow claimed, as a part of Rumania. He registered his biggest success in Hungary; Rome and Budapest signed a treaty of friendship on April 5, 1927. Albania was, in effect, an Italian protectorate. Italy and Albania signed the Tirana pact on November 27, 1926, providing for aid to Albania, and a year later the two neighbors negotiated a military alliance. Yugoslavia, next door to Albania, felt alarmed and crept closer to France.

Foreign Commissar Chicherin, the passionate Easterner and Anglophobe, watched over Turkey's interest. Iran and Turkey had been feuding over border territory. Chicherin wrote a memorandum to his colleagues in the Commissariat explaining that Moscow should act as "conciliator" between the two. "Unlike England," he declared, "which egged on every eastern state against every other eastern state, we shall act as a power that makes peace between them." Iran and Turkey accordingly concluded a treaty of friendship in April, 1926, which "eliminated various issues in dispute between them and strengthened the front of the struggle against imperialism."[6] "The struggle against imperialism" was a euphemism for Russia's agelong and continuing competition with Britain to achieve security or supremacy—the two terms are often interchangeable—in Central Asia, one more manifestation of balance-of-power politics which no government, Conservative, Labour, Liberal, Fascist, or Communist, could escape. Chicherin buttressed Turkey against Britain.

Due to the absence of principles—except the principles of physics—the United States, both by design and inadvertently, supported the Soviet Union against Japan. Communist Russia was weak and the ideological enemy. Japan was militarily strong. She concerned Washington more.

Whereas all European troops had left Russia in 1920, the Japanese army and navy did not evacuate the Amur and Maritime Provinces (of Siberia) until October, 1922; on October 31 Lenin, in the first public appearance after his first stroke, announced this development to a jubilant congress. Immediately the Far Eastern Republic, or Chita Republic, a fictional buffer state which served Moscow's purpose, received permission to enter the Soviet Union.

Japan's military withdrawal introduced a chain of dozens of fruitless Nipponese-Soviet conferences. Tokyo wanted to remain in northern Sakhalin, rich in oil and coal, and offered to buy it for 150 million yen. Adolf A. Yoffe asked a billion gold rubles, and when the poker-faced Japanese negotiators did not bat an eyelid he asked a billion and a half gold rubles. This meant Moscow was not selling.

United States policy helped Moscow. Japan left Siberia in 1922 when occupation no longer made any sense, but also because Secretary of State Charles Evans Hughes, anti-Soviet to the extreme and adamantly opposed to recognition of the Soviet government, obeyed the rules of balance-of-power politics and pressed Japan to leave. During the 1921-22 Washington Arms Limitation Conference, moreover, Britain agreed to break her 1902 alliance with Japan which "was unwelcome to some of the Dominions, in particular to Canada, as well as to the United States. It was somewhat embarrassing to Great Britain herself to be allied to a potentially aggressive power, and one which might come into conflict before long with the United States."[7] American diplomats no doubt reminded the British of the dilemma. Now Tokyo had no friends in the West, except perhaps France; "Briand believed in the League [of Na-

[6] A. A. Gromyko, N. N. Zemskov, V. A. Zorin, and others, *Istoria Diplomatii* (The History of Diplomacy), Vol. III, p. 473. Chicherin's memorandum is quoted from unpublished Soviet archives.

[7] Lord Strang, *Britain in World Affairs. A Survey of the Fluctuations in British Power and Influence from Henry VIII to Elizabeth II*, p. 306. Lord Strang had been Permanent Under-Secretary of the British Foreign Office.

tions]. He saw possibilities of making it a continental instrument against the United States and England."[8]

To make matters worse, and wound Japan's pride, the United States Senate, on April 17, 1924, adopted the anti-Japanese immigration bill. This event helped to mitigate Japanese hostility to the Soviet government. In September, 1923, a national calamity, a disastrous earthquake struck Tokyo and nearby areas. Japan for the moment forgot expansion abroad and concentrated on rehabilitation at home. The Mikado's diplomats were interested in fishing rights off the Soviet Far Eastern coast and oil and coal concessions in northern Sakhalin. These were granted, after long negotiations, on condition that Japan evacuate the upper half of Sakhalin by May 15, 1925. The treaty was signed in Peking by Soviet Ambassador Karakhan and Japanese Ambassador Yoshizaya in the latter's sick-chamber, January 20, 1925. So isolated was Japan in international politics that the treaty inspired rumors of a Japanese-Soviet alliance. "Utter rubbish," Feodor Rothstein, the Soviet spokesman, exclaimed in his denial.

In a balance-of-power world treaties do not denote friendship, neither do alliances promote permanence. The opportunities in the 1920's and 30's for bargaining, changing sides, and compromise were therefore numerous. Early in that period, Russia's freedom to maneuver was limited. Toward its end she could choose, and Stalin chose—fatefully.

XV THE FALL OF TROTSKY

British Chancellor of the Exchequer Winston Churchill: The Russian Bolsheviks are "miscreants" and Russia is "an ignorant slave state." The Bolsheviks believed that "the same sort of stuff with which they bamboozled their own mujhiks would suit Britain."

Lord Birkenhead, Secretary of State for India: The Soviet government is "a discredited junta."[1]

Even the Conservative, mass-circulation London *Daily Express* of June 21, found Churchill's language offensive; "it was such as would draw a protest from any other Government in the world." The *Express*

[8] Louis Fischer. *The Soviets in World Affairs*, Chap. XXI, based on Christian G. Rakovsky's report of his first conference with Briand.

[1] London *Times*, *Daily Telegraph*, and other newspapers of June 21, 1926.

did not yet realize that Churchill and Birkenhead were not concerned with Moscow's reactions, they wanted a rupture of diplomatic relations with Moscow. "I hope to see the day when either there will be civilized Government in Russia, or we shall have ended the present pretence of friendly relations with men who are seeking our overthrow," Churchill said in the same speech.

Three days after the speeches Sir William Joynson-Hicks, the Home Secretary, gave the House of Commons a Blue Book entitled *Communist Papers*.[2] These papers had been seized nine months earlier during the arrest of several British communist leaders and search of their headquarters. Now they were published in an effort to force a break with Russia which Baldwin and Chamberlain did not want.

A packed House of Commons laughed uproariously as David Lloyd George lampooned Sir William Joynson-Hicks's revelations. "Well now," the former Prime Minister said, trying to hide a smile, "I thought really that at last the Home Secretary had dug something out. He has been very active. He evidently came to the conclusions before he got his evidence. That happens sometimes in politics. I think this is a remarkable document, but it is a document that, if anything vindicates the Labour Party [in recognizing the Soviet government]. What is it? Here is the correspondence which is supposed by some of my honourable friends here to justify the breaking off of relations with this great country on the ground that that country is spending unlimited gold to overthrow our institutions. In the first place the complaint throughout is that the gold is very limited. Here are letters from the Communist Party getting unlimited gold to say that they are running into debt because they owe £14. . . . Another of these gentlemen who is receiving this stream of gold complains that he has not got a stenographer. He says he has to turn the office boy on to copying his letters. He says the arrears of his correspondence are so great that he cannot go out to address meetings. So he applies for a typist. He does not ask for poison gas, machine guns, rifles—only one poor typist. And this is the Russian gold that is pouring into the coffers of the Communist Party. . . . Here is another great phrase: 'We must adopt merciless measures.' What to do? To overthrow the Government, to overthrow the British Empire? No. 'We must adopt merciless measures to fight the Labour Party.' . . . Trade that runs into millions—£34 million last year, and it will be more when we take what we want in the way of timber and other essential commodities from Russia—trade that is growing year by year, is to be thrown away for this miserable abortion of a book."[3]

[2] British Blue Book, *Communist Papers,* Cmd. 2682.

[3] *Official Reports, Parliamentary Debates, House of Commons, June 25, 1926,* Vol. 197, No. 90.

Joynson-Hicks made Lloyd George's task easy by the inept, badly timed publication of the *Communist Papers*. What had provoked the Churchill-Birkenhead poisoned philippics was a true flow of so-called "Red gold" from the Soviet Union to the British coal miners who went on strike in May, 1926. In sympathy with the miners, the British Trade Union Council declared a General Strike. Coal was a major industry and a major item of British exports. The General Strike paralyzed the economy. Russia thrilled to these events. Soviet communists and the Soviet public do not understand strikes in the western world; they regard them as preludes to the breakdown of capitalism. The Soviet press usually reports the beginning of a strike abroad but rarely if ever its settlement on favorable terms for the workers. In 1926, with the procapitalist NEP in full flower and believing Bolsheviks in appropriate depression, a strike of hundreds of thousands of miners augmented by an unprecedented General Strike in Britain, the mother and citadel of capitalism, stirred sudden high hopes that the Russian revolution might still be saved from decay by world revolution. Genuine enthusiasm swept Russia, and while voluntary contributions were not always voluntary, less pressure was needed to collect large sums for the British strikers than usually accompanies "spontaneous" actions in communist nations. Between May 22 and June 17, 1926, Sir William Joynson-Hicks told Parliament on June 17, the All-Russian Central of Trade Unions forwarded four remittances to British strikers totaling 380,128 pounds sterling. This was a huge sum from a country like Russia which would soon be selling Rembrandts to meet its financial obligations abroad. They were of course made through the Soviet State Bank with government sanction.

Churchill, who helped suppress the General Strike, felt outraged by Muscovite encouragement of the strikers. In him and Birkenhead the hatred of the old Russia, "the bear that walks like a man" and threatened India, was now intensified. But cooler heads in the government realized it would be a grave psychological error, and therefore a political blunder, to antagonize the British working class in its hour of bitter wrath by punishing those who came to its aid. They counseled patience; a better conjuncture for a rupture with Russia was sure to come.

It came the next year.

Sir Austen Chamberlain, the Foreign Secretary, on February 23, 1927, warned the Soviet government in a note addressed to Soviet Chargé d'Affaires Rosengoltz (who had negotiated secretly with General Hans von Seeckt about German rearmament in the U.S.S.R.) that the abrogation of the 1921 Anglo-Soviet trade agreement and "even the severance of ordinary diplomatic relations" threatened if "the continuance of such acts as are here complained of" did not cease. In Appendices to the note

Sir Austen quoted statements, reported in Soviet newspapers, by Bukharin: "During the great English strike and during the great Chinese revolution our [Bolshevik] party—we can and dare assert this—has shown itself in the forefront"; and by Commissar of War Voroshilov. Chamberlain also resented "a mendacious cartoon" of himself in *Izvestia,* and alluded to the view expressed by the Commissar of Health on the significance of physical culture as a factor in the revolutionary labor movement.[4]

Litvinov replied in effect that Chamberlain wished to interfere with freedom of the press in the Soviet Union. He also drew Sir Austen's attention to "insults and defamations" leveled by British leaders and Conservative dailies at the Soviet regime.[5] His reply was too early to comment on Lord Birkenhead's February 26 description of the Soviet government as "a junta of swollen frogs."

Such verbal slugging matches between governments boded only ill. Many forces, overt and hidden, were working against normal relations between London and Moscow. Sir Henri Deterding, chief of the Royal-Dutch Shell Oil Company, had lost properties in the Caucasus petroleum fields as a result of the revolution. Between 1922 and 1926 he purchased and resold exported Soviet oil. From 1926 to 1929 his powerful organization campaigned against the use of Soviet oil as "stolen." General Max Hoffmann, commander of the Kaiser's army on the eastern front, had met Deterding, according to the general's wife, in The Hague in 1925. The next year Deterding invited Hoffmann to London where the military man exposed to the oil magnate plans for military intervention in the U.S.S.R. He hoped to recruit Ukrainian émigrés for an effort to tear the Ukraine from the Soviet Union.[6] It was a wild scheme which took oxygen from the anti-Soviet air of London. Other owners dispossessed by the Bolsheviks dreamed idly of revenge.

The major factor in the coming event was China. Rivalry in Central Asia, assistance to British strikers, abhorrence of communist expropriators, oil imperialism, the King's hostility to the men who had executed his cousin Nicholas II and the tsarist family, all these and more elements went into the bomb about to explode. China triggered it.

On April 6, 1927, the Peking Metropolitan Police, responsible to Marshal Chang Tso-lin, the Manchurian warlord, sent armed agents into the diplomatic quarter to raid the offices of the Soviet Dalbank, the Chinese Eastern Railway, and the Soviet military attaché. The latter

[4] British Blue Book, *Russia No. 3 (1927). A Selection of Papers dealing with the Relations between His Majesty's Government and the Soviet Government, 1921-7,* Cmd. 2895, p. 45 ff.

[5] *Ibid.,* p. 64 ff.

[6] Frau Hoffmann in the Berlin *Vossische Zeitung,* Feb. 2, 1929.

threw many of his documents into a fire in the fireplace, but some were retrieved and published in facsimile and English translation.[7]

The documents, at least some of which were authentic, proved what was generally known: that Moscow had sent military advisers and money to South China, given ammunition to General Feng Yu-hsiang, and fomented a national revolution in China with the help of Chinese communists. "Immediately, rumors of a raid on the Soviet Embassy in London began to circulate, and the writer knows that Soviet officials were warned by friendly British business men."[8]

The Soviet Embassy in London was not raided. Scotland Yard, on May 12, 1927, came instead to the offices of Arcos (All-Russian Co-operative Society, Limited), a British firm operated by Soviet citizens under British laws, and to the official Soviet Trade Delegation at 49 Moorgate, London, and proceeded to search the premises and employees. The police remained in complete charge of the building for four days. Pneumatic drills were brought to open safes and strongboxes. Hinchuk, Chairman of the Soviet Trade Delegation, enjoyed diplomatic immunity "from arrest and search" under Article V of the Anglo-Russian Trade Agreement of March 16, 1921, and was "allowed to send and receive sealed bags." Nevertheless, the police broke open his safe and read papers it contained. They also opened and read sealed diplomatic mail that lay on his desk. Scotland Yard, according to official announcements, was looking for an important secret document that had disappeared from the British War Office. Did the police think Moscow had mailed the document to Mr. Hinchuk in London? In the parliamentary debate on the search, Sir William Joynson-Hicks, who ordered it, said the document "had left Arcos some days at all events before the search took place." He gave no proof.

The debate of May 26, 1927, centered on the White Paper containing papers found in the raid.[9] "What is the first charge brought by the Prime Minister on this document?" asked Lloyd George. "It is espionage for the purpose of obtaining information about our Army and Navy. Are we not doing that? If the War Office and the Admiralty and the Air Force are not obtaining by every means every information about what is being done in other countries, they are neglecting the security of this country. . . . As for employing agents to stir up trouble, that is not a new experience of Governments to bring pressure on others." He knew.

[7] Peking Metropolitan Police, *Soviet Plot in China,* Documents 1 to 32. Also, Wilbur and How (Eds.), *Documents on Communism, Nationalism, and Soviet Advisers in China. 1918-1927. Papers Seized in the 1927 Peking Raid.*

[8] Louis Fischer, *The Soviets in World Affairs,* Chap. XXIV.

[9] British White Paper, *Russia No. 2 (1927), Documents Illustrating the Hostile Activities of the Soviet Government and the Third International against Great Britain,* Cmd. 2874.

Arthur Ponsonby, Deputy Foreign Secretary under Ramsay MacDonald, continued the political education of the British public: "We must really face the facts when we are getting on our high moral horse, that forgery, theft, lying, bribery, and corruption exist in every Foreign Office and every Chancellory of the world. I say that according to the recognized moral code our representatives abroad would be neglectful in their duty if they were not finding out secrets from the archives of other countries." And as Members of Parliament and ambassadors in the diplomatic gallery leaned forward, Ponsonby continued, "I have during my career seen a document which was taken from the archives of a foreign country." In fact the debate called attention to documents in the White Paper seized neither in the London raid of May 12 nor in the Peking raid of April 6.

The purpose of the raid and of the debate was the rupture of Anglo-Soviet diplomatic relations. On the day of the debate Sir Austen Chamberlain informed the Soviet Embassy that relations had been severed. Arcos, he added, could stay and do business. The Soviet Naphtha Syndicate and other Soviet commercial organizations likewise continued as before.

The rupture of diplomatic relations leads to no good. Just as recognition is inevitable so is the resumption of ruptured relations. Commenting on Sir Austen Chamberlain's speech in the House of Commons debate, Lloyd George said, "He did not point out a single advantage that would be gained to this country by a rupture." Perhaps this omission was due to Sir Austen's lukewarm support of the rupture. "I think," Lloyd George told the House, "the Foreign Secretary has had his hand forced in regard to the breach of relations. In my judgment, I do not think the Foreign Secretary came to the conclusion before the Home Secretary acted that the time had arrived to have a rupture with the Soviet Union." "The Government," said the *Manchester Guardian* of May 25, "have once more surrendered to the continuing pressure of their own Die-Hards." This may have been so; rifts in Cabinets are not uncommon even in dictatorships.

Two weeks after the severance of Anglo-Soviet diplomatic relations, on June 7, 1927, a young Russian anticommunist named Boris Kaverda, lurking in the central railway station of Warsaw, shot and killed Peter L. Voikov, the Soviet Ambassador to Poland. Kaverda immediately surrendered to the Polish police. Years later he was reported living in New York.

Voikov, some believed, participated in the execution of Nicholas II, the Tsarina, and their children and physician in the cellar of a house in Yekaterinburg (now Sverdlovsk) on July 17, 1918. Trotsky states in his *Diary in Exile, 1935* that on returning once from the Civil War front,

President Yaakov M. Sverdlov told him he and Lenin had approved the decision of the local authorities to exterminate all the Romanovs lest one of them become the rallying point for a restoration. It is conceivable that Kaverda wished to punish Voikov for his reputed part in the murders.

Moscow saw the situation differently. Moscow saw conspiracy. Deputy Foreign Commissar Maxim M. Litvinov, writing under his pen name, said the Soviet leadership did not know who was responsible for Voikov's assassination, but he recalled that Soviet envoy Vatslav V. Vorovsky had been killed by a White Russian in Geneva a few days after the Curzon ultimatum; "instinctively one feels there is some kind of inner connection, some kind of evil logic" in these events. The raid on the Soviet offices in Peking, the raid on the Soviet Consulate in Shanghai, the raid on Arcos and the London Soviet Trade Delegation, he declared, create the atmosphere which encourages assassins. And there is no doubt that assassinations do flourish in congenial political weather. But Litvinov went beyond speculation on the circumstances that armed Boris Kaverda's mind. He said Poland might make war again on the Soviet Union.

Marshal Pilsudski had returned to power in Warsaw in May, 1926. "Pilsudski—is war," Litvinov wrote. England will help Poland more than she did in 1920, though England herself would not fight. Neither would France or Italy. But France will help, and Italy would take advantage of a Soviet-Polish war to move into the Middle East. "The possibility of American support (the delivery of arms and money) is not at all excluded." Rumania, Estonia, Latvia, and Finland, on the other hand, might fight. That is "quite probable but not at all inevitable." War would be more dangerous to Russia's little neighbors than to her. If the Soviets strengthen their army, navy, and air force, all will be well.[10]

Without reference to the Soviet political scene and the Stalin-Trotsky feud then nearing its climax, there is no understanding of what Litvinov was trying to do in this book whose introduction is dated September, 1927. For reasons he knew well, he blew hot and cold. On June 9, two days after Voikov's assassination, the Soviet government published a statement saying in part, this "murder is one of the links in the chain of events all of which signify an ever increasing threat of war."[11] Litvinov did not agree. But he could not say so directly. Therefore he indicated that while a war was "probable" it was not "inevitable" and even if it came only Russia's small neighbors, not the big powers, would partici-

[10] M. Tanin, *Dyesat Let Vneshnei Politiki SSSR, 1917-1927* (Ten Years of the Foreign Policy of the U.S.S.R.), pp. 200-204.

[11] U.S.S.R. Ministry of Foreign Affairs, *Dokumenty Vneshnei Politiki SSSR,* (Documents on the Foreign Policy of the U.S.S.R.), Vol. X: *January 1-December 31, 1927,* p. 639.

pate although, to cede a point to Stalin, he wrote that England, the United States, and France would send supplies. All this did not add up to "the world bourgeoisie" attacking the U.S.S.R. Moreover Moscow's "relations with Germany are one of the basic factors that determine our entire international situation," and while Germany "will swing between London and Moscow" she has taken no anti-Soviet obligations; Chamberlain was no more than partially successful in drawing Germany "into the anti-Soviet game of British imperialism. . . . If England, however, succeeds in pushing Poland into a war with the Soviet Union" Germany "in all probability" will be under pressure from the imperialist powers. But Germany would act against Russia if the West gave her what she wanted: the Polish Corridor and the right to arm. That would so frighten Poland that she would refrain from attacking Russia. Should the Versailles victors reduce German reparations, Berlin would incline still further toward the West. "We repeat, however, that the direct participation of Germany in military action against the U.S.S.R. must be considered quite unlikely."

In effect this meant that Poland, knowing Germany must take advantage of a Russo-Polish war to regain her lost territory in the East, would not invade Russia. While seeming, therefore, to give importance to the official Kremlin view of impending war, Litvinov refuted it. In 1929, when I discussed the 1927 war scare with him, Litvinov said, "That was mere idle gossip by some people here and the press. It is wrong to suppose, as many of us do, that Russia is the center of all international affairs. England broke with us because she hoped others would follow her example and that as a result the Soviet government would become more amenable to British pressure."

"Some people" included Stalin. And he controlled the press.

Chicherin agreed with Litvinov. In 1929 I spent eight days with Chicherin in Wiesbaden where he was taking a cure. "I returned home in June, 1927, from western Europe," he recalled. "Everybody in Moscow was talking war. I tried to dissuade them. 'Nobody is planning to attack us,' I insisted. Then a colleague enlightened me. He said, 'Shh. We know that. But we need this against Trotsky.' "

Though Trotsky was nearing the end of his career in the Soviet Union he possessed enormous strength. He had opposed Lenin for many years in the emigration and did not join the Bolshevik Party until 1917, but he made the revolution with Lenin and was considered by many party members and the youth as the heir of Lenin and the guardian of the revolution against mounting mass apathy, cynical communist careerism, and spreading bureaucracy. After more than three years of world war, three and a half years of civil war, and long undernourishment capped by the 1920-21 famine, the nation was tired, the party uninspired. The

NEP created hope of better material conditions and despair over the possibility of keeping alive the spirit of the revolution. By 1927 the hope had been fulfilled and the despair justified.

Trotsky warned of the imminent death of the Soviet revolution. His tocsin to a renewed faith found an echo among intellectuals, in the Red Army which he had organized and led, in the League of Communist Youth (Komsomol), and, to the extent that they were interested in politics or anything but daily bread and heat, among workingmen. The proletariat in whose name the communist party governed was haggard from heavy labor and family worries and had abdicated in its disillusionment to the few who were fighting for power. After several good harvests due to favorable weather and the freedom to enrich themselves, the peasants began to feel new pressures, for the Trotskyist opposition charged the Stalin administration with fostering dangerous village capitalism by permitting the hiring of labor and the renting of land (practices formerly forbidden by law), and Stalin reacted by squeezing more taxes out of the muzhik and reverting to grain confiscations. As a result the "union" between workers and peasants, which Lenin considered the foundation stone of Soviet stability, was dissolving. "In regard to the peasant problem there has emerged the tremendous defect that the peasantry, having received land, no longer feels the sharp need of its ally the proletariat."[12] The peasants preferred their union with the new class of Nepmen merchants who, never numerous but ingenious at making a quick ruble and vanishing only to reappear for another transaction, were now being driven into bankruptcy by the tax collector and into prisons where they often met friends, the more prosperous and usually more diligent peasants or kulaks with surpluses to sell through the Nepmen. Russia had been making moderate economic progress thanks in part to Soviet heavy industry but in larger part to the kulaks, the less successful middle peasants, and the agile Nepmen all of whom Stalin, goaded by Trotskyist criticism, was persecuting, killing the hands that grew the golden grain and brought it to market.

In foreign affairs too the Soviet situation looked bleak. The British rupture of diplomatic relations with Moscow in May, 1927, threatened to reduce commerce and prestige; in June it became clear that Chiang Kai-shek, Stalin's favorite, had converted the Chinese revolution into an anticommunist counterrevolution. A June 25, 1927, manifesto signed by G. Zinoviev, L. Trotsky, K. Radek, and G. Yevdokimov and directed to the Soviet Communist Party and to the Comintern rang with wrath and revolutionary determination. Assuming that Moscow could still lead in China, it called for "the immediate exit of the communist party from the

[12] Tanin, p. 230.

Kuomintang," denounced Chiang Kai-shek, Feng Yu-hsiang, and other noncommunist allies of the Kremlin, rejected "the charlatan promise of agrarian 'reform' [in China]" and demanded an "agrarian revolution." "Down with army-officer landlords!" the manifesto shouted. "Immediate execution of officer-traitors." "Down with the imperialists! . . . Only a union of workers and peasants, under proletarian leadership, can liberate and unite China. Only Soviets can organize that union, strengthen it, and bring it to power! . . . Long live the union of independent, free, united worker-peasant China with the U.S.S.R.!"[13]

Seen by a communist, the Stalin administration was a picture of compromise and muddle at home and defeat abroad. The opposition's heavy oratorical artillery took every advantage of Stalin's failures. But if Stalin had few arguments he also had few scruples. In the end intellect and eloquence succumbed to bureaucratic devices and deceit. As an introductory device, Stalin scattered his enemies. Leo Kamenev was "exiled" to the Rome Embassy. Yuri Pyatakov, a foremost industrial organizer praised by Lenin in his last testament, was sent to the Paris Embassy together with Yevgeni A. Preobrazhensky, a noted economist and coauthor with Nikolai Bukharin of *The ABC of Communism*. Ivan T. Smilga, a leading planner and industrial manager, one of the heroes of the November 7, 1917, revolution, received a mission to remote Khabarovsk on the Amur River. Vladimir A. Antonov-Ovseyenko, who led the assault on the Winter Palace on the night of November 7, 1917, and thus completed the seizure of power in Petrograd, was dispatched to Prague. Georgy I. Safarov, who tamed Turkestan for Bolshevism, went to Istanbul. All of these generals of the small oppositionist army irked Stalin by their criticism, and he used the party tradition of obedience to get rid of them.

This left Trotsky, the lone lion. In October, 1926, addressing the supreme Politburo, Trotsky pointed his finger at Stalin and exclaimed, " 'The First Secretary poses his candidature to the post of gravedigger of the revolution.' Stalin turned pale, rose, first contained himself with difficulty, and then rushed out of the hall, slamming the door. The meeting, at which many members of the Central Committee happened to be present, broke up in a hubbub. The next morning the Central Committee deprived Trotsky of his seat in the Politburo."[14]

Therewith commenced the precipitous descent to the end. Personal venom could no longer be wrapped in political circumlocutions. "I think," Stalin told a Comintern meeting on May 24, 1927, "Trotsky does not deserve so much attention. Especially since he reminds one of an

[13] Trotsky Archive in Harvard University, T. 962. Copy supplied. The document has a handwritten comment by Trotsky reading, "I think Zinoviev wrote this. L.T."

[14] Isaac Deutscher, *The Prophet Unarmed. Trotsky:1921-1929*, Vol. II, p. 296.

actor rather than a hero. . . ."[15] (This suggests Stalin knew Trotsky was a hero.) And when the British government broke off diplomatic relations with Moscow, Stalin said, "Something like a united front from Chamberlain to Trotsky is being created."[16]

This was an ominous formula and Stalin soon filled it with sinister meaning. An ear-splitting, never-ceasing crescendo campaign was unleashed to convince Soviet citizens that their country was about to be attacked. Though Chicherin and Litvinov discounted the danger of war they could say little in private, for their words would reach Stalin, and nothing in public except in veiled form, as Litvinov did in his book. The war scare hurt the economy: peasants hoarded grain and bought salt, traditional muzhik reactions to impending calamity. But to cripple Trotsky Stalin was ready to pay the cost. A very long article by Stalin in *Pravda* of July 28, 1927,[17] supplied fuel for the nationwide bonfires signaling the coming of war. "It cannot be doubted," he began, "that the basic question of the present is the question of the threat of a new imperialist war. This is not a matter of some kind of indefinite, vague 'danger' of a new war. This is a matter of a real and actual *threat* of a new war in general—of a war against the U.S.S.R. in particular." Obviously, he continued, the British "conservative party, preparing to make war on the U.S.S.R., has, for some years, conducted preliminary work for the establishment of 'a holy alliance' of large and small countries." After attacking British Labour Party leaders, Stalin turned to the Trotsky-Zinoviev opposition. "What can one say . . . about our ill-fated opposition in connection with its new attacks on the [communist] party in the face of the threat of a new war? What is one to say about the fact that it, this same opposition, has found it appropriate on the occasion of the threat of war to intensify its attacks on the party? . . . is it possible that the opposition is against the victory of the Soviet Union in the coming battles with imperialism, against improving the defensive capacity of the Soviet Union, against the reinforcement of our rear?"

Stalin's next move followed inexorably. What would Trotsky do in the event of Russia's involvement in a war? The question was put to Trotsky. Did he, in his fury, not see the trap? The trap was clearly marked. It faced Trotsky with two alternatives: Would he continue to oppose the party leadership in case of war or would he desist and collaborate? Trotsky answered frankly in a letter on July 11, 1927, to Sergo Orjonedikze, presiding officer of the Central Control Commission, the inspectorate and judiciary of the communist party. In it Trotsky expounded his views in harsh terms: "Thus, for instance, if someone says

[15] J. V. Stalin, *Sochinenia*. Vol. 9. p. 283.
[16] *Ibid.*, p. 311.
[17] *Ibid.*, pp. 322-361.

the political line of ignorant and unscrupulous cheats should be swept away like dirty trash in the interests of the victory of the workers' government then this does not at all make him 'a defeatist.' On the contrary, in the present concrete circumstances he is the authentic expression of the will to revolutionary defense: ideological trash does not bring victory." Trotsky offered one illustration of what he would try to do if war came: at the beginning of the first world war the French government "lacked rudder and sail." Clemenceau and his followers were in the opposition. The German army was "eighty kilometers from Paris." Clemenceau said he would overthrow the government of Viviani and Painlevé "for that very reason." He did, and led France to victory.[18] Trotsky would act like Clemenceau.

Trotsky knew what he was doing. He had nothing to lose. "None of us is scared by firing squads. We are all old revolutionists," he cried defiantly at a July 24, 1927, session of the Central Commission called to expel him from the Central Committee of the party. He was given eighty minutes to defend himself and asked for more. "The war danger," he declared, "is now being exploited by you in order to hound the opposition and to prepare for its physical annihilation. . . . We will continue to criticize the Stalinist regime as a worthless regime. . . . If you were seriously mindful of the war danger, as you claim"—he obviously doubted it—"how could there possibly have been the wild internal repressions which are now becoming more and more unbridled? How can you at the present time discard first-class military officers who are being removed from military activity because, though they are ready and able to fight for the Socialist fatherland, they consider the present policy of the Central Committee false and ruinous."[19] Trotsky named some of them.

The Central Control Commission was controlled by Stalin, yet it could not decide to expel Trotsky; he was still the revolution maker. Five days later Stalin convened a joint plenary meeting of the Central Control Commission and the Central Committee. It lasted from July 29 to August 9. Other business was transacted, but its urgent business was Trotsky. Stalin and Trotsky spoke the same day—August 1.

Stalin's speech lasted a little less than two hours.[20] He attacked not only Trotsky but also Zinoviev and Kamenev who, after Lenin's death, constituted the ruling triumvirate with Stalin. He dug into numerous controversial episodes in the history of the Soviet Communist Party. He insisted that the ideological authority of the U.S.S.R. was greater than

[18] *Ibid.*, Vol. 10, p. 52.
[19] Trotsky, *The Stalin School of Falsification*, pp. 125-159.
[20] Stalin, Vol. 10, pp. 3-59.

ever in China and in western Europe. Then he presented a proposition which, for a man who would make Soviet foreign policy for the next quarter of a century, was astonishing. "Zinoviev thinks," Stalin said, "that once there is [capitalist] stabilization it means the business of revolution is lost. He does not understand that the crisis of capitalism and the preparation for its death grow out of its stabilization." And in an attempt to prove this strange thesis he continued, "Is it not a fact that of late capitalism has perfected and rationalized its technology, thus creating a tremendous mass of goods which cannot be sold? Is it not a fact that capitalist governments are becoming more and more fascist, taking the offensive against the working class and temporarily strengthening their positions?" All this, Stalin stated, led to "the birth of conditions making for a new war, a new division of the world."

To indicate that he had learned his simplistic Marxism, Stalin added, "Capitalism could solve this crisis if it could increase workers' wages several fold, if it could seriously improve the living conditions of the peasantry, if it could in this manner appreciably raise the purchasing power of the millions of toilers and broaden the capacity of the domestic market. But then capitalism would not be capitalism." (Until his death in 1953 Stalin continued his search for the final, fatal crisis of capitalism. Western visitors were asked for clues.)

"Why," Stalin inquired of his high-ranking communist audience, "do certain imperialist circles look askance at the U.S.S.R. and organize a united front against it? Because the U.S.S.R. represents a very rich market for goods and the export of capital. Why do the same imperialist circles intervene in China? Because China represents a very rich market for goods and the export of capital. And so forth and so on.

"That is the basis and the source of the inevitability of a new war, it's all the same—whether it breaks out among various imperialist coalitions or against the U.S.S.R."

Stalin used the occasion to formulate definitions which later became standards for foreign communists. "*A revolutionist,*" he affirmed, "is one who unreservedly, unconditionally, frankly and honestly . . . will defend the U.S.S.R., for the U.S.S.R. is the first proletarian revolutionary state in the world that builds socialism. *An internationalist* is one who is unreservedly, unwaveringly, unconditionally ready to defend the U.S.S.R., for the U.S.S.R. is the base of the world revolutionary movement and it is impossible to defend, to advance that revolutionary movement apart from and against the U.S.S.R."

But what does the opposition say? Stalin asked rhetorically. Trotsky, "this operatic Clemenceau, will try, we learn, first to overthrow the present majority [in the party] just because the enemy stands eighty kilometers from the Kremlin and then undertake the defense. . . . And what is this 'dirty trash'? This, we learn, is the majority in the party, the majority of the Central Committee, the government majority." Stalin advised Trotsky not to talk so much about sweeping out the trash, the idea might occur to someone else.

Nevertheless, even this joint meeting, overwhelmingly Stalinist yet mindful of Trotsky's role in the revolution and civil war, did not expel him. He denounced as "brazen impudence" the question whether the opposition is opposed to the victory of the U.S.S.R. "in the coming battles with imperialism." The opposition does think that "the leadership of Stalin makes victory more difficult."

"What about the party?" Molotov heckled.

"You have strangled the party," Trotsky shot back.

"For the Socialist Fatherland? Yes!" Trotsky concluded, "For the Stalinist course? No!"[21]

In retrospect it is clear that Trotsky made two basic errors in the 1927 debate. He put his trust in foreign revolutions. "We . . . are surrounded by capitalist countries more advanced than we are with respect to technology and industry, and with a more powerful and cultured proletariat. We may expect revolutions in these countries in the comparatively near future. In consequence the international position of our revolution, despite the fact that imperialism is mortally hostile to us, is in a wide historical sense far more favorable to us."[22]

Stalin was skeptical.

Trotsky's second error was his belief that Stalin would permit him and his opposition colleagues to continue their criticism now, much less during a war.

Stalin was a cynic with no interest in party democracy.

Once again, on October 23, Trotsky addressed the Central Committee. He was heckled from the platform. A member threw a book at him. Another member threw a glass at him. The Central Committee expelled him after his speech. On November 14 he was deprived of party membership. In January, 1928, the secret police came to his apartment, carried him bodily downstairs, and shipped him off to Alma-Ata in Central Asia. Stalin had strengthened his stranglehold on the party.

Trotsky finished his brilliant book *Literature and Revolution* in July, 1924. There he wrote: "To accept the Workers' Revolution in the name of a high ideal means not only to reject it, but to slander it. All the social illusions which mankind has raved about in religion, poetry, morals or philosophy served only the purpose of deceiving and blinding the op-

[21] Trotsky, pp. 162-167.
[22] Ibid., p. 158.

pressed. . . . The Revolution is strong to the extent to which it is realistic, rational, strategic, and mathematical."[23]

Trotsky's vision of the workers' revolution had been fulfilled. It was shorn of high ideals, it was realistic and mathematical. His own handiwork now devoured him.

XVI TRIAL AND ERROR

In the late summer of 1923 Trotsky, Stalin, Zinoviev, and Bukharin had joined with several German communist leaders to form a Comintern commission which "made a series of concrete decisions regarding direct aid to German comrades for the purpose of seizing power."[1] At that time the Soviet government was helping the German Reichswehr rearm. In October, 1923, the Reichswehr suppressed the German Communist Party's attempt to seize power. As Commissar of War Trotsky, nevertheless, continued to promote the Reichswehr's rearmament in Russia. Stalin pursued the same policy when Trotsky's power declined. Support of the Reichswehr was one of the few constants in Kremlin foreign policy toward the West, for its roots ran deep into the soil of mutual necessity. It too, however, could not escape the effects of stormy weather or a dry season.

One circumstance that plagued Soviet-German relations and Soviet foreign relations generally was the chasm between the purposes of the Soviet Foreign Commissariat and the powers whom Litvinov, sitting in the old commissariat office on Kuznetsky Must, would indicate by inclining his head toward the left, toward the huge building of the secret police across the street, and refer to it as "our neighbors." These "neighbors" gave Chicherin and Litvinov frequent headaches.

When the Germans arrested General Peter A. Skoblevsky (alias Goryev), who had been sent to Germany to play a major part in the October, 1923, revolution, the GPU began to plan his rescue. In October, 1924, three young Wandervoegel or hitchhikers—Karl Kindermann, Theodore Wolscht, both German, and Max von Ditmar, an Estonian of German origin—arrived in Moscow and were arrested.

[23] Trotsky, *Literature and Revolution,* p. 88.
[1] J. V. Stalin, *Sochinenia,* Vol. 10, p. 63.

After Skoblevsky had been tried in February, 1925, in Leipzig and sentenced to death, Moscow informed the German government that the three hitchhikers would be tried for plotting to assassinate Trotsky and Stalin. At the trial in Moscow, in June, 1925, Ditmar turned state's witness and incriminated the others. It was widely assumed that he had lured them into Russia. All three were sentenced to be shot. A Foreign Commissariat official told me at the time that the trio had been arrested and condemned so they could be exchanged for Skoblevsky. The exchange took place. German public opinion, mirrored in the press and at meetings, exploded in wrath. But the tempest died and military collaboration lived on.

In 1922 and 1923 arrangements had been concluded not only for a Junkers airplane plant at Fili, near Moscow, and a poison gas factory at Trotsk in Samara province but also for German technical aid in Soviet munitions making in Tula, Petrograd, and Zlatousk; Germany would receive a share of the output. In 1924 Moscow and Berlin agreed to equip a school for pilots at Lipetsk in the central Russian province of Tambov. A Captain Vogt and a Major Fischer represented the Reichswehr in these transactions. From 1924 to 1928 Colonel von der Lieth-Thomsen, German Chief of Staff of the Air Force in the first world war, served in the Moscow German Embassy as military coordinator with the Kremlin. German Reichswehr officers took frequent "vacation" trips to the Soviet Union, and numerous Red army officers, later generals and marshals, attended training academies in Germany.

The German Social Democratic Party, socialist but vehemently anti-communist, opposed this Reichswehr-Russian entente. In September, 1926, three Soviet freighters, carrying 300,000 artillery shells for the Reichswehr, docked at the German ports of Stettin and Pillau. Some longshoremen accidentally on political purpose, it seems, dropped several boxes and the contents and the news spilled out. The *Manchester Guardian* of December 3, 1926, published detailed information from its Berlin correspondent, who had excellent connections with Social Democrats, regarding Soviet-German military cooperation. Two days later these sensational revelations were duly reprinted in the Berlin SPD *Vorwaerts* and made the subject of an unruly debate in the Reichstag on December 16, in which the socialist deputy Philipp Scheidemann attacked the government of Chancellor Wilhelm Marx of the Catholic Center Party and moved a vote of nonconfidence. Marx fell.

Politicians came and went, but the partnership of armies enjoyed a hallowed life. Nothing could impair it, for it grew from Germany's wish to rearm in violation of the Versailles treaty and her desire to have a balance, sometimes a synonym for diplomatic blackmail, against the West. The Soviets needed German help because the country was industrially ruined, technologically backward, and eager to build a modern army. General Hans von Seeckt, chief of the Reichswehr, remained the master mind of the relationship. He wrote a memorandum in 1915 urging Germany's expansion at Russia's expense: "Once there are 200 millions of healthy and mostly German people on 200 thousand square miles of soil, say in the year 2000, we shall be at least somewhat secure against this Russia that might one day give birth to another Peter the Great. . . . This war will probably cost us a million men, among them the best. . . . Against this what does it mean to expel 20 million men, among them a lot of riffraff of Jews, Poles, Masurians, Lithuanians, Letts, Estonians, etc.?"[2] Defeat in the world war and the creation of an independent Poland altered his attitude. "Germany cannot be against Russia," he declared on January 15, 1925; the Kremlin knew how to appreciate this. Alexei Rykov, Lenin's successor as Chairman of the Council of People's Commissars, told Ambassador Brockdorff-Rantzau on February 24, "We see here in the general one of the safest supports of the truly cordial understanding between Germany and Russia."[3]

So attached was Seeckt to the partnership with Moscow he had fathered, so certain was he of receiving a warm welcome from the Kremlin that early in 1927, only a few months after the *Manchester Guardian* disclosures, the general, now retired—President Hindenburg replaced him as the military king of the Republic—proposed to travel to the Soviet Union. Rantzau, who fervently disliked him, wrote the Foreign Ministry in Berlin on March 10, 1927, saying the visit was highly undesirable, the Soviet government would "ostentatiously acclaim him" and thus confirm all "rumors regarding a military treaty between us and Russia"; the German government should dissuade Seeckt in its name "and without reference to me." (The same "strictly secret letter" announced that GPU chief Menzhinsky planned to come to Germany for a cure under an assumed name and the ambassador would of course give him a German visa "as I had at the time in the case of Trotsky.")

Seeckt abandoned the idea of touring the Soviet Union. But the military partnership prospered. The flying school at Lipetsk near Voronezh was expanded, and German chemists arrived in Orenburg in the Ural region to conduct experiments in chemical warfare.[4]

On August 10, 1927, Rantzau sent a telegram, marked "Secret," through State Secretary Carl von Schubert in Berlin for Colonel (formerly Major) Fischer saying the Soviet War Office had granted permission for German officers to join in Red Army maneuvers in Dretun and Novosibirsk during the last nine days of August, artillery

[2] Gustav Hilger and Alfred G. Meyer, *The Incompatible Allies*, Note, pp. 191-192.
[3] Francis L. Carsten, *Reichswehr und Politik 1918-1923*, p. 257.
[4] Hilger and Meyer, p. 207.

practice at Kiev in the first fifteen days of September, and maneuvers outside Odessa between September 20 and 28. Rantzau added: "No confrontation with foreign military attachés who participate in other maneuvers."

A second Rantzau telegram to Schubert for "Frank," that is, Fischer, dated September 24, 1927, reported that student pilot Haring had been seriously hurt in a flying accident and student pilot Gasshar slightly hurt.[5]

The Soviets constantly pressed for more military cooperation. Dr. Gustav Stresemann, Foreign Minister in the new Cabinet of Chancellor Hans Luther, Reichswehr Minister Dr. Otto Gessler, General Wilhelm Heye, commander of the Reichswehr in succession to Seeckt, Colonel Werner von Blomberg, and Dr. Gerhard Koepke, representing Schubert, met in an off-the-record conference on Russian affairs on May 18, 1927. General Heye reported that Moscow was insisting on explicit German Foreign Ministry agreement to the projected establishment of a tank school at Kama near Kazan; moreover, Litvinov urged that the school be given a commercial disguise. Stresemann agreed.

Deputy Commissar of War Joseph S. Unschlicht had informed Thomsen of the German Embassy in Moscow that the Soviet government wished to coordinate its disarmament proposals with Germany. The secret conference did not object.

The Reichswehr had intended to conduct large exercises at Orenburg in anti-gas defense. The Soviets, Reichswehr Minister Gessler said, demanded total participation in the exercises and access to the chemicals used. "In the discussion the Reichswehr Minister himself voiced misgivings about this project. He expressed his fears," the minutes of the conference read, "that the Russians who, after all, might someday become our enemies, would receive too valuable material without any significant quid pro quo." Gessler therefore proposed that the exercises be held in Germany and that the Soviets be told the reason for the change was to save money.[6]

The conference proposed but circumstances disposed. It transpired, as the Reichswehr Ministry wrote the Foreign Office on December 29, 1927, that the gas attack exercises could not be conducted in Germany. In addition, the Russians wanted them on Soviet soil. The Reichswehr Ministry asked the Foreign Office for permission to accede to Soviet wishes. Stresemann could not deny both the Reichswehr and the Kremlin.

[5] Politisches Archiv, Auswaertiges Amt. Buero Staatssekretaer. Akten betreffend 'Fischertelegramme,' von April 1927 bis Dezember 1928. Bd. app 3. s. Bd. 3 Osec. Photocopied in Bonn summer of 1966. Rantzau's letter about Seeckt's trip to the U.S.S.R. is in the same file.

[6] Same file. The minutes are signed "Koepke" and numbered E 163884.

The Russo-German military program brought mutual benefits. During the crisis precipitated in 1927 by the rupture of Anglo-Soviet diplomatic ties, Stresemann rejected a proposed reorientation of German foreign policy to exclude friendship with Russia. The Kremlin, as well as the Wilhelmstrasse, was in the market, or on the street, ready to be bought by France or England, but the price was never right. Rantzau described Soviet-German relations as "a community of fate." Necessity had married them. Germany without Russia might have been subjected to much heavier western pressures. Russia without Germany would be isolated.

The communist leaders were aware of these facts. In all countries, however, domestic politics may distort the implementation of foreign policy, and the natural laws of the Soviet dictatorship gave a high priority, often autonomy, to the internal needs of the regime irrespective of the effects on its foreign position.

A dictatorship must have enemies. When it cannot find them it creates them. Incessant attacks on the domestic rivals of the dictator and on real or fancied foreign adversaries enable him to summon the citizenry to accept added privations and rally around the government, their shield against those who threaten. By striking down the internal dissident and denouncing the hostile outsider the ruling oligarchs proclaim themselves the vigilant guardians of the people's interests and hope thereby to establish an identity between the dictatorship and the nation. All government failures and blunders can then be blamed on near-at-hand scapegoats. The infallible dictator remains without sin and with fewer critics.

This technique of administration goes far to explain why the Kremlin staged the important Moscow trials of the 1920's and 1930's when the totalitarian state was not yet stabilized. The first of these, the Shakhti trial, enveloped Soviet-German relations in a black cloud.

Fifty Soviet and five German engineers employed in the Donets Coal Basin in the Ukraine and Rostov region were arrested on March 7, 1928, and charged with espionage for the former owners and of starting fires and floods in the mines.

Economics is politics in a communist country, and all executive, legislative, and judiciary powers are jointly vested in the party hierarchy. The Shakhti trial therefore released a tremendous nationwide propaganda crusade. Long before the proceedings began millions of men and women throughout the land marched from their factories and offices to party and government headquarters demanding the death penalty for the accused. Chairman Rykov declared them guilty before the verdict was rendered, and during the trial Stalin himself expressed his opinion about the alleged crimes.

Until November 7, 1917, Lenin trained the Bolshevik party as a conspiratorial organization. Conspiracy suited Stalin's mentality and purpose. The note of a capitalist conspiracy to crush the Soviet state has probably been the loudest and longest in the communist propaganda symphony. The Shakhti trial, like several that followed it, was accordingly presented to the masses as an instrument for the condign punishment of Soviet plotters whose actions were the more sinister because they conspired with agents of capitalism. The involvement of foreigners —in the Shakhti case, Germans—served to sow suspicion of all aliens and to emphasize the gulf that yawned between Fortress Communist Russia and the scheming, rapacious capitalist world.

Chicherin and Litvinov were horrified when their "neighbors" arrested the five German engineers. They anticipated the effect in Germany. And indeed the storm in Germany threatened to disrupt Soviet-German relations right after the rupture of Anglo-Soviet relations. For not only were the five German engineers indicted as individuals, their firms were implicated in the espionage and sabotage. One of these, the A.E.G., or Allgemeine Elektritsitaets Gesellschaft (General Electric Company), had contracted for much work in the Soviet Union, and its Chairman of the Board, Felix Deutsch, championed massive Soviet-German trade. Four of the five arrested German engineers were A.E.G. employees. Deutsch telegraphed Rantzau that the A.E.G. would cease operating in Russia unless its men were released immediately. The Foreign Commissariat pressed for their release. Two were released fourteen days after their arrest and returned to Germany.

One of the liberated men, Senior Engineer Goldstein, reported to the German Foreign Office that "In his considered opinion, the catastrophic decline of production, as well as the numerous accidents and disturbances in the Donets Basin area, were due to the Soviet system and not to sabotage . . . control of production was left to inept party members . . . the ever-present threat of arrest for the merest bagatelles seriously curtailed the efficiency of nonparty Russian specialists. The workers, disinterested in their jobs and poorly supervised, accomplished one third or one fourth of what was expected of German workers on similar jobs. . . . Equipment is utilized in the most haphazard way. As a consequence, it rusted or otherwise deteriorated in a short time."[7]

When all these factors caused breakdowns, fires, and floods, inept party members could not be blamed; that would undermine the prestige of the party. They made out a case against Soviet "wreckers" and foreign "counterrevolutionaries." The GPU did the rest.

Rantzau protested to Chicherin and emphasized that he would resign as ambassador unless Moscow made amends. Stresemann protested. The

[7] Kurt Rosenbaum, *Community of Fate. German-Soviet Diplomatic Relations 1922-1928*, p. 254.

three German engineers were being held incommunicado. Rantzau threatened to go to Rostov himself to find out "whether one would dare to refuse the German ambassador access to his countrymen." The GPU yielded and allowed visits by German officials.

The trial began on May 18, 1928, not in a courtroom but in the great Hall of the Trade Unions which seats some two thousand persons. Rantzau sat conspicuously in the diplomats' box. For days and weeks thereafter he repeated his warning that if the defendants were punished German-Soviet relations would be undermined. On June 2 President Mikhail I. Kalinin stated publicly, "We do not want to discredit German industry, because we value it very highly." He added that only three Germans stood in the dock, not their firms. The verdict was handed down by the Supreme Court of the U.S.S.R. on July 7. Of the fifty Soviet defendants, eleven were sentenced to death, others to long terms of imprisonment. Two of the Germans were acquitted and immediately released. The third German was sentenced to a year in prison and immediately released.

Rantzau had been suffering from throat cancer. Nervous tension caused by the Shakhti trial aggravated his condition. He left Moscow on July 18. His innate pessimism, once relieved by a sense of humor and haughty cynicism, now took possession and he saw the future of German-Soviet relations wreathed in black. He died in Berlin on September 8, 1928.

Just four days after the Shakhti trial ended the German government demonstrated its good will toward the Kremlin. French Foreign Minister Briand and United States Secretary of State Frank B. Kellogg had proposed an international treaty to outlaw war as an instrument of national policy. "But this amounts to nothing," Soviet President Kalinin commented. The pact's only purpose, he declared, was to fool the worker and peasant masses. "War," Chairman Rykov asserted, "is the violation of all treaties," and when war came the Briand-Kellogg pact would go the way of all scraps of paper.

Moscow's misgivings were heightened by Britain's attitude. Responding to Kellogg's invitation to join, Sir Austen Chamberlain wrote on May 19, 1928, "There are certain regions of the world the welfare and integrity of which constitute a special and vital interest for our peace and safety. Their protection against attack is to the British Empire a measure of self-defense." The Foreign Secretary did not name the "certain areas." They might have included most of the globe. Moscow read his reservation to mean Persia, Afghanistan, India, and China.

Furthermore, Chamberlain opposed Kellogg's wish to make the treaty universal. He argued that "universality would, in any case, be difficult of attainment, and might be inconvenient, for there are some states that have not been universally recognized"—obviously the Soviet Union—"and some which are scarcely in a position to ensure the maintenance of good order and security within their territories." China?

Chicherin abhorred the proposed pact for these and an additional reason: he contended that the French reservations tied the treaty to the League of Nations, to Locarno, and the French chain of anti-Soviet alliances in Eastern Europe. Since last December, Chicherin said in a press interview on August 4, 1928, the powers have been discussing a pact to outlaw war. Yet they had not asked Russia to participate. Was it not patent, then, that the pact is "an instrument for the isolation of the Soviet Union and the struggle against Bolshevism"?

Further to strengthen his hand in the inner councils of the communist party where he was fighting hard to defeat those who wished to adhere to the Briand-Kellogg treaty, Chicherin argued that if Russia was to sign she had to share in the talks regarding the nature of the document. He knew the Secretary of State would not negotiate with a Soviet representative. Bukharin supported Chicherin. Litvinov was not averse to joining.

The controversy in the Kremlin revolved around a reality and an illusion. On July 11, 1928, Acting German Foreign Minister Schubert, in the absence of Stresemann, inquired of Kellogg what his attitude would be if Russia were ready to adhere to the pact. Kellogg replied he would not accept Moscow as one of the fifteen original signatories, but it could sign later. When Schubert informed the Soviets of his interest in Russia's adherence nobody in the Kremlin believed he had acted on his own initiative and out of Germany's good will. The Bolshevik leaders assumed the United States wanted Russia to sign; this put a new color on the entire situation. For Stalin eagerly desired U.S. recognition. Stalin's foreign policy, moreover, favored being present, making Russia's presence felt.

Fifteen powers signed the Briand-Kellogg pact in Paris on August 27, 1928. The same day Jean Herbette, French Ambassador in Moscow, called on Litvinov to inquire whether the Soviet government wished to sign. Herbette said he was acting for his own and the United States government. Litvinov asked for all official correspondence relating to the pact.

Two days later Herbette again came to Litvinov's office. Litvinov subsequently repeated to me the contents of their amusing dialogue. Litvinov said his government wished to make reservations. Herbette replied that he could receive no Soviet reservations, no reservations were valid unless all signatories accepted them. Litvinov repeated Herbette's phrase: No reservations are valid unless all accepted them. This meant that Russia could make reservations, Herbette would transmit them for rejection or approval by the powers. No, Herbette insisted, he had no authority to transmit Soviet reservations, only Moscow's readiness to sign. Playfully Litvinov said, "And suppose I give you a negative reply?" Herbette, somewhat embarrassed by Litvinov's crushing logic, agreed to transmit that too.

On August 31 Litvinov handed Herbette the Soviet government's note. It contained Moscow's agreement to adhere, and Herbette therefore had to send it to Paris and Washington. It also contained Moscow's reservations. Herbette could not delete them. The first reservation was the Kremlin's refusal to recognize the British and French reservations. The second, that pacts outlawing war had no value unless accompanied by disarmament.

The entire Briand-Kellogg pact episode was an exercise in futility: many meetings, diplomatic comings and goings, long oceanic cablegrams, high officials acting as though they were doing something important—and the god of war smiling down on it all without concern. The Soviet aspect, however, was not without significance. The German move to bring a Soviet pen to the document was appreciated in Moscow and helped dissipate the gloom spread by the Shakhti trial. Kremlin adherence to the worthless pact showed that the Chicherin period was drawing to a close. Stalin and Litvinov would try to pursue a more active and more positive foreign policy.

XVII DIPLOMACY AMIDST TURMOIL

In 1928 the Soviet standard of living commenced to fall.

The New Economic Policy (NEP), adopted in February, 1921, announced in March, 1921, had given Russia six relatively fat years. The peasants, permitted to market their surpluses, responded by producing more surpluses. In 1916 Russia, within the same boundaries as the Soviet Union in 1928, had had 28.8 million cows, according to a speech by Khrushchev published in *Pravda* on September 15, 1953. By January 1, 1928, he said, the number of cows had risen to 33.2 million. The national herd of large-horned cattle was 58.4 million in 1916, and 66.8 million on January 1, 1928. In the same period, Khrushchev declared, sheep and goats increased from 96.3 million to 114.6 million; pigs 23 million to 27.7 million. Grain and flax yields also mounted. Workingmen, seeing there was something to buy, worked harder to earn money. Small private shops began turning out women's underwear, shoes, dresses, belts. Stocks hidden since 1917 appeared in the stores of the new businessmen, the Nepmen.

Such capitalism was too good to be allowed. Stalin moved against it for reasons more compelling than anticapitalism. The Trotskyites were insisting that the prosperous kulaks would soon dominate the villages, and Russia was largely village. This, the opposition held, threatened the dictatorship of the proletariat.

But could the Kremlin defeat nature? A middle peasant owned two cows; if one cow calfed he owned three next year and became a kulak. Tax the peasantry heavily, the Trotskyites proposed, and use the proceeds to finance rapid industrialization. Stalin fought the opposition but, in 1927, he stole its clothes and clamped a tax-squeezing press on kulaks and Nepmen. Often a storekeeper, taxed more than the value of his goods and resources, abandoned the enterprise—which is what the Kremlin wanted.

The NEP died in the autumn of 1928. Neither anticapitalism nor Trotskyism explains its demise. The peasant was producing more and enjoying it less. The government had too few consumer goods to give the peasant in exchange for his produce, it had only dirty paper rubles which he spurned. The peasants in 1927 accordingly began feeding grain to their horses while Moscow and other cities were short of bread. The armed tax collectors came to a village once and took away what they found, then they came again, seized a likely informer, and dug out hidden supplies from earth-covered pits. The next year the peasants planted less.

This crisis called forth Stalin's talent for drastic action irrespective of cost. On October 1, 1928, he launched the first Five Year Plan of rapid industrialization, and early in 1929 he sent in the Red Army and the secret police to collectivize Russia's reluctant peasantry.

Tsarist oppression had taught the muzhik to be docile yet wily. The news that Stalin's gunmen were herding peasants into the corral spread quickly. The muzhiks knew they had no choice. But why enter and deliver their livestock to the collective as required? Instead, they slaughtered their animals, ate what they could, and hawked the rest in the streets and squares of city and town. The results plagued the Soviet Union for many years. According to Khrushchev's speech in *Pravda* of September 15, 1953, the number of cows in the Soviet Union dropped from 33.2 million on January 1, 1928, to 27.8 million on January 1, 1941, before Russia was at war. In the same thirteen years of collectivization the number of sheep and goats shrank from 114.6 million to 91.6 million, horses from 36.1 million to 21 million, pigs from 27.7 million to

27.5 million, large-horned cattle from 66.8 million to 54.5 million. Harvests too were inadequate.

The peasants regretted the passing of the NEP and of the free trading that came with it. They gave the collective their worst effort, for they regarded it as a new serfdom, this time not under an approachable man in a visible manor house, but under a remote, unattainable state represented by a fearful bureaucrat who stiffly observed Kremlin rules. To several million Soviet communists, however, the collectives, though involuntary, spelled socialism. Combined with accelerated industrialization it promised "Socialism in one country" and would inspire other nations to take the same road. Communists rejoiced. Relieved of the NEP-capitalist nightmare, they threw themselves with bouncing enthusiasm into the work of building "socialism." Few then foresaw that the conjunction of forcible collectivization with giddy industrialization would culminate in a grim totalitarianism that would send many scores of thousands of those fervent communists to death in the dungeons of the secret police.

Though collectivization was a herculean task and industrialization an equally giant enterprise, Stalin undertook both simultaneously. This was wise. Collectivization gave the Soviet government millions of "free" laborers—the recalcitrant kulaks who refused to enter the collectives were arrested and put to work digging canals and building roads and railroads, minus pay. Many other peasants migrated to cities. They left because collectivization disrupted village society. Traditionally, and far into the Soviet period, land in the countryside was periodically redistributed by the village assembly in accordance with the increase by births or the decrease by deaths or departures in each family. The head of the family therefore objected to any of its members resettling in towns. The Russian village was consequently overpopulated and land in short supply. But with all land pooled for common cultivation in the collective and only a small private plot of an acre or half acre or quarter acre (depending on the fertility and availability of arable soil) reserved for a family, the restraint on cityward migration ended and hordes of young men flocked to urban centers. They lived twelve in a room in hovels or by hundreds in barracks, slept in their dirty clothing, went to the public baths once or twice a month, where they flailed one another with bundles of twigs, changed their underwear, and then took in a movie. This was the good life, better than the despised collective. It supplied the government with a fresh supply of cheap labor and gave a fillip to industrialization.

Work commenced on spectacular hydroelectric power plants, steel mills, ball-bearing factories, tractor factories, and machine-tool factories. Consistently the emphasis was on these heavy industries, while the production of consumer goods lagged. Though total industrial output rose precipitately over the decades, the light industries, which made things people eat, wear, live in, and otherwise enjoy, remained the Kremlin's orphan child. As late as 1960, to take a year at random, and again in 1963 light industries had registered only one-sixth as much growth as heavy industry.[1]

Heavy industry was preferred because, among other things, it made armaments. Under the watchful eye of Stalin and the direct guidance of General (in 1935, Marshal) Mikhail N. Tukhachevsky, the Red Army, rich in manpower, gradually achieved greater firepower and mobility through mechanization. The military aspect of industrialization possessed Stalin's mind.[2]

Unlike most developing countries before and since, the Soviet Union received no foreign loans, grants, or gifts, and though she always paid her bills, she obtained foreign credits only at excessive interest rates. The outside world exacted this price partly because of what Bolshevism was and partly because the Bolsheviks talked so much about what Bolshevism was. Ironically Germany, the country whose government the Kremlin tried hardest to overthrow, maintained the best commercial and financial relations with Moscow. The others needed Russia less and swore undying enmity to her until they needed her.

Without foreign help the wherewithal for the intense investment in heavy industry and armaments was at the expense of the food, clothing, housing, and leisure of the Soviet people. The 1928-29 collectivization-industrialization upheaval inaugurated a period of robber-baron, monopoly-state-capitalist exploitation of the workers, peasants, and middle class which lasted for decades. Chairman Nikita S. Khrushchev, propaganda genius, occasionally blurted out the truth. Returning to Moscow from a visit to Mao Tse-tung in Peking after a stay in America, he stopped at several places in Siberia to confront huge audiences. At Bratsk, where the Soviets claimed to be building the world's largest hydroelectric power station, he spoke on October 8, 1959 (*Pravda* of October 10, 1959), about his visit to the United States, his meeting with President Eisenhower, and his proposal for complete disarmament at the United Nations. If that proposal had been adopted the Soviet Union "could have commenced much earlier to begin the transition to the six-hour day. Our country grows and waxes stronger every year. Every year the Soviet people live more richly and better." The sooner the collectives

[1] Tsentralnoye Statisticheskoye Upraleniye (Central Statistical Directorate) of the Council of Ministers of the U.S.S.R. *SSSR v Tsifrakh v 1960 godu.* (The U.S.S.R. in Figures for 1960.) *Natzionalnoye Khozaistvo SSSR v 1963 godu.* (The National Economy of the U.S.S.R. in 1963.)

[2] J. V. Stalin, *Sochinenia,* Vol. 13. pp. 38-39.

and state farms raised their production, the sooner the great new industrial enterprises were completed, "the sooner we shall arrive in this country at the great goal—communism." Khrushchev urged them to work harder. They were working for themselves, for their children. "What else would you wish to hear from me?"

A Voice: "When will the prices of consumer goods be reduced?"

This heckle, as quoted by *Pravda*, brought the plump Khrushchev down with a jolt from the heights of imaginary communism to the flat reality of everyday Soviet living conditions.

He replied, "Of course it is possible to reduce prices rashly, but then where would we get the means to develop the national economy?"

If as late as October, 1959, Soviet workers and others still had to pay high prices out of meager wages to finance the national economy, it is easy to see the misery of Russian life thirty years earlier—in 1929 and the 1930's—when the country was much poorer. The economic essence of Stalinism consisted in compelling more and more generations to forfeit a considerable portion of their earnings in the name of the greater glory and military power of the Russia of the undefined future. De-Stalinization did not abolish this policy.

The end of the NEP and the advent of collectivization and the first Five Year Plan were regarded at the time as a swerve to the left. Concern for neatness in politics induced some to say that, by eliminating the Trotskyist left, Stalin, once the center between left and right, had now become the left. But peasant servitude, proletarian exploitation, and economic nationalism have little in common with radicalism. "Left" and "right" are often misleading terms; certainly they veiled the Soviet truth. Chairman Rykov, stormy petrel Bukharin, and Mikhail Tomsky, trade union chieftain, were grouped as rightist opponents of Stalin. They did indeed fear the disastrous effects of Stalin's 1928-29 headlong plunge into the new economics. What they feared more was that Stalin would crush them after having crushed Trotsky. They tried to organize against Stalin when collectivization and hasty industrialization were still only a gleam in his narrow eyes.

At 9 A.M. on July 11, 1928, former Finance Commissar Gregory Sokolnikov rang the bell at Leo Kamenev's Moscow home. He came so early, and without telephoning, in the hope of eluding the GPU. Sokolnikov acted for Bukharin. Stalin had combined with Bukharin and Kamenev to oust Trotsky. Later he used Bukharin to help oust Kamenev. Now Bukharin felt he was next. He hoped with the aid of Rykov and Tomsky to bring Kamenev and Zinoviev back into the supreme Politburo and thereby wrest power from Stalin or at least curb him.

By agreement with Sokolnikov, Bukharin appeared at Kamenev's apartment after Sokolnikov had been there for almost an hour. Bukharin talked nervously for forty-five minutes without stopping. "Stalin," he said, "has no scruples. He is an opponent of the Genghis Khan variety, loving revenge, and expert in knifing comrades in the back. . . . He will antagonize the peasantry. The result will be civil war. . . . Recent sessions of the Politburo had been stormy with members calling one another 'liar' and 'scoundrel.' You cannot put a single document in Stalin's hands without his using it against you. . . . He has no principles, he merely wishes to control everybody. He will destroy us all."[3]

In 1928 and 1929 Stalin did not yet possess the power to destroy them. But Bukharin was right: their years were numbered.

The convulsions within the Soviet Union revealed the existence of several debilitating conditions: the countryside had been torn asunder socially by collectivization, which Rykov, Bukharin, and Tomsky called "the military-feudal exploitation of the peasantry"; the communist party, depleted by the long joust with Trotsky, was floundering under the leadership of its feuding, intriguing oligarchy; the armed forces were weak. The situation conduced to a blurred view of world affairs and a barren foreign policy.

Whenever Moscow faced a major domestic crisis it put on its Comintern hat and took a leap into unreality. Throughout 1928, 1929, and 1930 the Kremlin followed the line laid down by the Sixth Congress of the Comintern which met in the Soviet Union for a month and a half, from July 17, 1928, to September 1, 1928. Nikolai I. Bukharin, keynote speaker for the Soviet Communist Party, saw the capitalist camp heading for world war. Anglo-American cooperation had turned into fierce competition and the two powers were hurtling toward a colossal collision. Germany was growing increasingly anti-Soviet.

The Congress program adopted on September 1 asserted: "The epoch of imperialism is the epoch of dying capitalism." Capitalism was moving to "inevitable destruction." However, the basic revolutionary tendency of the world proletariat was "temporarily crippled" because certain sections of the American, European, and Japanese working classes were being "bribed" by the capitalists. (The bribes took the form of higher wages.) Nevertheless, "The ultimate aim of the Communist International is to replace the capitalist world economy by a world communist

[3] Kamenev wrote a memorandum on the Bukharin-Sokolnikov visit. Several days after the event a Soviet communist friend brought a copy to me in Moscow. There were few secrets in those days of battle. Stalin already had the memorandum, probably from Kamenev himself. Stalin referred to the Bukharin-Kamenev-Sokolnikov meeting in a speech in April, 1929: ". . . why did Bukharin conspire with former Trotskyists against the Central Committee [of the party] and why did Rykov and Tomsky support him in this matter?" Stalin, Vol. 12, p. 3.

system." Developments in the Soviet Union would accelerate capitalism's fall.

But it was wrong to wait; communists must fight their enemies, the social democrats, Labourites, and moderate socialists, whom they labeled "social fascists." Thus the Kremlin sanctioned anew the campaign, so welcome to reactionaries and Nazis, of splitting the working class, a key bulwark against fascism. "A communist party can develop only by fighting social democracy," read a communist resolution of May 4, 1928, regarding elections in Japan.

The other hat Moscow wore was a top hat, and with it went the de rigueur striped trousers and an attempt to walk the crooked and narrow path of diplomacy. In May, 1927, the Soviet government, breaking precedent, had sent a delegation, headed by Valerian V. Ossinsky-Obolensky, a member of the Central Committee and of a princely family, to the World Economic Conference in Geneva. In November of the same year Litvinov went to Geneva to attend the fourth session of the preparatory disarmament commission. On the eve of his departure from Moscow the blunt Commissar explained that the Soviet government "has never concealed its disbelief in the willingness and ability of capitalist countries to abolish the system of wars among nations, and consequently to achieve disarmament."[4] This would have been more correct if he had omitted the word "capitalist."

At the November 30, 1927, session of the disarmament commission Litvinov, speaking in heavily accented English to a hall of uncomfortable delegates and an applauding public in the galleries, again voiced his conviction that capitalist nations could not disarm and then proposed that the twenty-six governments represented in the commission immediately disband all their armed forces, immediately destroy all their weapons, fleets, fortresses, and bases, and immediately close their war ministries, air ministries, and admiralties. Having thrown this bolt of lightning, Litvinov relented; if his proposal was extreme, the governments could carry out complete disarmament in four years, but "the first stage of disarmament must be effected in the coming year."[5]

Litvinov did not look particularly downcast when none of his proposals was adopted. His address was propaganda. He had come to Geneva to establish diplomatic contacts and, chiefly, to be present, not to allow British diplomacy to push Russia off the international stage. In

[4] Jane Degras (Ed.), *Soviet Documents on Foreign Policy,* Vol. II; *1925-1932,* pp. 278-280.

[5] U.S.S.R. Ministry of Foreign Affairs, *Dokumenty Vneshnei Politiki SSSR* (Documents on the Foreign Policy of the U.S.S.R.), Vol. X: *January 1-December 31, 1927,* pp. 504-510.

fact the Deputy Foreign Commissar paid a visit to Foreign Secretary Sir Austen Chamberlain in his Geneva hotel despite the rupture of Anglo-Soviet relations. Sir Austen did not mention Russian debts or Soviet subversive activities in Central Asia and China. He spoke only of the Comintern. Litvinov gave the usual Soviet reply: the Soviet government did not belong to the Comintern, which was an organization of many communist parties including the Soviet Communist Party. That party could never withdraw from the Comintern. Chamberlain's position, Litvinov contended, meant that Great Britain would not resume relations with Russia as long as a communist government existed there, "in other words, until a counterrevolutionary insurrection in the U.S.S.R."[6] The impasse remained.

Back in Geneva for another useless session of the disarmament commission, Litvinov complained on March 16, 1928, that his proposal for complete disarmament had received inadequate attention the previous November. This time the proposal was discussed, but no one supported it except the German delegate—in accordance with the prior confidential understanding which formed part of Russia's secret agreement to help Germany rearm. Litvinov wanted the Turkish delegate to testify to the close relations between Moscow and Ankara by approving the Soviet Union's stand, or at least remaining silent. The Turk, however, declared he was no pacifist and his government fought pacifism at home.[7] So did the Soviet government.

Meanwhile Moscow endeavored to expand trade with Japan, Germany, Italy, the small Baltic nations, and the United States. In one of two extended interviews in the summer of 1927, Foreign Trade Commissar Anastas I. Mikoyan said to me, ". . . after the break with Britain, contacts with the United States must become broader . . . Our American purchases of oil equipment, coal-cutting and mining machinery, electrical appliances, automobiles, tractors, and agricultural machines should increase year by year."

But it was Britain that obsessed the Soviet official mind. Partly this was a legacy of the Tsarist period. Partly it reflected Kremlin fears that England, through her power in world banking and trade, might close the already narrow foreign credit and commercial channels open to the Soviets. At all times a Russian scratched by the lion's paw enjoyed the next occasion when he could stick a pin in his tail.

One such occasion came with the May 3 to May 18, 1928, visit to the Soviet Union of King Amanullah of Afghanistan. Red Moscow, Mecca of world communism, did not blush to play host to the padishah of a tribal

[6] *Ibid.*, pp. 532-536.

[7] *Ibid.*, Vol. XI: *January 1-December 31, 1928*, p. 18, and editorial note, pp. 709-710.

Islamic state and his beautiful Queen Souriya, for Afghanistan bordered on the Soviet Union and on British India and both competed for her favor. The British had paid an annual subsidy to Amanullah's father but withdrew it from the son. Thereupon Moscow paid him an annual subsidy of $500,000, sometimes in gold, sometimes in goods, sometimes in reduced installments, sometimes in arms.

En route to the West Amanullah voiced his sympathy in India for Indian nationalism and in Egypt for Egyptian independence. His reception in London consequently was less than warm. The Soviets greeted him with pleasure. Several times the Padishah asked Deputy Foreign Commissar Karakhan about Peter the Great; he fancied himself the Peter of Afghanistan, tearing the veils from women's faces as Peter had torn the beards from Russian men. He hoped to modernize his country. President Kalinin presented him with two Soviet-built tractors.

On May 7, four days after his arrival in Moscow, Amanullah had a lengthy audience with Foreign Commissar Chicherin, who deposited a record of the talk in the secret archives. Among other things, Chicherin said the anti-Soviet press was alleging that "our government wished to incite Afghanistan against England. . . . Given England's might, this would be absurd." It was not known whether England would make war on the Soviet Union, "but at present England was waging a constant, daily economic warfare against us. . . . Undoubtedly, the western governments told the Padishah that the Soviet government was about to fall on account of its economic difficulties." Amanullah protested that nobody dared to attack the Soviet government in his presence, and when any person tried, "he broke off the conversation."

Chicherin contended that other powers were growing weaker while Russia was getting stronger. Moreover, the other powers engaged in "so-called peaceful penetration" of weak nations, whereas the Soviet system precluded such action. Here Amanullah declared "it was necessary to use his visit in order to achieve something concrete." In the several countries on his itinerary he had bought machines or arms or come to an agreement regarding the enrollment of Afghan students or inviting engineers to Afghanistan. "He would be disappointed if in the country friendliest to him something would not be done for Afghanistan. . . . He especially raised two current questions: on the laying of a paved road," presumably from the Soviet frontier to Kabul, "and a commercial treaty." Both involved the matter of transit through the Soviet Union, for Afghanistan was landlocked.

Chicherin told the Padishah he had information that Poland wanted to undertake cotton planting in Afghanistan. "Some of our officials have talked about forming a mixed company for cotton planting" there. The Afghan government had also expressed a desire to retain Soviet specialists for oil exploration in the Herat region.

Amanullah replied that he was deeply interested in cotton planting "and he would never agree to any decision which would give foreigners dominion over anything in his country, so there is nothing to fear from the Polish gentry. As to the exploration of the oil regions, he would first like to see petroleum mining in Baku. Only then would he think about this question."

The King gave a similar evasive answer when Chicherin suggested that Afghan pilots train in the Soviet Union. He made everything dependent on a satisfactory solution of the transit problem.

Chicherin now cited a report in a Berlin daily that Amanullah in London had agreed to officer the Afghan army with Englishmen. "Amanullah laughed loudly and said he urgently begged him not to believe such gossip." In leaving, the Padishah again thanked the Foreign Commissar for the fine welcome given him by the Soviets and "again asked to believe him and not to listen to any rumors spread by enemies and not to fear anything."[8]

The Soviet government agreed "in principle" in October, 1928, to build the highway to which Amanullah attached so much importance. But there is many a slip between principle and practice. The agreement to construct the road was not signed until December, 1955, and on September 3, 1964, the highway from Kabul to the Hindu Kush was opened with pomp.[9]

From the Soviet Union Amanullah went to Turkey where, on May 21, 1928, the government of Ataturk invited the diplomatic corps to a dinner in honor of the royal visitor. The next day Soviet Ambassador Jacob Suritz wired the Foreign Commissariat from Ankara that Amanullah talked to him at the table about the excellent impression he had gained in the Soviet Union, about his enthusiasm for the Red Army "and the wisdom of our statesmen. Hearing all this, the British Ambassador, sitting near me, completely lost his appetite."[10] Another pin into the lion's tail.

On a more serious level Leo M. Karakhan, Deputy Foreign Commissar for Asian Affairs, appraised the King's visit in a telegram to Soviet Ambassador L. N. Stark in Kabul, which remained secret until 1966. Karakhan had probably had the best opportunities to observe the Padishah—he and Amanullah were doubles partners in tennis (the King played in a felt hat, necktie, vest, white flannels, and street shoes)—to talk informally with the monarch and comprehend his motives. Uppermost in the Afghan ruler's mind, Karakhan informed Stark, was a four-

[8] *Ibid.*, pp. 302-307.
[9] *Ibid.*, editorial note, p. 730.
[10] *Ibid,,* pp. 330-331.

power pact binding the Soviet Union, Turkey, Iran, and Afghanistan in a military alliance for mutual defense. The Soviet leaders reacted coldly. Any such combination should be preceded, they intimated, by two-power treaties between Afghanistan and Turkey and between Afghanistan and Iran. The first of these was signed in Ankara during Amanullah's stay there. In Tehran he was less successful. The Iranian Shah was appalled by Queen Souriya's attire in a Paris dress that revealed almost as much as it concealed and by Amanullah's insistence on driving his own car through the streets of the capital. Iran was not ready for so much progress. Moreover, as Karakhan stated in his telegram, "We made clear" to Amanullah "our restrained attitude to any far-reaching commitments binding these four countries in one way or another. We pointed to the impossibility of a military alliance or mutual guarantees among those four states, explaining that to give official form to the relationships between the four powers would be regarded as creating an aggressive combination against other powers and that thus our best intentions would be misunderstood."[11]

Amanullah could only have been seeking defense partners against Great Britain, his strong neighbor in India. Moscow, however, refused to be drawn into an entente that might involve it in armed hostilities with England or bring it into a system of alliances which could be interpreted as directed against the British raj.

The Soviets refused to move a finger even when Amanullah's crown was in jeopardy shortly after his return home. The Afghan Peter modernized too fast; mullahs, imams, and perhaps British agents accordingly conspired to overthrow him. Escaped to Kandahar, he sent his foreign minister flying over the Hindu Kush to Moscow, where, in the Sugar King's Palace opposite the Kremlin, a small group of Bolshevik leaders heard Amanullah's call for help but turned a deaf ear. (The dethroned King, age thirty-seven, thereupon fled to Italy; he lived there and in Zurich in quiet retirement until his death in 1960.)

Collectivization and the first Five Year Plan had churned the Soviet Union into a chaotic mess. All energies were needed at home. Abroad, the Kremlin wanted less trouble, least of all with Britain, and more trade, first of all with Britain.

Trade with England suffered as a result of the 1927 break in diplomatic relations with Moscow. Soviet orders placed in Britain fell from 20 million pounds sterling in 1925-26 to 14 million pounds in 1926-27, and 5 million pounds in 1927-28. Even the largest of these sums did not weigh heavily in England's world commerce, but Soviet purchases were often concentrated in machine-tool industries which needed the business

[11] *Ibid.*, pp. 386-389.

most. The United States benefited. For the fiscal year ending September 30, 1929, Soviet-American trade reached a record total of $149 million, compared with $113 million the previous year and $48 million in 1913. Of the $149 million, $109 million represented Russian imports from the U.S.A.[12]

In addition the Soviet agreement of October, 1928, with the International General Electric Company, an affiliate of the American General Electric Company, provided for Soviet purchases of massive machinery, and a nine-year contract signed by Henry Ford and Saul G. Bron on May 31, 1929, paved the way for the construction of a huge automobile factory at Nizhni Novgorod (now Gorki) with the help of Ford blueprints, personnel, machine tools, automobile parts, and trucks and cars.

By October 1, 1929, thirty such agreements for technical aid in the implementation of the first Soviet Five Year Plan had been signed with American firms like Du Pont de Nemours and the Radio Corporation of America, and with Colonel Hugh L. Cooper to supervise the erection of the great Dnieperstroi Dam. Diplomatic relations between Moscow and Washington might have strengthened economic ties, but the absence of an embassy in Moscow and consulates elsewhere caused little inconvenience to Americans working in or visiting Russia. "Americans," Chicherin said to me in 1928, "in fact enjoy extraterritoriality in our country." What protected them was Stalin's desire for U.S. recognition.

There would be a long wait before Ambassador William Christian Bullitt presented his letters of credence to the Kremlin, but the British political system permits rapid change. As a result of the General Elections a second Labour government, again led by Prime Minister Ramsay MacDonald, took office on June 7, 1929. Moscow felt relieved. More than interest in trade was involved.

The resumption of diplomatic relations between Great Britain and the Soviet Union was preceded by months of official discussions on debts and propaganda. Neither issue ever reached a satisfactory settlement. Nevertheless, the House of Commons on November 5, 1929, approved the agreement to restore relations. Gregory Sokolnikov, appointed ambassador to London in accordance with Stalin's practice of getting opposition leaders out of the country until he could try them for treason, presented his credentials to the Prince of Wales on December 20. Sir Esmond Ovey, his chest covered with flowery gold braid and his white teeth aglitter, handed his to President Kalinin on December 22. In Moscow the refusal of King George V to attend Sokolnikov's presentation ceremony was regarded as an indication that relations would be impeded by powerful forces outside the Labour government. More

[12] Report by Saul G. Bron, president of Amtorg, the Soviet trading company in New York, in *The Economic Review of the Soviet Union*, New York, Oct. 1, 1929.

likely, George V declined to receive a Bolshevik associated with those who had ordered the execution of his cousin, Nicholas II.

Despite clouds and doubts the re-establishment of Anglo-Soviet diplomatic relations after a two-and-a-half-year rupture gave Moscow some sense of ease at a time when the strain of the domestic economic upheaval and hot trouble on the China frontier combined to create a crisis atmosphere.

XVIII THE RISE OF HITLER

Mahatma Gandhi was morally strong; he therefore had no fear of appearing weak. Some weak persons, on the other hand, try to create an impression of strength. Similarly, a powerful nation need not be apprehensive if its behavior strikes outsiders as weak, whereas a weak country dreads giving neighbors the feeling that they can take too many liberties with it.

In 1929 the Soviet Union was in economic disarray, politically distraught by fights within the ruling communist party, and not prepared for major military combat. It consequently reacted with vigor when the "young" Marshal Chang Sueh-liang, son of Marshal Chang Tso-lin, warlord of Manchuria, seized the Chinese Eastern Railway on July 10, 1929. The railway was the property of Russia, hence of the Soviet government, and had been managed by Russians and Chinese with the former in controlling positions. In addition to its economic advantages, the possession of the railroad kept Moscow's hand in Chinese politics.

After Borodin's withdrawal from China in 1927 and the failure of Russia to guide the Chinese revolution, Marshal Chiang Kai-shek entrenched himself in south and central China and established his capital in the city of Nanking. Between Chiang's large fief and the "young" Marshal's Manchurian domain lay two rivals of both: Feng Yu-hsiang, the "Christian" general, and Yen Shi-shan, the warlord of Shansi Province who in 1928 and 1929 dominated Peking. Chiang Kai-shek and the "young" Marshal of Manchuria apparently believed that the seizure of the Chinese Eastern Railway would so strengthen Chang Sueh-liang that he could eliminate Feng and Yen. Moreover, the "young" Marshal did not enjoy seeing the Russian giant sitting astride the chief east-west railroad of his vast industrial region.

The take-over of the Chinese Eastern was motivated, almost exclusively, by these endlessly complicated Chinese domestic considerations. But Moscow did not think so. Nor did Japan. Tokyo had ambitions in Manchuria and designs on the Chinese Eastern; it suspected that Chiang Kai-shek was under United States influence and that he and the "young" Marshal would welcome American power in Manchuria as a counterweight to Soviet and Japanese power. Moscow shared these suspicions and found confirmation in notes sent by Washington to the Soviet and Chinese governments on July 18, eight days after the seizure of the Chinese Eastern, urging a peaceful settlement of the dispute. The State Department's action, as self-appointed guardian of the Kellogg-Briand Pact, aroused Moscow's apprehension, and while Litvinov promised to abide by the obligations under the pact, he wondered what impended.

The newly formed "Special Far Eastern Army," under the command of Vasili K. Bluecher, was put in combat readiness. Mukden and Nanking offered to negotiate a settlement. The Kremlin insisted on the return of the Chinese Eastern. Weeks passed, then months. On November 18 the Red Army moved into Manchuria and bombed and shelled Chinese towns and military concentrations. During the next three days the Russians advanced thirty-eight miles against negligible opposition. The Soviet peace terms were communicated to Marshal Chang Sueh-liang on November 22; four days later he accepted them. The Red Army withdrew to Soviet territory.

The Chinese Eastern Railway was returned to the Soviet government.

The swift Soviet blow indicated that Russia intended to assert her rights. The quick retirement precluded international complications. Moscow now negotiated bilaterally with Mukden; this was Moscow's preferred procedure.

Throughout the brief episode Germany, which protected Soviet interests in China after the April, 1927, rupture of relations, and, amazingly, Japan, took Moscow's side in the dispute. President Herbert C. Hoover's Secretary of State, Henry L. Stimson, on December 2, 1929, again reminded Moscow and Nanking of their obligations under the Kellogg Pact, and, in a second note, invited the chief pact signatories to cooperate for peace. The German government replied that it knew of "direct negotiations for the peaceful composition of the conflict." Japan declined to join any move for foreign mediation on the ground that an antiwar pact could not be invoked after the war had ended and when talks were in progress. Japan wanted no American finger in the affairs of Manchuria where she hoped her own boot would soon tread uncontested.

Litvinov, in a rejoinder to Stimson dated December 4, said, "The Government of the Soviet Union cannot abstain from expressing its astonishment that the government of the United States of America which, at its own wish, maintains no official relations with the Government of the Soviet Union, finds it possible to address advice and directions to the latter."[1]

Litvinov's ten-year tenure as Foreign Commissar would be enlivened by many such barbs. They were the spice of his work.

Chicherin had been Foreign Commissar, in succession to Trotsky, from March, 1918. He held Lenin in the highest regard and worked closely with him. But he had only contempt for Stalin's mind and methods, and Stalin was too sensitive to denigration not to notice it. During 1929 Chicherin spent a number of months in Germany on cure. Litvinov acted for him. On July 25, 1930, Stalin dismissed Chicherin and appointed Litvinov Commissar. Chicherin told me he first learned of the change when he read his morning newspaper. In the ensuing years he could be seen, a lonely, haggard figure walking Moscow streets, usually along the Arbat, books in hand—he was a voracious reader—and head down to avoid being recognized. He died on July 7, 1936, age sixty-four. At the memorial service in the conference room of the Foreign Commissariat he lay in an open coffin, his contorted face and clenched hands mute witnesses to the physical pain and mental agony he had suffered for years. With officials of the commissariat and a few foreigners standing in dense ranks in the chamber, Deputy Foreign Commissar Nikolai N. Krestinsky, former ambassador in Berlin, pronounced an unusual funeral oration: a denunciation of Chicherin's conduct of Soviet foreign affairs. It was Stalin's wish and Krestinsky could not disobey (but obedience failed to save him from the death sentence at the third, March, 1938, Moscow trial, and execution). However, *Pravda* of December 5, 1962, the ninetieth birthday of Chicherin, noted that "The reason for his dismissal was not only illness but Stalin's displeasure with Chicherin's critical remarks." This belated obituary erased the shame of Krestinsky's tirade and hailed Chicherin as "a diplomat of the Lenin school who gave all his knowledge, abilities, and energy to the cause of communism." His reputation in Russia is now secure.

* * *

Maxim M. Litvinov's decade as Soviet Diplomat Number One lies between two earth-shattering explosions. The first was the Wall Street crash of October, 1929; the second the Soviet-Nazi pact of August, 1939. They were related.

The Wall Street boom of the 1920's was a purely American phenomenon; all strata, from bankers to stenographers, speculated on the

[1] Max Beloff, *The Foreign Policy of Soviet Russia, 1929-1941,* Vol. I, p. 75.

stock market in a get-rich-quick frenzy. Big and little fortunes were made until, in October, 1929, the prices of stocks stumbled, tumbled, rallied, wavered, and finally dropped so precipitously as to wipe out many fortunes and some lives. A depression followed. John Kenneth Galbraith writes, "After the Great Crash came the Great Depression which lasted, with varying intensity, for ten years. In 1933 Gross National Product (total production of the economy) was nearly a third less than in 1929. . . . Until 1941 the dollar value of production remained below 1929. Between 1930 and 1940 only once, in 1937, did the average number unemployed during the year drop below eight million. In 1933 nearly thirteen million were out of work, or about one in every four of the labor force. In 1938 one person in five was still out of work."[2]

The United States had become the biggest national economy in the world. A major business earthquake in America communicated itself of necessity to all the developed countries of the globe and not a few of the underdeveloped. In a sense the Soviet Union benefited because U.S. firms were more eager for Russian orders and U.S. engineers and technicians for jobs in the U.S.S.R. Germany felt the repercussions most keenly because she had become an American financial dependency in the consequence of the Dawes Plan and Young Plan for the collection of reparations. German banks and industrialists had been receiving enormous loans from the United States. The Wall Street crash stopped the golden flow. German democracy crashed.

Economic factors were not the only reason for the rise of Hitler, but they contributed enormously. In July, 1930, Chancellor Heinrich Bruening, a conservative Catholic, facing a budget deficit, proposed new taxation. When he found no Reichstag majority for this urgent measure he warned that the Weimar Constitution of the German Republic, in Article 48, permitted emergency legislation by presidential decree. President Hindenburg issued the taxation decree on July 16. The Social Democrats, resentful of this disregard of Parliament, moved to annul the edict. The motion passed 236 to 221 on the votes of the Social Democrats who believed in democracy and of the Nazis, communists, and Nationalist Party who did not. Bruening and Hindenburg thereupon disbanded the Reichstag and ordered new elections on September 14, 1930. The communists, who had 54 deputies in the previous Reichstag, elected 76; the Nazis polevaulted from 12 to 107; the Social Democrats dropped from 153 to 143. The Berlin stock market collapsed. On December 15, 1930, Germany counted 3,977,000 unemployed.

At the end of 1931 the army of unemployed numbered 5,773,000. Wages fell, capital fled abroad for fear of inflation, big banks closed,

[2] *The Great Crash 1929*, p. 173.

small businesses failed. The next year, 1932, would determine the fate of Germany and of hundreds of millions of people outside Germany, for Adolf Hitler waited in the wings of the world stage.

Litvinov's Foreign Commissariat was active. The Soviet government signed a nonaggression treaty with Finland on January 21, 1932, with Latvia on February 5, 1932, with Estonia on May 4, 1932, with Poland on July 25, 1932, and with France on November 29, 1932. (A nonaggression treaty with Lithuania had been negotiated earlier.) They reflected nervousness about Germany's future.

Soviet-German military collaboration continued, but Germany was showing less enthusiasm for the enterprise. Ambassador Herbert von Dirksen, Rantzau's successor in Moscow, had written his Foreign Office on December 19, 1929, that "The Soviet government intends to create a special industry because it feels that without it its security is threatened. . . . Since the Soviet government is unable to create this special industry with its own resources" it asked German aid.[3] However, a German Foreign Office letter dated January 6, 1930, speaks of "the known decision of the [German] Cabinet regarding military restraint in regard to Russia."[4]

Several circumstances account for the cooling of Germany's zeal. Despite Moscow's eagerness to expand the secret military collaboration inaugurated by Seeckt, the Germans found Russian suspicion of foreigners irksome and work with the Soviets blocked by myriad bureaucratic hurdles. Moreover, time, money, and ingenuity tended to loosen the restrictions imposed by the Versailles peace treaty on German armaments. During the 1920's Krupp of Essen acquired an ever-expanding portfolio of shares in the Bofors Arms Factory of Sweden whose patents and unpublicized technical processes became available to the Reichswehr. Krupp and other Ruhr and Rhineland firms were producing special steels which interested only the German armed forces. American loans had permitted German armament industries to modernize their equipment with an eye to a bright future. The departure of Seeckt as commander of the Reichswehr on October 9, 1926, and his replacement by Colonel General Wilhelm Heye was followed, on January 31, 1927, by the withdrawal of the Allied Commission of Control of German disarmament on the assumption—false—that Germany had disarmed or that there was no way of disarming a country like Germany that wished to elude foreign inspectors. Under the Dawes Plan Germany had grown more prosperous and could afford greater hidden expenditures on arms and armed men. President Hindenburg considered Russia Germany's hereditary enemy, and his appointment on January 20, 1928, of Wilhelm

[3] From the secret files seen in Bonn, June, 1929-May, 1930, Bd. 5. E 163978.
[4] *Ibid.*, E 163997.

Groener, a general, as Minister of Defense, strengthened anti-Russian tendencies in the German political high command. (Groener had been commander in chief of the German army of occupation in the Ukraine in 1918.)

General Groener received me in his Berlin apartment on the afternoon of December 20, 1932, and read to me from the diary he kept in the Ukraine. The passages documented his intense anti-Bolshevism and interest in Ukrainian separatism. The next day, through Groener's intervention, I had an interview in the Grunewald section of Berlin with Hetman Pavel P. Skoropadsky, a former Tsarist general and the Germans' puppet ruler of the Ukraine during their occupation. The tall, soldierly Hetman still wondered—in 1932—how long the Soviet regime would last and when he might return to the Ukraine. He was fifty-nine years old. I inquired whether he was not happy in his Grunewald villa.

Hitler had been hypnotizing hundreds of thousands throughout Germany with his anti-Versailles philippics and anti-Bolshevik harangues. He wanted "Lebensraum" for Germans in the Ukraine, release from reparations, and the expulsion of foreign troops. The Young Plan, adopted in January, 1930, and inaugurated September 1, not only reduced reparations, it provided for the evacuation of the Rhineland by the French and Belgian garrisons. They left Cologne in June. (Litvinov sent a telegram of congratulations.) No longer able to coerce Germany, the western powers courted her. Formerly they might proscribe, now they could merely protest.

Logically, the Young Plan's liberation of Germany from some heavy impositions of Versailles should have weakened Hitler's movement. But logic is the least component of politics. The departure of all foreign troops and foreign arms inspectors from Germany gave free rein to the Nazis and militarists. With a field marshal in the President's palace and a general as Minister of Defense and with Hitler's anti-Bolshevik propaganda buzzing in the nation's ears, Germany undertook an accelerated program of undisguised rearmament at home. One of the most sensational acts of 1931 was the launching of the first German "pocket battleship." Held within the restrictions of the Versailles treaty—10,000 tons displacement and 11-inch guns—this Panzerkreuzer A, later christened the *Deutschland,* was furnished with the finest armor plate, powerful engines, and many ingenious devices so it could outrun and outgun any foreign cruiser of its size. It was the first of a family. Rearmament on a grand scale—preparation for the second world war—had commenced inside Germany. Moreover, Ambassador von Dirksen explains in his memoirs,[5] Chancellor Bruening's deeply religious feelings held Soviet-

[5] Herbert von Dirksen, *Moskau Tokio London. Erinnerungen und Betrachtungen zu 20 Jahren deutscher Aussenpolitik 1919-1939,* pp. 115-120.

German collaboration to a minimum. Personnel changes in the German Foreign Office, according to Dirksen, compounded Berlin's negative attitude. The secret arrangements for rearmament in the Soviet Union remained in force, but the Cabinet decision of January 6, 1930, "regarding military restraint" in Russia limited its effectiveness.

By 1930 some one hundred German aviation observers had received their training in the Soviet Union. Then these studies were transferred to Braunschweig in Germany. However, the training of fighter pilots continued at Lipetsk, Russia, until 1933. In 1932 a group of Soviet officers, led by General Tukhachevsky, visited Reichswehr installations and were received by President Hindenburg. German officers were attached to Soviet divisions for protracted periods. On the other hand, the German navy decided to refrain from contact with its Soviet counterpart; it feared the infectious effect of Bolshevism.[6] That this consideration was not lacking in validity may be judged from the startling fact that the three daughters of General Kurt Hammerstein-Equord, Commander in Chief of the Reichswehr, were active communists.[7] Germans, especially young Germans, wove back and forth, from the communists to the Nazis and from the Nazis to the communists. Usually their gyrations reflected the rapid oscillations in the fortunes of the two extremist movements and, also, changes in economic conditions. In the second half of 1932, partly as a result of Soviet orders (Soviet imports from Germany rose from 353 million marks in 1929 to 625 million marks in 1932), but more because reparations had ceased, German business improved and unemployment in the machine-tool industries working for Russia dropped. The elections in November, 1932, registered the change: the Nazis received 11,737,391 votes, or 33.2 percent of the total; this represented a loss for them of 1,995,386, compared with the previous balloting. The communists, on the other hand, increased their vote to 5,980,540, or 17 percent of the total. But both extremes were eating at the vitals of German democracy. Violence filled the streets. Most Germans yearned for law and order. They got lawlessness and terror from Hitler.

The Nazi losses and the communist gains frightened industrial magnates and the military. They had money and power, but they saw that the working class and large sections of the middle class were deserting the German state which rocked from simultaneous blows by Nazis and communists in the Reichstag, in strikes which both parties supported (for instance, the Berlin city transport strike), and in the deliberate stimulation by the two parties of confusion and discontent (communists, for example, on party instruction, made running raids on food shops, stealing geese, chickens, and so forth, with a view to enhancing middle-

[6] Francis L. Carsten, *Reichswehr und Politik 1918-1933*, pp. 406-410.
[7] *Ibid.*, p. 362.

class resentment against the government). German communist leaders of my acquaintance did not conceal the intent of their Made-in-Moscow political strategy: "Yes, these actions will bring Hitler to power; he will be finished in six months and then our turn will come."

They got the first part of their wish; Hindenburg appointed Hitler Chancellor on January 30, 1933. The communist illusion of the quick political demise of Hitler was matched by the illusion of big business that this would help induct "the little corporal with the ridiculous mustache" into office the better to control him, and through him the unhappy masses. Accordingly Chancellor Franz von Papen, who had flirted with Hitler, was ousted by that military genius at intrigue, General Kurt von Schleicher, an intimate of Nazi leaders, on December 3, 1932. During eight and a half weeks Schleicher warmed the Chancellor's chair for Hitler. Then Hitler made the German state supreme ueber alles, above all classes, as a prelude to an attempt at lifting Germany Ueber Alles in der Welt.

German-Soviet relations languished until the secret talks which led to the Stalin-Hitler Pact of August 23, 1939.

XIX THE NEW RUSSIA

Russia resembled a busy beehive. The year 1928 was the great divide. Professor Abram Bergson asserts that "by 1928 the country had largely if not entirely recovered from the devastating losses suffered under the successive blows of world war, revolution, and civil war, and probably was producing a total output similar to that of Tsarist times."[1]

Then came the first Five Year Plan and the huge losses from agrarian collectivization. By 1932 the Soviets began boasting that they would "overtake and surpass America" (a Russian wit commented, "when you overtake America, leave me there and go on without me"). *Pravda* explained how overtaking would be achieved: "While we are advancing steadily toward higher levels they are dropping back to meet us." Life turned bragging into folly, but progress was undeniable.

Toward the end of 1932, however, Russia's foreign trade balance grew sharply unfavorable and the Soviet government had to curtail its pur-

[1] *The Real National Income of Soviet Russia Since 1928*, p. 7.

chases abroad and dispense with all except the absolute minimum of foreign technical assistance. Now began the Soviet sale of Rembrandts, Rubens, and other masters to eager European and American buyers.

The first Five Year Plan divided the commentators. Lord Beaverbrook, visiting the United States, told the *New York Times* of August 22, 1931: "England is as terrified of what the Soviets will do to her as America is, but it is a groundless fear. The Soviet and her plan are doomed to the worst sort of failure, for it is impossible to turn a race of peasants into an industrial nation. . . . Russia has no leaders. All the key positions in industry are filled by politicians with no qualifications. The country is producing nothing but the shoddiest sort of goods."

Leslie Urquhart, who had owned vast mining properties in the Urals and Siberia before the revolution: The Five Year Plan was not a success; its motives were political rather than economic; industries were being established which were liabilities; the Ford Motor Car Works at Nizhni Novgorod (Gorky) had a capacity of 100,000 automobiles annually, but the number of cars in the Soviet Union did not exceed 18,000; it would be more economical to buy cars in America; besides, the entire country did not possess more than 100 miles of motor roads outside of cities; several tractor plants had been or were being erected, but tractors were not needed when the muzhik earned 35 cents a day for his labor. "The purpose of the industrialization of Russia," he continued, "was to create work for ten million to twelve million people of the towns at the expense of one hundred and forty million who live on the land."[2]

In London Alexander F. Kerensky, Chairman of the 1917 Provisional government, likened people who helped the Bolsheviks to lunatics. He opposed the granting of credits to the Kremlin: "The Five Year Plan not only is not needed, but it is extremely damaging. It has destroyed the very foundations of the national economy" and "thrust Russia into a bottomless pit of destitution."[3]

The statements of Beaverbrook, Urquhart, and Kerensky, typical of numerous others, contained an ounce of truth, a ton of regrets, and a lack of perspective. Stalin supplied the perspective because he knew the central motivation of the plan. In an address to the first Conference of Industrial Managers in Moscow on February 4, 1931, he said, "To slacken the speed of advance—that means to fall behind. And those who are backward get beaten. But we do not want to be beaten. No, we don't want it! The history of old Russia, incidentally, is one unbroken record of the beatings she suffered for falling behind, for her backwardness. She was beaten by the Mongol khans. She was beaten by the Turkish beys. She was beaten by the Swedish feudal lords. She was

[2] *New York Times*, Nov. 1, 1931.
[3] *Ibid.*, Nov. 11, 1931.

beaten by the Polish and Lithuanian gentry. She was beaten by the British and French capitalists. She was beaten by the Japanese barons. All beat her—because of her backwardness. For her military backwardness, for her cultural backwardness, for her political backwardness, for her industrial backwardness, for her agricultural backwardness. . . . We are fifty to a hundred years behind the advanced nations. We must run this distance in ten years. Either we do it or they will crush us."[4]

In ten years Hitler invaded Russia.

Soviet goods were shoddy when Beaverbrook spoke; they continued to be shoddy for decades. Every industrial nation began with a race of peasants and village craftsmen who had to be retrained and taught the discipline of a factory at the expense of the community. The price Russia paid for industrialization is beyond calculation; the Kremlin bans social bookkeeping, and nobody knows how many lives were lost and shortened, nerves destroyed, careers ruined, so the nation might grow mighty. Kerensky's cry of "destitution" was mild compared with the widespread famine, the serious undernourishment, the rationing that followed in the wake of the first Five Year Plan, the waste from inefficiency, political mismanagement, terror, bureaucratic timidity and apathy, and just plain cultural backwardness, the poor housing, illnesses, and premature aging—especially of women—all in the interest of not being beaten in war. Urquhart missed this point. An automobile plant can manufacture trucks for the army and a tractor factory can produce tanks. The high price of military strength never deterred the Kremlin. It has always been Soviet policy to keep military men far from the summit of power but to give militarism at home maximum support. Communism, like Tsarism, trained the Russian people to pay big bills.

If Lord Beaverbrook spoke the truth when he said England and America were terrified of what the Soviets would do to them, here is evidence of how misguided foreigners and their governments can be. Beaverbrook found comfort in the conviction that the fears were "groundless" because of Russian weakness; but as a member of the British government in the second world war he took comfort from Russian strength. Nor can Britain's loss of empire be attributed to the Soviets. Chicherin, speaking from a text meticulously edited by Lenin, stated at the Genoa Conference in 1922 that "As a result of the [first] world war the independence movements of all oppressed and colonial peoples have been strengthened."[5] He paid no similar compliment to the Bolshevik revolution. Indian nationalists often referred to the 1904-5 victory of the colored Japanese over Russia as a source of inspiration to them, but the effect of the 1917 Bolshevik revolution was rarely men-

[4] *Pravda*, Feb. 5, 1931. J. V. Stalin, *Sochinenia*, Vol. 13, pp. 38-39.
[5] Louis Fischer, *The Life of Lenin*, p. 573.

tioned. Objectively, it was the blood and treasure Britain lost in the two world wars and her recognition of the pervasive influence of nationalism in Asia and Africa that led her statesmen to liberate the colonies from Britain and liberate Britain from the colonies. Britain's terror of what the Soviets would do to her was groundless.

In the United States some people always take to underground shelters when the new and incomprehensible appears. But it cannot be said that the mass of the American people or even their government officials were terrified by what Bolshevism would do to them. Many abhorred its principles and actions on religious or other grounds. Many used the issue of U.S. recognition of Soviet Russia as a convenient political hand grenade to throw at domestic enemies. Serious observers discovered good things to report. One of them, Colonel W. N. Haskell, director of the Hoover American Relief Administration (ARA) in Russia during the 1921-22 famine, who visited Russia in 1926, wrote after a second tour in 1931: "Five years ago a machine was a mystery, now it is an idol. . . . Perhaps the most marked change is in the railroads, in the freight they carry." Formerly it had been grain and general merchandise, now it was structural steel, castings, transformers, automobiles. The latest type of machinery was being installed in place of obsolete equipment; he also noted better organization in the shops. The standard of living had not improved in five years; this was according to plan, with ruthless disregard of the people. The dictatorship rested on military force.[6]

This was a fair summary acceptable to Americans who remembered the remarkable transformation of their country in less than a half century. Not a few U.S. social scientists, industrial managers, and liberal or radical intellectuals were impressed—overimpressed, one might say in hindsight—with Soviet economic planning. A whole nation wrapped in a central blueprint was a thrilling phenomenon. Stalin had married Russia to modernization for war or peace, in hunger or plenty, with an ample dowry of promises, propaganda, and low piecework wages for the many, privileges for an upper caste, and prison, concentration camp, or murder for those who displeased him. The future had arrived, the new, Stalinist Russia destined to mingle economic creativity with blood, fear, and cultural stagnation.

[6] *New York Times*, June 21, 1931.

XX THE U.S.A. RECOGNIZES THE U.S.S.R.

Emil Ludwig had an interview with Stalin in Moscow on December 13, 1931. When the German writer asked whether Stalin saw any parallel between himself and Peter the Great, he answered no, he was a pupil of Lenin and "As regards Lenin and Peter the Great, the latter was a drop in the ocean, but Lenin was an entire ocean." On another matter Stalin declared that Trotsky had been forgotten in the Soviet Union.

"Altogether forgotten?" Ludwig wondered.

"He is sometimes remembered in anger."

"By everybody in anger?"

"As far as our workers are concerned they all remember Trotsky in anger, with irritation and with hatred."

Later Ludwig remarked on the respect he had noticed in the Soviet Union for all things American. "I would even say obeisance to everything American, that is, to the land of the dollar, the most consistent capitalist country. . . . How do you explain this?"

Stalin: "You exaggerate. . . . But we respect American efficiency in everything—in industry, technology, literature, and life. . . . Although America is a highly developed capitalist country her morals in industry and practices in production contain something of democracy—an affirmation that cannot be made of the old European capitalist countries where the spirit of feudal overlordship still persists." America, Stalin continued, is a country of " 'free colonists,' with no estate owners, no aristocrats." In American factories it is difficult "to distinguish an engineer from a workingman in outward appearance."

Having paid this tribute, Stalin turned to Ludwig and, without being prodded by a question, said, "However, if one is to speak of our sympathies for any nation, or, more correctly, for the majority of any nation, then of course one must mention our sympathies for Germans. Our feelings for Americans cannot compare with these sympathies."

Ludwig asked why, and Stalin recalled that Marx and Engels were Germans. Not content with this lame explanation, Ludwig spoke of Moscow's nonaggression pact negotiations then in progress with Poland

and stated that if the Soviet government recognized Poland's frontiers and thereby the Versailles peace system, Germans would be profoundly disillusioned.

Stalin denied that the nonaggression pact with Poland would constitute a guarantee of the Versailles system. "Our friendly relations with Germany remain the same as they have been until now. That is my firm conviction." Rumors to the contrary had been spread by certain Poles and Frenchmen. All fears will disappear, he added, when we publish the text of the pact. "Everybody will then see that it contains nothing against Germany."[1]

Thus Stalin at the end of 1931 was praising the United States while avowing sympathies for Germany. He wanted U.S. recognition and German friendship. He was not the man to put all his foreign policy eggs in one basket. Diplomatic relations with Washington loomed large in his wishes because of America's economic power, because he feared Japan and expected the U.S. to check Nipponese expansion in China, especially in Manchuria, and because recognition would enhance the Kremlin's prestige. Friendship with Germany, the pivot of Soviet foreign policy, served to keep Poland peaceful; it was assumed that if the Poles moved against Russia Germany would move to retrieve the lands Versailles had granted Poland. Moreover, Soviet-German collaboration blunted the effects of French hostility born of the never-to-be-solved debt problem now augmented by Soviet dumping. (Moscow, in dire need of foreign currency to pay its bills abroad, had been exporting goods at prices lower than those prevailing on the world market. This proved a windfall to propagandists who maintained that dumping was intended to undermine capitalism. France and several other countries embargoed Russian products.) The resumption of diplomatic ties with London did not make England any friendlier to Russia than France was. Beginning in 1931 and 1932, therefore, Stalin's interest in world affairs centered on the United States and Germany.

Franklin D. Roosevelt assumed the office of President on March 4, 1933, thirty-two days after Hitler became German Chancellor. Japan's mounting aggressiveness in China and the tensions in Europe caused by Hitler's accession created an atmosphere favorable to U.S. recognition of the Soviet Union. Roosevelt lent an ear to the intellectuals in his entourage who had always urged recognition and were now impressed by the Russian economic revolution in contrast to capitalist stagnation after the 1929 stock market crash. Apart from these considerations, the reason for recognition was the absence of any reason against recognition. The new President, elected in November, 1932, by a huge majority and

[1] J. V. Stalin, *Sochinenia*, Vol. 13, pp. 104-123. Excerpt in Jane Degras, *Soviet Documents on Foreign Policy*, Vol. II: 1925-1932, pp. 517-518.

expecting to remain in the White House for eight years, could overlook the opposition of certain churchmen, trade unions, and Republicans to diplomatic relations with Moscow.

Incongruously, yet in a strange way logically, the official U.S. documentary history of American recognition of the U.S.S.R.[2] begins with a letter by Secretary of State Henry L. Stimson stating the case against recognition. The letter, dated September 8, 1932, was a reply to Senator William E. Borah, Chairman of the Senate Foreign Relations Committee and an avowed, active proponent of recognition. Borah's inquiry to Stimson had mentioned rumors of a possible Russo-Japanese agreement if U.S. recognition were withheld. Stimson said any such understanding would be "very transitory. The rivalry between those two countries in respect to Manchuria is so keen and the lack of confidence of each in the promises of the other so real, that it is very unlikely that they have entered into any substantial or permanent relation of mutual support and assistance. Their interests are far too antagonistic for that."

Stimson committed the error of assuming that the relations between any two countries are unalterable or that negotiations between them aim at permanence. The first law of foreign politics is fluidity.

On February 23, 1933, nine days before Roosevelt's inauguration, the Soviet military attaché talked at length with the U.S. military attaché, Lieutenant Colonel J. G. McIlroy, at an official luncheon in Tokyo. The Soviet officer told the colonel, "It is to the interest of both the United States and the U.S.S.R. to come to some friendly understanding. The Soviets would be glad to pay the small debt owed to America, but that would necessitate the recognition of debts elsewhere, the total of which is very large." Therefore the Soviet government would prefer not to recognize the debt but to pay under some equivalent arrangement. ". . . propaganda," the Soviet military attaché added, is a difficult question and "difficult for them to control." Then came the significant communication: ". . . two years ago, Japan could have taken the [Soviet] Maritime Province and Amur Province, but now he doubted very much their ability to do so. In this connection, he mentioned their [the Soviet government's] superiority in tanks and their ability to produce many times the number of tanks that the Japanese can produce." The colonel's communication to his superiors in Washington ended with the last tidbit the Soviet attaché had offered him: "the Japanese now have about 300 tanks."[3]

No Soviet ambassador, let alone a Soviet military attaché, would speak on so important a matter to a foreign official except under ver-

[2] U.S. Department of State, *Foreign Relations of the United States. Diplomatic Papers, 1933*, pp. 778-840. (Hereafter referred to as *FR, 1933*.)

[3] *Ibid.*, pp. 770-771.

batim instructions from the highest Kremlin authority. That the conversation took place in Tokyo, that its core was information about Soviet military strength vis-à-vis Japan, and that the Soviet representative gave his American colleague a sample piece of the military intelligence about Japan which might be shared in the future portrays Moscow thinking: Stalin looked forward to Soviet-American collaboration in the Far East.

A momentous event had occurred across the Soviet Union's Far Eastern border. The Japanese military, seeing that China was weak, decided to occupy Shanghai and other areas in southern and central China, and, most important, Manchuria. The campaign in Manchuria commenced on September 19, 1931. By the beginning of 1932 all of the region's coal, iron, timber, and industries were under Japanese control. On March 1, 1932, Japan officially unveiled the "independent state" of Manchukuo with Chinese "Emperor" Henry Pu'yi as her Manchurian puppet. When, on January 12, 1932, the Soviet Ambassador in Tokyo, Alexander A. Troyanovsky, proposed a nonaggression pact to the Japanese government, his overtures were repulsed. Japan did not dispute Russian ownership of the Chinese Eastern Railway, but in all other respects Manchuria (Manchukuo) had become a satellite state. (China, reacting to this loss, restored diplomatic relations with Russia on December 12, 1932.)

The Kremlin wondered whether the birth of Manchukuo would usher in a second Japanese intervention in Siberia. U.S. recognition of the U.S.S.R. assumed paramount importance to Stalin; only America could give Japan pause.

Until Roosevelt's election as President recognition was precluded. On March 3, 1933, the last day of the Hoover Administration, Acting Secretary of State W. R. Castle, Jr., saw fit to expound once again the Hoover-Stimson hostility to relations with Moscow. Castle's letter, a reply to an inquiry by Fred L. Eberhardt, president of Gould and Eberhardt, manufacturers of machine tools, said, "this government has taken the position that it would be unwise to enter into relations with the Soviet regime so long as the present rulers of Russia persist in aims and practices in the field of international relations that are inconsistent with international friendship." Secretary Castle added that no real or lasting benefit to the American people would be "attained by the establishment of relations with Russia until the present rulers of that country have given evidence that they are prepared to carry out in good faith the international obligations which experience has demonstrated are essential to the development of friendly intercourse and commerce between nations."[4]

When a government refuses to come to grips with reality it feels free

[4] *FR, 1933*, pp. 780-782.

to indulge in generalities about morality. The reality was Japanese expansion. Roosevelt saw the connection between Japan's forward drive and relations with Russia, and even before he entered the White House he had cleared his mind of Hoover-Stimson-Castle cobwebs and decided to recognize the Soviet government.

On January 11, 1933, James A. Farley, Democratic Party leader, gave a dinner in his New York home in honor of Roosevelt. The President-elect said most Filipinos wanted independence but "The Philippines must have security against Japan. After extending herself in China, Japan will be casting her eyes about for new fields of conquest. It is likely she will move southward and try to extend her possessions along a chain of islands as far as Australia. Japan will give a lot of concern to the world generally within the next ten years."[5]

A statesman does not have to be a prophet. If he is, all the better. His duty consists in discerning dangers and opportunities. Roosevelt was right about Japan; she gave the world a lot of concern in the next twelve and a half years.

As soon as Roosevelt entered the White House the State Department, aware of his inclination to recognize, busied itself supplying the new President with data on the obstacles to recognition. Robert F. Kelley, Chief of the Division of Eastern European Affairs and a passionate enemy of diplomatic relations with Moscow, prepared a memorandum dated July 27, 1933, in which he itemized the Russian debt to the U.S. showing a total of $636,177,226. He raised the problem of communist world revolutionary activity. Most cogently, he contended that "if the questions of repudiated debts and confiscated property are not settled prior to recognition, there is little likelihood that subsequent negotiations would result in a mutually satisfactory settlement."[6]

The new Secretary of State, Cordell Hull, a silver-haired, courtly Southern gentleman and former Senator, also took the position that, since the Soviet authorities "are apparently convinced that recognition by the United States would be a factor in preventing a Japanese attack on the Maritime Provinces" and "open the private banking resources of the United States to the Soviet government," the President should use these "two powerful weapons" to obtain Moscow agreement on "some, if not all, of our outstanding problems with the Soviet government."[7]

The State Department made the President impatient. Franklin D. Roosevelt was a man of towering confidence in his dexterity and destiny. He had been elected to the highest office of the land though his legs were paralyzed and he could not walk, would never walk, and stood

[5] James A. Farley, *Jim Farley's Story. The Roosevelt Years*, p. 34.
[6] *FR, 1933*, pp. 782-788.
[7] *FR, 1933*, pp. 789-790.

only when propped up. He knew his charm and the appeal of his smile and mellifluous voice. He believed in the efficacy of personal confrontation. Robert H. Jackson, Associate Justice of the U.S. Supreme Court, told me that when he was Attorney General he would come to Roosevelt and say he had sufficient evidence to convict a certain company of violating federal antitrust legislation. "Aw, Bob," the President used to reply, "bring them in to me, I'll take care of it." This trust in his power to overcome political difficulties as he had overcome his own physical handicap served him well on innumerable occasions at home and abroad and spelled disaster when he met Stalin during the second world war. But as the State Department littered his desk with memoranda on what to do and what not to do so as to squeeze every advantage out of U.S. recognition of Russia, he yearned for a man-to-man discussion to settle everything without a lengthy exchange of lengthy notes. "If I could only, myself, talk to one man representing the Russians," he told Henry Morgenthau, Jr., later Secretary of the Treasury, "I could straighten out the whole question."[8]

After outlining the nonrecognition policy of the three Republican administrations which succeeded Woodrow Wilson—those of Warren G. Harding, Calvin Coolidge, and Herbert C. Hoover—George F. Kennan, former U.S. Ambassador to the Soviet Union, writes, "F.D.R., of course, was a bird of a different feather. He had as little interest in collecting debts from Russia as he did in Soviet propaganda or in the theory of the Soviet outlook on international affairs. He therefore promptly yielded the United States position on both issues, the valid one and the dubious one alike, and conceded to Moscow the recognition it sought without obtaining satisfaction on either count."[9]

Roosevelt was shrewd and lucky. He knew that if the State Department were permitted to discuss the conditions of recognition it would take years and perhaps never achieve his goal. He accordingly addressed a telegram on October 10, 1933, to President Mikhail I. Kalinin of the Soviet Union drawing attention to the anomalous absence of relations between "the hundred and twenty-five million people of the United States and the hundred and sixty million people of Russia" and, while mentioning the difficulties, added that they can be removed "only by frank, friendly conversations." These were to be conducted "with me personally" if Kalinin would send "a representative to Washington."[10] Thus F.D.R. bypassed the State Department. Secretary Hull was leaving

[8] Quoted by Beatrice Farnsworth, *William C. Bullitt and the Soviet Union,* pp. 91-92. This is a valuable book on U.S. recognition and the early history of Soviet-American relations.

[9] George F. Kennan, *Russia and the West under Lenin and Stalin,* p. 207.

[10] *FR, 1933,* pp. 794-795.

for Montevideo on November 5 to attend a Pan-American conference. Kalinin responded affirmatively on October 17, and Foreign Commissar Maxim M. Litvinov arrived in Washington on November 7, the sixteenth anniversary of the Bolshevik revolution.

In the interval between Kalinin's acceptance and Litvinov's appearance, Japan reacted. Koki Hirota, the Japanese Foreign Minister, had a way of saying several contradictory things in the same paragraph. Referring to Litvinov's impending arrival in the U.S. capital, he told the press, "It is doubtful whether the matter will develop into American recognition of the Soviet Union." In the next sentence, he said, ". . . if those two countries continue in favorable relations for years to come, they will teach a lesson to the world that capitalism and communism can agree. . . . And if that is realized, it will be unnecessary for Japan to fear communism." Finally he asserted, "If there is a man who observes that the possible American-Soviet agreement means pressure on Japan's position in the Far East, he knows nothing of the Far Eastern situation." In telegraphing the text of Hirota's interview, Ambassador Grew informed Hull that newspaper dispatches to Japanese newspapers from Paris and Berlin reported editorial opinion in those two capitals as seeing Roosevelt's invitation to Litvinov in anti-Japanese terms.[11]

A Grew-to-Hull telegram the next day, October 24, described a subtle Nipponese move: a Japanese Foreign Office official intimated indirectly to Grew that U.S. recognition of Russia would give the Japanese military the impression that the United States, England, Russia, and China were combining against Japan. Hirota would then encounter greater obstacles in cutting the military budget and curbing expansionist actions by the army and navy.[12] Hirota wished the U.S. government to know he believed recognition might unleash the military. He was offering the State Department, free of charge, an argument to dissuade F.D.R.

Nothing could dissuade Roosevelt, not even Maxim Litvinov. The Commissar would have preferred recognition before negotiation; a sixteen-year-old government was entitled to be recognized. But the President had his public and his bureaucracy to consider. He wrestled with the Commissar about debts, and they finally entered into what both, in a document dated November 15, 1933, called a "gentlemen's agreement" which "eliminated" all claims of the U.S. government and of U.S. citizens, and of the U.S.S.R. and its nationals, except that "the Soviet government will pay to the Government of the United States on account of the Kerensky debt or otherwise a sum of not less than $75,000,000 in the form of a percentage above the ordinary rate of interest on a loan to be

[11] *FR, 1933,* pp. 796-797.
[12] *FR, 1933,* pp. 797-798.

granted to it by the Government of the United States or its nationals."[13]

The next day the President informed Litvinov that the U.S. government had decided to establish diplomatic relations and exchange ambassadors with the Soviet government. Litvinov acquiesced.[14]

One day later eleven agreed documents on U.S.-U.S.S.R. relations were given the press, but the gentlemen's agreement was kept secret and remained secret for years. It became an apple of discord between Litvinov and William C. Bullitt, the first U.S. ambassador to Moscow who was present, together with Acting Secretary of the Treasury Morgenthau, when the two gentlemen accepted it. Roosevelt, according to James A. Farley, told a subsequent Cabinet meeting that he expected the gentlemen's agreement to result in the collection of $150 million. This was a misreading of Soviet mentality. To anybody in the Kremlin "not less than $75,000,000" meant not more than $75 million. Why pay more when you can pay less—unless the Soviets obtained very large loans in the United States. For the gentlemen's agreement provided that if Russia received a loan she would pay more than the current rate of interest, say 9 percent instead of 6 percent, and the difference, or 3 percent, would go to repay the $75 million. However, it would take a considerable loan to create a fund of $75 million out of the 3 percent surcharge. But when the time came for concrete talks in Moscow Ambassador Bullitt argued that in America commercial credits and loans were synonymous and that a loan was never intended.[15] Litvinov, accustomed to Kremlin casuistry, recognized Bullitt's.

Apart from its vagueness the gentlemen's agreement was unfortunate in another respect: of all Russia's debts the Soviets were asked to pay, the Kerensky debt was the most obnoxious, because it was negotiated to finance the first world war, which Bolsheviks regarded as imperialist and predatory. Indeed, Litvinov had told Roosevelt that most of the Kerensky loan bought equipment in America for the army of Admiral Kolchak, chief of Bolshevism's domestic enemies. And how could Moscow pay for guns which shot down its own Red Army soldiers? This is probably the main reason why Litvinov did not want the gentlemen's agreement published. Roosevelt too saw the wisdom of secrecy because he realized how many persons and purses would be hurt by his cancellation of all U.S. claims except the Kerensky debt to the U.S. government. Moreover, cancellation of debts set a costly precedent. Finally, the manner in which the gentlemen's agreement suggested that a sum "between $75,000,000 and $150,000,000" might be extracted from Moscow

[13] *FR, 1933,* p. 804.
[14] *FR, 1933,* p. 805.
[15] Farnsworth, Note, p. 211.

would have struck many as frivolous, if not ludicrous.

Unlike Coolidge, who believed debts were debts and had to be paid, Roosevelt the patrician was more interested in politics than in money. The time for recognition had arrived and he did not propose to let dollars bar the way.

No loan was ever granted, no debt was ever paid.

In consideration of his constituency, the American voting public, Roosevelt took up another matter with Litvinov: the rights of Americans temporarily or permanently residing in Soviet Russia to "enjoy in all respects the same freedom of conscience and religious liberty which they enjoy at home." Religious liberty was defined by Roosevelt in a letter to Litvinov as embracing baptism, confirmation, communion, marriage, burial, and of course worship. But "freedom of conscience"? Suppose an American resident of the U.S.S.R. followed the dictates of his conscience and went out into a street to condemn Stalin's dictatorship? Litvinov had no objection; he quoted chapter and verse from the Soviet Constitution to show that everybody in the Soviet Union, citizen and foreigner, enjoyed religious liberty and freedom of conscience. Diplomacy, when diplomats wish, ignores facts. Pursuant to the F.D.R.-Litvinov agreement Americans in Moscow had their own church and usually the services of a clergyman.

Most important for a considerable segment of the American public and for Bullitt's fate was the issue of communist propaganda. The eleven documents given the press on November 16, 1933, included a letter from Litvinov to the President undertaking, on behalf of the Soviet government, "to refrain from interfering in any manner in the internal affairs of the United States, its territories or possessions." And more explicitly, "Not to permit the formation or residence on its territory of any organization or group—and to prevent the activity on its territory of any organization or group, or of representatives or officials of any organization or group—which has as an aim the overthrow or the preparation of the overthrow of, or the bringing about by force of a change in, the political or social order of the whole or any part of the United States, its territories or possessions."[16]

Bullitt helped phrase this pledge and it helped end his career in the Soviet Union.

The European press, especially that of Britain, Germany, and France, saw U.S. recognition as a new factor in the unstable Far Eastern situation and noted that Troyanovsky would be the first Soviet Ambassador in Washington. The Japanese press, on the other hand, tried to minimize

[16] *FR, 1933,* pp. 805-806.

the probable effect on Far Eastern developments of the Roosevelt-Litvinov agreements.

When news of U.S. recognition reached Stalin he issued a characteristically cryptic order in two words which went out to all editors, party leaders, and government offices: "Nye Raskhlyabatsya," which may be translated, "Don't slip into high gear." He himself was pleased; he demonstrated it later. He knew others would be highly pleased. But Russia was a great power and she had to behave with dignity when another great power recognized her after so many years. *Izvestia* in its issue of November 20 demonstrated how this should be done editorially, and in the process displayed the customary mixed proud-Russian-Marxist approach: The United States had believed that because it was so strong and vast "it could manage to get along without the establishment of normal relations with the U.S.S.R." But this was "purely imaginary." In the current world crisis "not even the strongest capitalist power can solve its economic problems in isolation." The remarkable expansion of the Soviet Union's productive powers had "compelled" the most stubborn representatives of capitalism to wonder whether they could prosper without the Soviet market. (Actually, the Soviet market had been open to U.S. firms and Roosevelt was under little pressure from businessmen to establish diplomatic relations with Moscow. But "compelled" and "compulsion" by objective circumstances are key words in the communist lexicon.)

Izvestia stated furthermore that "the U.S.S.R. is not only a great European, but also a great Asiatic power." As a Pacific power, the U.S. is a partner with the U.S.S.R. in maintaining peace in Asia. "The United States could not continue its former policy of a refusal to establish normal relations with the U.S.S.R. without causing the greatest injury to itself and to the cause of peace."

Soviet partnership with America against Japan was Stalin's hope. It can scarcely have been Roosevelt's intention. He recognized Russia because he was at the beginning of a long tenure in the White House and thought it a proper and easy thing to do. Moscow, however, could never accept such an uncomplicated explanation. Stalin expected a loan, more business, and partnership in the Far East. Roosevelt would not fulfill these hopes. Bullitt's mission to Moscow was consequently ruined in advance. Whatever the objective circumstances failed to ruin, his personality did.

It is noteworthy that on November 20, 1933, when the fiercely anticommunist regime of Adolf Hitler had been in office for more than nine months, the long *Izvestia* editorial discussed U.S. recognition without any mention of or allusion to the new situation in Germany.

Maxim Litvinov "was clearly more disturbed by the prospect of trouble between the Soviet Union and Japan than between the Soviet Union and Germany, if only because, as he remarked, the Soviet Union had no common frontier with Germany," William Strang of the British Embassy in Moscow wrote in a report to Sir John Simon about his interview with the Foreign Commissar on September 25, 1933. Germany's foreign policy, Litvinov told Strang, "spoke with two voices," one the mollifying voice of the Foreign Ministry, the other of the eastern expansionists. Litvinov also said he could only wish that relations with Great Britain might acquire the stability which had always characterized, for example, Soviet relations with Italy. No doubt Litvinov hugely enjoyed the comparison of Moscow's unsatisfactory ties with democratic England and good relations with fascist Italy. But the Commissar's emphasis throughout the talk with Mr. Strang was on Japan. "The Germans were arming and would continue to arm," he stressed. Irrespective, however, of Germany's actions, Japan would refuse to limit her armaments. "How," he asked, "could the Soviet Union disarm so long as an aggressive neighbor like Japan remained free to arm herself as she pleased?"[17] (Copies of Strang's letter were sent to the King, the Cabinet, and the Dominions.)

Fear of Japan as well as of Germany, and the low ebb of relations with England, affected Soviet domestic affairs in the 1930's. The need to arm meant emphasis on heavy industry and hence a lowering of the standard of living, except that of the upper class. This, and tensions abroad, intensified terror at home.

Soviet foreign policy was influenced by domestic conditions and influenced domestic policy.

XXI KIROV, GORKY, AND STALIN

Stalin, the revolutionist, was a genius of gradualism. Slowly, brick by brick, just as he had built up his power in the communist party, he began to build his popularity with the population which did not know him as it had known Lenin and Trotsky. This early phase of the "cult of personality" assumed the relatively innocent form of "thickly smeared

[17] Foreign Office Archives N7400/748/38/. Copy supplied by the Public Record Office, London.

praise, fawning adulation, and tasteless obeisance," as I described it in an article sent from Moscow to the *Nation* (New York) of August 13, 1930. "I have gone back over the newspapers from 1919 to 1922; Lenin never permitted such antics . . . it is as un-Bolshevik as it is politically unwise. . . . He could stop it by pressing a button." But these extravagant odes to his person evidently answered some deep need of Stalin's sick psychology. He pressed a different button. On November 7, 1922, the fifth anniversary of the revolution, when Lenin was still alive, *Pravda* mentioned Lenin twelve times, Trotsky four times, Stalin not once. On November 7, 1937, *Pravda* mentioned Stalin eighty-eight times, Lenin fifty-four times, "Stalinist" fifteen times, Trotsky not once.

Marshal Voroshilov, Commissar of Defense, gave a party at his home on the evening of November 9, 1932. Stalin and his young wife, Nadiezhda Alliluyeva—she thirty-one, he fifty-three—attended. So did many Kremlin leaders and their wives. It was the period of horror and hunger in Russia's villages and privations and pressures in the cities. Stalin had not said a word in public since June 23, 1931; when things were bad he remained silent. At the annual celebration of the revolution in the Bolshoi Opera House on November 6, 1932, he was expected to speak but did not. Voroshilov received more applause on that occasion than Stalin, who sat on the stage in black gloom.

Seventy-two hours later they gathered at Voroshilov's. Stalin's wife knew more about the people's suffering than her Kremlin-tower husband and felt it keenly. During the evening someone alluded to the Five Year Plan and collectivization, and Nadiezhda voiced her pain. Stalin, who had once cursed Lenin's wife over the telephone (Lenin broke off personal relations with him as a result), was no more tender toward his own wife that evening. They quarreled openly at the party and continued the quarrel at home.

The next morning rumors ran through Moscow that Nadiezhda was dead, and indeed, an official bulletin stated that she had succumbed during an operation. But a Foreign Commissariat diplomat, pledging me to protracted secrecy, said she had committed suicide or been shot by Stalin. "In either case," he asserted, "it was murder. Now," he added, "everything will be black."

Stalin grew more morose, more cruel, more suspicious, more unloved, more paranoic. He saw enemies assailing him from all sides at home and assailing the country from all sides abroad. In a lengthy report delivered on January 7, 1933, to the Unified Plenary Session of the Central Committee and Central Control Committee Stalin dilated on the successes of the Five Year Plan and of agrarian collectivization, yet warned of internal and foreign foes. Some comrades, he said, interpreted the theory of a classless society and the withering away of the state "as a justification of laziness and complacency, as justification of the counterrevolutionary idea of the extinction of the class struggle and the weakening of the government's power." Such hypocrites should be driven from the communist party. "The withering away of the state will come not by weakening the state's power but through its maximum reinforcement which is necessary finally to exterminate the dying classes and to organize the defense against the capitalist encirclement which is still far from being destroyed and will not soon be destroyed."[1]

The advantage of dialectics is that in the mouth of the unscrupulous it turns dictatorship into democracy and the withering away of the state into a withering state terror of unprecedented proportions. This is not to say, however, that Stalin's statement about the "capitalist encirclement" of the Soviet Union lacked foundation. He exaggerated, he did not invent. Eiji Amau, the Japanese chargé d'affaires in Moscow, obeying instructions from Tokyo, told Leo Karakhan on December 11, 1932, "The Japanese government is responsible for maintaining order in Manchukuo."[2] This tore the transparent mask from the regime in Manchuria; Japan stood fully armed on Siberia's frontier. Stalin had no evidence that the Japanese intended to go to war with Russia; in fact everything pointed to their prolonged preoccupation with China. Yet the new Manchurian situation made the Kremlin uncomfortable.

Stalin feared a simultaneous Japanese-Polish attack. Karl Radek, Lenin's adviser on European affairs, who had been exiled as a Trotskyite but, in common with other opportunists, recanted and returned to serve the Kremlin, was advising Stalin on world affairs and writing in the Soviet press on international politics. He told me of Stalin's fears. In part his apprehensions were a reaction to reality, in part they sprang from his paranoia, in part they reflected Russian national megalomania. One reason for the communist complex of Soviet encirclement was the conviction that the U.S.S.R. was the navel of the universe. "It does not require special perspicacity or knowledge of internal affairs to know that relations with the U.S.S.R. did not play the least important role in the negotiations which have taken place in London and Paris, or in the subsequent conferences of representatives of the capitalist world," wrote *Izvestia* on July 29, 1931. "The U.S.S.R., thanks to its size, its social structure, and the rate of its development is a tremendous force. Therefore, whenever the capitalist powers undertake to regulate their mutual affairs, they cannot ignore the question of relations with the Soviet Union."

If Soviet Russia was the center of the world, she was easily encircled. But Tokyo scoffed at the idea of a Japanese-Soviet war. According to

[1] J. V. Stalin, *Sochinenia*, Vol. 13, pp. 210-211.

[2] Jane Degras, *Soviet Documents on Foreign Policy*, Vol. II, p. 548.

a dispatch from Tokyo to the *New York Times* of December 29, 1933, the Soviet forces in eastern Siberia far outnumbered Japan's in Manchuria and were superior in fighting quality to the tsarist army. This, and Japanese long-term involvement in China, guaranteed Soviet security. Stalin misread Tokyo's intentions. But even with better political literacy he could not have been sure which way Japan would march.

Uncertain weather in the East coincided with mist in the West. Adolf Hitler was the ominous new factor in the West. But for a long time Stalin gave no indication that he thought so. Hitler's totalitarianism did not repel the leader of an older totalitarianism. Nor did Nazism. "Certainly we are far from being enthusiastic about the fascist regime in Germany," Stalin declared in his report to the Seventeenth Congress of the Soviet Communist Party on January 26, 1934. "But the point here is not fascism, if only because fascism in Italy, for instance, did not prevent the U.S.S.R. from establishing excellent relations with that country."[3]

For Stalin the only question was whether Germany intended to do political, military, and commercial business with Russia. The signs were negative. The final doubt-dispelling blow came two months after Stalin addressed the Seventeenth Party Congress. A five-year Soviet contract with Krupp for the training of technicians and the sale of complicated machinery and special steels had remained in force. But in March, 1934, Krupp's representatives arrived in Moscow to cancel the agreement. Sergo Orjonekidze, member of the Politburo and Commissar for Heavy Industry, instructed the Soviet negotiators to offer every inducement for the retention of the contract: Moscow would place additional orders with the firm, compensate it for the loss in the value of the dollar (all payments were made in U.S. currency), et cetera. "We need so much of everything," Sergo exclaimed. But the Krupp men could not be budged. "Special circumstances compel us to do this," they stated.[4] The special circumstances were Hitler's hostility.

For a full year, while liberals, democrats, socialists, progressives the world over roared in horror against Hitler's regime, Moscow was silent. Many of my Soviet communist friends, some in high places, privately condemned the Kremlin's veto on the expression of anti-Nazism in print. To the foreigner they said "Wait, it will come." It came only after Stalin abandoned hope of establishing "excellent relations" with Nazi Germany.

When I asked Radek whether Stalin was reading Hitler's speeches, he

[3] Stalin, Vol. 13, p. 302.

[4] V. Yemelyanov, Member-Correspondent of the Soviet Academy of Science and one of the negotiators, tells the story in the Moscow monthly *Novy Mir* of January, 1967.

replied, "Yes, we translate all Hitler's speeches for him, and I know he reads our translations. He has also read translated excerpts from *Mein Kampf.*" But words never impressed Stalin. Hitler's *Mein Kampf,* the Book of Hate by the Great Hater, seemed like the ravings of a prisoner, age thirty-five, whose mad push for power in a Munich beer saloon had fizzled. Subsequently, however, Stalin learned to respect Hitler, indeed in one major domestic policy to imitate him and to take *Mein Kampf* seriously.

Hitler, born in Austria near the German frontier, abominated his native land and in particular Vienna: "I was repelled by the conglomeration of races which the capital showed me, repelled by this whole mixture of Czechs, Poles, Hungarians, Ruthenians, Serbs, Croats, and everywhere, the eternal mushroom of humanity—Jews and more Jews." The future was Germany's, and Germany's future was in Russia. He opposed the acquisition of colonies in Africa or elsewhere. "For Germany, consequently, the only possibility for carrying out a healthy territorial policy lay in the acquisition of new land in Europe itself. . . . If land was desired in Europe it could be obtained by and large only at the expense of Russia, and this meant that the new Reich must again set itself on the march along the road of the Teutonic Knights of old, to obtain by the German sword sod for the German plow and daily bread for the nation." This presupposed England's acquiescence. To obtain it Germany should be ready to renounce world trade, colonies, and a fleet for "concentration of all the state's instruments of power on the land army."

Marxism was Jewish, Bolshevism Jewish, and, Hitler continued, "the Bolshevistic present is embodied in a cubistic monstrosity." The Jew obsessed him; the Jew aimed to subjugate. "The most frightful example of this kind is offered by Russia where he killed or starved about thirty million people with positively fanatical savagery, in part amid inhuman tortures, in order to give a gang of Jewish journalists and stock exchange bandits domination over a great people."

France constituted a "menace. . . . *In the predictable future there can be only two allies for Germany in Europe: England and Italy.*" But toward the end of this erratic volume he came back to Russia: "If we speak of soil in Europe today, we can primarily have in mind only *Russia* and her vassal border states." (Hitler's emphasis.)

Nine years after he penned this prison prose the author, having become Nazi dictator, turned Germany's back on cooperation with the Soviet Union and gave free rein to rearmament. On October 12, 1933, German Foreign Minister Baron Konstantine von Neurath announced that Germany would no longer participate in the disarmament conference in Geneva, and exactly one week later Germany withdrew from the League of Nations. (Japan had left the League on March 28, 1933.)

Japan's encroachments in China to the very gate of Siberia and Moscow's delayed recognition of the Nazi German threat produced changes within the Soviet Union which had repercussions on her foreign policies. The year 1934 was the hinge year in Soviet history, but the hinge was a free hinge and the door might have swung toward relaxation or increased terror. Stalin's psychology pushed him in the direction of bestial totalitarianism, yet he saw the value of winning popular support by experimenting with a milder course.

Stalin did not become the despot dictator the moment Lenin died. He climbed to the peak of the Soviet power pyramid over innumerable obstacles. One of the greatest was the secret police. "Two years ago," I wrote in the *Nation* of August 9, 1933, "Akulov was appointed Vice-President of the GPU. As such he superseded Yagoda, the active head of the organization, and became chief of the institution. Apparently, however, friction developed between Akulov and the permanent officials, and before long the newcomer with a penchant for reform was sent to a rather inferior post in the Donets coal basin." Stalin had been defeated. Characteristically he waited and tried again. "Akulov, an old Bolshevik and former associate of Lenin," I wrote in the same article, "has been appointed Attorney General of the Soviet Union. This is a new office. . . . The most surprising of Akulov's functions is his right to watch over the activities of the GPU." I knew Soviet citizens who were arrested by Yagoda and liberated by Akulov. In the latter half of 1933 and throughout 1934 the country witnessed a perceptible easing of the atmosphere. For the first time under Bolshevism the secret police could not, without consulting higher authority, arrest an important engineer or a Red Army officer. In January, 1934, some of the judicial functions of the GPU were transferred to the courts and the GPU was renamed the People's Commissariat of Internal Affairs, or NKVD. For six months, however, the Commissariat remained without a Commissar, a condition without precedent; Stalin was resisting the appointment of Yagoda. In the end, in July, 1934, Yagoda became Commissar. He had won again.

Curbing the secret police brought a little relief to a population sorely tried by seventeen years of hardship under communism, but it did not suffice to unite the nation. And national unity is what Stalin needed most in the face of the possibility of war. Here he took a page out of Hitler's book. Dictators learn from one another. The Italian Embassy in Moscow had instructions from Mussolini to send him all data showing how Stalin ruled. In 1933 and 1934 Stalin saw that Hitler had whipped the German people into a frenzied nationalistic unity by haranguing them endlessly, hysterically, about foreign and domestic enemies. In the Soviet Union, on the contrary, the effect of Bolshevism had been divisive; it set class against class and the party against the nonparty majority; it preached autonomy for national minorities who constituted nearly half the country's population. Though communism centralized power it decentralized the nation. There was no Soviet nationalism or Russian nationalism—except in what the government did, and this was never admitted. The original internationalism of Marxist dogma had been robbed of reality by the resistance of other countries to revolution, and nothing inside Russia had taken its place. The Soviet Union consequently was an emotional vacuum enlarged by fatigue and flabby apathy and filled by occasional flashes of enthusiasm for construction under the Five Year Plan.

Stalin accordingly decided to give the nation nationalism. An official U.S. report on the wartime Tehran Conference in December, 1943, contains this memorandum on Stalin's views: "He did not share the view of the President [Roosevelt] that Hitler was mentally unbalanced and emphasized that only a very able man could have accomplished what Hitler had done in solidifying the German people whatever we thought of the methods."[5] Stalin, beginning in 1934, intended to solidify the Soviet people. Bolshevism-Leninism was a protest against Russia's tsarist past, and tsarist history was therefore taught in Soviet schools with hatred if taught at all. Lenin had popularized the statement, "Tsarist Russia is the prison of nationalities." But the decree of May 16, 1934, changed this. Stalin wanted links with the Russian past. Later he found heroes in it for the new generation: General Alexander V. Suvorov (1730-1800), who suppressed foreign revolutions; Field Marshal Prince Mikhail I. Kutuzov (1745-1813), who fought Napoleon; and Bogdan M. Khmelnitsky (1595-1657), who waged war on Poland and massacred Jews. During the second world war Red Army decorations were named for these three.

Until 1934 Red Army and navy officers were designated by their tasks: Commander of Battalion, Commander of Brigade, and so forth, because titles like lieutenant, captain, major, and especially colonel had a pejorative connotation reminiscent of the class which served the oppressive monarchy. "General" and "Admiral" were not introduced until May, 1940.

Further to fortify the loyalty and esprit de corps of the army and navy officer class Stalin, on May 4, 1935, drank a toast at a Kremlin reception of Red Army commanders to "nonparty Bolsheviks." Theretofore "Bolshevik" meant a communist party member; a nonparty person could not be a Bolshevik no matter what his convictions. The dictator intended to identify the officers with the ruling caste. He succeeded in watering

[5] U.S. Department of State, *Foreign Relations of the United States, Diplomatic Papers, The Conferences at Cairo and Tehran, 1943*, p. 513. Also in Robert E. Sherwood, *Roosevelt and Hopkins, an Intimate History*, p. 782.

down the concept of party member until, at the zenith of Stalinist totalitarianism, the one-party system became a no-party system; the party was a supine instrument in the hands of the despot.

Stalin's greatest innovation in 1934-35 was the decision actively to inculcate nationalism. Suddenly a new word appeared in the Soviet press, a word never used since November 7, 1917: "rodina," or fatherland. Not socialist fatherland but plain fatherland. Poets sang "to our beautiful country." On May 1, 1935, an article by Vasilkovsky said, "There is no more grateful task and no more important political task than to encourage the sacred flame of love of fatherland." Such words were once anathema to communists. David Zaslavsky, often Stalin's echo in *Pravda,* declared that these words "formerly hated by millions, have lost their old meaning. . . . They sound different now." They had been hated by millions because they were part of the vocabulary of Tsarism, the "cake" when there was too little bread and too much bloodshed.

Meanwhile a process had begun which became repressive in the vast regions populated by the non-Russian minorities. For instance, an editorial in *Pravda* January 15, 1937, entitled "The Great Russian People" declared, "We love our fatherland. We love our great, strong, picturesque Russian language. It is becoming an international language." In the early years of the Soviet regime this was unheard of. The Kremlin assiduously taught the national minorities to cultivate their own tongues and dialects. Peoples who had never had a written language were given one by Moscow. The complicated, cursive script of the Moslem ethnic populations of the Soviet East, so conducive to illiteracy, was abolished, and a Latin alphabet substituted, as in Turkey. But now their Latin alphabet—bridge to Turkey and the West—was abolished and the Cyrillic, or Russian, alphabet substituted. Russification, an ugly phenomenon of Tsarism, reared its head.

Stalin was trying to teach the nation patriotism, to rally the non-Russians around the Great Russians who would lead in the event of war. Ethnically a Georgian, Stalin was politically a Great Russian who regarded Great Russians as the Soviet Union's superior race.

The courtship of the people went a step further in 1935 when a commission was selected to draft a new constitution giving the individual larger liberties and eliminating the discrepancy between the votes of peasants and those of urban residents. (The previous constitution gave a worker's ballot five times the weight of a peasant's.) For the first time since 1917 priests were enfranchised. Direct inheritance of wealth was legalized. The draft also contained a resounding bill of rights. Most of the constitution was written by Bukharin, the secretary of the commission who, immediately after the Seventeenth Party Congress, became editor in chief of *Izvestia,* and inaugurated the verbal war on Nazism.

Nothing is easier than to dismiss these measures as a ruse. To do so would ignore one of the most fascinating situations in Soviet history. It emerged in 1933 and 1934 coincidentally with the rise of Sergei M. Kirov, the communist boss of Leningrad and the Number Two man in Russia.

Kirov, a communist with an impeccable record, was mysteriously assassinated in Leningrad on December 1, 1934, at the age of forty-eight. Kirov's murder was dealt with in Khrushchev's secret speech in the night of February 24-25, 1956, to the Twentieth Communist Party Congress. There is no doubt about the authenticity of the speech. In the summer of 1956 I asked Anastas I. Mikoyan in Moscow why the speech had not been published. "It's too early," he replied, "but hundreds of thousands have read it." The speech, unpublished still, is mentioned in Khrushchev's biography in the *Large Soviet Encyclopedia*.[6]

"It must be asserted," Khrushchev said, "that to this day the circumstances surrounding Kirov's murder hide many things which are inexplicable and mysterious and demand a most careful examination. There are reasons for the suspicion that the killer of Kirov, Nikolaev, was assisted by someone from among the people whose duty it was to protect the person of Kirov.

"A month and a half before the killing, Nikolaev was arrested on the grounds of suspicious behavior, but he was released and not even searched. It is an unusually suspicious circumstance that when the Chekist [secret policeman] assigned to protect Kirov was being brought for an interrogation on December 2, 1934"—a day after the assassination —"he was killed in a car 'accident' in which no other occupant of the car was harmed. After the murder of Kirov, top functionaries of the Leningrad NKVD were given light sentences, but in 1937 they were shot. We can assume that they were shot in order to cover the traces of the organizers of Kirov's killing."[7] Addressing the Twenty-Second Congress of the Soviet Communist Party on October 27, 1961, Khrushchev stated that Leonid V. Nikolaev, the murderer, was arrested "twice" while loitering around the Smolny Institute in Leningrad, headquarters of the communist party; each time a loaded revolver was found in his briefcase. Each time he was released. That he should have been released in these circumstances seems very odd indeed to anybody who knows the Soviet Union. Borisov, the man killed in the auto "accident," was Kirov's orderly and must have been a witness to the assassination in the party boss's office. The car, the driver, and the other occupants of the car in which he met his death belonged to the NKVD. All these matters were

[6] Second edition, Vol. 46, p. 391.

[7] Nikita S. Khrushchev, *The Crimes of the Stalin Era. Special Report to the 20th Congress of the Communist Party of the Soviet Union,* S 22.

known to Stalin; he traveled to Leningrad the day after the assassination to conduct the investigation in person. The top functionaries of the Leningrad NKVD were sent to Kolyma concentration camp. This too, like the car "accident," erased the evidence. Their subsequent execution finally destroyed it. Remembering that Khrushchev's secret speech was directed against Stalin and knowing that the NKVD would not have acted as accomplices in Kirov's murder without orders or intimations from Stalin, Khrushchev's suspicions confirm the view widely accepted in the Soviet Union at the time and since that Stalin wanted Kirov out of the way.

Kirov, a party bureaucrat with more charm than most, became chief of the Leningrad party organization in 1926, replacing Zinoviev, and entered the Politburo in 1930. His star began to rise in 1932 when, at a Politburo meeting, he defied and defeated Stalin who had proposed executing Riutin, a prominent party figure and open critic of Stalin's personality and of his ruthless, expensive policy of collectivization. Kirov maintained that a death sentence for a dissident communist offended the Leninist ethos. A majority in the Politburo upheld him.

At the Seventeenth Party Congress in January-February, 1934, Kirov received an ovation and was elected to the Central Committee and then to the Politburo by the most votes, in contrast to Stalin who received the least votes. It was agreed at the Congress that Kirov would move from Leningrad to Moscow and serve as party secretary by the side of Stalin. Stalin delayed the move on the ground that Kirov remained indispensable to the Leningrad party apparatus. Stalin presumably feared that Kirov might replace him. "Many delegates to the Seventeenth Party Congress," reads *Kratkaya Istoria SSSR*[8] (A Short History of the U.S.S.R.), "especially those who knew Lenin's testament considered that the time had come to transfer Stalin from the post of general secretary [of the party] to some other work." Stalin's sensitive antennae and spies would have carried this information to his suspicious brain. He took revenge on the Seventeenth Congress. Of its 1,966 delegates, 1,108 were subsequently "destroyed," according to an article in *Pravda* of February 7, 1964; of the 139 members and deputy members of the Central Committee elected by that Congress, 98 were "ruined." "Stalin," the article states, "cleared the path for the further reinforcement of the cult of his personality." "Cult of personality" is a socialist-realist synonym for the unbridled terror conducted by Stalin from the death of Kirov to his own death with disastrous effects on Soviet foreign relations.

Light is thrown on the Stalin-Kirov relationship by the *Letter of an Old Bolshevik,* first published in the Russian-language Menshevik

[8] Part Two, p. 270.

journal, *Sotzialistichesky Vestnik* (Socialist Courier) of December, 1936, and January, 1937.[9] The title was a disguise; the "letter" was not a letter but the notes made by Boris I. Nicolaevsky, a Russian Menshevik and the best authority on Soviet domestic politics in the western world, after his talks in Paris in the spring of 1936 with Bukharin, who had come to see him ostensibly to purchase Nicolaevsky's invaluable Karl Marx archives but in fact to pour out his heart and "write" a kind of political testament. The "letter" was subsequently printed in a book by Nicolaevsky,[10] thus establishing the authorship.

"In the winter of 1933-34," Bukharin told Nicolaevsky, "Kirov had so strengthened his position that he could afford to follow his own line. He aimed not only at a 'Western orientation' in foreign policy but also at the conclusions which would follow logically from this new orientation as far as home policy was concerned." Bukharin said, "It was clear that a new orientation in the direction of the democratic parties of Western Europe"—the Popular Front—"would inevitably lead to considerable changes in the *internal policy* of the Soviet Union. It was at this time that Kirov began to gain great influence." However, the "Western orientation" met with considerable resistance: "It was not easy to overcome the old, deeply rooted orientation for an alliance with Germany, even with a reactionary Germany."

"There were two alternatives," Bukharin explained. "To pursue the former policy of crushing all dissenters, with the administrative pressure ruthlessly tightened and the terror intensified, or to try 'reconciliation with the people,' to gain their voluntary cooperation in the political preparation for the coming war. The most convinced and most prominent advocates of the *second alternative* were Kirov and Gorky."

Maxim Gorky, the popular Russian author, friend of Lenin, courted by Lenin, had left the Soviet Union in anger because of the persecution of intellectuals, but began to return for visits in the late 1920's and settled in Moscow in 1933. Stalin wooed him. Gorky wrote long articles in the Soviet press in praise of Stalin and at the same time used his influence to moderate Stalinism, for Gorky, though deeply Russian, deeply appreciated European culture and wished to weave a web between his country and the West. He sided with Kirov. This made a mighty combination, for neither sought to depose Stalin, that would have been impracticable in 1933 and 1934; the objective was to mold Stalin's mind. One of the fruits of their labors was Soviet entry into the League of Nations on September 18, 1934. Stalin, in an interview he

[9] In English, *Letter of an Old Bolshevik. The Key to the Moscow Trials,* Rand School Pamphlet, 1937.

[10] Boris I. Nicolaevsky, *Power and the Soviet Elite. "The Letter of an Old Bolshevik" and Other Essays.*

gave Walter Duranty of the *New York Times* on December 25, 1933, had anticipated this sharp reversal of Soviet policy when he said, "If the League can become a slight obstruction in the path of war and aiding, to some extent, the cause of peace, then we are not opposed to the League." Circumstances favored this development: Japan and Germany had left the League; Nazi Germany was now openly anti-Soviet, and storm warnings—of war—were out all over Europe. Litvinov also favored joining the League; he took pleasure in twisting capitalism's tail at Geneva. Largely through his efforts at several meetings of the League disarmament commission, diplomatic relations were established with Hungary on February 4, 1934, and with Bulgaria on July 23, 1934. Litvinov, the westerner, rejoiced in the Kirov-Gorky line.

* * *

Four scholars set out for Africa to gather material on the elephant. The Englishman returned and wrote a book entitled *Hunting the Elephant in Africa.* The Frenchman authored a book on the love life of the elephant. The German spent four years compiling a two-volume opus called *An Introduction to a Study of the Evolution of the African Pachyderm.* The Pole wrote a book entitled *The Elephant and the Polish Question.*

The point of the last quip in this political anecdote was to mock the penchant of Poles to relate all matters to the painful problem of their country wedged between the two mammoths: Germany and Russia. Yet the fact is that from 1931 to 1939 Poland did occupy a central position on the European stage. On July 24, 1931, U.S. Secretary of State Henry L. Stimson talked in Paris with Premier Pierre Laval. In his report to the President, Stimson wrote: "We discussed the Franco-German situation first of all. . . . He . . . told me of his talks with [Chancellor] Bruening [of Germany]. The underlying problem which could solve everything else was the question of the Polish corridor. If that could be solved France would have no other real trouble with Germany."[11] The rising frenzy of nationalism, which swept Hitler into power on January 30, 1933, gave many discerning persons in all countries the uncomfortable feeling of impending war. The Poles, knowing Hitler's hostility to the Versailles peace treaty system that transferred considerable German territory to Poland, were so deeply alarmed that Marshal Joseph Pilsudski, the Polish leader, decided to act even before Hitler became Chancellor of the Reich.

The ice in Soviet-Polish relations following the 1920 war and the assassination of a Russian ambassador in Warsaw quickly melted, and

[11] U.S. Department of State, *Papers Relating to the Foreign Relations of the United States, 1931,* Vol. I, p. 549.

on July 25, 1932, the two governments signed a nonaggression treaty; it was ratified on December 25, 1932. While Poland thus formally secured her eastern frontier with a paper rampart, the Kremlin secured Russia's western frontier. This rounded out the Soviet diplomatic offensive which had already achieved a nonaggression treaty with Finland on January 21, 1932, with Latvia on February 5, 1932, and with Estonia on May 4, 1932.

Pilsudski was a resolute man of action. He knew Germany would rearm fast, but believed that in 1932 the Polish army was stronger than the Reichswehr. The Marshal therefore intended to launch a preventive war against Germany. For this purpose he needed French support and the assurance that Russia would not take advantage of Poland's position and stab her in the back. He accordingly sent Count George Potocki, a senator, to Paris early in 1933 and Colonel Boguslav Miedzinski, editor of the *Gazeta Polska*, a member of Parliament, and at one time chief of the Polish Intelligence service and president of the Senate, to Moscow in April, 1933. Count Potocki was to inform the French General Staff on the speed of German rearmament and to interview political leaders; he saw, among others, Foreign Minister Joseph Paul-Boncour.[12] He made little impression. In March, 1933, Pilsudski sent his friend, M. Vieniawa-Dlugoszowski, on a similar mission to Paris. Premier Daladier and Paul-Boncour told him in so many words, "Nous ne marcherons pas." "This," says Colonel Miedzinski, "was the situation when I arrived in Moscow." In April, 1933, Pilsudski ordered the Polish army to occupy the Westerplatte, a peninsula in the harbor of the free city of Danzig. He made other preparations for war in the expectation, one must assume, that only Polish military action, not words, would precipitate French participation in the invasion of Germany.

Meanwhile in Moscow, Miedzinski held talks with Karl Radek. To Radek and to several Soviet newspaper editors and high Foreign Commissariat officials who came to a dinner, Miedzinski said, "Poland will never join with Germany against the Soviet Union."

"How many Poles think as you do?" Radek asked.

"Many. But perhaps it's enough that Pilsudski does," Miedzinski replied.

"Oh, yes," Radek agreed, "that's enough."

"If we cooperated with the Nazis," Miedzinski explained, "it would be the end of us." The Germans would stay. On the eve of Miedzinski's departure for Moscow Pilsudski had revealed his thoughts to his emis-

[12] Ministère des Affaires Etrangères. Commission de Publication des Documents Relatifs aux Origines de la Guerre 1939-1945, *Documents Diplomatiques Français 1932-1939*, Ire Serie (1932-1935), Tome II (15 Novembre 1932-17 Mars 1933), p. 451.

sary: Russia was menaced by Japan in the Far East; Stalin was not yet "strong in the saddle"; Ukrainian nationalism gave the Kremlin much concern; therefore Stalin should facilitate Polish action against Germany by keeping hands off Poland.[13]

Stalin would have welcomed Polish preoccupation with Germany; it deflected Pilsudski from Russia and lessened the Soviet dictator's fear of a Japanese-Polish attack on the U.S.S.R. Radek was accordingly commissioned by Stalin to proceed to Warsaw in May, 1933, and continue the talks begun by Miedzinski. Radek raised a central question: "What if the Poles are faced with a German ultimatum: either you join us against Russia or we march through and occupy Poland?" Miedzinski conveyed this to Foreign Minister Joseph Beck and Beck conveyed it to Pilsudski. The Marshal answered: "We'll fight." Radek suggested joint general staff discussions. He mentioned the possibility of Soviet oil and armament supplies to Poland in case of war.

Pilsudski's preparations for preventive war did not remain a secret. On May 16, 1933, President Hindenburg left a note for Otto Meissner, chief of the Presidential Chancery, saying "In these days you can of course get in touch with me at any time of the day or night." The octogenarian Chief of State slept a great deal and normally was not to be disturbed. But the times were not normal; Germany expected Polish armed action which might trigger western intervention. The day after Hindenburg wrote the note Hitler delivered a pacifist speech. "No new European war," he declared, "could create better conditions than the unsatisfactory conditions of today. . . . Germany is ready to assume further security obligations of an international character. . . . Germany would be prepared to abolish her entire military establishment."

Tension persisted. Though the big lie was soporific music to western ears, Pilsudski did not desist. In fact Germany's withdrawal from the Geneva disarmament commission alarmed some western politicians and there was a moment of nervousness in Berlin: would the powers take action in concert with Poland? The cloud passed quickly. At a Cabinet Ministers' meeting on October 17, 1933, Hitler reported that "Threatening steps against Germany had neither persisted nor were they to be expected. . . . Germany could now let events take their course. . . . Germany," he added, "was finding herself in the pleasant position of being able to watch how the conflicts between the other powers turned out."[14]

[13] Colonel Miedzinski read to me from ancient notes when we met in London in the summer of 1966 and again in the summer of 1967.

[14] U.S. Department of State, *Documents on German Foreign Policy 1918-1945*, Series C (1933-37): *The Third Reich: First Phase*, Vol. II: *October 14, 1933-June 13, 1934*, pp. 11-12.

This shrewd remark is the key to many secrets of the 1933-1939 period in world affairs.

Poland hesitated to act alone. Berlin made further friendly sounds to Warsaw. Negotiations for a nonaggression pact were begun; it was signed on January 26, 1934. "Germans and Poles," Hitler told the Reichstag on January 30, 1934, "will have to accept the fact of each other's existence."

Moscow seemed stunned by Poland's sudden volte-face from preventive war to hands-across-the-Polish-Corridor. In conversations with Foreign Minister Joseph Beck, Litvinov said the German-Polish agreement was "directed against the U.S.S.R." German hostility to Poland had been the keystone of Soviet military and political collaboration with Berlin for twelve years. If now Hitler gave Pilsudski even a temporary sense of safety along Poland's western boundary she might indeed indulge her old expansionist ambitions once more and strike at Russia simultaneously with Japan.

Neither Poland nor Japan attacked the Soviet Union. The Soviet Union attacked them. But this is hindsight. Stalin had to weigh all contingencies. Nevertheless, a less alarmist view of the evolving world situation might have conduced to a more refined Soviet foreign policy, for Japan was sinking deeper and deeper into the great bog of China and Warsaw paid attention to Hitler's armaments rather than to his "pacifism" which simply meant he was not ready.

Japan was a consuming Soviet obsession. Moscow expected no help from isolationist America. It feared German cooperation with Japan in case of an armed attack. Even German Ambassador Rudolf Nadolny, in a dispatch from Moscow to his Foreign Minister dated January 9, 1934, urged "that the Soviet Government must be convincingly reassured as to our imperialistic intentions in the East and, in particular, as to the intention to take advantage of possible difficulties with Japan to launch attacks on Russian territory or even to support the Japanese against Soviet Russia . . . any conspicuous sympathizing with the Japanese should be avoided for the time being."[15] An ambassador often succumbs to the atmosphere of the capital in which he sojourns.

Presently Stalin took a drastic step: he decided to sell the Chinese Eastern Railway (CER). The line ran through Manchukuo territory under Japan's control. Operations had already been impeded by the Japanese army; managerial controversy could grow into military confrontation. Soviet ownership in these circumstances was of doubtful value. This was not lost on the Japanese who, when Moscow offered

[15] *Ibid.*, pp. 322-323.

them the railway on May 2, 1933, proposed paying a sum which Litvinov called "contemptuous."[16] The Soviet government argued: on July 3, 1933, it informed Manchukuo that Russian expenditures on the railway amounted to 411,691,976 gold rubles, a sum that "does not include 178,529,618 rubles loaned by the former tsarist government to the CER" or "the cost of various CER properties which are in themselves of great economic value. . . . The railroad, as is well known, owns an enormous area of land." Adding all these amounts the Kremlin arrived at a selling price of 210 million gold rubles,[17] or approximately $105 million. But the negotiations, which were an exercise in subtraction, lasted almost two years and ended on March 23, 1935, when Russia sold the Chinese Eastern to Manchukuo for $35 million.[18] In effect Moscow gave away what it no longer had.

By selling the Chinese Eastern Railway Moscow removed its foot from China's closing door and felt that it had thereby appeased Japan. But, with good reason, nobody trusted anybody else; the double-tracking of the Trans-Siberian Railroad was accelerated and, under Bluecher, the Special Far Eastern army was reinforced and mechanized until it became the crack segment of the Soviet armed forces. Stalin could now concentrate more attention on European affairs.

* * *

King Alexander of Yugoslavia and French Foreign Minister Jean-Louis Barthou were assassinated in Marseilles on October 9, 1934. Barthou had tangled with Chicherin at the 1922 Genoa Conference where he was regarded as an enemy of the Soviet regime. Yet the Soviets, after his death, praised him as they would a friend and blamed the assassination variously on Mussolini, Hitler, and Croatian terrorists acting for the first or the latter. A Soviet treaty with France had been under discussion. Barthou, watching Hitler, pressed for its conclusion. His successor, Pierre Laval, was less interested in the pact, but public opinion, divided though it was—embryo fascists had tried to storm the Chamber of Deputies in February, 1934—forced him to sign it on December 5, 1934. Its central purpose was to improve relations between Moscow and Paris and, more to the point, move toward an "Eastern Locarno" which would guarantee the western frontiers of the U.S.S.R. and the frontiers of Russia's neighbors. Czechoslovakia adhered to the Franco-Soviet agreement on December 11, 1934. "Thereby Soviet diplomacy succeeded not only in disrupting the conclusion of an aggressive pact between France,

[16] Dispatch from Moscow by Walter Duranty, *The New York Times*, Dec. 30, 1933.
[17] Degras, Vol. III, pp. 23-28.
[18] Max Beloff, *The Foreign Policy of Soviet Russia, 1929-1941*, Vol. I, p. 173.

Germany, and Poland, but also in taking an important step forward toward European security."[19]

In conformity with the Kremlin's western inclination, the Seventh Congress of the Third International, the first since 1928, sitting in Moscow in July and August, 1935, made history first because this was the International's last congress and because it adopted the policy of the Popular Front, that is, common action by communists in bourgeois countries with social democrats who thereby ceased to be "social fascists," with liberals, and even with conservatives, Catholics, and anybody else who would work with them, obviously not to make a social revolution but to reinforce the efforts of Soviet diplomacy against war. Characteristically zealous, the communists of course tried to control the Popular Front organizations, this was necessary to bend them to Moscow's purpose, but clearly Stalin had now altogether abandoned the idea of fomenting revolution abroad and was determined to win support for the Soviet Union in the West.

U.S. Ambassador Bullitt regarded the Third International's Congress as a personal insult. He felt, rightly, that the presence at the Congress of American communist delegates and their participation in the proceedings violated the pledge Litvinov, on behalf of the Soviet government, had given President Roosevelt: ". . . to prevent the activity on its territory of any organization or group, or of representatives or officials on its territory of any organization or group which has as an aim the overthrow or the preparation of the overthrow of, or the bringing about by force of a change in, the political or social order" of the United States. Taken literally, Bullitt was justified in protesting. But the American Communist Party had not the minutest chance of overthrowing the United States government or changing the social order by force, and a politically minded ambassador would have welcomed rather than resented a Congress that adopted the policy of Popular Front which bore a promise of better relations with the West and which was antirevolutionary in intent and result.

Bullitt, however, had been disappointed in his mission to Moscow. He, as an old champion of good relations with the Soviets, had received a hearty reception from the Kremlin; Stalin himself attended a dinner in Voroshilov's apartment in honor of Bullitt at which President Kalinin, Molotov, and Litvinov also were present. But Litvinov disliked Bullitt. He told me several times it would have been better had the United States sent a businessman, a general, or career diplomat instead of an emotional well-wisher. Perhaps the full-blooded Jew from the Russian-Polish ghetto in Byalostok and the rich man's son born in Rittenhouse

[19] A. A. Gromyko and others, *Istoria Diplomatii* (The History of Diplomacy), Vol. III, pp. 604-605.

Square in Philadelphia and psychoanalyzed by Freud were destined to rub one another the wrong way. "F.D.R., John Reed, and I," Bullitt said to me in his residence in Moscow, "belong to the same American strain." On a deeper level the Soviet sale of the Chinese Eastern Railway indicated that Moscow did not expect American support against Japan. Nor had U.S.-U.S.S.R. trade expanded sufficiently to alter policy. Recognition had been weighed in the balance of power and found wanting. Against this background Bullitt's protest about the Third International's Congress was regarded in the Kremlin as petty politics instead of high diplomacy and was rejected on the formal ground that the Soviet government did not control the Third International. The ambassador's conduct thereafter in urging the United States and other countries, especially Poland, through his close colleague the Polish envoy in Moscow, to freeze their relations with the U.S.S.R. made his further presence in the Russian capital impossible; he left in a cloud of hate.

The policy of Popular Front, the Soviets in the League of Nations, the work of a new constitution, the rapprochement with France and Czechoslovakia, the restraint on the secret police were products of Stalin's mind influenced by Kirov, Gorky, and objective facts: a good harvest in 1933, the menace of Hitler, and the end of opposition within the party. In 1933 and 1934 more Trotskyist and other oppositionists recanted and returned from exile to cooperate in the grandiose schemes for the reformation of Soviet society. During March, 1934, former Ambassador Christian G. Rakovsky recanted and accepted a position in the Commissariat of Health. In 1928, when I spent eight days with him at his place of exile, he showed me a telegram from opposition colleagues asking that he join them in repenting. But he said he would never betray Trotsky. In 1934, however, Rakovsky wrote from Baranaul in Siberia, "The differences which separate me from the party lose their significance in view of the growth of international reaction." Hitler had brought him back to Stalin.

Then came the assassination of Kirov. The assassin, Nikolaev, according to Bukharin's statement to Nicolaevsky in Paris, was a "nervous and undisciplined individual" who "frequently spoke quite openly" of his dread intention. It is at least conceivable that the assassination of King Alexander and Barthou on October 9, 1934, prompted him to kill Kirov on December 1, 1934, for like riots and suicides, assassinations, which are equally irrational, may be infectious.

Kirov's assassination unleashed a furious wave of terror; persons long in prison who could have had no connection with the murder were shot as participants; party leaders were accused, then secret police officials, then foreigners, especially if they had German-sounding names. In London Soviet Ambassador Ivan Maisky told a British trade union delegation that some of those executed in various towns had "entered the Soviet Union illegally from abroad. . . . In court they confessed."[20] Pure nonsense. Maisky knew better but he obeyed orders.

Nevertheless, 1935 was a relatively good year; Soviet citizens associated more freely with foreigners and the coming Constitution was the subject of joyful comment in private. The dictatorship remained vigilant, however. Nobody in his fondest dreams expected the secret police, the "flaming sword of the revolution," to be dismantled. Nor, however, was there reason to expect an intensification of terror. The new Constitution appeared in draft form on June 12, 1936, and the Eighth All-Union Congress of Soviets adopted it, without dissent, on December 5, 1936. Its announced purpose was to "democratize" the previous Constitution of 1923.

All of these processes and the western tilt of Soviet foreign policy that grew with them were set in train by Stalin. Yet presently he had second thoughts. Or he may have had them all the time. He had a two-track mind. From Sochi in the Caucasus, where he was vacationing with Andrei A. Zhdanov, the successor to Kirov as Leningrad boss and heir apparent, he sent a telegram signed by Zhdanov too, dated September 25, 1936, and addressed to Lazar M. Kaganovich, Molotov, and other members of the Politburo in Moscow. Khrushchev supplied the text in his secret speech of February 24-25, 1956: "We deem it absolutely necessary and urgent that Comrade Yezhov be nominated to the post of People's Commissar for Internal Affairs. Yagoda has definitely proved himself incapable of unmasking the Trotskyite-Zinoviev bloc. The OGPU is four years behind in this matter."

No sooner wired than done. The next day, September 26, 1936, Nikolai I. Yezhov replaced Yagoda as chief of the secret police. The Trotskyites as an opposition had long been suppressed and many of them, like Radek and Rakovsky, were working within the government or party apparatus. The so-called Right Opposition had also laid down its arms. At the Seventeenth Party Congress in January-February, 1934, Rykov, Bukharin, and Tomsky, as well as Zinoviev, and Kamenev, delivered apologetic speeches and praised Stalin's industrialization plans. The farm collectives were an accomplished fact. Traveling through the Soviet Union in the summer of 1936 I found that the peasants' mood was quieter than it had been one year and two years earlier; they knew there was no escape from collectivization, refusal to cooperate would mean death for millions of them, as in the recent famine.

Yet the appointment of Yezhov marked the beginning of the worst terror in Soviet history. The terror came when it was no longer necessary

[20] Degras, p. 100.

and because it was no longer necessary, because there existed no opposition to criticize Stalin for indulging in terror or to obstruct his massacre of talent in 1936, 1937, and 1938.

The peasant problem lay at the root of all opposition in the late 1920's and the beginning of the thirties. Now Stalin had crushed the peasant (without solving the farm problem) and thereby eviscerated political opposition. The influence of Kirov and Gorky should have been dominant after 1933, and for a time it was—in domestic as well as in foreign affairs.

From the point of view of political power Kirov could not compete with Stalin. But a man like Stalin, who allowed himself to be venerated as a god, to be likened unto the sun and the stars, to be quoted ad nauseam as an authority on subjects on which he was a mere layman, would have been jealous of Kirov's popularity and fearful of him as a rival. Stalin was no ordinary person in ability or cruelty or envy or venom. All his capacities were intense, and Kirov intensified the worst of them.

This aspect of Stalin's attitude to Kirov, and to Gorky, must not conceal the political core of the matter. Continued liberalization at home and a prowestern policy abroad would have meant giving full meaning to the new Constitution and more liberalization inside, and in the end the diminution of the dictatorship and of Stalin as dictator. But Stalin considered dictatorship good for Russia. He was not the first, nor would he be the last, Russian statesman who feared that democracy, imperfectly practiced in the West, would corrode not only Russian autocracy but also the essence of Russia. In September, 1936, in quiet contemplation with Zhdanov, surrounded by the beauty of the Caucasus, Stalin decided, the Constitution notwithstanding, to escalate the terror. The democratic West had lost.

However, Stalin permitted his prowestern foreign policy to run its course. Stalin was a pluralist. He believed in one party but not in one policy. Even as he allowed Litvinov to cultivate the West he began, as early as 1935, to probe the possibility of an understanding with Hitler.

XXII PRELUDE TO THE PACT

Historians and others in many lands have wondered about the origins of the Soviet-Nazi pact of August 23, 1939. Who took the initiative and when? The signing of the pact is one of the most significant events of modern times. Nine days later Hitler launched the second world war. The pact and the attached secret protocol set in train a series of acts which led to the Nazi invasion of Russia. The contents of the two documents shaped Stalin's diplomacy toward the United States and England during the war. Archive material made specially available reveals the first steps that led to the agreements between Hitler and Stalin.

"What, in your opinion, could improve German-Soviet relations?" Sergei A. Bessonov, counselor of the Soviet Embassy in Berlin, said during a talk in Moscow on October 7, 1935, with Dr. von Twardowski, counselor of the German Embassy in Moscow. The 200-million-mark credit granted to the Soviet Union will soon be exhausted, Bessonov added, and David V. Kandelaki, the Soviet trade representative in Berlin, who enjoyed "extraordinary connections here"—in Moscow—had "great plans" for the expansion of Soviet-German trade "if no political incidents intervened."[1]

This first probing step toward better Soviet relations with Nazi Germany was followed by a further démarche undertaken by the same Bessonov on December 20, 1935. The Counselor of the Soviet Embassy in Berlin this time began with commerce and moved on to the major political issue. Speaking to a German Foreign Office official who reported the conversation the next day to Hans Dieckhoff, the right-hand man of the Foreign Minister, Bessonov said the way was open to an agreement for a half-billion-mark German credit to Russia, the only misunderstanding being that Dr. Hjalmar Schacht, President of the government's Reichsbank, wanted a debt of some 65 million marks paid in gold or stable currencies, whereas David Kandelaki of the Soviet Trade Delega-

[1] Private letter of Twardowski in the archives of the Auswaertiges Amt, *Abteiling IV Ru Akten betreffend deutsch-russische Wirtschafts- u. Zolltarif Verhandlungen*, E 664278-664300, *vom September 1935 bis 21 Dezember 1935*, Bd 8, Handel 13: Russland A. #E664281.

tion in Berlin offered 25 million marks in gold or stable foreign currencies. The German and the Russian agreed that one must be patient when conducting financial-commercial discussions.

Thereupon Bessonov referred to the recent meeting between the "Fuehrer" and Sir Eric Phipps, the British Ambassador in Berlin, in which, according to information the Soviet Embassy had from German sources, Chancellor Hitler said "he had no intention of attacking Russia." On the other hand, the Soviet Embassy had learned from diplomats in the German capital that Hitler was displeased with the "Franco-Soviet military treaty." Bessonov's German interlocutor confirmed this and said the "Fuehrer" regarded that treaty "as directed against the Reich." Hitler also objected to the proposed "Eastern Locarno," designed to guarantee the western frontiers of Russia and the frontiers of Russia's western neighbors (Poland and the Baltic States). Hitler believed it would freeze the situation in Europe. Bessonov then suggested a German-Soviet nonaggression pact. This, the German official remarked, would be difficult; one had to be patient in political affairs too.[2]

A year of patience passed. German-Soviet diplomatic relations remained congealed. The next initiative also came from the Soviets. In the last days of December, 1936, Kandelaki, accompanied by an assistant named Leo K. Friederichson went to see Dr. Hjalmar Schacht. "During the conversation," Schacht reported to Foreign Minister von Nuerath, "I asserted that I could see a quickening of trade between Russia and Germany only if the Russian government made an unmistakable political gesture, and the best would be in the form of assurances through the [Soviet] ambassador in Berlin to refrain from all communist propaganda outside Russia." Kandelaki was not taken aback by Schacht's suggestion; on the contrary, he showed some "spontaneous sympathy" for it. Since then, the February 6, 1937, Schacht report to Neurath continued, Kandelaki had been in Moscow, where he saw Stalin, and Molotov and Litvinov. On January 29, 1937, he again visited Schacht, accompanied by Friedrichson, and reading from notes spoke as follows: "The Russian government has never refused to engage in political negotiations with us [with Germany]. . . . The Russian government is prepared to enter into negotiations with us concerning the improvement of mutual relations and about peace in general. . . . The Russian government is always ready to meet the wishes of the German government to keep all talks and negotiations confidential and not to give them publicity."

[2] *Ibid.*, same number: E664281.

Schacht told Kandelaki that these démarches should be made by the Soviet Embassy to the Foreign Office. Kandelaki agreed, but requested Schacht to ascertain whether such conversations would have the least chance of success. "Then he will see to it that further steps are taken." Kandelaki was a Georgian and a youthful friend of Stalin, and was acting on Stalin's personal instructions.

Schacht concluded his report to Foreign Minister von Neurath with the expression of his own view that Kandelaki should be answered in only one way: Germany was ready to talk with Moscow after "an unequivocal declaration, accompanied by the necessary guarantees" about Soviet dissociation from Comintern propaganda.[3]

Neurath replied to Schacht in a letter dated February 11, 1937: "Yesterday, during a personal report to the Fuehrer, I spoke to him about your discussions with Mr. Kandelaki, and especially about the declaration he made to you in the name of Stalin and Molotov. . . . I am in agreement with the Fuehrer that at present these [talks with the Russians] could lead to no result at all, and rather would be used by them to reach their desired goal of a close military alliance with France and, if possible, a further rapprochement with England. A declaration by the Russian government that it dissociates itself from the Comintern would, after the experience with such declarations in England and France, have not the least practical use and would therefore be insufficient. It would be quite different if things in Russia moved further in the direction of an absolute despotism based on the military. In that case we should certainly not miss the opportunity to connect again with Russia. . . . Heil Hitler! Your Neurath."[4]

Kandelaki was received by Stalin and Molotov during his frequent visits to Moscow. In his talks with Dr. Hjalmar Schacht he spoke for Stalin, who preferred to avail himself of the services of an intimate rather than to act formally through the Soviet Embassy in Berlin. This indirect approach had several advantages: it sounded out Hitler without committing the Soviet government, it could be denied as unofficial or untrue if the Germans chose to publish the news, and if Hitler had shown interest Stalin could have used the fact to convince Politburo comrades, and Litvinov, that an alternative existed to their prowestern orientation. But Hitler was not yet ready to go to war, and therefore had no need of Russia unless a military despotism was established in Moscow which would march with him against the rest of Europe.

[3] German Auswaertiges Amt, Politische Abteilung, *Akten betreffendi: Politische Beziehungen Russlands zu Deutschland vom 12 Maerz 1936 bis Dezember 1938*, Bd 1, forts, Bd 2: *Politik Russland* 2. #212210 and 212211.

[4] *Ibid.*, #212215.

Hitler rebuffed Stalin. Yet these Soviet feelers must have been filed away in the "Fuehrer's" mind. The Kremlin gate was shut, but not locked. Someday it might be opened. To this extent the Bessonov-Kandelaki effort was the prelude to the Soviet-Nazi Pact of August 23, 1939.

Part Two

Hitler and Stalin

XXIII DOWN THE ESCALATOR TO WAR

Hitler was no ordinary national leader; he lied more than most. His lies, however, were not pathological, they were psychological, they answered to a widespread yearning for peace. He addressed France on October 14, 1933, and declared, "After the Saar Territory"—a rich German mining area held by France—"had been returned to the Reich, only a madman would be able to think of the possibility of war between the two countries for which, from our point of view, there would be no longer any moral or rational reason."[1] If he got his way, he was saying, he would reward France with peace.

Thanks to hands-off isolationism, the United States was tens of thousands of thought-miles from the territorial balance-of-power conflicts whose outcome shaped the future. Checking Mussolini and Hitler therefore rested with England and France, both still under the shock of the bloodletting in the first world war when France counted 1,357,800 dead, Britain 908,371 dead, and many more wounded and maimed in the trenches of the Continent. The poppy fields of Flanders, fertilized with rich red blood, grew a large crop of pacifists. The human brain is so constituted that it thinks of a possible impending experience in terms of an earlier and similar experience. In the 1930's, as soon as British and French men and women saw signs of a new world war, they recoiled in anguish. "Anything, but not war" expressed the ruling mood. It was the root of appeasement.

Germany had had 1,773,000 dead after the first world war. She lost territory too and was subjected to foreign occupation and reparations.

[1] U.S. Department of State, *Documents on German Foreign Policy, 1918-1945* Series C: *The Third Reich; First Phase*, Vol. II: *October 14, 1933-June 13, 1944*, p. 11.

Foreign troops, predominantly French and Belgian, quit the Rhineland on June 30, 1930, and reparations ended in the midst of the global financial crisis of the summer of 1932. For fourteen years the victors' feet on German soil and their fingers in the German exchequer had fed Hitler nationalism. Such is the twisted logic of politics, however, that the lifting of some of the peace treaty's punitive arrangements removed German fear of foreign military and monetary sanctions and encouraged embittered Germans to join the Hitler movement.

Hitler held the western nations in low regard; they were decadent. "None of these people," he said in 1932 with reference to the French, "any longer want war or greatness."[2] He intended to exploit their decline. He would deceive them with lies and impress them with strength. Immediately he became Chancellor, therefore, he proposed to increase the size of the German army to 300,000. When on December 8, 1933, Sir Eric Phipps, the British ambassador in Berlin, obeying instructions from London, contended that this was "excessively high" and the acquisition of a commensurate air force "formidable," Hitler replied that he based his plans on "the fact that none of the heavily armed states wanted to disarm" and that he was demanding merely one fourth of what Germany's neighbors possessed.[3] This was part transient truth, part loud lie; France and England were not in a war-preparedness temper.

Socially prominent Englishmen believed in Hitler's innocence. The Marquess of Lothian was one of them. As Philip Kerr he had been Prime Minister Lloyd George's secretary; he would soon be ambassador to Washington. The *Times* of London on January 31 and February 1, 1935, published two articles by Lothian on his visit to Germany. "National Socialism," he wrote, ". . . is a movement of individual and national self-respect. . . . The central fact in Europe today is that Germany does not want war and is prepared to renounce it absolutely as a method of settling disputes with her neighbors, provided she is given real equality." This is what Hitler told Lothian in a two-hour interview and Lothian believed Hitler, and many believed Lothian, who also reported "finally and most vital, that he will pledge Germany not to interfere in his beloved Austria by force." Lothian commented: "I have not the slightest doubt that his [Hitler's] attitude is perfectly sincere."

"Slightest" and "perfectly sincere" are superlatives no person who has been in politics should use about a politician. "Hitler does not want war," Lothian continued, "not because he is a pacifist, but because he knows what war means, because he can only carry out his plan for training and disciplining and uniting the young generation in peace." Lothian therefore urged the influential readers of the influential *Times*

[2] Quoted by Alan Bullock, *Hitler, A Study in Tyranny*, p. 225.
[3] *Documents on German Foreign Policy*, Series C. Vol. II, p. 189.

to treat Germany "as a friend." For Germany, Lothian asserted, "is not imperialist in the old sense of the word. . . . Its very devotion to race precludes it from trying to annex other nationalities." Lastly, according to Lothian, and perhaps most revealing, "it is an open secret that Hitler, while unconcerned about the Russia of today, is deeply concerned about the Russia of tomorrow. . . . What will Russia be when it is organized, strong, and equipped and Stalin is no longer there?" When is "tomorrow"? Or why not attack a weak Russia before tomorrow?

Lord Lothian's views had been submitted previously to Sir John Simon, who distributed them to the Cabinet. Statements like Lothian's were abundant; they gave Moscow propagandists cause to contend that appeasement was designed to turn Hitler's aggression eastward. Stalin saw no reason why he should not turn it westward. He had as few loyalties as Hitler.

Hitler's principal purpose was isolation—of others, and above all of France. On March 25 and 26, 1935, British Foreign Secretary Sir John Simon and Lord Privy Seal Anthony Eden added to Hitler's prestige by visiting the "Fuehrer" in Berlin. On that occasion, as Sir John the appeaser admitted in the House of Commons on April 3, Hitler told the visiting Englishmen, "We have reached parity with Great Britain" in air strength. This did not prevent the British ministers from taking up Hitler's suggestion of an Anglo-German naval agreement.

On May 21 Hitler placed Dr. Hjalmar Schacht in charge of secret preparations for war. The same day he delivered an antiwar discourse. European nations had warred upon one another for three centuries: "If these States had applied merely a fraction of their sacrifices to wiser purposes the success would certainly have been greater and more permanent." The speech made a good impression on sleeping England. Early in June Joachim von Ribbentrop, suave champagne salesman, flew to London where, on June 18, the British government—without informing France, her ally, and Italy—both naval powers—signed a treaty which permitted the Reich to build surface ships up to 35 percent of the strength of the British navy and submarines equal in number to those of the entire British Commonwealth.[4] Hitler was true to his word—until he reached the agreed tonnages.

The British government had apparently expected Hitler to build more ships and welcomed his signed and sealed assurance to build fewer. This was the unreality. Appeasement had reared its ugly head. Appeasement assumed that a tiger fed some meat would not want more. Appeasement also bore overtones of fairness and justice. "Germany's claim to equality of rights," Sir John Simon told the House of Commons on February 6,

[4] Bullock, pp. 337-338.

1934, "ought not to be resisted. There is little likelihood of peace in the world if you try to put one country or one race under an inferior jurisdiction." This principle, applied to post-1918 Germany, might have saved the world from Hitler. Instead, Lloyd George launched his ludicrous "Hang the Kaiser" election slogan and the Allies adopted a policy of reparations and territorial annexations which bred vindictive nationalism and ruined the promising democracy of the Weimar Republic. (The West showed greater wisdom toward Germany, and the United States toward Japan, after World War II.) Hitler made the second world war but non-Germans as well as Germans made Hitler. England, then the greatest world power, bestowed a civilized policy on the uncivilized Nazis, who took what they were given, considered it a sign of weakness, and armed to get more by diplomacy or war.

While Germany armed fast, the British League of Nations Association, led by Lord Robert Cecil, conducted a nationwide voluntary "peace ballot" in which 11,559,165 persons enjoying official adult franchise participated; this equaled more than half the number of votes cast in British national parliamentary elections. Of the total, according to results published on June 27, 1935, almost everybody—more than 10.5 million—voted for a general reduction of armaments and dependence on League of Nations economic sanctions to punish Mussolini for invading Ethiopia. The British people's abhorrence of war had led them to think armaments would produce a war, not prevent one.

When, in October, 1935, the Italian army invaded Ethiopia, British politicians divided. Some said: Stop Mussolini. Anthony Eden wanted Il Duce's scalp; in Ethiopia Mussolini threatened Egypt, a British semi-protectorate. Others, like Churchill and Vansittart, regarded Hitler the greater menace. Sir Robert Vansittart, Permanent Under Secretary of the British Foreign Office, a poet, scenario writer, and his country's top career expert on international affairs, hoped to keep Italy in the British camp. If Mussolini, as he put it to me, were forced to fight in deserts 3,000 miles away he could not protect the green garden in his backyard: Austria. (Mussolini had kept Hitler out of Austria in July, 1934.) Sir John Simon agreed. He would have been glad to appease Mussolini as well as Hitler. In June, 1935, Simon and Prime Minister Ramsay MacDonald, of whom Vansittart had said, "You can't make two empty sacks stand upright," stepped down from their posts in favor, respectively, of Sir Samuel Hoare and Stanley Baldwin. Appeasement continued to prosper.

French politicians, irritated by the Anglo-German naval accord, were delighted by Britain's discomfiture and division. They hoped to retain Mussolini's friendship. Hitler as an enemy was problem enough without inciting another fascist foe on the French flank. Moreover, France had her own social cleavages; her leaders could not afford to take drastic action against Italy. In the circumstances the economic sanctions imposed on Italy by the League of Nations for invading Ethiopia were bound to fail, especially since the sanctions were not extended to oil without which Il Duce's expedition into Africa would have starved.

Great Britain was mistress of the Suez Canal; all Mussolini's men and materials, except airplanes, had to traverse the canal to reach Abyssinia. Britain might have closed the canal. But that would have contravened the 1888 Constantinople Convention governing the use of Suez.

In the end Mussolini won Abyssinia, won enemies in England, saw himself weakened, and, reconciled to the inevitable German annexation of Austria, became the Axis partner of Hitler.

Stalin watched from afar.

* * *

Historians differ in fixing the date of the beginning of the second world war. Some argue that it commenced during the first world war, and, in a sense, the second was the child of the first. Others hold that the second world war was born with the Versailles peace treaties. Certainly January 30, 1933, the day Hitler assumed the Chancellorship of Germany, is entitled to stand as a candidate for the doubtful honor of marking the start of the second world war. Or Mussolini's "success" in Abyssinia and other events of 1935 might compete for the prize. But there is little question that March 7, 1936, is the chief contender.

Hitler watched the western democracies. Their acts, of commission but usually of omission, fed his gambler's instinct. In contrast to their irresolution he had audacity, faith in his intuition, and a strong belief in the efficacy of bluff. All these qualities brought him an extraordinary triumph on March 7, 1936, when German troops entered the Rhineland in violation of the Versailles treaty and of the Locarno treaty, which was initiated by the German government. "More than once, even during the war," writes Hitler's interpreter, "I heard Hitler say, 'The forty-eight hours after the march into the Rhineland were the most nerve-racking in my life.' He always added, 'If the French had then marched into the Rhineland, we would have had to withdraw with our tails between our legs, for the military resources at our disposal would have been wholly inadequate for even a moderate resistance.' "[5]

The German military, including General Werner von Blomberg, Minister of Defense and Commander of the Armed Forces, Colonel General Werner von Fritsch, Commander in Chief of the Army, and Colonel General Ludwig Beck, Chief of Staff of the Army, opposed Hitler's plan

[5] Dr. Paul Schmidt, *Hitler's Interpreter,* p. 41.

to remilitarize the Rhineland. He brushed aside their argument that the German army, though enlarged, was not ready for war. "According to General Jodl" at the Nuremberg trial, "the German occupation forces which moved into the Rhineland consisted of approximately one division, and only three battalions moved across the Rhine."[6] France "concentrated thirteen divisions in the East, but they only manned the Maginot Line and stood on the defensive. . . . In view of this concentration, von Blomberg, at the instance of von Fritsch and Beck, urged the Fuehrer to withdraw the three battalions. . . . Hitler scornfully refused. . . . All that Hitler would concede to his uneasy generals was his contemptuous assent to the withdrawal of the troops sent across the Rhine in the event of serious military opposition being offered by the French."[7]

Danton called for "toujours de l'audace," but Hitler's audacity consisted of equal portions of his own mendacity and other men's gullibility. The very hour those three battalions crossed the Rhine Hitler addressed the Reichstag and lied, "At no moment of my struggle on behalf of the German people have I ever forgotten the duty incumbent on me and on us all firmly to uphold European culture and European civilization. . . . Why should it not be possible to put an end to this useless strife" between Germany and France? "Why not replace it with the rule of reason?"[8]

All Hitler's steps toward the second world war were accompanied by idealistic words against war. Yet multitudes in France and Britain nodded their heads approvingly. The Rhineland was German territory, Englishmen argued; how could you keep it demilitarized eighteen years after war? But Warsaw was alarmed, for with the entry into the Rhineland Hitler commenced building the Siegfried Line to prevent France from striking at Germany in the event of a Nazi assault on Poland. The Poles suddenly saw that without French aid they would be exposed to Hitler's arrogant aggressiveness. France, however, had abdicated. Her thirteen mobilized divisions sat in the underground forts of the Maginot Line and did not move against the German division in the Rhineland. Yet how could France invade Nazi Germany? She had invaded the Ruhr in 1923 to no effect. The new Germany was not only stronger, she was aroused. A military riposte to the remilitarization of the Rhineland would have sown myriad dragon's teeth. To be sure, Hitler had, after ordering German soldiers into the Rhineland, told the French and other ambassadors that Locarno no longer existed. France now had no German guarantee of her eastern frontier. Nor had she a heart for war. This was the French dilemma; her loss was enormous and she could do

[6] Bullock, p. 343.
[7] John W. Wheeler-Bennett, *The Nemesis of Power,* p. 352.
[8] Munich *Voelkischer Beobachter,* March 8, 1936.

nothing about it. The situation suited Hitler's plans.

It did not suit Moscow's. Moscow blamed England. "The British are paying the French back for not supporting them on Ethiopia," Litvinov said to me in London during the special session of the Council of the League of Nations summoned to deal with the Rhineland emergency. "A few more blows like this and where is the League?" he added. The Soviet Ambassador in London, Ivan Maisky, told Foreign Secretary Eden, "Germany has committed a clear act of aggression fraught with tremendous consequences. And what do we see? Instead of acting firmly against Germany, England is actually supporting her."[9]

The French too blamed the British. Albert Sarraut, French Premier when Hitler's units marched into the Rhineland, subsequently told a French friend in Vienna that France did not react forcefully in March, 1936, for two reasons: the British refused to support an armed response and General Maurice Gamelin said the response would require complete mobilization. Pierre Etienne Flandin, French Foreign Minister at the time, likewise sought to transfer the guilt to Britain's broad shoulders. The truth is France was sick, divided, and incapable of action.

* * *

Litvinov characterized the situation as "a half-peace that is not peace but war." He summoned Hitler's possible victims—all of Europe—to concert their political efforts to thwart fascist expansion. The logic of Litvinov's foreign policy was reflected in a secret telegram to Berlin by Fritz von Twardowski, the German counselor in Moscow, on December 27, 1933: "Since the Soviet need for peace and security makes a cooperation with our revisionist policy problematical, the prerequisites for cooperation between Germany and the Soviet Union in larger European policy do not exist at the present time."[10] Moscow, worried about Japan's intentions, wanted tranquillity in Europe. Hitler's policy, on the other hand, was "revisionist." At whose expense? Of Poland and Czechoslovakia, first of all. Of Austria too. Subsequently of France. Since Britain's traditional concern was to prevent one power from dominating the Continent and thus threatening England, the Anglo-French should, in Litvinov's concept, oppose revisionism and favor collective security. In the final analysis, however, a government looks to its own interests, and the Soviet government, knowing the contents of *Mein Kampf,* (holy scripture after Hitler's accession to power), was concerned with Nazi revisionism in Russia. Revisionism meant conquest.

Litvinov's antirevisionism marked a basic change in Soviet foreign

[9] V. I. Popov, *Diplomaticheskiye Otnosheniya Mezhdu SSSR i Angliyei (1929-1939)* (Diplomatic Relations Between the U.S.S.R. and England), citing a document from unpublished Soviet archives, p. 256.

[10] *Documents on German Foreign Policy,* Series C. Vol. II, pp. 278-280.

policy from hostility to the Versailles peace treaty—the concomitant of Moscow's earlier collaboration with Germany—to acceptance of the European territorial status quo in preference to its alteration by Nazi force. The new Soviet collective security policy aimed to prevent Hitler, or Hitler and Mussolini, from knocking down the targets of their aggression one by one. It made sense. Unity brings strength. Yet the period from 1933 to 1939 is remarkable for the obstacles that prevented nations in peace from pooling their power for survival.

Collective security was the antidote to appeasement. Nevertheless, governments preferred the poison. A government which called itself communist prescribed an antidote to enable the democracies to survive the plague of Hitler, who proclaimed his undying enmity to communism. This had the effect of creating skepticism about Stalin's motives and credibility for Hitler's. Nobody yet understood that the Kremlin was the citadel of Russian nationalism, no longer of world communism. It required the Soviet-Nazi pact of August, 1939, to convince bourgeois-democratic governments that the Soviet Union could compact with Nazi Germany and that Hitler could forget his anticommunism and sign secret treaties with Stalin. Until then western politicians, whose own democratic ideology did not prevent them from cooperating with dictators, believed that ideologies guided those who preached them so vociferously.

Collective security was conceived as a means of preventing a war, not of fighting one. The history, however, of the descent from 1933 into the hell of 1939 demonstrates the difficulties of inducing governments to avert disaster in the nations they rule. Poland is the prime example.

Throughout 1934 French Foreign Minister Barthou and Foreign Commissar Litvinov worked for an "Eastern Locarno" to guarantee all frontiers in Eastern Europe. Barthou had intended to include Germany, Poland, Finland, Estonia, Latvia, Lithuania, Rumania, Czechoslovakia, France, Britain, and the Soviet Union. On June 9, 1934, Czechoslovakia and Rumania recognized the Soviet Union and established diplomatic relations with Moscow.

Rumania's recognition of the Soviet Union crowned a prolonged effort by Foreign Commissar Litvinov and Foreign Minister Nicolas Titulescu to conquer the mountain-high barrier of Bessarabia, seized by Rumania in 1918 and claimed by Russia. Moscow did not recognize Rumania's ownership. Rumania feared Russian irredentism and Bolshevik propaganda. Titulescu on June 12, 1934, told the British Minister, Michael Palairet, that "He had had a hard struggle with King Carol, but His Majesty had given way with a good grace. . . . Queen Marie would no doubt be less tractable, and His Excellency [Titulescu] admitted that he looked forward to his next meeting with her with some apprehension. It would, he feared, be impossible to expect Her Majesty to receive the new Soviet Minister in Bucharest, and some means would have to be found to spare her this embarrassment without offending the Soviet Government."

It is not likely that the Kremlin would have been offended.

During their negotiations Litvinov said he had information that in case of war Poland would try to persuade Rumania to permit the passage of German troops through her territory into the Soviet Ukraine. When Titulescu reported this to King Carol "he was dismayed to find" that the King "showed the keenest interest in the proposal." Since then, Titulescu told the British Minister, King Carol "had seen much more of various Germans here."

Sir Robert Vansittart on reading this dispatch, now deposited in the Public Record Office (FO 371/18448), made a handwritten comment: "King Carol would be a very disturbing factor if his country were not so incapable."

Rumania's, and Czechoslovakia's, recognition of the Soviet government was the logical prelude to an eastern collective security pact, for France could come to the aid of Russia and Russia to the aid of France and both to the aid of the small nations of eastern Europe only if Czechoslovakia, Rumania, and Poland were on friendly terms with them and granted transit rights to their armed forces. But on September 10, 1934, Hitler rebuffed Barthou—for obvious reasons: he had designs on the frontiers of Poland and Czechoslovakia. Deaf and dumb to this warning, Poland four days later announced that she too would not adhere to an Eastern Locarno. Britain also refused to guarantee Eastern Europe's frontiers. They seemed too remote; Germany might resent England's participation. To mitigate London's resistance to the Eastern pact, Moscow had offered to join the Eastern Locarno-to-be with the western Locarno of 1925: "Thus the Soviet government would guarantee the western boundary of Germany and the eastern boundary of France. The French government would guarantee Germany's eastern and the Soviet western boundary, and Germany would guarantee the Soviet western and the French eastern boundary." British reaction was negative. On the other hand, Nazi Germany and Polish Foreign Minister Beck intimated, according to unpublished Soviet documents, that Germany might be interested in an eastern pact with Russia but without France and Czechoslovakia (and therefore at their expense). Litvinov informed the French government of this "perfidious" proposal.[11]

The crux of the situation was Poland. Colonel Beck contended that

[11] B. N. Ponomaryov, A. A. Gromyko, V. M. Khvostov (Eds.), *Istoria Vneshnei Politiki SSSR, Part I, 1917-1945* (The History of Soviet Foreign Policy, Part I, 1917-1945), pp. 286-287.

Warsaw already had nonaggression treaties with Germany and the Soviet Union, and therefore needed no further guarantees. But his "main point" was Germany's rejection of an Eastern Locarno. "Our principal thesis," Beck wrote after the second world war wrecked his Poland, "was that the participation of Germany in this pact represented for us a condition *sine qua non* for the maintenance of our policy of equilibrium between the two great powers which we had for neighbors."[12] Beck did not want Poland to participate in a multilateral treaty which included communist Russia but not anticommunist Nazi Germany.

Beck was described as "this tall, elegant, and rather Mephistophelean figure" who "conveyed an impression of hardness without depth." There was certainly no depth in the fatuous ambition of the Foreign Minister of the weak state of Poland to maintain an "equilibrium" between her two great neighbors who, on the propitious day, moved away from the ends of the equilibrated seesaw and shook hands at the fulcrum where Beck had stood so unsteadily. Without Poland an Eastern Locarno was impossible. In many respects this set the stage for the Soviet-Nazi pact and the second world war.

Diplomacy is the visible skin of the body politic. Beneath the integument, beneath the publicized trips and talks of ministers and ambassadors, are the bones, muscles, and organs of the nation or, in most cases, of that part of the nation, sometimes the very small part, which shapes policy. The Poland of the second half of the 1930's had opposition parties and an opposition press as well as trade unions and other instruments of democracy. Yet Marshal Pilsudski was dictator; the accouterments of freedom rarely impeded his exercise of power. When he died on May 12, 1935, the Marshal's mantle fell on a group of colonels led by Edward Smigly-Rydz and Beck, whose pulse beat in unison with that of the Polish aristocracy. U.S. Ambassador John Cudahy liked to hunt with them on their huge estates in eastern Poland which escaped the imperfect land reform of the 1920's.

I had several extended conversations with Cudahy in January, 1936. He described the intimate relations of the Polish nobility with Prussian Junkers who came to shoot and Nazi officials who came to intrigue. The Polish upper class feared the Soviet Union because they feared their own peasants. Polish Finance Minister Kwiatkowski said in parliament that Polish peasants who owned twenty-five acres of land and spent an average of $22.40 a year in 1929 were now spending an average of $8 a year. Peasants who owned ten to twelve acres and constituted 38 percent of the nation's population spent next to nothing. "Ten million per-

[12] Quoted from Beck's memoirs, *Dernier rapport*, by Professor Henry L. Roberts in his chapter on Beck in Gordon A. Craig and Felix Gilbert (Eds.), *The Diplomats, 1919-1939*.

sons," the minister explained, "stand completely outside the realm of economic life." A peasant insurrection had erupted in the province of Volhynia in May, 1935, and another in central Poland in December, 1935. Ambassador Cudahy hunted with Polish peers and observed Poland's poor. The landlords, who feared Russia most, exercised most influence on their country's foreign policy.

Between talks with Cudahy and visits to miserable villages I interviewed Beck. I found him eel-like, so much so that I decided, contrary to custom, to take notes lest his words slip away. He said, "Always have a fluid foreign policy. . . . People formerly exaggerated the Polish-German problem. . . . I am sure that when the present atmosphere clears Franco-Polish relations will improve. . . . I don't believe Europe is in crisis. . . . There is too much nervousness. . . . Poland will not join the Soviet-French bloc."

This meant: The Polish-French alliance had lapsed and Poland now rested her security on Hitler promises. Poland's death was casting its shadow before. If war came, I wrote in the *Nation* of March 18, 1936, "Poland might easily be the battlefield and be ruined. Poland . . . is playing a doubtful diplomatic game based on the idea that since war is inevitable she might as well get something out of it. . . . Poland would undoubtedly prefer German expansion in the direction of Austria and Czechoslovakia." (Poland coveted the Teschen region in Czechoslovakia.)

It is not unnatural for shortsighted politicians, assuming war inevitable, to try to direct it away from their own country. But after the Nazis expanded into Austria and Czechoslovakia they expanded into Poland. The expectation of such one-by-one plucking lay behind Litvinov's all-for-one collective security program. Beck thought otherwise. He did not wish to invite Hitler's wrath and the Polish nobility's hostility by participating in a political coalition with Russia and other nations alarmed by Hitler's rapid rearmament.

Poland's death blow to the Eastern Locarno was a row of nails in her coffin. Nobody can say for certain what would have happened if Beck had pursued a different policy. Perhaps Poland was doomed. One knows for certain that the policy he did follow ended in disaster.

* * *

The defection of Poland made it all the more important for France to ally herself with the Soviet Union.

Since the simultaneous inauguration of rapid industrialization and agrarian collectivization in 1928-29, Soviet economy—and hence domestic politics—had been churned into chaos. The upheavals in city and farm in backward bureaucratized Soviet Russia resulted in inefficiency, waste, failure to fulfill Moscow-made plans, and numerous industrial accidents. Lest the infallible Kremlin be blamed, the Kremlin blamed others. This goes far to explain the famous major and minor Moscow trials of the 1930's. One of these performances was staged between April 12 and April 19, 1933. A group of important officials of the Commissariat of Heavy Industry was arrested on March 2; with them the secret police jailed five employees of the British firm of Metro-Vickers; all were accused of "wrecking" activities in large Soviet electric power stations. In court the British defendants were charged with military espionage and causing accidents at the stations. That the British and Soviet governments were just then in the process of negotiating a new commercial treaty was immaterial; the needs of Soviet internal politics always take precedence over foreign affairs. The British defendants were found guilty, as expected, but three were sentenced merely to banishment from the Soviet Union and the other two men to three years' imprisonment. London retaliated by placing an embargo on a considerable percentage of Soviet imports.

The Metro-Vickers trial, as it came to be known, followed a pattern set by an earlier trial in December, 1930. Indeed, the frustrated Soviet novelists who wrote the scenarios of the Moscow trials lacked the talent to deviate from the plot. In the 1930 trial a number of Soviet industrial specialists, notably Professor Leonid K. Ramzin, were accused of having plotted with France (and Britain) to wreck the first Five Year Plan and restore capitalism to Russia. Needless to say, the prosecution, with the aid of most of the defendants, proved its case, and Ramzin and his fellow defendants were sentenced to death. The purpose of the trial having thus been achieved by means of millions of square inches of publicity in the Soviet press and thousands of hours on the radio, Ramzin's sentence was almost immediately commuted to ten years and he was soon quietly released "for research work essential to the national economy." In 1943 he received the Stalin Prize for theoretical studies in thermal, aerodynamic, and hydrodynamic calculations of boiler installations and the properties of fuel. He died a natural death in 1948.

The Soviet judicial process begins and ends in the centers of political power. Soviet courts do not dispense justice; they obey instructions. The Ramzin trial was born when Stalin, addressing the Central Committee of the Soviet Communist Party on June 27, 1930, described the world capitalist crisis in detail and with relish, and added, "Every time the contradictions among capitalist nations commence to sharpen the bourgeoisie turns to look at the Soviet Union: Is it not possible to resolve one or the other contradiction of capitalism or all those contradictions at the expense of the Soviet Union . . . ?" He accordingly saw "a tendency toward adventurous attacks on the U.S.S.R. and toward intervention."

Finally, to be specific, he said, "The clearest expression of this tendency is now to be found in bourgeois France . . . the most aggressive and militaristic country."[13]

The secret police and the judges now had their orders. With such alarmism went the intimation that the opposition—this time the so-called Rightist Opposition of Bukharin, Rykov, and Tomsky—was assailing the Soviet state at the very moment the capitalists threatened to make war on it.

As the Metro-Vickers trial infuriated British public opinion, so the Ramzin trial caused a grave deterioration in Soviet-French relations, particularly since Stalin castigated not only France but the socialists who exercised considerable power in France.

However, time and the rise of Hitler helped blur the impressions of 1930. The first Five Year Plan, as well as the second, and the third, was a war-preparedness plan. Their emphasis was on heavy industry which produces armaments. France, a nation divided and sick, needed an ally in Eastern Europe. The Soviet Union was the only candidate.

In Berlin, on August 9, 1929, Foreign Commissar Litvinov, expressing his own views and the Kremlin's said to me, "France is our enemy; we hate her." But on December 29, 1933, addressing the VTSIK (Central Executive Committee or parliament of the Soviet Union), he poured some sense and moderation into Stalin's unmodulated talk about war against Russia. ". . . you would get a wrong idea of the international situation if you concluded . . . that all capitalist states are now anxious for war and are preparing for it," he declared. "Side by side with the small handful of countries which have either already replaced diplomacy by military operations, or which, not being ready to do so, are preparing to make the change in the near future, there are others which have not yet set themselves such tasks." Here he mentioned, as factors for peace, U.S. recognition of the Soviet government and "our relations with the great Turkish Republic as a model of relations with foreign states." Then he came to France: "In speaking of the gradual improvement in relations with other states, France comes first of all to mind . . . this is due both to the absence of any political antagonisms between us, and particularly to our common desire to work actively for the preservation of peace."[14]

Litvinov also devoted a few sentences to the signing of the Franco-Soviet Treaty of Nonaggression—on November 29, 1932—in Paris and of a Conciliation Convention. This was a short step in the direction of better future relations. It reflected fear combined with hesitation.

[13] J. V. Stalin, *Sochinenia,* Vol. 12, pp. 255-256.

[14] Jane Degras, *Soviet Documents on Foreign Policy,* Vol. III: *1933-1941,* pp. 48-61.

Germany stood on the threshold of Nazism. Russia and France were troubled, yet both felt disinclined as yet to antagonize Berlin or to forfeit the possibility of closer relations with Berlin. The French Communist Party anticipated no alteration in its attitude to the French government. "If it is necessary to change something in our activity we will make it even more ardent against French imperialism," wrote André Ferrat in the Paris communist daily *l'Humanité* of December 1, 1932, and here he echoed Stalin's words of 1930: French imperialism was "the most aggressive and the most militarist of imperialisms, the gendarme of Europe and the bloody tormentor of sixty million colonial slaves."[15] Europe, including the French communists, waited on events in Germany.

Hitler's accession to power on January 30, 1933, should have ended the waiting. *Mein Kampf* had branded France as an enemy and Russia as the victim of coming Nazi territorial acquisitions. But the ways of diplomacy are devious. Instead of banding together against Hitler, France and Britain accepted Mussolini's proposal of March 18, 1933, to include Germany in a four-power pact. The document, dead in infancy, was a gift of time to Hitler. It also frightened Poland, Czechoslovakia, and Moscow: Was the West giving Hitler carte blanche in the East? At least Poland and Czechoslovakia, neighbors of one another and of Germany and allies of France, might have concerted their efforts. Yet Pilsudski and Beck disliked Czechoslovakia, and when Hitler shrewdly bought off Poland with the ten-year nonaggression treaty of January, 1934, Czechoslovakia was isolated. So were the Poles, though they did not yet know it.

German communists of my acquaintance regarded Hitler as a passing phenomenon. "He will ruin himself in six months and then come we," they used to say. Some of this nonsense rubbed off on the Kremlin; the Russian communists long clung to the hope that Germany would go communist. On the other hand, Stalin had no intention of cutting his ties with Germany and allying the Soviets with France until Hitler had closed the door in Moscow's face. Unready for war, Hitler, no maniac, though he could often act like one in public and private, tried to delay the marriage between Russia and France which might follow their engagement (the November 29, 1932, nonaggression treaty) by extending the life of the Soviet-German Berlin Treaty of May, 1926. He did this in May, 1933.

But the hyena did not change its stripes. On June 16, 1933, Alfred Hugenberg, German Minister of Agriculture, presented to the World Economic Conference in London a memorandum which gained con-

[15] Quoted by William Evans Scott, *Alliance Against Hitler. The Origins of the Franco-Soviet Pact,* pp. 70-71.

siderable notoriety. In it he advocated giving the "people without land" —Germany—"space for the settlement of its vigorous race," and, in the spirit of *Mein Kampf*, he mentioned Russia where "War, revolution, and internal decay had made a beginning of this destructive process. . . . It is necessary that it be stopped." This bid for an international mandate to rip away portions of the Soviet Union roused Moscow to quiet fury. In these circumstances Soviet-German military cooperation soon ceased. By September, 1933, all German Reichswehr personnel had quit Russian soil.

No ambassador is happy in a country hostile to his. So it was that Rudolf Nadolny, German envoy in Moscow, wrote Berlin on February 6, 1934, suggesting that "we must proceed both with sweetcake and whip in order to quiet the maddened Soviet beast." Hitler might release to the Soviets Ernst Thaelmann, the German communist leader, "and possibly other Communists." That would be the "sweetcake." As for the whip, Nadolny urged "countermeasures very soon"[16] against the arrest of Germans accused of fomenting separatism in the Ukraine with a view to finding Lebensraum for Germans in accordance with the Hugenberg Memorandum.

Hitler refused to liberate Thaelmann. Stalin had no inclination to harbor another foreign communist whom he himself might want to liquidate. Ukrainian separatism was fed by Russification, Muscovite terror, collectivization, and other Kremlin-imposed hardships, and least by Nazi propaganda.

Nadolny wrote to express his disquiet over the emerging Franco-Soviet rapprochement. Bernhard von Buelow, State Secretary in the German Foreign Ministry, replied reassuringly. He said "we are convinced that the trees of the Franco-Russian afforestation will not reach the sky and we therefore do not wish to rush into expense in order to drain off their water. . . . If Herriot instead of Daladier had recently become Premier and Foreign Minister, and if he, unlike Daladier, had been able to master the difficult domestic situation, then we would have to count on serious French attempts in that direction." But with Rightists in the new French government, "Russia swinging or swerving into the French camp . . . alignment of the Soviet Union with the front of our opponents . . . etc., are slogans with no reality behind them." French consent "to keep Russia free from behind in case of East Asiatic involvement"—French consent, in other words, to neutralize Germany and Poland in case of war between Russia and Japan—"is exceedingly difficult to formulate in a treaty." What could Russia give France in return? "In any case the Russo-French rapprochement must not in-

[16] *Documents on German Foreign Policy,* Series C. Vol. II, pp. 452-454.

timidate us; it cannot . . . become really dangerous to us."[17]

This secret document, dated February 12, 1934 was prescient: Nazi Germany had no need to fear a Russo-French entente. Paris too remained skeptical about the dividends that might flow from a combined effort with Soviet communism, and while small moves were made in the direction of a rapprochement with the Kremlin (military attachés were exchanged and the nonaggression treaty of November, 1932, was ratified), two main factors interfered with dressing the treaty in the clothes of reality. France and her ever-changing governments declined to resist Germany diplomatically or to prepare to stop her militarily. The ghosts of the first world war filled too many French houses. The Rightists hated the Leftists, "Hitler rather than Blum" was one of the Right's silly slogans, and pacifist socialists and antirearmament communists, thanks to Muscovite stupidity, were still enemies.

Moscow intensified its courtship of Paris. Courting Paris was neither a simple procedure nor a short one. Because France was fractured socially and politically, French Cabinets were unhomogenized coalitions which fell apart at the touch of a rightist riot or a financial scandal. The dissent of one or two ministers sufficed to thwart policy. Procrastination or inaction was therefore preferred to a clear-cut stance. This suited the apathy of the country. While Moscow courted Paris, London and Berlin tried to block the courtship, and Paris was too busy courting Mussolini and Hitler to pay much attention to Soviet blandishments. Europe was undergoing a reshuffling of relationships caused by the advent of Nazism. Was it not better to unite with Hitler for peace than to unite against him for war? Poland had answered this question in the affirmative and thereby wrecked Barthou's endeavors to achieve an Eastern Locarno. When Pierre Laval became French Foreign Minister after Barthou's assassination, he began all over again to negotiate an Eastern Locarno.

Laval failed just as Barthou had. Germany's rapid rearmament lent urgency to the entente with Moscow. Nevertheless, Laval spent much time preparing for his visit to Rome between January 4 and 8, 1935, where accords were reached by him and Mussolini regarding Africa and on the protection of Austria from Hitler's appetite. Lest Hitler take umbrage, Laval moved on to London, where he and Foreign Secretary Sir John Simon agreed (February 3, 1935) on the necessity of a settlement which "would replace the provisions of Part V of the Treaty of Versailles at present limiting the arms and armed forces of Germany."[18] They thus planned to acquiesce in what Germany had been doing without their acquiescence.

[17] *Ibid.*, pp. 474-477.
[18] Quoted by Scott, p. 221.

While Laval wasted time, Hitler practiced blitz diplomacy. France transferred the overwhelmingly German Saar territory to Germany on March 1, 1935. Having won what he wanted from France without force, the "Fuehrer" on March 9, 1935, announced the extent of his force: Germany, in contravention of the Versailles peace treaty, had an air force; on March 16 the German government introduced universal military service. The same day, Paul Joseph Goebbels, Minister of Enlightenment and Propaganda, informed the press superfluously that the military provisions of Versailles were no longer valid; Germany's peacetime army, he said, would consist of thirty-six divisions, or more than half a million soldiers. The beginning.

Moscow reacted with a shell from its biggest military gun: Mikhail N. Tukhachevsky, Russia's top general and Deputy Commissar of Army and Navy, wrote an article in *Pravda* of March 31, 1935. Frederick Kuh, correspondent of the United Press in Berlin, and I had an interview in Moscow that same year with Klimenti Voroshilov, Commissar of Army and Navy, on the Far Eastern situation. In normal course Kuh delivered his dispatch on the interview to the post office, where foreign correspondents' telegrams were censored. The censor, uncertain whether the Commissar had made the statements attributed to him, submitted Kuh's telegram to the Press Department of the Foreign Commissariat. An official of the department, who told me of the subsequent developments, took the telegram to Voroshilov. The Commissar carried it to Stalin. Apart from the political contents, which had to be approved by Stalin, Kuh described Voroshilov's office and, incidentally, noted that a revolver lay on the desk. Voroshilov suggested to Stalin that mention of the revolver should be excised. "What of it?" Stalin replied. "A military man, a revolver."

When a commissar and member of the Politburo does not dare censor the story of his own interview and feels he must show it to Stalin, there can be no question that Tukhachevsky's *Pravda* article was sanctioned by Stalin if not by the entire Politburo. "In fact," the article reads, "the French army, with its twenty divisions, its hastily assembled units and slow rate of expansion by stages during mobilization, is already incapable of active opposition to Germany." Prophetically, Tukhachevsky affirmed that "Hitler's imperialist plans are directed not only against the Soviet Union. That is merely a screen for his plans to seek revenge in the West (against Belgium and France) and in the South (Poznan, Czechoslovakia, and Anschluss with Austria). . . . By the summer of this year Germany will have an army of 849,000 at least; that is, 40 percent greater than the French army and nearly as large as that of the Soviet Union (whose forces total 940,000)" (although the U.S.S.R. was ten times bigger than Germany, had two and a half times the population and a land frontier of some 12,500 miles).

The article told the French government that France was weak and in greater peril than Russia. It contained warnings to Poland ("Poznan"), Czechoslovakia, and Austria. It mirrored Moscow's eagerness for a military alliance with France but also puzzlement at French hesitation to forge the bond. French friends of the alliance could read into the article an intimation that the Kremlin was somewhat disenchanted. But if "France is already incapable of active opposition to Germany," why did the Soviet Union need the alliance? At the time Soviet diplomats said an alliance with a militarily inferior France was better than complete isolation. Japan constituted a threat, Germany too; Poland sided with Germany; Britain flirted with Germany; France would do likewise unless linked with Russia. In case of a German attack on Russia through Poland, the French army might at least render passive opposition by sitting in the forts of the Maginot Line or moving into Belgium—if (a big if) Belgium agreed.

But why should France act to save Communist Russia?

Edouard Herriot, leader of the Radical Socialist Party, which was neither radical nor socialist and served as the keystone of most French governments of the period, had always pursued a pro-Soviet policy and insisted on the alliance now. Pierre Cot, Minister of Aviation and a progressive, considered the Soviet air force a powerful potential reserve for France at war. But the central factor which conduced to French acceptance of the mutual defense treaty with Russia was psychological rather than strategic. In a political crisis, when nerves are frayed and panic threatens, governments tend to do something just in order to do something, it would prove they were neither asleep nor insensitive to the national peril. There was not much an unstable French Cabinet could do in the face of the mounting menace of Germany rearmed. It allowed a mutual assistance treaty to be signed in Paris on May 2, 1935, by Foreign Minister Laval and Soviet Ambassador Vladimir Potemkin.

The treaty was one-legged at birth. Four times in its brief text it stressed the European nature of the arrangement: it came into effect only if either country were attacked by a European power; in other words, France would not help Russia in a war with Japan.

With the document in his pocket Laval journeyed to Moscow. The Russians know how to produce stage effects. Pierre Laval, looking like a small provincial tradesman, was received with pomp. There were dances and drinks and little congratulatory speeches. Laval seized the opportunity to talk politics with Stalin. Now that France and the Soviet Union were partners, he submitted, was it not in Russia's interest to enhance French military strength? And how could this be done in the face of French communist opposition to French rearmament? (Communists in the Chamber of Deputies had refused, for instance, to vote appropriations for the construction of the Maginot Line.) Stalin saw the justice of Laval's contention, and the communiqué on the results of Laval's May 13 to 15 visit included these words: "Comrade Stalin expressed complete understanding and approval of the national defense policy pursued by France with the object of maintaining its armed forces at a level consistent with security requirements."

The French Communist Party read Stalin's statement as an order. It had already initiated a program of collaboration with socialists (the former "social-fascists") and liberals. The Third International's Congress of July-August, 1935, confirmed this Popular Front policy: communists would fraternize with noncommunists of all hues, from pink to black, in the interest of Russia's national security. Revolution would wait—perhaps forever, for advanced industrial states do not make revolutions.

The Franco-Soviet treaty of mutual defense should have had another logical sequel: joint General Staff talks. None took place. The British government frowned on them. "Are we still quite satisfied that the French have no intention of entering into any paramilitary commitments with Russia?" a high Foreign Office official asked on January 7, 1936.[19] London feared being drawn into Continental quarrels from which it felt remote. The same official therefore proposed to Foreign Secretary Eden that "we should make this clear to the French Government by stipulating forthwith that before they make any change in their relations with Russia they will consult us and give us an opportunity of expressing our view. . . . France's policy in Europe must always be a matter of direct concern to H.M. Government."

His Majesty's government aspired to a veto over French foreign policy and was often permitted by the irresolute French to use it. Great Britain did not object to the signing of the Franco-Soviet treaty because the Foreign Office regarded it as a means of blocking a rapprochement between Nazi Germany and Soviet Russia: "and supposing we had broken the project of the treaty," Vansittart wrote in the margin of an October 22, 1936, Foreign Office paper on this subject, "and in a few years there *had* been some sort of Russo-German rapprochement?" But when it transpired that such a rapprochement was more unlikely than at any time since Hitler's accession to office, when the French General Staff showed no desire for collaboration with the Red Army, the British lost interest in Franco-Soviet relations. The treaty, in which so much work and hope had been invested, had no effect on Hitler, on the course of international affairs from May, 1935, to September, 1939, or on the second world war. Another scrap of diplomatic paper.

[19] Foreign Office Secret Files, F.O. 371, No 19880, Registry 7262/92/62, p. 74.

General Staff talks in any case were impractical. If the Soviet Union was to help France after a German attack, Red forces would have to traverse Poland or Rumania or both in order to strike the Nazi flanks. Poland refused to adhere to the Eastern Locarno because she wanted no Soviet armed units on her territory. Rumania had a seventeen-year-old dispute with Moscow which, despite the establishment of diplomatic relations, would not recognize Rumanian sovereignty over Bessarabia, seized by Rumania in January, 1918, when Bolshevik Russia was weak. If the Red Army went through Rumania it might retain Bessarabia for Soviet rule, and, in any case, even after Russian troops crossed Rumania they would still have to cross Czechoslovakia in order to assist a France that had been the victim of German aggression. Accordingly, the Soviet Union and Czechoslovakia signed a mutual defense pact on May 16, 1935, the day of the Stalin-Laval communiqué. It was similar to the Franco-Soviet treaty except for Article 2 of the appended Protocol which stipulated that the contracting parties would come to the aid of one another only after France had come to the aid of the victim of aggression. This meant that Russia would wait until France had moved to the assistance of Czechoslovakia under German attack. "It is interesting," comments an official Soviet diplomatic history, "that this condition was made on the insistence of the Minister of Foreign Affairs of Czechoslovakia, Beneš."[20]

Why did Beneš take this stand? The answer that springs immediately to mind is fear of being occupied by communist troops likely to implant a communist regime. But Czechoslovakia had another reason, which emerged in subsequent secret negotiations between Beneš and Nazi Germany.

Remained the question of how France could help Russia in the event of invasion. Only by taking the offensive against Germany in the West. But France was not offensive-minded; her generals conceived only of passive inaction. Hitler, moreover, began building the Siegfried Line as soon as his meager battalions entered the Rhineland on March 7, 1936. This dissuaded France from contemplating military action benefiting Russia or Poland, Czechoslovakia, and Rumania.

Not only was the Franco-Soviet treaty stillborn. By the spring of 1936 Germany had in effect nullified all French alliances in Eastern Europe. With Britain more inclined to appease Hitler than to antagonize him, the sole barrier on his path to conquest was Germany's unpreparedness, as yet, for war.

The situation challenged Stalin's ingenuity. Hitler was fiercely anti-Soviet, the West was flabby and unfriendly.

[20] A. A. Gromyko and others (Eds.), *Istoria Diplomatii* (The History of Diplomacy), Vol. III, p. 607.

XXIV MOSCOW'S HAND IN THE SPANISH CIVIL WAR

Historians and diplomats, and many others, have been puzzled by Stalin's foreign policy from 1934 or 1935 to August 23, 1939. They wonder whether he was sincere in his prowestern orientation. Or did he intend from the beginning to sign with Hitler?

The issue of sincerity does not arise. Like Lenin, Stalin believed in practicing "practicality." Morality plays a minor role in international affairs and least of all in Moscow. It would not have seemed wrong to Stalin to sign alliances with France and Czechoslovakia and to launch the Popular Front, which foreign communists loved because it enlarged their field of action, and in the same and the next year inquire through Sergei A. Bessonov and David Kandelaki whether Hitler wanted better relations with Soviet Russia. Playing two hands of cards is not an uncommon diplomatic gambit when the future is opaque and the present so capricious.

By proximate control Stalin simultaneously ran two trains, one headed via Prague for Paris and perhaps London, the second going to Berlin. Either might be wrecked before reaching its destination. Both might. But with two on the tracks he had a better chance to get somewhere.

The events of 1934, 1935, 1936, 1937, and 1938 put a premium on alternatives. Most governments sought alternatives. Schizophrenia was king of policy—except in the realm of the schizophrenic Hitler, who followed a single path toward suicide by rearmament and demonic diplomacy.

* * *

The world of sport gathered in the giant Berlin stadium in August, 1936, for the Olympic Games. One of the British visitors was Sir Robert Vansittart. He had gone to Berlin at the invitation of Ribbentrop, the new Nazi Ambassador in London. Ribbentrop took Sir Robert to see Hitler in the Wilhelmstrasse Chancellery.[1] Hitler knew Vansittart's pervasive influence in London and his furious anti-German sentiments.

[1] Ian Colvin, *Vansittart in Office. The Origins of World War II*, p. 109.

He tried to moderate them by a favorable reference to the British Empire, which he "admired," and an expression of alarm over the "communist menace in Europe." He supposed, Hitler said, that "the Left" would win in the Spanish civil war.

There is every indication that Vansittart did not budge a millimeter.

Hitler and Mussolini had already taken steps to prevent the victory of the "Left." Hitler delivered a speech on June 6, 1939, in which he said he had decided as early as July, 1936, to answer General Francisco Franco's appeal for help to overthrow the government of the Spanish Republic.[2]

The lying commenced immediately after the rebel generals struck on July 18. The German Consulate in Tangier telegraphed the Berlin Foreign Office on July 24 that, "The Nationalist uprising was necessary in order to anticipate a Soviet dictatorship, which was already prepared."[3] No fact supported this invention. The Spanish Communist Party was weak and the Soviet government had not yet intervened in Spain. The German consul in Tetuán took the same lying line when he wired Berlin on July 25, "After the Rightist military faction learned that Soviet ships had arrived in Spanish harbors with arms and ammunition for an uprising planned by the Communists, they believed they should no longer delay the military uprising."[4] That day the German Embassy in Madrid pleaded for help to the military rebels intent on ousting the democratically elected government to which it was accredited.[5]

On visits to Spain in 1934 and in the spring of 1936 I saw a nation deeply divided between poor and rich. The urban and village poor were desperate, the rich inflexible. As I drove with colleagues and friends along the highways, some Spaniards gave us the clenched-fist antifascist salute and others the outstretched-arm fascist salute. The civil war was already present in embryo. Civil wars occur where governments are weak. The Spanish Republican government was weak in resolution. Spain, like Tsarist Russia, had resisted Napoleon and missed the bourgeois revolution. She needed a land reform to break up the vast estates of aristocrats who wasted their lives in Madrid and Paris, distribute the land among peasants or landless farm laborers, and help them acquire animals and machinery. She needed modern industry. She needed to join Europe from which the Pyrenees and history separated her. She needed to be awakened from her feudal sleep by leaders capable of stern action on behalf of change. But Prime Minister Manuel Azaña was a politician in whom an excess of intellect paralyzed will. Educated in a

[2] U.S. Department of State, *Documents on German Foreign Policy. 1918-1945. (1937-1945)*, Vol. III: *Germany and the Spanish Civil War, 1936-1939*, p. 11.

[3] *Ibid.*, p. 8.

[4] *Ibid.*, p. 9.

[5] *Ibid.*, pp. 11-13.

famous Catholic monastery, he became a prominent jurist and author of several plays, three novels, an autobiography of his youth entitled *The Garden of the Monks* esteemed for its literary brilliance, and a Spanish translation of Borrows' *The Bible in Spain.* When I interviewed him on April 4, 1936, he knew what was wrong, "The reactionaries of the Right have lost the capacity to rule Spain. They are half-republican, half-monarchist and they agree among themselves upon the necessity of squeezing labor and perpetuating outmoded forms of landownership and industrial management." Rejection of the obsolete had brought the Popular Front to power on February 16, 1936. The Right, defeated by ballots, decided on bullets.

Prime Minister Azaña knew the army was plotting against his government. He had therefore transferred Franco from Madrid to the Canary Islands, General Manuel Goded to the Balearic Islands, and General Emilio Mola to Navarre Province in northern Spain. Forewarned by this half measure, the military plotted to destroy the Republic. Francisco Largo Caballero, chief of Spain's socialists, put the situation in a sentence, "The reactionaries can come back into office only by a coup d'état." That was their purpose when they attacked on July 18, 1936.

The Spanish civil war sprang from Spain's poverty, economic backwardness, and the narrow-mindedness of her thin military, industrial, feudal, and ecclesiastical upper crust. It was rooted in the soil and rocks of Spain. But it had enormous international significance. It opened the prospect of extending Italian influence to the western Mediterranean and a corresponding contraction of British power. To Hitler it meant that France, with Nazi Germany on one of her borders and fascist Italy on another, would, if Franco won, be almost totally surrounded on land by fascist states. It would give wings to the idea that fascism was the world's wave of the future.

For Moscow the chief consideration in Spain was France. "It is obvious," Count Johannes von Welczeck, German Ambassador in Paris who had been ambassador in Spain from 1926 to 1936, wrote his Foreign Office on August 2, 1936, "that after a victory of the Nationalists—as the rebels are wont to call themselves—their relations with present-day France will probably be very cool, but very cordial to us and Italy."[6]

A France handicapped by hostile neighbors on three sides and perhaps succumbing in whole or part to a surge of fascism or defeatism would leave the Soviet Union isolated and a prey to the pressures of Japan, Germany, and Poland. Germany and Italy committed themselves early to the task of imposing Franco on Spain. If France and England permitted this operation to succeed, it would be clear that appeasement

[6] *Ibid.*, p. 22.

in those countries was so deeply entrenched as to enable the Hitler-Mussolini Axis to dominate Europe and imperil Russia. The Kremlin hoped, even after March 7, 1936—perhaps because of it—that the Spanish civil war might persuade London and particularly Socialist Léon Blum's Popular-Front French government to resist aggressors and abandon appeasement. It was a slim chance, but too much was at stake not to try. It could not have occurred to Stalin that the Soviet Union alone might defeat Franco. For if Russia had augmented her aid to the Loyalists, Mussolini and Hitler would have sent as much or more to the "Nationalists." Stalin's only political strategy was to help until England and France saw the wisdom, in self-interest, of helping the legitimate government defeat the rebels. They, not he, could have turned the tide in Spain. And having decided to defy fascism in Iberia they would, presumably under firmer leadership, have taken measures to check it wherever it encroached on their territories or spheres of influence.

* * *

The German Consulate in Seville transmitted, via Lisbon, a request to Berlin from General Queipo de Llano, one of the three rebel chieftains (the other two were Franco and Mola) for "10 large and 5 small planes. . . . The General stated that several Italian planes had already arrived in [Spanish] Morocco with Italian pilots who nominally joined the Spanish Foreign Legion."[7] Ambassador Welczeck telegraphed from Paris on July 31, "Reports in the press this evening that the Italian planes which crashed in French Morocco were military planes are correct, as I hear confidentially from a good source." They had taken off from Sardinia "for delivery to Franco."[8]

Mussolini intervened in the Spanish civil war before it began and in order to make sure it would begin. Italy's contribution to the "Nationalists" was greater than Germany's. Dr. Ernst Woermann, German chargé d'affaires in London, informed Berlin on February 4, 1938, that "The Italian Ambassador [Dino Grandi] told me . . . the maximum number of Italian volunteers [in Spain] had been 60,000 to 70,000 in March, 1937. The number had now been reduced to some 30,000 men."[9]

It is not necessary to take these figures or the name "volunteers" at face value. The relations between the Axis partners in Spain were delicate; Hitler wished to avoid the impression of poaching on Mussolini's sphere of influence. But he did not repose excessive confidence in Italy's combative efficiency. Grandi would therefore have tended to minimize Italian participation lest Germany reinforce her contingent. Moreover,

[7] *Ibid.*, p. 15.
[8] *Ibid.*, p. 17.
[9] *Ibid.*, p. 580.

the truth about the extent of Italy's aid to Franco might hurt the Spanish Nationalists' pride and alarm Britain where Rome was hoping to float a loan. A British Foreign Office memorandum of October 2, 1938, quoted a British War Office estimate of 40,000 Italian fighting men in Spain as well as 250 planes, 2,200 aviation personnel, and "about 2,000 civilian lorry drivers."[10]

The reliability, never even approximately complete, of official statistics on intervention in Spain depends on the date of their publication. During the Civil War the Italian government would wish to conceal, after it to boast: "Italian aid to the Nationalists was named by the semiofficial Stefani News Agency in 1941 and its figures may be accepted as approximately accurate. Thus Italy may be supposed to have sent 763 aircraft to Spain, 141 aircraft motors, 1,672 tons of bombs, 9,250,000 rounds of ammunition, 1,930 cannon, 10,135 automatic guns, 240,747 small arms, 7,514,537 rounds of artillery ammunition, and 7,663 motor vehicles. According to the Italian press in 1939, Italian pilots flew in 135,265 hours in the war, participated in 5,318 air raids, hit 224 ships, and engaged in 266 aerial combats in which they brought down 903 aeroplanes."[11] The last figure is suspect. The Spanish Republic did not, throughout the civil war, possess a total of 903 airplanes.

Germany's main help to Franco was in the air. "The strength of the Germans in Spain reached about 10,000 at its maximum in the autumn of 1936." The majority of these belonged to the Condor Legion, which consisted, with few exceptions, of airmen. It "was accompanied by thirty antitank companies."[12]

Italo-German assistance weighed most heavily at the beginning, when the major portion of the territory of Spain remained in the Republic's hands and the major portion of the population rallied to the government. "Under good military leadership; numerically weak, for it lacks support among the broad masses," reads an official German military assessment of the Spanish rebel situation as of August 22, 1936.[13] But Germans, Italians, Franco's Moors, as well as 20,000 Portuguese tipped the balance in favor of the Nationalists and helped push back the untrained militiamen who leapt to arms in defense of the Republic against military insurgents and foreign intruders.

Soviet aid came late.

The Italian and German governments charged that considerable arms shipments were going into Republican (Loyalist) Spain from France.

[10] E. L. Woodward and Rohan Butler, *Documents on British Foreign Policy 1919-1939,* Third Series: *1938-1939,* Vol. III, p. 315.

[11] Hugh Thomas, *The Spanish Civil War,* p. 634.

[12] *Ibid.*

[13] *Documents on German Foreign Policy,* Series D. Vol. III, p. 50.

The Republic had money, and armaments merchants are always ready to make an easy penny. On August 4, 1936, however, the French Ambassador in Berlin called on Foreign Minister Baron von Neurath to suggest "a joint declaration of the interested powers regarding nonintervention in the affairs of Spain." Great Britain had already agreed. Italy and Germany procrastinated while they accelerated their arms shipments to the military junta. "Our reply to the French note verbale—informing us of the agreement between the French and the British governments as to their attitude toward events in Spain—has, I am reliably informed," the Nazi chargé in Rome wrote Berlin on August 20, 1936, "caused great satisfaction in the Foreign Ministry here; it fits perfectly into the policy followed here, since it makes possible a further delay in the conclusions of the proposed nonintervention agreement."[14] During the delay more Italian and German munitions went into Spain.

No sooner had Germany agreed to nonintervention in Spain than she began to plan intervention. The Spanish rebels sent a request to Lisbon on August 27 "to pass on an order for 2,000 aerial bombs. . . . Delivery could be made through Holland which had not joined the pact."[15] Four days later—August 31, 1936—the German Foreign Ministry explained to its diplomatic missions abroad that the French proposal of nonintervention committees caused German "uneasiness lest the committees . . . might gradually develop into an agency of extended competence with control functions."

Hitler did not object to committees without control functions. Rome too wanted a nonintervention committee of "a purely platonic character." Twenty-seven countries ultimately joined the Nonintervention Committee with headquarters in London and with a permanent British chairman. Among them Portugal, a latecomer, served as a sieve for shipping arms to the rebels, and Italy and Germany were never deterred by the Committee's deliberations or decisions from propping up Franco with their arms.

The Soviet government agreed to nonintervention on August 23. At once the Soviet representative on the Committee proposed that a commission be sent to examine the situation on the Spanish-Portuguese frontier. Since fascist infiltration of men and munitions continued, the Soviet government declared on October 23, in a note to the Committee chairman, that "it cannot consider itself bound by the Agreement for Nonintervention to any greater extent than any other of the remaining participants of the Agreement."[16]

[14] *Ibid.*, p. 47.
[15] *Ibid.*, p. 59.
[16] Ivan Maisky, *Spanish Notebooks*, p. 49. Maisky was the Soviet ambassador in London and the Soviet delegate to the Committee.

Moscow's formal position was that without international inspection there would be violations. In reality the Soviet government saw that without its military assistance the rebels, aided by Hitler and Mussolini, would soon rule Spain. Marcel Rosenberg, the Soviet Ambassador in Madrid, and Mikhail Koltsov, *Pravda* correspondent in Spain and unofficially Stalin's eyes and ears in that country, had been bombarding Moscow with gloomy prognostications of the Spanish government's impending demise. (I was in Madrid and in touch with both of them.) The Soviet note of October 23 did not foreshadow a policy change; the change had already taken place. It was announced by Stalin on October 15 in his usual elliptical manner: "The workers of the U.S.S.R. are doing no more than their duty in giving the help they are able to give to the Spanish revolutionary masses. They are well aware that the liberation of Spain from the oppression of the fascist reactionaries is not merely the private business of the Spaniards but the common cause of all advanced and progressive mankind."[17] At the hour of his announcement Soviet tanks were aboard vessels bound for Spanish harbors. The cause of Spain aroused intense enthusiasm throughout Russia. Many communists and noncommunists hoped that events in Spain might lend new life to the dying flame of the Russian revolution.

Not Stalin. He had consented to sell the Spanish Republic arms. But not to make a revolution. He intended in the near future to snuff out the flame with Russian blood. Help to Spain was for Stalin essential to his prowestern foreign policy: given time France and England might recognize the folly of appeasement and join the Soviets in blocking fascist-Nazi-Japanese aggression. If, furthermore, Italy and Germany were testing new weapons and gaining experience in actual warfare, the Soviet Union should do likewise. The instantaneous explosion of affection in Russia for the Spanish Republic also propelled Stalin in the direction of intervention. He was about to discover and destroy untold thousands of "fascist spies" and "enemies of the people" inside Russia. He could scarcely ignore the avowed fascist enemies of the U.S.S.R. outside who were poised to bury antifascist Spain. Soviet public opinion counted for little, but it still counted for something, and Stalin's itch for popularity grew worse by the day. All governments like to be liked. Foreign communist parties, notably the French, were clamoring for Soviet action against fascism in Spain, and although Stalin abhorred international communists he expected to need their services in the immediate future and did not wish to alienate them completely by remaining aloof from the direct fascist-antifascist confrontation in Spain. He made it clear, however, that neither Soviet assistance nor that of foreign communist

[17] Jane Degras, *Soviet Documents on Foreign Policy*, Vol. III: *1933-1941*, p. 212.

parties implied a desire to make Spain communist or socialist. Rather the contrary. The Kremlin wanted no communist revolution or communist government in Spain and said so in clear terms. This message was conveyed to Spanish Prime Minister Largo Caballero in a letter dated December 21, 1936, and signed by Defense Commissar K. Voroshilov, Chairman V. Molotov, and J. Stalin. The letter and one that followed on February 4, 1937, were in French and appeared in facsimile and English translation in the *New York Times* of June 4, 1939, in an article by Luis Araquistain, a Spanish socialist, former Loyalist ambassador in Paris, a close friend of Caballero (from whom he obtained copies of the letters), an angry enemy of the Spanish communists, and a biting critic of Soviet conduct in Spain.

After promising in the first letter that "We have deemed and we shall always deem it our duty, within the measure of our possibilities, to go to the aid of the Spanish government . . . against the military and fascist clique which is only an instrument of international fascist forces," the three Kremlin leaders introduced the advice they intended to give Caballero by saying, "The Spanish revolution plots its course, different from many viewpoints from the course followed by Russia. This is determined by the difference in social, historical, and geographical conditions and by the needs of the international situation, different from those the Russian revolution had to contend with."

Having laid down this proposition, Voroshilov, Molotov, and Stalin affirmed that "It is very possible that the parliamentary way will show itself to be, in Spain, a more efficient means for revolutionary development than in Russia."

Stalin and his colleagues had not suddenly been converted to the virtues of parliamentary democracy nor were they early discoverers of the law of polycentrism in communism. Still less can it be supposed that they were following the precept of Karl Marx, rejected by Lenin, that in countries like England, the United States, and Holland socialism could be achieved by democratic means. The key to the introductory statement of the three is in the words "determined by the international situation." They knew that if the Spanish Republic went communist all hope of bringing England and France to its rescue would be vain. This is borne out by the last of the four "counsels" in the Kremlin letter: "the government of Spain will not allow any one attempt against the property rights and legitimate interests of foreigners in Spain who are citizens of nations not supporting the rebels." Those property rights belonged, chiefly, to British subjects, Frenchmen, and Americans.

Stalin, Molotov, and Voroshilov submitted three other "friendly pieces of advice." The Spanish government, they suggested, "should take into consideration the peasants." Spain was "an agrarian country." The interests of the peasants should be "furthered" in matters of taxation. "It would be well also to attract peasants into the army."

Secondly, "It would be necessary to attract to the side of the government the small and middle bourgeoisie" who were to be protected against "attempts at confiscation and guaranteeing them, within possible limits, freedom of trade. Otherwise these groups will become fascist."

And third, "The chiefs of the Republic [liberal bourgeois] party should not be repudiated but, on the contrary, they should be attracted to the side of the government. . . . It is above all necessary that the government should be assured of the continuance of [President Manuel] Azaña and his group in power. . . . This is necessary in order to prevent the enemies of Spain from considering her a communist republic."

The second letter, dated February 4, 1937, and signed by the same three Soviet leaders, was brief and less revealing. It merely said, "We wish you [Prime Minister Caballero] and the Spanish people a complete victory over the external and internal enemies of the Spanish Republic. We deem it our duty to continue to help you in the future, within the measure of our possibilities. We shake your hand as your friends."

On domestic matters the Kremlin's advice amounted to: Avoid, or at least shelve, the class war until the civil war shall have been won. This put the obedient Spanish communists in one political cubicle with the Republicans. But Moscow moderation encountered furious opposition from the anarchists who, though they had joined the Caballero government, were by nature and in principle untamed, and from the POUM (Partido Obrero de Unificación Marxista), a semi-Trotskyist party, strong in Barcelona, who took the opposite view: that civil war was by definition class war and could only be won by throwing the torch of revolt into the villages and arousing the peasants to seize the land; then they would fight to retain it. The POUM and the anarchists were organizing farm collectives on confiscated estates.

In April, 1937, when the Stalin blood purge in the Soviet Union was going into high gear, civil war between the communists and POUM erupted within the larger civil war between fascists and antifascists. Barcelona, the capital of Catalonia, was its battlefield. George Orwell, author of *Homage to Catalonia,* who had joined a POUM battalion at the front in January, 1937, arrived in Barcelona on April 26 and found the two parties in fortified buildings ready for combat. City streets and boulevards, always so teeming with people, particularly men, were empty. Anarchists and POUM members, laden with hand grenades, machine guns, revolvers, and rifles, attacked government and communist strongholds. Government and communist troops attacked POUM and anarchist strongholds.

British destroyers appeared in Barcelona bay; nobody knew why. Tension increased. Firing increased. Caballero in Valencia, Spain's new capital—for Madrid continued under tight siege—hesitated to intervene. But War Minister Indalecio Prieto, a man with an immense bald head and a flabby paunch, and intensely anticommunist, as I know from talks with him, prevailed: he dispatched two cruisers and a battleship and 4,000 reliable Republican soldiers to Barcelona. The fighting ceased. Hugh Thomas, in his book, *The Spanish Civil War,* gives the official estimate of casualties as 400 killed and 1,000 wounded. He cites H. N. Brailsford in the London *New Statesman* of May 21, 1960, who put the number of dead at 900 and wounded at 2,500. A gift to Franco.

The communists pursued their anti-POUM vendetta. At a Cabinet meeting on May 15, in Valencia, Vicente Uribe and Jesús Hernández, the two communist members, demanded POUM's suppression. Caballero declared that as a worker and an old socialist he could not outlaw a workingman's party. At this the communists, and several socialist ministers who realized that the Republic would lose Stalin's valuable arms aid unless the POUM was proscribed, withdrew their support from Caballero. Juan Negrín, a physician and professor of medicine in the University of Madrid, who spoke Russian—his wife, whom he had met in the 1920's, was a Russian—and cared little about ideology, in fact cared little about party politics although he had been elected a socialist member of parliament, became Prime Minister. I spent many long evenings with Negrín in Valencia, later in Barcelona, and in his countryside hideaway where he went to rest and think. He was a compassionate liberal democrat and scholar, liked to live the good life, disliked dictatorship, had not the least sympathy with communism or Stalin's terror in Russia, but knew that the war could not be won without Soviet munitions and men and without communist support in the Cabinet and at the front.

Negrín told me how, on several occasions, he traveled incognito to Paris to beg Premier Léon Blum for help. Blum would literally weep and say that as a socialist he of course wished to assist the Spanish Republic, but if he did, civil war would erupt in France as it had in Spain. Shipments from the Soviet Union and the Third International (Comintern) were therefore the Republic's only hope. Negrín, cool and practical, cultivated the Russians and the communists.

Negrín wanted French arms because the Loyalists needed arms. By avoiding complete dependence on Russia, moreover, he hoped to achieve political elbow room at home and abroad. But he failed to commit France to the cause of the Republic. Moscow remained his sole foreign support.

Mussolini boasted of Italy's aid to Franco. Hitler hailed his contribution and reviewed the veterans of the Condor Legion when they paraded in Berlin. Moscow was and remains laconic. An official Soviet diplomatic history published in Moscow in 1965 limits itself to these words: "Soviet volunteers fought in Spain in units of the International Brigades. Aviators and tankists and Soviet technical weapons were sent in aid of the Spanish Republican Army."[18] An official Soviet history (all Soviet histories are official) of Soviet international relations uses almost the same words as the diplomatic history, adding only that "The Soviet Union opened a credit of $85 million for the Spanish government."[19] Comments to come.

* * *

Traveling to the front one day—it was October 24, 1936—I saw, ten miles from Madrid, two tanks, one towing the other. A man stood in the turret of the first tank. The black monsters had stopped at a crossroads. I got out of my car, walked over to the man in the turret, and addressed him in Russian. The Loyalists had had no tanks; the man was unmistakably Slav. He answered in Russian. These were the first Soviet tanks to reach Spain.

Somewhat nearer the front I sought out the little white house where General Enrique Lister had established his forward headquarters. With Lister was a short thin individual in a blue serge suit which was obviously new and to which he was obviously unaccustomed. He put out his hand and introduced himself: "Fritz." I addressed him in Russian; his pronunciation of his own name proved he was no "Fritz." He was a Soviet officer, Lister's chief of staff. "Fritz" briefed me on the situation at the Madrid front.

One evening Mikhail Koltsov took me to dinner in the special Soviet restaurant in Madrid's elegant Palace Hotel. It was unusually full. Soviet military personnel had arrived—all dressed in ill-fitting, Moscow-made blue serge suits. "Who," Koltsov asked, "is the top officer here? Guess." I indicated a tall, gaunt man with a thick mat of gray hair. "No," Koltsov corrected, "that's General Jan Berzin. The commanding general is this one," and he nodded in the direction of a shorter person with a ruddy,

[18] A. A. Gromyko and others, (Eds.), *Istoria Diplomatii* (The History of Diplomacy), Vol. III, pp. 638-639.

[19] V. G. Trukhanovsky (Ed.), *Istoria Mezhdunarodnikh Otnoshenii i Vneshnei Politiki SSSR, 1917-1939* (The History of International Relations and the Foreign Policy of the Soviet Union, 1917-1939), Vol. I, p. 462.

kindly face and silver hair. I subsequently met him, General "Grishin," in the headquarters of the Spanish General Staff. I watched him as he received a telephone report from the front and issued orders in Russian in reply. Then he talked with me.

During September, 1936, the Loyalists laid siege to the Alcazar fortress in the ancient Moorish city of Toledo forty-seven miles from Madrid. I went there every day. One afternoon I encountered the Soviet military attaché, General Goriev. "With a thousand fellows of the Red army I would take the Alcazar in twenty-four hours," he said. The Spanish Republic had four to six thousand men surrounding the citadel to no avail. The "Nationalists" relieved the Alcazar and then laid siege to Madrid. General Goriev took charge of the defense of Madrid. In November I came to his apartment in the Ministry of War. The capital was almost entirely surrounded by four columns of troops under General Emilio Mola y Vidal who boasted that a "fifth column" of Franco sympathizers inside the city would soon enable Franco to capture it. But Goriev behaved as though he were at home in a peaceful suburb. He had been bathing and entered brushing his flaxen hair. Then he put a black net over it and ordered a light breakfast. After the meal he lit his pipe and talked calmly about the situation.

A man in civilian clothes appeared who introduced himself as Charles Loti. A Russian Jew named Rosenfeld, he spoke perfect French and some Spanish and when I accompanied him to the University of Madrid front he met Spanish officers to whom he gave instructions on improving the trenches and building fortifications.

"What is your job here?" I inquired.

"I am second assistant to our commercial representative here," he replied with a laugh. He was a Russian army officer.

Three Soviet colonels were attached as advisers to the International Brigade. One called himself Valois, which was surely not his name. At a training camp I saw Russians teaching Spaniards how to operate Soviet machine guns.

All the Soviet military I met were fervently devoted to the Spanish Republican cause. I do not know how they were chosen. Probably for ability. If, at an assembly of Soviet defense force officers, they were asked who wished to go to Spain many hands went up and some were selected. Only in this sense were they "volunteers." In all other respects they were regulars. They did not fight in units of the International Brigades though they occasionally advised them. Some of the foreign communists who joined the Brigades may have been long-term residents of the Soviet Union and hence Soviet citizens, but in Spain they were regarded as German or Yugoslav or Polish, and so forth. Soviet airmen functioned as a special unit and had their own airfields; by chance I once landed on one at Alcalá de Henares.[20] The tankists fought in support of the Loyalist army and of the International Brigades. A large number of the Soviet military in Spain served as advisers.

There were never more than five hundred Soviet military in Spain at any given moment. The total number active throughout the civil war probably did not exceed nine hundred.

When Franco mutinied, the legitimate government took arms where it could find them in the country and outside. In September, 1936, a Mexican ship landed 20,000 Mexican rifles and a large supply of bullets at Cartagena in Loyalist territory. One hundred and fifty Mexican volunteers came to fight for the Republic. André Malraux, the gifted French novelist, organized a cosmopolitan air force for the Loyalists with volunteer fighter pilots from France, England, Latin America, and elsewhere, and bought or otherwise obtained the planes which they flew. This heterogeneous organism saved antifascist Spain during the early months of the Civil War. Not until the advent of the Russians, however, did the Loyalists enjoy organized professional foreign military aid in men and material.

How much material is not known.

Soviet Ambassador Maisky writes that "a comparatively small stream of arms—including tanks and aeroplanes—came from the Soviet Union. From October 1936 to September 1937 only 23 shipments of arms went by sea from the U.S.S.R. to the Spanish Republic. . . . The Soviet government could, of course, have chosen to make a considerable increase in the delivery of arms to Spain. The Republic had sufficient means at its disposal to have paid for such deliveries. The limiting factor was the difficulty of transporting them."[21]

Maisky's book is a record of the infractions of the Nonintervention Agreement by Germany, Italy, and Portugal. He would therefore tend, in contrast, to minimize Soviet deliveries. Moreover, his statement that "only 23 shipments of arms went by sea from the U.S.S.R. to the Spanish Republic" shrewdly omits shipments to France and then overland to the Spanish Republic. Then too his cutoff date—September, 1937—is premature.

Thomas, in an appendix to *The Spanish Civil War,* writes, "As for Soviet aid by sea, the only report which even purports to be comprehensive is the analysis made by the German military attaché in Ankara." The military attaché presumably employed Turkish or German observers at the Turkish Straits who perhaps had access to the ships' mani-

[20] Louis Fischer, *Men and Politics, an Autobiography,* p. 396.

[21] Maisky, pp. 116-117. This book was first published in 1962 in Moscow under the Russian title of *Ispanskie Tetradi* by the publishing house of the Soviet Ministry of Defense.

fests or visual means of discerning what goods the vessels en route from Soviet ports were carrying to Spain. His total, from September, 1936, to March, 1938, was: 164 vessels loaded with 242 aircraft, 703 guns, 27 antiaircraft guns, 731 tanks, 1,386 trucks, 69,200 tons of other war material, 29,125 tons of ammunition, as well as 28,049 tons of petrol, 100 rifle-machine guns, 500 howitzers, 187 tractors, 325 tons of medical stores 32,278 tons of crude oil, 5,650 tons of lubricants, 450 tons of clothing—and 920 officers and men.

The German attaché conceivably tried to be objective. Hugh Thomas, however, regards his "analysis" as "incomplete . . . because it does not deal with shipments after March, 1938, and it is certain that some did arrive after that date." It is incomplete for an altogether different reason, given me by General M. Uritzky, a high-ranking army intelligence officer charged with the expedition of arms to Spain. I spent three hours in his Moscow office and then several informal hours in his suburban dacha at the end of 1936. He explained that a special unit of experts was busy devising means of deceiving the curious. Tanks and guns were immersed in petroleum-filled tankers; equipment was concealed between the real deck of a freighter and a built-in false deck; some guns were completely dismantled and the parts dispersed throughout the ships. Even the most clever German military attaché could not penetrate these and other disguises.

The British government attempted to ascertain the extent of shipments to Loyalist Spain. H.M.S. *Woolwich,* docked at Valencia, relayed a message on May 1, 1937, from Cartagena that the Spanish ship *Romeu* had arrived there on April 29 with oil, bombs, and sugar. On May 4 the *Woolwich* received another message from Cartagena, which it forwarded to Gibraltar, to the effect that the steamer *Tome* had arrived in Cartagena with a cargo of 100 airplanes, 100 airplane motors, 62 guns, 15 torpedo motor boats, and 20 tanks. The Military Branch of the British Admiralty informed C. A. E. Shuckburgh of the Foreign Office on June 14, 1937, regarding recent sailings from Soviet Black Sea ports for Republican Spain. Between March 24 and June 2 thirty-eight Spanish ships, ranging from the 12,589-ton *Tome* to the 1,194-ton *Celta,* passed through the Turkish Straits with munitions for the Loyalists. In the month of May alone "over 12,000 tons of war material left Soviet Russian ports for the Spanish Government . . . carried in thirteen ships." The First Lord of the Admiralty complained that "Great publicity is given in this country to reports, not always substantiated, of arrivals of Italian volunteers in Spain but there is very little attention paid to these continuous and very large breaches of the [Nonintervention] Agreement by the Soviet Government." The War Office, however, objected on two grounds: the summary of arms traffic contained in the list of ships "comes from a source in Istanbul who supplies similar information to Germany and Italy" and the information on the nature of the shipments was not always reliable. Moreover, Spanish government ships were not subject to the Nonintervention Agreement.[22]

Arms also reached the Spanish Republic via Gibraltar. I had personal knowledge of one such vessel,[23] and indirect information of others. Some munitions were purchased by the French Communist Party on Comintern instructions from the anticommunist Polish government. The Comintern paid in irresistible U.S. dollars or gold. These and other arms were unloaded in French ports and transshipped.

Ambassador Maisky confirms this. For months in 1937 the London Nonintervention Committee had been discussing ways of reducing the temperature of the Spanish civil war by withdrawing all "volunteers" from Spain: German, Italian, Russian, and the International Brigade. The British proposed a composite plan. Nazi Ambassador von Ribbentrop and Rome's Ambassador Dino Grandi delayed a decision. As a result, "the French government [since June 20, 1937, of Premier Camille Chautemps] had found itself obliged, under the pressure of democratic circles in the country, to open the frontier between France and Spain completely from the middle of July 1937 until such time as the discussions of the British plan could be concluded. . . . And since that discussion dragged on until 5 July 1938 . . . the Spanish Republic was able to receive arms through France. True, not everything was plain sailing. . . . None the less, by making free use of a system of bribes to persons on whom depended the granting of passes for transport of arms across France, the Spanish government succeeded in replenishing its arsenals considerably during the winter of 1937-8."[24]

The bulk of those shipments came from the Soviet Union and were paid for by the Spanish government. In September, 1936, I went to see Dr. Juan Negrín, then Loyalist Finance Minister. I had established friendly relations with him in 1934 and in the spring of 1936, and when I asked him in September how much money the Republic possessed he swore me to secrecy ("Our cause would suffer if this became known"), unlocked a drawer in his desk, and pulled out a card with figures written in ink in his hand. "We have 2,446,000,000 pesetas in gold, 25 million pesetas in foreign currency," he read. "And 656 million pesetas in silver." This, he calculated, totaled 600 million gold dollars or 1 billion paper dollars. Fleeing rebel sympathizers had left behind jewels and stocks and bonds; the government, moreover, was taking over the assets of

[22] Foreign Office, 371/21340-371/21345. Copies supplied by the Public Record Office, London.

[23] Fischer, pp. 392-393.

[24] Maisky, p. 164.

banks owned by Franco friends.

In October, 1936, after Toledo had fallen and "Nationalist" troops moved to encircle Madrid, the Spanish government transferred its gold hoard—500 tons—to the naval base at Cartagena whence it was taken under Spanish warship escort to Odessa, where the Soviet secret police transported it to Moscow by train. The Kremlin duly sent a receipt. From that fortune the Soviets subtracted what the Spanish government owed it for arms and other materials and services, and opened accounts in London and Paris banks on which the Loyalist authorities drew.

Soviet arms did not suffice to save the Spanish Republic. Distance was a contributing factor. Germany and Italy flew planes to Franco territory. Russia could not do that. There was another reason. In May, 1938, I transmitted an oral message from Prime Minister Negrín to Foreign Commissar Litvinov in Moscow. Negrín had said, "If we got 500 planes we could defeat Franco."

"Five hundred airplanes!" Litvinov exclaimed. "Five hundred airplanes would do us more good in China." The Soviet Union was already conducting a low-temperature war on two fronts: in Spain against Germany and Italy, in China against Japan. The 500 airplanes would have gone to Chiang Kai-shek for his flabby war against the Japanese invaders. Stalin, always cautious, was averse to becoming too deeply involved in Spain, a remote country access to which presented problems. The Soviet steamer *Komsomol* was burned and sunk by a Spanish insurgent warship near Gibraltar on December 14, 1936; the Soviet vessel *Stepan Kalturin* was boarded by a rebel gunboat in the Straits of Gibraltar; the Soviet S.S. *Kuzbas* was seized; the Norwegian S.S. *Lago* was halted by Franco men-of-war and forced to discharge its cargo at Fernando Po.[25] The Soviet S.S. *Soyuzvodnikov* was captured by the Franco fleet. The Soviet S.S. *Chubar* was seized by the Spanish insurgents on the high seas. The S.S. *Kharkov* was captured and its cargo examined.[26] The Soviet S.S. *Timiriazev* was sunk on August 31, 1937, and the *Blagoev* on September 1, 1937. Many foreign ships bringing food to the Loyalists were bombed from the air by planes serving Franco. Foreign and Soviet vessels carrying Soviet supplies to the Republicans were torpedoed in the Mediterranean by "unknown"—Italian—submarines. In 1937 and more so in 1938, Stalin's increased interest in his blood purges coincided with mounting Anglo-French-American appeasement of the aggressors. The two factors doomed the Spanish Republic.

Stalin had issued an order to the Russians he committed to Spain:

[25] British Foreign Office Archive, 409/59. Index p. 156.

[26] *Ibid.*, p. 155.

"Stay out of range of the artillery." As a substitute for Soviet infantry, the Comintern organized the International Brigade, the best fighters on the Loyalist side. The vast majority were communists; some socialists and other noncommunist antifascists came from Scandinavia, Italy, the United States, Britain, and from German social democrats in exile. Approximately 40,000 foreigners enlisted in the Brigade and entered Spain. Because they were brave, convinced, and often experienced, the command used them in the hottest battles, and their casualties reflected this necessary circumstance. The largest contingent was French, 10,000 of them, of whom 3,000 were killed. The Germans and Austrians numbered 5,000; they suffered 2,000 killed. Nine hundred of the 2,800 Americans met death in battle. Of the 2,000 British volunteers, 500 were killed and 1,200 wounded. "Perhaps 3,000 members of the Brigades were Jewish in origin."[27]

During the decades of its existence, the Comintern rallied hundreds of thousands of idealists throughout the world. The ranks of those who remained to witness its demise in 1943 were far thinner than the legions who had fled in angry frustration. The high-minded came to change an imperfect world. They found themselves in the service of an evil oligarchy committed to aggrandizement-in-one-country. Some were enmeshed in the despicable trade of spying. Thousands died, as in Canton in 1927, to prove Stalin a revolutionary. Yet all the Kremlin's base purposes could not prevent the idealists from writing a golden page of glory in Spain. They traversed oceans and continents in secret, crossed mountains on foot, and underwent endless hardships to fight for a foreign country under fascist attack. Too many lie today in her hard soil.

One of the noncommunists in the International Brigade was Randolfo Pacciardi, a liberal Republican and Minister of Defense in post-Mussolini Italy. As leader of the Garibaldi Battalion of Italians he fought Mussolini in Iberia. Pietro Nenni, the Italian socialist, served under Pacciardi. Another noncommunist in the Brigade was a Czechoslovak artillery captain (subsequently major) named F. O. Miksche. His 1941 book, *Blitzkrieg,* is dedicated "to the heroes of the International Brigades who sacrificed their lives for the freedom of the Spanish people between 1936 and 1939, in the first battles of the present war." He fought in Spain to save "my beloved homeland, the Republic of Czechoslovakia," and to prevent the second world war and its dire human and political consequences. All those who worked for Loyalist Spain had the conviction that if only the western democracies awakened to the dangers inherent in appeasing the Nazi-fascists in Spain a second world war might be avoided.

[27] Thomas, p. 637. The casualty data also are his.

In Chapter I of *Blitzkrieg* Major Miksche declares, "The Germans learned from Spain that war had changed." The French did not. "In one country outside Germany the experiences of the Spanish War were studied and corrected values. The Russian military press . . . gave almost as much space to a discussion of the fighting in Spain and the lessons to be drawn from it as the German military journals." The Soviet military in Spain functioned, of course, as professionals, sometimes ignoring Spanish government orders, but their zeal and dedication to the Spanish cause went beyond the call of duty. In a special sense they too were fighting to save Russia. For Loyalist Spain in wartime was a free country where people feared enemy bombs but not their own government. The high Soviet officers and officials felt the difference between Spain and their native land and some were particularly incensed when Moscow introduced into Spain the very instrument, the NKVD, which spread fear in Russia.

The Soviet secret police was richly represented in Republican territory and extremely active. Not only did it spy on and interfere with Soviet citizens of all ranks, it killed and kidnaped Spaniards and foreigners. It liquidated Andrés Nin, leader of the POUM. It kidnaped Mark Rein, the son of the Russian Menshevik Rafael Abramovich, and José Robles, Professor of Spanish literature at Johns Hopkins University who had been General Goriev's interpreter. They have not been heard of since. Suspected Trotskyites of all nationalities vanished. André Marty, a leading French communist and the commissar of the International Brigade, a hysterical paranoic, imitating NKVD practices, ordered early-morning arrests of members of the Brigade on the charge of Trotskyism; usual punishment—posting to the most dangerous segment of the fighting front.

Soviet generals and diplomats in Spain complained to Moscow; Spain was not Russia and Soviet methods alienated top-rank Loyalists. To no avail. The Moscow hand is a heavy hand. However, Stalin habitually purged the purgers. In 1938 Alexander Orlov, chief of the NKVD in Spain, received a summons to come to Moscow. He knew his masters too well to comply. Instead he moved quickly to a town in French territory near the Spanish border where his wife and daughter resided, sped with them to a French port, boarded a steamer for Canada, and thence made his way to the United States. There he wrote a book on Stalin's crimes—in Russia.

Most of the important Soviet diplomats and military who worked with so much devotion in Spain were executed as they returned to the Soviet Union. This cast a pall over their comrades still in the front line and over the Spanish officials who learned of their fate.

After the Czechoslovak crisis and the surrender of the Anglo-French appeasers to the Nazi-fascists at Munich in September, 1938, Soviet aid to the dying Spanish Republic ceased. World War II, the European civil war, was only one year away. Claude G. Bowers, the United States ambassador to Spain, asserted that "the Spanish war was the beginning of a perfectly-thought out plan for the extermination of democracy in Europe, and the beginning of a Second World War with that as the intent."[28] In the seats of the mighty they heard not neither did they see this. Millions paid.

"It is my firm opinion," Anthony Eden, former Foreign Secretary, said in the House of Commons on November 2, 1938, during the debate on Munich, "that, had it been possible for His Majesty's Government to adopt a firmer attitude in respect to these Spanish problems in the early part of this year, the subsequent deterioration of the international situation which we all lament would not have taken place."

The fall of Spain and the shame of Munich had the same parents.

XXV PURGES AND FOREIGN POLICY

During the third Moscow show trial in March, 1938, when the waters of defeat had reached to Loyalist nostrils, Spanish communists, obeying Kremlin orders, tried to collect the signatures of the Republic's leaders under a petition demanding death sentences for Bukharin, former Chairman Rykov, Rakovsky, Krestinsky, Yagoda, Khodjayev, and other defendants.

"What sort of country is Russia?" Spaniards asked.

Such bewilderment, and the fact that Soviet officers were being executed after their return from Spain, damaged Loyalist morale at the highest well-informed level.

Stalin's blood purges hurt the cause of Spain and had a disastrous effect on Soviet foreign relations. They continue to this day to depress Soviet life.

By the time the purges began in 1935 the freedom of discussion tolerated within the communist party during the early years of Lenin's rule had retreated into the dim past. Stalin fulfilled a prophecy which Trotsky made in 1904 in a polemic with Lenin: "The apparatus of the

[28] *My Mission to Spain. Watching the Rehearsal for World War II*, p. 411.

party will replace the party, the Central Committee will replace the apparatus, and finally, the dictator will replace the Central Committee."[1]

The question of unitary power had been decided in Stalin's favor. Now the purges could begin. No power inside the country and certainly no power or influence or consideration outside would, or did, mitigate, much less stop, the horror of the blood purges. Reputation and previous service were no impediment. On the contrary, the bigger the man, the better the communist, the more likely he was to get a bullet in the medulla oblongata. Stalin was intent on standing alone, unchallenged, unassailable. He succeeded. By 1936 major foreign policy and domestic policy decisions were his.

Stalin's blood-and-poison purges have only one rival in history: Hitler's gas chambers for the extermination of Jews. Compared with the two modern totalitarian tyrants, Caracalla, Genghis Khan, Tamerlane, and Robespierre were mini-scale murderers. There are now more people available for killing and better techniques for killing them than in the backward days of old. In India and in Indonesia and elsewhere hundreds of thousands have been slaughtered one by one by their neighbors; all peoples, even the most gentle, can take lives wholesale when aroused by religious or nationalistic hate or a thirst for revenge. But in Stalin's Russia, as in Hitler's Germany, it was the government that perpetrated the monstrous crimes at the behest of one man. Soviet citizens knew only a fraction of the truth; even given full information they could not have stayed the hand of the executioner in chief.

Russia had lived under autocracy throughout the thousand years of her history. The seven-and-a-half-month hiatus after the last Tsar's abdication in March, 1917, was a flash of freedom across Russia's dark past. Lenin then spoke of his country as "the freest in the world." But immediately he acquired the power to do so he extinguished the light and plunged Russia back into tyranny. Bolshevism was an absolutist code. In keeping with its ambition to improve on the past it improved on Tsarist absolutism. The first day of the Bolshevik revolution Leo Kamenev, one of its leaders, urged the abolition of the death penalty. Trotsky urged its retention. When Lenin, emerging from his hiding place, heard of the discussion he exclaimed, "Nonsense! How can you safeguard a revolution without executions?"[2] Lenin, whose own brother had been hanged by the Tsar's government, frequently threatened people with hanging—and with shooting. Lenin introduced the Soviet terror. Trotsky justified it. But they directed it against enemies or alleged enemies of

[1]From the Trotsky Archive at Harvard University, quoted by Trotsky in the unpublished manuscript of the Stalin biography.

[2] Leon Trotsky, *Pravda*, April 23, 1924.

the new regime. The unique aspect of Stalin's terror was that he directed it against communists. He never liked communists. They were revolutionists. They believed in something. He was a nonbelieving powerman.

Stalin suffered from inbuilt insecurity. Whether it was his withered arm or his lack of personal magnetism or because he was no orator like Trotsky, no thinker like Bukharin, no crunching debater like Lenin—whatever the reason, he was psychologically insecure. It would have seemed odd to him, as it certainly did to others, that he should sit in the seat of Lenin. He therefore, according to Khrushchev's secret speech on February 24, 1956, originated the slogan "Stalin Is the Lenin of Today." Those who knew Lenin must have laughed bitterly when alone, and he must have squirmed in their presence. They had to go to the death dungeon. He had to reduce the size of all survivors in order to seem taller than they. Toward the same end he sought to add a cubit to his public image. Stalin's self-deification, the incessant campaign of saccharine praise by which he himself glorified himself, was the counterpart of the purges.

The purges sprouted not only from Stalin's mentality. Had Stalin emigrated to America in young manhood he might have become a certain type of boss, but he could not have supervised the death of millions of Americans by a secret police, any more than Hitler as a British subject could have set up gas chambers for millions; the political system does not provide for such action.

It was what Thucydides called "the thralldom of some fatal and master passion" that drove Stalin to murder millions. He was not insane. But sane men are capable of one act or, if not apprehended, of many acts of insanity. The fear of punishment deters many. Stalin reckoned, correctly, that if he punished enough, none could punish him. He sowed death in the army, the secret police, the party, and in government. The more he killed and banished the more he had to kill and banish, lest their cumulative wrath attain him. The terror thus fed itself.

The shootings ended the day Stalin died; this should be sufficient proof of his personal culpability. Beria was the lone exception. After Stalin's death he was quickly dispatched.

Many of Stalin's victims have been officially rehabilitated as not guilty, and those still unrehabilitated have been left in limbo not because their innocence is in doubt but for fear of destroying the last shreds of faith in the political system responsible for snuffing out the lives of tens of thousands of prominent communists and hundreds of thousands of others who had committed no crime. The Kremlin is faced, and will long be faced, with an anguishing dilemma: Either it admits that the communist party went along with Stalin in annihilating most of the leaders who had made the revolution with Lenin and millions of others equally innocent—and in that case the "infallible" party is proved fallible and criminal—or it concedes that Stalin brushed the party aside and established a personal tyranny; this would negate the Soviet dictatorship's basic principle that the communist party is all-powerful and irreplaceable.

Those in the party leadership (the neo-Stalinists) who disapproved of Khrushchev's secret speech dethroning Stalin and who seek to restore at least a fraction of Stalin's reputation as well as to whiten some of his black record, are not so much interested in history or in him as they are in safeguarding what is left of the party's authority. That authority is threatened in all communist-ruled countries by new generations whose scientific training and modern outlook rob Marx's dogmas of credibility and whose meager contact with the outside world gives them a thirst for more freedom. The neo-Stalinists feel, rightly, that to reveal all of Stalin's crimes (Khrushchev's secret address was only a teasing preview) would rock the Kremlin.

One of the services that suffered most in the purges was the Commissariat of Foreign Affairs. A majority of the Soviet ambassadors and ministers were purged, some shot, some shipped to concentration camps, all unheard from after their expulsion from office. They were: Yurenyev, Ambassador to Japan; Davtyan, Ambassador to Poland; Rosenberg, Ambassador to Loyalist Spain; Marchenko, his successor there; Gaikis, Rosenberg's counselor; Antonov-Oyseyenko, who had served in Spain and other countries; Sokolnikov, former Ambassador in London; Karsky, Minister to Lithuania; Asmus, Minister to Finland; Brodovsky, Minister to Latvia; Skvirsky, formerly unofficial Soviet representative in Washington, then Minister to Afghanistan; Bogomolov, Ambassador to China; Tikhmenev, Minister to Denmark; Bekzadian, Minister to Hungary; Yakubovich, Minister to Norway; and Ostrovsky, Minister to Rumania. Alexander Barmine, Soviet chargé d'affaires in Athens, ordered to return to Moscow at the height of the purge, went instead to the United States, where he published his book, *One Who Survived.* Leon B. Gelfand, chargé d'affaires in Rome, received instructions to proceed with his wife and little daughter to Genoa and there board a Soviet vessel for a Russian port. Knowing what that meant, he and his family took the train to Genoa but descended at a small station before Genoa and, with assistance from Mussolini's Foreign Minister Ciano, proceeded via Spain to the United States, there to become a rich businessman. On April 5, 1938, Feodor F. Raskolnikov, Minister to Bulgaria, received a summons to come to Moscow. He refused and forfeited his Soviet citizenship. A former officer in the Tsarist fleet, he brought one of the Russian cruisers over to the Bolshevik side in November, 1917. Later he took command of the Soviet flotilla in the Caspian Sea and fought with daring in

Persian waters. Captured by the British, he was exchanged for eight British officers. He had served as Soviet envoy to Afghanistan and Denmark before assuming his duties in Sofia. He was also a prominent revolutionary writer. On being ousted from his post in Bulgaria he fled to Belgium and the next year published an open letter to Stalin accusing him of disregarding the new Soviet Constitution, degrading socialism, destroying the Red Army's leaders, and acting as a tyrant. Several months later he died in mysterious circumstances in a hospital in Nice.

Addressing the Twenty-Second Congress of the Soviet Communist Party on October 24, 1961, Nikolai M. Shvernik, a member of the party's supreme presidium, cited an instance of the "inhuman attitude of Molotov to the fate of people. In 1937," Shvernik declared, "one of the professors working in the People's Commissariat of Foreign Affairs wrote to Molotov as Chairman of the Council of People's Commissars. He wrote that his father had been arrested, apparently through a misunderstanding, and requested intervention on behalf of his father. Instead of investigating the humane request, Molotov made this marginal note: 'For Yezhov. Can it be true that this professor is still in the Foreign Commissariat and not in the NKVD prison?' After that the author of the letter was arrested illegally."

Tens of thousands of anonymous innocents lost years of their lives or went to their deaths as a result of such inhuman acts by Stalin's servitors.

On a higher level than professorial expert, minister, or ambassador, Deputy Foreign Commissar for Asia Leo M. Karakhan, former Ambassador to China, Poland, and Turkey, was shot without trial in December, 1937. Nikolai N. Krestinsky, another Deputy Foreign Minister, was executed after the third Moscow Trial in March, 1938; he has been rehabilitated as innocent.

In addition, several of Litvinov's personal secretaries, stenographers, and translators were executed. Most heads of departments in the Foreign Commissariat disappeared.

Ivan Maisky, Soviet Ambassador to Britain since 1932, was called to Moscow in 1938. Suspecting the worst, and for good reason, he paid a visit to David Lloyd George and asked the former Prime Minister to write him a postcard to Moscow.[3] The card, evidence of friendship in the highest British circles, would, presumably, act as a shield against the NKVD's bullet. Whether it was the postcard or Stalin's shrewd calculation that he needed Maisky in London, no harm came to him until 1951, when he was sent to a concentration camp. Stalin's death in 1953 brought Maisky's release.

[3] Lloyd George told me this when I saw him on his farm at Churt, near London.

Amid the grim harvest in the Soviet foreign service, Litvinov remained unscathed. Deputies, ambassadors, and ministers fell to the left and right of him, but he lived to die a natural death on the last day of 1951. Litvinov's escape from the hands of the Red executioner has puzzled Soviet citizens, including his close friends, and numerous foreigners.

Stalin had shorn Litvinov of power. At Geneva, in September, 1938, Litvinov said to me, "I am merely a messenger boy; I hand up papers." Yet he was kept in office probably so that he might be dismissed at the desired time with the proper effect. He was dismissed in May, 1939, on the eve of negotiations leading to the Soviet-Nazi pact. His removal then served as an indication to Hitler that Stalin wanted the pact. Litvinov, a Jew, would have been an embarrassment to the Nazi negotiators. He was not executed at that juncture because the purge had abated under Beria and because Stalin must have thought that Litvinov, with his enormous prestige abroad, might be useful someday if it again became necessary to woo the West. He was when Germany invaded Russia. Stalin then summoned Litvinov and said, "Have you kept your tuxedo? Take it out of the mothballs." He went to Washington as ambassador.

In his last book of memoirs, the late Ilya Ehrenburg quotes Litvinov as saying to him that Stalin "does not know the West. . . . If our opponents were a bunch of shahs and sheiks he would outwit them." Ehrenburg also reports that at the session of the Central Committee when Litvinov was ousted from that power body, Litvinov—outraged—addressed Stalin, saying, "Well, so you regard me as an enemy of the people." "Enemies of the people" were shot. Stalin took the pipe out of his mouth and replied, "No, we don't."

Ehrenburg tells too of an ambassadorial conference in 1936 at which Litvinov outlined his views on the international situation. Stalin walked over to him and, putting his hand on the Foreign Commissar's shoulder, said, "You see, we can agree." Litvinov lifted Stalin's hand, dropped it, and replied, "Not for long."[4] He knew Stalin was contemplating an alternative to the then prowestern orientation of Soviet foreign policy.

Stalin, insecure himself, would have respected the courage and independence of Litvinov. The tyrant, like the bully, is impressed by strength. Litvinov's inner strength helped to save him.

The slaughter in the Soviet foreign service was negligible compared to the massacre of key men in other branches of the state and party apparatus. Chairman Chervyakov of the Byelorussian government "committed suicide" in June, 1937, and the entire Cabinet of Byelorussia was

[4] Ilya Ehrenburg, *Post-War Years 1945-1954*, p. 278.

arrested at the same time. A tornado of terror ripped through the Ukraine and Uzbekistan carrying thousands of front-rank communists to their deaths. Valeri Mezhlauk, Chairman of the State Planning Commission and Deputy Chairman of the Soviet Union, recognized at home and in the United States as an outstanding industrialist, disappeared forever. So did his brother, also a prominent Soviet industrialist. Kraval, assistant to Mezhlauk, likewise fell victim to the purge. Dibetz, former director of the Kharkov tractor factory, later director of the automobile and tractor industry of the Soviet Union, was attacked by *Pravda*, discharged from his post, and never heard from again. From May to December, 1937, I checked three Soviet provincial newspapers; they listed 1,313 executions in the districts they served.

These are a minuscule sample of the holocaust. The industries of the whole country were decapitated, and the men who remained at their jobs were so paralyzed by the fear of what impended (no one felt safe) that they worked with half a heart and half a brain; the other halves were absorbed in nervous worry. For numberless communists the ignominy of being arrested by their own communist government and the tension of waiting for death in an NKVD dungeon was so unbearable that they committed suicide.

The dictator's keenest sword is fear. To be effective, fear must strike the innocent. If only the guilty are given condign punishment, the innocent can relax and feel free. But relaxation and freedom are unwanted in a totalitarian state. The Stalinist technique therefore consisted in blind injustice. The secret police cast its net with deliberate indifference to the lives it caught. Lack of evidence mattered not, because it could be manufactured by mystery-story writers inside the prisons and presented to helpless inmates for signature. Some signed. Some resisted, were tortured, and executed. Some resisted and survived to tell. There were no rules to create consistency or certainty, for the certainty of death might have been a comfort. The future, whether it was tomorrow or the next decade, remained dark by official design.

Marshal Tito, the communist President of Yugoslavia, recalled in the autumn of 1951 that he had been in the Soviet Union in 1935 and for a few months in 1936: "even in 1935 there were no end of arrests, and those who made the arrests were later themselves arrested. Men vanished overnight, and no one dared ask whether they had been taken. I witnessed a great many injustices. One morning the militia summoned a Yugoslav worker, who had been living in the Soviet Union and working in a factory for many years, with his wife. They informed him he was sentenced to eight years' exile in northern Siberia, and his wife to five years in southern Siberia. They were not even allowed to return to their flat to take their things, but were sent to Siberia directly. No one dared ask how they had offended."[5] This was common procedure.

Moshe Piyade, a member of the Politburo of the Yugoslav Communist Party and translator of Marx into Serbo-Croatian, declared in an address on August 6, 1951, "In 1936, 1937, and 1938, in the Soviet Union there were killed over three million people. They didn't belong to the bourgeoisie, because it had long ago been liquidated in that country. They were Communists, from Russia and the other republics in the Soviet Union."[6]

The late Boris I. Nicolaevsky, a Menshevik expert on Soviet domestic affairs, put the figure at seven to ten million. Others have offered higher estimates. Academician Andrei D. Sakharov, a Russian nuclear physicist, said in a manifesto which circulated underground in the Soviet Union and was published on two full pages of the *New York Times* of July 22, 1968, "At least 10 to 15 million people perished in the torture chambers of the N.K.V.D. from torture and execution, in camps . . . in the mines," etc. Nobody knows the exact number except the Soviet secret police. It does not tell.

The three famous Moscow show trials (August 19-24, 1936; January 23-30, 1937; and March 2-13, 1938) were merely the sharp visible peak of an enormous iceberg of terror that crushed the lives of untold communists, Soviet and foreign, whom Stalin "liquidated" through the agency of the secret police headed first by Genrich G. Yagoda, secondly by Nikolai I. Yezhov, the worst purger, and last, by Beria. Trotsky wrote in the manuscript of a second, unpublished, volume of his Stalin biography, "Yagoda was a pharmacist in his youth. In a peaceful epoch he might have died the owner of a small-town drugstore. Who would have thought that the greatest revolution in history would turn this provincial pharmacist into the court poisoner of a modern Borgia!" Yagoda, Yezhov, Beria, and the "modern Borgia" were all short men.

The most crashing blow of the Stalin-Yezhov terror struck the military.

Nothing—not the death of Lenin, the banishment of Trotsky, the assassination of Kirov, not the three Moscow show trials, nothing in Soviet history that one can recall before June 22, 1941—sent such a shattering shock through the people of the Soviet Union as the announcement in the entire Soviet press of June 12, 1937, that "yesterday" a special military tribunal of the Supreme Court of the U.S.S.R., sitting in secret session, had examined the case of Marshal M. N. Tukhachev-

[5] Vladimir Dedijer, *Tito*, p. 105. Dedijer was a prominent Yugoslav communist and a friend of Tito.

[6] *Ibid.*, p. 106.

sky, Deputy Commissar of Defense and the highest ranking officer in the Red Army; Marshal I. Z. Yakir; Marshal I. P. Uborevich; General A. I. Kork, head of the Frunze Military Academy and former military attaché in Berlin; General R. P. Eideman; General B. M. Feldman; General K. M. Primakov, deputy commander of the Leningrad district; and Vitovt K. Putna, former military attaché in Tokyo, Helsinki, Berlin, and London, and had "established" that the accused, "while in the service of the military intelligence agency of one of the foreign nations that is pursuing an unfriendly policy toward the U.S.S.R. systematically supplied the military circles of that nation with espionage information, carried out wrecking activities designed to undermine the strength of the Workers and Peasants Red Army and aimed to partition the Soviet Union and restore a government of landlords and capitalists in the Soviet Union."

The announcement declared further that all the accused "confessed" themselves "fully guilty" of the enumerated "crimes." The tribunal thereupon sentenced them to death. The eight men were immediately shot. Marshal Y. V. Gamarnik, chief of the Political Administration of the Soviet army forces, committed suicide—so the Kremlin press stated —when the secret police came to arrest him on May 31, 1937.

Tukhachevsky was the nation's hero. No Soviet leader was better known and more popular with all generations, especially the youth, than he. The other military victims were outstanding either nationally or in their districts. Photographs of a group of marshals, including Tukhachevsky, hung in many schools, offices, and homes.

The best treatment of the military purge is in a book by a British university professor, John Erickson, entitled *The Soviet High Command; a Military-Political History, 1918-1941*; it is often used for reference in Russia. In biographies appended to the book, Erickson states that Tukhachevsky and his comrades were shot "without trial." No evidence has ever been adduced that a trial or trials occurred. U.S. Ambassador Joseph E. Davies writes that "It is difficult to associate his [Stalin's] personality . . . with these purges and shooting of the Red Army generals, and so forth. His friends say, and Ambassador Troyanovsky [the Soviet envoy in Washington] assures me, that it had to be done to protect themselves against Germany—and that some day the outside world will know 'their side.' "[7] The disclosure "some day" might have been appropriate when Hitler attacked the Soviet Union or, later, during the second world war, or after Nazi Germany had vanished. Yet the outside world has never been given "their"—the Soviet—"side." The Ameri-

[7] *Mission to Moscow*, p. 357.

can and British armies and the Red Army captured carloads of official documents, whole libraries of which have been published. They contain no scintilla of evidence of the guilt of the purged army and navy officers. Soviet jurists functioning at the Nuremberg trial had ample opportunity to question the Nazi leaders in the dock about German collusion with the executed Soviet military. They never mentioned the subject. Instead, Chairman Khrushchev has exonerated the victims. He told the concluding session of the Twenty-Second Congress of the Soviet Communist Party on October 27, 1961: "Such prominent military commanders as Tukhachevsky, Yakir, Uborevich, Kork, Yegorov, and others were victims of repression. They were distinguished men of our army, especially Tukhachevsky, Yakir, and Uborevich, they were outstanding commanders. And then they were repressed. . . . Many excellent commanders and political officers of the Red Army were annihilated. Here among the delegates there are comrades—I don't want to cause them pain by naming them—who spent many years in prisons. They were 'persuaded,' persuaded by particular methods, that they were German or British or some other spies. And some of them 'confessed.' Even in cases when such persons were told that the accusation of espionage had been lifted they felt that it would be better to insist on their false testimony so as to get the torture over with and die as soon as possible. . . .

"I knew Comrade Yakir well. I knew Tukhachevsky, but not as well as Yakir. This year, during a conference in Alma-Ata his son, who worked in Kazakstan, came to me. He asked me about his father. What could I say to him? When we in the Presidium of the Central Committee examined these cases and the report was that neither Tukhachevsky, nor Yakir, nor Uborevich had committed any crime against the party or the government we asked Molotov, Kaganovich, and Voroshilov:

" 'Are you in favor of rehabilitating them?'

" 'Yes, we are in favor,' they replied.

" 'But you executed these people!' we said to them in indignation. 'So when did you act according to your conscience: then or now?'

"But they gave us no answer."[8]

Khrushchev knew the answer. "They" did not "execute these people." Stalin did, and he did it by the usual Politburo (Presidium) procedure of having members sign all decisions in order to implicate them. If they had refused to sign they would have been executed. Khrushchev himself showed no more courage and carried no less guilt than they. His attack on them was part of a successful 1956-1959 campaign to oust the three veteran leaders from the Kremlin.

[8] *XXII Syezd Kommunisticheskoi Partii Sovietsovo Soyuza* (Twenty-Second Congress of the Communist Party of the Soviet Union, October 17-31, 1961). Official Stenographic Record, Vol. II, pp. 585-586.

On the same occasion Khrushchev mentioned a few of the leading communists: Stanislav V. Kossior, a member of the Politburo and Moscow's Viceroy in the Ukraine; Vlas V. Chubar, Deputy Chairman of the Soviet government; Jan E. Rudzutak, a member of the Politburo; Pavel P. Postishev, a former secretary of the Ukrainian Communist Party, and Robert I. Eikhe, deputy member of the Politburo, who were arrested and shot in 1938 and rehabilitated posthumously. (He also named Nikolai A. Voznesensky, a member of the Politburo executed in 1950 and posthumously rehabilitated.) Khrushchev had no time to call the roll of all innocent victims.

Members of the Politburo and of the Central Committee were at the same time rulers of republics or regions or managers of great industries. Sergo Orjonekidze was a member of the Politburo and Commissar for Heavy Industry. He committed suicide on February 18, 1937, after his brother had been executed and because he "saw that he could no longer work with Stalin although he had been one of his closest friends," Khrushchev told the Twenty-Second Party Congress.

One can easily imagine the dislocation, disorganization, depression, and demoralization that fastened upon the Soviet economy as a result of the blood-and-poison purges. These negative phenomena in factory and farm were in turn the stimulus to further purges.

It would be a mistake, however, to think of the purges as limited to marshals, generals, Kremlin leaders, key industrial managers and planners, diplomats, and other notables. If a chief was purged, the entire system he had supervised was purged. When, for instance, the foreign affairs editor of *Izvestia* disappeared, the foreign correspondents whom he had chosen were recalled and liquidated. Even this method of sinking the crew with the captain gives only a small idea of the horror and havoc of the purges of the late 1930's. The persecution mania spread to every town, county, and village of the Soviet Union—as large as North America. The Kremlin slogan was "Vigilance," and "vigilance" required anyone who wished to survive to distinguish himself by hunting down and destroying a maximum number of victims as "spies," "Trotskyites," "secret fascists," and "two-faced enemies of the people." In numerous cases the hunter himself succumbed to a secret police bullet.

By chance, history has a detailed record of exactly how all this happened in one Soviet province—Smolensk. Soviet provincial archives have never been made available to scholars of any nationality. In mid-July, 1941, when the Nazi hordes swept into the western city of Smolensk, German intelligence officers found an official archive of approximately 200,000 pages of documents. These were transported back to Germany where, at the end of the war, they were seized by the Americans. This Smolensk Archive was subsequently placed at the disposal of a distinguished expert on Soviet affairs, Professor Merle Fainsod of Harvard University, for study and presentation.[9]

The Smolensk Archive shows that Kirov's assassination on December 1, 1934, was followed by a "hailstorm of indiscriminate denunciations in which listening to an anti-Soviet anecdote . . . was assimilated to membership in an opposition group . . . the net was spread wide, and many who were caught in it found themselves the victims of inventive busybodies who saw an opportunity to prove their devotion and improve their fortunes by zealously denouncing their colleagues. . . . As the year 1935 wore on, the heresy hunt gathered momentum." Angry letters from the party's Central Committee in Moscow warned the provincial communists of spies and "wreckers" lurking behind every party card. "By the end of 1936 a mood of panic and hysteria was beginning to sweep through Party ranks, and this time not even the leadership of the oblast [region] was immune. At a top-secret meeting of the bureau of the Western oblast, Rumyantsev, the first secretary, acknowledged his guilt in having earlier defended and expressed confidence in one Klyavin who had been expelled from the Party as a 'Trotskyite double-dealer.' " The party leadership was accordingly accused of the "dulling of vigilance" and the "failure to prevent 'enemies of the people' from worming their way into responsible posts."

The day of reckoning "came hard on the heels of the *Pravda* announcement . . . of the execution of Marshal Tukhachevsky and seven other prominent generals. . . . One of the executed was General Uborevich, the Commander of the Western Military District. . . . This time [Lazar M.] Kaganovich [Chairman of the party's Control Commission] was the chief executioner. Toward the end of June, 1937, he appeared in Smolensk . . . and announced the decision of the Central Committee to purge the obkom [regional committee] leadership. Rumyantsev, Shilman, Ratikov, and their associates were coupled with Uborevich as 'traitors' and 'spies' of 'German-Japanese fascism,' as members of the right-Trotskyite band of enemies of the people . . . who committed infamous crimes directed toward the preparation of the military defeat and the restoration of capitalism in the U.S.S.R." Presumably, Fainsod continues, "Rumyantsev and company were arrested and either executed or sent to forced-labor camps. In any case, they left no trace behind."[10]

Rumyantsev's successor as party leader in Smolensk was D. Korotchenkov. "Less than three months after coming to office, Korotchenkov reported . . . that 'according to incomplete data,' about 1,000 new people had been promoted to leading posts, including 188 to leading Party work." This means that at least an equal number of leading communists

[9] Merle Fainsod, *Smolensk under Soviet Rule.*
[10] *Ibid.*, p. 59.

had disappeared. "The files of the Archive contain long lists of people previously occupying junior posts who found themselves lifted by the Purge of 1937-38 to positions of far greater responsibility." Often they were not equal to their new assignments.

"As the hysteria of the Great Purge mounted, the Komsomol [League of Communist Youth], like the Party, found itself caught in the holocaust of mutual denunciations. Many Komsomols lost their jobs with the loss of their Komsomol cards; some lost their lives when their records were turned over to the NKVD. Desperation accelerated the suicide rate, and the pall of suspicion which enveloped the organization stifled hope and enthusiasm. . . .

"The Komsomol purge reached its climax in 1937 when the central [Moscow] leadership was decimated and the Western oblast apparatus in turn was largely destroyed in the wake of the purge of Rumyantsev and the group that surrounded him. The mood of the period is perhaps best conveyed by some extracts from a report to an oblast Komsomol conference held on October 11, 1937." The report said, "Train wrecks with loss of human lives, poisoning of workers, terror, wrecking of factories, arson, and diversion—these are the paths traveled by our enemies, who are trying . . . on the instructions of the German and Japanese intelligence service to undermine the might of the first socialist state. . . . These Fascists penetrated even into the Central Committee of the Komsomol—trying to restore the rule of landowners and capitalists."

The train wrecks, the poisoning of workers by spoiled food in communal cafeterias, and the wrecking of factories were not invented; they were true and due to ancient equipment, inexperienced personnel, and poor management. Also to bad nerves caused by fear. Officials and technicians were so afraid of making mistakes that they made them. They thus became spies, fascists, and enemies of the people. There was only one enemy of the people—Stalin, aided by a handful of henchmen who perforce submitted to his maniacal will.

Smolensk region (population 6.5 million) was less industrialized than many other Soviet regions. One is therefore entitled to assume that its "wreckers" and purge victims were far fewer than in scores of more advanced provinces. The eyes of the purge storm were the big cities like Moscow, especially Moscow, Leningrad, the second largest target, Kharkov, Kiev, Baku, and numerous other towns and industrial centers.

But no greater disaster befell the Soviet Union than the purge of the military. Tukhachevsky and his seven colleagues executed on June 11, 1937, were "judged," according to the lying communiqué, at a "trial" that never took place, by nine of their military peers. Of the nine, General Y. I. Alksnis, Chief of the Soviet air force, was arrested in 1937, probably before the "trial," and died in 1940; Marshal Alexander I.

Yegorov, former Chief of Staff of the Army and Deputy Commissar of Defense in 1937, disappeared immediately after the military purge; Marshal Vasili K. Bluecher, commander of the special Far Eastern Army, also vanished with his executed colleagues and is reported to have died on November 9, 1938: "Perfidiously maligned during the years of Stalin's cult of personality, he perished tragically," wrote *Pravda* of November 19, 1964, "at the height of his creative powers"; and Pavel E. Dybenko, prominent in the 1917 Bolshevik coup, commander of the North Caucasus Military District, disappeared with the men he allegedly sentenced to death. Thus at least four of the nine "judges" died with or soon after the loyal accused.

It is estimated that between 15,000 and 30,000 army, navy, and air force officers below the rank of marshal and general were likewise purged. "From May, 1937, to September, 1938," according to the official communist party history of Russia's participation in the second world war, "repression [a synonym for capital punishment] was applied to almost half of the commanders of regiments, almost all the commanders of brigades and divisions, all commanders of corps and commanders of troops in military regions, members of military soviets, and directors of the political administration of districts, the majority of the political officers of corps, divisions, and brigades, nearly a third of the commissars of regiments, and many instructors in superior and middle military academies."[11]

One officer who survived told his story graphically in the Moscow *Novy Mir,* March-May, 1964. An abridged edition in English translation was published in New York and London under the title *Years Off My Life, The Memoirs of General of the Soviet Army A. V. Gorbatov.* Born in 1892 into the large family of a poor peasant, he fought in the civil war, joined the communist party in 1919, rose gradually to the rank of general, was relieved of his command in the Tukhachevsky purge without any explanation, arrested in Moscow at 2 A.M. on October 16, 1938, and taken to a cell in the NKVD central prison on Lubyanka Square. He had seven cellmates. "I was all the more horrified to hear that during their interrogation every single one of them had written the most unmitigated rubbish, confessing to imaginary crimes and incriminating other people. Some had given way under physical pressure, some had been terrified by the threat of torture."

Gorbatov was tortured. Stolbunski was his chief interrogator. "Apart from him, two brawny torturers took part in the interrogation. Even now my ears ring with the sound of Stolbunski's voice hissing, 'You'll

[11] Institute of Marxism-Leninism of the Soviet Communist Party, *Istoria Velikoi Otechestvennoi Voiny Sovietskovo Soyuza 1941-1945* (The History of the Great Fatherland War of the Soviet Union in 1941-1945), Vol. VI, pp. 124-125.

sign, you'll sign!' as I was carried out, weak and covered with blood."

An NKVD court sentenced Gorbatov to fifteen years in prison and concentration camps, and five years' deprivation of civil rights thereafter; he was transported to the Kolyma concentration camp in northeastern Siberia. There he was robbed and beaten by criminals. He fell ill "so I went to see the doctor. He was in fact a doctor's assistant, sentenced to ten years for some trifle." Gorbatov's neighbor on the plank bed had been the head of the political department of a railway. "He prided himself on having incriminated some three hundred people." He urged Gorbatov to commit suicide. "The next morning he was found dangling from a rope."

Gorbatov was released on March 5, 1941, after "I had signed a promise to be silent." He was not silent. He wrote his book "to tell the younger generation." Soon he was commanding a division sent to stem the Nazi invasion on the western front. There "my earlier fears made my hair stand on end; how were we going to be able to fight when we had lost so many experienced commanders even before the war had started? Undoubtedly that was one of the main causes of our failures, although no one talked about it."

The purges, beginning in 1935 and continuing mercilessly and unremittingly through 1936 and 1937 until they reached maximum crescendo in 1938, robbed the Soviet Union of the physical and psychological capacity to wage war in 1939. The Soviet-Finnish Winter War of 1939-40 is one proof. The effects of the purge lingered on throughout the Soviet-Nazi war and took a hideous toll in Russian battlefield casualties.

It has been reported that files purporting to document treasonable acts by the Soviet marshals and generals had been planted by the German intelligence agency with the Czechoslovak secret service which it had infiltrated. President Beneš allegedly sent the papers on from Prague to Stalin. Some would have it that the German Gestapo allowed imprisoned German communists to purloin the forged files and escape with them from concentration camps to Moscow. But these and still more fantastic versions assume that Stalin needed documentation for execution. He merely needed imaginary confessions or "confessions" extracted by brutal torture (see Khrushchev's 1956 secret speech) or by refined torture such as promises to spare the lives of wives and children or by compelling a prisoner to stand in a confined space under bright lights for forty-eight or more hours or, frequently, by making a deal with the defendant and then not keeping the bargain. Confessions, however, were not a prerequisite to death. The fifty-four defendants in the three Moscow show trials confessed and were therefore tried publicly; sometimes it took eight or more months to break them. Untold thousands of iron-willed communists remained unbroken and were done to death without confessions. False documents and faked confessions do not explain Stalin's purges. Moreover, the tale of the German counterfeit documents refers only to the military purge. It would not explain why tens of thousands of important civilian communists were executed.

The question "Why?" assumes that there was a reason. But in the mad Soviet world of the late 1930's people did not ask "Why?" They expected no "because." Life was a lottery. Men and women were shot because they were there. Leonid Leonov, a well-known Soviet novelist, asked in the 1950's by Yugoslav communist writers in Belgrade why Boris Pilnyak, a fellow Soviet writer, had been shot, replied, "It is pure accident that Pilnyak is not sitting here and you are not asking him why Leonov was shot." Ilya Ehrenburg, who knew a great deal about the contorted methods of the Kremlin, wrote in his last memoirs, "When I think about the fate of my friends and acquaintances there seems to be no logic to it. Why, for example, did Stalin spare Pasternak who took his own independent line, but destroy Koltsov who honorably carried out every task assigned to him? Why did he do away with Vavilov and spare Kapitsa?"

One must not look for logic in a lottery.

The purge is a substitute for elections in a democracy. It goes on permanently, bloody in Stalin's time, bloodless yet painful since. It kills men and keeps fear alive. It arrests some so that the rest may quake.

The big man is rare who wants big men around him. He prefers sycophants and puppets. No surer way has been discovered of reducing the size of subordinates than to behead their predecessors.

The wielders of the ax or revolver acquire power and secret knowledge. They must not last too long. While they last they brook no competition.

The Soviet secret police and the Red Army had a long history of angry rivalry. For the Cheka, the GPU, the NKVD—every incarnation of the Soviet secret police was more than an intelligence agency and more than a punitive organization. It was also an army. It, not the regular army, guarded the frontiers, telephone, telegraph, and railway lines, and bridges. In the Russian Far East the NKVD maintained 40,000 troops equipped with artillery, tanks, and airplanes operating autonomously under separate command. The Red Army commanders resented that. Nor did the soldiers, from marshal to private, relish being spied upon by unknown members of their units who collected information or misinformation and purveyed it to headquarters for misuse.

This situation long antedated the Spanish civil war but was exacerbated by it. Soviet army officers in Spain told me they were being "pushed around" and "spied upon" by the NKVD. They carried their complaints to Stalin and they were executed.

The 1936-37-38 purge gave maximum extension to the NKVD's functions and hence to its powers. If an accident occurred in a factory, a fire in a mine, an explosion on an oil field, if a machine was ruined, output spoiled—the NKVD proclaimed that "wreckers" and spies were at work. It carried away engineers, plant managers, foremen, workingmen. As a result production dropped. This was attributed to an "enemy of the people" in the district or regional government. He disappeared. Finally the big communist chief—he might have been a member of the Politburo or of the party's Central Committee—was summoned to Moscow and given a furious scolding by Stalin or a Stalin henchman. "But," he remonstrated, "how can my republic fulfill its plan when the NKVD arrests so many of my best technicians, managers, and directors?"

Between the communist chief and the NKVD Stalin sided with the latter. In the summer of 1956 in Moscow Anastas I. Mikoyan, a member of the Politburo under Stalin and subsequently, said to me, "But you understand, Stalin held us in his hand. Only one escape was left to us—what Orjonekidze did when he committed suicide. I stood before the same decision. At the end of Stalin's life I was about to be executed." He was not executed and lived on for many years abominating Stalin. The story is that his and Molotov's names were included on a list for execution, but at the last moment Stalin crossed them out. Why? Ask not the reason why.

Once the terror commenced it achieved a momentum of its own which gave the NKVD great latitude. But Stalin could have stopped the secret police murders by pressing a button. He stopped most of them during the second world war. He not only permitted and ordered the executions. He supervised them. He specifically gave instructions in 1937, according to Khrushchev's secret speech, for physical torture to extract confessions. The secret police was Stalin's political right arm and he was in touch with it several times a day in person or by telephone. He even advised the manner in which certain executions were to be announced. Thus, when Solomon M. Mikhoels, the actor-director of the Yiddish State Theater, who had traveled to the United States and England in 1943 as head of a war propaganda delegation of the Soviet Jewish Antifascist Committee, was executed in 1948, Stalin received the news by telephone at home and, apparently in reply to a question about how the death of such a prominent figure was to be announced, said, "Well, an automobile accident." This version then circled the globe. Many men administered the terror with fervor. One man bears the supreme responsibility for it.

Stalin's slow-moving body and slow-moving mind gave him the air of deliberative wisdom. But his wisdom was prudence and his prudence born of fear and a realization of his inadequacies. Trotsky was brilliant,

Lenin perceptive, Stalin cunning. He had a keen eye for the weaknesses of others. Envy was a consuming passion. His successes were due to the power over life, death, and promotion which he achieved through guile and used without mercy. Impetuosity governed his decisions, hesitation his actions. He had the good fortune to rule over a population taught by centuries of tyranny the habit of servile obedience which the brief Kerensky hiatus could not break. Stalin built on the despotism of his imperial predecessors and being politically illegitimate—witness Lenin's last will and testament—surpassed them in irrational jealousy and wanton cruelty. Citizens and communists alike awaited their fate in passive despair, for they could not resist or seek a redress of grievances or escape. An eyebrow raised in spontaneous horror or a shrug of the shoulders in impatient incredulity might sign one's death warrant. Ubiquitous professional policemen and an army of voluntary informers eager for transitory reward cast the shadow of the grave over every hour of life. Armed with such methods Stalin created national might and killed creativity. He never loved, neither was he loved. He was feared. His victims were not proved guilty; their trials were circuses or secret nontrials. But in their place he would have conspired against a usurper like himself; hence the punishment for fancied conspiracy. He purged so that the successors of the purged would be his craven, adulating servitors. The true measure of the man is his insatiable hunger for fawning flattery. He hoped that self-inspired panegyrics would erase all the records of his crimes. History has uncovered some of the truth. Much more remains concealed.

Death, discord, disorganization, hate, and fear filled the Soviet Union as Europe moved toward war in 1939. Soviet friends in Soviet cities told me in the secrecy of their homes during visits in 1956 and 1961 that when the war reached Russia it came almost as a relief: they knew why they had to suffer and die.

XXVI THE ORIGINS OF THE SOVIET-NAZI PACT

Some have argued that Stalin's purges were necessary to remove possible opponents of the Soviet-Nazi pact of August 23, 1939. The reverse is more plausible: the purges helped make the pact necessary. Litvinov objected to the pact but was not purged. Yet even he and probably most of the purged leaders were disgusted with Anglo-French-American appeasement of the aggressors. After the collapse of the Spanish Republic, Mussolini's victory in Ethiopia with western connivance, Hitler's conquest of his "beloved Austria," and the Anglo-French surrender to Hitler at Munich, few Kremlin communists would have put much reliance in the West. In any case, Stalin was the autocrat. Hence the purges. Nobody in the Soviet Union dared to say him nay. Hence the pact.

Russia in Europe has no natural defenses and is open to invasion. Japan had access to Siberia by land, air, and sea. With the Soviet economy and morale weakened by the purges and in view of the military unpreparedness and supine diplomacy of the western powers it is not difficult to understand Stalin's fear of an assault by Germany and Japan. His fear would have been shared by the persons he purged.

Wars, they and Stalin knew, had been fateful to Russia—in 1917 and in 1905, for instance. Stalin's response to this circumstance was characteristic of his native caution. In a speech to the plenary session of the Soviet Communist Party's Central Committee, far back on January 19, 1925, he noted "that the preconditions for war are maturing and that war may become inevitable, not tomorrow or the day after, of course, but in a few years' time. . . ." This is a sample of Stalin's safe generalities. "I think," he continued, "that the forces of the revolutionary movement in the West are strong, that they are growing and will continue to grow, and here or there may succeed in kicking out the bourgeoisie. That is so. But it will be very difficult for them to hold out. That is clearly shown by the example of the border countries, Estonia and Latvia, for instance. The question of our army, and its might and preparedness, will certainly face us as a burning question in the event of complications in the countries around us." (Did this imply that if war came Russia might annex "the countries around us"?)

Now the essence: "That does not mean that in such a situation we must necessarily undertake active operations against somebody or other. That is not so. If anybody shows signs of harboring such a notion—he is wrong. Our banner is still the banner of *peace*. But if war breaks out we shall not be able to sit with folded arms. We shall have to take action, but we shall be the last to do so. And we shall do so in order to throw the decisive weight into the scales, the weight that can turn the scales."[1]

This Stalin "peace" statement is a far better clue than the purges to the Soviet-Nazi pact. The dictator thought he could sit out the war until both sides had almost spent themselves, and then throw Russia's "decisive weight" to one side or the other, whichever promised larger accretions of territory and power.

The strategy of sitting it out until he could tip the scales was congenial to Stalin's mentality and appropriate to Russia's weakness in general, and after the purges in particular. The question is whether the pact with Germany conduced to the success of Stalin's strategy.

* * *

Western appeasement has been blamed for the Soviet-Nazi pact. It is not the explanation.

Neville Chamberlain, who became Prime Minister of Great Britain on May 28, 1937, in succession to Stanley Baldwin, was "the archpriest of appeasement,"[2] writes Iain Macleod, Chairman of Chamberlain's Conservative Party and Conservative Leader of the House of Commons—a Cabinet post.

Neville Chamberlain, half brother of Sir Austen and son of Joseph, was the true conservative. "The late Victorian age for me, before the days of motors [automobiles] and telephones," Macleod quotes him as exclaiming in the 1920's. ". . . even so simple an amenity as a modern fountain pen," Macleod adds, "he found an instrument of torture, preferring all his life to write letters, diaries and speeches with a plain steel nib." Macleod had access to his diaries.

Chamberlain appeased Hitler. Yet he was not pro-German. "On the whole I loathe Germans," he noted on a vacation in the Black Forest in 1930. After the Nazis came to power he declared, "I am horrified by the German behavior to the Jews." In 1936 and 1937 he favored measured, belated rearmament. But he was a skeptic and a pessimist. "I say," he

[1] J. V. Stalin, *Works*, Vol. 7, pp. 13-14. The speech was first published in Russian in 1947 in Moscow in Vol. 7 of Stalin's *Sochinenia*. The English translation quoted here was first published in Moscow in 1954.

[2] *Neville Chamberlain*, p. 206.

told the House of Commons on February 22, 1938, "we must not try to delude ourselves, and still more, we must not try to delude small weak nations, into thinking that they will be protected by the League [of Nations] against aggression and acting accordingly when we know that nothing of the kind can be expected." Nor could the United States be relied upon for "President Roosevelt was struggling against a strong isolationist tide which was actually strengthened by the famous Chicago speech of October [5], 1937, in which he urged that aggressors be 'quarantined.' If Japanese planes could shell and sink an American gunboat with impunity and General Franco obtain three quarters of his oil from American producers, reiteration of American moral principles was unlikely to make rulers tremble in Berlin and Rome."[3]

Chamberlain likewise doubted the value of France as an ally: "She can never keep a secret for more than half an hour, nor a government for more than nine months," he wrote in January, 1938. "Therefore our people see that in the absence of any powerful ally, and until our armaments are completed, we must adjust our foreign policy to our circumstances, and even bear with patience and good humor actions which we should like to treat in a very different fashion."[4]

Two months later, on March 13, 1938, the German army arrived in Vienna. "It was the Russians who now sounded the alarm, and on March 18 proposed a conference. . . . They wished to discuss if only in outline," writes Winston Churchill, "ways and means of implementing the Franco-Soviet Pact within the frame of League action in the event of a major threat to peace by Germany. This met with little warmth in Paris and London. . . . Chamberlain was both skeptical and depressed. He profoundly disagreed with my interpretation of the dangers ahead and of the means of combatting them."

Churchill had been advocating a "Franco-British-Russian alliance" as the "only hope" of checking the "Nazi onrush." Chamberlain scoffed at the notion. "You have only to look at the map to see that nothing that France or we could do could possibly save Czechoslovakia from being overrun by the Germans, if they wanted to," Chamberlain wrote in a letter to his sister on March 20, 1938. ". . . I have therefore abandoned any idea of giving guarantees to Czechoslovakia, or to the French in connection with her obligations to that country."[5]

What Churchill (and many others) failed to understand was the Chamberlain logic of giving a guarantee to Poland *"within a year,"* he

[3] *Ibid.*, p. 207.
[4] *Ibid.*, p. 207.
[5] Winston Churchill, *The Second World War. The Gathering Storm*, p. 274. Churchill quotes the Chamberlain letter from Sir Keith Feiling, *The Life of Neville Chamberlain*, pp. 347-348.

emphasizes, "after all the strategic value of Czechoslovakia had been cast away, and Hitler's power and prestige had almost doubled."[6]

The "Fuehrer" announced in an address on April 28, 1939, after Czechoslovakia was his, that Germany had come into the possession of 1,582 Czech planes, 501 antiaircraft guns, 2,175 light and heavy cannon, 785 mine throwers, 469 tanks, 43,875 machine guns, 114,000 automatic pistols, 1,090,000 rifles, 1 billion rounds of rifle ammunition, 3 million artillery shells, and vast quantities of searchlights, bridgebuilding equipment, motor vehicles, and automobiles. Any planes, tanks, and other arms produced, any divisions trained and equipped by Britain and France between the end of September, 1938 (Munich), and September 1, 1939, when the war began, could not nearly match the power of Czechoslovakia's armed forces which the Anglo-French lost when Hitler dismembered that state.

Churchill mentioned Hitler's doubled prestige. He was equally aware of Czechoslovakia's strategic importance; the Czechs might have struck at Germany's rear in the event of war. Or the mere existence of a Czechoslovak state would have forced Hitler to keep a sizable fraction of his military strength on duty to watch the Czechs.

Hitler preferred to take Czechoslovakia and Austria by force. He could have established peaceful relations with Prague at the expense of France and Russia. Late in 1936 Czechoslovak President Eduard Beneš, cognizant of the turmoil in Europe resulting from Hitler's remilitarization of the Rhineland, conducted secret negotiations with the German government designed to settle all difference between the two states. In interviews with Beneš and Foreign Minister Krofta in Prague on November 13 and 14, 1936, Albrecht Haushofer, a close collaborator of Joachim von Ribbentrop, who had set up a kind of personal foreign office behind the back of Foreign Minister von Neurath whom he would soon supplant, discussed trade, a nonaggression treaty, Prague's alliances, and the artificially superheated problem of the Sudeten German minority in Czechoslovakia.

The ostensible issue which precipitated the Nazi conquest of Czechoslovakia was Hitler's alleged distress over the mistreatment of Germans in that country. But when Haushofer submitted to Hitler the written report of his talks in Prague indicating Czech willingness to grant the Sudeten Germans economic equality, cultural autonomy, and legal cultural and political relations between them and the Reich, the "Fuehrer" made no marginal comment. He needed the grievances of the Sudeten Germans to destroy Czechoslovakia.

"Beneš," Haushofer wrote, "was almost violent in his assertions of

[6] *Ibid.*, p. 275.

independence of Moscow and in the repudiation of all insinuations that the Soviet Union could influence Czech policy against a rapprochement with Germany. Similarly he insisted that there was no internal opposition to him—he could sign with Germany at any time." On a second visit to Prague, on December 18, 1936, Haushofer, son of the renowned German geopolitician, reported that "Beneš wanted a guarantee of the existence of his state. . . . In return for such a guarantee, Beneš offered to refrain from adopting a pro-Russian foreign policy."[7]

Hitler's marginal notes on Haushofer's reports show that the Nazi dictator wanted no peace with Czechoslovakia. He cried aloud that Germany was "being encircled" by the Czech and French alliances with Russia. But when Beneš proposed to breach the encirclement the "Fuehrer" showed no interest. He had an undisguised preference for military solutions. Those British editorial writers, notably in the *Times* and the *New Statesman and Nation,* who asked Chamberlain to assent to the cession of the Sudetenland to Germany as a means of avoiding war misunderstood Hitler. It was not necessary to have secret documents to understand him. His public utterances and violent acts at home provided sufficient insight. Today, however, reading Hitler's mind has been facilitated by the publication of many of his secret speeches. One on November 5, 1937, is particularly revealing.

That evening he assembled War Minister Field Marshal Werner von Blomberg; Colonel General Baron Werner von Fritsch, Commander in Chief of the Germany army; Admiral Dr. Erich Raeder, Commander in Chief of the German navy; Colonel General Hermann Goering, Commander in Chief of the German Luftwaffe; Foreign Minister von Neurath; and Colonel Hossbach, Hitler's adjutant, who kept the minutes.

Blomberg, Fritsch, and Raeder were professional military men, yet Hitler, the ex-corporal of the first world war, presumed to give them a lengthy "exposition" which "was the fruit of thorough deliberation and the experience of his 4½ years in power." He proposed to lay before them his thoughts on the development of German foreign policy "and he asked . . . that his exposition be regarded, in the event of his death, as his last will and testament."

"Germanism" in Austria and Czechoslovakia was in "decline." Even in Germany "sterility" was setting in. "Germany's future was therefore wholly conditional upon the solving of the need of space." Germany could not live on her own resources of metals and food; Hitler accord-

[7] These secret German-Czech negotiations are recorded in papers seized in Germany by the U.S. authorities and now deposited in the Manuscript Division of the Library of Congress under Accession Number 11,249. The documents and related material were used by Professor Gerhard L. Weinberg of the University of Michigan for his article, "Secret Hitler-Beneš Negotiations In 1936-37" in the *Journal of Central European Affairs,* Vol. 19, December-January 1959-60, Boulder, Colorado.

ingly rejected autarchy as a solution of the nation's problems. Despite the use of fertilizers Germany's soil "was showing signs of exhaustion. . . . We are living in an age of economic empires: . . . in the cases of Japan and Italy economic motives underlay the urge for expansion, and with Germany, too, economic need would supply the stimulus."

World trade offered no solution. "The only remedy . . . lay in the acquisition of greater living space." This space "can only be sought in Europe, not, as in the liberal-capitalist view, in the exploitation of colonies. . . .

"The history of all ages—the Roman Empire and the British Empire—had proved that expansion could only be carried out by breaking down resistance and taking risks . . . the attacker always comes up against a possessor. The question for Germany ran: where could she achieve the greatest gain at the lowest cost?

"German policy had to reckon with two hate-inspired antagonists, Britain and France, to whom a German colossus in the center of Europe was a thorn in the flesh. . . . Germany's problem could only be solved by means of force . . . there still remain to be answered the questions 'when' and 'how.' . . .

"The equipment of the army, navy, and Luftwaffe, as well as the formation of the officers' corps, was nearly completed." Other countries were rearming. "It was while the rest of the world was still preparing its defenses that we were obliged to take the offensive. . . . If the Fuehrer was still living, it was his unalterable resolve to solve Germany's problem of space at the latest by 1943-45" or earlier if France should develop an internal crisis which would absorb the attention of her army, or if she were involved in war with another country.

"For the improvement of our politico-military position," Hitler continued, according to Colonel Hossbach's record, "our first objective, in the event of our being embroiled in war, must be to overthrow Czechoslovakia and Austria simultaneously in order to remove the threat to our flank in any possible operations against the West."

Hitler "believed that almost certainly Britain, and probably France as well, had already written off the Czechs. . . . Britain's attitude would certainly not be without influence on that of France. An attack by France without British support, and with the prospect of the offensive being brought to a standstill on our western fortifications, was hardly probable."

Poland, "with Russia at her rear," would not fight a victorious Germany. "Military intervention by Russia" to help Austria and Czechoslovakia "must be countered by the swiftness of our operations; however, whether such an intervention was a practical contingency at all was, in view of Japan's attitude, more than doubtful."

Civil war in France "must be seized upon *whenever it occurs,*" Hitler stressed, "for the blow against the Czechs." Tensions in the Mediterranean between Italy and France and between Italy and Britain might lead to war and "he was resolved to take advantage of it whenever it happened, even as early as 1938." The war in Spain might last three more years. ". . . a 100% victory for Franco was not desirable either; from the German point of view . . . our interest lay more in the prolongation of the war in Spain." It might draw France or Britain into war with Italy; Germany would then send munitions to Mussolini, whom he called "a genius." A war in the Mediterranean would create a favorable situation for Germany to pounce on Czechoslovakia. "This descent upon the Czechs would have to be carried out with 'lightning speed.' "

Finally the military had their say. It did not conform with Hitler's speculations. Their own, however, were no more correct. Blomberg and Fritsch feared the French and the British who "must not appear in the role of our enemies." The French army "would not be so committed by the war with Italy that France could not at the same time enter the field with forces superior to ours on our western frontier." Fritsch thought the French might invade the Rhineland . . . "and it must be remembered, apart from the insignificant value of our present fortifications—on which Field Marshal von Blomberg laid special emphasis—that the four motorized divisions intended for the West were still more or less incapable of movement." As to Czechoslovakia, Blomberg "drew particular attention to the strength of the Czech fortifications . . . which would gravely hamper our attack." Hitler, nevertheless, remained unconvinced by the mistaken prognostications of the professionals. He had his own. He regarded "an Anglo-French-Italian conflict" possible in the summer of 1938. Whereupon Goering, the practical one, proposed that, since Franco must not be allowed to win too soon, "we should consider liquidating our military undertakings in Spain." Hitler agreed, but thought "he should reserve a decision for a proper moment."[8]

[8] U.S. Department of State, *Documents on German Foreign Policy,* Series D (1937-1945), Vol. I: *From Neurath to Ribbentrop (September, 1937-September, 1938),* pp. 29-39. In his sparsely documented book, *The Origins of the Second World War,* A. J. P. Taylor of Oxford University tries to deny any foreign policy significance to this Hossbach document and condemns historians for not asking themselves why Hitler convened the conference. Hitler answered that himself by saying the speech was his "last will and testament." Taylor, however, failed to mention this in his book and did so only as a " 'second thought' " in answer to criticisms of the published work. Instead, Taylor believes that the significance of the speech is limited to domestic politics. His lame explanation pretends that Hitler feared Schacht. Schacht, who had been responsible for the economic aspect of rearmament, "was jibbing at further expansion of the armament program. Hitler feared Schacht . . . [and] aimed to isolate Schacht from the other Conservatives [Blomberg, Fritsch, and Raeder] . . . and to win them for a program of increased armaments." When did the military have to be won for more armaments? What

Such were the muddled mini minds of men who held the lives of millions in their hands. The military exaggerated the strength of France. Hitler's war-attuned brain saw wars that never were. Even his deeply desired war on Czechoslovakia would be denied him by the weak-kneed leaders in London and Paris. And in the end the space he craved was sowed with death and drenched with blood but yielded no food for the German people.

In his November 5, 1937, "last will and testament" Hitler devoted little time to Bolshevism and Russia. He hoped the Spanish civil strife would be prolonged so as to involve his friend Mussolini in hostilities with the French and British. He could take advantage of that situation to seize Czechoslovakia, although he believed France and England had already written her off. For this illogic a high school teacher would give him a low grade for common sense, prophecy, and intuition. And zero for loyalty and friendship. The Rome-Berlin Axis had been formally constituted on October 25, 1936. By November, 1937, Italy was in such a state of exhaustion from her efforts in Abyssinia and Spain that war with France or England or both would have caused the southern end of the Axis to collapse unless Germany went to Italy's defense. But the "Fuehrer's" brain remained obsessed with Czechoslovakia. He had no sooner annexed Austria than preparations began for the breakup of Czechoslovakia. "We are now on the eve of the attempt to realize the German programme in Czechoslovakia," Sir Nevile Henderson, British ambassador in Berlin, wired Foreign Secretary Lord Halifax on May 14, 1938. The ambassador thought it would be the better part of wisdom for Czechoslovakia, "a small and defenceless country," to compose her difficulties with Hitler "disagreeable though it may be." He was "convinced that [this] is in the interests not only of European peace, but of the existence of Czechoslovakia."[9]

How wrong can a diplomat be?

French Ambassador André François-Poncet telegraphed Yvon Delbos, his new Foreign Minister, on March 12, 1938—the day German troops invaded Austria—that "Field Marshal Goering, during a reception he gave last night, had a conversation with the Czechoslovak Minister. He gave assurances that Germany had no evil intentions whatever towards Czechoslovakia and that the latter state had therefore nothing to fear from the Reich, and he gave his word of honor to that effect. He then

proof that Hitler "feared" Schacht or the brakes of the military? His entire career shows that he either overpowered them with his oratory, convinced them by his "intuition," or dismissed them.

[9] E. L. Woodward and Rohan Butler (Eds.), *Documents on British Foreign Policy 1919-1939*, Third Series, Vol. I: *1938*, pp. 294-297.

gave expression to the hope that Czechoslovakia would not mobilize."

Mastny, the Czech minister, left the reception and telephoned his government what Goering had said. Then he hurried back to the party and informed Goering that Czechoslovakia would not mobilize. Thereupon Goering "repeated what he had said before, adding that he was not only speaking for himself, but in the name of the Fuehrer."[10]

Goering's word of honor was good for sixty-nine days. Henderson informed Halifax on May 19, 1938, that "German troops are concentrating in Southern Silesia and Northern Austria." Two days later Sir Nevile called on Foreign Minister von Ribbentrop "and found him in a highly excitable and pugnacious frame of mind. . . . Herr Ribbentrop listened but merely repeated that M. Beneš could not be trusted. . . . Germany would act."

President Beneš acted. On May 20 Czechoslovakia announced "partial mobilization." It was, as diplomats told me that day in Prague, complete mobilization. Soviet Ambassador Sergei S. Alexandrovsky, whom I had known for many years, said, "Between ourselves, they have summoned to the colors not only the classes mentioned in the official communiqué, but all their reserves." Alexandrovsky had been consulted, he had consulted Moscow, and Moscow had advised Czechoslovakia to order a general mobilization. The Kremlin promised assistance.

Hitler recoiled. Nothing happened. But on May 30, 1938, Hitler issued a detailed "Top Secret" order which began: "It is my unalterable decision to smash Czechoslovakia by military action in the near future." But one of the "necessary prerequisites for the intended attack" was "a convenient apparent excuse."[11] In the face of this and other documentation a shopful of A. J. P. Taylors will find it difficult to mend Hitler's reputation as a warlover.

A Soviet history of Russian foreign relations published in Moscow in 1961 states: "In the second half of May, 1938, J. V. Stalin informed President Beneš through K. Gottwald, the leader of the Czechoslovak Communist Party, that the U.S.S.R. is ready to assist Czechoslovakia militarily even if France does not do so and even if Poland and Rumania refuse to permit Soviet troops to pass in transit to Czechoslovakia."[12] This meant that Moscow would fly planes to the Czechs.

Soviet histories distort and lie, but they would not invent a specific act by Stalin. In fact, Soviet President Kalinin made a public statement on

[10] Ministère des Affaires Etrangères, *French Yellow Book,* p. 2.

[11] *Documents on German Foreign Policy.* Series D. Vol. II: *Germany and Czechoslovakia, 1937-1938,* pp. 357-362.

[12] Prof. V. G. Trukhanovsky (Ed.), *Istoria Mezhdunarodnikh Otnoshenii i Vneshnei Politiki SSSR 1917-1939* (The History of International Relations and of Soviet Foreign Policy 1917-1939), Vol. I, p. 535.

April 26, 1938, avowing his country's readiness to come to the aid of Czechoslovakia.[13] Stalin's encouragement to Czechoslovakia sprang from an endeavor to prove that French and British appeasement was unnecessary. The conquest of Czechoslovakia by Hitler would imperil Russia, and Stalin must have hoped to show the West how the Nazis could be blocked. Between the May, 1938, crisis that evaporated and the Munich crisis that crippled democratic Czechoslovakia, the Soviet Union, according to a statement to me by Pierre Cot, French Minister of Aviation, delivered three hundred airplanes to Czechoslovakia. Count Werner von der Schulenburg, the German Ambassador in Moscow, reported to Berlin on August 31, 1938, that "a member of the Italian Embassy" told the secretary of the German Embassy he knew from "an absolutely reliable informant" that "forty Soviet aircraft had flown to Czechoslovakia over Polish territory at a great height some time ago. . . . The Poles noticed the flight too late to take practical measures against it."[14]

Just one day earlier Andor Hencke, the German chargé in Prague, reported that the Czech and Rumanian governments were discussing the passage of Soviet troops in the event of war. "It looks as though Rumania," he wired Berlin, "would permit transit of, at most, 100,000 Soviet soldiers in civilian clothes should Poland agree to this."

Unpublished Soviet archive documents referred to by the Soviet *History of Diplomacy* (Vol. 3) state that the Kremlin had moved 30 infantry divisions to Russia's western border, "put her air force and tanks on a war footing," and prepared "246 bombers and 302 fighters for dispatch to Czechoslovakia."

The question of Soviet aid to Czechoslovakia is germane to the tragedy of Munich; it also bears on the negotiations leading to the Soviet-Nazi Pact. Grigore Gafencu, former Rumanian Foreign Minister and former ambassador to Moscow, wrote in 1948 that the Kremlin was approached in March and in June, 1938, on assistance to the Czechs, and on both occasions Litvinov replied that the assistance would not be refused "if Poland and Rumania first undertook to allow Soviet armies to pass through their territories. As neither Poland nor Rumania intended to make such an anticipatory engagement, it could not be expected that Russia would intervene."[15]

Since Gafencu was a diplomat, his diplomatic language is subject to interpretation. Clearly neither Poland nor Rumania would make an "anticipatory" engagement, but Rumania might have consented at the moment of crisis by closing her eyes without an "engagement." When

[13] A. A. Gromyko and others (Eds.), *Istoria Diplomatii*, Vol. III, p. 733.
[14] *Documents on German Foreign Policy*, Series D. Vol. II, p. 667.
[15] *Last Days of Europe. A Diplomatic Journey in 1939*, p. 15.

Schulenburg saw Litvinov on August 27, 1938, and said, "Poland and Rumania were unlikely to grant transit rights to Soviet troops," Litvinov replied that Rumania was "very greatly worried about the future." She was "afraid of being next on the list, when once Czechoslovakia had been settled by Germany."[16]

Five days earlier the German ambassador had had a "conversation . . . of long duration" with Litvinov. But his "efforts to make Litvinov state what form possible Soviet help to Czechoslovakia would take were in vain. The Foreign Commissar repeatedly avoided answering this question." Perhaps Litvinov did not know the answer. Perhaps he did not intend telling Hitler's envoy what Russia proposed to undertake against Hitler. In the same dispatch, however, Schulenburg summarized the conclusions reached by the German military and naval attachés in Moscow after examining how the Soviet Union might fulfill her promise, which the ambassador regarded of "importance," to support Czechoslovakia. "The Soviet Union can attack Germany from the air. . . . By employing U-boats, light naval forces and naval aircraft, and also by laying mines, the Soviet Union can considerably disrupt German shipments of ore from Sweden and northern Norway. . . . The Soviet Union can attack East Prussia across the Baltic by naval and land aircraft, and also interrupt sea communication between the Reich and East Prussia by means of U-boats. . . . The Soviet Union will make use of every opportunity to supply Czechoslovakia with war material in considerable quantities, in particular with aircraft. . . . The dispatch of military technicians is not out of the question. . . . Wherever it can harm Germany, the Soviet Union will incite the workers against Germany."[17]

Schulenburg was a good German, hence anti-Nazi. (He paid for it with his life.) It might therefore be said that he tried to deter Hitler by exaggerating the dangers to Germany in case of war. But he was no exception. A British Foreign Office communiqué of September 26 affirmed that "if, in spite of all efforts made by the British Prime Minister, a German attack is made on Czechoslovakia, the immediate result must be that France will be bound to come to her assistance and that Great Britain and Russia will certainly stand by France." Such statements pulled taut the strings on which Hitler played. The nearer war appeared the greater the fear and the more reason there seemed to appease. Baron Ernst von Weizsaecker, State Secretary of the German Foreign Office, took cognizance of this situation in an August 30, 1938, memorandum he sent up to Foreign Minister von Ribbentrop. In the coming weeks, he wrote, there will "no longer be any doubt that if Germany invades Czechoslovakia she will have the Western Powers as

[16] *Documents on German Foreign Policy,* Series D. Vol. II, p. 632.
[17] *Ibid.,* pp. 629-631.

her enemies. . . . This war would sooner or later end in German capitulation." He therefore offered some sage advice: ". . . there is no need for us to sacrifice the fruits of our previous policy if we change our warlike tactics. What can be achieved at present can be obtained by negotiation."[18]

This may be the key to Munich. In May, 1938, Hitler had recoiled before Czech mobilization. But he did not relent. He launched a psychological campaign stupendous in magnitude and skillful in quality to break the will of the Czechoslovaks and win the acquiescence of the Anglo-French. The Sudeten German territories must be united with the Reich, he insisted. He threatened war if thwarted. Hitler blew hot.

Hitler also blew cold. When he claimed the Saar he said it was his last territorial ambition. Now too. "And now we are confronted with the last problem which must be solved and which shall be solved," he told a howling crowd in the Berlin Sportspalast on September 26, 1938, on the eve of Munich. "It is the last territorial claim which I have to make in Europe, but it is a claim from which I shall not swerve, and which I will satisfy, God willing. . . . I am grateful to Mr. Chamberlain for all his efforts; and I assure him that the German people want nothing but peace; but I also told him that I cannot extend any further the limits of our patience. I assured him, moreover, and I repeat it here, that when this problem is solved, there will be no more territorial problems for Germany in Europe; and I further assured him that from the moment when Czechoslovakia solves its problems, that is to say, when the Czechs have come to an arrangement with their minorities, peacefully, without oppression, I shall no longer be interested in the Czech state. And this I guarantee. We don't want any Czechs at all."

The lover of minorities and of peace, the opponent of oppression, wanted no Czechs (until March, 1939), no more territory in Europe (except Poland less than a year later).

Millions of Europeans saw war within hours. Londoners saw bombs crash into their undefended city. The French feared another German invasion. And Hitler seemed so reasonable: give me the Sudeten and all will be well. Those who desired nothing and peace agreed to negotiate. This time the appeasers made sure, by intimidation, that Beneš would not order a second mobilization. Chamberlain and Daladier met Hitler and Mussolini at Munich.

Hitler had kept the world so feverishly frightened that when the agreement was reached at Munich to give Germany the Sudeten territory western humanity exploded in a spasm of joy. It was "peace with honor," Chamberlain cried. "I believe it is peace for our time." He

[18] *Ibid.*, pp. 662-663.

received "a hero's welcome. 'Come straight to Buckingham Palace,' bade the King, 'so that I can express to you personally my most heartfelt congratulations on the success of your visit to Munich.' All the way from Heston airport to the palace, the streets, as the Prime Minister described to his sisters, 'were lined from one end to the other with people of every class, shouting themselves hoarse, leaping on the running board, banging on the windows, and thrusting their hands into the car to be shaken.' "[19]

As Premier Daladier looked out of the airplane that flew him from Munich he saw an immense crowd at the Paris airport and thought it was a hostile demonstration. But the crowd had come to cheer.

Czechoslovakia had not been invited to her vivisection at Munich. Nor was the Soviet government asked to attend because it would have tried to impede the surrender. Moscow interpreted Munich as an attempt by the western powers to channel Nazi aggression eastward against Russia. Moscow usually interpreted international developments in this manner. The interpretation was contradicted by subsequent events.

An enormous and neglected episode now unfolded which determined the course of the second world war.

The Soviet Union sprawls across Eurasia from the Baltic to the Pacific; its military and foreign-political problems are correspondingly great. In recent decades politics has changed Soviet geography, and technology has altered the nature of these problems. But during the late 1930's geography gave Russia two potent possible enemies: Germany and Japan. Germany might advance from East Prussia via Lithuania and Latvia into the Soviet Union. The Soviet military watched that front but considered it too narrow for full-scale aggression. They did foresee Germany traversing Czechoslovakia and Poland or Rumania to attack them. Munich looked like the first leap. There remained the hurdle of Poland or Rumania. But in the Far East the Red Army and the Japanese army stood nose to nose on the border between the Soviet puppet state of Outer Mongolia and the Japanese puppet state of Manchukuo. They had fought skirmishes in that region from 1935—113 in 1937 alone, by a Japanese count. Soviet military aviation and "volunteer" pilots and advisers had been sent to Chiang Kai-shek in 1938 to bolster his resistance to Japanese encroachment in central China. Litvinov, speaking in Leningrad on June 23, 1938, referred to "Japan's unlimited aggressiveness in China and occasional dreams of annexing Soviet territory. However, we do not want Soviet soil to become the object of anyone's dreams and fancies."

In July and August, 1938, combat quickened between Japanese and

[19] Macleod, p. 268. Macleod publishes the text of the Munich Agreement and its annexes in Appendix B of his book.

Soviet forces in the vicinity of Lake Khasan. Tanks, planes, artillery, and infantry were used by both sides in this Changkufeng Incident. "As it turned out," says a Japanese authority, "the encounter ended in a disastrous defeat for the Japanese forces, and cost approximately 1,350 casualties."

Sporadic fighting continued throughout the next twelve months. The Japanese Kwantung army, stationed in Manchukuo, kept the battle boiling in order to win attention and reinforcements that might otherwise go to Nipponese forces operating against Chiang Kai-shek. The Soviets did not avoid combat, they wished to divert Japanese strength from Chiang and teach Tokyo a lesson. In 1938 the number of border skirmishes rose to 166. The "Nomonhan Affair" opened on May 12, 1939, on the poorly marked boundary between Outer Mongolia and Manchukuo near the Khalka River (Khalkin-Gol). "On May 28 a Japanese force of 200 men and ten light armored cars was wiped out by enemy tanks . . . on June 18 and 19, Soviet bombers raided Japanese outposts, and their infantry penetrated Nomonhan under the cover of Soviet artillery and mechanized forces." The Japanese command thereupon threw two full divisions into the fight and asked Tokyo for 120 fighter planes. "By the end of June . . . the core of the Japanese forces were supposed to consist of thirteen infantry battalions, 112 antitank guns, seventy tanks, 400 motor vehicles, and 180 warplanes." Now the Red Army brought up reinforcements "so that its forces . . . amounted to three rifle divisions, five mechanized and armored regiments having 860 tanks and armored cars and two Mongolian cavalry divisions." General (later Marshal) Georgi K. Zhukov launched this immense accumulation of firepower against the Japanese on August 20. ". . . by the end of August the 23rd [Japanese] Infantry Division was almost completely destroyed, having sustained over 11,000 casualties. The fighting continued into September."[20] The Kwantung Army thirsted for revenge. Tokyo said no; the Soviet-Nazi pact had been signed: World War II had opened in Europe. A truce was concluded in Moscow between Molotov and Japanese Ambassador Shigenori Togo providing for a cease-fire on September 16. The Japanese had been routed and expelled from Outer Mongolian territory.

Zhukov's brilliant success against the crack Kwantung Army contributed considerably to Tokyo's decision not to invade Siberia when Hitler invaded European Russia, and instead, to move south, against British,

[20] Katsu H. Young, "The Nomonhan Incident. Imperial Japan and the Soviet Union," *Monumenta Nipponica. Studies In Japanese Culture.* pp. 81-102. Further details in John Erickson, *The Soviet High Command; A Military-Political History, 1918-1941,* pp. 534-537. The History of Soviet Foreign Relations edited by V. G. Trukhanovsky gives the number of Japanese engaged in the Khalkin-Gol battle as 38,000 (Vol. I, p. 593).

French, and Dutch possessions as well as against the United States. In the summer of 1939, however, Stalin could not have known this; Japan was a bellicose neighbor, a fact that would of course enter into his calculations as he pondered what policy to contrive when the second world war loomed.

* * *

Never since November 7, 1917, had the Soviet government been able to establish even normal formal relations with Japan. Despite the first world war, on the other hand, the Kremlin had collaborated intimately with Germany in military and economic fields. As a second international conflict appeared above the horizon Moscow would naturally think of an accommodation in Europe the better to cope with Japan. But skillful diplomacy always tries to open two doors simultaneously. An impressive military defeat administered to Japan would reduce Hitler's eagerness for a crusade against Bolshevik Russia. As a result the Soviet Union might indeed "sit it out" while others bled, thus granting Stalin time to mend the amputations among the military, the industrialists, and the party leaders.

This would have been a legitimate Soviet policy. In view of the appeasers' apathetic acquiescence in the conquest of Ethiopia, Austria, and Czechoslovakia and, above all, in the destruction of Loyalist Spain, Moscow had no moral debt to them. Nor is any government under an obligation to invite an invasion of its country.

Yet a Soviet policy of paying back the appeasers in their own coin of appeasing the aggressors could not have succeeded so long as the western powers continued to appease. For when, in March, 1938, Hitler had taken Austria and in March, 1939, completed the conquest of Czechoslovakia, neither England nor France did anything to stop him. Now only Poland and Rumania lay between him and Soviet territory. If he destroyed only one of these he would be under the irresistible temptation to rip from Russia the "living space" he coveted since writing *Mein Kampf*. His attitude toward the Soviets had not changed: on January 30, 1939, he called the Soviet Union a "satanic apparition" and "a menace to the peace and civilization of the world."

Even before Germany's total occupation of Czechoslovakia commenced on March 15, 1939, Hitler turned his attention to the Poles. Poland had long been the target of German nationalists; they accused her of annexing German territory, cutting East Prussia off from the body of Germany, and extracting the city of Danzig, largely German in population, from German rule. Poland appeared to be marked as Hitler's next victim.

Tension gripped Moscow.

Events in Europe followed bumper to bumper. On February 28, 1939, Britain and France recognized Franco the rebel as the government of Spain. Paris appointed Marshal Pétain its ambassador to Madrid. On March 22 Germany forced Lithuania, by an ultimatum, to cede the Baltic port of Memel and surrounding territory. On April 7 Italy invaded Albania and on April 14 Albania was incorporated into the Italian kingdom.

London and Paris groped for a policy.

Moscow was in the same quandary. It must not be supposed that the Soviets play diplomatic chess and know their own and their opponents' moves several moves ahead. Only Hitler knew where he was going. Stalin did not. "The new imperialist war has become a fact," he told the Eighteenth Party Congress of the Soviet Communist Party on March 10, 1939.[21] ". . . war is inexorable." Analyzing the world situation Stalin found that the nonaggressive states, "Primarily England, France and the U.S.A.," pursued "the policy of nonintervention" which he interpreted as "an eagerness, a desire, not to hinder the aggressors in their nefarious work: not to hinder Japan, say, from embroiling herself in a war with China, or, better still, with the Soviet Union; not to hinder Germany, say, from enmeshing herself in European affairs, from embroiling herself in a war with the Soviet Union." He accused the "nonaggressive states" of lying about the weakness of the Red Army and of "egging the Germans on to march further east." "Just start a war on the Bolsheviks," he paraphrased them as saying, "and everything will be all right." Stalin called this "conniving at aggression."

He then formulated the four principles of Soviet foreign policy. "We stand," he said, "for peace and the strengthening of business relations with all countries. That is our position; and we shall adhere to this position as long as these countries maintain like relations with the Soviet Union, and as long as they make no attempt to trespass on the interests of our country."

These words have been widely described as the green light which opened the road to the Soviet-Nazi pact. Indeed Vyacheslav Molotov, Soviet Chairman and Foreign Commissar, stated on August 31, 1939, eight days after the pact was signed, that on March 10, 1939, "Comrade Stalin posed the question of good neighborly relations without enmity between Germany and the Soviet Union. It can be seen now that the declarations of Comrade Stalin were, in general, correctly understood by

[21] *The Land of Socialism Today and Tomorrow. Reports and Speeches at the Eighteenth Congress of the Communist Party of the Soviet Union* (*Bolsheviks*), March 10-21, 1939. (Published in English in Moscow in 1939.) Russian text in *Pravda,* March 11, 1939, and in I. V. Stalin, *Sochinenia* (Works), Vol. 1 [XIV], edited by Robert H. McNeal.

Germany, and that Germany drew political conclusions from them."

This sounds like the false logic of "post hoc, ergo propter hoc." Hitler did not take Stalin's hint. The talks leading to the pact began in April, 1939, but not on Germany's initiative—on Moscow's. Hitler knew all along he could have a pact with Stalin. The Bessonov and Kandelaki probes of 1935 and 1936 made that clear. What changed the situation was not Stalin's bland statement of March 10 which could have meant everything or nothing but Hitler's decision to attack Poland after taking Czechoslovakia; he thought he needed Russian nonintervention. Moreover, Stalin, after enunciating the first principle of Soviet foreign policy, added the second: "We stand for peaceful, close and friendly relations with all neighboring countries which have common frontiers with the U.S.S.R. That is our position; and we shall adhere to this position as long as these countries maintain like relations with the Soviet Union, and as long as they make no attempt to trespass, directly or indirectly, on the integrity and inviolability of the frontiers of the Soviet state."

Principle Number Three clad Number Two in a promise: "We stand for the support of nations which are the victims of aggression and are fighting for the independence of their country." That would soon mean Poland.

Fourth, Stalin said, "We are not afraid of the threats of aggressors, and are ready to deal two blows for every blow delivered by instigators of war who attempt to violate the Soviet borders."

Concluding his presentation on foreign affairs, Stalin urged "caution" so as "not to allow our country to be drawn into conflicts of warmongers accustomed to having others rake the chestnuts out of the fire for them."

Stalin's speech can rather be read as a warning to Hitler that if he invaded Poland or Rumania the Soviet government would come to their aid, and if he dared to assault Russia he would meet furious resistance. This might have impressed Hitler and inclined him to welcome the Soviet proposals of April, 1939. But since the initiative came from Moscow the more plausible thesis is that the negotiations leading to the Soviet-Nazi pact were precipitated not by Stalin's address of March 10, 1939, but by the British government's decision of March 31, 1939, to give a guarantee to Poland. It was to honor this guarantee that Britain and France entered the second world war on September 3, 1939. Stalin knew that the March 15 dismemberment of Czechoslovakia had caused a revolution in British politics and turmoil in Neville Chamberlain. The British Prime Minister had talked with Hitler and trusted him. The trust was gone.

Chamberlain was scheduled to speak on March 17 in Birmingham, a city whose mayor he had been. His speech, on "domestic questions and social service," was prepared. He threw it into the trash basket when he learned of the death of Czechoslovakia. "Is this the last attack upon a small state to be followed by another?" he asked angrily. "Is this in fact a step in the direction of an attempt to dominate the world by force?" England heard that speech and recognized a new Neville Chamberlain. On March 31 he informed the House of Commons that "in the event of any action which threatened Polish independence and which the Polish Government accordingly considered it vital to resist with their national forces, His Majesty's Government would feel themselves bound to lend the Polish Government all support in their power. . . . I may add that the French Government have authorized me to make it plain that they stand in the same position as His Majesty's Government."

Polish Foreign Minister Colonel Joseph Beck arrived in London on April 3 and was received by Chamberlain, Foreign Secretary Lord Halifax, and the King. Britain was now firm and determined. The Dominions, which supported Munich because they believed war should and could be avoided, now shared Chamberlain's disillusionment and resolution.

Appeasement had flown out the window.

This was the signal to Stalin that he could appease. So long as the British and French "connived" at Nazi and Italian aggression Moscow was compelled to urge collective security in self-defense. The moment England and France committed themselves to the defense of Poland Stalin believed he could "sit it out." The war would turn west.

If, as Soviet historians still insist, the Anglo-French-American imperialists had wished to incite Hitler to make war on Russia they would have remained passive and rejoiced when he prepared to engulf Poland; he would quickly conquer Poland and menace the Soviet Union. But they behaved quite differently. England and France pledged themselves to go to war in the event of a German attack on Poland. ". . . between night and morning," in Churchill's words, Chamberlain "turned his back abruptly upon his past." Chamberlain also acted. On March 29 he told Parliament the Territorial Army would be doubled. On April 27 Britain introduced conscription.

Once more, as in the first world war, Germany's wrath poured forth on England. ". . . it is exclusively England and England alone," wrote Ribbentrop on December 3, 1939, "that bears the guilt of the war and wanted it in order to destroy Germany."[22] Hitler had set the anti-British tone in an address to the Reichstag on April 28, 1939: "Since England today . . . upholds the view that Germany should be opposed in all circumstances, and confirms this by the policy of encirclement known to

[22] German Information Bureau, *100 Dokumente zur Vorgeschichte des Krieges. Auswahl aus dem Amtlichen Deutschen Weissbuch,* Introduction by Foreign Minister von Ribbentrop, p. 9.

us, the basis of the [Anglo-German] Naval Treaty [of 1935] has been removed." He tore it up.

It might be said, therefore, that Neville Chamberlain was the unwitting author of the Soviet-Nazi pact of August 23, 1939. He fathered it by discarding appeasement. Stalin was its coauthor. On his instructions Soviet diplomats sounded out the German government in mid-April, 1939, about the possibility of improved relations.

* * *

In March, 1936, I had a long discussion with Soviet Ambassador Jacob Suritz in Nazi Berlin about the world situation after Hitler's remilitarization of the Rhineland. He rejected my contention that the three "revisionist" nations: Germany, Japan, and Italy, had interests in common and would try to coordinate their activities. During the argument he summoned his counselor, Bessonov, who sided with Suritz. When the Rome-Berlin Axis and the anti-Comintern treaty were concluded, Suritz sent me a message saying he had been wrong. We met for many friendly talks when he was transferred to Paris during the Spanish civil war. On a Saturday morning, August 19, 1939 he said to me, "There will be no second Munich." Three days later Ribbentrop flew to Moscow, and within twenty-four hours he and Molotov signed the Soviet-Nazi pact.

The frequently encountered sequence: appeasement at Munich, hence Soviet-Nazi pact, has no validity. It would be nearer the truth to say: antiappeasement after Munich, hence pact.

The day before the signing of the Soviet-Nazi pact the "Fuehrer" addressed the German commanders in chief. He made no reference to Stalin's speech of March 10, 1939. He gave a more convincing explanation. "Litvinov's replacement," he said, "was decisive."[23] Litvinov the Jew and eager anti-Nazi, the champion of collective security, was dismissed by Stalin on May 3, 1939, and replaced by Chairman Molotov. Then Hitler knew Stalin was ready for a far-reaching agreement with Germany.

[23] *Documents on German Foreign Policy*, Vol. VII: *The Last Days of Peace, August 9-September 3, 1939*, p. 204. German text in the record of the Nuremberg trial: International Military Tribunal, *Trial of the Major War Criminals*, Vol. XXVI, Document 798-PS, p. 343 ("Litvinovs Abloesung war ausschlaggebend"). In his *Russia at War*, 1941-1945, Alexander Werth quotes Hitler as saying, "Litvinov's dismissal was decisive. It came to me like a cannon shot" (p. 4). The second sentence makes Hitler's declaration even more dramatic, but Werth gives no source and I have not been able to discover any.

XXVII THE ROADS TO THE PACT

David Low, the unforgettable British cartoonist, recorded the signing of the Soviet-Nazi pact in a famous cartoon. It showed Hitler tipping his hat, bowing to Stalin, and saying, "The scum of the earth, I believe." Stalin, tipping his hat and bowing to Hitler with the same obsequiousness, replied, "The bloody assassin of the workers, I presume."

The Soviet regime, considered revolutionary, signed a far-reaching agreement with Hitler whom it had pilloried as counterrevolutionary. Together they partitioned Poland, and Stalin, with Nazi permission, annexed the independent Baltic States, part of Finland, and parts of Rumania.

Throughout his political career, anticommunism was the burden of Hitler's propaganda and the proclaimed inspiration of his actions. Communists regarded Nazism and fascism as their ugly enemies. This proved no barrier when Hitler wanted war and Stalin coveted territory.

Soviet ideology lay on a shelf where it had already collected years of dust.

* * *

The Soviet-Nazi pact had many facets. Primarily it was an operation on the body of Poland. The patient would die.

After a series of conversations in Moscow between Foreign Commissar Litvinov and Polish Ambassador Waclav Grzybowski, the Soviet and Polish governments issued a joint communiqué on November 26, 1938, saying that "relations between the two countries are and will continue to be based to the fullest extent on all existing Agreements, including the Polish-Soviet Pact of Nonaggression dated July 25, 1932" which had been prolonged to December 31, 1945. This pact, the communiqué asserted, "has a basis wide enough to guarantee the inviolability of peaceful relations between the two States." In the spirit of the statement, a Soviet-Polish commercial agreement was signed in Moscow on February 19, 1939, providing "for a considerable extention of trading operations between the two countries."[1]

[1] General Sikorski Historical Institute, *Documents on Polish-Soviet Relations 1939-1945*, Vol. I: *1939-1943*, pp. 23-24.

On the Soviet-Polish front all seemed quiet.

However, much was new on the German-Polish front. Joachim von Ribbentrop visited Warsaw on January 26, 1939, and told Polish Foreign Minister Joseph Beck that the Free City of Danzig had to come back to Germany. He likewise demanded an "extraterritorial autobahn and railway connection between the Reich and its East Prussian province." As compensation, the Nazi Minister offered "a guarantee of the German-Polish frontier." Beck promised to take the matter under advisement. In closing his report on this encounter, Ribbentrop stated that he "again" brought up the issue of the treatment of Germans in Poland.[2]

The pressure had commenced. On March 21, 1939, Czechoslovakia having been broken up and swallowed piece by piece, Ribbentrop called in Polish Ambassador Lipski and complained of anti-German student demonstrations in Danzig and Poland's apparent reluctance to accept the Nazi proposals for a general settlement. The matter was "important because the Fuehrer has been astonished by the remarkable stance of Poland on a number of questions; everything depended on his not getting the impression that Poland simply did not wish" to cooperate.[3]

Poland ordered a partial mobilization on March 24.

Two days later Ribbentrop once more summoned Lipski to the Wilhelmstrasse and repeated Germany's demands for Danzig and extraterritorial communications through the Polish Corridor. "Mr. Lipski replied that he had the unpleasant duty to indicate that any further pursuit of this German plan, particularly as far as the return of Danzig to the Reich was concerned, meant war with Poland."[4]

It was in these circumstances that Prime Minister Chamberlain informed the House of Commons on March 31 that Britain had given Poland a guarantee of aid in case of war. A week later Britain gave similar guarantees to Rumania and Greece. France did likewise. Hitler cried, Encirclement.

Chamberlain on September 27, 1938, had referred to the Czechoslovak crisis as "a quarrel in a far-away country between people of whom we know nothing." Now, in a country just as far away, a quarrel about the little-known city of Danzig and a strange "Corridor" brought a totally different reaction from the same Prime Minister. Meanwhile, however, Czechoslovakia, a strong country, had been lost to the West and Hitler felt encouraged to try the trick again.

The British guarantee to Poland had brought Joseph Beck to London where, on April 4, he conferred with Foreign Secretary Lord Halifax in

[2] German Auswaertiges Amt., 1939, Nr. 2, *Dokumente zur Vorgeschichte des Krieges*, pp. 186-187.

[3] *Ibid.*, pp. 187-189.

[4] *Ibid.*, p. 191.

the presence of Sir Alexander Cadogan, Permanent Under Secretary of the Foreign Office, William Strang, a high Foreign Office official, Count Edward Raczynski, Polish Ambassador in London, and Count Joseph Potocki of the Polish Ministry of Foreign Affairs. To judge by the official British record,[5] Halifax and Beck spoke while the audience listened or took notes.

Beck began by saying that the German threat was serious and Poland would fight if attacked. He proposed to clarify the situation. "He would start with Soviet Russia . . . in view of the grave tension between Moscow and Berlin, it would be dangerous to bring Russia into any discussions. He recalled what Marshal Pilsudski had said, namely, that when thinking of Germany and Russia it was necessary to take into account not only their interests but their ideologies. For this reason the question of Soviet Russia required to be handled with great caution and by special methods.

"There were two things which it was impossible for Poland to do, namely, to make her policy dependent upon either Berlin or upon Moscow."

Beck also alluded to the basin of the Danube. Poland's alliance with Rumania, he said, applied only to "an attack from the East." That is, from Russia, not from Germany. If Poland extended the alliance so that it applied to a German attack, Hungary, on bad terms with Rumania, would be thrown "into the arms of Germany." Hungary and Italy, according to Beck, "were seriously perturbed by Germany's designs of domination." Nothing should be done that "would diminish the possibility of a joint Italo-Hungarian effort against Germany."

This possibility was pure fantasy.

Halifax reverted to the Russian issue. Beck had no objection to Britain's "having good relations with Soviet Russia." Poland had good relations with Russia. Beck "wished, however, to say that any pact of mutual assistance between Poland and Russia would bring an immediate hostile reaction from Berlin and would probably accelerate the outbreak of a conflict."

Halifax, persisting, asked, "Was the appropriate course not, therefore, to look upon the problem facing Poland and Great Britain and France as the problem of how to get the maximum degree of collaboration from Soviet Russia without entailing dangerous consequences?"

Beck "appreciated this argument, but insisted that the aim of the efforts which were now being made should be the maintenance of peace. . . . Poland, for her part, was ready to improve her relations with Soviet Russia, but not to extend them. . . . If France and Great Britain now

[5] E. L. Woodward and Rohan Butler (Eds.), *Documents on British Foreign Policy 1919-1939*, Third Series. Vol. V: *1939*, pp. 1-9.

undertook obligations towards the Soviet Union, Poland would find it necessary" to declare that these obligations did not involve any extension of Poland's obligations to Russia. Beck added that the Soviet-French pact was "a bad bargain which brought few concrete results and made a *détente* with Berlin and Rome more difficult."

So on April 4 Beck dreamed of a détente with Berlin and Rome and discouraged an Anglo-Soviet pact. The day before Hitler had ordered the German army to prepare for an attack on Poland "at any time from September 1, 1939 onwards."[6] (The detailed plan of invasion was given to the Wehrmacht on April 11.)

The Beck-Halifax colloquy occurred in the morning. That afternoon Beck met with Prime Minister Chamberlain and Halifax. Chamberlain began by expressing his suspicion of Hitler's methods and intentions: "The Prime Minister asked whether M. Beck felt, as His Majesty's Government did, that German action in Czechoslovakia was in flagrant contrast with Germany's assurances as to the limits of her action, and that it did seem to point to a desire on the part of the German Government to extend this process to other States."

This was the new antiappeasement Chamberlain. The conversion came late, at the cost of Czechoslovakia, but now the task before them was to save Poland.

When Chamberlain asked Beck for his appraisal of the situation, the Pole gave it as his "personal view . . . that the gravest question was the colonial question." In Germany "there was temporarily a kind of lull."

Beck was wrong.

The Prime Minister quickly came to the Russo-Polish dilemma. "Supposing," he said, "that Great Britain and France and Poland were at war with Germany, he asked himself how Poland could carry on the conflict. She had a fine army and certain air resources, but he understood her artillery was not very strong. . . . Poland's forces would no doubt put up a gallant fight, but if her munitions were exhausted, where could they replenish them except from Soviet Russia . . . ?"

Beck said he wished to do nothing to precipitate an armed conflict. "From conversations he had had in Germany, he had acquired the conviction that a decision to open a war against Poland would be a very difficult one for Germany to take. Any association between Poland and Russia would bring that decision nearer." Therefore "he was not in a position to accept any agreement which would have the effect, if even only indirectly, of linking Poland with Soviet Russia."

Chamberlain "quite understood" Beck's objection. "But the question he wished to ask was, was there any other reason against accepting help

[6] Full text of order in Gerhard L. Weinberg, *Germany and the Soviet Union 1939-1941*, p. 21.

from Soviet Russia if war actually takes place?"

Here Chamberlain pressed Beck hard. "Would it be embarrassing to Poland if His Majesty's Government now tried to improve their relations with the Soviet Government?" Not an agreement; merely "to establish such relations as would enable them to expect help from Soviet Russia in case of war."

Beck, politely adamant, wanted to "utter the warning that, if Russia were brought in, this might well precipitate a conflict." For the rest, Beck remained optimistic. Poland had enough oil supplies and did not depend on Rumania. He "desired to come to some arrangement with Germany."[7]

During this tense period when Moscow was on the eve of formulating its policy in the event of war, Soviet Ambassador Ivan Maisky interviewed Lord Halifax often. On March 29, informed of Britain's intention of giving guarantees to Poland and Rumania, Maisky said "this would be a revolutionary change in British policy and . . . would increase enormously the confidence of other countries."[8]

On April 11 Maisky again saw Halifax. "Beck," the Soviet envoy charged, "had always been pro-German." And Maisky "did not readily see why, if we and France wished to help Poland and Rumania, we could not make such help conditional on their adopting a reasonable attitude towards the acceptance of help from Russia."[9]

Sir William Seeds, the British Ambassador in Moscow, received coded telegraphic reports of the Maisky-Halifax talks and of Beck's conferences in London. From time to time Seeds saw uncommunicative Soviet officials. Daily he and his foreign colleagues took in one another's diplomatic washing—rumors, facts, speculations, thoughts. For the most part ambassadors are reporters and guessers. Sir William sat down at his desk on April 13, 1939, four days before the Soviets made the first decisive step toward their pact with the Nazis, and wired Halifax a long guess of what the Kremlin would do in the ripening European crisis. Given the thick cloud that shrouded Moscow's policy-making summit, the ambassador must be credited with considerable radar insight.

Sir William Seeds began by telling Lord Halifax "it is difficult to see how the Soviet government can effectively contribute towards a solution of our difficulties so long as the countries where the Soviet contribution could be effective resolutely refuse to consider any idea of co-operating with or even consulting this country."

This was not so much sight as sense.

"Moreover," the ambassador continued, "an obvious temptation to the

[7] *Documents on British Foreign Policy*, Third Series. Vol. V, pp. 9-19.
[8] *Ibid.*, p. 21.
[9] *Ibid.*, p. 83.

Soviet government to sit back and do nothing is presented by the situation which is developing." This was insight. One does not expect precise prophecy in such complicated circumstances. But Sir William did envisage two possibilities: either Rumania and Poland would "provide a bulwark" for Russia or, "should Germany overrun these two countries she would halt at the Soviet frontier rather than add the Soviet Union to her Western enemies."

The ambassador refused to join "those foreign observers" (including a British historian and many deluded communists) who regarded the coming war as one "where all capitalist Europe will destroy itself for the benefit of Soviet Russia." Nevertheless, he thought that the U.S.S.R. "can quite properly be tempted to stand aloof and in case of war confine its advertised support to the victims of aggression to the profitable business of selling supplies to the latter. Such an attitude," he believed, "would be consonant with Stalin's known caution" and with his principle of not pulling other people's chestnuts out of the fire.

That was one plausible Soviet policy, and Stalin would have been wise to adopt it. "I am bound however," Sir William continued—here he almost predicted what happened—"to point to a possible danger arising either now or in case of war at the stage where Germany had reached the Soviet frontier through Poland, namely an offer by Germany to the Soviet Union of Bessarabia and parts of Poland not to mention perhaps Estonia and Latvia." He did not rate this danger as more than "possible." Yet in his concluding sentence he warned that Russia "might be tempted to follow counsels of prudence or worse."[10]

"Temptation" and "tempted" are, in the light of history, the key words in the British Ambassador's dispatch. The temptation was so strong that Stalin did abandon caution and prudence and adopted a worse course, in fact, the worst.

* * *

In speeches at Wilhelmshaven on April 1, 1939,[11] and before the Reichstag on April 28, 1939,[12] Hitler turned his fire on the West, especially on England; the usual fulminations against communism were muted. He was reacting to the Anglo-French guarantees to Poland, Rumania, and Greece. The anti-Bolshevik tone of the Nazi press and the anti-Nazi tone of the Soviet press were lowered an octave. But there was no indication that Berlin had as yet formulated a new policy toward the U.S.S.R. Hitler still hoped to achieve a Polish "Munich" with the help of London and Paris.

[10] *Ibid.*, p. 104.
[11] German Auswaertiges Amt., 1939, Nr. 2, pp. 188-190.
[12] *Ibid.*, pp. 197-198.

A Polish "Munich" that carried the German army effortlessly to the Soviet border would have been to Russia's acute disadvantage. In the circumstances, Stalin's strategy consisted in impressing England and France with Soviet eagerness to resist Hitler. This was done when Maisky persisted with Halifax that Poland and Rumania be induced to accept assistance from the Soviet Union. The mirage of Soviet collaboration was designed to make sure that the Anglo-French remained firmly antiaggression in the face of intensified Nazi pressure and the threat of war.

At the same time, Stalin could have permitted himself to approach the German government with a view to an improvement of Soviet-Nazi relations so that, in the event of war, Hitler, after conquering Poland, turned west instead of attacking Russia. This would have been perfidious, but perfidy is not an unusual feature in the life of nations.

Stalin went beyond perfidy.

* * *

The first tentative conversation that led to the Soviet-Nazi pact took place in Berlin on April 17, 1939, when Soviet Ambassador Alexei Merekalov visited State Secretary Weizsaecker in the Auswaertiges Amt. Merekalov had presented his credentials on June 5, 1938. After Ribbentrop, Weizsaecker was the highest official in the German Foreign Office. Yet for more than ten months Merekalov had never come to see Weizsaecker. He came on April 17 to discuss a matter of secondary importance not normally handled by top diplomats: the fulfillment of Soviet contracts for war material with the Skoda Works in crucified Czechoslovakia. "Toward the end of the discussion," Weizsaecker wrote in his memorandum on the talk, "I casually mentioned to the Ambassador that even granted goodwill on our part, a favorable atmosphere for the delivery of war materials to Soviet Russia was not exactly being created at present by reports of a Russo-British-French air pact and the like. Herr Merekalov seized on these words to take up political matters." The two diplomats sparred for a few minutes after which "the Russian asked me frankly what I thought of German-Russian relations." Weizsaecker noted the constant German desire for better commercial relations and the more subdued tone of both the Soviet and German press in commenting on their respective countries. "The Ambassador thereupon stated approximately as follows:

"Russian policy had always moved in a straight line. Ideological differences of opinion had hardly influenced the Russian-Italian relationship, and they did not have to prove a stumbling block with regard to Germany either. Soviet Russia had not exploited the present friction between Germany and the Western democracies against us, nor did she desire to do so. There exists no reason why she should not live with us on a normal footing. And from normal, the relations might become better and better."[13] Therewith the ambassador ended the conversation. Several days later he left for Moscow.

"The present friction between Germany and the Western democracies" is the key to the pact. "In preparation for the big war in the name of imperialist Germany's annexationist aims," reads the official *History of Diplomacy,* edited by Foreign Minister A. A. Gromyko and others and published in Moscow in 1965, "Fascist Germany planned its first stage as a war against the western powers. 'The adjustment' with Poland was regarded by the Hitlerites as an important step in the preparation for that war and indispensable from the point of view of the strengthening of the strategic and economic position of the Reich."[14]

Ambassador Merekalov took the friction between Germany and the West as the point of departure for his proposal to make Soviet-Nazi relations "better and better." It was Moscow's conviction that Germany would turn west after engulfing Poland that explains the Russian initiative in Berlin. If Stalin had thought the Wehrmacht would keep going eastward after conquering Poland he would have sought safety with the Anglo-French. Stalin would not have trusted himself alone in Eastern Europe with Hitler except in the belief, justified by events, that Germany intended to engage in hostilities against the West.

While making soundings in Berlin the Kremlin opened talks with Paris and London. Brilliant or Byzantine, Soviet diplomacy intended, in the spring and summer of 1939, to extract maximum benefits from the European crisis by negotiating simultaneously with Hitler and with the West.

The Soviet-Nazi treaty negotiations and the Soviet-Western negotiations ran on parallel monorails until Stalin threw a switch. The Soviet-Nazi train then swerved, crashed into the Soviet-Western train and crushed it. The fault was not altogether Stalin's. The Soviet-Western train offered poorer accommodations at a higher price. Nor were the western personnel eager to make the trip. Chamberlain, writes his biographer, "had as little taste for what he called 'the Bolshies' as he had for the Nazis. He distrusted their motives 'which seem to me to have little connection with our ideas of liberty and to be concerned only with getting everyone else by the ears,' and he suspected that 'they are chiefly concerned to see the "capitalist" Powers tear each other to pieces whilst they stay out themselves.' His political judgment made him doubt Russia's willingness to defend the common cause; less reliably, his advisers

[13] U.S. Department of State, *Nazi-Soviet Relations 1939-1941. Documents from the Archives of the German Foreign Office,* Raymond James Sontag and James Stuart Beddie (Eds.), pp. 1-2.

[14] Vol. III, p. 765.

provided him with a consistently low estimate of her military capacity to do so."[15]

Chamberlain did not at Munich distrust Nazi motives although they too had "little connection with our ideas of liberty." And a nation's "willingness to defend the common cause" is a phrase that mocks reality. Did the United States belatedly enter the first world war to "make the world safe for democracy" or was that slogan "brainwashing" on a national scale? Anticommunist America gave communist Russia over $11 billion in Lend-Lease during the war and $2 billion in military and economic aid to communist Yugoslavia after she defected from the Soviet bloc. Leaders like to fool themselves, governments like to fool their people, and people like to be fooled.

Chamberlain, his biographer asserts, "was reluctant to acquiesce in the opening of negotiations with the Soviet. He did so only under strong pressure from the French Government and from public opinion at home as reflected in the Press, in Parliament and in the anxieties of his Cabinet colleagues. He was neither elated when the negotiations seemed to go well, nor cast down when they seemed to be going badly, nor shaken when the Communist preference for an accommodation with the Nazis became apparent."[16]

Such (surely somewhat pathological) divorce from reality on the part of His Majesty's First Minister would affect the Anglo-French-Soviet negotiations adversely even if all other conditions had favored them—which they did not.

The Anglo-Soviet negotiations began haphazardly under the handicap of Chamberlain's reluctance to negotiate. On April 14, 1939, the day after Halifax had received Sir William Seeds' intelligent appraisal of Soviet policy, the Foreign Secretary wired back saying he still hoped to achieve "some measure of cooperation" from Moscow. But the Soviet proposal for an Anglo-French-Russian-Polish conference as well as "our own suggestion for a Four-Power declaration had to be abandoned . . . when it was clear that the attitude of the Polish Government made its conclusion impossible." Halifax added that he had read Stalin's speech of March 10, and the British Cabinet had noted his statement regarding Moscow's readiness to support the victims of aggression. Would not the Soviet government therefore issue a "public declaration" that "its assistance would be available, if desired"?[17]

Litvinov brusquely rejected the idea. Instead, on April 18 he handed Seeds a written five-to-ten-year plan of Anglo-French-Soviet collabora-

[15] Iain Macleod, *Neville Chamberlain*, p. 273.
[16] *Ibid.*, p. 273.
[17] *Documents on British Foreign Policy*, Third Series. Vol. V, pp. 205-206.

tion which obliged the three contracting partners "to render mutually forthwith all manner of assistance, including that of a military nature, in case of aggression in Europe against any one" of them. They, in turn, undertook to give the same kind of help to "East European States situated between the Baltic and Black Seas and bordering on the U.S.S.R." Early tripartite General Staff consultations would follow.

The Soviet document went further. It asked the British government to assert that "the assistance recently promised to Poland concerns exclusively aggression on the part of Germany." Such an explanation was necessary, Litvinov stated, lest the British guarantee to Poland "be read as implying the possibility of aggression by [the] Soviet Union." Formally, therefore, England would not aid Poland if Soviet aggression occurred. Moreover, the Kremlin wanted the Polish-Rumanian alliance, "originally aimed at the Soviet Union only," to be made operative against aggression from any quarter, in other words by Germany, "or else [that the Polish-Rumanian alliance] be revoked altogether as one directed against U.S.S.R."[18]

Litvinov was asking the impossible from Poland and Rumania who had little sympathy for the U.S.S.R. and feared Germany. Did Stalin instruct Litvinov to present Moscow's maximum desires in order to have them rejected? It was too soon in Stalin's double game to invite a western rebuff; he still needed negotiations with both sides. I incline to the view that Litvinov, Stalin and Chairman Molotov approving, named Russia's highest price as the beginning of a long bargaining procedure during which, despite price-cutting, Litvinov might have hoped for a favorable arrangement with the West while Stalin and Molotov, hedging their bets, would not break with the West until they were certain they could get a big deal from Hitler.

Litvinov's April 18 program maximum was the Soviet reply to Halifax's April 14 program minimum of a mere unilateral "public declaration" by the Kremlin. Now they would haggle.

Western officials, drenched with problems, did not know when and where or if Hitler would strike. Thus on April 13, 1939, the French ambassador in London told the British Foreign Office that Premier Daladier expected Germany to attack Rumania; this would give the Nazis oil supplies for a long war. "M. Daladier did not pay too much attention to troop concentrations in the neighborhood of the Polish frontier; they might be only a feint, and it might be quite easy to turn them quickly against Rumania in a lightning attack."[19] On the other hand, French Foreign Minister Bonnet expected that Italy would go to

[18] *Ibid.*, pp. 228-229.
[19] *Ibid.*, p. 114.

war simultaneously with Germany "and if we could inflict a crushing blow upon her in early days of the conflict it would insure our general victory."[20]

Far worse than wrong guesses were the difficulties the British had in understanding the Soviet position as defined on April 18 by Litvinov. Lord Halifax could not see why the "Soviet Government should affect to believe that His Majesty's Government are not committed by the Declarations they have made to Poland and Rumania. The language of those Declarations (as also of the Declaration to Greece) makes it clear that in the event of any action being taken which clearly threatened the independence of these countries . . . His Majesty's Government would feel themselves bound at once to lend them all the support in their power. . . . It was on the strength of that definite commitment on our part that I suggested that the Soviet Government should for their part make a declaration in respect of their Western neighbours. It would of course have been for them to decide whether to include Latvia, Estonia, and Finland as well as Poland and Rumania though it was the two latter which I have particularly in mind. If the Soviet Government wished to include Turkey also, so much the better. . . . I would add that it was no part of the intention of His Majesty's Government that the Soviet Government should commit themselves to intervene on behalf of Poland, Rumania (or Turkey) irrespective of whether Great Britain and France had already intervened. If the Soviet Government wished to make their own intervention contingent on that of Great Britain and France (at all events in respect of the countries which had been made the subject of declarations by Great Britain and France), His Majesty's Government for their part would have no objections."[21]

This was the nub of the matter. Russia would enter the war after England and France. In the postwar era Soviet leaders and political writers charged the western powers with evil intent. For instance: "The ruling circles of Britain and France, who are accustomed to having others pull the chestnuts out of the fire for them, on this occasion too attempted to inveigle the Soviet Union into assuming commitments under which it would have taken upon itself the brunt of the sacrifice in repulsing eventual Hitler aggression, while Britain and France would not be bound by any commitments toward the Soviet Union."[22]

Halifax answered this argument by saying that "The primary task must be to erect the first essential barrier against aggression in Eastern Europe by making arrangements for the safety of those States most directly menaced. It is only after we have completed this stage that we

[20] *Ibid.*, p. 160.
[21] *Ibid.*, pp. 266-267.
[22] Soviet Information Bureau, *Falsifiers of History (Historical Survey)*, p. 29.

should be in a position to consider extending any arrangement to other States, like the Soviet Union itself, which are not so immediately threatened. . . .

"This does not mean to say that His Majesty's Government do not wish the Soviet Government to be associated with their efforts. On the contrary they are conscious that the support that might be afforded by the Soviet Government to the small Eastern European countries might be of the utmost value in case of war. The difficulty is that the Governments of those countries are reluctant either to engage themselves in a treaty of mutual assistance with the Soviet Union or even publicly to admit that Soviet assistance would be welcome to them." This is why, Halifax said, the British government had proposed that Moscow limit itself to a declaration of intention to assist victims of aggression "who wish to take advantage" of Soviet aid.

These were the instructions Halifax sent to the British Ambassador in Moscow on April 21. "You should speak to M. Litvinov on the foregoing lines," Halifax concluded.[23]

France showed greater comprehension than England for the Soviet position. The French response to Litvinov's document, drawn up by the Foreign Ministry and communicated to the British Foreign Office on April 21, asserted: "The Quai d'Orsay think that Russia is entitled to ask for the same kind of guarantee from Great Britain and France as Poland is receiving and that she could hardly be expected to undertake any obligations without receiving such a guarantee." Paris believed that the Litvinov proposal went further than the Franco-Soviet treaty in that it provided "for automatic and immediate assistance" and expanded that treaty "by bringing in a guarantee of mutual assistance between Great Britain and Russia."[24]

This stance reflected French weakness as well as Daladier's bitterness and anger. When Sir Eric Phipps, the British Ambassador in Paris, visited the Premier on April 22 and attempted to persuade him to mend French relations with Mussolini, Daladier remained obdurate. "He is convinced," Sir Eric reported to Halifax, "that the present Italian Government are gangsters. They are in with Herr Hitler up to the hilt. They were so even before Munich. Prime Minister [Chamberlain] and he himself had been bluffed and lied to at Munich. He almost regretted that we had not made war then, or rather he felt that, if we had been sufficiently firm, Herr Hitler and Signor Mussolini would have given way."[25] But Foreign Minister Bonnet, who had been no less an appeaser than Daladier, remained so to the end. The Quai d'Orsay felt that

[23] *Documents on British Foreign Policy*, Third Series. Vol. V, pp. 267-269.
[24] *Ibid.*, p. 273.
[25] *Ibid.*, pp. 276-277.

the negotiations required to reach the kind of alliance outlined in Litvinov's April 18 document would be "too lengthy." This may have been one of the document's purposes. Bonnet took the position that any public stipulation of Soviet aid to Poland "would provoke on the part of the Polish government reactions that risked compromising profoundly the very object of the proposed agreement." The French government accordingly wished to limit the Anglo-French-Soviet agreement to three propositions: If France and Great Britain found themselves at war with Germany the Soviet Union would immediately come to their assistance. If as a result of Soviet collaboration with France and England the Soviet Union found itself at war with Germany, France and Great Britain would immediately come to Russia's aid. Thirdly, the three governments would without delay study the means of implementing this agreement.[26]

On April 25 Sir William Seeds wired Halifax from Moscow that "M. Litvinov's proposals are not of a hard and fast nature but are meant as a basis for discussion."[27] The ambassador would have sent such a telegram only on clear information from a high Soviet source.

Halifax frankly explained the British government's dilemma in telegrams to Sir H. Kennard and Sir R. Hoare, British Ambassadors in Warsaw and Bucharest respectively. The British government, Halifax asserted, did not wish to forgo the chance of receiving help from the Soviets in case of war and yet did not want to jeopardize the common front by disregarding the feelings of Poland and Rumania which refused that help. The British government, further, did not want "to forfeit the sympathy of the world at large by giving a handle to Germany's anti-Comintern propaganda." (It would do so, he thus intimated, by allying itself with Russia.) Nor did it wish to "jeopardize the cause of peace by provoking violent action by Germany."[28]

This was a perfect formula for doing nothing.

The British and French governments had been discussing the April 18 Litvinov document between themselves for a fortnight without giving an answer to Moscow. Presently lightning struck: Maxim Litvinov was dismissed. A four-line inconspicuous notice on the last page of the Soviet dailies of May 4 announced that he was released "at his own request." Litvinov had been guest of honor on the Red Square during the First of May parade standing "right next to Stalin," the German chargé in Moscow reported.[29] The next day Litvinov received the British Ambassador, who wrote: "He gave me no inkling" of his intention to resign. The

[26] *Ibid.*, pp. 316-317.
[27] *Ibid.*, p. 319.
[28] *Ibid.*, p. 357.
[29] *Nazi-Soviet Relations 1939-1941*, pp. 2-3.

Commissar probably did not know he would resign.

The suddenness with which Litvinov was dropped enhanced the significance of the act. This May 3 signal from the Kremlin tower, a surprise to all, foreshadowed an imminent change of policy. "Molotov (no Jew)," the German chargé wired Berlin, "is held to be the 'most intimate friend and closest collaborator' of Stalin."[30] Chairman Molotov, highly acclaimed by the Soviet press, took over the Foreign Commissariat.

The dismissal of Litvinov may have been precipitated by a report from a Soviet spy in Tokyo. Richard Sorge was no ordinary spy. Born near Baku on October 4, 1895, of a Russian mother and a father who was a German mining engineer working for the Swedish firm of Nobel which had holdings in the Baku oilfield, young Sorge fought in the German army during the first world war and was severely wounded. According to the Moscow *Izvestia* of September 5, 1964, he returned to the land of his birth and joined the Russian Communist Party in 1925. In 1934 he joined the German Nazi Party while acting as correspondent in Tokyo of the *Frankfurter Zeitung*. In that disguise he became the confidant and close collaborator of Major General Eugen Ott, the Nazi Ambassador in the Japanese capital. He was also on friendly terms with the German military attaché there and with high Japanese officials. He used these connections to serve Moscow. "In the spring of 1939," wrote *Pravda* of September 4, 1965, "Sorge reported to Moscow that the Hitlerite invasion of Poland would take place on September first." (He was executed by Japan on November 7, 1944. The Soviet government gave him posthumously its highest decoration: Hero of the Soviet Union.)

The knowledge, available as early as spring, 1939, that war impended against Poland profoundly affected Soviet foreign policy and particularly relations with Germany.

On May 5 the Soviet chargé in Berlin, Georgi Astakhov, a pale, mild, ascetic-looking communist with a sparse Ho Chi Minh beard, called on Dr. Karl Schnurre, chief of the East European Department of the Economic Section of the German Foreign Office, at the latter's request to be told that the Skoda Works would carry out their Soviet contracts. "Counsellor of Embassy Astakhov was visibly gratified. . . . Then Astakhov touched upon the dismissal of Litvinov and tried without asking direct questions to learn whether this event would cause a change in our position toward the Soviet Union. He stressed very much the great importance of the personality of Molotov, who was by no means a specialist in foreign policy, but who would have all the greater importance for the future of Soviet foreign policy."[31]

Astakhov again visited Schnurre on May 17, ostensibly to discuss

[30] *Ibid.*, p. 3.
[31] *Ibid.*, p. 3.

Soviet-Czechoslovak trade relations. After dealing with that matter, "Astakhov stated in detail that there were no conflicts in foreign policy between Germany and Soviet Russia, and that therefore there was no reason for enmity between the two countries. It was true that in the Soviet Union there was a distinct feeling of being menaced by Germany. It would undoubtedly be possible to eliminate this feeling of being menaced and the distrust in Moscow. During this conversation, he also again mentioned the Treaty of Rapallo. In reply to my incidental question, he commented on the Anglo-Soviet negotiations to the effect that under the present circumstances the result desired by England would hardly be achieved."[32]

Three days later, May 20, German Ambassador Count von der Schulenburg had an interview with Molotov. Although the Count characterized it as "friendly," he and his Foreign Ministry considered it unsatisfactory. It began with references to the economic negotiations between the two countries which, Molotov said, "had faded out." Now the "Soviet Government could only agree to a resumption of the negotiations if the necessary 'political bases' for them had been constructed." The German, on the other hand, believed that the successful conclusion of the commercial discussions "would also help the political atmosphere." Moreover, what did he mean by "the construction of political bases"? the Count inquired. Here Molotov proved evasive: "All my determined efforts to bring Herr Molotov to make his wishes more definite and more concrete were in vain. Herr Molotov had apparently determined to say just so much and not a word more."

At this stage of the pact negotiations Molotov obviously thought it wise, by being vague, to provoke his protagonist into taking the initiative. Any German eagerness would put Moscow in a better position to make larger demands. But Molotov's stance had the opposite effect. As soon as Schulenburg's telegraphed report had been read and pondered in Berlin, Weizsaecker instructed him on May 21 to "sit tight" and "wait to see if the Russians will speak more openly."[33]

In a telegram dated Moscow, May 22, Schulenburg amplified the report he made immediately after his meeting with Molotov on May 20. Ribbentrop, he recalled, had instructed him, "to maintain extreme caution" in talking with Molotov. Therefore he said as little as possible "all the more because the attitude of Herr Molotov seemed to me quite suspicious . . . he apparently wants to obtain from us more extensive proposals of a political nature." Then Schulenburg exposed German strategy: he advised caution "as long as it is not certain that possible proposals from our side will not be used by the Kremlin only to exert

[32] *Ibid.*, pp. 4-5.
[33] *Ibid.*, pp. 5-7.

pressure on England and France." Yet the Count knew that the German situation required action before the imminent attack on Poland. "On the other hand," he therefore added, "if we want to accomplish something here, it is unavoidable that we sooner or later take some action."

Schulenburg had eagerly sought information on the Anglo-French-Russian talks. But the British Ambassador, he reported, "preserves an iron silence. . . . Even neutral diplomats have not been able to learn anything." The French Ambassador was away and the chargé too was about to leave Moscow.[34]

The Germans were perplexed. Molotov's secretiveness, native to him, congenial to totalitarianism, and a necessary concomitant—at this stage—of the two-track-two-train diplomacy, intensified their concern. The condition was somewhat reminiscent of Rapallo where Chicherin and Litvinov created an impression of success with the British in order to induce the Germans to sign.

Weizsaecker had instructed Schulenburg to "sit tight." But Hitler felt he must know what Russia would do when he went to war. Nazi impatience propelled Ribbentrop into sending Schulenburg a 1,400-word telegram of instructions on May 26.[35] Explicit and detailed, this "strictly secret" message blazed the trail to the Ribbentrop-Molotov pact.

The reason for Nazi impetuosity is revealed in the introductory paragraph: "Since the latest reports indicate that the English-Russian treaty negotiations could soon lead to a favorable result in one form or another, it seems the time has come, in our further talks with the Russians, to step out of our reserve much more than had hitherto been intended. I therefore ask you to seek out Molotov as soon as possible and have a conversation with him in the following terms . . ."

Molotov had made the extension of Soviet-German commercial trade contingent on a clarification of the political relationship between Germany and Soviet Russia. The German government did not object to exposing its ideas about German-Soviet relations. "In past years German foreign policy was conducted, first of all, under the sign of hostility to the Comintern. It had been the primary purpose of National Socialism to establish a new, strong Germany completely secure against any inroads of communist tendencies. This purpose has been achieved. We will, of course, in future relentlessly suppress all communist stirrings inside Germany as well as any Comintern influence from outside.

"But the question of shaping the foreign political relations between

[34] *Ibid.*, pp. 7-9.

[35] This telegram, not included in *Nazi-Soviet Relations 1939-1941* or published in any collection of official documents or quoted anywhere else, was found by me in the German Foreign Office archives in Bonn in the summer of 1966, Nr. 111334-111345.

Germany and Soviet Russia is another matter provided we in Germany can assume that the Soviet government, for its part, has renounced the aggressive struggle waged against Germany through the introduction of communist and world revolutionary ideas into Germany. Certain events in recent months have led us to believe that in this respect a change has taken place in Russian views. We could quite understand this if one takes into consideration the course of the Spanish civil war [Franco's victory], for instance, and on the other hand, the extraordinary strengthening of Germany abroad and at home. We believe we recognized certain indications of the Soviet Russian trend in this direction in Stalin's speech in March.

"If this assumption is correct we can affirm without hesitation that no real foreign political conflict of interest exists between Germany and Soviet Russia. On our part, in any case, we see no aggregate of issues in which our mutual interests are directly opposed to one another. For this reason we can quite see that the time has arrived to envisage the tranquilization and normalization of German-Soviet Russian foreign political relations."

As proof of a new German attitude toward Russia Ribbentrop cited the improved tone of the Nazi press toward Soviet Russia. Moreover, "any intention to expand into the Ukraine is completely foreign to our thoughts. . . . The central factor in German foreign policy is now the close relationship to Italy which has been sealed by a treaty of alliance. This alliance is, in the obvious nature of things, not directed against Soviet Russia and does not even indirectly affect her interests. It is aimed exclusively against the Anglo-French combination. As far as our relation to Japan is concerned we declare quite openly that we intend to continue to cultivate and deepen this relationship. It is also a fact that the German-Japanese relationship was a historic development of the Anti-Comintern motto. This motto, however, does not characterize the actual political essence of what we have in mind in cultivating German-Japanese relations. We rather think in this connection of our mutual opposition to England. On the basis of our good relations with Japan we quite believe to be in a position to counteract Japanese-Russian hostility; in any case we are not interested in intensifying this hostility, and we also believe that we can help see to it that Japanese foreign policy gradually moves more and more in a direction which will not bring it in conflict with Russia.

"Our differences with Poland are known. We take the view that the problems of Danzig and the Corridor must some day be solved; on our part we do not intend to impose this solution by military means. But should military complications with Poland arise contrary to our wishes, we are firmly convinced that this too need not lead in any way to a conflict of interest with Soviet Russia. Today we can already say that in the settlement of the German-Polish question—no matter how this occurs—we would give every possible consideration to Russian interests. From the purely military viewpoint Poland represents no problem for us at all. As things stand now the military decision would be achieved in so short a time that Anglo-French assistance would be illusory.

"This is altogether decisive for an understanding of the present military-political situation in Europe. In view of our own military strength and of the completed construction of our western defenses, England and France would be faced with a question of life or death if they undertook military action against Germany. We have legitimate doubt of the extent to which, in the final analysis, these two states are even determined to attempt any effective intervention in favor of Poland. In any event it is clear to us that even if this attempt were seriously made by them the decision of the Polish question would not thereby be affected. Help would come too late because our western defenses could be penetrated by no one.

"When one weighs the practical situation of power and interest soberly we cannot understand what might actually induce Soviet Russia to participate actively in Britain's game of encirclement. Available reports seem to indicate that it is clear to Moscow too that what is involved here is a one-sided burden for the Soviet Union without any really worthwhile British compensation. We also take the view that England is not at all in the position, no matter how the treaties might be worded, to offer any truly valuable reward. While the West Wall makes all aid impossible in Europe, England would not be in a position to move effectively in the Far East against Japan which possesses an absolute maritime superiority there. We are therefore convinced that England again remains true to her traditional policy of allowing other powers to rake the chestnuts out of the fire for her. We furthermore regard the entire direction of English policies at present as a sign of weakness, and we do not believe, no matter how the treaty and guaranty agreements will finally be phrased, that any concrete political realities will emerge.

"Thus we in no way fear England's attempts at encirclement. But we deem it proper to inform the Soviet government of our political intentions and conceptions at this moment in order to prevent the Soviet government from reaching its decisions in ignorance of the real situation. Should the Soviet government consider it proper, despite the information about our intentions and conceptions, to join firmly in a bloc with England and France against Germany she would make Germany and Japan her enemies and would have to bear the consequences . . .

"Russia's alliance with England against Germany would be comprehensible, from the point of view of Russian interests, only if the Soviet government feared Germany's aggressive intentions against Russia. As stated above, such intentions are far from our minds." If Moscow mistrusted German statements, the two governments might attempt to reestablish trust through commercial negotiations and the normalization of political relations. The Nazi Foreign Minister added that the Japanese and Italians had been informed in general terms of this German-Russian conversation. Finally, he instructed Count von der Schulenburg to conduct his dealings with Molotov by word of mouth "and nothing written should be handed" to Chairman and Foreign Commissar Molotov.

Literacy had risen sharply in the Soviet Union—even among innocents. Certainly the crafty Kremlinmen knew how to read Ribbentrop's comprehensive message. It said: Germany would soon be at war with Poland. In the "settlement" of the Polish question Russia's interests would be given "every possible consideration." (A share of the booty?) England and France were unlikely to want to intervene on behalf of Poland and if they tried they could only fail. They themselves would be in peril. Why then should Russia ally herself with the West? Germany could help the Soviet Union in the Far East by directing Japan's expansionist urge away from Siberia and toward British and French colonies; England lacked the power to confer such benefits on Russia. Germany herself, Ribbentrop added, had forsworn any hostile intentions against the U.S.S.R.; she no longer coveted the Ukraine. *Mein Kampf* was outdated.

If all this was so, why did Hitler need Stalin? Germany's ability to crush Poland quickly and Anglo-French inability to aid Poland or break through Germany's newly built Siegfried Line should have made a Nazi link with the Kremlin superfluous and Ribbentrop's clumsy courtship of Russia unnecessary. Apparently Hitler still feared the West and a West-Soviet Union league. "We are of the opinion here that the English-Russian combination certainly will not be easy to prevent," Weizsaecker wrote Schulenburg the day after Ribbentrop sent his long wire to Schulenburg.[36]

Confusion reigned in Berlin. The day Ribbentrop sent his long telegram to Schulenburg, Weizsaecker wired Schulenburg confirming his May 21 order to "sit tight." Four days later, on May 30, Weizsaecker rescinded his "sit tight" instructions: "Contrary to previously planned tactics we have now nevertheless decided to establish some contact with the Soviet Union."[37] Fear is a poor diplomatic counselor.

The Soviet government took no pains to calm German fears. It fed them. Molotov praised the British in an address on May 31, 1939. He said, "It must be admitted that the mutual-assistance pact between Brit-

[36] *Nazi-Soviet Relations*, p. 9.

[37] I found Weizsaecker's telegrams of May 26 and May 30 in the German Foreign Office archives in Bonn.

ain and Poland alters the European situation. . . . There are a number of signs that the democratic countries of Europe are coming to realize that the non-intervention policy has collapsed."

That change in the European situation drastically altered Soviet foreign policy.

By granting guarantees to Poland and Rumania the western powers gave Russia all they had to give her. They would go to war—as they did on September 3—because Germany threatened to seize Poland—the access route to Soviet territory. Was there anything else Moscow could extract from the Anglo-French? If not, what more could be extracted from Hitler? This was the heart of the two-way negotiations Stalin conducted from May to August, 1939. To extort the maximum from Germany Moscow had to foster false impressions of success in Paris and London where there was none. Hence Molotov's words on May 31.

Winston Churchill urged a triple alliance: "If, for instance, Mr. Chamberlain on receipt of the Russian offer [of April 18] had replied, 'Yes. Let us three band together and break Hitler's neck' . . . history might have taken a different course. At least it could not have taken a worse."[38]

Who knows? The brighter the prospects of an agreement between Russia and the West the greater the nervousness in Berlin and the greater the concessions Stalin could wring from Hitler.

On May 6 Britain finally replied to the Litvinov offer of April 18.[39] It was a disappointing reply. If that offer still stood, Halifax instructed Sir William Seeds, and if "no change in the outlook" of the Soviets had taken place, the ambassador was to tell Molotov that the western allies were prepared, not for an alliance, but to welcome Moscow's "unilateral declaration" of readiness to help the West in war. Halifax also wanted everything done "to prevent the negotiations from breaking down. . . ."

A unilateral declaration gave Russia nothing, yet might involve her in war. Why then make such a declaration? On the other hand, a continuation of the negotiations with the Anglo-French would conduce to just the atmosphere in Berlin the Kremlin needed for its deal with Hitler.

Robert Coulondre, the French ambassador in Berlin, tried to penetrate the diplomatic mist. "The Fuehrer," he wrote Georges Bonnet on May 7, "will come to an understanding . . . with Russia." Coulondre sketched the possibilities. Hitler might wish to assure himself of "the benevolent neutrality of that country [the U.S.S.R.] in the event of a conflict, and perhaps even of her complicity in the partition of Poland."[40] The Ambassador and his informers envisaged other variations of Nazi policy, but he at least confronted Paris with the grim prospect of

[38] Winston S. Churchill, *The Second World War. The Gathering Storm,* p. 365.
[39] *Documents on British Foreign Policy,* Third Series. Vol. V., pp. 443-444.
[40] Ministère des Affaires Etrangères, *French Yellow Book,* pp. 132-134.

a far-reaching Soviet-Nazi agreement.

However, Polish-Rumanian aversion to Soviet military aid, Chamberlian's hostility to the "Bolshies," and the atmosphere of appeasement and pacifism that hovered over London and Paris paralyzed Anglo-French diplomacy and left it little room for maneuver. Moreover, Coulondre's information and speculations were vague. Given the western reluctance to form an alliance with Moscow, his report fell on fallow ground.

In this long period of uncertainty as to which card the Kremlin would play, which Soviet train would arrive at its destination, hundreds of telegrams, now resting in the archives of various governments, indicate the vast amount of groping that went on. Coulondre saw signs of a Soviet-Nazi rapprochement. On the other hand, William C. Bullitt, U.S. Ambassador in Paris, purveyed information to Sir Eric Phipps, the British Ambassador in Paris, according to which Litvinov's dismissal "does not in the least imply the intention of the Soviets to isolate themselves from Europe and still less to flirt with Hitler. . . . Mr. Bullitt, who knows M. Litvinov and M. Molotov, thinks," Phipps wired Halifax, "that we can only have gained by the change. The latter in any case has the advantage of being a pure Russian."[41] Perhaps Bullitt was requiting Litvinov's unconcealed dislike of him. Even ambassadors are not immune to pettiness and prejudice in the midst of a lowering world crisis.

Thirty minutes past midnight on May 15 Molotov handed Sir William Seeds the Soviet reply to the British proposal of a unilateral Russian declaration. The proposal would not do. It lacked reciprocity. France and England and Poland had given one another reciprocal guarantees: if one was attacked the other two would come to its defense. No such guarantee was being offered the U.S.S.R. Moreover, the British and French had guaranteed only Poland and Rumania, not Finland, Estonia, and Latvia. (Lithuania did not border directly on Russia.) As a result, the "north western frontier of the U.S.S.R. remains uncovered" and this "may serve to provoke aggression in the direction of the Soviet Union." Molotov asked a "concrete agreement" on the forms and extent of the assistance to be rendered.

The British Ambassador made one point in his tentative reply. Finland considered herself a Scandinavian nation, had certain "unpleasant historical associations with Russia," and was disturbed already by mere rumors that Russia wished to guarantee her security. The British and French had never contemplated such action.[42]

Britain regarded the prospect of a German attack on Russia via the Baltic States and Finland highly unlikely. "The front would be far too narrow for any effective result," Vansittart told Maisky at lunch on May 16. "No German attack on Soviet Russia was conceivable except by the

41 *Documents on British Foreign Policy,* Third Series. Vol. V, p. 505.

42 *Ibid.,* pp. 558-559.

broader front of Poland and Rumania, and it was on that that we had better concentrate now."[43] In any event, the Baltic countries wanted no Russian guarantee. They feared the bear's embrace.

The French government objected to England's stance. Sir Alexander Cadogan, who replaced Vansittart as Permanent Under Secretary of State for Foreign Affairs on January 1, 1938 (Vansittart was kicked upstairs to the honorific position of "Chief Diplomatic Adviser"), met Premier Daladier and Foreign Minister Bonnet in Geneva on May 20. Cadogan contended that a three-power alliance "might well provoke Germany to violent action" and "divide opinion in Great Britain which was at present firmly united behind the policy which His Majesty's Government had been pursuing during the recent months."

Daladier scoffed at this logic of appeasement: Don't anger the tiger. Unless France and England concluded a triple alliance with Russia "we should increase rather than diminish the risk of an act of force by Germany." (This had been Litvinov's consistent reasoning.) "Without the collaboration of Russia," Daladier continued, "assistance could not be effective."

Cadogan then asked Daladier and Bonnet whether a danger existed "of the Soviet Government saying at any moment that in view of the delay in accepting their ideas they could not discuss the matter any further and would drop the whole thing. M. Daladier thought that was a serious danger. M. Litvinov's departure meant something . . . the Soviet government might retire into isolation and let Europe destroy itself. . . . I asked the French Ministers," Cadogan reported to Halifax, "whether they thought there was a serious danger of an accommodation between Germany and Russia if we failed to close with the Russians now. They replied that this danger could not be ignored since there was a party in Germany which was in favour of such a rapprochement. Russian policy was quite incalculable and was liable to sudden changes. It was impossible to follow the workings of the Soviet mind from day to day."[44]

In fact, they were following the workings of the Soviet mind with some accuracy. Stalin was walking the long well-trodden lane linking the Soviet and German military and adding a political path. Hitler came to meet him. Coulondre reported to Bonnet on June 13 about the "Fuehrer's" address during a review of the Condor Legion which fought for Franco. It would have been normal on such an occasion to attack communism. Hitler "never uttered the word 'Bolshevism' or 'Communism.' It was against the 'Democracies,' the 'warmongers and war profiteers,' the promoters of 'encirclement,' that his thunderbolts were directed."[45]

By this time anybody with ears to hear and eyes to read should have

[43] *Ibid.*, pp. 564-565.
[44] *Ibid.*, pp. 623-625.
[45] *French Yellow Book*, pp. 158-159.

had no difficulty following the workings of the Soviet mind, that is, of Stalin's mind. To most observers, experts and Soviet ambassadors included, the Soviet-Nazi pact nevertheless came as a complete and shocking surprise.

Moscow pursued its negotiations with the Anglo-French. On June 3 Molotov handed Sir William Seeds and Paul-Emile Naggiar, the French Ambassador, his plan for the tripartite alliance: Britain, France, and the U.S.S.R. "would render to each other immediately all effective assistance" if one of them was attacked by a European power or if a European aggressor attacked Belgium, Greece, Turkey, Rumania, Poland, Latvia, Estonia, and Finland—countries which the three great nations agreed to defend.[46] They would not wait for League of Nations approval.

Sir Nevile Henderson, the British Ambassador in Berlin, wired Halifax on June 6 that "Hitler is not immediately seeking a quarrel which may lead to world war."[47] This assurance would have tended to make London even more antagonistic to involvement in Molotov's proposed blanket guarantee to so many small European countries, especially since the majority of them wanted no Russian guarantee because they felt the Soviets would defend them by devouring them.

By this time, however, the British government, as Chamberlain told the House of Commons on June 7, had overcome many of its inhibitions and was prepared to conclude the triple alliance with reciprocal guarantees to one another. The contractual guarantee to the small countries presented the last remaining obstacle. To deal with it Britain sent William Strang, later Permanent Under Secretary of the Foreign Office, as well as Frank Roberts, subsequently Ambassador to Yugoslavia and West Germany, to Moscow. Lord Strang told me in London in the summer of 1966, confirming Chamberlain's statement in the House of Commons on June 7, 1939, that he and Roberts did not go to the Soviet capital to conduct the negotiations but to help Sir William Seeds in the negotiations. I asked him on that occasion and again in the autumn of 1967 whether the outcome would have been different had Prime Minister Chamberlain gone to Moscow to negotiate. He said, "That would have been inconceivable."

Chamberlain in the "Bolshie" Kremlin!

"Suppose Halifax or Eden had gone to Moscow?" I persisted.

"The result would have been the same," Lord Strang replied.

The same or worse.

Strang recalled that he and his diplomatic colleagues in Moscow knew in the summer of 1939 that something was afoot between Stalin and

[46] *Documents on British Foreign Policy,* Third Series. Vol. V, pp. 753-754.
[47] *Ibid.,* p. 782.

Hitler but they did not know exactly what. The Soviet-Nazi talks were secret. The Anglo-French-Russian negotiations were not. Moscow used open diplomacy with the West to frighten Berlin into making maximum concessions to Russia. If Chamberlain or Halifax or Eden had been on the scene in Moscow the Bolsheviks, I suspect, could have won more territorial "adjustments" from Hitler.

Had Stalin wanted an agreement with the West he would have negotiated openly with Berlin and secretly with the Anglo-French; then London and Paris might have been more prone to make concessions. He did the reverse.

Aware that the two-track negotiations gave it a strong position, the Soviet government's talks with Germany were characterized by a toughness bordering on rudeness calculated to impress. But the Russian negotiators mingled brutality with subtlety. Stalin wanted none of his lieutenants to display an eagerness that would reduce his rewards for entering into a deal with Hitler.

As Hitler's deathline for Poland drew near, Nazi diplomacy grew tense. Count von der Schulenburg had been in Berlin and on his return to Moscow made an appointment with Molotov for June 29. "The conversation lasted over an hour and proceeded in a friendly manner." The ambassador offered proof that Germany's attitude to Russia was cordial: the Nazi press was reserved, and Berlin sought a resumption of commercial discussions and had concluded nonaggression treaties with the Baltic countries; these treaties showed that Germany had no hostile intentions against Russia. But what, Schulenburg inquired, did the Chairman mean when in their last conversation he had called for "the creation of a new basis of our relationship"?

Molotov pocketed the goodwill assurances but counterattacked. Germany, he said, concluded the nonaggression agreements with the Baltic States "in her own interests, and not out of love for the Soviet Union." Besides he doubted "the permanence of such treaties." Had not Hitler just canceled Germany's nonaggression treaty with Poland? "My impression is," Schulenburg informed his Foreign Ministry, "that the Soviet Government is greatly interested in knowing our political views and in maintaining contact with us."[48]

It was now the turn of the Nazis to feign disinterest. Hitler gave orders on June 30 that "further activities in Moscow were to be stopped in view of the conduct of the Russians."[49]

The Russians remained reserved for four weeks and continued their slow-motion talks with the Anglo-French. A peculiar article on these talks appeared on the front page of *Pravda* of June 29, 1939. It was

[48] *Nazi-Soviet Relations,* pp. 26-27.
[49] *Ibid.,* p. 31.

signed by A. Zhdanov (Andrei A. Zhdanov, member of the Politburo and regarded as close adviser of Stalin on foreign affairs). Zhdanov wrote that he expressed his "personal opinion although my friends do not agree with it." The unidentified friends continue to believe "that the British and French governments, having commenced the negotiations with the U.S.S.R. about a pact of mutual assistance, had serious intentions of creating a mighty barrier against aggression in Europe." But he asked why the British would not guarantee certain Baltic nations irrespective of whether they wished to be guaranteed, and, citing newspaper reports, suggested that the western powers were preparing the way for "a deal with the aggressors. The next few days," the article concludes, "should prove: is this so or is it not."

Zhdanov's article aroused multiple reactions. Was the Politburo divided? Did Zhdanov speak for Stalin? Was this really a personal view? On a major issue the Politburo might argue at its weekly sessions but once a decision had been adopted no member stepped out of line to air his own misgivings. The Kremlin had not suddenly permitted freedom of speech. In retrospect the article seems like a segment of the double track Soviet diplomacy calculated to speed British concessions and thereby stir the Nazis to still more concessions. Zhdanov's subsequent record is that of a Russian nationalist-expansionist. Expansion would be possible in collusion with Germany.

The nervous Nazis could not stand the tension. The Soviet-German talks had been frozen as a result of Hitler's June 30 order. He unfroze them. Dr. Karl Schnurre, chief Foreign Ministry economic diplomat for eastern Europe, invited Soviet Chargé Astakhov and Deputy Director Babarin of the Russian Trade Mission in Berlin to dinner on July 26 "in accordance with my instructions. . . . The Russians stayed until about half past twelve." Schnurre told his guests that "despite all the differences in Weltanschauung, there was *one* thing in common in the ideology of Germany, Italy, and the Soviet Union: opposition to the capitalism of the West. Therefore, it would appear to us quite paradoxical if the Soviet Union, as a Socialist state, were to side with the Western democracies."

Schnurre did not record the Russians' reply. Perhaps they showed no interest in philosophical disquisitions. Knowing full well that time was of the essence to Germany, Astakhov declared that the tempo of the Russo-German rapprochement "must probably be very slow and gradual." If encirclement worried the Germans it troubled the Soviets too after the dismemberment of Czechoslovakia, the anti-Comintern pact, and the peril of Japan. In particular, Germany's "assumption that the Baltic countries and Finland, as well as Rumania, were in our

[Germany's] sphere of influence completed for the Soviet government the feeling of being menaced."

This was an exquisite gambit worthy of framing for a museum of diplomacy. The Kremlin habitually makes important pronouncements through its telegraphic agency or a newspaper editorial or in an ostensibly casual remark by a fourth-rank official over a glass of wine. Astakhov had skillfully shown the Russian hand. Stalin had named his price. The Soviet Union would not feel menaced and would not join the Anglo-French if Germany retired from her sphere of influence in the Baltic, Finland, Poland, and Rumania and allowed Russia to replace her.

"During the subsequent discussion," Schnurre noted, "Astakhov came back again to the question of the Baltic countries and asked whether, besides economic penetration, we had any far-reaching political aims there. He also took up the Rumanian question seriously. As for Poland, he stated that Danzig would return to the Reich in one way or another and that the Corridor question would have to be solved somehow in favor of the Reich. He asked whether the territories which once belonged to Austria were also tending toward Germany, particularly the Galician and Ukrainian territories."

No Soviet diplomat, even of a higher rank than Astakhov, would have spoken in this vein without specific instructions from the Kremlin summit. Astakhov was actually giving a preview of the territorial settlement that emerged from the Soviet-Nazi pact: the Baltic countries and parts of Rumania as well as the Galician and Ukrainian territories of eastern Poland would—after Germany had taken Danzig and the Polish Corridor "in one way or another"—be consigned by Hitler to the U.S.S.R.

Throughout the long dinner, Dr. Schnurre insisted on stressing ideology. He explained that the Nazis were bound to be opposed to communism, but now "Communism had been eradicated in Germany." The Soviet government was not the Comintern, in his opinion. "The amalgamation of Bolshevism with the national history of Russia, which expressed itself in the glorification of great Russian men and deeds (celebration of the battle of Poltava, Peter the Great, the battle on Lake Peipus [against Teutonic knights], Alexander Nevsky), had really changed the international face of Bolshevism, as we see it, particularly since Stalin had postponed world revolution indefinitely. In this state of affairs we saw possibilities today which we had not seen earlier, provided that no attempt was made to spread Communist propaganda in any form in Germany.

"At the end Astakhov stressed how valuable this conversation had been to him. . . . The Russians were silent about the status and chances of the English pact negotiations . . . it looks as if Moscow, for the time being, is following a policy of delay toward us as well as England."[50]

This was correct. Stalin was in no hurry. The British and Germans felt the urgency of the situation. He could wait.

"It is we, not the Russians, who took the initiative in starting negotiations," William Strang wrote from Moscow on July 20, after weeks of futile toil assisting Sir William Seeds in his talks with Molotov. "Our need for an agreement is more immediate than theirs. Unlike them we have assumed obligations which we may be obliged to fulfill any day; and some of the obligations we have undertaken are of benefit to the Soviet Union since they protect a good part of their western frontier. . . . The Russians have, in the last resort, at least two alternative policies, namely the policy of isolation, and the policy of accommodation with Germany. We are being urged by our press and by our public to conclude an agreement quickly; and the Russians have good reason to assume that we shall not dare to face a final breakdown of the negotiations. This is the strength of their negotiating position, and this makes it certain that if we want an agreement with them we shall have to pay their price or something near it."

The price was much the same as the Kremlin was demanding from the Germans. "Where their own special interests are at stake and where they claim to regard themselves as being especially vulnerable," Strang's letter continued, "namely in the Baltic states, they are determined to ensure that our assistance shall be forthcoming not only in the event of aggression of the classical type, but also in the event of aggressive action undertaken according to the new technique with which the Axis Powers have made us familiar. If we wish to understand how they feel about the Baltic States," Strang asserted, sympathetically, "we have only to imagine what our own attitude would be to the establishment of German influence over Holland and Belgium."[51]

Molotov had raised the fateful issue of "indirect aggression." Ambassador Maisky casually dropped the term "indirect aggression" into a talk with Halifax on May 9, 1939, and when the British Foreign Secretary asked the Soviet Ambassador on June 23 why it was necessary to include in the projected treaty of alliance a list of the countries where domestic political changes might constitute "indirect aggression" and thus warrant foreign intervention, "M. Maisky could offer no explanation except that what was aimed at was a sort of Monroe doctrine in Eastern Europe."[52]

It was a Monroe doctrine with a difference, for "indirect aggression" was subsequently translated into outright annexation.

Molotov pursued the theme of "indirect aggression" in his relentless,

[50] *Ibid.*, pp. 32-36.

[51] *Documents on British Foreign Policy*, Third Series. Vol. V, pp. 422-426.

[52] *Ibid.*, p. 152.

plodding, "stone bottom" way. He had great staying power which exhausted his opponents but appeared to give him rich satisfaction. The Anglo-French political negotiations with Moscow foundered on the problem of indirect aggression. The two words implied that Russia might be imperiled not only by military aggression via the Baltic countries—the Anglo-French accepted that as a legitimate reason to implement the alliance guarantees—but also by undefined and, in the nature of the circumstances, indefinable changes in the nations to be enumerated. Moscow might, for instance, regard the appointment of an anticommunist minister of interior or chief of army staff in Riga or Tallinn as indirect aggression and invoke the treaty to justify intervention with or without Anglo-French aid. The British felt they could not make a gift of small foreign countries to a great power like Russia.

As subsequent developments demonstrate, Stalin expected that Hitler's invasion of Poland, followed by Nazi attacks on the West, would unscramble the map of eastern Europe and grant Moscow a unique opportunity to restore the Soviet Union to the dimensions of the Tsarist Empire and perhaps beyond.

The Soviet-Nazi talks now moved quickly to their explosive climax.

XXVIII THE PACT

Trust is the essential ingredient of any worthwhile personal, professional, commercial, industrial, or political relationship. Few governments have ever completely trusted one another. Nations try to spy out the secrets of their best friends. Mistrust characterized the relations of foreign countries to the Soviets and of the Soviets to the outside world from the very beginning of the Bolshevik revolution. It waned in periods of diminished international tension and rose crescendo during crises. From September, 1938, to September, 1939, was a year of unending crises and hence of mounting mistrust. "If we do not trust them," William Strang, referring to the Soviets, wrote from Moscow on July 20, 1939, "they equally do not trust us. They are not, fundamentally, a friendly Power; but they, like us, are driven to this course by force of necessity. If we are of two minds about the wisdom of what we are doing, so are they."

The lack of trust was not merely diffuse and atmospheric. Molotov, who, as Strang declared in the same letter, "does not become easier to deal with as the weeks pass," had been demanding military talks immediately—before the forging of the triple alliance. ". . . it is, indeed, extraordinary," Strang commented, "that we should be expected to talk military secrets with the Soviet Government before we are sure that they will be our allies." Nevertheless, Strang favored this procedure and, he concluded, "The Ambassador has read this letter and agrees with it."[1]

So did Halifax—reluctantly.[2]

On July 25 Halifax instructed Sir William Seeds to inform Molotov that the British government was ready for the "immediate initiation" of military conversations in Moscow among the three powers.[3] This represented a major concession by London, for Halifax was afraid to enter into military talks before they knew what Moscow meant by "indirect aggression." It might mean "naked interference in the internal affairs of the Baltic States. Apart from the immorality of this proceeding, reports from the Baltic States indicate that the effect is likely to be to drive these countries into the arms of Germany."[4]

The French government followed the example of Britain.

By now—the fourth week of July—the British and French governments had acquiesced in the Soviet demand for a reciprocal treaty of alliance; if Russia were attacked by Germany via Poland, Rumania, or the Baltic States, the Anglo-French would go to war against Germany. The two governments were prepared to engage in military talks before the signing of the reciprocal treaty. There remained, ostensibly, one hindrance: the definition of indirect aggression. Masters of diplomatic language worked on the formula to no avail. The loophole of Soviet intervention in the Baltic nations in case Stalin disliked a given turn in their domestic policy could not be closed.

At this juncture a new and equally revealing difficulty arose. The western powers, having agreed to military talks pending a political settlement and consensus on the definition of indirect aggression, wished to inform their citizens that military conversations were about to begin. Molotov objected. "The Soviet government might be prepared to consider a joint communiqué announcing the fact of the arrival of British and French Military Missions, but only after the Missions had arrived," Seeds quoted Molotov as telling him and his French colleague on the afternoon of July 27. However, if the British and French governments wanted to make unilateral statements now that "was a matter for those governments to decide."[5] Later in the same meeting Molotov went fur-

[1] E. L. Woodward and Rohan Butler (Eds.), *Documents on British Foreign Policy*. Third Series, Vol. VI: *1939*, pp. 422-426.

[2] *Ibid.*, p. 430.

[3] *Ibid.*, p. 478.

[4] *Ibid.*, p. 430.

[5] *Ibid.*, pp. 509-510.

ther and declared his opposition to any announcement by Paris and London. "It would be desirable," he said, "to finish military conversations before making any announcement to the public about the negotiations. The important point was to see how many divisions each party would contribute to the common cause and where they would be located . . . he did not approve either of a joint communiqué or of individual statements."

Did the Chairman intend to prevent democratic governments from "informing their public opinion as to the state of affairs"? the French Ambassador asked.

"The Soviet Union," Molotov replied, "was the most truly democratic country but it would be a mistake to run the risk of misleading the public." It would, he explained, "be a mistake to excite public opinion in the Soviet Union before we were sure there would be no serious divergence of view on military questions."[6]

Was that the reason? Did the Kremlin ever give primary consideration to its public opinion? The real explanation would have had some relation to the simultaneous negotiations with Germany. The arrival in Moscow of the Anglo-French military missions could not, of course, remain a secret to the Nazis. Nor would the Soviets be interested in concealing the fact. Western willingness to engage in staff talks with Moscow might impel Berlin to grant larger concessions. On the other hand, too much publicity might impel Hitler to cut his contacts with the Kremlin. He could afford to overlook rumors or private reports by informers. But an open Soviet avowal of military discussions with the Anglo-French might have been interpreted by him as a defiant breach of faith.

The acrid argument about an announcement reflected the essential difference between systems, however delinquent in foreign affairs, that owed their people an account of political developments and a state whose control of all communications media and the entire economy absolved it from paying such debts and prevented the people from making claims. The discussion over the announcement also led to puzzlement and suspicion in the western camp. A public declaration about Anglo-French readiness to engage in military talks would have committed the West and should therefore have pleased the Soviets. But the argument took place on July 27, the day after Schnurre's long dinner with Astakhov and Babarin. Astakhov's detailed report of the meal had been read by Stalin and Molotov and was discussed by them at Stalin's dinner table before Molotov received the British and French ambassadors. At the end of their evening together, Astakhov had asked Schnurre "whether we would maintain similar opinions [similar to those expressed

[6] *Ibid.*, pp. 521-524.

by Schnurre] if a prominent Soviet representative were to discuss these questions with a prominent German representative." To this undisguised invitation Schnurre "answered . . . essentially in the affirmative."[7] It was no moment to announce Soviet military talks with the West.

Schnurre's reply to Astakhov was confirmed in a telegram from State Secretary Weizsaecker to Ambassador von der Schulenburg directing him to speak to Molotov and "use the line of thought" enunciated by Schnurre at the dinner. No matter how the Polish question was settled, in peace or through war, Weizsaecker said, "we would be prepared to safeguard all Soviet interests and to reach an understanding with the Moscow government." If Schulenburg's conversation with Molotov "proceeds positively in the Baltic question too," Weizsaecker wrote, "the idea could be advanced that we will adjust our stand with regard to the Baltic in such a manner as to respect the vital Soviet interests in the Baltic."[8]

While nervousness in Berlin mounted, Molotov remained calm and cantankerous. In a 1 1/4 hour talk with Schulenburg on August 4 Molotov paid little discernible attention to the ambassador's declarations about the Baltic states (yet he did inquire whether Germany regarded Lithuania as one of them) and about Poland. Instead he querulously blamed Germany for the deterioration of Soviet-German relations, denounced the anti-Comintern pact although Schulenburg had said it was directed against the western democracies, and advocated "the gradual resumption of cultural relations. . . . Proofs of a changed attitude of the German Government were for the present still lacking," Molotov charged.

In a final paragraph Schulenburg stated that "the old mistrust of Germany still persists." He gave it as his "over-all impression" that "the Soviet Government is at present determined to sign with England and France if they fulfill all Soviet wishes. It will . . . take considerable effort on our part to cause the Soviet Government to swing about."[9]

This, no doubt, was precisely the impression Molotov intended to create. The Soviet government had taken the initiative in opening the negotiations with Germany in April. But as September 1 approached the Germans became the impatient, impassioned suitors while Molotov, relaxed in confidence, skillfully toyed with Schulenburg on the brink and held the Anglo-French at bay; he was waiting for their military missions to arrive. That would surely drive the Germans into a paroxysm of anguish.

Schulenburg naturally kept his ears open for any news of the Anglo-

[7] U.S. Department of State, *Nazi-Soviet Relations 1939-1941*, p. 36.
[8] *Ibid.*, p. 36.
[9] *Ibid.*, p. 41.

French-Soviet talks. "The British military men here," he wrote in a letter dated August 7, "regard the prospects of the pending military negotiations . . . with considerable scepticism." During meetings with the British and French ambassadors "we hear that throughout Herr Molotov sat like a bump on a log. He hardly ever opened his mouth, and if he did it was to utter only the brief remark, 'Your statements do not appear to me entirely satisfactory. I shall notify my Government.' The British and French Ambassadors are both said to be completely exhausted and glad that they now have a breathing spell ahead of them." A breathing spell during the military discussions. "The Frenchman said to one of my informants, 'Thank God that that fellow—Molotov—will not participate in the military negotiations.' "[10]

It is not certain whether Schulenburg was pitying his Anglo-French colleagues or feeling sorry for himself after undergoing experiences similar to theirs. He was not inventing British skepticism about the military talks. Seeds wired Halifax on July 24: "I am not optimistic as to the success of military conversations, nor do I think they can in any case be rapidly concluded, but to begin with them now would give a healthy shock to the Axis Powers." Shock yes, but not one the British or French would enjoy. Molotov, it seems, was deliberately wasting time waiting for the arrival of the British and French military negotiators. That would be the final proof that London and Paris were serious and hence the final turn of the screw on Germany.

Those negotiators dawdled. It was first agreed that the British and French military missions should meet in London or Paris not later than August 2 to coordinate their views. On July 29 the French government proposed that the missions travel by train through Nazi Germany. The British preferred a plane trip to Moscow. The French rejected the idea. London then suggested that the military staffs go by cruiser to Leningrad. The French thought travel by cruiser too "spectacular"; better move by steamer to some port near Russia and then by train. Finally the British government chartered a passenger ship which would sail from London on Friday, August 4. However, Daladier still "hankered" for a rail journey via Germany because that would cut the travel time to Moscow by two days. As an alternative, Alexis Leger, Secretary-General of the French Foreign Ministry, proposed that the ship go to Riga instead of Leningrad and thence by train to the Soviet capital; that too would reduce travel time. If the French wished to go via Germany, the British stated, they could go alone and arrive in Moscow first; no objection to that.

* * *

[10] *Ibid.*, pp. 42-44.

The slow-motion negotiations between the Anglo-French and Soviets rekindled German hopes for a Polish "Munich." Ambassador von Dirksen, reporting from London June 24, 1939, said it was "within the bounds of probability" that Chamberlain "will approach Germany with new proposals directly after the completion of the negotiations with the Russians . . ."[11]

But only sixteen days later—July 10—Dirksen was despondent: "antagonism to Germany is on the increase," he found, "the readiness to fight has hardened . . . the feeling has gained ground: 'We must not put up with this any more. Our honour is at stake; we must fight; the Government must not give way.' " The "broad masses," Dirksen wrote, were in no "Munich" mood; in September, 1938, they were "passive, now they have taken over the initiative from the Government and drive the Cabinet on."[12]

"Public opinion is so aroused and the warmongers and intriguers have gained such ascendancy," Dirksen reported on July 24, "that publication of such plans for negotiations with Germany would immediately be torpedoed by Churchill and other agitators with the cries of 'No second Munich.' "[13]

Nevertheless hope bubbled eternally in the hearts of German diplomats and it no doubt murmured softly in the veins of the Chamberlain circle. Indeed an opportunity to test Britain's resistance to further appeasement had presented itself when, early in June, Helmuth Wohltat, a high official on special assignment in the Berlin Office of the Commissioner for the Four Year Plan came to London in June for "business connected with Jewish emigration" and went far afield and talked about an Anglo-German rapprochement with a Foreign Office official and with Sir Horace Wilson, Chamberlain's chosen expert on international affairs who had no previous experience with such affairs. Wohltat, Sir Horace, and Sir George Joseph Ball of Conservative Party headquarters met in the home of the Duke of Westminster in June. They met again in London on July 18 and again on July 21, and Wohltat saw Robert S. Hudson, Parliamentary Secretary to the Department of Overseas Trade, on July 20. Sir Horace was known as Chamberlain's appeasing right arm. Now the right arm could still be raised in a salute to Hitler: he had "had an opportunity," Wilson said to Wohltat, "of observing the Fuehrer"—at Munich—"and he thought that the Fuehrer could, as a statesman for peace, achieve even more than he had already accomplished in the building up of a Greater Germany. He believed that the Fuehrer wished

[11] U.S. Department of State, *Documents on German Foreign Policy*, Series D, Vol. VI: *The Last Months of Peace, March-August 1939*, p. 783.

[12] *Ibid.*, p. 892.

[13] *Ibid.*, p. 970.

to avoid the outbreak of a world war caused by the Danzig question . . ." But Wilson was also aware of the turn against appeasement in British politics. Talks would have to be secret, preferably in Switzerland. "Certainly," he explained, "the British Government would not like to create the impression that they desired to negotiate in all circumstances. If no other solution was possible, Britain and the Empire were ready for, and determined upon, an armed conflict."[14]

Sir Horace Wilson gave Wohltat the outline of an ambitious peace-and-alliance scheme which the German took to Field Marshal Goering. Goering talked to Hitler three times in August, 1939, "earnestly urging him to avoid getting entangled in a war, seeing that a complete compromise with Britain on the basis of Wohltat's reported offers would bring to Germany the fulfillment of her claims. Hitler, of course, repulsed him."[15]

"To give the discussions an official status," Dirksen states in his reminiscences, "Sir Horace Wilson invited me to a conference" on August 3 when he repeated what he had told Wohltat. The first proposition was a "joint German-British declaration that forcible aggression will not be employed by either country." This would make Britain's guarantees to Poland and Rumania "superfluous" (Hitler would consequently lose the sense of being "encircled"). "The Danzig question after a broad German-British agreement," Wohltat had reported, "would play a minor part for Britain." In other words, Germany could have Danzig. Secondly, the colonial question would be opened; Nazi Germany might rule Africans. Armaments would be limited. Britain and Germany would cooperate in trade, in developing foreign markets, and in developing retarded countries.[16]

"The program developed by Sir Horace Wilson" seemed to Dirksen to embrace "in its entirety the mutual relations of both countries. . . . The decisive question was: would Hitler authorize the appointment of a suitable person to take charge of the negotiations?"[17]

This was not the only question. The British press learned of the Wilson-Wohltat-Dirksen talks and, says Dirksen, "a crossfire began." He ascribed the leak to the French Embassy. British journalists obtained from Robert S. Hudson "some rather unwise statements which were to stir up British public opinion."

Appeasement no longer enjoyed popular support. Neither Chamberlain, and much less Sir Horace, could proceed without the good will of

[14] *Ibid.,* p. 980.

[15] Herbert von Dirksen, *Moscow Tokyo London. Twenty Years of German Foreign Policy,* p. 226. Dirksen, who had been German ambassador in the three capitals, wrote his memoirs after World War II.

[16] *Documents on German Foreign Policy,* Series D. Vol. VI, pp. 977-983.

[17] Dirksen, pp. 226-227.

Parliament, press, and public. But Dirksen kept trying. He went to Berlin in the middle of August, 1939. He asked to see Ribbentrop and was refused. He asked to see Hitler and was rebuffed. He resigned and retired to his East Prussian estate.

"The historical significance of Chamberlain's last peace efforts," Dirksen concludes, "consists in this: they placed the onus on Hitler's shoulders." Correct. Hitler faced the choice between peace-and-entente with England or war-and-entente with Russia. He chose communist Russia.

The Chamberlain government had been negotiating with Moscow on the assumption of an impending war. Sir Horace Wilson, undoubtedly speaking for his Prime Minister, had sought to avert war and harness Hitler to normal political and economic procedures. The enterprise was futile. Hitler lived for aggression.

Soviet historians make much of the Wilson-Wohltat-Hudson-Dirksen episode. Chamberlain, they charge, negotiated with Germany while negotiating with Moscow. The pot calling the kettle black. The fact is Stalin and Molotov negotiated with Hitler behind the backs of the Anglo-French while the British merely attempted to negotiate with Germany but never got far because Hitler preferred Stalin the appeaser to Chamberlain who was no longer free to appease.

* * *

Peacefully sailing the blue sea during this storm in a teakettle, the Anglo-French military missions arrived in Leningrad by the S.S. *Exeter* on August 10 (the trip is described by Captain [later General] Beaufre in *Drame de 1940*), in Moscow the next day, and held their first meeting with the Soviet delegation on August 12. Admiral The Honorable R. A. R. Plunkett-Ernle-Erle-Drax led the British mission. His associates included Air Marshal Sir Charles Burnett, Major-General T. G. G. Heywood, and Colonel F. H. N. Davidson. The French mission consisted of General of the Army Joseph Doumenc, General Valin, Captain André Beaufre, Navy Captain Willaume, and Captain de Willcot de Rincquese. The Soviet military were presided over by Marshal Voroshilov, a member of the communist party's Politburo. He was assisted by Marshal Boris M. Shaposhnikov, Admiral Nikolai G. Kuznetsov, who had been active in Spain, and Army Commander A. D. Loktionov.

The Soviet members of mission declared on August 12 that they were empowered to negotiate and sign a military convention "dealing with aggression in Europe." The French stated they could negotiate and sign a draft convention; the final decision rested with their government. Admiral Drax said he had no written credentials but would "take steps to obtain credentials forthwith." He too would have to consult London before signing. The Soviet mission enjoyed the advantage of being able to get instructions from Stalin on short notice.

In the first three sessions of the missions on August 12 and 13 the Soviet officers drew from the French and British considerable precise information on the size of their armed forces, the state of their armaments, and the condition of their fortifications. "The Maginot Line," General Doumenc reported, "now extends from the Swiss Frontier to the sea." At the fourth session on August 14, with Voroshilov in the chair, the Soviet military continued their interrogation of the Anglo-French.

When, however, the westerners pressed the Soviet representatives for comparable information on their preparedness for war, Voroshilov put these questions to the visitors: "Do the British and French General Staffs think that the Red Army can move across North Poland, and in particular the Wilno [Vilna] Salient, and across Galicia in order to make contact with the enemy? Will Soviet troops be allowed to cross Roumanian territory?"[18]

"It was on this . . . point that the negotiations broke down. The Poles declined to give their assent," writes Lord Strang.

"Naturally enough," Strang commented: "if the Russians ever entered upon the wide non-Polish areas acquired by Poland from Russia at the time of Russia's weakness under the Treaty of Riga in 1921, would they ever go out again?"[19]

Admiral Drax argued that as operations against Germany developed the Poles and Rumanians would "solicit" Soviet support. General Doumenc agreed. Voroshilov, in the Molotov manner, repeated his question: "Marshal Voroshilov said that he wanted a definite answer to his question 'Do the French and British General Staffs think that the Soviet Army will be able to operate through Poland and Roumania?' "

Voroshilov knew the answer in advance.

In their August 22 report from Moscow on the military talks, Admiral Drax and General Heywood recorded details of the discussions and charged that "During the long negotiations between M. Litvinov, M. Molotov, Sir W. Seeds, and Mr. Strang, extended over several months, the question of the passage of Russian troops across Poland was never mentioned. We spent more than an hour with M. Maisky at the Russian Embassy before we left London and saw him again at the station before departing. He spoke of many subjects but never said a word to us about what the Soviet Military Mission call their cardinal point."[20]

Neither Molotov nor Maisky mentioned "the cardinal point" because

[18] *Documents on British Foreign Policy,* Third Series. Vol. VII, Appendix II, pp. 558-572. The Soviet minutes of the military talks are published in the Moscow monthly *Mezhdunarodnaya Zhizn* for February, 1959, and March, 1959.

[19] *Britain in World Affairs,* p. 325.

[20] *Documents on British Foreign Policy,* Third Series. Vol. VII, p. 594.

they knew it would wreck all negotiations—and they wanted negotiations continued while the Kremlin bargained with Hitler. Even after Voroshilov, on August 14, raised the question of the Red Army's transit through Polish and Rumanian territories the Soviet military mission did not break off the negotiations. Although Voroshilov remarked at the same session that "without a solution of this question, all the discussions . . . are doomed to failure," he did not disrupt the military conference. In fact on August 15 Marshal Shaposhnikov reported on Soviet troop strength and armaments, and on August 16 the missions heard a statement on the British and French air forces and on British and French airplane production. But when French General Doumenc suggested at the end of the day that they might save time by beginning to draft the military agreement while waiting for the Polish and Rumanian replies, Voroshilov said, "It is my view that, until the Soviet Military Delegation has an answer to its question which we all know, it will be useless to continue our conversations."

Nevertheless, the three missions met on the 17th and listened to a report on the Soviet air force. Voroshilov, as the meeting neared its close, "advised the other Delegations to amuse themselves by seeing the sights of Moscow" until the receipt of replies to his "cardinal point." He was prevailed upon, however, to fix the next session for 10 A.M. on August 21. When they met on the morning of August 21, Voroshilov urged a recess "not for three or four days but for a longer period." The members of his delegation were busy men, he explained. Pressed for some notion of how long the adjournment might last, Voroshilov made the answer dependent on replies from Poland and Rumania.

Here Admiral Drax protested with some vehemence. Why, he demanded, had the Soviet government invited the British and French missions to Moscow when it intended to pose "difficult political questions" beyond the competence of military men? These were matters for their governments; the answers entail delays. Why, he implied, had these questions not been put to their governments long before the admirals, generals, and marshals assembled?

Voroshilov asked a recess to formulate a reply. On reconvening the Soviet marshal asked why the French and British governments had not given them instructions on such an elementary issue as the passage of Russian troops through Poland and Rumania. The Anglo-French might have asked in turn why the Soviets had not put their cardinal question at the beginning of the political negotiations in April. And so the delegations would have gone 'round and 'round the mulberry bush. Instead they talked about adjournment. Drax suggested a meeting on the 27th when they should have an answer to the political question of troop transit. "Marshal Voroshilov said he thought it would be better not to fix a date."[21]

The British and French governments sought to persuade Poland to accede to the Soviet request for troop passage. ". . . every effort should be made to persuade Poland and Roumania to agree to the use of their territory by Soviet forces . . ." Halifax wired the British ambassador in Warsaw on August 17. ". . . Without early and effective Soviet assistance, neither Poland nor (still less) Roumania can hope to stand up to a German attack on land or in the air for more than a short time. . . . To defer a decision until war breaks out will be too late."[22]

The French ambassador in Warsaw received similar instructions from Paris. He saw Beck first and found the Polish Foreign Minister adamant; he did not trust the Russians. The British ambassador's interview with Beck was even less fruitful. (On September 2, according to *Documents on Polish-Soviet Relations 1939-1945,* Vol. I, published by the General Sikorski Historical Institute, Soviet Ambassador Sharonov called on Beck and asked why Poland was not negotiating with the Soviets regarding munitions supplies. This time—a day after the Nazi invasion—Beck was no longer negative. He instructed the Polish envoy in Moscow "to investigate the situation." Molotov told the envoy it was too late. It was too late. Sharonov had apparently not heard of the secret Soviet-Nazi protocol.)

The failure of the Anglo-French-Soviet military talks was due to the success of the German-Soviet political talks. It does not follow that the failure of the talks with the Nazis would have led to the success of the talks with Britain and France. Russia had a third alternative: no agreement with either, for agreement with the Anglo-French meant Soviet participation in the war, and Stalin intended to avoid war as long as possible. (The idea that Hitler would have been deterred from attacking Poland if Moscow had not signed with him is untenable; he was committed to the defeat of the Poles.)

On the record, the Anglo-French-Soviet talks broke down because the Kremlin asked western support for Soviet intervention in the Baltic countries in case of indirect, nonmilitary, aggression. On the record the military talks broke down owing to the Kremlin's demand for transit rights through Poland and Rumania. But sometimes the essence remains unspoken and therefore cannot be found in the archives. The essence is that Russia could not and would not go to war against Germany in 1939, and agreement with the western powers involved going to war. This

[21] *Ibid.,* pp. 575-593. General Beaufre's account in *Le Drame de 1940* adds some details and quotations from the sessions.

[22] *Ibid.,* p. 39.

explains the failure of the discussions with the West and the success of the talks with Germany.

The first week of August brought considerable progress in German-Soviet relations. The second week registered more progress. Dr. Schnurre of the German Foreign Ministry continued his discussions with Soviet Chargé Astakhov on August 10. Schnurre said "one question was quite ripe, namely Poland." The Poles, he contended, entertained "delusions of grandeur" and, "shielded by England," constantly engaged in "new provocations." Schnurre saw no good reason for the military talks in Moscow. "It would, of course," he stated, "be a poor start for the German-Soviet conversations, if, however, as a result of the military negotiations in Moscow, a sort of military alliance were contemplated against us." Schnurre again assured Astakhov "that, even in the event of a solution by force of arms, German interests in Poland were quite limited. They did not at all need to collide with Soviet interests of any kind. . . . If the motive behind the negotiations conducted in Moscow with England was the feeling of being threatened by Germany in the event of a German-Polish conflict, we for our part were prepared to give the Soviet Union every assurance desired, which would surely carry more weight than support by England, which could never become effective in Eastern Europe."[23]

Astakhov sent a full report to Molotov.

On August 14, the day Voroshilov raised his "cardinal point" with the British and French military missions about Soviet troop passage through Poland and Rumania, Astakhov informed Dr. Schnurre, on instructions from Molotov, that the Soviet government was interested in discussing with Germany a number of questions: economic relations, "cultural collaboration, the Polish question, the matter of the old German-Soviet political agreements." The Kremlin suggested Moscow as the place for these discussions.[24]

That same day Ribbentrop telegraphed a long dispatch to Ambassador von der Schulenburg. The Nazi Foreign Minister declared he was "prepared to make a short trip to Moscow in order, in the name of the Fuehrer, to set forth the Fuehrer's views to Herr Stalin. . . . In addition to a conference with Molotov, an extended conference with Stalin would be the condition for making the trip."[25]

Schulenburg read this telegram to Molotov on the evening of August 15. The Chairman and Foreign Commissar listened "with close attention." He would naturally have to ask Stalin. He "could state at once,

[23] *Nazi-Soviet Relations*, pp. 44-46.
[24] *Ibid.*, pp. 48-49.
[25] *Ibid.*, pp. 51-52.

however, that the Soviet government warmly welcomed the intention expressed on the German side." For years, Molotov affirmed, Berlin had given no evidence of a desire to improve relations with Moscow. "Now the situation had changed. From the conferences that had taken place in the last few weeks [between Astakhov and Molotov and the Germans] the Soviet Government had gotten the impression that the German Government was really in earnest. . . . He regarded the statement which had been made today as decisive. . . . As regards the Soviet Government, it had always had a favorable attitude to the question of good relations with Germany and was happy that this was now the case on the German side too. . . . Herr Molotov was quite unusually compliant and candid," Schulenburg reported further. The Chairman asked three questions: would Germany be ready to sign a nonaggression pact with the U.S.S.R., guarantee the Baltic States jointly with Russia, and influence Japan to improve her relations with the Soviets?[26]

The next day Voroshilov told the British and French military delegations "it will be useless to continue our conversations" until they had an answer to his "cardinal point."

At 1 A.M. on the following morning—August 17—Schulenburg received Ribbentrop's reply to Molotov's three questions. All were answered in the affirmative. The Reich Foreign Minister added that he wished to fly to Moscow on Friday, August 18. At the close of the military discussions on the 17th, Voroshilov recommended a tour of Moscow's sights to the British and French officers and a recess until the 21st.

Molotov told Schulenburg on August 17 that the "principle of a peaceful existence of various political systems side by side represents a long established principle of the foreign policy of the U.S.S.R." Moscow wanted economic agreements first, and, "after a short interval," a nonaggression treaty. The Soviet government was "very gratified" by the proposal to dispatch "such a distinguished public figure and statesman" as Ribbentrop. This "emphasized the earnestness of the intentions of the German Government" and was in "noteworthy contrast with England who, in the person of Strang, had sent only an official of the second class to Moscow." Nevertheless, it would be better if the first-class Ribbentrop did not come immediately; the text of the treaty and of the attached protocol needed additional preparation. "With regard to the protocol," Schulenburg stated, "it would be desirable to have more exact information about the wishes of the Soviet Government." Molotov asked for the German drafts of the treaty and protocol.

[26] *Ibid.*, pp. 52-57.

It was August 17, and the date of September 1, Moscow knew, hung alarmingly over the head of Hitler. He was impatient, therefore Stalin delayed.

And indeed, on August 18, Ribbentrop wired Schulenburg to see Molotov again "without any delay." The "Fuehrer" wanted "quick results. German-Polish relations were becoming more acute from day to day." The German-Soviet trade agreement would be signed the next day. Hence Ribbentrop's desire for "my immediate departure for Moscow" with "full powers from the Fuehrer, authorizing me to settle fully and conclusively the total complex of problems." Ribbentrop appended the draft text of the nonaggression treaty: "No resort to war or any other use of force" against one another; the treaty to come into effect "immediately on signature and shall be valid and undenounceable thereafter for a term of twenty-five years." Ribbentrop was empowered, he said, to arrange matters "to comply with Russian wishes. I am also in a position to sign a special protocol regulating the interests of both parties in questions of foreign policy. . . : for instance, the settlement of spheres of interest in the Baltic area." Ribbentrop concluded by instructing Schulenburg to press "emphatically" for "a rapid realization of my trip. . . . In this connection you must keep in mind the decisive fact that an early outbreak of open German-Polish conflict is probable." Germany accordingly had "the greatest interest" in his going to Moscow "immediately."[27]

Events now moved hastily. While the French and British military officers cooled their heels and wrote reports, Schulenburg saw Molotov twice on August 19. At the first encounter, from 2 to 3 P.M, Molotov asked for more specific drafts of the nonaggression treaty and the protocol. "The attitude of the Soviet Government toward treaties which it concludes was a very serious one," he asserted; "it respected the obligations which it undertook and expected the same of its treaty partners." He proposed that Ribbentrop arrive in Moscow on August 26 or 27.

Schulenburg came again to the Kremlin at 4:30 P.M. Molotov handed him the Soviet draft of the nonaggression treaty but refused to advance the date of the Foreign Minister's visit. The Soviet draft reduced the period of the life of the treaty from twenty-five to five years but made it renewable for another five-year period if it was not renounced one year before its expiration. There were other modifications and elaborations of the German draft. The most important change was a proviso that the nonaggression pact would become valid "only if a special protocol is signed simultaneously covering the points in which the High Contract-

[27] *Ibid.*, pp. 58-63.

ing Parties are interested in the field of foreign policy. The protocol shall be an integral part of the Pact."[28]

The protocol was the heart of the Soviet-Nazi pact.

Now Hitler took a hand directly. Ribbentrop telegraphed Schulenburg, on August 20, the text of a message to "Herr Stalin" signed "Adolf Hitler" in which the German dictator told the Soviet dictator, "I accept the [Soviet] draft of the nonaggression pact" but some questions needed clarification. So did the supplementary protocol. By signing the pact and protocol, Hitler declared, "Germany . . . resumes a political course that has been beneficial to both states during by-gone centuries." The tension "between Germany and Poland," the "Fuehrer" added, "has become intolerable. . . . Germany is determined . . . from now on to look after the interests of the Reich with all the means at its disposal." It was desirable, in view of the intention of Russia and Germany "to enter into a new relationship to each other, not to lose any time. I therefore again propose that you receive my Foreign Minister on Tuesday, August 22, but at the latest on Wednesday, August 23." Because of the international situation, Hitler stressed, Ribbentrop could not remain in Moscow longer than "one or two days at most."

After quoting this Hitler-to-Stalin communication, Ribbentrop added, without explanation, "Please deliver to Herr Molotov the above telegram of the Fuehrer to Stalin in writing, on a sheet of paper without letterhead."[29]

Would Hitler disavow the message to Stalin if nothing came of it?

Stalin wired Hitler on August 21 saying he would receive Ribbentrop on August 23.

Ribbentrop wrote—while waiting at Nuremberg to die—that he suggested Marshal Goering instead of himself as Hitler's emissary to Moscow, but the "Fuehrer" preferred the Reich Foreign Minister. On arrival at the Moscow airport in Hitler's plane on the afternoon of August 23 he saw the Nazi swastika flag and the Bolshevik sickle-and-hammer flag flying from neighboring poles. Less than two hours later he was received in Stalin's office by Stalin and Molotov. Schulenburg, who accompanied his Minister, had never spoken to Stalin. Gustav Hilger, translator for the Germans, and Vladimir N. Pavlov, translator for the Russians, were the only other persons present.[30]

No Soviet record of the ensuing conversation is available. "Finland, the greater part of the Baltic countries, as well as Bessarabia, were recognized as belonging to the Soviet sphere of influence," Ribbentrop

[28] *Ibid.*, pp. 63-66.
[29] *Ibid.*, pp. 66-67.
[30] Joachim von Ribbentrop, *Zwischen London und Moskau*, pp. 177-179.

writes. "In the event of the outbreak of a German-Polish conflict which, in the existing state of affairs did not seem precluded, a line of demarcation was agreed upon." The arrangements thus arrived at were to be recorded in a secret protocol.

Actual political developments coincided with Ribbentrop's description and make it credible. "Stalin promised me," Ribbentrop affirms, ". . . that he would not alter the internal structure of these countries" which fell into the Soviet sphere. This promise was not kept.

After conferring for three hours "affirmatively in our sense," the summit meeting was recessed so that Ribbentrop could wire Hitler that Stalin demanded the inclusion of the Baltic ports of Libau and Windau in the Soviet sphere of influence. That same evening the Foreign Ministry, after consulting Hitler, telegraphed, "Answer is Yes. Agreed."[31]

At 10 P.M., accordingly, the four men and their interpreters met once more. All difficulties had been ironed out. The pact, and the secret protocol which was not published until after the second world war, were signed before midnight on the 23rd. Then waiters entered to serve "a simple supper," as Ribbentrop called it. In the traditional Russian-Georgian manner, toasts were drunk. Stalin's toast came first: he drank to Hitler, a man "for whom he had always had an extraordinary respect," to quote Ribbentrop.[32] "I know how much the German people loves its Fuehrer; I should therefore like to drink to his health."[33]

The following morning Ribbentrop dictated an account of a long exchange of views the previous night between him and Stalin and Molotov. The Nazi reassured Stalin about German-Japanese relations. They were not directed against the Soviet Union. On the contrary, he would use his best offices to strengthen the ties between Moscow and Tokyo. "Herr Stalin replied that the Soviet Union indeed desired an improvement in its relations with Japan, but that there were limits to its patience with regard to Japanese provocations. If Japan desired war, it could have it. . . . If Japan desired peace—so much the better." German help to improve Soviet-Japanese relations would be useful, "but he did not want the Japanese to get the impression that the initiative in this direction had been taken by the Soviet Union."

Stalin asked about Italy's ambitions. Did Mussolini covet Greek territory? Was Rome's conquest of Albania a step in that direction? Ribbentrop gave no direct answer. He merely said Mussolini "had expressed himself as gratified with the conclusion of the Nonaggression Pact."

Stalin then inquired about Germany's attitude to Turkey. Ribbentrop reported that Turkey had been "one of the first countries to join the

[31] *Nazi-Soviet Relations,* pp. 71-72.
[32] Ribbentrop, p. 182.
[33] *Nazi-Soviet Relations,* p. 75.

encirclement pact against Germany. . . . Herren Stalin and Molotov hereupon observed that the Soviet Union had also had similar experiences with the vacillating policy of the Turks." Ribbentrop mentioned that England "had spent five million pounds in Turkey in order to disseminate propaganda against Germany." Stalin, with a smile which showed his short blackened teeth, said that according to his information Britain had spent "considerably more than five million pounds . . . buying Turkish politicians."

Subject matter changed rapidly. Stalin and Molotov "commented adversely on the British Military Mission in Moscow, which had never told the Soviet Government what it really wanted." Ribbentrop gave it as his expert opinion that England was weak and let others fight to assure her world domination. "Herr Stalin eagerly concurred and observed . . . the British Army was weak; the British Navy no longer deserved its previous reputation. England's air arm was being increased, to be sure, but there was a lack of pilots. If England dominates the world . . . this was due to the stupidity of other countries that always let themselves be bluffed. It was ridiculous, for example, that a few hundred British should dominate India." On the other hand, Stalin volunteered, "France had an army worthy of consideration."

And so they went on far into the night rambling over the globe and drinking toasts. Stalin sipped his wine drop by drop. He closed the long nocturnal dialogue with these words: "The Soviet Government takes the new Pact very seriously. He could guarantee on his word of honor that the Soviet Union would not betray its partner."[34]

Stalin meant this. Some years later he said all would have been well had the Germans remained Russia's ally. He believed they would. As events showed, he trusted Hitler—at Russia's great cost.

XXIX INTO THE PIT OF EMPIRE

On the evening of August 23, 1939, when Hitler knew that the German-Russian pact had been signed, he gave the signal for the attack on Poland at 4:30 A.M. on August 26.[1] Then he delayed the invasion in the

[34] *Ibid.*, pp. 72-76.
[1] Alan Bullock, *Hitler. A Study in Tyranny*, p. 527.

hope that the pact would produce a Polish "Munich." But August, 1939, was not September, 1938. England had changed; Poles were not Czechs. Hitler ordered the attack for September 1. The Senate of the city of Danzig, with a large German majority, might have voted itself a part of Germany and thus provoked Polish military action to which Hitler could have replied with his army and air force "in self-defense." He chose to be the aggressor. He chose 1939 for the opening of another world war. "He was now fifty" according to Sir Nevile Henderson's account of his talk with the "Fuehrer" on August 23, "therefore, if war had to come, it was better that it should come now than when he was fifty-five or even sixty years old."[2]

Hitler and Ribbentrop congratulated themselves on the pact with Stalin. They thought it a tremendous coup; both said so. It was a gigantic folly. For the essence of the pact was that Hitler paid Stalin heavily to do what Stalin wanted to do, had to do. The military and economic dislocation caused by the purges merely reinforced Stalin's inclination, as enunciated in his 1925 speech, to stay out of the war in its early and middle phases and enter when the exhausted belligerents would acquiesce in his decisions about the shape of the peace.

For this reason historians doubt that the Soviets ever contemplated joining England and France in war if Hitler invaded Poland. Stalin, like most statesmen, was guilty of enormous mistakes; but it would have been the crowning error of his career to send a Russian army crashing through the Vilna Gap and a hostile Poland into the deadly fire of Hitler's legions. The Kremlin craved neutrality. The pact gave it that. It provided that neither of the contracting parties would attack the other, nor would it join a third power in attacking the other. It also contained an article promising that the two governments "shall in the future maintain constant contact with one another for the purpose of consultation in order to exchange information on problems affecting their common interests."[3] This is the usual formula for an alliance.

The price Hitler paid for Soviet neutrality which he could have had for nothing was fixed in the "Secret Additional Protocol" annexed to the pact. It placed Finland, Estonia, and Latvia in the Soviet sphere of influence while Lithuania, including Vilna, fell to the German sphere. The line of demarcation between the German and Russian spheres in Poland would be that formed by the Narev, Vistula, and San rivers. In southeastern Europe "attention is called by the Soviet side to its interest in Bessarabia. The German side declared its complete political disinterestedness in these areas.

[2] *Ibid.*, p. 529.

[3] U.S. Department of State; *Nazi-Soviet Relations,* pp. 76-77, for full text of treaty; text of secret protocol, p. 78.

"This protocol shall be treated by both parties as strictly secret."[4]

Ribbentrop and Molotov signed the pact and the protocol.

Much later, on June 24, 1940, Ribbentrop explained in writing that before leaving for Moscow Hitler "authorized me to declare Germany's disinterestedness in the territories of Southeastern Europe, even, if necessary, as far as Constantinople and the Straits. However, the latter were not discussed."[5]

From Finland to Constantinople Hitler was ready to give away what did not belong to him. Yet Germany could have occupied the Baltic countries and Bessarabia with little effort, and Russia annexed them only after obtaining Hitler's consent. In this double sense they were Hitler's gift to Stalin.

The Soviet-Nazi pact started the Soviet Union down the road to empire. The pact and the war which followed in a week made Russia a great power again. The seduction was irresistible to the Kremlin rulers. But empire in Europe in the anti-imperialist age when almost all of Asia and most of Africa have achieved national independence is not an unalloyed blessing. For the Soviet government it has brought prestige and trouble, for the Soviet people waste and war.

Referring to Courland, a part of Latvia, and to Poland, Lenin had said on May 27, 1917, "Together these three crowned brigands [the rulers of Russia, Prussia, and Austria-Hungary] partitioned Courland and Poland. They partitioned them for a century, they tore the living flesh, and the Russian brigand tore away more because at that time he was stronger."[6] Now the two uncrowned brigands engaged in a fourth partition of Poland, and the German brigand assigned Latavia, Estonia,

[4] *Istoria Mezhdunarodnikh Otnoshenii i Vneshnei Politiki SSSR 1917-1939* (The History of International Relations and the Foreign Policy of the U.S.S.R. 1917-1939), Vol. I, published in Moscow in 1961, gives the full text of the nonaggression treaty but does not mention the protocol. *Istoria Diplomatii* (The History of Diplomacy), Vol. III, published in Moscow in 1965, gives a detailed if biased account of the negotiations in the summer of 1939 and describes all features of the treaty but is still loyal to the 1939 agreement that the protocol remain secret. *Istoria Vneshnei Politiki SSSR, Chast Pervaya 1917-1945* (History of the Foreign Policy of the U.S.S.R., Part I, 1917-1945), published in Moscow in 1966 also under the editorship, among others, of Foreign Minister A. A. Gromyko, likewise pretends to know nothing about the protocol although its authors had access to foreign sources. Nor is the protocol mentioned in P. A. Zhilin's heavily documented book, *Kak Faschistkaya Germania Gotovila Napadenie Na Sovietskii Sovuz* (How Fascist Germany Prepared the Attack on the Soviet Union), published in Moscow in 1966, despite the fact that Zhilin made use of and cites in a footnote the volume of *Documents on German Foreign Policy, 1918-1945,* which gives the text of the protocol. The protocol was the charter of the Soviet empire. Hence probably the reticence. "Socialist diplomacy," writes A. Kovalyov in *Azbuka Diplomatii* (The ABC of Diplomacy) published in Moscow in 1965, "has no need to conceal or disguise its purposes."

[5] *Nazi-Soviet Relations,* pp. 157-158.

[6] Cited in Louis Fischer, *The Life of Lenin,* p. 145.

and Finland and a segment of Rumania to the Russians. Lenin had foreseen it. A victorious proletarian revolution, he declared in 1916, might be motivated by "selfish motives," might "ride on somebody else's back."[7]

Down the ages imperialism has been the cause of wars hot and cold. It is impossible to prove a proposition about something that has not happened. It is impossible to prove that if Stalin had adopted the ideal policy—neutrality without annexations—Russia would have been spared the numerous expensive difficulties stemming from her new Soviet-made empire; the record does show that little over half a year after the wedding of August 23, 1939, bridegroom and bride commenced quarrels which resulted in the most disastrous war in Russian history.

Immediately following the marriage the two partners were touchingly considerate, indeed unnaturally forgiving and helpful. Then began minor irritations, conflicts over the dowry, and finally the divorce and the great fight in which they tore their own living flesh.

* * *

The Poles fought with romantic bravery, but they were no match for German organization, military leadership, numbers, and equipment. Soon Hitler's divisions were slicing through Poland. On the third day of the Polish campaign Ribbentrop wired Schulenburg that the Polish army would be beaten decisively "in a few weeks." He accordingly urged Molotov to have Soviet forces occupy the part of Poland assigned to Russia in the secret protocol of August 23. The Soviets replied that "this time has not yet come." The German army might find it necessary to cross the line of demarcation and enter the Russian sphere of influence but "that must not prevent the strict execution of the plan adopted." Molotov received information on September 9 that German troops had entered Warsaw. "Please convey my congratulations and greetings to the German Reich Government," he said in a telephone message to Schulenburg.

Schulenburg reported on September 9 that the Red Army was preparing to intervene in Poland. Reservists up to the age of forty-five had been called up (for a minor military operation against a dissolving Polish army); "important foods" suddenly disappeared; gasoline sales had been curtailed. "Over three million men were being mobilized," Molotov told Schulenburg on September 10; the Kremlin was taken by surprise by the speed of the German advance. Schulenburg "explained emphatically . . . how crucial speedy action of the Red Army was at this juncture."

[7] *Ibid.*, p. 93.

So little did the Kremlin share its politics with the Soviet people, so confused were Soviet citizens that many thought Russia was going to war against Germany. Savings were withdrawn from banks; panic buying commenced; huge queues formed at all shops. In villages around the capital, and probably elsewhere too, peasants rushed to buy salt. Molotov realized the importance of a public announcement on the cause of Soviet intervention in Poland. To make that action "plausible to the masses," he told Schulenburg, and to avoid making Russia look like an aggressor, Moscow, Molotov asserted, wished to announce that the Polish state was disintegrating and it had therefore become necessary for the Soviet Union "to come to the aid of the Ukrainians and White Russians threatened by Germany" in the zone assigned to Russia by the secret protocol. Ribbentrop objected strenuously. Molotov "conceded," Schulenburg wired on September 16, that his desire to justify Soviet intrusion into Poland by claiming the need of protecting the minorities in eastern Poland "was jarring to German sensibilities," but Moscow "unfortunately saw no possibility of any other motivation" since it had hitherto "not concerned itself about the plight of the minorities in Poland and had to justify abroad, in some way or other, its present intervention."

The next day, at 2 A.M. on September 17, Stalin received Schulenburg in the presence of Molotov and Voroshilov to inform the ambassador that the Red Army would invade Poland that morning at 6, but he wanted no joint communiqué on the event for several days. On September 18 Stalin, in a conversation with Schulenburg, and the German military attaché, wondered whether the German army, which had already crossed the line of demarcation between the German and Soviet spheres in Poland, would withdraw before the advancing Red Army. Schulenburg affirmed the Nazi government's loyalty to its pledged word. "Stalin replied that he had no doubt at all in the good faith of the German Government. His concern was based on the well-known fact that all military men are loath to give up occupied territory." The German army "would do just what the Fuehrer ordered," the German military attaché interjected.

Remained the problem of the joint communiqué. Berlin submitted its draft on September 17. Molotov said he would "have to consult with Herr Stalin on the matter." Stalin, however, rejected the German draft "since it presented the facts all too frankly."

An examination of the German and Stalin's drafts—he wrote it in his own hand—reveals what was uppermost in his mind. The German version spoke of "the incapacity of the Polish State," "the dissensions of the populations," and of the "joint duty" of Germany and Russia to restore "peace and order in these areas which are naturally of interest to them

. . ." These matters did not trouble Stalin. His draft emphasized that German and Soviet military operations in Poland "do not involve any aims which are contrary to the interests of Germany and of the Soviet Union" —this was his primary concern. He wished "to avoid all kinds of unfounded rumors concerning the respective aims of the German and Soviet forces which are operating in Poland." A statesman like Stalin, on the morrow after his great leap into a career of military intervention, would not be bothered by future rumors. He was bothered by possible German charges that the Red Army's operations in Poland were contrary to German interests "or," he added, "to the spirit or the letter of the Nonaggression Pact." He was mistrustful.

Having marched in against little Polish opposition, Russia's appetite grew. Molotov hinted to Schulenburg on September 20 that "the original inclination entertained by the Soviet Government and Stalin personally to permit the existence of a residual Poland had given way to the inclination to partition Poland along the Pissa-Narev-Vistula-San Line." The Nazis liked the idea, and Ribbentrop "decided to fly to Moscow myself."

"Stalin and Molotov asked me to come to the Kremlin at 8 P.M. today"—September 25—Schulenburg wired Berlin. "Stalin stated . . . In the final settlement of the Polish question anything that in the future might create friction between Germany and the Soviet Union must be avoided. From this point of view, he considered it wrong to leave an independent Polish rump state." (Germany and Russia would surely have competed for dominion over it.)

Further, Stalin suggested an exchange of territory: from its share of Poland Russia would surrender to Germany the entire province of Lublin in the southeast and part of the Warsaw province to the Bug River. In return "we"—Germany—"should waive our claim to Lithuania . . . the Soviet Union would immediately take up the solution of the Baltic countries in accordance with the Protocol of August 23, and expected in this matter the unstinting support of the German Government. Stalin expressly indicated Estonia, Latvia, and Lithuania, but did not mention Finland."

With Stalin "immediately" meant that it had already begun. Russian planes flew over Estonia the very day—September 25—the Soviet leader told Schulenburg of his intentions in the Baltic countries. Simultaneously Moscow demanded a naval base and an air base in Estonia.

Ribbentrop arrived in the Soviet capital at 6 P.M. on September 27. His initial meeting with Kremlin leaders took place the same evening and was resumed the next afternoon. After a dinner with toasts in the Kremlin, Ribbentrop saw the first act of *Swan Lake* while Stalin absented himself and made on Latvia demands similar to those he had made three days earlier on Estonia. After the ballet Ribbentrop went to the Kremlin where he negotiated with Stalin from midnight to 5 in the morning when the Nazi and Molotov signed a "German-Soviet Boundary and Friendship Treaty." The following day Ribbentrop departed.

The new treaty and its supplementary secret protocols wiped out the Polish state and provided for the exchange of Lublin and Warsaw lands for Lithuania as Stalin had outlined. "Both parties will tolerate in their territories no Polish agitation which affects the territories of the other party. They will suppress in their territories all beginnings of such agitation and inform each other concerning suitable measures for this purpose."

No one has ascertained whether the Gestapo learned more from the NKVD about such measures, or vice versa. We do know that a "Confidential Protocol" executed on September 28 for an exchange of nationals was interpreted by the Kremlin as carte blanche to return forcibly into German hands German communists who had fled from Nazi Germany in the 1930's. Memoirs on the atrocity have been published.

Another document signed by Molotov and Ribbentrop on September 28 declares to all the world that, the Polish problem having been settled by the two governments, it was desirable to end the state of war between Germany and France and England. Moscow and Berlin would try to achieve this goal. "Should, however, the efforts of the two Governments remain fruitless, this would demonstrate the fact that England and France are responsible for the continuation of the war, whereupon, in case of the continuation of the war, the Governments of Germany and of the U.S.S.R. shall engage in mutual consultations with regard to necessary measures."[8]

The close relationship with the intolerant Nazi regime made the intolerant Soviet regime seem tolerant. The Soviet government had sentenced many of its subjects to years in Siberian concentration camps for listening to an anti-Soviet anecdote or working in the same newspaper editorial office with an alleged Trotskyite (see, for instance, *Journey Into the Whirlwind* by Eugenia S. Ginzburg, who served eighteen years in prisons and camps for such an offense). Yet on October 9, 1939, *Izvestia*'s editorial reeked of what communists call "rotten liberalism." "Every man," it wrote, "is free to express his relationship to this or that ideology and has the right to defend or reject it. . . . One can respect or hate Hitlerism as one can respect or hate any other system of political thought. That is a matter of taste."

A Soviet person who, as a matter of taste, manifested respect for

[8] Events from September 17 to 28 documented in *Nazi-Soviet Relations*, pp. 96-108.

Hitlerism or social democracy would soon find himself in the NKVD's death dungeon or in a cattle car bound for the Arctic. The editorial was addressed to Hitler.

In the same spirit of understanding for Nazidom, Chairman Molotov told the Supreme Soviet of the U.S.S.R. on October 31, 1939, "Such concepts as 'aggression' and 'aggressor' have acquired a new concrete connotation. Today Germany is in the position of a state that is striving for peace while England and France are opposed to the conclusion of peace. You see the laws are changing."

The laws were changing for the Soviet Union too. The Soviet Union forced pacts of mutual aid on Estonia on September 28, 1939, on Latvia on October 5, and on Lithuania on October 10. Stalin was a master of dosage, of politics by installments. That was his first move in the Baltic region. "The chatter about the sovietization of the Baltic countries is profitable only to our enemies and all anti-Soviet provocateurs," Molotov asserted in his October 31, 1939, address. The treaties, he said, "firmly stipulate the inviolability of the sovereignty of the signatory nations as well as the principle of noninterference in the affairs of the other nation." This statement was designed to dissipate Nazi suspicions. Yet it is repeated in history of Soviet foreign affairs published in Moscow in 1966.[9]

In the spring of 1940, while Hitler concentrated on the conquest of Norway and Denmark, Moscow sent troops into the three Baltic countries and established ground, naval, and air bases there. That was move number two. On July 21, 1940, with Hitler busy digesting France, Estonia, Latvia, and Lithuania were annexed by the Soviet Union, sovietized as Molotov said they would not be, and ceased to exist as sovereign nations although the Soviet government had recognized their independence, maintained diplomatic relations with them, signed nonaggression treaties with them, and promised in the pact with Hitler not to violate their sovereignty. That was move number three. Subsequently, many thousands of Estonians, Latvians, and Lithuanians were carried away to Siberia and replaced by Great Russians.

Stalin had not been disloyal to the legacy of Lenin. At a conference that debated the Brest-Litovsk peace on January 21, 1918, Lenin said "no Marxist who has not abandoned the basic ideas of Marxism and in general of socialism can deny that the interests of socialism stand higher than the interest of the right of nations to self-determination."[10] And since, of course, the Soviet government which signed secret pacts with

[9] A. A. Gromyko and others (Eds.), *Istoria Vneshnei Politiki SSSR 1917-1966. Chast Pervaya 1917-1945* (The History of Soviet Foreign Politics 1917-1966, Part One, 1917-1945), p. 357.

[10] Fischer, p. 193.

Hitler's National Socialist government was socialist, the interests of socialism were served by the violent seizure of the three independent Baltic nations, whose peoples are not Russians, and of the eastern half of Poland, whose people are not Russians.

Nobody can expect a Soviet leader on the brink of an important decision to ask himself whether he will be affronting the ideas Marx propagated in the middle of the nineteenth century. Neither does the President of the United States consult Thomas Jefferson before adopting a policy. The British Empire was not built according to the rules of British democracy and France did not acquire its African and Asian colonies in conformity with the high ideals of the French Revolution.

Stalin was motivated by considerations far removed from the proletarian internationalism of Marx and Engels. Through weakness in 1917 and 1918 Russia had lost the Baltic region and Poland. Through diplomacy in 1939 and power in 1940 Stalin retrieved most of what had been lost. He took back the Baltic states in order to claim the support of patriotic Great Russian nationalists; he was restoring the empire. Nationalism thrives on the protein of territory.

Stalin wanted the Ukrainians of eastern Poland in order to bid for the loyalty of the Soviet Ukrainians, the largest national minority in the U.S.S.R. Many times in the 1920's and 1930's he had purged and re-purged Ukrainians, including Ukrainian communists, on charges, true or false, of favoring an independent Ukraine. Now, having shown himself to be a good Great Russia by returning the wayward Baltics to the bosom of Mother Russia, he intended to prove himself a good Ukrainian. Not only did he seek and gain Hitler's permission to annex the seven million Ukrainians of eastern Poland, in June, 1940, the Soviets decided to carry out the part of the secret protocol of August 23, 1939, that assigned Bessarabia to them. Bessarabia, detached from Russia by Rumania in 1918, housed a Ukrainian minority. For both reasons the Kremlin wanted it. At the same time Moscow demanded Bukovina, another province of Rumania with a Ukrainian minority. "The claim of the Soviet Government to Bucovina is something new," Ribbentrop wired Schulenburg on June 25, 1940, when apprised of the Soviet demand. "Bukovina was formerly an Austrian crown province and is densely populated with Germans." It never belonged to Russia. When Schulenburg made this point to Molotov the Chairman said that "Bukovina is the last missing part of a united Ukraine and that for this reason the Soviet Government must attach importance to solving this question simultaneously with the Bessarabian question."

In the face of German opposition Molotov compromised. He told Schulenburg the next day—June 26—that Moscow would content itself with the northern part of Bukovina and the city of Czernowitz. The

Chairman requested German support for these claims on Rumania. Ribbentrop accordingly telegraphed the following instructions to Bucharest: "In order to avoid war between Rumania and the Soviet Union, we can only advise the Rumanian Government to yield to the Soviet Government's demand." There is a note of resignation in these words and of malaise. But Stalin wanted all the Ukrainians of eastern Europe united under Moscow rule. Why after that would a grateful Ukraine yearn for separate sovereignty?

To complete the unification under Soviet rule of all Ukrainians Stalin coveted a small, backward slice of Czechoslovakia called Carpatho-Ukraine inhabited by some 750,000 persons. President Beneš told me on May 17, 1943 when he was the guest of the United States government in Blair House, Washington, D.C., that he thought he had dissuaded the Soviet leadership from tearing the area from his tortured country. This was one of his illusions. Russia annexed Carpatho-Ukraine on June 29, 1945.

(Stalin's grand design failed to win the soul of the Ukraine. In his secret speech of February 24-25, 1956, Chairman Nikita S. Khrushchev stated that during the second world war Stalin deported the Karachai, the Chechen and Ingushi peoples, and the Balkars [he did not mention the Crimean Tartars] from the lands on which they and their ancestors have lived for centuries. "The Ukrainians," Khrushchev added, "avoided meeting this fate because there were too many of them"—some thirty million—"and there was no place to which to deport them. Otherwise he would have deported them also." Despite the unification of all Ukrainians under the red flag of communism many Soviet Ukrainians were not exactly loyal to Russia when Hitler invaded the Soviet Union on June 22, 1941. A number of factors contributed to Ukrainian discontent: collectivization and the famine it brought in its wake; memories of the purges; exploitation of the working class and the decline in living standards since 1928; Russification. Ukrainian nationalism made in Moscow by the "Great-Russian" Georgian responsible for these wounds was no balm.)

Russian expansion into the Baltic countries and Poland raises the question of the role of small nations and the wisdom of maintaining them intact. Soviet annexation of Lithuania gave the Soviet Union a common frontier with East Prussia, and the partition of Poland made Russia a neighbor of Germany-in-Poland. Is such proximity conducive to peace? Would it be desirable for great powers to wipe out weaker nations and face one another across a line of demarcation? They might live in amity. But the balance would be precarious and they might fall, and fall upon one another.

* * *

Joseph Stalin said at the Sixteenth Soviet Communist Party Congress on June 27, 1930, "We want not a single inch of others' territory. But we will surrender to no one a single inch of our own."[11] (Nine years are a long time in the life of a statesman's words; appetite comes with opportunity.) Karl Radek, Stalin's adviser on international politics, quoted the words of his leader in the January, 1934, *Foreign Affairs* quarterly and commented, "The attempt to represent the foreign policy of the Soviet Union as a continuation of Tsarist policy is ridiculous. . . . It used to be an axiom of Tsarist policy that it should strive by every available means to gain possession of the Dardanelles. . . . Not only have the Soviets not attempted to seize the Dardanelles, but from the very beginning they have tried to establish the most friendly relations with Turkey; nor has Soviet policy ever had as one of its aims the conquest of Port Arthur and Dairen. Again, Tsarism, or any other bourgeois regime in Russia, would necessarily resume the struggle for the conquest of Poland and the Baltic states. . . . The Soviet Union, on the contrary, is most anxious to establish friendly relations with these countries, considering their achievement of independence a positive and progressive historical factor. It is silly to say that geography plays the part of fate, that it determines the foreign policy of a state."

Not only geography but the political character of the state. And opportunity. Stalin evidently subscribed to the principle of strike while the war is hot. He applied it in Asia as well as in Europe. Radek wrote the truth when he said that the Soviets tried from the start to establish friendly relations with Turkey—and succeeded because Soviet Russia was too weak to harbor aggressive intentions. At the 1923 Lausanne conference on the Straits Chicherin was more Turkish than the Turks. By defending Turkey's rights he defended Russia's too, for if the Dardanelles (and the Sea of Marmora and the Bosporus) remained closed no enemy could enter the Black Sea which washes the shores of South Russia.

Foreign Commissar Maxim M. Litvinov played a similar role at the Montreux conference on the Turkish Straits held in mid-1936 at the invitation of the Ankara government to revise the Lausanne agreement. Litvinov spoke of "the Soviet Union's special interest arising from its geographical situation, from the lack of communication between the seas which wash its shores"—a reference to absence of internal passages between the Black and Baltic seas and between the Black Sea and the Pacific coast of Russia. ". . . for us the Straits represent a vital nerve which not only attaches my country to the outside world, but also ties the different parts of the country itself to each other." He therefore argued for the right of exit and entry of Soviet warships through the

[11] J. V. Stalin, *Sochinenia*, Vol. 12, p. 261.

Turkish Straits and also, in the interest of Turkey, for the closing of the Straits to the warships of countries without Black Sea coasts except when, in limited numbers, they paid ceremonial visits to riverian states. Commercial vessels should enjoy the right of ingress and departure at all times. Turkey ought to fortify and defend the Straits.[12]

These proposals were incorporated into the Montreux Convention signed by the powers on July 20, 1936. The document stipulated that in time of peace the total nonriverian tonnage in the Black Sea not exceed 30,000; the total tonnage of any one nonriverian country was not to exceed 20,000. In time of war, however, and with Turkey neutral, no warships were to pass through the Straits into the Black Sea.[13]

Litvinov told the conference that Moscow's attitude stemmed from having renounced "completely all imperialist designs . . ." and from "invariably and systematically" pursuing a policy of peace. That was in 1936.

In September, 1939, Germany feared that Turkey might go to war on the side of the Anglo-French. This would have caused grave inconveniences to Hitler in the Balkans, especially in Rumania, source of grain and oil for the Nazi regime. Berlin asked Moscow's assistance in keeping Turkey neutral. Rumor had it that Britain intended to send a fleet through the Dardanelles and land troops in Rumania. ". . . it was in the interests of the Soviet Government," Schulenburg told Molotov, "to prevail upon Turkey to close the Dardanelles completely."

Turkish Foreign Minister Sükrü Saracoglu was summoned to Moscow. He stayed from September 23 to October 18, an inordinately long period. During much of the time he had no contact with Stalin or Molotov or any high official. The Kremlin's purpose was to prevent Turkey from signing with England and France. It proposed, instead, that the Turks conclude a mutual assistance pact with the Soviet government which, however, would not aid Turkey if she were attacked by Germany. (The Soviet-Nazi pact made this proviso implicit.) But since Germany was the only power whose attack Turkey feared, Saracoglu scorned the Kremlin's proposal. He went home empty-handed. On October 19, 1939, Turkey, alarmed, entered into a mutual assistance treaty with England and France which stated that Turkey would not assist the western powers against the Soviet Union.

"The Soviet Government regards Turkey with deep suspicion," Schulenburg wired his superiors in Berlin on June 16, 1940. Stalin had always

[12] Jane Degras, *Soviet Documents on Foreign Policy*, Vol. III: *1933-1941*, pp. 190-194 and 200-202.

[13] V. G. Trukhanovsky (Ed.), *Istoria Mezhdunarodnikh Otnoshenii i Vneshnei Politiki SSSR 1917-1939* (The History of International Relations and the Foreign Policy of the U.S.S.R.), Vol. I, pp. 453-456.

viewed Turkey with deep suspicion. His native Georgia shared the Black Sea with Turkey, and the Turks had once occupied Soviet Batum, Georgia's chief Black Sea port. The suspicion grew when Saracoglu did not bow to the Kremlin's wishes. Schulenburg referred to "Turkey's unfriendly atttitude toward Russia and other countries," by which Molotov obviously meant Germany and Italy. "Soviet suspicion of Turkey was intensified by the Turkish attitude in regard to the Black Sea, where Turkey desired to play a dominant role, and the Straits, where Turkey wanted to exercise exclusive jurisdiction. The Soviet Government was reducing a Turkish threat to Batum."

This Schulenburg report gave the gist of a conversation between Molotov and Italian Ambassador Augusto Rosso. The Soviet Chairman concluded the interview by saying that "In the Mediterranean, the Soviet Government would recognize Italy's hegemony, provided that Italy would recognize the Soviet Government's hegemony in the Black Sea."[14] Hegemony at the expense of Turkey.

The deterioration of Turko-Soviet relations, the truncation of Rumania, and Russia's yearning for Black Sea supremacy burst open the Balkan hornet's nest. Soon Moscow and Berlin-Rome would be rasping rivals in that traditional incubator of wars. This was one of the central causes of the Nazi invasion of the U.S.S.R.

Before that happened Stalin ordered the invasion of Finland.

XXX BLOOD ON THE SNOW

Chairman and Foreign Commissar Vyacheslav M. Molotov spoke on May 31, 1939, of Czechoslovakia as a "large Slav nation." It was the first time a Soviet leader had used the word "Slav" to characterize a country. *Pravda* and *Izvestia* of September 22, 1939, referred to the "millions of brother Ukrainians and brother Byelorussians of the same blood as ours," formerly Polish citizens, who were now safe in the Soviet Union. The Nazis based policy on race and blood, or so they said. Now the communists were doing it. Not on class, on blood.

Early in the life of the Soviet regime the Bolsheviks gave a Latin alphabet to Turkoman, Turkish, and other Moslem minorities whose

[14] All quotations from Schulenburg and Ribbentrop's dispatches are from *Nazi-Soviet Relations 1939-1941*.

complicated cursive Arab script conduced to illiteracy. Lenin in 1922 termed Latinization "the great revolution of the East." It brought Asiatic peoples closer to western culture. Kemal Pasha Ataturk had introduced a similar innovation in Turkey.

But 1937 saw an officially inspired Soviet move away from Latinization. It reached crescendo after the Soviet-Nazi pact, and especially after the friction with Turkey. For while Turkey was a friend, Moscow did not fear Turkish influence on the Turanian or Turkish minorities in Central Asia and the Caucasus. With the Kremlin seeking Black Sea hegemony and Ankara reacting unfavorably to this new expansionism, the communists needed a linguistic iron curtain to break the contact with the Anatolian Turks. *Pravda* of October 14, 1939, reported "a meeting of the intelligentsia of Tashkent" which unanimously adopted a resolution asking "the party and government of Uzbekistan to hasten the transfer to an alphabet based on the Russian script." The government and party of Uzbekistan acquiesced in Moscow's wishes as obediently as the "unanimous" Uzbek intelligentsia. Russification marched in step with Russian nationalism and Soviet imperialism.

The Estonians, Latvians, and Lithuanians are not Slavs, nor is their language cognate to Russian. Their territory was required for Russia's "security." The Finns, with their unique language and culture, are still further removed from the Russians. Here too the Kremlin pleaded "security" to justify conquest. At the October 31, 1939, session of the Supreme Soviet, Molotov declared that "Leningrad, which after Moscow is the most important city of the Soviet State, is situated at a distance of only 32 kilometers [20 miles] from the Finnish border. This means that the distance of Leningrad from the border of a foreign State is less than that covered by modern long-range artillery. . . . I must remind you that the population of Leningrad has grown to 3½ million, which almost equals the entire population of Finland, amounting to 3,650,000." The Soviet government, Molotov said, had opened negotiations with Finland with a view to the conclusion of "a Soviet-Finnish pact of mutual assistance approximately on the lines of our pacts of mutual assistance with the other Baltic states."[1]

First, Finland considered herself a Scandinavian, not a Baltic, state. Secondly, she had a premonition of what "mutual assistance" implied. The Finns refused.

Thereupon, according to Molotov, "We proposed an agreement to shift the Soviet-Finnish frontier on the Isthmus of Karelia a few dozen kilometers further to the north of Leningrad. In exchange for this we proposed to transfer to Finland a part of Soviet Karelia, double the size

[1] Jane Degras, *Soviet Documents on Foreign Policy*, Vol. III: *1933-1941*, p. 395.

of the territory which Finland would transfer to the Soviet Union." This seemed eminently reasonable except to those who knew that the "few dozen kilometers" contained part of Finland's main defenses against Russia: the Mannerheim Line. The rest was to be dismantled. "We also proposed to Finland the demilitarization of the fortified zones along the entire Soviet-Finnish border on the Isthmus of Karelia," Molotov added. Moscow, furthermore, demanded that "Finland lease to us for a definite term a small section of its territory near the entrance of the Gulf of Finland where we might establish a naval base."

It was by such an installment plan that Latvia and Estonia died.

The exchange-of-territory offer fooled no Finn. With the same shoddy generosity Moscow persuaded Nazi Germany to assign Polish Vilna to Lithuania, only to sovietize all of Lithuania.

"The ladies of St. Petersburg could not sleep peacefully as long as the Finnish frontier ran so close to our capital," Peter the Great wrote in explanation of his seizure of Viipuri (Vyborg) and Karelia. From Leningrad, Andrei A. Zhdanov, the communist boss of the city, declared on November 29, 1936, he could "hear, ever more loudly, the howling of the fascist beasts and the snapping of their jaws" in Finland.[2] Tsar and commissar had the same goal, only the latter's rhetoric was fiercer.

Assuming the likelihood of an assault by the hostile midget on the peace-loving tiger, how does one arrive at the margin of safety? Finnish airplanes might rain bombs on Leningrad from a distance of several hundred miles. To calm Zhdanov's ears and fears Finland would have to efface herself entirely. But Leningrad could be destroyed by bombers from Norway, Sweden, or Denmark. Long-distance bombers could destroy Leningrad, Moscow, London, Paris, Rome, New Delhi. Absolute insurance against attack in the age of propeller planes, and certainly in this age of jets and missiles, would require one power to take over the planet and put all other powers in chains. The spectacle of a timorous Soviet Union seeking security at the expense of Finnish soil and sovereignty would be comic had it not become tragic for both countries. In twenty-one years of the life of independent Finland no Finnish gun had shelled Russia's second city. But on August 23, 1939, Germany assigned Finland to the Soviet sphere of influence. After this Nazi nod Stalin decided on drastic steps to protect the Soviet beast from the Finnish flea.

Significantly, the first Kremlin approach to Finland regarding the issues that ended in blood on the snow was made, in mystery, on April 14, 1938, when Boris Yartsev, a second secretary of the Soviet Legation in Helsinki, speaking not in the name of the Commissariat of Foreign

[2] Both quotations from Max Jakobson, *The Diplomacy of the Winter War. An Account of the Russo-Finnish War, 1939-1940*, pp. 14 and 18.

Affairs but apparently for the Communist Party's Politburo or at least several of its members, told Finnish Foreign Minister Rudolf Holsti that Hitler intended soon to attack Russia using Finland as a base. The Red Army, Yartsev explained, did not propose to wait for the invasion. It wanted to advance through Finland to meet the aggressor. Yartsev was suggesting that the Finns drop neutrality and accept Russian troops into their land. He spoke in this sense to Prime Minister A. K. Cajander and Finance Minister Vainoe Tanner. He also lobbied in pro-Soviet circles. For months he made no progress. Finally, in December, 1938, the Finnish Foreign Ministry sent two high officials to negotiate in Moscow without knowing whom they would meet. Only after the two Finns had passed through the gates of the Kremlin did they learn that their appointment was with Anastas I. Mikoyan, member of the Politburo and Commissar of Foreign Trade. They were told that Litvinov's Foreign Commissariat knew nothing about Yartsev's activity or of the conference with Mikoyan.

The conference failed totally.[3]

Finnish Minister of Interior Urho Kekkonen, later President for many years, banned the People's Patriotic Movement, a semifascist party, on November 22, 1938. His motive, he subsequently admitted, was to demonstrate to Moscow neutral Finland's ability to deal with a potential pro-German fifth column which won only eight seats in a parliament of 200. The electorate was more than 90 percent democratic and 40 percent socialist; the Soviet Union had nothing to fear. At the same time Marshal Baron Gustav Mannerheim, a former Tsarist army officer now Chairman of Finland's Defense Council, called for a much larger military budget; Finland would fortify her neutrality.

True to neutrality, Finland also rejected Germany's offer of a nonaggression pact. Sweden and Norway rejected similar offers.

Finland's fate depended on Sweden, her neighbor.

Napoleon wrenched Finland from Sweden in 1809 and presented her to Alexander I as a reward for Russia's cooperation. The Tsars permitted Finland a murky autonomy. A Swedish minority still lives in Finland and most educated Finns speak or at least read Swedish. Finland always tried to nestle close to the Swedish bosom lest her personality be submerged in Russian tyranny.

Just where the Baltic Sea forks and turns east to form the Gulf of Finland while continuing north into the Gulf of Bothnia lie tiny isles, 6,500 of them, known as the Aaland Islands. Situated twenty-five miles from Sweden and fifteen miles from Finland, they belong to the Finns.

[3] *Ibid.*, pp. 7-52. Max Jakobson, for many years Finland's Permanent Representative at the United Nations in New York, describes this episode from unpublished Finnish archives.

Napoleon said Aaland in the possession of a great power was "a pistol aimed at the heart of Sweden."

As the European crisis darkened in 1938, the Swedish and Finnish military drew up plans to fortify the Aalands. "But the real driving force behind Swedish participation in the defense of Aaland was the Foreign Minister. Richard Sandler was dedicated to the idea of Scandinavian unity."[4]

Swedish collaboration in defending the Aaland Islands would imply a determination to defend all of Finland and serve as a barrier to Soviet expansion. Sweden, the leader of the Nordic bloc, was a strong, industrialized nation with approximately twice the population of Finland. Moscow accordingly undertook to separate Sweden from Finland. Molotov argued before the Supreme Soviet on May 31 that "for more than a hundred years those [Aaland] islands belonged to Russia. . . . In fact the remilitarization of the islands affects the interests of the Soviet Union more than those of Sweden." The next day *Pravda* and *Izvestia* referred to "Russia's historic rights" in the Aalands. "Historic rights" are a nationalistic, antisocialist principle.

Molotov's words took immediate effect in Stockholm. The day after he spoke the bill requesting the Swedish parliament to authorize the Aaland fortification scheme was withdrawn never to be returned.

Finland now stood alone.

Stalin wanted no war. Having isolated Finland from Sweden and having sent Boris Stein, Soviet Ambassador in Rome, on a second mission to Helsinki, which failed in March, 1939, as Boris Yartsev's had in 1938, the Kremlin experimented with a leaf out of Hitler's book. Hitler had summoned Chancellor Kurt von Schuschnigg to the Berghof, subjected him to a humiliating tirade on February 12, 1938, and forced him to sign a document which, in effect, surrendered Austria to the Nazis. Then the German army marched in. He repeated the performance with President Emil Hacha of Czechoslovakia in March, 1939. Compared to Hitler, however, Stalin and Molotov were gentlemen. Moscow imposed treaties "of mutual aid" on Estonia on September 28, 1939, and on Latvia on October 5, 1939. The day Latvia submitted Molotov invited the Finnish Foreign Minister to come to Moscow within forty-eight hours. The Finnish government let the time expire without an answer. When it did reply, on October 8, it stated that the Foreign Minister's place was in Helsinki to advise his Cabinet colleagues. Instead it was sending Juho Kusti Passikivi, Finnish Minister in Stockholm, who spoke Russian.

Passikivi and his assistants arrived in Moscow on October 11. His

[4] *Ibid.*, p. 38.

instructions were "to reject any proposal for a mutual assistance pact . . . as contrary to Scandinavian neutrality. He was to refuse to discuss demands for changes in Finland's historic frontiers or for military bases on the mainland of Finland or on the Aaland Islands." Finland would fortify them. "The only concession he was allowed to make was giving up three smaller islands in the Gulf of Finland" in exchange "for a bigger piece of territory in Soviet Karelia."[5]

Finland mobilized her armed forces.

An official inquiry in Berlin elicited the response that Nazi Germany had washed her hands of Finland because she lay in the Soviet sphere of influence. The three Scandinavian kings met at Stockholm with the Finnish President in a show of solidarity which showed that they would give sympathy, and Sweden might send arms, but nobody was ready to fight for the Finns. Nevertheless, the Kremlin hesitated to take precipitate action. A small war sometimes has the same effect as the moving of a rock which starts an avalanche. Twice the Finnish delegation journeyed to Moscow, each time it talked at length with Stalin and Molotov, made tiny concessions, extracted tiny concessions, but reached no agreement. On both occasions Stalin let the Finns leave the conference chamber and drive to their legation only to be summoned by a telephone call to return for more debate about this island or that base. After such fruitless discussions the Finns each time took the train back to Helsinki to report and consult. The Soviet proposals seemed "reasonable and modest," as Finnish Foreign Minister Eljas Erkko put it. But were they the first installment?

For this reason the Finnish delegation's third trip to Moscow early in November, 1939, also ended in failure. The Finns stood firm not because they were prepared to go to war for a naval base demanded by Russia or against an exchange of territory which pushed the frontier away from Leningrad. "The [Finnish] government as a whole did not believe that he [Stalin] would be content with making Finland only 'to some extent' dependent on the Soviet Union," writes Jakobson. "It was convinced that once the Red Fleet had anchored off the coast of Finland, its guns would be used to force Finland into servitude to Moscow . . ."[6]

Distrust was the crux. The Soviet-Nazi pact conveyed a lasting impression of a Kremlin that had doffed the red robes of communism and revealed Stalin as an emperor without clothes. The treatment accorded Estonia and Latvia filled Finland with fear of similar treatment. Hence Finnish intransigence. Yet Stalin probably contributed to it by his moderation. He did not talk to the Finnish diplomats like a man about to order his army into battle. His flexibility induced the Finns to hope for a

[5] *Ibid.*, p. 109.
[6] *Ibid.*, p. 139.

peaceful settlement. After all, they had made three journeys to and from Moscow. Why not a fourth? It seemed clear to them that Stalin did not want war. On the other hand, to be defied by little Finland would hurt his pride and damage his prestige at home and Russia's abroad. Such a turn of events might invite an attack by Germany or the West. Stalin, always suspicious of individuals and nations, could not be sure. Bleeding the Red Army in a minor war and rousing the country's patriotism, moreover, had military as well as political advantages. The Tass correspondent in Helsinki reported to Moscow that the Finnish working class was on the verge of revolution, mobilization meant economic ruin for Finland, and soldiers were deserting in droves. He "quoted statements of numerically insignificant and politically impotent leftist groups as evidence of popular resentment against the government position. . . .

"Such reports were read in Finland with amusement." But they "ought to have been taken more seriously, for it is unlikely that the dispatches of the Soviet Legation in Helsinki were substantially different. The result was that the Soviet leaders apparently were led to believe that the Finnish 'masses' were ready to receive the Red Army with flowers and banners."[7]

The proposition, stoutly defended by Andrei A. Zhdanov, that the armed forces of the Leningrad Military District would suffice to reduce the Finnish defenses and the illusion of a "proletarian" fifth column inside Finland overcame Stalin's caution. The new military commanders, freshly promoted over the graves of their recently executed comrades and eager to prove their mettle, reinforced Zhdanov's arguments. The scales were tipped to war. But Moscow marched against Finland in camouflage. On November 26 Molotov charged that that very day seven cannon shells from the Finnish side of the border struck a Soviet unit stationed near the village of Mainila, killing four men and wounding nine. The Finnish minister in Moscow, handed this information, reminded Molotov that the Soviet-Finnish treaty of 1928 provided for investigation of border incidents by a joint commission. Surely Russia would not go to war because of one frontier shooting?

The Finns sent a study group to the frontier and reported to Moscow that the shots could not have come from Finnish territory. They nevertheless proposed a withdrawal of armed forces from both sides of the border. But throughout the Soviet Union the propagandists began to bang the drums of hate. Fascist Finland, it was asserted, had committed aggression against the Soviet Union (population 190 million).

In an attempt to avoid being considered foolish the Kremlin decided that the camouflage of going to war to defend the Soviet Union against

[7] *Ibid.*, pp. 142-143.

Finland was too transparent. It accordingly proclaimed that Russia was not at war with Finland. To be sure, Soviet airplanes dropped bombs upon Helsinki on the morning of November 30; the same day Soviet troops crossed the Finnish frontier, and the Red navy shelled Finnish islands in the Gulf of Finland. The war had commenced. Finnish Foreign Minister Holsti asked for a meeting of the League of Nations Security Council which was convened by Secretary General M. J. Avenol for December 9. The General Assembly would meet two days later. But Molotov responded with flagrant casuistry to Avenol's invitation to appear in Geneva. "The U.S.S.R.," he telegraphed, "is not in a state of war with Finland and is not menacing the people of Finland with war."

The sophistry was explained in the next sentence. "The Soviet Union," it read, "maintains pacific relations with the Finnish Democratic Republic whose government, on December 2, signed a pact of assistance and friendship with the U.S.S.R. This pact regulated all the questions which the Soviet government discussed without result with the former government of Finland now out of office."

Further in explanation of the camouflage intended to convert war into un-war, Molotov stated that "By its December 1 declaration the Democratic Government of Finland applied to the Soviet government asking it to offer this republic armed assistance with a view to the united and speediest liquidation of the most dangerous hearth of war created in Finland by her former leaders." Therefore Mr. Holsti had no right to ask for a meeting of the League Council and Assembly.[8]

"The Democratic Republic of Finland" led a placid existence in the small office of Otto W. Kuusinen in the Moscow headquarters of the Comintern. It was furnished with a desk and a filing cabinet and several chairs piled high with newspapers. That was the "Republic" sprung full-blown from the brow of Joseph Stalin. Kuusinen, age fifty-eight at the time, had lived in the Soviet Union for nine years since Finland banned her communist party in 1930. "The Republic," like so much else in Russia, was born in bureaucracy far from the popular will. On November 13, 1939, Kuusinen wrote to Arvo Tuominen, secretary general (address: Stockholm) of the illegal Finnish Communist Party, inviting him to come to Moscow "to do a job he would like." Disaffected by the Stalin-Yezhov purges of 1937-38 and their withering toll of Finnish and other foreign communists, disillusioned by the Soviet-Nazi pact and its after-

[8] Through the kindness of U Thant, Secretary General of the United Nations, I was given access to the League of Nations archives in Geneva during the summer of 1966. But since the League's activities were public, I found only a few thin folders, one of which contained the original, in French, of Molotov's telegram. A League official supplied the photostat.

math, Tuominen remained in Stockholm. A courier brought a second letter on November 21, this time from the Soviet Politburo, summoning him to Moscow to become the Prime Minister of the new "Democratic Republic" of Finland. (Kuusinen would be its president.)

On December 14, 1939, the League of Nations, which had not expelled fascist Italy for invading Abyssinia, expelled the Soviet Union for invading Finland. It paid no attention to the fictional "Democratic Republic of Finland." Neither did Tuominen. Instead he moved to Helsinki to work for the government Molotov had declared dead.[9] He joined the social democrats. He was not the only Finnish communist who helped his country with words or weapons to resist aggression. The Finnish communists had been pro-Soviet. How could a Finn be pro-Soviet now? They had been communists less for reasons of doctrine than because they were in opposition. How could they oppose the government fighting invasion? A number of illegal communist leaders immune to this logic were arrested.

In diplomatic negotiations the Soviet demands had been relatively modest: the island of Hogland in the eastern Gulf of Finland; the little peninsula of Hanko at the western end of the gulf; the destruction of the Mannerheim Line, Finland's chief defense against Russia. War removed the restraints. The Red Army was to occupy all of Finland up to the Swedish border; Soviet officers taken prisoner carried orders not to cross that frontier. And it would be over, Moscow said, in three days. A march rather than a battle. Propaganda was to smooth the road. Russian airplanes dive-bombing Helsinki dropped leaflets promising an eight-hour day—enforced in Finland since 1917. The endemic professional disease of propagandists is self-deception.

The war did not end in three days, it lasted more than three months, long enough to elicit sympathy and admiration for the Finns from most of the noncommunist world, and plans to aid them which might have changed the course of the second world war and the future of the Soviet Union.

Conceived by the Soviets as a pushover, the Finnish War threatened to draw Russia into World War II, thus annulling the effect of the Soviet-Nazi pact and Stalin's policy of abstention. This was due, primarily, to the courage and skill of the Finnish soldier. Finns are born on skis. The troops had skis and the appropriate clothing and were defending every inch of their small country because its heart was not many inches from where they stood, fought, and died. The Red Army, on the other hand, lacked enough skis and skiers, and the men clad in traditional rough wool uniforms were soon soaked to the skin, their knee-high boots full of

[9] In 1956-57 Tuominen published his three-volume autobiography telling the story.

water as they trudged through the deep snow while snipers took deadly aim at them from behind every tree and every hillock. The Finns had plenty of guts but not enough guns, especially antitank guns. They therefore filled bottles with kerosene, gasoline, or other combustible liquids and hurled the "Molotov cocktails" at advancing Soviet tanks. A white landscape dotted with these blackened monsters in a variety of awkward poses testified to the ingenuity of the Finnish invention.

The Russian soldiers, unprepared for such vehement resistance and for the conditions underfoot, were likewise ill-prepared politically. They had invaded a foreign nation for no officially supplied reason except that Finland was "fascist." So was Germany, with whom Stalin had so recently concluded a pact of friendship. And had not *Izvestia* of October 9, 1939, said that "to start a war to 'destroy Hitlerism' is to commit a criminal folly in politics"? Why then start a war to destroy "fascism" in Finland? Confusion of mind does not lift fighting morale.

Maxim M. Litvinov asserted in New York at a Russian War Relief Rally on June 22, 1942, the first anniversary of the Nazi invasion of Russia: "Incorrect conclusions were also probably drawn by Hitler from the initial setbacks of the Soviet Army during the Finnish campaign. He did not understand that these temporary failures were due to the fact that the Soviet Army had never prepared for war against Finland, that no plans for that had been made." Litvinov blamed this on "Hitler's own aggressive plans." But Litvinov, like Lenin, grew up in the prerevolutionary Russian school in which he learned "the Aesopian language." Where he said "Hitler" read "Stalin."

Stalin was more forthright because he did not intend to have himself shot. He said during the Tehran conference in November, 1943, "that in the winter war against Finland, the Soviet Army had shown itself to be very poorly organized and had done very badly; that as a result of the Finnish war, the entire Soviet Army had been reorganized; but even so, when the Germans attacked in 1941, it could not be said that the Red Army was a first class fighting force."[10]

(Nobody was so impolite as to ask whether this costly condition stemmed from the 1937-38 army purge.)

Official Finnish figures support Stalin's statement. On the 88-mile front from the Gulf of Finland to Lake Ladoga—the Karelian Isthmus front—six Finnish divisions or 84,000 men faced twelve to fourteen larger Soviet divisions—210,000 to 245,000 men—backed by more than a thousand Russian tanks and several regiments of heavy artillery. North of Lake Lagoda, two Finnish divisions manned a 60-mile front against

[10] Robert E. Sherwood, *Roosevelt and Hopkins. An Intimate History*, p. 790. The occasion was a dinner attended by President Roosevelt, Prime Minister Churchill, Stalin, Harry Hopkins, and others.

seven Soviet divisions and a brigade of armor. From there to the Arctic Ocean, a distance of 625 miles, scattered Finnish battalions and companies endeavored to stop five Red divisions from reaching the Swedish border. The Soviets had complete control of the air. Yet throughout December the Finns held the Russians at bay. (In the very far north, in the nickel mining Petsamo region, Finland could spare no men to check the Red intrusion.)

Where the enemy did advance the Finns outflanked him and cut him to pieces. North of Lake Ladoga several Soviet divisions were "largely annihilated in ferocious and pitiless battles. The tenacious resistance of some of the trapped Soviet troops was worn down by hunger and the intense cold, and the northern forests were soon dotted with ghastly statues of Russian soldiers frozen solid in the deep snow."[11]

The stand of the Finns stirred the western world's admiration. It also inspired expectations and, in some capitals, pet schemes to alter the entire strategy of the second world war.

Italian Foreign Minister Galeazzo Ciano, son-in-law of Mussolini, wrote in his diary on December 2, 1939, that "the whole of Italy is indignant about Russian aggression against Finland, and it is only a sense of discipline that checks public demonstrations." Two days later the "sense of discipline" had apparently been allowed to evaporate, for Ciano noted on December 4: "In all Italian cities there are sporadic demonstrations by students in favor of Finland and against Russia. But we must not forget that the people say 'Death to Russia' and really mean 'Death to Germany.' " The Duce resented the Soviet-Nazi pact. In speaking to German Ambassador Hans Georg von Mackensen, the Italian leader, according to Ciano, "clearly reaffirmed the anti-Bolshevik orientation of our policy." Mussolini went so far as to give "instructions to our Consul in Prague to advise the Bohemians to side with the Communists. This will make German repression harder and will accentuate the causes for disagreement between Moscow and Berlin."[12]

Mussolini had two fears: if Hitler marched west instead of attacking Russia Italy might have to go to war before she recuperated from her adventures in Abyssinia and Spain. Secondly, after Russia smashed the Finns she would seize Bessarabia and thereby become involved in the Balkans where Mussolini in wild dreams saw himself the painless conqueror.

Again and again Ciano stressed that the Italian government was less interested in the ordeal of Finland than in breaking the Berlin-Moscow axis: "The fate of the Finns would be of much less concern to the Italians if the Russians were not from all practical points of view the

[11] Jakobson, p. 174.
[12] *The Ciano Diaries. 1939-1943,* pp. 174-175.

allies of Germany." The Italian students therefore continued to demonstrate. Molotov, who understood dictatorship, told Count von der Schulenburg that the student demonstrations "under a totalitarian regime could not be other than prearranged."[13]

Demonstrations were the visible froth. Ciano received the Finnish Minister on December 8 and said, "No objection [exists] on our part to the sending of arms; some planes have already been sent. This, however, is possible only so long as Germany will permit the traffic." In retaliation the Soviets suspended oil shipments to Italy. On December 8 the Grand Fascist Council "reaffirmed the continuity of Italy's interest in all the problems of the Danubian basin."[14] The next day Ivan Gorelkin, the new Soviet Ambassador to Italy, left Rome without having presented his letters of credence to the King, without bidding farewell to the Foreign Ministry, and without explanation. Three weeks later Mussolini withdrew his ambassador from Moscow. But he did not wish to sever relations with the Kremlin. In January, 1940, he asked Germany to use her good offices to improve them.[15] He merely wished to chill Soviet-German relations. He tried persuasion. He had not exchanged a communication with Hitler since September 4, 1939, the day after Britain and France declared war on Germany. That event then monopolized his attention. Now he vented his restrained wrath on the Ribbentrop-Molotov pact. "You will not be surprised if I tell you," he wrote in a letter dated January 3, 1940, "that the German-Russian agreement has had painful repercussions in Spain. The Civil War is too recent. The earth which covers the dead—yours and ours and the Spanish—is still fresh. Bolshevism is a memory that obsesses Spain and the Spaniards; with their passionate and fanatical logic they do not understand the tactical necessities of politics." Franco did when he stayed out of the second world war. The unsentimental Mussolini plying the unsentimental Hitler with sentiment is comic relief from the darkness of the year that had just commenced. Neither Hitler nor Mussolini counted the dead when they decided on war.

As to Finland, "Fascist Italy is favorably disposed toward this brave little nation. . . . There has been talk of immense aid given by Italy to Finland. That is a matter of 25 fighter planes ordered before the war and nothing else. Thousands of volunteers have presented themselves individually at the Finnish Legation in Rome and at the Consulates, but the offers have to date been declined by the Finns."

Poland deserved better treatment, the Duce proceeded. "It is my conviction," he told Hitler, "that the creation of a modest, disarmed Poland

[13] Mario Toscano, *Una Mancata Intesa Italo-Sovietica Nel 1940 E 1941*, p. 14.
[14] *Ibid.*, p. 13.
[15] *Ibid.*, pp. 18-19.

which is exclusively Polish, liberated from the Jews—for whom I fully approve your project of gathering them all"—all three million—"in a large ghetto in Lublin—can no longer constitute any threat to the Greater Reich." This would deprive the big democracies, he argued, "of any justification for continuing the war."

Did this "genius" believe that the western democracies would quit the war because Hitler had established a truncated puppet Poland? Or was he afraid of war in the West which would drag him in and down? He soon revealed his true emotions. "I am profoundly convinced," he continued, "that Great Britain and France will never succeed in making your Germany, assisted by Italy, capitulate, but it is not certain that it will be possible to bring the French and British to their knees or even divide them. To believe that is to delude oneself. The United States would not permit a total defeat of the democracies."

After this brief excursion into common sense, the Duce came to his major point. The Soviet-Nazi pact had enabled Germany to avoid a second front and Russia, "without striking a blow," to profit in Poland and the Baltic. "But I, a born revolutionist who has not modified his way of thinking"—he had been a Leninist antiwar socialist and then a prowar western propagandist in World War I—"tell you that you cannot permanently sacrifice the principles of your Revolution to the tactical exigencies of a certain political moment. I feel that you cannot abandon the anti-Semitic and anti-Bolshevist banner which you have been flying for 20 years and for which so many of your comrades have died; you cannot renounce your gospel, in which the German people have blindly believed. It is my definite duty to add that a further step in your relations with Moscow would have catastrophic repercussions in Italy, where"—here the balcony bombast—"the anti-Bolshevik unanimity, especially among the Fascist masses, is absolute, solid as a rock, and indivisible."

First, sentiment. Second, western invincibility. Then the appeal to ideology. Finally, advice on strategy: "The solution of your Lebensraum problem is in Russia and nowhere else; in Russia, which has an immense area of 21 million square kilometers and 9 inhabitants per square kilometer. Russia is alien to Europe. In spite of her extent and her population, Russia is not a power but a weakness. The mass of her population is Slavic and Asiatic. In olden times the element of cohesion was furnished by the people of the Baltic; today, by the Jews; that explains everything. Germany's task is this: to defend Europe against Asia. . . . Until 4 months ago Russia was world enemy number one; she cannot have become, and is not, friend number one . . .

"The day when we shall have demolished Bolshevism we shall have kept faith with our two Revolutions. It will then be the turn of the big democracies, which cannot survive the cancer which is gnawing at them . . ."[16]

The Duce was trying to bring Hitler back to *Mein Kampf*. The attempt failed. Hitler did not reply to Mussolini's letter until March 8. He cannot have been that busy. The delay of more than two months was a snub and a sign of disagreement. The "Fuehrer's" letter, rambling into irrelevancies, assured Mussolini that "sooner or later fate will force us after all to fight side by side, that is, that you will likewise not escape this clash of arms. I do not, however, believe, Duce, that any danger will threaten the Balkans from Russia." The Soviet Union under Stalin "has without doubt experienced a modification of the Bolshevist principle in the direction of a nationalist Russian way of life . . . if Bolshevism in Russia is developing into a Russian national state ideology and economy, it constitutes a reality which we have neither interest nor reason to combat. On the contrary! . . ." There followed a long defense of Russian actions against Finland, concluding with the statement that "we have no cause to champion Finland's interests."[17]

Within several months Russia's expansionist aims in the Balkans proved irritating to both Hitler and Mussolini. Before 1940 was out Hitler gave orders for the invasion of Stalin's Russian national state. Mussolini won most of the points in the debate. On the other hand, Hitler was right in predicting that Italy would enter the "clash of arms," in the event sooner rather than later, and as a result Italy lost the war and Mussolini his life. The Nazis, moreover, would champion Finland's interests.

In the 1939-40 Russo-Finnish war, however, Germany remained unalterably loyal to the secret protocol of August 23, 1939, which gave Finland to the bear. On December 2, two days after the war commenced, Weizsaecker, State Secretary in the German Foreign Ministry, instructed all German missions abroad as follows: "In your conversations regarding the Finnish-Russian conflict please avoid any anti-Russian note." England was to be blamed for Finnish resistance. "England's guilt in the Russo-Finnish conflict should be especially emphasized," Weizsaecker wired Schulenburg on December 4.[18] The German government, which had, before the winter war, exchanged arms for Finnish nickel, stopped that traffic when hostilities commenced. It also barred arms shipments in transit from Belgium, Hungary, and Italy to Finland. "The German navy agreed to supply Soviet submarines operating in the Baltic against Finnish shipping."[19]

[16] U.S. Department of State, *Documents on German Foreign Policy,* Series D, Vol. VIII: *The War Years, September 4, 1938-March 18, 1940,* pp. 604-609.

[17] *Ibid.,* pp. 871-880.

[18] *Nazi-Soviet Relations,* pp. 127-129.

[19] Jakobson, pp. 184-185.

As soon as the Soviet Union attacked Finland a new Finnish Cabinet was selected with Risto Ryti, Governor of the Bank of Finland as Prime Minister, and Vainoe Tanner, leader of the social democrats, as Foreign Minister. The Ryti government immediately asked Sweden to mediate a peaceful settlement with Moscow. It asked Germany to support this démarche. Molotov told Count von der Schulenburg on December 4 that the Soviets not only rejected negotiations, they would not allow Sweden to represent Finland's interest in Moscow:[20] a new Finland had been born and its president was Otto Kuusinen, the Secretary-General of the Comintern. Thereafter Germany remained aloof from all aspects of the Russo-Finnish struggle.

Sweden, however, was deeply involved.

"Finland's Cause Is Ours" read posters which papered Sweden as soon as the Soviet assault began. A strong spontaneous swell of sentiment swept Sweden. There was also a supremely practical issue: if Moscow took Finland the Swedes would be uncomfortable with the Russians as neighbors. On the other hand, Sweden treasured her neutrality. As a result of being caught on the sharp horns of this dilemma the Swedish government was divided; the Conservatives favored considerable aid to Finland, the social democrats none, the in-between parties vacillated. Volunteers were allowed to go to Finland but without weapons from government stores. Soldiers who wished to volunteer had to ask permission. *Pravda* of January 15, 1940, published a statement by the Commissariat of Foreign Affairs that "According to information of December 28 up to 10,000 'volunteers' have arrived in Finland from Sweden. Later it was reported that two corps of 'volunteers' had arrived in Finland from south and central Sweden, under the command of General Ernest Linder. To this . . . should be added the direct supply of arms from Sweden to the Ryti-Tanner Government, and permission for the passsage through Sweden to Finland of all kinds of military supplies."

The Swedish government denied the accusations, said the figures for volunteers were grossly exaggerated, and noted that Swedish law permitted individuals to act, travel, and write as they pleased. Similar Soviet charges against the Norwegian government were rebuffed in Oslo.

In the United States feelings against communist Russia's invasion of Finland rose just as high as in Scandinavia. But isolationism prevailed over anticommunism, and neither President Franklin D. Roosevelt nor Congress offered anything more than kind words until the end of February, 1940, when the Senate and the House of Representatives approved a $20 million loan for nonmilitary imports by Finland. The sum was too little and by that time too late.

[20] *Documents on German Foreign Policy*, p. 487.

The situation in France and England was different.

The Russo-Finnish winter war coincided with the "phony war" in the West. Anglo-French forces tangled sporadically with Germans at sea and in the air but on the ground all remained serene. The French and British reacted emotionally much as the Americans and Scandinavians to the assault on Finland. They, however, were still smarting under Russia's betrayal in signing with Hitler, and they now realized that "indirect aggression" meant aggression by Russia. The war in the north, far from their own territories, beckoned. It opened a possibility of doing something, of striking a blow at Russo-German unity under the guise of assisting gallant Finland. Strategy joined to sentiment makes a powerful stimulant.

The operation envisaged was complicated politically and militarily. Churchill, then First Lord of the Admiralty in Neville Chamberlain's Cabinet, schemed to aid the Finns. His mind preferred adventures far removed from his native isle. In the first world war it was Gallipoli. Now it was Narvik.

The British Ministry of Economic Warfare found that in the first year of the war Germany had to import nine million tons of iron ore from Sweden in order to stave off "a major industrial breakdown." The ore was shipped from the Swedish far north through the ice-free Norwegian port of Narvik, above the Arctic Circle, or, from mid-April to mid-December, through the Swedish port of Lulea at the top of the Gulf of Bothnia. Before the war and in its early months various departments in Whitehall had studied means of interrupting this supply. The outbreak of the Finnish-Russian conflict gave a mighty fillip to the project. Enormous possibilities emerged which staggered the imaginations of the imaginative—like Churchill: help the Finns resist Russia, paralyze the German war effort, create a northern front where few skilled men could compete with German numbers, and win Swedish and Norwegian support by presenting them with the grim prospect of a Soviet victory over the Finns that might culminate in a Russian advance through northern Sweden and Norway to the Atlantic Ocean.

On December 16, 1939, Churchill laid a detailed note before the Cabinet proposing the mining of the Narvik harbor and, when the ice melted, of Lulea. The Swedes and Norwegians would conceivably take economic countermeasures and the Germans more violent measures. The Scandinavians, however, had much to lose from economic warfare against Britain, and "with our command of the sea there is no reason why French and British troops should not meet German invaders on Scandinavian soil." As for the moral aspect of violating Norwegian and Swedish neutrality, "The final tribunal is our conscience. We are fighting to re-establish the reign of law and to protect the liberties of small countries. Our defeat would mean an age of barbaric violence, and would be fatal, not only to ourselves, but to the independent life of every small country in Europe."[21] The end justified the means.

The French authorities were even more eager than the British to see their armed forces in action. Premier Daladier favored a landing at the Arctic ice-free Finnish port of Petsamo, captured by the Russians in default of any defense by the Finns who were hard-pressed on other fronts. General Maurice Gustave Gamelin, Chief of the French General Staff, proposed an offensive in the Caucasus to deprive Russia of oil. If this succeeded, he submitted, "it may decisively weaken the military and economic power of the Soviet Union and perhaps even lead to the collapse of the entire Soviet system." Russian émigrés, in all seriousness, suggested to Finnish Foreign Minister Tanner that he invite Trotsky and Kerensky to Helsinki to form a Russian government-in-exile.[22]

The prosaic military and civilians of Whitehall had no more qualms than Churchill about the morality of their contemplated operations. But the British Chiefs of Staff considered Swedish and Norwegian acquiescence indispensable to any military action at Narvik or to the mining of the Norwegian coastal waters where the Germans avoided English patrols at sea. When the Scandinavian governments were informed on January 6, 1940, of the contemplated moves they protested furiously. They did not know then that Hitler had, in mid-December, 1939, authorized preparations for a plan to occupy Norway.[23] But they feared that Anglo-French violation of their neutrality might invite Nazi, and perhaps (though far less likely) Soviet, retaliation. The Anglo-French, however, continued to plan to help themselves by ostensibly helping the Finns.

Throughout January, 1940, the Soviets escalated their attack with heavy artillery, larger tanks, more men, and more frequent air bombardments. Finnish defenses held. Red casualties mounted. Clearly, nevertheless, the Finns would crack under the ponderous assault if assistance did not come soon. Some arms did arrive, notably from Sweden, France, England, and the United States, according to Tanner's memoirs. But the quantities were in no way commensurate with the reinforcements Russia had brought up from as far away as Siberia and the Caucasus.

When British Military Attaché Ling returned to London from Helsinki on January 12 with a letter from Mannerheim asking for 30,000 men and considerable munitions the Anglo-French accelerated their

[21] Winston S. Churchill, *The Second World War. The Gathering Storm,* pp. 544-547.

[22] Tanner reveals this in his Finnish-language memoirs: *Olin Ulkoministerina Talvisodan Aikana* (I Was Foreign Minister during the Winter War), p. 219.

[23] J. R. M. Butler (Ed.), *History of the Second World War,* United Kingdom Series: *Grand Strategy,* Vol. II: *September 1939-June 1941,* p. 105.

plans for carrying the war to Scandinavia.

General Sir Edmund Ironside, the British Chief of Imperial General Staff (CIGS), was eager to seize "the initiative from Hitler." He wrote in his diary, "if we can keep Finland on her legs we shall certainly stop any combined advance in the Balkans. If we can transfer the scene of action to Scandinavia, then the Middle East will be quiet." He, like Churchill, expected to cut off Germany's supply of Swedish ore. "Intervention in Scandinavia is our first and best chance . . . of shortening the war." The British War Cabinet did not want "the odium of having allowed Finland to be crushed." On February 5 the Anglo-French Supreme War Council agreed on landings at Narvik and Trondheim in south-central Norway. "If we can bring this off we shall have carried out a great coup," Ironside exclaimed in his diary. ". . . It may bring in Norway and Sweden." The Germans "will have to come out in the open and declare themselves for or against the Russians" in Finland.[24]

The Supreme War Council, attended by Chamberlain, Foreign Secretary Lord Halifax, Churchill, and the armed service chiefs with their French opposite numbers, agreed "that Finland must be saved." Her capitulation would be "a major defeat for the Allies." They gave favorable consideration to Mannerheim's request for 30,000 troops with adequate arsenals. Chamberlain said he wished "to kill two birds with one stone": help the Finns and stop the supply of iron ore to Germany. Daladier agreed. The bulk of the troops would be British. As soon as the expedition was ready the Finns, according to the plan, would appeal to the world for help. Then "the Allies would use this moral lever to overcome the opposition of the neutral Powers [Sweden and Norway] to allow them passage, assuring the neutrals that a force stood ready to assist them against German retaliation." Daladier was more skeptical than Chamberlain about winning the neutrals' acquiescence and recommended his brain-child: a landing at Petsamo. He nevertheless fell in with British plans. "The move involved 100,000 troops and 11,000 vehicles in all and was expected to take eleven weeks." (The French were to contribute 5,000 additional men.) The expedition would be in place and ready for combat on or about March 23.

In the weeks that followed the February 5 Supreme War Council session "Assistance to Finland was a daily item on the Cabinet agenda." The Finns, who had commenced to falter, pleaded hourly for fighter aircraft, antiaircraft artillery, and other arms. While the Allies planned and procrastinated Finland bled and retreated foot by foot before the ever-more-massive Russian onslaught, and on February 22 "the Finnish President appealed to the Allies . . . to bring pressure on the U.S.S.R. to

[24] Colonel Roderick Macleod and Denis Kelly (Eds.), *Time Unguarded. The Ironside Diaries 1937-1940*, pp. 188-197.

agree to peace negotiations. This suggestion was not at all to the liking of the Allies; they desired neither war with Russia nor a patched-up peace between Russia and Finland which would enable Russia to give more extensive economic aid to Germany." (Total British aid amounted to 53 aircraft and heterogeneous armaments. Volunteers from all countries numbered 11,300.)[25]

Bled white, faint from fatigue, the Finns could not wait until March 23. On March 7 Prime Minister Ryti flew from Stockholm to Moscow to negotiate a peace settlement.

The Finns knew they were beaten. Yet they did not throw themselves at the mercy of Moscow. And Anglo-French plans to help Finland played a role in the peace.

Merely the fact that Chairman Molotov condescended, through the mediation of Madame Alexandra Kollontai, the Soviet envoy in Stockholm, to receive Prime Minister Ryti erased the fiction of Kuusinen's "People's Republic." A gain for realism. Finland, unlike Estonia, Latvia, and Lithuania, would survive as a free state. Ryti's talks with Molotov, Zhdanov, and Soviet generals began where the prewar peace negotiations with Passikivi and Tanner left off: what islands and bases the Soviet Union could win from the Finns. The Finnish blood that colored the snow red had not been shed for nothing; the nation was saved. Yet was there not a failure of statesmanship here? Multitudes died—48,745 Soviet military, according to figures Molotov gave the Supreme Soviet on March 29, 1940 (200,000 according to Finnish estimates), and 20,000 Finns (60,000 by Molotov's count). In addition, 158,863 Soviet soldiers and officers were wounded but survived, according to Molotov, and, from the same source, 250,000 Finns. But now the two sides were back where they were before the shooting started.

Yet not quite. Anglo-French intentions could not have remained a secret from Soviet spies and other informers in London and Paris and especially in Stockholm and Oslo, the centers of protest. Molotov told the Supreme Soviet on March 29, 1940, that "when the war began in Finland, the British and French imperialists were prepared to make it the starting point of war against the U.S.S.R. in which not only Finland but likewise the Scandinavian nations—Sweden and Norway—were to be used."

The next day Count von der Schulenburg telegraphed Berlin: "All our observations, particularly the speech of Molotov on March 29, confirm that the Soviet Government is determined to cling to neutrality in the present war and to avoid as much as possible anything that might in-

[25] Butler, pp. 105-109. All facts concerning Allied conferences and aid are from Butler who, according to a statement prefacing his government-published volume, was "given in full access to official documents."

volve it in a conflict with the Western powers. This must have been the main reason why the Soviet Government broke off the war with Finland, abandoning the People's Government."[26]

The Kremlin was in a hurry to conclude peace. So was Helsinki. The negotiations commenced on March 8 and the negotiators signed the treaty of peace on March 12. It was humiliating but not annihilating. Russia got Viipuri (Vyborg) where, on the day before the signing, exhausted Finns fought the enemy to a standstill in the suburbs; most of the Karelian Isthmus, and a thirty-year lease to the tiny Hanko peninsula, less than a hundred miles from Helsinki, as well as several islands in the Gulf. Moscow promised to evacuate Petsamo in the north but forced the Finns to cede territory at the "waist" of Finland between the White Sea and the Gulf of Bothnia. This pushed the Russian border westward. From that new border the Finns had to undertake to build a railway for Russia across their country to the head of the Gulf of Bothnia, close to the Swedish iron ore mines and the Swedish port of Lulea.

The next morning at eleven fighting ceased. "It was a day of quiet, bitter mourning in Finland," writes Max Jakobson. When the Finnish Parliament met to ratify the peace treaty, 42 of the 200 deputies absented themselves, 9 abstained, 3 voted no.

* * *

Occasionally it is revealing, if impractical, to ask a question that cannot be answered.

When the Russo-Finnish war commenced the Swedes said, "Finland's cause is ours." What if they had said this before the war started?

Sweden on June 1, 1939, abandoned the plan to join with Finland in fortifying the Aaland Islands. The Swedish government could not have feared an attack by the Soviet Union. Stalin had hesitated to attack Finland, a smaller, weaker country. Nor would Germany have attacked Sweden. Hitler needed Swedish iron ore, and the Swedes could have sabotaged its production and its transportation on the only railroad from the mines to the sea (there was no road). If the Soviets made war on Sweden, the western Allies, unencumbered by a Swedish-Norwegian veto, would have hastened to intervene in Scandinavia on a scale as great or greater than that approved by the Supreme War Council of February 5, and Russia would have become the central arena of the second world war.

Swedish diplomats encountered in Stockholm, Helsinki, and elsewhere cite, in defense, their long tradition of neutrality and the benefits of peace in terms of living standards and social legislation. Finns reply that

[26] *Nazi-Soviet Relations*, p. 136.

the point was to prevent a war, not to fight one. Swedish identification with Finland from May to November, 1939, it is contended, would have intensified Kremlin caution. A leadership that was in doubt about assaulting Finland would have been triply uncertain about the wisdom of taking on Finland and Sweden with the prospect of inviting a spreading conflict.

This does not quite answer the unanswerable question. It does suggest that governments often lack the capacity to foresee even the short-term effects of their policies of omission or commission. Policy-making must necessarily be based on a calculation of immediate or remote results or both. That is the definition of policy. Otherwise, governing is merely a shopping basket of decisions forced on the leadership by today's pressures. To direct a state is to anticipate. Sweden did not anticipate. She looked backward. By looking forward she might have preserved Finland's neutrality and her own, prevented a war, and compelled Stalin to make a more sober study of the Soviet Union's international problems.

Part Three

The Origins of the Soviet-German War

XXXI GENESIS

The how, who, and when of history are highly important; without facts there is nothing. But the why of history is its most fascinating aspect. Fortunately, Nazi-Soviet relations give clear clues to the reasons for Hitler's invasion of Russia on June 22, 1941, twenty-two months to the day after the signing of the Ribbentrop-Molotov pact and protocol. It is possible not only to trace the descent from the summit of friendship to the hell of war. It is possible to apportion the blame between the two governments and between the persons and circumstances.

Throughout the Russo-Finnish war Germany remained strictly loyal to the Ribbentrop-Molotov pact and protocol. Nine months after the close of that war Hitler issued precise instructions for Operation Barbarossa designed *"to crush Soviet Russia in a quick campaign."*

From the signing of the pact and protocol on August 23, 1939, to November 18, 1940, the Soviet and German governments strove mightily to avoid friction. Moscow's efforts exceeded those of the Wilhelmstrasse; it curried favor with the Nazis. But Berlin was not far behind. The friendship reached its apogee in November, 1940, with Molotov's visit to Berlin when Hitler proposed to induct the Soviet Union into a four-power alliance with Germany, Italy, and Japan. Baron Ernst von Weizsaecker told all German missions abroad on November 18, 1940, "that speculations of the foe as to a disturbance in the Russo-German relationship of trust and friendship are based on self-deception."[1]

Exactly a month later, December 18, 1940, Hitler gave orders for Operation Barbarossa.

* * *

[1] U.S. Department of State, *Nazi-Soviet Relations 1939-1941*, p. 255.

Similarity of traits brings clashes. The love of territory and low regard for human beings common to the two totalitarianisms threatened their relations when diplomacy gave them proximity. They knew this, and resolutely tried to avoid difficulties. One instance: Weizsaecker reported to his superiors on December 5, 1939, that Wehrmacht chief Colonel General Wilhelm Keitel "telephoned me today on the following matter: Lately there have been repeated wrangles on the boundary between Russia and the Government General"—the German-held region of Poland. "The expulsion of Jews into Russian territory, in particular, did not proceed as smoothly as had apparently been expected. In practice, the procedure was, for example, that at a quiet place in the woods, a thousand Jews were expelled across the Russian border; 15 kilometers away, they came back, with the Russian commander trying to force the German one to readmit the group." Keitel seems to have been naïvely surprised. He requested the Foreign Ministry to take the necessary measures.[2] Herewith the shuttle-herding of the helpless homeless vanishes from the diplomatic record.

Territory was more important to both governments than persons.

When Ribbentrop agreed, in Hitler's name, to the Soviet sphere of influence in the Baltic and Rumania as demarcated in the August 23, 1939, secret protocol he felt sure that "spheres of influence" did not mean annexation; countries have exercised dominion over foreign lands without annexing them. This helps explain why Stalin took Latvia and Estonia in three installments and hesitated so long to attack Finland. He wondered what might be Germany's reaction.

During Ribbentrop's second hurried stay in Moscow he and Molotov, on September 28, 1939, signed a "Secret Supplementary Protocol" which transferred Lithuania from the German sphere of influence to the Russian in exchange for a piece of Poland in the Soviet zone. This was done on Kremlin insistence; Lithuania had been part of the Tsarist Empire.

The Lithuanian barter deal awarded the southwest corner of Lithuania to Germany. At the same time Moscow "gave" Vilna to Lithuania. (Lithuania had claimed it; Poland had held it; Russia had seized it under the August 23, 1939, agreement.) Ambassador Schulenburg protested. He found the arrangement "harmful" because "it would make us appear as 'robbers' of Lithuanian territory, while the Soviet Government figures as the donor." Schulenburg proposed a different settlement: Russia would occupy Lithuania but not the southwest corner; Russia would owe the area to Germany as an "obligation." Some day Germany would collect the debt from Russia (which would then be the "robber"). Germany did not want Lithuania informed about this arrangement. Molotov

[2] *Ibid.*, p. 128.

informed the Lithuanian Foreign Minister.

October 5, 1939—enter Stalin. He "*personally* requested the German Government *not* to insist *for the moment* upon the cession of the strip of Lithuanian territory." This seemed to be just what Germany wanted.

Molotov confirmed in writing that the Lithuanian corner would not be occupied "in case forces of the Red Army should be stationed [in Lithuania]." Molotov also pledged that "It shall be left to Germany to determine the date" when she would take over the strip. All looked deceptively good. Events proved that Stalin, while ostensibly acceding, intended never to let Germany have the strip.

The Red Army occupied the strip. On August 3, 1940, Russia officially annexed all of Lithuania. Germany protested the breach of written promise. On September 13, 1940, Molotov told Schulenburg Stalin had "examined the problem" and saw the justice of Germany's stance. But Molotov pleaded the difficulty of reversing possession. Outfoxed, Germany bowed.[3] Moscow offered to pay $3,860,000 in gold as compensation. Ribbentrop argued, on December 28, 1940—ten days after Hitler ordered Operation Barbarossa—that this was too little. The sale price of Alaska could not be used as a standard; that was long ago. Lithuanian land had a high value. He asked $13 million in gold to be paid in nonferrous metals, oil, flax, manganese, and cotton over and above delivery programs fixed earlier.[4] Finally, Molotov signed a secret protocol on January 18, 1941, which provided for a payment by Moscow to Germany of 31½ million Reichsmarks—roughly $7 million.[5] Ribbentrop had agreed to this price reduction on condition that the sum be paid "not in two years but by immediate delivery of nonferrous metals" or, if that presented difficulties, half could be paid forthwith in gold.

After the first world war Germany had considered the Baltic her inland sea and the Baltic countries her area of interest. Hitler signed them away to Russia in 1939. He kept his word. But he did not like what happened. Regrets bred resentments. Hate began to simmer. Stalin realized this and sought to apply verbal balm to Nazi wounds.

Pravda of August 23, 1940, celebrating the first anniversary of the pact and protocol, wrote, "The news of the Soviet-German pact was a last warning to the organizers and inspirers of the imperialistic war. The warning, however, had no effect. The war commenced."

Several times in September and October, 1939, Hitler offered to conclude peace with Britain and France. The Nazi python wanted a respite

[3] *Ibid.*, pp. 112-117.

[4] Original seen in German Foreign Office, Bonn, in the summer of 1966; copy supplied: Politisches Archiv., Auswaertiges Amt. *Buero des Staatssekretaer, Akten betreffend Sowjet-Union. III: vom Oktober 1940 bis Mai 1941*, Bd. 3, #24425.

[5] Gustav Hilger and Alfred G. Meyer, *The Incompatible Allies*, p. 319.

to digest Poland. The Soviet government too tried to end the war after the conquest of Poland. But, Stalin charged in *Pravda* of November 30, 1940, "the ruling classes of England and France rudely declined Germany's peace proposals as well as the Soviet Union's attempts to achieve the earliest termination of the war."

There was a contradiction here. The pact, *Pravda* wrote on August 23, 1940, "has guaranteed Germany undisturbed security in the East." Security to do what? To attack the West. Then why should anybody have taken seriously Hitler's peace offers to the West? Or the Soviet Union's attempts to end the war?

Stalin's attacks on the western powers and *Pravda*'s praise of the pact were not intellectual exercises. Moscow wished to remind Hitler of Russian support and its value to Germany. Moscow had abandoned neutrality and become Hitler's advocate. *Pravda* proclaimed on August 23, 1940, that "the basis of the new good-neighborly and friendly relations between the Soviet Union and Germany is not accidental considerations of a passing nature but the fundamental interests of the Soviet Union and Germany." The voice of the Kremlin was trying to convince Hitler that this was so.

Russia and Germany could now be friends or enemies; "no third path," as Lenin used to say. Russia was eager not to become Germany's enemy; that might mean war. Germany too wanted good relations with Moscow; Hitler was on the verge of expanding the war in the West. Yet with both partners conscious of the need of collaboration neither forgot the potential of hostility. The scales were too delicately balanced to warrant complacency. Ribbentrop sensed the need of courting the Kremlin. He wired Schulenburg on March 28, 1940, that during his recent visit in Rome he had tried to improve Soviet-Italian relations. This information would be passed on to Molotov. Ribbentrop hoped to see Molotov soon in Berlin. The Reich Foreign Minister added, "it would suit our own needs better, as well as our really ever-closer relations with Russia, if Herr Stalin himself came to Berlin. The Fuehrer would not only be particularly happy to welcome Stalin in Berlin, but he would also see to it that he would get a reception commensurate with his position and importance, and he would extend to him all the honors that the occasion demanded."[6] Hitler had authorized this message.

Alas, the world was denied the delicious spectacle of Stalin and Hitler riding together in an open car down Unter den Linden to the acclamation of the Brownshirt SA, the Blackshirt SS, and other Nazis. At the moment even Molotov would not go. He had never, Schulenburg explained, been abroad, did not like to fly, and "had strong inhibitions

[6] *Nazi-Soviet Relations,* pp. 134-135.

against appearing in strange surroundings." Strange indeed. "This applies as much if not more to Stalin," Schulenburg stated. The two dictators might nevertheless meet "in a border town."[7]

The subject was dropped for months.

Just about the time of Ribbentrop's invitation to Stalin and Molotov a dark cloud passed over Russo-German relations. Shipments of oil and grain to Germany were suspended and "the deportation of German citizens long imprisoned in Soviet jails" ceased. Schulenburg found no explanation. He interviewed Mikoyan, who shed no light on the new situation. He asked on April 8 for an appointment with Molotov. The appointment took place the morning of the next day, April 9. On April 9 Germany invaded Denmark and Norway. Armed forces under Colonel General Nikolaus von Falkenhorst quickly occupied Denmark and in twenty-three days subdued opposition in Norway where the Nazis established a puppet government under Vidkun Quisling whose surname became a synonym for traitor.

The inauguration of these events drove away the dark cloud. Molotov told Schulenburg on the 9th that the suspension of petroleum and grain shipments were due to the "excessive zeal of subordinate agencies"—something that could not happen in the Soviet Union—and "would be immediately remedied." Molotov "was affability itself." All issues were settled "in a positive sense." Ambassador Schulenburg could not suppress his surprise: "I must honestly say that I was completely amazed at the change."

Schulenburg tried to explain the change. The German invasion of Norway and Denmark, he ventured, "removed a great burden of anxiety" from the Soviet government which, he declared, had expected the Anglo-French to carry out the plans laid during the Russo-Finnish winter war for attacks on Norway and Sweden, and thereby reopening the Finnish front. "Apparently this fear was relieved by us . . . Today's long and conspicuous article in *Izvestia* on our Scandinavian campaign . . . sounds like one big sigh of relief."[8]

Or the real explanation was exactly the reverse: the *Izvestia* editorial of April 11 can also be read as a kowtow to Hitlerite military might as it moved dangerously near Russian interests in the Baltic. Germany, the editorial stated, reacted to the aggressive intentions of England and France. The Nazi invasions were "countermeasures." Germany's aviation was brought closer to British industrial centers, thus improving her chances of subduing Britain.

Not content with welcoming Nazi aggression, the organ of the Soviet government clothed the German "countermeasures" in a principle whose

[7] *Ibid.*, p. 136.
[8] *Ibid.*, pp. 138-140.

acceptance would justify Russia's imperialistic acts past and impending. *Izvestia* asserted that " 'Absolute neutrality,' as experience has shown, is a fantasy when unaccompanied by real power capable of maintaining it. And small nations do not possess such power. It would be unintelligent to think that a situation in which great powers are engaged in a war to the death and the small nations, decking themselves in the flag of neutrality, enrich themselves from the war, can continue endlessly." The policy of several small neutral nations "which contributed to the outbreak and inflaming of the war can only be described as a policy of suicide."

But two days after the *Izvestia* editorial appeared, Schulenburg saw Molotov at the latter's request to hear the Soviet Chairman declare that "in his opinion" Germany and the Soviet Union "were vitally interested in Swedish neutrality." Sweden was a small nation, undoubtedly destined to enrich herself in the war, yet Molotov told the ambassador the violation of Swedish neutrality "was frowned upon by the Soviet Government, and that it hoped that the inclusion of Sweden in our operations would not take place, if this could at all be avoided."[9]

What sounded to Schulenburg's ears as "a big sigh of relief" was perhaps a long gasp of fear. Norway was still resisting; Sweden would defend herself. Reluctant as they had been to admit the Anglo-French on the excuse of aiding Finland they would, if attacked, invite western military aid. Finland might be drawn into the conflict on one side or the other, whichever proved faster or stronger. Stalin would find the second world war on his doorstep. Therefore Sweden's "absolute neutrality," the object of heavy scorn in the editorial, became the subject of supreme concern in secret conclave.

There was another arrow in the Kremlin's quiver: the Comintern. The May 12, 1940, issue of the New York *Sunday Worker*, and numerous other communist publications throughout the world, carried a text of a long loud diatribe by Georgi Dimitrov, head of the Comintern, against the Anglo-French. Its essence is stated in two sentences: "The British and French war incendiaries are exerting unparalleled pressure on the small neutral states and have openly trampled the neutrality of the Scandinavian countries under foot. Germany has retaliated by occupying Denmark and a large part of Norway." Dimitrov, lion of the Reichstag fire trial, exculpated Hitler and Goering! As a prisoner in the dock he had defied Goering. As a leading communist he did not dare defy Stalin. He wept tears for neutrals where the government's *Izvestia* spat on their neutrality.

The same issue of the *Sunday Worker* and its communist cousins

[9] *Ibid.*, p. 140.

published an article by André Marty, the French communist, telegraphed from Moscow. It too attacked the Anglo-French: "Like filthy animals, the monstrous imperialists are at one another's throats and are preparing to tear one another to pieces. Already the Lofoten Isles are under the protection of Chamberlain." The Lofoten Isles are dots in the harbor of Narvik. It apparently escaped Marty's notice, sitting in Moscow, that Hitler had invaded Norway and Denmark; he saw only the dots. The Comintern and all foreign communist parties were now harnessed to the Soviet-Nazi pact and secret protocol and to the implications of those documents. The day the Wehrmacht erupted into Holland and Belgium (May 10, 1940) Schulenburg brought the information to Molotov, who was grateful and said "he understood that Germany had to protect herself against Anglo-French attack. He had no doubt of our success," the telegram concluded. World communist parties took the same line.

Communist parties made a creditable record in the 1930's combating fascism and the Nazis. They supported Litvinov's collective security policy and reveled in the Popular Front strategy of collaboration with everybody who would collaborate with them—including the German Nazis before January 30, 1933. The Soviet-Nazi pact caught them with their dialectics down; they could not imagine that when the western Allies became anti-Hitler, Hitler would become pro-Soviet, and the communists would become anti-Allies. If communists outside the Soviet Union had advocated an alliance between Hitler and Stalin or foreseen it one might understand their enthusiasm for it when Moscow dictated enthusiasm. But they had indignantly denied such a possibility. One communist leader promised to "eat my hat" if the rumor proved true. Ambassador Ivan Maisky declared the news false when it first reached him in London. (The Kremlin rarely shared important secrets with its envoys.) Such, however, was then Moscow's status as Mecca and Mt. Sinai that all foreign communists who did not fall by the wayside fell into step. The depth of their subservience is illustrated by the case of Harry Pollitt, secretary-general of the British Communist Party. A true proletarian, simple in manner and devoted to the cause, he wrote a penny pamphlet, published by his party on September 3, 1939, entitled *How to Win the War,* in which he declared that, though the war was an imperialist war, "the present rulers of Britain and France [are] actually for the first time challenging the Nazi aggression which has brought Europe into crisis after crisis for the last three years." Therefore the British working class "will do everything it can to bring the war to a speedy conclusion, but only by the defeat and destruction of Hitler and the Nazi rule. . . .

"To stand aside from this conflict," Pollitt continued, "to contribute only revolutionary-sounding phrases while the fascist beasts ride roughshod over Europe would be a betrayal of everything our forebears have fought to achieve in the course of long years of struggle against capitalism." Pollitt's brochure had been approved by the party leadership in London. In mid-September, however, instructions came from Moscow. The party leadership bowed while many members bolted. The pamphlet was withdrawn and the party succumbed not to "revolutionary-sounding phrases" but to counterrevolutionary pro-Nazi, proaggression phrases. In France and elsewhere communists openly opposed the war effort. The United States Communist Party discontinued its boycott of German goods.

The behavior of the Comintern and its foreign branches was a Kremlin contribution to Nazi strength. By inference this flowed as an obligation from the Ribbentrop-Molotov pact. Soviet practices, moreover, were too rigidly bureaucratic and inflexibly consistent to permit foreign-communist policy to deviate from Moscow policy. It would not do for Molotov to brand the Anglo-French as aggressive imperialists against whom Hitler had to defend himself while communist parties abroad supported those aggressive imperialists and excoriated Hitler. There was no precedent, yet, for foreign communist acts which implied that Moscow was mistaken or reactionary. But surely Stalin would have sacrificed consistency to safety had he thought the country in danger. Consistency was permissible because he saw no peril. He trusted Hitler and exaggerated French powers of resistance.

May 10, however, wrote "Crisis" in letters of fire on the face of Europe: the Wehrmacht's unprovoked assault on Belgium and the Netherlands meant that the road to France lay open to Hitler; the Chamberlain government fell. The same evening the King asked Winston Churchill to form a new Cabinet. Churchill brought the Labour Party into a national coalition to save Britain.

German troops occupied Paris on June 14.

A silence of nervous apprehension gripped Moscow. Press and radio, in their confusion, said little about the war in the West. During the second half of June, 1940, the Soviet Union completed its conquest of the three Baltic nations and marched an army into Rumanian Bessarabia and Bukovina. This might be the last chance to expand.

When I interviewed Churchill in October, 1939, he growled, "We shall not flinch" several times and agreed that some day the Soviet Union could be forced by circumstances to fight on the side of the West. Had the propitious condition been brought nearer by the collapse of France? If Britain surrendered, Russia would stand alone facing a Hitler dizzy with triumphs. Churchill decided to probe for a change of mood in the Kremlin. He sent Sir Stafford Cripps as ambassador to Moscow. Cripps was ascetic and idealistic, characteristics not highly prized in the Kremlin. He was a left-wing Labour Party dissident. If Churchill thought this would give Sir Stafford a warmer communist welcome he erred; Moscow always preferred a banker, a general, or a big capitalist, a "representative of the ruling class." Nevertheless Molotov told the Supreme Soviet on August 1, 1940, that "the appointment of Sir Stafford Cripps as ambassador to the U.S.S.R. does, possibly, reflect a desire on the part of England to improve relations with the Soviet Union."

Cripps, an eminent barrister, arrived in Moscow on June 12 in the same plane with Erik Labonne, Ambassador of France, who held a similar post in Barcelona during the Spanish Civil War and was, as I knew from interviews with him, pro-Loyalist. But in June, 1940, France fell and Labonne's politics did not matter in Moscow. However, Stalin received Cripps on July 1 for a long talk and felt constrained to report its contents to Germany. Molotov informed Count von der Schulenburg on July 13 that Cripps had propounded several propositions to Stalin and requested the dictator's responses. The British government, Cripps stated, was convinced that "Germany was striving for hegemony in Europe. . . . This was dangerous to the Soviet Union as well as England. Therefore both countries ought to agree on a common policy of self-protection against Germany and on the re-establishment of the European balance of power."

Stalin replied that he "did not see any danger of the hegemony of any one country in Europe and still less any danger that Europe might be engulfed by Germany." He "knew several leading German statesmen well" and "had not discovered any desire on their part to engulf European countries." Germany's military successes did not menace the Soviet Union. As to the old European balance of power, it had "oppressed not only Germany, but also the Soviet Union. Therefore, the Soviet Union would take all measures to prevent the re-establishment of the old balance of power in Europe."

Cripps also raised the question of Anglo-Soviet trade. Britain was ready to export to Russia provided her exports were not resold to Germany. Stalin "contested the right of England or any other country to interfere with German-Soviet commercial relations. The Soviet Union would export to Germany part of the non-ferrous metals she bought abroad, because Germany needed those metals for the manufacture of war matériel she delivered to the Soviet Union."

Sir Stafford next touched on the Balkans. The British government, he said, believed the task of unifying and leading the Balkan countries "for the purpose of maintaining the status quo" rightly belonged to Russia and could only be carried out by Russia. Stalin acknowledged that the Soviet Union "was interested in Balkan affairs" but claimed no such mission as described by the ambassador. ". . . no power had the right to an exclusive role in the consolidation and leadership of the Balkan countries."

Finally, Cripps brought up the question of the regime in the Turkish Straits with which, the British government knew, "the Soviet Union was dissatisfied." Russia's interests in the Straits "must be safeguarded." To this Stalin replied that "the Soviet Union was in fact opposed to the exclusive jurisdiction of Turkey over the Straits and to Turkey's dictation of conditions in the Black Sea. The Turkish Government was aware of that."[10]

This is a strange document. It was unusual for Stalin to render the German government an account of his discussion with the ambassador of a great power. Hitler, as far as we know, never gave Stalin a similar record. But Cripps spoke for Britain, and Stalin wished to convey to the "Fuehrer" that he remained loyal to his alliance with the Nazi Goliath: he did not negotiate behind the back of Germany.

The document expressed Soviet interest in the future configuration of Europe. No one country would enjoy hegemony over Europe, Stalin said. He thus intimated that he would not like to see Germany dominant. He rejected the old balance of power and wished to share in the new.

Stalin took a parallel position on the Balkans. Russia had no ambition, he stated, to unite and lead the Balkan countries. Neither should any other power play that role, neither, in other words, should Germany. He feared German designs on the peninsula. He seemed to sense that Soviet-Nazi friction in the Balkans might strike a spark that would blow up the keg of hot powder which was gradually accumulating under the cover of the "cordial" relations between Berlin and Moscow. German greed for Soviet deliveries of grain, oil, and other products helped fill the keg.

Lastly, Stalin served notice of his hostility to Turkey's "exclusive jurisdiction" over the Turkish Straits. This stance had spoiled Russo-Turkish relations in 1939, caused serious complications in 1945 and 1946, and explains Turkey's alignment with the West in the postwar period. (A nonexpansionist Soviet Union had always championed Turkey's exclusive jurisdiction over the Straits.)

Stalin had communicated to Hitler the contents of his talk with Cripps and, what was perhaps more important, that the talk had taken place; Britain was represented in Moscow. Although the Kremlin remained in the Nazi alliance it could choose to go elsewhere unless its waxing desires were satisfied by Germany. This may have been a blunder. Hitler

[10] *Ibid.*, pp. 166-168.

might have read the account as an avowal of loyalty. Or the fact that Stalin discussed serious international problems with a British ambassador might have intensified Hitler's irritation over Russian behavior in the Balkans. With brilliant insight Churchill had chosen the right moment to delegate Cripps to the Kremlin.

XXXII DUAL DISAPPOINTMENT

In his euphoria over the Soviet-Nazi pact Hitler exclaimed, "We need not fear a blockade. The East will furnish us with grain, cattle, coal, lead, and zinc."[1] Out of the communist cornucopia Hitler hoped to pluck victory.

Provision for Soviet-German exports and imports was made in the trade agreement signed in Berlin on August 19, 1939. Germany granted the Soviet Union a credit of 200 million Reichsmarks for the purchase of machinery and industrial installations, and, to a lesser extent, of "armaments in the broader sense (such as optical supplies, armor plate and the like) . . ." Russia would repay the credit by delivering to Germany, in the next two years, "lumber, cotton, feed grain, phosphate, platinum, raw furs, petroleum, and other goods" which had a gold value for Germany.[2]

The Soviet politicians were willing but the Soviet bureaucratic economic system was weak. The Germans complained of "inadequacies of transportation, of organization, of production methods, etc."—endemic Russian plagues. But the fault did not lie on the communist side only. With the expansion of Nazi military operations in the West, Germany needed more imports than planned and realized that these enlarged programs must be carried out "at the expense of their own Russian consumption."[3]

Difficulties multiplied. Foreign Minister Ribbentrop reminded the So-

[1] Speech on Aug. 22, 1939. German text in International Military Tribunal, *Trial of the Major War Criminals*, Vol. XXII, p. 343. English translation, Department of State, *Documents on German Foreign Policy*, Series D, Vol. VII: *The Last Days of Peace, August 9-September 3, 1939*, p. 204.

[2] U.S. Department of State, *Nazi-Soviet Relations 1939-1941*, pp. 83-85.

[3] *Ibid.*, pp. 119-120.

viet ambassador in Berlin on December 11, 1939, that "Germany was at war and that certain things were simply not possible." A Soviet trade delegation had brought from Moscow a supplementary list of military goods. Ribbentrop told the ambassador that "there was certain material which we could not supply during the war."

The Germans wanted raw materials quickly and contended that the manufacture of machinery took a long time. In the beginning the Soviets asked that their exports be balanced against imports from Germany every three months. Later this was extended to six months. On January 10, 1940, Molotov informed Schulenburg that the Soviet Union "was prepared to begin its deliveries at once" on condition that the account be balanced by the end of 1940. One way of tipping the trade balance in Germany's favor, Molotov asserted, would be the sale to Russia of two cruisers previously requested. Some sample German planes would be another way of paying for Soviet raw materials.[4]

Planes had been promised and sold, according to Dr. Karl Schnurre who supervised German commercial transactions with Russia, but "the Reich Ministry for Air will not release the aircraft." No deliveries of German cruisers are recorded and it is doubtful that any were made. The military collaboration between the Nazi and communist allies remained at a minimum: as late as May 15, 1941, Schnurre reported that the "Construction of the cruiser 'L' in Leningrad is proceeding according to plan, with German supplies coming in as scheduled. Approximately seventy German engineers and fitters are working on the construction of the cruiser in Leningrad under the direction of Admiral Feige."[5] The Nazi navy assisted the Russians in the Baltic during the winter war against Finland. The Soviet government gave the German navy a base on the Murmansk coast which was relinquished with thanks in September, 1940, because such bases were then available to Germany in Norway.[6] For the rest Soviet-Nazi cooperation was restricted to territorial "adjustments," diplomatic support, helpful propaganda, and trade. Trade relations were never smooth.

To facilitate commercial exchanges a new trade treaty was concluded on February 11, 1940. When the results were examined six months later by specialists from both countries Germany was found to have fallen short of her commitment by "roughly 73 million Reichsmarks." For the next half year—until February 11, 1941—Germany's commitments under the treaty amounted to 233 million marks. From February 11 to

[4] *Documents on German Foreign Policy*, Series D, Vol. VIII: *The War Years, September 4, 1939-March 18, 1940*, pp. 641-643.
[5] *Nazi-Soviet Relations*, pp. 339-341.
[6] *Ibid.*, p. 185.

May 11, 1941, shipments to Russia amounting to 78 million marks were called for by the treaty. But Schnurre noted in Berlin on September 28, 1940, that deliveries of such magnitude would not be possible if the armaments program ordered by Hitler was to be fulfilled. "In addition," Schnurre wrote, "there is the directive issued by the Reich Marshal [Goering] to avoid shipments to Russia which would directly or indirectly strengthen Russia's war potential." As a consequence, "the suspension of Russian shipments to Germany must shortly be expected." Thus far, according to Schnurre, Russia had delivered "one million tons of grain" to Germany. No country could replace Russia as a supplier of grain or petroleum, nonferrous metals, and cotton. Moreover, it was through the Soviet Union that Germany imported soya beans from Manchukuo and other essential commodities from Iran, Afghanistan, Japan, and even South America.[7]

An air of unreality enveloped Soviet-German trade during 1940. The Goering order proscribing armaments aid to Russia actually came from Hitler through Goering to General Georg Thomas, Chief of the Army War Economy and Armaments Office, on August 10, 1940, and instructed him to interdict the sending of war materials to Russia after the spring of 1941.[8] General Thomas occupied a key post which required him to be apprised of coming changes in major strategy developments, yet Goering's order was the first intimation he received that the Nazi leadership was thinking of war on Russia instead of trade with Russia.

Germany's inability to invade Fortress Britain bristling with guns and beach traps and stoutly defended by the Royal Air Force—Hitler had not learned to be a cross-Channel swimmer, Litvinov said—called for a decisive shift of plans that would enable Germany to win the war. She could not stand still. The to-and-fro battles of the Axis forces across the hot sands of North Africa yielded few victories and no economic gains. Openly and secretly, the United States was giving increasing aid to England. Hitler now reverted to his dream of dismembering Russia and using her natural wealth to sustain him in a world war which, he belatedly realized, would last longer than he had expected. In August, 1940, German troops were admitted into Finland by the Helsinki government. Moscow knew this immediately. It felt threatened but could do nothing.

Nevertheless, the Nazi government put maximum pressure on the Soviets to increase deliveries to Germany, in effect to finance a share of Germany's war at the expense of Russia's military preparedness. Schu-

[7] *Ibid.*, pp. 199-201.

[8] Trumbull Higgins, *Hitler and Russia. The Third Reich in a Two-Front War 1937-1943*, p. 66.

lenburg reported to Berlin on November 27, 1940, that Commissar of Trade Mikoyan had agreed to augment Russian grain shipments to Germany in the period ending May 11, 1942, from 1,250,000 tons to 1,500,000 tons. (By May 11, 1942, the German army was fighting deep in the heart of the Soviet Union.) Schulenburg then went to Molotov and requested an increased tonnage out of Russia's reserves. The ambassador won. The next day Schulenburg informed Ribbentrop by telegram that Molotov, in the presence of Mikoyan, had told him the total for the next eighteen months would be raised to 2½ million tons. The ambassador suggested a special message of thanks from Ribbentrop to Molotov.[9] Mikoyan had insisted, at a session with the ambassador on November 2, 1940, on the delivery of armor plate and tank turrets as the irreducible condition for any further commercial concessions from the Soviets.[10] Molotov ruled out such a stance.

Schulenburg did not know Hitler's plans for the war on Russia. He did his duty and obeyed Ribbentrop's instructions which read to extract the maximum from Russia for a minimum German return.

In consequence of German needs and Russian fears, trade between the two countries rose sharply. German imports from the Soviet Union, which constituted 5.8 percent of total imports in 1932 and fell to 0.9 percent in 1938, mounted steeply to 7.5 percent in 1940. Germany's exports to the U.S.S.R. were 10.9 percent of her total exports in 1932, only 0.6 percent in 1938, and 4.4 percent in 1940. The tempo of trade was even faster in 1941: German imports from Russia were valued at 327 million Reichsmarks in the first five-plus months of 1941 compared to 391 million Reichsmarks in all of 1940; German exports to the Soviets in the same period climbed to 269 million Reichsmarks against only 216 million Reichsmarks in all of 1940. As a result, Hitler Germany's commercial deficit to Moscow amounted to 239 million Reichsmarks when the Nazis invaded Russia on June 22, 1941. After the war the Kremlin ignored this debt; it would have drawn attention to Russian support of the Nazi war effort against the West.

In the seventeen-plus months of German-Russian trade reactivated by the August 23, 1939, pact, the Soviet Union exported to Germany 160,000 tons of rye, 193,000 tons of wheat, 793,000 tons of barley, 302,000 tons of oats, and 14,000 tons of corn for a total of 1,462,000 tons of grain; 101,000 tons of raw cotton; 11,000 tons of flax; 942,000 tons of timber (and 103,000 tons in the last four months of 1939); and 865,000 tons of petroleum; 140,000 tons of manganese; 26,000 tons of chro-

9 Both telegrams seen and copied in the Bonn Foreign Office. Politisches Archiv Auswaertiges Amt, Buero des Staatssekretaer. *Akten betreffend Russland, vom 25 Juni 1940 bis 31 Dezember 1940,* #112683 and 112684.

10 *Ibid.,* #112629.

mium; 15,000 tons of asbestos; 14,000 tons of copper; 3,000 tons of nickel; 1 ton of zinc; 184,000 tons of phosphate of lime; and 2,736 kilograms of platinum.[11]

During May and June, 1941, according to Alexander Werth, "important raw materials such as copper and rubber [in transit] were being rushed to Germany by express trains from the East and Far East to keep Hitler happy in an effort of 'appeasement' that was as frantic as it was futile. A few weeks later this copper, after processing, was used to kill thousands of Russians."[12] "I am under the impression," Schnurre wrote on May 15, 1941, "that we could make economic demands on Moscow . . . beyond the extent now contracted for. The quantities of raw materials now contracted for are being delivered punctually by the Russians, despite the heavy burden this imposes on them, which, especially with regard to grain, is a notable performance, since the total quantity of grain to be delivered under the agreement of April 10 of this year . . . amounts to three million tons up to August 1, 1942."[13]

Schnurre, like Schulenburg, would have expanded commercial relations with Russia for the benefit of Germany. Hitler's attack on the Soviet Union came to them as a surprise and disappointment. But they were officials. The top Nazi politicians took a different view. It humiliated them to beg for bread, metals, oil, and fiber from the Kremlin after they had given it an empire. The communists, on the other hand, felt bitter because they were afraid to antagonize Germany by refusing her growing demands. It afforded them no pleasure to fuel the Nazi war machine to the detriment of their own. For the Soviet Union, rich potentially yet poor actually, the deliveries to Germany were large. It disappointed them that Hitler, with a movement of his forearm across a shining desk, brushed all this to the carpet and wrote "War."

[11] All data from Ferdinand Friedensberg, "Die sowjetischen Kriegslieferungen an das Hitlerreich," *Vierteljahreshaefte zur Wirtschaftsforschung*. Published by the Deutsches Institut fuer Wirtschaftsforschung, Berlin and Munich, Fourth quarter, 1962, pp. 331-338.

[12] Alexander Werth, *Russia at War, 1941-1945*, p. 114.

[13] *Nazi-Soviet Relations*, p. 341.

XXXIII "MY DEAR HERR STALIN"

To judge whether a war might have been prevented one should know when it began. No war begins when the shooting starts. The Soviet-Nazi war resulted from acts and policies in Germany, Russia, and elsewhere between August 23, 1939, and June 22, 1941.

When Ambassador Count von der Schulenburg came to Chairman Molotov's office on the morning of June 22, 1941, to announce that Nazi troops had crossed the Soviet frontier several hours earlier, Molotov said, "This is war. Do you believe we deserved that?"[1] The communist leader's self-righteous exclamation suggests he thought his government's conduct throughout the pact period had been above reproach; Hitler was requiting good with evil. Molotov made the remark soon after daybreak and, coming from an old Bolshevik who had witnessed over two decades of violence, domestic but also foreign, by his own government (and so recently against Finland) it seemed rather naïve even if spontaneous. The Kremlin had flattered and fawned on Hitler. It had deprived its population and defense forces of essential commodities to please the Nazis. It had lent them the strident propaganda voice of foreign communist parties. Had it deserved war?

Stalin deliberately sought to avoid an armed clash with Nazi Germany. Whether his deeds conduced to peace is another question.

In the telegraphic Ribbentrop instructions which Schulenburg read to Molotov in the early dawn of June 22, 1941, announcing the Nazi invasion, the Reich Foreign Minister declared that the U.S.S.R., "contrary to the declaration made at the conclusion of the treaties that she did not wish to Bolshevize and annex the countries falling within her sphere of influence—was intent on pushing her military might westward wherever it seemed possible and on carrying Bolshevism further into Europe. The action of the U.S.S.R. against the Baltic States, Finland, and Rumania . . . showed this clearly. The occupation and Bolshevization by the Soviet Union of the sphere of influence granted her clearly violated the Moscow agreements, even though the Government of the Reich for the time being accepted the facts."[2]

[1] Alexander Werth, *Russia at War*, p. 127.

[2] U.S. Department of State, *Documents on German Foreign Policy*, Series D, Vol. XII: *The War Years, February 1-June 22, 1941*, pp. 1063-1065.

This smacks of the same sort of innocence, feigned or sincere, that Molotov exhibited in exclaiming, "Do you believe we deserved that?" Had Hitler expected Moscow to support democracy in the Baltic countries? Or resist the temptation to occupy them? It would have been just as fatuous to expect Hitler to bolster the Beneš regime in Czechoslovakia and leave that country intact and free. The "Fuehrer" knew something about Stalin if only because he understood a little about himself.

It is usual for a person, whether peddler or dictator, to regret after the fact what he did mistakenly under stress. That probably describes Hitler's feeling in 1940 about his 1939 deal with Moscow. Soviet sovietization of Bessarabia and northern Bukovina was in a special category. While Muscovite behavior in the Baltics and against Finland made the Nazis helplessly irate the eruption of Russia into Rumania called for immediate German countermeasures.

The Balkans were like a child's house of blocks. Remove one block and all blocks move. In her new postpact-and-protocol imperialist phase, Russia resumed her interest in the Balkans. Hitler wished to keep her out. He also wished to keep out his "genius" friend Mussolini whose dreams of empire included the Balkans. The Duce had engulfed Albania on April 7, 1939. He coveted Yugoslavia. Admiral Miklos Horthy, the dictator Regent of Hungary, uncomfortable in what he called the "German-Slav sea," would have liked to lean on Italy with a view to breaking up Yugoslavia and establishing a common Italo-Hungarian border. Moreover, Hungary took an irredentist attitude toward Transylvania and wanted help from Italy, or Germany, to wrest that border territory from Rumania. It follows that Russia's entry into Rumania, by weakening that state, excited the appetite of Hungary, aroused the interest of Italy, and the attention of Hitler who needed Rumanian grain and oil.

Mussolini heroically advanced into the second world war on June 10, 1940, when he thought it was over; he would now try to determine the fate of the wooden blocks of the Balkans. Stalin's occupation of Bessarabia and northern Bukovina late the same month met with a quick response from Rome and Berlin.

Italy's first move was to send her handsome Foreign Minister Ciano to Berlin. Mussolini, his father-in-law, "charges me," Ciano wrote in his diary on July 5, 1940, "to tell Hitler that he intends to land on the Ionian Islands and to tell him about splitting up Yugoslavia, a typical Versailles creation . . ." Five days later he met "the Hungarians at Hitler's residence." Hitler explains the "restless Magyars" to Ciano: "If they are certain they can do it alone, and if they are sure they must not expect any aid from Italy and Germany, who are involved elsewhere, let them attack." Whom? Rumania.

Ministers of the Rumanian government went to Salzburg to confer with Hitler on July 23 and were in Rome on July 27 where they saw the Duce and Ciano. "The Hungarians are nervous about the Rumanians' trip . . ." Ciano wrote in his diary. "They fear that Rumania . . . might ask and obtain admission to the Axis." The Axis, presumably, would protect Rumania against Russia and Hungary.

An August 3, 1940, entry in Ciano's diary reads: "Four agents of Our Military Information Service (SIM) were surprised this evening in the Yugoslav legation. We must encourage the rumor that they were only common burglars." August 6: "Mussolini talks very much about an Italian attack on Yugoslavia during the second half of September." August 11: Mussolini "speaks of a surprise attack against Greece toward the end of September." But on August 17 Dino Alfiere, the Italian ambassador in Berlin, reported to Ciano that Ribbentrop advised against any attack on Yugoslavia or Greece and against "too close" an Italian rapprochement with Russia. Mussolini obeyed and abandoned his Yugoslavia schemes and ordered General Graziani "to march on Egypt as soon as a German patrol lands in England." No German patrol landed in England.

Britain or no Britain, the Balkans refused to be ignored. The controversy between Hungary and Rumania had become so fierce that Ribbentrop summoned Ciano to Vienna. On August 30 the two Axis Foreign Ministers signed the Vienna Award. Ciano: "The Hungarians can't contain their joy when they see the map" on which Ribbentrop and Ciano had arbitrarily drawn the new Hungarian-Rumanian frontier. "Then we heard a loud thud. It was [Mihal] Manoilescu [the Rumanian Foreign Minister] who fainted on the table. Doctors, massage, camphorated oil. Finally he comes to, but shows the shock very much."[3]

The Vienna "arbitration" award tore more than 40,000 square kilometers from Rumania and gave them to Hungary. In addition, Rumania, acceding to a German demand, surrendered the southern Dobruja to Bulgaria. Crisis in Bucharest. King Carol abdicated. As compensation for submitting to multiple surgery Germany and Italy guaranteed all the frontiers of the Rumanian rump against further mutilation by Hungary and Russia.[4] To implement the guarantee Hitler put armed forces into what remained of Rumania. From north to south on Russia's western frontier, Germany now had troops in Finland, Poland, and Rumania.

Consternation in Moscow. Molotov complained to Schulenburg on September 1 that the Vienna Award violated Article III of the Soviet-Nazi nonaggression treaty which provided for consultation. Ribbentrop

[3] Count Galeazzo Ciano, *The Ciano Diaries 1939-1943*, pp. 273-289.

[4] *Documents on German Foreign Policy*, Vol. X: *The War Years, June 23-August 31, 1940*. Text of award, pp. 583-584. Record of negotiations and discussions, pp. 570-585.

instructed Schulenburg to reply that the Article called for consultation on matters of interest to both parties. But the Soviet government, having taken Bessarabia, had no further interest in Rumania, he alleged. Or in Hungary which had no common frontier with Russia. Then for good measure he added a tu quoque: The Kremlin had annexed the Baltic nations before consulting Germany, and in Lithuania it had seized the southwest corner which was assigned to Germany.[5]

Nobody was fooled by the emphasis on these formal aspects. Schulenburg came closer to the heart of the issue when he suggested that the Soviet government, "by its settlement of the Bessarabian matter with unexpected speed" had "forced" Germany, "in order to avoid military complications in the Balkans, to take quick decisioins in the matter of the Rumanian-Hungarian dispute."[6] In other words, Germany was shutting the door to additional Soviet encroachments into the peninsula and opening the gate to encroachments of her own. Molotov, however, was not to be put off. He insisted that Germany and Russia faced a real dispute. He told Schulenburg on September 10 that in Vienna the German government's conduct "had not been entirely in good faith, for it could not have been in doubt that the Soviet Government was interested in Rumania and Hungary." So, he admitted, was Germany.[7] He thereby intimated that the time had come for top-level talks between Moscow and Berlin about the Balkan tangle.

Everyone has pride in his own handiwork. The Soviet-Nazi entente was Ribbentrop's. He did not want to see it crumble. Nor did he want to face trouble with Russia while Britain shattered all German prophecies by standing firm after France's fall. On October 13, 1940, accordingly, Ribbentrop addressed a very long letter to "My Dear Herr Stalin" urging him to send Molotov to Berlin for meetings with Hitler and himself.[8]

The United States was siding more openly with Britain: on September 3 Washington announced the delivery to Britain of fifty "over-age" American destroyers which were youthful enough to do battle throughout the war. Hitler wrote to Mussolini on September 17, 1940, explaining how bad weather had delayed the invasion of England. That day Operation Sea Lion, the conquest of Britain, was postponed until the spring of 1941.

Ribbentrop's long letter offered Stalin a German eye-view of world problems. To cope with them Germany, Italy, and Japan were entering into a triple alliance. They signed it in Berlin on September 27. Ribben-

[5] *Ibid.*, Vol. XI: *The War Years, September 1, 1940-January 31, 1941*, p. 1; pp. 8-10.
[6] *Ibid.*, p. 18.
[7] *Ibid.*, p. 47.
[8] U.S. Department of State, *Nazi-Soviet Relations 1939-1941*, pp. 207-213.

trop invited Russia to join. "In summing up," the Nazi Foreign Minister wrote in a penultimate italicized paragraph, "I should like to state that, in the opinion of the Fuehrer, also, it appears to be the historical mission of the Four Powers—the Soviet Union, Italy, Japan, and Germany—to adopt a long-range policy and to direct the future development of their peoples into the right channels by the delimitation of their interests on a world-wide scale."

Nothing less than a division of the planet among the Four.

Stalin accepted for Molotov on October 22.[9]

XXXIV MR. MOLOTOV GOES TO BERLIN

Enraged by British resistance, Hitler became obsessed with Russia. Her exports could never satisfy. Her desire for expansion irritated. Standing on the Lenin Mausoleum in Moscow's Red Square, Marshal Semyon K. Timoshenko, Commissar of Defense, addressed the November 7, 1940, military parade, the Soviet leaders, as well as the diplomatic corps, and adverting to Russia's territorial gains in the past year which the "capitalist world" was forced to accept, he declared, "But however great have been our successes . . . it would not become us to . . . be content with what has been achieved. . . ." These were Molotov's marching orders. Two days later he left Moscow by train for talks with Hitler, Goering, Hess, and Ribbentrop.

The Soviet Chairman's meetings with Hitler were extraordinary. Molotov, a stolid, stubborn stammerer, Hitler glib and impassioned. Molotov, hugging the earth, eager to determine the shape of things to come tomorrow, Hitler partitioning the planet for future ages among the Four (Germany, Japan, Italy, and Russia) when they had vanquished Britain. Molotov talked back to Hitler as nobody dared since 1933. After almost fifteen months of Muscovite flattery and commercial favors Hitler would have been justified in expecting the Russian to be pliant. He found him defiant. For Molotov the problem was to hold and enlarge the empire gained. For Hitler the purpose was to restrain Russian expansion.

Molotov went to Berlin for forty-eight hours accompanied by sixty-five persons including thirteen bodyguards, two interpreters, a physi-

[9] *Ibid.*, p. 216.

cian, a cook, a waitress, and a barber. The day after he left Moscow the German Embassy wired a detailed biography for the Nazis he would encounter: Molotov means hammerer. (The party pseudonym suited him well.) He was born in a village in the province of Vyatka—now Kirov—to a father who helped keep a store. At the age of sixteen he joined the revolutionary movement. The Tsarist police arrested him repeatedly for antiwar and other communist activities. November 7, 1917, inaugurated his climb up the Soviet government and party hierarchy until, in 1930, he succeeded Rykov (also a stammerer) as Chairman of the Council of People's Commissars. On March 9, 1940, his fiftieth birthday, he was awarded the coveted Order of Lenin and showered with accolades and honors; the city of Perm, near his birthplace, was rechristened "Molotov." Molotov, the embassy's biography added, was a Russian. His wife was "a 100% Jewess." In 1939 (during one of the anti-Semitic waves) she lost her important post in the government and, according to the embassy's information, was separated from her husband.[1]

Two accounts are available of Molotov's visit to Berlin, one, a literary effort, by Valentin Berezhkov, Soviet interpreter, published in the Moscow *Novy Mir* of July, 1965, the other, the minutes kept by Gustav Hilger and Dr. Paul Schmidt, Hitler's translators. (Schmidt devotes several pages of his book, *Hitler's Interpreter,* to the Bolshevik-Nazi encounters.)

The Molotov train arrived at Anhalter Station in Berlin at 10:45 A.M. on November 12. Berezhkov writes that they were met by Ribbentrop, Heinrich Himmler, chief of the Gestapo, and Field Marshal Keitel, among others; as a band struck up "The International" Nazi generals clicked heels and stood at attention. After inspecting the guard of honor Molotov moved about shaking hands and tipping his felt hat, smiling faintly, to all and sundry. The Soviet delegation was housed in the Bellevue Palace, formerly owned by the Kaiser's family.

Hitler gave a preview of the Molotov talks when he and Ribbentrop met Mussolini and Ciano in Florence on October 28, 1940.[2] Gibraltar would soon be taken, and the Suez Canal blocked, by the Axis. This, together with action in the Balkans, particularly in Rumania, Hitler explained, "would have a favorable influence on Russia. . . .

"The Fuehrer pointed out that Italy and Germany were natural allies, while the partnership with Russia had sprung purely from considerations of expediency." He was as mistrustful, he said, of Stalin as Stalin

[1] The biography and the names of the persons who entrained with Molotov were photocopied in the Bonn Ministry of Foreign Affairs in 1966.

[2] U.S. Department of State, *Documents on German Foreign Policy,* Series D, Vol. XI: *The War Years, September 1, 1940-January 31, 1941,* pp. 411-422.

was of him. "Molotov would now come to Berlin (this communication was received by the Duce and Count Ciano with evident surprise and great interest) and it would perhaps be possible to divert the activity of the Russians to India. There was a danger that they would again turn to their old goal, the Bosporus, and they had to be kept away from it. It had become necessary to point out to them that they might not step beyond certain definite boundaries.

". . . it must be made clear to the Russians," Hitler elaborated, "that there was little sense in their expanding in areas where they would collide with Italy's and Germany's interests. . . . Stalin was shrewd enough to realize this and then, if possibly a world front against England was formed from Japan via Russia to Europe, the effect on the island empire, which was in desperate straits and still living only on hopes and psychological considerations, would be shattering."

With fine German precision a draft of the agreement between the Tripartite Bloc (Germany, Italy, and Japan) and the Soviet Union was laid on Ribbentrop's desk on November 9, 1940. The pact would continue for ten years. "Done in four originals, in the German, Italian, Japanese, and Russian languages. Moscow, 1940."[3]

To the pact, in the tradition of the Soviet-Nazi treaty of August 23, 1939, was attached a draft of "Secret Protocol No. 1." Germany would content herself with "territorial revisions in Europe" and territories in Central Africa. Italy wanted gains in Europe and in northern and northeastern Africa. Japan "declares that her territorial aspirations center in the area of eastern Asia to the south of the island Empire of Japan." And, "The Soviet Union declares that its territorial aspirations center south of the national territory of the Soviet Union in the direction of the Indian Ocean."[4]

"Secret Protocol No. 2" took account of Russia's known interest in the Turkish Straits and Turkish territory. Germany, Italy, and the Soviet Union "would recognize the extent of Turkey's possessions." In other words, they would limit or shrink Turkey's possessions. The Montreux convention on the Straits shall be modified to permit Soviet naval vessels to pass through them into the Mediterranean "at any time," whereas every other country, Germany and Italy included, but not the lesser Black Sea riverian nations, "would in principle renounce the right of passage through the Straits for their naval vessels."[5]

On paper, all was ready for Molotov. If he accepted Russia's slice of the world and her control of the Straits, the Big Four could advance over the dead body of the British Empire toward the gratification of

[3] *Ibid.*, pp. 508-509.
[4] *Ibid.*, pp. 509-510.
[5] *Ibid.*, pp. 509-510.

their aspirations. A telegram from Tokyo to Ribbentrop indicated the far-flung implications of Hitler's plan to parcel the planet. Japan's conditions for approving Russian entry into the select company of the Three was a Soviet-Japanese nonaggression pact and Moscow agreement "to stop supporting Chiang Kai-shek."[6] To give China to Japan.

On the morning of November 12, Molotov, joined by Deputy Commissar for Foreign Affairs Vladimir G. Dekanozov and several counselors and two interpreters, drove to the Wilhelmstrasse Foreign Ministry for his first meeting on German soil. Ribbentrop opened with a long discourse on the war. "England was beaten," read Dr. Schmidt's minutes, "and it was only a question of time when she would finally admit defeat. It was possible that this would happen soon, because in England the situation was deteriorating daily. . . . If, however, the English did not make up their minds in the immediate future to admit their defeat, they would definitely ask for peace during the coming year. Germany was continuing her bombing attacks on England day and night. Her submarines would . . . inflict terrible losses on England. . . . If, however, England were not forced to her knees by the present mode of attack, Germany would, as soon as weather conditions permitted, resolutely proceed to a large-scale attack and thereby definitely crush England. . . .

". . . England hoped for aid from the United States, whose support, however, was extremely questionable. Regarding possible military operations by land the entry of the United States into the war was of no consequence at all to Germany. Germany and Italy would never again allow an Anglo-Saxon to land on the European Continent."

Thanks to German submarines, American arms shipments to England would arrive "only in very meager quantities. . . . In these circumstances, the question of whether America would enter the war or not was a matter of complete indifference to Germany."

Molotov listened with poker-player eyes behind his old-fashioned pince-nez to Hilger's translation into perfect Russian. (The Moscow-born German spoke the language like a native.) Ribbentrop then outlined the partition of the globe among the Big Four. Germany, Italy, and Japan were determined to turn south for empire—away from Russia. Ribbentrop "wondered whether Russia in the long run would not also turn to the south for the natural outlet to the sea that was so important for Russia."

"Which sea?" Molotov interrupted.

The Reich Foreign Minister required several hundred words to recover and give the answer: ". . . the Persian Gulf and the Arabian sea" toward Asian areas "in which Germany was completely disinterested."

[6] *Ibid.*, pp. 512-513.

Molotov sat opposite Ribbentrop "with an impenetrable expression," Dr. Schmidt writes in his book.

Ribbentrop finally came to a halt.

Molotov declared that "as a representative of a non-belligerent country . . . he had to ask for a number of explanations." The concept of a "Greater East Asian Sphere [for Japan]" was "quite vague, at least for a person who had not participated in the preparation of the [German-Italian-Japanese] Pact." He hoped to receive "a more accurate definition of this concept. And the participation of the Soviet Union in the actions envisaged by the Reich Foreign Minister must be discussed in detail, and not only in Berlin, but also in Moscow."[7] No decision without Stalin.

The Russians withdrew for lunch before their afternoon session with Hitler.

"When greeting Molotov on November 12th," writes Hilger, "Hitler was surprisingly gracious and friendly. After a few words of welcome he launched into a long-winded speech."[8] He began with a compliment to Stalin, another to Russia, and a third to the "systems of government of both countries which did not wage war for the sake of war, but which needed peace more than war in order to carry out their domestic tasks."

Molotov agreed.

"One must give him his due," Valentin Berezhkov, present as Soviet interpreter, wrote in *Novy Mir* of Hitler. "He knew how to speak." He knew how to speak for long periods without saying anything. His speech, with translation, lasted an hour. Germany was at war, Russia was not, but both countries, Hitler said, had gained "great advantages" from their political collaboration.

"Molotov stated that this was quite correct," Schmidt noted.

If "the two great peoples of Europe" went along together they would, "in any case, gain more than if they worked against each other."

This startling revelation met with Molotov's assent.

Hitler also described the military situation: "Britain's retaliatory measures [the air raids] were ridiculous. . . . As soon as atmospheric conditions improved, Germany would be poised for the great and final blow against England." In view of that prospect Hitler had been examining his relations with Russia "and not in a negative spirit, but with the intention of organizing them positively—if possible for a long period of time." Germany needed space. "Some colonial expansion in Central Africa was necessary. Germany needed certain raw materials. . . . She could not permit the establishment by hostile powers of air or naval

[7] *Ibid.*, pp. 533-541.

[8] Gustav Hilger and Alfred G. Meyer, *The Incompatible Allies*, p. 323.

bases in certain areas. In no event, however, would the interests of Russia be affected. The Russian empire could develop without in the least prejudicing German interests. (Molotov said this was quite correct.) . . .

"There were in Europe a number of points of contact between Germany, Russia and Italy," Hitler proceeded. "Each one of these countries had an understandable desire for an outlet to the open sea. Germany wanted to get out of the North Sea, Italy wanted to remove the barrier of Gibraltar, and Russia was also striving toward the ocean." The question was how to achieve these aims without conflict among the beneficiaries.

"Germany had no political interests whatsoever in the Balkans and was active there at present exclusively under the compulsion of securing for herself certain raw materials. . . . For similar reasons the idea was intolerable that England might get a foothold in Greece in order to establish air and naval bases there.

"In addition," Hitler remarked, "there was the problem of America. The United States as now pursuing an imperialistic policy. It was not fighting for England, but only trying to get the British Empire into its grasp." The countries that might suffer from "the extension of the sphere of influence of this Anglo-Saxon power" should work together—not in 1945 but perhaps in 1970 or 1980 "when the freedom of other nations would be seriously endangered" by America. The United States should be kept off the European continent. "Therefore, he had undertaken an exchange of ideas with France, Italy, and Spain, in order with these countries to set up in the whole of Europe and Africa some kind of Monroe Doctrine." In regions where Russia was the foremost power her interests would come first.

This brought Hitler back to German-Russian relations and to the Balkans. Germany "would at once oppose by military action any attempt by England to get a foothold in Salonika."

Molotov asked why Salonika.

Because of its "proximity to the Rumanian petroleum fields," Hitler explained. But after the war "German troops would immediately leave Rumania again." Meanwhile "Germany would be prepared at any time to help effect an improvement for Russia in the regime of the Straits."

Hitler, accustomed to orate before frenetic multitudes and deferential diplomats and colleagues, found Molotov a chilling listener. When the "Fuehrer" had finished his tour of the horizon Molotov said that "the statements of the Fuehrer had been of a general nature and that in general he could agree with his reasoning." Of course it would be better if their two countries collaborated. "Upon his departure from Moscow,

Stalin had given him exact instructions and everything he was about to say was identical with the views of Stalin. He concurred in the opinion of the Fuehrer that both partners had derived substantial benefits from the German-Russian agreement. Germany had received a secure hinterland that, as was generally known, had been of great importance for the further course of events during the year of war. In Poland, too, Germany had gained considerable economic advantages. By the exchange of Lithuania for the Voivodeship of Lublin, all possible friction between Russia and Germany had been avoided. The German-Russian agreement of last year could therefore be regarded as fulfilled, except for one point, namely Finland." Was the Soviet-German agreement regarding Finland still in force? Molotov demanded. "What was the meaning of the new order in Europe and in Asia, and what role would the USSR be given in it?" These matters had to be examined in Berlin and again when Ribbentrop came to Moscow. "Moreover, there were issues to be clarified regarding Russia's Balkan and Black Sea interests with respect to Bulgaria, Rumania, and Turkey."

Hitler offered more generalities.

"Molotov expressed agreement with the statements of the Fuehrer regarding the role of America and England. The participation of Russia in the Tripartite Pact appeared to him entirely acceptable in principle, provided that Russia was to cooperate as a partner and not be merely an object. In that case he saw no difficulties in the matter of participation of the Soviet Union in the common effort."

At this point Hitler looked at his watch, and, "In view of a possible air raid alarm"—one of those "ridiculous" British air raids—closed the session with a promise of a meeting on the morrow to discuss questions in greater detail.[9]

The same day—November 12—"The Fuehrer and Supreme Commander of the Wehrmacht" issued his "Top Secret Military" Directive No. 18.[10] Under the heading "Russia" he stated: "Political discussions have been initiated with the aim of clarifying Russia's attitude for the coming period. Regardless of what results these discussions will have, all preparations for the East which already have been orally ordered, are to be continued."

The oral orders were issued by Hitler at his Berghof hideaway on July 31, 1940, and are recorded in the diary of Colonel General Franz Halder, Chief of the Army General Staff, who was present with Admiral Raeder and others. Viewed against the background of these oral orders, Hitler's talks with Molotov on November 12 and 13 and the commercial

[9] *Documents on German Foreign Policy,* Series D. Vol. XI, pp. 541-549.
[10] *Ibid.,* pp. 527-531.

negotiations between Moscow and Berlin in the last months of 1940 and into 1941 seem like the acme of deception, and Molotov's visit to Berlin and the draft treaty bringing Russia into the Tripartite alliance appear to be a monstrous hoax, a huge smokescreen to conceal from Moscow, from Mussolini, and even from superior Nazi officials that Hitler had already decided to invade the Soviet Union.

General Halder noted Hitler's exact words, some in italics: *"Russia the factor on which England is mainly betting. . . .* Russia never need say more to England than that she does not want Germany to be great, then the English hope like a drowning man that things will be entirely different in 6-8 months. *Should Russia, however, be smashed, then England's last hope is extinguished.* Germany is then the master of Europe and the Balkans.

"Decision: In the course of this contest Russia must be disposed of. Spring '41.

"The quicker we smash Russia the better. Operation only makes sense if we smash the state heavily in one blow. Winning a certain amount of territory only does not suffice. A standstill during the winter hazardous. . . .

"Aim: Annihilation of Russia's vital energy."[11]

So on the day Molotov talked with Hitler and Ribbentrop these oral orders for Russia's destruction were confirmed by the "Fuehrer." Preparations for the Armageddon of the East would continue.

In the evening of Molotov's first day in Berlin, Ribbentrop gave a dinner in his honor. Toasts of friendship were exchanged.

The morning after, Molotov went to see Rudolf Hess, Hitler's deputy as leader of the Nazi Party. Hitler had decreed, like a monarch, that in the event of his death Goering was to succeed him, and if Goering died Hess would succeed Goering. Molotov and Hess talked at length "about the relations between party and state in their respective countries" and on the precise functions of the "Deputy Fuehrer." There were parallels. Hilger interpreted.

With Goering Molotov weighed the problem of trade. "On the whole the tone of the conversation was quite friendly, and Goering revealed all the jovial character traits with which he impressed so many Western statesmen." Molotov thanked Goering for the "friendly reception."[12]

On Molotov's second day in Berlin—November 13—Hitler did a rare

[11] Generaloberst Halder, "Kriegstagebuch, Band II: Von der geplanten Landung in England bis zum Beginn des Ostfeldzuges," p. 49. The translation used here is taken from *Documents on German Foreign Policy,* Series D. Vol. X: *The War Years, June 23-August 31, 1940,* p. 373.

[12] Hilger and Meyer, pp. 322-323.

thing; he invited Molotov to lunch. (Hitler disliked being seen while eating.) A three-hour discussion between Chancellor and Chairman followed the meal. This time Hitler did not declaim, he protested: Russia annexed the sphere of influence assigned her in the secret protocol of August 23, 1939; Germany had not. Nor had Germany occupied "any territory that was within the Russian sphere of influence"; Russia took the corner of Lithuania promised to Germany. The Soviets had changed the original agreement and Germany acquiesced. Germany also accepted a revision of the secret protocol in regard to Bukovina—and Russia benefited. She adhered to the protocol on Finland although this had brought her odium in the rest of the world and expense. Hitler recognized Russia's "primary interest" in Finland, but "For the duration of the war" Germany was "very greatly interested in the deliveries of nickel and lumber from Finland. She did not desire any new conflict in the Baltic Sea. . . . It was completely incorrect to assert that Finland was occupied by German troops." Some German troops were passing through Finland en route to Norway. Germans "were somewhat annoyed" by the position of their government during the Russo-Finnish war. Germany "did not wish any new Finnish war because of the aforementioned considerations. . . . For the duration of the war, [German] interests in Finland were just as important as in Rumania."

After this long hiss of protest came the short lullaby: Germany "had no political interest of any kind in Finland, and she fully accepted the fact that that country belonged to the Russian zone of influence."

Molotov "agreed with the remarks of the Fuehrer on the revisions made" in the August 23, 1939, secret protocol. "However, if he drew a balance sheet of the situation that resulted after the defeat of France, he would have to state that the German-Russian agreement had not been without influence upon the great German victories." If Germany had vetoed the exchange of Lithuania for a piece of Poland "the Soviet Union would not have insisted." Ribbentrop interjected that Moscow had strongly urged the modification. Molotov retorted that Moscow would have allowed matters to stand had Germany objected strenuously. "At any rate, however," Molotov asserted, "Germany, for her concession in Lithuania, had received compensation in Polish territory." Hitler called the economic compensation "inadequate." Molotov conceded that the annexation of northern Bukovina was not provided for in the secret protocol. But Russia had subsequently asked for southern Bukovina too, and Germany, instead of responding to this request, had guaranteed all of Rumania (thus rejecting Russia's attempt at further dissection of Rumania). Hitler alluded to "an oral agreement" to leave all former Austrian territory, all of Bukovina, in the German sphere of influence. Molotov insisted that the revisions desired by Russia "were insignificant" compared with "the revisions which Germany had undertaken elsewhere by military force." Hitler said revision by force of arms had not been the subject of agreements with Russia. Molotov again maintained that the Russian revisions had been insignificant. Hitler said "that if German-Russian collaboration was to show positive results in the future, the Soviet Government would have to understand that Germany was engaged in a life and death struggle." He hoped Russia would "not now seek successes in territories in which Germany was interested for the duration of the war."

Molotov stammered a soft answer: the Soviet leaders "and Stalin in particular" wished to "strengthen and activate the relations between the two countries. In order to give those relations a permanent basis, issues would have to be clarified which were of secondary importance . . . there must be neither German troops in Finland nor political demonstrations in that country against the Soviet Russian Government."

Hitler declined debate. Germany "had nothing to do with these things. Incidentally, demonstrations could easily be staged, and it was very difficult to find out afterward who had been the real instigator." (Was this an intimation that Moscow might have been the instigator?) As to the German troops, "if a general agreement were made, no German troops would appear in Finland any longer." Molotov answered testily that "No new agreements were needed. . . . The old German-Russian agreement assigned Finland to the Russian sphere of influence." Hitler assured Molotov that the transit of German troops through Finland to Norway would soon end. "The decisive question for Germany was whether Russia had the intention of going to war against Finland." (The demonstrations might have served as the excuse.)

Molotov declared "everything would be all right if the Finnish Government would give up its ambiguous attitude toward the USSR, and if the agitation against Russia among the population . . . would cease." Hitler, reading that as a threat, suggested that this time Sweden might intervene in a Russo-Finnish war. He could "imagine that in the case of a new conflict a sort of resistance cell would be formed in Sweden and Finland, which would furnish air bases to England or even America. This would force Germany to intervene."

The atmosphere grew heated in the Chancellor's office with Molotov contending that the Finnish question must be settled "within the framework of the agreement of last year" which assigned all of Finland to Russia and Hitler saying "he could only repeat that there must be no war in Finland." Sweden might intervene in such a war and America too. "Would Russia declare war on the United States, in case the latter should intervene in connection with the Finnish conflict?" Molotov said this question had no relevance now. Hitler shot back that "it would be too late for a decision" when it was relevant. What did Moscow want of Finland? Hitler asked. Molotov replied "that he imagined this settlement on the same scale as in Bessarabia and in the adjacent countries." That meant Russian annexation of Finland. Hitler reiterated that there must be no war against Finland.

The dialogue which turned into a debate had become a dispute. Molotov's demand for southern Bukovina poured oil on Hitler's red-hot ire. In an effort to reduce the temperature Ribbentrop, summarizing the conversation, declared that "Demonstrations in a conquered country were not at all unnatural"; he repeated Hitler's statement regarding the temporary nature of the presence of German troops in Finland, and finished by saying "if one considered matters realistically, there were no differences between Germany and Russia."

Did he know of the military preparations for the invasion of the Soviet Union? Presumably he did not. Higher Nazi Party members than he were kept in ignorance. His summary offered Hitler an opportunity to revert to a favorite theme. Conceding that "in principle Finland belonged to the Russian sphere of influence," he preferred, he said, to discontinue the "purely theoretical discussion" and "turn to more important problems.

"After the defeat of England," Hitler explained, "the British Empire would be apportioned as a gigantic world-wide estate in bankruptcy of 40 million square kilometers. In this bankrupt estate there would be for Russia access to the ice-free and really open ocean. Thus far, a minority of 45 million Englishmen had ruled 600 million inhabitants of the British Empire. He was about to crush this minority." He wanted no diversions from this central task, no Italian invasion of Greece, no Russian war on Finland. "All the countries which could possibly be interested in the bankrupt estate would have to stop all controversies among themselves and concern themselves exclusively with apportioning the British Empire. This applied to Germany, France, Italy, Russia, and Japan."

Molotov said he had listened with interest and agreed "with everything that he had understood." But he would not comment because he had thought about these matters less than the "Fuehrer." "The decisive thing was first to be clear regarding German-Russian relations." Hitler returned to the subject of British real estate: "It was a matter . . . of assigning to nations large areas where they could find an ample field of activity for fifty to a hundred years."

Molotov again endeavored to bring the debate down to earth and territory. "He wanted first to discuss a problem closer to Europe, that of Turkey." He expressed displeasure at Rumania's acceptance of the Italo-

German guarantee without consulting Moscow. The guarantee was aimed "against the interests of Soviet Russia, if one might express oneself so bluntly." He hoped the guarantee would be revoked. Hitler said that was "impossible." Then what, Molotov inquired, would be Hitler's view, "if Russia gave Bulgaria . . . the independent country located closest to the Straits, a guarantee under exactly the same conditions" as the Italo-German guarantee (imposed on Rumania)? Russia, Molotov averred, would not interfere in the internal affairs of Bulgaria. "Not a hairsbreadth" would Moscow deviate from this promise.

Hitler said he knew of no request by Bulgaria to be guaranteed. Molotov hammered away at the guarantee. The Soviet Union needed it for national security and as a step to settling her differences with Turkey. What was Germany's attitude? "The Fuehrer replied with a counter-question as to whether the Bulgarians had actually asked for a guarantee, and he again stated that he would have to ask the Duce for his opinion." In other words, Hitler rejected a Soviet takeover of Bulgaria disguised as a guarantee.

"The talk then turned again to the great plans for collaboration between the powers interested in the British Empire's bankrupt estate. . . . At this point in the conversation the Fuehrer called attention to the late hour and stated that in view of the possibility of English air attacks it would be better to break off the talks now."[13]

That evening Ribbentrop and his colleagues supped at the Soviet Embassy on Unter den Linden. At 9:40 they adjourned to Ribbentrop's office in the Wilhelmstrasse, but five minutes later the air-raid warnings sounded and the Germans and Russians descended to the Reich Minister's sumptuous shelter; the "bankrupt" British Empire's Royal Air Force was summing up the Hitler-Molotov discussions. Ribbentrop showed Molotov the German draft of the Four-Power Pact and asked for comments; "he could only repeat that the decisive question was whether the Soviet Union was prepared and in a position to cooperate with us in the great liquidation of the British Empire."

"If England is beaten," Valentin Berezhkov quotes Molotov as saying, "why are we sitting in this air-raid shelter? And whose bombs are those that are falling so close that their explosions are heard even here?"

Ribbentrop did not reply. He pressed Molotov on the pact. Molotov evaded the issue and put questions about Japan, the Baltic Sea, and Turkey. ". . . the fate of Rumania and Hungary are also of interest to the Soviet Union. . . . It would further interest the Soviet Government to learn what the Axis contemplated with regard to Yugoslavia and Greece, and, likewise, what Germany intended with regard to Poland."

[13] *Documents on German Foreign Policy*, Series D, Vol. XI, pp. 550-562.

"I am being queried too closely," Ribbentrop protested. He would "have to consult Hitler." (And when Hitler listened to the report he raged.)

The two foreign ministers did not emerge aboveground until midnight.

The next morning Molotov and comrades left for home by train.

* * *

Napoleon, another ex-corporal thwarted by the English Channel, encouraged Russia's ruler to strike at his archenemy England by invading India; subsequently he invaded Russia and met disaster.

Stalin preferred the bird near at hand, the loot nearer home than India. He could have had no desire to liquidate the British Empire. Soviet safety lay in Britain's continued successful defiance of Nazi power; her surrender would have filled Moscow with mortal fear.

In 1939 Stalin miscalculated; he counted on the prolonged resistance of the mighty army and fortifications of France; subduing them would cost Hitler much time and blood. Hitler made the same mistake. Hence the high price he paid for Russian neutrality.

Now England stood like a rock. When Molotov met Hitler the German invasion of Britain had been postponed to the spring of 1941. The invasion of Russia was scheduled for the spring of 1941. Germany could not do both. But whereas the preparations for Operation Sea Lion, the assault on England, "shall be continued," according to Keitel's order dated October 12, 1940, "solely for the purpose of maintaining political and military pressure on England,"[14] the preparations for Operation Barbarossa, the invasion of Russia, proceeded at an accelerated pace. Sea Lion soon retreated into the dim background. Barbarossa took the center of the military stage. Yet at the center of the diplomatic stage Hitler "was surprisingly gracious and friendly" to Molotov.

Military concentrations can always be dispersed and warlike preparations suspended. None can say whether, if, instead of revealing Moscow's intention to resume the war against Finland and debauch into the Balkans toward the Straits, Molotov had accepted the role of fourth wheel to Germany's war chariot, Hitler might not have turned toward Africa and seized Gibraltar and Suez. Such a plan existed.

Why should Hitler have engaged in two long acrimonious arguments with Molotov? Valentin Berezhkov, one of Molotov's interpreters, found that Hitler spoke like an actor. Perhaps the "Fuehrer" had studied his part to perfection in order to confuse the Kremlin and conceal his bellicose purpose. Yet perhaps he really wanted Russia as a member of the Big Four. England would then be an isolated island and, with Europe

[14] Quoted by Alan Bullock, *Hitler. A Study in Tyranny*, p. 596.

behind (or under) Germany, America blocked by U-boats, Japan and Russia attacking the British Empire in Asia, and Germany and Italy attacking it in Africa, the British would surrender. It was not a mad conception for the twentieth-century micro-Bonaparte.

After Molotov had reported to Stalin and after the entire situation had been surveyed, Molotov called in Reich Ambassador Schulenburg on November 26 and informed him that "The Soviet Government is prepared to accept the draft of the Four Power Pact which the Reich Foreign Minister outlined in the conversation of November 13, regarding political collaboration" and economic relations "subject to the following conditions:

"Provided that the German troops are immediately withdrawn from Finland. . . . At the same time the Soviet Union undertakes to ensure peaceful relations with Finland and to protect German economic interests in Finland [export of lumber and nickel].

"Provided that within the next few months the security of the Soviet Union in the Straits is assured by the conclusion of a mutual assistance pact between the Soviet Union and Bulgaria, which geographically is situated inside the security zone of the Black Sea boundaries of the Soviet Union, and by the establishment of a base for land and naval forces of the U.S.S.R. within range of the Bosporus and the Dardanelles by means of a long-term lease." At the same time Molotov proposed to Schulenburg that in case Turkey refused to join the Big Four, Germany, Italy, and Russia would sign a secret protocol fixing the "required military and diplomatic measures" to compel Turkey to give Moscow what it wanted.

Schulenburg was also told that before Russia entered the Big Four Japan must renounce her oil and coal concessions in northern Sakhalin and that "the area south of Batum and Baku in the general direction of the Persian Gulf is recognized as the center of the aspirations of the Soviet Union."

This then was the charter of the new Soviet Empire: Communist Russia aspired to the control of Bulgaria and the Turkish Straits and hegemony over Iran and Afghanistan in the direction of India while maintaining that "Finland, under the compact of 1939, belongs to the Soviet Union's sphere of influence."[15]

The German government never replied to this Molotov démarche. Hitler disliked the Muscovite conditions. He had disliked Molotov's demeanor. In fact, he reacted with fury to the two Molotov days in Berlin and immediately launched a spectacular campaign of blitz-diplomacy to counteract the Kremlin's expansionist designs which conflicted with his own.

[15] U.S. Department of State, *Nazi-Soviet Relations 1939-1941,* pp. 258-259.

XXXV FROM DEFIANCE TO COMPLIANCE

A few days after Molotov's return to Moscow he asked the German government to accept Foreign Commissar Vladimir G. Dekanozov as the new Soviet ambassador in Berlin. Ribbentrop telegraphed his agreement on November 21 and in the message to Schulenburg added, "We assume Dekanozov is Aryan."

"As a Georgian," Schulenburg replied the next day, "Dekanozov is no Jew."[1] (The information was correct; Stalin, aware of Nazi racism, would not have appointed a Jew. But Schulenburg apparently did not know that Jews had lived in Georgia for centuries.)

When weather permitted Dekanozov took his family on Sunday picnics to one of the many delightful lakes-and-woods areas in the environs of the German capital. But his life in Germany was no picnic. It was a diplomatic hell. For soon after Molotov left Berlin Hitler released a hurricane of events designed to check Russian expansion in the Balkans and Finland. King Boris of Bulgaria came to the Berghof on November 18 at Hitler's invitation to discuss the entry into his country of German troops. Hungary joined the Tripartite Pact (Germany, Italy, and Japan) on November 20, Rumania on November 23, and Slovakia on November 24. The Soviet official telegraphic agency Tass complained on November 22 that Hungary had signed the pact without Moscow's approval. This indicated Moscow's disapproval. Hitler paid no attention. He was building the Balkans into a rampart against Russia.

Sweden sensed new dangers to Finland from Russia. Finland had similar premonitions. The Stockholm and Helsinki governments knew about the mounting tension between Moscow and Berlin and were encouraged by it to engage in consultations. This time the Swedes realized that further Soviet encroachments on Finland would be disastrous for them. The consultations did not escape the Kremlin. Molotov warned the Finnish Minister in Moscow on December 7 (Finland's Independence Day) that Russia would regard a Finnish agreement with Sweden as tantamount "to a liquidation of the Russo-Finnish peace treaty of March 12, 1940": the two countries would again be at war. A week later

[1] From the German Foreign Ministry archives in Bonn, #112662.

the Swedish Minister in Moscow explained to Molotov: Sweden had "considered inaugurating a political exchange of views with Finland, as a result of which the foreign and defense policies of the two countries would be coordinated." This was just the support for Finland the Kremlin abominated especially since the Swedish diplomat said the basis of the agreement "would be the status quo of Finland."[2] Molotov had revealed Stalin's hand: it was opposed to the geographic status quo in Finland.

During December the German and Finnish General Staffs planned operations together, and on December 31, 1940, Germany and Finland signed a treaty[3] whose contents remained secret, but which, in context, could only have provided for Finnish collaboration with the Wehrmacht against Russia.

The Balkan situation was more complicated. Operation Barbarossa, in the definite shape it took on December 18, 1940, anticipated that "On the flanks of our operation we can count on the active participation of Rumania and Finland in the war against Soviet Russia." German troops began moving into Rumania through Hungary early in January, 1941, "with the full concurrence," Ribbentrop informed the German envoys in Moscow, Ankara, Yugoslavia, and Greece, "of the Hungarian and Rumanian Governments." Ribbentrop's statement that, "For the time being the troops will be quartered in the south of Rumania" was designed to give plausibility to his explanation that these "troop movements result from the fact that the necessity must be seriously contemplated of ejecting the English completely from all of Greece." The number of troops entering Rumania, Ribbentrop added, should be kept vague to leave room for "stimulating exaggeration."[4] The exaggeration was not slow in appearing; it was intended for Moscow. "In Rumania," the German Foreign Ministry wired Schulenburg on February 22, 1941, "there are 680,000 (six hundred eighty thousand) German troops in readiness." Among them, technical units abounded. Behind them "are inexhaustible reserves in Germany." Schulenburg and his staff were instructed to disseminate this information "in an impressive manner" in Soviet official circles and in the diplomatic corps. German forces in Rumania, Ribbentrop concluded, sufficed to meet any eventuality in the Balkans "from any side whatsoever."[5] Not only from the British in Greece.

Ribbentrop's contention that German troops were needed in far-off Rumania to eject the British from Greece was specious and designed to

[2] U.S. Department of State, *Documents on German Foreign Policy*, Series D, Vol. XI: *The War Years, September 1, 1940-January 31, 1941*, pp. 925-926.

[3] U.S. Department of State, *Nazi-Soviet Relations 1939-1941*, p. 264.

[4] *Ibid.*, pp. 264-265.

[5] *Ibid.*, pp. 274-275.

save Mussolini's pride and army. There were no British ground forces in Greece except on the island of Crete, and assistance in the air, at sea, and in war materials was meager.[6] But Mussolini's stab at Greece had been a disaster, and Hitler was committed to rescue him. A German army moving down the Balkan peninsula to Greece, however, would have to traverse Bulgaria, and to be comfortable in Bulgaria it would have to secure its flank by seizing Yugoslavia.

Whereas Finland and Rumania welcomed Nazi troops because the Soviets had robbed them of territory, Bulgaria feared Russia's frown and an attack by her Turkish neighbor. Yugoslavia was reluctant to become Hitler's doormat and corridor. The "Fuehrer" pressed both countries hard. He told Parvan Dragonov, the Bulgarian Minister in Berlin, on December 3, 1940, that "The attitude of the Turks was stupid and provocative and there was nothing behind it. To utter threats was simply crazy. . . . The Turks knew full well that the Bulgarian attitude was guided only by self-defense against the Russian danger and that they certainly would not be better off if Bolshevism took over." Hitler urged Bulgaria, through the Minister, to join the Tripartite Pact; such a step had checked Soviet encroachment on Rumania. Molotov had promised him (Hitler) that if the Soviet government guaranteed Bulgaria it would not remove "the regime and the King." But Hitler called the Minister's attention to what happened to the Baltic countries: first a guarantee, then Bolshevik propaganda and annexation. He "was concerned only because . . . Italy certainly did not wish to see Russia sitting at the Straits, and, because he did not want to see the whole Balkan Peninsula Bolshevized."[7]

Hitler aspired to mastery of the Balkans, a consummation that required corkscrew diplomacy and constant deception. To win Yugoslavia for the Tripartite Pact the "Fuehrer" told her Foreign Minister that he wanted nothing of her; he wanted a strong Yugoslavia; she had nothing to fear from Italy; Italy had met disaster in Greece, "a classic example of the recurrent case . . . of a big power underestimating a smaller nation's ability to resist." He had not asked Italy to go to war in June, 1940, and now that "the exuberance of certain Italian patriots and public opinion had been somewhat dampened as a result of the events in Greece," Rome would be amenable to Germany's policy toward Yugoslavia. Hitler said he would intervene in Greece with massive military power but he did not intend to use Yugoslavia for transit. Bulgaria would be the passageway and would receive territorial compensation at the expense of Greece. So would Yugoslavia if she joined the Tripartite Pact; she could annex the Greek port of Salonika and therewith an exit to the

[6] *Documents on German Foreign Policy*, Series D, Vol. XI, p. 810 and p. 1115.
[7] *Ibid.*, pp. 767-773.

Aegean Sea. To make this palatable to Mussolini, who had dreamed of gaining Yugoslav territory, Yugoslavia must demilitarize her Adriatic coast. "Regardless of Yugoslavia's attitude toward these proposals," Germany intended to "carry out the measures she had planned. . . . In 3 months the situation would possibly be less favorable for Yugoslavia." This was only one segment of Hitler's brutal scheme. "The sooner order was brought to the Balkans," he told the Yugoslav leader, "the sooner it would be possible to reach an agreement with Russia on this point. Stalin was a shrewd statesman. He wanted to succeed. He was attempting it first along the traditional Russian roads. If, however, he saw that he was not making any progress there, he would certainly shift his expansion in other directions."[8]

This conversation, which laid bare Hitler's intentions in the Balkans, took place on November 29, 1940, before Moscow had sent Berlin its conditions for joining the Tripartite Pact, conditions abhorrent to the "Fuehrer." It suggests that though secret preparations for Operation Barbarossa were proceeding on a vast scale and at great speed Hitler was not unalterably wedded to the plan for an invasion of Russia. Franco had met Hitler at Hendaye and resisted pressure to join Germany in the war by taking Gibraltar. Mussolini wept on Hitler's shoulder (in a letter) and complained that the Greek mud blocked his armored division, that "almost all the Albanian troops . . . threw away their arms and went over en masse to the enemy" (what else did he expect?), and that Bulgaria's pro-Greek attitude enabled Greece to withdraw eight divisions from the Greco-Bulgarian frontier and hurl them at the nine Italian divisions. The Duce was now a military liability to Hitler. Would it be wise to attack the Soviet Union?

The immediate German problem was to establish "order" in the Balkans. Despite Hitler's threat that the Yugoslav situation would be worse in three months the Yugoslav Foreign Minister played for time; he would have to consult Prince Regent Paul. Bulgaria, equally hesitant, told Berlin she feared a Russian landing on her Black Sea coast and therefore preferred to remain neutral. At the same time Bulgaria held Russia at arm's length by contending that any rapprochement with Moscow would alarm the Turks and bring harassment if not invasion.

Undaunted, Russia courted the Bulgars. She would support them "in the realization of Bulgaria's well-known claims in the European part of Turkey." She would give Bulgaria a loan and buy more Bulgarian goods. The Soviet Union would drop its objections to "the accession of Bulgaria to the well-known Tripartite Pact . . . on condition that the mutual assistance pact between the Soviet Union and Bulgaria be concluded. It

[8] *Ibid.*, pp. 728-735.

is entirely possible in that case that the Soviet Union will join the Tripartite Pact."[9]

Stalin was prepared to adhere to the Tripartite Pact against Britain provided Russia could expand into Bulgaria and Turkey. Hitler, on the other hand, rejected Russia's candidacy because of her designs on those two countries. At stake was peace or war between Germany and the Soviet Union. Never was so much sacrificed for so little.

The Soviets persisted. After Bulgaria had refused on September 20, and on October 17, 1939, to sign a mutual-aid treaty with Russia "In order to close the road into the Balkans for the Hitlerites," the Soviet government "sent a delegation to Sofia on November 25, 1940" to "encourage Bulgaria to secure her independence in the face of the German threat" by concluding a mutual-assistance agreement with the Kremlin. "However, this time too the Bulgarian Tsar and his government rejected the Soviet proposal." Blame was laid on "the pro-fascist temper of the ruling circles of Bulgaria headed by the Tsar and Prime Minister [Bogdan] Filov." On January 17, 1941, "the Soviet government again declared to the German government that the Soviet Union regards the eastern part of the Balkan peninsula a zone of its security and cannot be indifferent to events in that region."[10]

The defiance riled Hitler. Ribbentrop was ordered to reply with stern vehemence, as he did on January 21: ". . . the German Army will march through Bulgarian territory should any military action be carried out against Greece." Hitler had already decided that such action was necessary to save Mussolini's gloomy face.

The climax came clear and unmistakable. Bulgaria joined the Tripartite Pact on March 1. Schulenburg informed Molotov of the event on the same day, adding that German troops would forthwith camp on Bulgarian soil. "Molotov received my communication with obvious concern" and said Moscow continued to regard Bulgaria as being "within the security zone of the Soviet Union." Diplomacy being what it is—part truth and part masquerade—Schulenburg assured Molotov in reply that "the accession of Bulgaria was in no way prejudicial to the interests of the Soviet Union."[11] Basically, this was correct. If the Soviet Union is translated the Soviet people, Bulgaria's acceptance of the Nazi embrace did not affect their interests. It actually deflected German military attention southward, away from Russia. But if the interests of the Soviet Union are interpreted as the interests of Soviet imperialism, Bulgaria's

[9] *Ibid.*, pp. 772-773.

[10] A. A. Gromyko and others (Eds.), *Istoria Vneshnei Politiki SSSR. Chast Pervaya 1917-1945* (The History of Soviet Foreign Policy, Part I, 1917-1945), pp. 375-376.

[11] *Nazi-Soviet Relations*, pp. 277-278.

act was indeed damaging. And Molotov and Schulenburg were not discussing human beings, they were discussing power relationships. In the joust for fair lady Bulgaria, Germany won.

With Bulgaria bagged Hitler trained his sights on Yugoslavia. Sir Stafford Cripps, the British Ambassador, his sensitive ear held close to the Kremlin wall, had not failed to notice the Soviets' mounting discomfiture; in mid-March he twice sought out Deputy Foreign Commissar Vyshinsky to suggest a meeting between Molotov and Foreign Secretary Anthony Eden. Vyshinsky said "Russia was not ready."[12]

Russia was constantly in Churchill's mind. The British had mauled Mussolini in the North African desert as the Greeks had mangled him in their homeland. Now "If Yugoslavia stands firm . . . the attitude of Russia may be affected favorably," Churchill prayed.[13]

Yugoslavia stood firm until she no longer could. As late as February 15, 1941, Dragisa Cvetkovic, Minister-President, and Alexander Cincar-Markovic, Foreign Minister, of Yugoslavia, told Hitler and Ribbentrop in a day of interviews that Yugoslavia "intended, jointly with the other Balkan States, to guarantee peace in the Balkans," and therefore did not need German or Russian intervention. Yugoslavia, the leaders emphasized, was anticommunist. She could mediate the Italo-Grecian dispute. Hitler ignored these statements which were tantamount to a plea to be spared German intervention; Yugoslavia "now had to take a clear position regarding the new order in Europe . . . by immediate accession to the Tripartite Pact. There was no time to lose . . . Germany's new methods of combat would, moreover, in the not too distant future make the Mediterranean into a real hell for England." Britain had to be driven out of Greece.

The Yugoslavs promised to consult Prince Regent Paul.[14]

March 1, the day Bulgaria succumbed to Nazi pressure and agreed to admit German troops, General Antonio Gandin of the Italian Armed Forces General Staff informed the German Embassy in Rome that "the Italian armed forces wish to defeat the Greek Army before a compromise peace might possibly be arranged." Here was the military mind—a universal phenomenon—shaping national policy in the mystic name of the "army" but hardly of the rank-and-file soldier. "The German Wehrmacht," the Italian general added, "will surely understand this."[15] To

[12] From the German Foreign Ministry archives in Bonn. Copy supplied, #24469. Cripps shared the information with the Finnish Minister in Moscow who informed Helsinki. Helsinki informed the Finnish Minister in Berlin who carried the news to State Secretary Weizsaecker on March 17, 1941. Weizsaecker passed the message to Ribbentrop.

[13] Winston S. Churchill, *The Second World War. The Grand Alliance*, p. 10.

[14] *Documents on German Foreign Policy*, Series D, Vol. XII: *The War Years, February 1-June 22, 1941*, pp. 79-96.

[15] *Ibid.*, p. 199.

save their mutilated face, the Italian generals wanted to smash the Greeks without German aid. Hitler, however, had no faith in the Italians —politicians or generals. He was establishing "order" in the Balkan peninsula. He asked Yugoslav acquiescence.

Prince Paul of Yugoslavia met Hitler at the Berghof on March 4 in the presence of Ribbentrop. The "Fuehrer" sang a familiar song: England had already lost the war; "the time had come for all European countries to adapt themselves to the coming new order in Europe. Today Yugoslavia was being offered the unique opportunity, which would not recur, to establish and secure her position in the reorganized Europe of the future." By acceding to the Tripartite Pact, Yugoslavia's territory would be guaranteed and she could annex the Greek port of Salonika.

Prince Paul said the decision was a difficult one for personal reasons: "the Greek descent of his wife, his personal sympathies for England, and his attitude toward Italy." Furthermore, Paul feared, in view of the Yugoslav internal situation, "that he would no longer be here in 6 months if he followed our [German] advice." To which Ribbentrop, always so subtle, replied he feared "the reverse might happen," the Prince "would no longer be here if he did not take our advice."[16]

Paul "reserved his decision."

Hitler wanted a decision within the next fortnight.

Storm warnings were up in the always turbulent sea of Yugoslav politics. The storm would alter the course of Soviet-German relations from defiance to compliance. The Yugoslav Crown Council decided on March 17 to accede to the Tripartite Pact. The government nevertheless procrastinated. Elements in the army and in the Cabinet were opposed to the move. Three members of the Cabinet resigned on March 21. This, Ribbentrop admitted, created an "awkward situation" for the Yugoslav government; yet he insisted that the Cabinet make up its mind one way or the other before March 26. It joined the Tripartite Pact on March 25. As a reward, Ribbentrop promised, in a note to remain secret, that when the Balkan frontiers were reshuffled Salonika would go to Yugoslavia.[17]

The storm broke loose two days later. Yugoslav troops occupied government offices and a proclamation by King Peter, age seventeen, was read over the radio announcing that he had ascended the throne, dismissed the Cvetkovic Cabinet, and appointed Dusan Simovic Minister-President.

Moscow immediately recognized the new anti-German government and on April 5 Molotov and Milan Gavrilovic, Yugoslav Minister in Moscow, signed the Soviet-Yugoslav treaty of amity.

March 28, the day after the Belgrade coup d'état, Churchill counted

[16] *Ibid.*, pp. 230-232.
[17] *Ibid.*, p. 353.

his chickens (divisions). "Together Yugoslavia, Greece, Turkey, and ourselves have seventy divisions in this theatre"—the Balkans. "The Germans have not yet got thirty," he wired Foreign Secretary Eden who had just arrived in Athens.[18] Field Marshal Sir John Dill arrived in Belgrade on March 31. Moscow was heartened. Sustained Yugoslav and Greek fighting against the Axis and British support for both armies might mean the difference between peace and war for the Soviet Union. There was a possibility that after crushing Greece the German Wehrmacht would continue southward—to Egypt, to Syria, to Iraq, to India to a junction with the Japanese and away from Russia. In April, 1941, Rashid Ali rose up against British rule in Iraq. The French puppet government in Vichy granted Germany permission to use the French airfields in Syria from which Rashid Ali could be helped.

Russian and British hopes fell quickly. The seventy divisions were never hatched. As Stalin and Milan Gavrilovic sat far into the night of April 5-6 analyzing the situation created by the treaty of amity, Nazi bombers from Rumania struck Belgrade. For seventy-two hours they rained death on human beings and animals alike. The zoo was struck and cages broke open. "A bear, dazed and uncomprehending, shuffled through the inferno with slow and awkward gait towards the Danube," Churchill wrote. "He was not the only bear who did not understand."

Churchill erred. The Russian bear finally understood.

By the end of April German armies had overrun Yugoslavia and Greece. The small British force which landed on the mainland in March, 1941, was expelled the next month. Crete was captured in May. Hitler immediately shifted more divisions to the Soviet frontier. But Bulgaria's delaying tactics, Yugoslavia's evasions and upheaval, and Hitler's inner compulsion to rescue Mussolini from the Greek mire postponed the attack on Russia for at least a month, probably for the five and a half weeks from May 15 to June 22, and thus saved Moscow, and perhaps Leningrad, from conquest by mobilizing General Furious Winter against the Wehrmacht.

Numerous signs pointed to an imminent Nazi invasion of the Soviet Union. Stalin tried to avert it. In contemplating the situation he would naturally have assessed the chances of a simultaneous Japanese assault. Many factors formed Japan's war policy. The United States was a primary consideration. Germany's plans were equally decisive. Some Japanese favored an intrusion into Siberia if Germany attacked Russia. Most Japanese powermen, however, were far more interested in China than in another wasteful Siberian adventure, and they assumed that Soviet preoccupation with German military might would compel the Kremlin to

[18] Churchill, p. 169.

cease supporting Chiang Kai-shek. That promised Japan freedom to defy America and lay hands on the immense natural resources of the British, Dutch, and German colonial empires in southeast Asia. Hitler wanted those resources denied to England. He did not think he needed Japanese assistance to defeat the Soviet defense forces. ". . . the Russian army," he said on December 8, 1940, "was no more than a joke."[19] "The Fuehrer," Ribbentrop told Japanese Foreign Minister Yosuke Matsuoka in Berlin on March 27, 1941, "was convinced that in case of action against the Soviet Union there would in a few months be no more Great Power of Russia."[20] Hitler's strategy and Japan's coincided in regard to the United States and Britain and hence to Russia; no need therefore to veto a Soviet-Japanese agreement.

En route to Berlin Matsuoka stopped in Moscow on March 25 and talked with Molotov and Stalin but, pending his meetings with Nazi leaders, avoided negotiations. In preparation for Matsuoka's visit, Ambassador Hiroshi Oshima saw Ribbentrop, who pressed Japan to attack Singapore. "This would wipe out England's key position in the Far East."[21] On March 5 Hitler ordered the closest military cooperation with Japan and, cautioning the High Command that "No hint of Barbarossa Operation must be given to the Japanese," declared, "*The seizure of Singapore*, England's key position in the Far East, would signify a decisive success for the combined warfare of the three Powers."[22] Hitler wished to encourage the Japanese who preferred southward expansion, but he withheld information about Barbarossa from those who might, if they knew of it, opt for an attack on the Soviet Union. The Nazi Foreign Ministry held the view that "The most important topic is naturally the time of *Japan's entry into the war against England.*"[23] Not against Russia.

In Berlin on April 1, Matsuoka accompanied by Ambassador Oshima met Hitler, Ribbentrop, and Eugen Ott, German Ambassador to Tokyo. The Number One Nazi assured Matsuoka that "the war had been decided, and the Axis powers had become a dominant combination." Resistance to their will had become impossible. England was left with nothing but hope. Her first hope was America but Germany "had taken such help into her calculations in advance. . . . The second help of England was Russia." Germany, however, "had at her disposal in case of necessity 160 to 180 divisions for defense against Russia . . . and would not hesitate a second to take the necessary steps in case of danger." Hitler believed "this danger would not arise."

[19] *Documents on German Foreign Policy*, Series D, Vol. XI, p. 770.
[20] Churchill, p. 185, quoting a captured German document.
[21] *Documents on German Foreign Policy*, Series D. Vol. XII, p. 144.
[22] *Ibid.*, pp. 219-220.
[23] *Ibid.*, pp. 348-349.

Now therefore was the best hour for Japan to intervene. "Such a moment would never return. It was unique in history. The Fuehrer admitted that there was a certain amount of risk, but it was extraordinarily slight at a moment in which Russia and England were eliminated and America was not yet ready."

Matsuoka agreed and revealed that he had presented the same argument at headquarters in the presence of two princes of the imperial family. But "the hesitant politicians in Japan would always delay and act partly from a pro-British and pro-American attitude." He told Hitler he had represented the Anglo-Saxons to Stalin as the "common foe of Japan, Germany, and the Soviet Union." But Stalin reserved his answer until Matsuoka passed through Moscow again. (Until he knew Hitler's view on a Russian pact with Japan.) Stalin did say that "Soviet Russia had never gotten along with Great Britain and never would."[24]

During Matsuoka's stay in Moscow on the journey back to Tokyo he and Molotov, for their governments, signed a treaty on April 13, 1941, which provided that if one of the parties became the object of attack the other would "observe neutrality throughout the entire duration of the conflict." An added declaration promised the two empires inviolability for their respective and neighboring puppet states: Japan for Manchukuo, Russia for Outer Mongolia.[25]

Matsuoka left Moscow the same day for the long trip via the slow Siberian express. His departure was delayed for an hour, nobody knew why—until, unexpectedly for all foreigners and Russians on the dingy station platform, Stalin and Molotov appeared to bid the Foreign Minister farewell. After greeting the Japanese effusively Stalin sought out Schulenburg, "threw his arm around my shoulder," the Ambassador reported, "and said, 'We must remain friends and you must do everything to that end.' Somewhat later Stalin turned to the German acting military attaché, Colonel Krebs, first made sure that he was a German, and then said to him, 'We must remain friends with you—in any event.' "[26] The words were overheard; foreign journalists rushed to their typewriters. The censor passed their dispatches.

Disquiet ruled the Kremlin. The Politburo met in extraordinary sessions. On May 6 Stalin removed Molotov as Chairman of the Council of People's Commissars and took his place. He had always had the power; he desired, in addition, to occupy the office, to have all the reins in one hand, his. The change was also an act of courage. The bear understood that Hitler could no longer be challenged, he had to be mollified by humiliating genuflections, compromise, and compliance. Stalin accepted

[24] *Ibid.*, pp. 386-394.

[25] Jane Degras, *Soviet Documents on Foreign Policy*, Vol. III: *1933-1941*, pp. 486-487.

[26] *Documents on German Foreign Policy*, Series D. Vol. XI, p. 537.

the unpleasant task for himself. What was there to do? Norway and Belgium were subjugated in 1940. Yet for a year their envoys remained in Moscow and enjoyed diplomatic privileges. On May 9 the Kremlin deprived them of their special status. At the same time Stalin withdrew recognition from the Yugoslav government with which Molotov had concluded the treaty of amity little more than a month earlier. In another gesture to appease Hitler the Soviets recognized the government of Rashid Ali, the anti-British, pro-German rebel of Baghdad. A Tass communiqué, published in *Pravda* of May 9, denied that the Soviet government was concentrating powerful armed forces on its western frontier. Everything to tame the Nazi tiger.

On May 10 Rudolf Hess flew to Scotland.

XXXVI HESS FLIES TO SCOTLAND

Stalin usually operated on the principle that others would do unto him as he would do unto others if he could. Suspicion and mistrust lie at the foundation of totalitarianism. When, therefore, Rudolf Hess made his spectacular solo flight from Germany to Scotland the Kremlin immediately leapt to the conclusion that this was an anti-Soviet plot: Hess intended to negotiate a peace with Britain so that the Nazis might hurl all their military strength against Russia. The conspiracy angle seemed all the more plausible since Hitler had long preached a crusade against Bolshevism and complained that the British were compelling him to fight them although he had never wished it.

Saturday, May 10, 1941, Churchill was spending the weekend in the country. After dinner "news arrived of a heavy air raid on London. There was nothing I could do about it, so I watched the Marx Brothers in a comic film. . . . The merry film clacked on, and I was glad of the diversion. Presently a secretary told me that the Duke of Hamilton wished to speak to me from Scotland. The Duke was a personal friend of mine, but I could not think of any business he might have with me which could not wait till the morning. However, he pressed to speak with me, saying it was an urgent matter of Cabinet importance. I asked Mr. [Brendan] Bracken to hear what he had to say. After a few minutes he came back with the news. 'Hess has arrived in Scotland.' I thought this was fantastic. . . . As the night advanced, confirmatory messages arrived. There was no doubt that Hess, the Deputy Fuehrer, Reich Minister without Portfolio, Member of the Ministerial Council for the Defense of the Reich, and the Leader of the Nazi Party, had landed alone by parachute near the Duke of Hamilton's estate in Scotland."[1]

Rudolf Hess, born in 1894 in Alexandria, Egypt, fought as a Luftwaffe pilot in the first world war; was wounded; heard Hitler speak at a meeting and fell under his spell; joined the Nazi Party in 1920; was arrested after the abortive Ludendorff-Hitler Putsch in November, 1923, and spent seven and a half months in prison where he occupied a cell with Hitler and wrote down from dictation a large part of the future "Fuehrer's" ravings later published as *Mein Kampf*. In 1932 Hitler appointed him chairman of the political central commission of the Nazi Party, and when the party came to power in January, 1933, Hess's star rose to zenith. He worshiped Hitler as an idolater would a god.

Hess, dressed in a flight lieutenant's uniform, took off from Augsburg at 5:45 P.M. in a Messerschmitt lent him by Willi Messerschmitt, the plane's inventor and producer, and came down a few miles from the Duke of Hamilton's estate where a farmer with a two-pronged pitchfork took him prisoner. After being hospitalized a few days for the treatment of minor injuries suffered in his fall he was moved to the Tower of London and subsequently to a military camp in the vicinity of Aldershot and in Wales.

Hess's arrival near the Hamilton estate was by careful design and remarkable navigation, not by accident. He had seen the Duke in Berlin at the 1936 Olympic Games and hoped, through him, to meet King George. The plan to establish contact with influential Britons did not come suddenly to Hess, it had germinated for many months behind his receding forehead and deeply sunken eyes. Documents and facts relevant to the plan offer a few clues to the two mysteries of Hess's flight: What precisely was his mission? And, did Hitler know?

The story begins in 1920 when Hess, having joined a nationalist and anti-Semitic group and fought against communists and socialists in Bavaria, enrolled in the Munich University and took courses in history, economics, and geopolitics. There he fell under the influence of Karl Haushofer, the famous geopolitician, who became his guru or mentor. Dr. Haushofer's "influence from this time on was to dominate much of his [Hess's] philosophy and his thought, and, eventually, as we shall see, was to be responsible for his flight to Scotland."[2]

[1] Winston S. Churchill, *The Second World War. The Grand Alliance*, p. 48.

[2] J. R. Rees (Ed.), *The Case of Rudolf Hess. A Problem in Diagnosis and Forensic Psychiatry*, p. 9. This book is a pedestrian, professional report by seven British physicians and psychiatrists who treated Hess between 1941 and 1946. It was published with Hess's permission given from Nuremberg where he stood trial.

After the November, 1923, Putsch that failed Dr. Haushofer concealed Hess until quiet was restored, then ordered the 29-year-old to report to the police. Hess obeyed. The geopolitician brought books to the prisoner and tried to break the bond with Hitler. Hess resisted; he and Hitler, he said, would live and die together. Dr. Haushofer nevertheless used his enormous prestige in Germany to obtain a reduction of Hess and Hitler's sentences. The visits alone of such a prominent man to their cells had improved their prison conditions. When Albrecht, his son, later asked him why he supported the Nazi regime so long, he replied in English, "Let us educate our masters." The masters were using Dr. Haushofer's books and geopolitical philosophy for their evil ends. In 1938, Albrecht told his posthumous biographer, the father changed. He had attended an Africa congress where representatives of European countries gathered to discuss colonial problems. Delegates, presumably British, who spoke with authority, told him of a readiness to give Germany colonies "provided Germany forswore all manner of expansion to the East." When Dr. Haushofer returned to Germany he reported to Hitler. The moment the visitor mentioned German renunciation of boundary revisions in the East, Hitler turned on his heel and walked out of the room. Hess's friendship with Dr. Haushofer did not suffer. He phoned his mentor the day the second world war commenced and said there would be "only a very brief thunderstorm." The geopolitician was skeptical; rains may bring floods, he warned. "Don't forget," he told Hess in conclusion, "who sits on a tiger can no longer jump off." The warm relations between Hess and Dr. Haushofer remained intact.

Albrecht Haushofer "inherited" these relations while his father was alive. Hess had been a regular guest at the Haushofer dinner table for a decade, and when the Nazis took office, Albrecht, age thirty and already a professor at the Berlin University and the publisher of a magazine, *Zeitschrift fuer Erdkunde* (he had stepped into his father's shoes and in addition wrote long plays in verse on Greek and Roman history), became Hess's unofficial adviser on international affairs.[3]

In this capacity he frequently visited England where his father's world reputation (even Stalin dipped into his works), his own talents, including a command of the English language, and his handsome face and gracious personality won him many firm friends. The Duke of Hamilton was one of these; Lord Lothian another. In 1936 Ribbentrop commissioned him to negotiate with President Beneš. The mission would have been successful had Hitler been interested in the fate of the Sudeten Germans or in peace. Albrecht, charting the trend to war, broke with

[3] Rainer Hildebrandt, *Wir Waren Die Letzten,* p. 38 ff.

Foreign Minister Ribbentrop in the spring of 1938, left the Foreign Ministry, and devoted himself to his students and his poetry. When the war broke out, however, Ribbentrop, in a mellow mood, brought him back to the information department of the Foreign Ministry.

Albrecht retained his contacts with Hess, yet through his students, notably Rainer Hildebrandt who wrote his life story, he became involved in 1940 in the secret movement to murder Hitler. He revealed his views to Hildebrandt with uncommon candor. His dual purpose was to save England from Germany and Germany from ruin at the hands of the "Fuehrer." High hopes rested on Hitler's generals. Many of them had opposed the militarization of the Rhineland, the subjugation of Austria, and the assault on Czechoslovakia. A coup d'état against Hitler had been planned in the spring of 1938 by several army colonels working under the guidance of Colonel General Ludwig Beck, Chief of the General Staff. The decision to act depended on General Walther von Brauchitsch, Wehrmacht Commander in Chief. He would not move. "I am a soldier," he declared hitching his collar; "it is my duty to obey."[4]

As Germany planned to invade Poland some top generals demurred. Even Hitler entertained a doubt. According to a dispatch of June 1, 1939 (printed in *Le Livre Jaune*), by Robert Coulondre, the well-informed French Ambassador in Berlin, "Hitler asked General Keitel, chief of staff, and General Walther von Brauchitsch, commander-in-chief of the Wehrmacht, if, under present conditions, Germany could win a general war. Both said it depended on whether Russia stayed out or came into the war. In case she stayed out Keitel's answer was 'Yes,' while Brauchitsch (whose opinion is worth more) answered 'Probably.' Both generals stated that if Germany had to fight against Russia she would have little chance of victory." The Soviet-Nazi pact reassured the generals. The quick collapse of Poland delighted them; "the brief thunderstorm" was over. But Britain's dogged resistance filled them with anguish. Nobody, not even Hitler, had counted on a war to the death with England. In 1940 Albrecht Haushofer told Hildebrandt that "Hitler was beginning to plan his Russian campaign for May of the coming year; therewith the generals would be gripped by another crisis which must be put to better use this time. Something had been learned from the unsuccessful attempts of the past."

Nobody doubted that the Nazi army could win victories in Russia but, Hildebrandt writes, ever-widening circles of the underground resistance movement were "convinced that, no matter how the campaigns went, Germany would win herself to death." Albrecht Haushofer knew that

[4] John W. Wheeler-Bennett, *The Nemesis of Power; The German Army in Politics, 1918-1945*, pp. 395-404.

"Hitler had already lost the battle against time." Hess was becoming increasingly impatient. He consulted his astrologer: Hitler's horoscope for April and early May showed "an unusual low." To save Hitler, Hess strained frantically to find means of ending the world war. Albrecht tried to channel his thoughts toward the Duke of Hamilton.

Dr. Haushofer on September 3, 1940, wrote Albrecht a letter whose length was designed to disguise nuggets of conspiratorial information in a mass of personal news and scholarly digressions. He had had a talk near Munich with "Tomo," Hess's family pseudonym, "from 5:00 o'clock in the afternoon until 2:00 in the morning, which included a 3-hour walk in the Gruenewalder Forest." Everything "is so prepared for the very hard and severe attack on the island in question [obviously England] that the highest ranking person [Hitler] only has to press a button to set it off . . . the thought once more occurs as to whether there is really no way of stopping something which would have infinitely momentous consequences. There is a line of reasoning in connection with this which I must absolutely pass on to you because it was obviously communicated to me with this intention." Hess had suggested to the elder Haushofer the desirability of getting in touch with Hamilton. Dr. Karl gave his son the name and address of a possible intermediary, an Englishwoman living in Lisbon who had recently written to Frau Dr. Karl Haushofer. "That the larger stage," the father added with pride, "has suddenly called for you again does not astonish me. Indeed, Tomo, too, on Saturday and Sunday almost expressed a wish to the same effect and was personally delightfully cordial. . . . Tomo seems to be staying here until Wednesday and wants to see me again."[5]

At Hess's request, Albrecht met him on September 8 at "Bad G." where they talked for two hours. "I was immediately asked," Albrecht wrote in a memorandum, "about the possibilities of making known to persons of importance Hitler's serious desire for peace. It was quite clear," Hess elaborated, "that the continuance of the war was suicidal to the white race. Even with complete success in Europe, Germany was not in a position to take over inheritance of the Empire. The Fuehrer had not wanted to see the Empire destroyed and did not want it even today. Was there not somebody in England who was ready for peace?"

"It is necessary to realize," Albrecht replied, "that not only Jews and Freemasons, but practically all Englishmen who mattered, regarded a treaty signed by Hitler as a worthless scrap of paper." Hitler had torn up several treaties; Albrecht named some. "What guarantee did England have that a new treaty would not be broken again at once if it suited us? It must be realized that even in the Anglo-Saxon world, the Fuehrer is

[5] U.S. Department of State, *Documents on German Foreign Policy,* Series D, Vol. XI: *The War Years, September 1, 1940-January 31, 1941,* pp. 15-18.

regarded as Satan's representative on earth and has to be fought. . . . The present war, I am convinced, shows that Europe has become too small for its previous anarchic form of existence; it is only through close German-English cooperation that it can achieve a truly federative order (based by no means merely on the police power of a single power), while maintaining a part of its world position and having security against Soviet Russian Eurasia." There was no security for Germany as long as the British fleet could blockade her. There was no security for England as long as the German air force could bomb her. "There is only one way out of this dilemma: friendship intensified to fusion, with a joint fleet, a joint air force, a joint defense of positions in the world—just what the English are now about to conclude with the United States."

Hess interrupted to ask why the British were prepared to seek such a friendship with America and not with Germany. "Because Roosevelt," Haushofer replied, "is a man, and represents a *Weltanschauung* and way of life, that the Englishman thinks he understands. . . . Hitler, however, seems to the Englishman the incarnation of what he hates, what he has fought for centuries—this feeling grips the worker no less than the plutocrats." Therefore, Haushofer junior told Hess, he did not believe seriously "in the possibility of a settlement between Adolf Hitler and England in the present stage of development."

Was not the difficulty that the right persons had not used the right words with the British?

Albrecht agreed that Ribbentrop's role in London had been a disaster and that the present Reich Foreign Minister had misinformed Hitler. But he again "stressed the fact that the rejection of peace feelers by England was today due not so much to persons as to the fundamental outlook" already mentioned.

Albrecht then named the Britons who might be approached. He especially recommended "the closest of my English friends: the young Duke of Hamilton, who has access at all times to all important persons in London, even to Churchill and the King."

Hess promised to consider the matter and send word to Haushofer senior. "From the whole conversation," Albrecht wrote at the close of his memorandum, "I had the strong impression that it was not conducted without the prior knowledge of the Fuehrer, and that I probably would not hear any more about the matter unless a new understanding had been reached between him and his Deputy."

Despite Albrecht's harsh words about Hitler, Hess had another conversation with him the next morning in the same place.[6] The implication, however, is not that Hitler knew in advance of Hess's flight, only that he

[6] *Ibid.*, pp. 78-81.

knew Hess was seeking information about the prospects of peace with Britain.

On September 10, writing to Dr. Karl from a place near Linz, Austria, and signing "R.H.," Hess referred to the matter "which is so close to the hearts of us both." He had considered the question of the contact "and arrived at the following conclusion:

"Under no condition must we disregard the contact or allow it to die aborning." Hess wanted Albrecht to write the Duke of Hamilton and ask him to come to Portugal, a neutral country, for a talk with Albrecht. ". . . the inquiry in question and the reply would not go through official channels. . . . Meanwhile let's keep our fingers crossed. Should success be the fate of our enterprise, the oracle given to you with regard to the month of August would yet be fulfilled since the name of the young friend [Albrecht] and the old lady friend of your family [in Lisbon] occurred to you during the quiet days of that month."[7]

Albrecht wrote his father on September 19 enclosing a letter to Hess for forwarding; it communicated cold pessimism: "the possibilities of successful efforts at a settlement between the Fuehrer and the British upper class seem to me—to my extreme regret—infinitesimally small." Nevertheless he suggested getting in touch with Lord Lothian, the British Ambassador in Washington, and Sir Samuel Hoare, the British envoy in Madrid. As for a letter to the Duke of Hamilton, this should be tried too, but the Scottish peer would certainly consult the government of his country before proceeding and, in effect, therefore, everything would depend on the attitude of Churchill—and that was no secret; he would entertain no peace proposal from victory-drunk Nazis bringing conditions. Albrecht nonetheless enclosed a brief yet very warm and personal letter to the Duke urging him to come to Lisbon. "I could reach Lisbon at any time (without any difficulty) within a few days after receiving news from you," Albrecht wrote. "There are some things I could tell you, that might make it worth while for you to try a short trip to Lisbon."[8] The reference was presumably to the dissent among German generals who knew about the massive transfer of troops to the Russian frontier. (By September, 1940, Albrecht could no longer have distinguished between his efforts, through Hess, to achieve an end of the war and his efforts, through generals and leading civilians like Dr. Carl Goerdeler, the former mayor of Leipzig, to overthrow the Nazi regime.)

On the receipt of this letter Hess telephoned Albrecht his approval of the draft letter to the Duke. Albrecht wrote Hess on September 23 saying the letter had gone off, via Lisbon, to Scotland. "It is to be

[7] *Ibid.*, pp. 60-61.
[8] *Ibid.*, pp. 129-132.

hoped," Albrecht added, "that it will be more efficacious than sober judgment would indicate." He sent his copy of the letter to Hess to his father who, being so eminent, would be less exposed to Gestapo intrusions. Then Albrecht poured out his heavy heart to his father. "Now as to the English matters," he wrote, "I am convinced, as before, that there is not the slightest prospect of peace." As for himself, "I do not see any possibility of any satisfying activity in the future. If our wild men obtain the well-known 'total victory' from Glasgow to Capetown, the drunken sergeants and corrupt exploiters will set the tone. . . . If this does not come about, if the English succeed in absorbing the first shock and then, with American help and by utilizing the Bolshevist uncertainty factor, are able to bring about a long-drawn-out balance in the war . . . there will be little enough left to save." He would go to Lisbon if Hess gave the order. "One thing I must be entirely clear about, however: *I* will have a political future only if I am *right* with my Cassandra predictions."[9] This is the mood that makes conspirators of scholars.

When news came of Hess's flight to the Duke's estate, Albrecht presented himself at Hitler's headquarters and, knowing the nature of totalitarianism, told some of what he knew. His memorandum first enumerated the influential, upper-class Britons "I have known well for years" and their connections with the Court and the Cabinet. These included the "present Under Secretary of State of the Foreign Office, Butler . . . he is not a follower of Churchill or Eden. Numerous connections lead from most of those named to Lord Halifax, to whom I likewise had personal access. . . . There was not one of those named who was not at least occasionally in favor of a German-English understanding. . . . Therefore when the Deputy of the Fuehrer, Reich Minister Hess, asked me in the autumn of 1940 about possibilities of gaining access to possibly reasonable Englishmen" Albrecht offered him advice on means of reaching several British diplomats or the Duke of Hamilton. Hess had preferred the Duke. Albrecht here mentioned his letter to the Duke sent via Lisbon. No reply came.

"Then in April, 1941, I received greetings from Switzerland from Carl Burckhardt, the former League of Nations Commissioner in Danzig and now Vice President of the International Red Cross whom I had known well for years." He had greetings for Albrecht "from someone in my old circle of English friends. I should please visit him sometime in Geneva." Albrecht assumed this was a response from the Duke and so informed Hess "who decided that I should go to Geneva."

Albrecht had a long conversation with Burckhardt on April 28. An

[9] *Ibid.*, pp. 162-163.

intermediary from London, whose name Burckhardt refused to disclose, had called on him in Geneva and "expressed the wish of important English circles for an examination of the possibilities of peace." In this connection Albrecht's name had been mentioned as an available channel of communication. Burckhardt had had other contacts with Britons in London and Geneva from which he had distilled the terms of a settlement: In southeastern Europe England's interest was limited to Greece; the restoration of "the western European system of states; and consideration of Germany's claims to her former African colonies provided "Italian appetites can be curbed."

Conscious of the fact that he was writing this memorandum for Hitler, Albrecht nevertheless stated in a concluding paragraph that "All of this" assumed that "a basis of personal confidence can be found between Berlin and London; and this would be as difficult to find as during the Crusades or in the Thirty Years' War . . . the contest with 'Hitlerism' was being considered, by the masses of the English people, too, to be a religious war with all the fanaticizing consequences of such an attitude." Burckhardt's outlook was just as grim.[10]

Since Hess had approved of Albrecht's trip to Geneva and probably helped to make it possible, it is safe to assume that he received a detailed report. Little over a week later he flew to Scotland.

When Albrecht finished his memorandum for Hitler and asked for a personal interview the Gestapo arrested him, took him to Berlin, but soon released him. Bravely, he returned to the underground and prepared for the July 20, 1944, abortive attempt on Hitler's life and the accompanying anti-Nazi coup. He paid for it. The Gestapo executed him on April 23, 1945, only fifteen days before Nazi Germany surrendered. Dr. Karl Haushofer committed suicide on March 10, 1946.

* * *

The day after Hess fell into Scotland the Duke of Hamilton, on air force duty nearby, called. Hess denied rumors of an impending attack on Russia. In all further interviews, until June 22, 1941, Hess said nothing about a possible invasion of Russia. He knew nothing about it. Hitler had kept the secret of Barbarossa from some of his closest aides. Only nine copies were made of Hitler's "Directive Number 21" for Operation Barbarossa of December 18, 1940, and, of these, six were locked in the safe of the General Staff. Lieutenant General Mueller testified in a prisoner-of-war camp in the Soviet Union that "already in April, 1941 it was absolutely clear to me and to others that things were moving toward

[10] *Documents on German Foreign Policy,* Series D. Vol. XII: *The War Years, September 1, 1940-January 31, 1941,* pp. 783-787.

a new aggressive war." One of the others was the commander of the German Seventeenth Infantry Army in the East.[11] Goering may have been perjuring himself when, in reply to questions by Soviet jurists at the Nuremberg trial, he stated on June 17, 1945, "I did not know until one and a half to two months before the beginning of the war" about the plans for the attack on Russia. Ribbentrop's declaration before the same tribunal that he "knew nothing in December [1940] about an aggressive war against Russia" is more plausible. Hitler deliberately concealed and distorted his purpose. Troops transferred from west to east were sent "on vacation," those shifted from Germany to the west were designated "for invasion." The agreed signal for the attack on Russia was "Albion." In these and other ways Hitler strove to keep the secret. He kept it even from Count von der Schulenburg who as German Ambassador in Moscow should have been informed. Schulenburg talked with Hitler on April 28, 1941, in Berlin. They discussed many subjects. When the Ambassador was about to leave, Hitler said suddenly, "Oh, one more thing: I do not intend a war against Russia." On his return to Moscow Schulenburg repeated the remark to Counselor of Embassy Hilger and added, "Well, he deliberately lied to me."[12] Such a thought would not have crossed Hess's mind; he deified the "Fuehrer." Moreover, from war's beginning he had been shunted off the main track of Nazi politics and replaced by Martin Bormann, a sinister figure who became Deputy "Fuehrer" after Hess's flight. Hess's eclipse by Bormann may have impelled him to the escapade to Scotland; he wished, by risking his life, to prove his devotion to Hitler and his love of the fatherland. Compared with other leading Nazis Hess was sentimental and soft, and if he had heard of the transfer of huge masses of German troops to the east he would have believed the version circulated by Hitler that they were for defense against a possible Russian attack. Hitler often explained how necessary it was to keep an army employed. After the conquest of Bulgaria, Yugoslavia, and Greece, and in view of the inability to cross the English Channel, the Wehrmacht had to be given a new task, and that, Hitler intimated, was to hold back the Russian hordes. If Hess heard this whisper he would have given it credence. All the correspondence and personal meetings with the Haushofers, all the interrogations of Hess in Great Britain and at the Nuremberg trial produced no scintilla of evi-

[11] P. A. Zhilin, *Kak Faschistkaya Germania Gotovila Napadenie Na Sovietskii Soyuz* (How Fascist Germany Prepared the Attack on the Soviet Union.), p. 120. Zhilin had access to the stenographic record of General Mueller's testimony.

[12] Gustav Hilger and Alfred G. Meyer, *The Incompatible Allies. A Memoir-History of German-Russian Relations 1918-1941*, pp. 328-329. Schulenburg, who was executed for participating in the July 20, 1944, plot against the Hitler regime, might have learned the truth from dissident generals.

dence that Hitler knew of Hess's intention to fly to Britain or that Hess knew about Barbarossa or had schemed to make peace between Britain and Germany so that Hitler could concentrate all German military might against the Soviet Union. Hess was eager to make history. He had fallen under the influence of the Anglophile Haushofers, both of whom feared for their country's fate if the war continued. Albrecht Haushofer had planted the name of the Duke of Hamilton in Hess's brain and the name buzzed and buzzed in that far from normal gray matter until it obsessed him and impelled him to fly and jump into a political void. The British government paid no attention to his proposals. He was a case for physicians and psychiatrists. From his descent on Scotland to his removal to Nuremburg in October, 1945, one or more of seven British doctors kept him under permanent observation. Three British medical experts and psychologists who submitted their conclusions on Hess to the International Military Tribunal on November 19, 1945, declared: "His mental state is of a mixed type. He is an unstable man, and what is technically called a psychopathic personality . . . he has had delusions of poisoning and other similar paranoid ideas. Partly as a reaction to the failure of his mission, these abnormalities got worse, and led to suicidal attempts. In addition, he had a marked hysterical tendency which had led to . . . a loss of memory. . . . At the moment he is not insane in the strict sense." Three Soviet specialists, Professor Krasnushkin, a physician, Professor Sepp, member of the Academy of Medicine, and Professor Kurshakov, chief therapist of the Commissariat of Health of the U.S.S.R., and Professor Jean Delay of the School of Medicine in Paris examined Hess in Nuremberg in the presence of British and American colleagues and reported on November 16, 1945, that, "His mental conditions are of a mixed type. He is an unstable person, who in technical terms is called a psychopathic personality. In addition . . . he had noticeable hysterical tendencies which caused . . . amnesia." All experts declared he was not insane and could stand trial.[13]

The fiasco of his flight no doubt produced some of Hess's symptoms and aggravated others. He reacted spasmodically to changes in his own and Germany's condition. When, for instance, he heard of the German army's catastrophe at Stalingrad in 1943, earlier delusions of persecution disappeared and were replaced by amnesia. But the brain and nervous system responsible for these pathological symptoms were there when he served as deputy to Hitler and when he decided to fly to Scotland. The key to some acts of politicians is found solely in their psychology. But Soviet authorities scorn psychology. They prefer to see conspiracy.

For Hitler the Hess episode lacked political significance; he merely

[13] Rees, pp. 217-224.

lamented the loss of a loyal comrade. He knew the purpose of the flight from a letter Hess had left behind for him. But, "Far from waiting to see whether Hess was successful in his mission or not, Hitler dismissed it as a mad idea, and on May 12, two days after Hess's flight, fixed the date for the opening of 'Barbarossa.' "[14]

XXXVII THE FUTURE BEGAN ON JUNE 22, 1941

No war in the history of mankind cost so many lives and caused so much damage as the Nazi invasion of Russia. Tens of millions of Soviet fighting men and several million civilians died. Even more millions were maimed. Germans too suffered enormous fatalities and casualties.

Europe was too small for two expanding totalitarian empires. The moment Germany guaranteed Rumania it should have been clear to the Kremlin that if communists and Nazis moved into the narrow arena of the Balkans they were bound to collide and come to blows. Yet Moscow persisted in pressing toward Bulgaria and the Turkish Straits. Hitler equivocated on Russia's surge to the Dardanelles. At times he acquiesced, in the end he sided with Mussolini who did not.

It was appropriate for Hitler to direct Russian expansion away from Europe toward Central Asia. Having heard the cliché that Russia always yearned for an outlet to a warm sea he offered her the Persian Gulf where, after traversing barren wastes and oil fields, she would find neither harbors nor commerce and only exacerbate British rivalry. A battle to the death between the lion and the bear would have delighted the "Fuehrer" and quickened his faith in victory. Stalin quite properly rejected the poisoned gift. But he insisted on intruding into the Balkans and the Baltic—traditional Tsarist objectives.

The word "tsarist" may be the key to the origins of the Soviet-Nazi war. Nothing other than the un-Bolshevik desire to retrieve all Tsarist territory can explain Stalin's appetite for Lithuania. It irritated Hitler and gave the Soviet Union another abrasive frontier with Nazi imperialism. The intention, unconcealed by Molotov in Berlin, to swallow the rest of Finland belongs in the same category.

Soviet history is a record of the struggle between Russia and commu-

[14] Alan Bullock, *Hitler. A Study in Tyranny*, p. 655.

nism. Russia won. Marxism-Leninism is Marxism modified by Lenin whose life shows he was Russocentric; it is Marxism adjusted to Russia after the 1917 revolution. In domestic affairs the Kremlin approach was Pavlovian, not Marxist. In foreign affairs Lenin applied a policy objectively nationalistic, and internationalistic only to the extent that it served Russia. Stalin was more of a nationalist and less of an internationalist than Lenin. Just as "democratic centralism" is the Soviet equivalent of dictatorship, so under Stalin "proletarian internationalism" meant imperialism and subordinating foreign communist parties to the whims and needs of Russia as a world power.

The history of Tsarist Russia is a history of expansion in all directions except north. The Soviet Union followed in the same channels when Hitler exaggerated the strength of the French army and paid exorbitantly for Russian neutrality. Stalin then undertook to regain the territories of the Tsar and extend Soviet power in the direction of Constantinople and the Straits, a thoroughly unnecessary exercise smacking of the mythology of the Romanov monarchy and the Orthodox Church.

Stalin's foreign policy, favored by the opportunities opened in 1939, became vigorously expansionist. But he overestimated the opportunities and landed his country in the great fatherland catastrophe, "The Great Fatherland War," as the Kremlin and its historians call it. Stalin assumed wrongly that Hitler would pursue the conquest of Britain. Since Germany's preoccupation with the Low Countries and France enabled Stalin to annex the Baltic republics and parts of Finland and Rumania, he expected that the greater task of subduing Britain would permit him to grab the rest of Finland and Bulgaria. Molotov's defiance of Hitler in Berlin in November, 1940, makes sense on no other premise, for Germany was stronger militarily than Russia in 1940-1941, and Stalin did not intend to challenge her in war. To have done so when she was not committed to Operation Sea Lion across the English Channel would have been deadly folly. But the consumption of territory loosed Stalin's lust for more and he forgot his native caution, forgot the practical sense of his 1925 "sit it out" speech. Advancing toward foreign objectives which interested Hitler was the reverse of sitting it out.

It follows that although Nazi Germany was clearly the aggressor on June 22, 1941, Stalin provoked the aggression by a Himalayan-high blunder. Once he realized the error he crawled before the "Fuehrer" to ward off the blow. But the die had been cast. By April-May, 1941, Operation Barbarossa was ready for launching.

Stalin's mistake stemmed, in large measure, from his wishful belief that the Ribbentrop-Molotov nonaggression treaty protected Russia from aggression. He himself had disregarded many nonaggression pacts (with Poland, the Baltic nations, and Finland), as had Hitler. Yet he trusted Hitler to observe this one. Surprised, Stalin characterized the Nazi invasion as "treachery," an expression repeated to this day by Soviet historians.

An official history by Pavel A. Zhilin, entitled *How Fascist Germany Prepared the Attack on the Soviet Union,* begins with the words, "A quarter of a century has passed since that memorable Sunday—June 22, 1941—when the hurricane of war suddenly and unexpectedly descended upon our country."[1] It should not have been unexpected. Stalin had received ample warning. But he closed his eyes to the truth, he pushed it away, for the coming of war marked the bankruptcy of his foreign policy, and since he did not want to face it he refused to believe it. The Nazi invasion stands today as Stalin's monumental defeat. He realized that this would be so and ignored every concrete indication of the impending attack.

President Roosevelt dispatched Harry Hopkins, his special envoy, to Moscow at the end of July, 1941, for discussions on American military aid for Russia. Hopkins talked at length with Stalin and saw Molotov and a Soviet general. "In Moscow, in the Kremlin," Hopkins reported in the December, 1941, issue of *American* magazine, the invasion "aroused hatred of Hitler that nothing but the death of the German Chancellor can lessen." This sounds like a precise echo of Stalin's mentality: hatred must be assuaged by death. "The invasion," Hopkins continued, "was regarded in Moscow as the treachery of a partner who suddenly revealed himself as a rabid dog." Stalin could not conceal his "sudden" disappointment with Hitler. "Once we trusted this man," Stalin said to Hopkins. "Stalin told me he had no intention of doing anything but be straightforward in his dealings with Germany," Hopkins wrote. Yet Hitler attacked without warning, without making any demands, Stalin complained.

There were warnings galore. U.S. Under Secretary of State Sumner Welles informed Soviet Ambassador Oumansky on March 1, 1941, of Hitler's preparations to invade Russia. Richard Sorge, the astonishing Soviet spy, sent Moscow on March 5, 1941, photocopies of top-secret telegrams from Ribbentrop to Eugen Ott, the German Ambassador in Tokyo, saying the Wehrmacht would attack Russia in the second half of June.[2] On April 18, 1941, Churchill, through Sir Stafford Cripps, informed Stalin, as Khrushchev disclosed in his secret speech of February 24-25, 1956, "that the Germans had begun regrouping their armed units with the intention of attacking the Soviet Union." Between April 21 and June 21, Deputy Commissar for Foreign Affairs Solomon A. Lozovsky told newsmen on June 28, 1941, German planes violated Soviet air space

[1] *Kak Faschistkaya Germania Gotovila Napadenie Na Sovietskii Soyuz.*
[2] Zhilin, p. 220.

180 times; some reconnaissance machines penetrated as much as 400 miles. One German plane, according to Zhilin, landed at Rovno inside the Soviet border as early as April 15; its cameras had exposed several rolls of film over Russia's frontier districts.

Soviet Deputy Military Attaché Khlopov in Berlin reported to Moscow on May 22, Khrushchev told the Twentieth Party Congress in his secret speech, "the attack of the German Army is scheduled for June 15, but it is possible that it may begin in the first days of June . . ."

British Foreign Secretary Eden informed Soviet Ambassador Maisky on June 2, 1941, that Germany "was making considerable concentrations of land and air forces against Russia." Maisky was skeptical. Eden had a "long talk with Maisky" on June 5 and again referred to "tremendous German pressure" on the Soviets. Five days later Eden broached the same subject with the Russian Ambassador. But Maisky, in the spirit of Stalin, said "Russia regarded her relations with Germany as governed by the Non-Aggression Pact of 1939 and felt no anxiety about the German concentration of troops."[3]

A week before the invasion, Sorge, "overcoming incredible difficulties and risking his life, was able to send Moscow," Zhilin writes, "one short but supremely important dispatch: 'War begins June 22.' "

Stalin refused to credit these and similar warnings. He appears to have believed that there was still room for diplomatic maneuvering and he tried such a maneuver in the famous Tass communiqué released June 14, 1941, which said the increasing number of "rumors" about "an early war" between Russia and Germany were nothing but clumsy propaganda by forces hostile to the Soviet Union and Germany "and interested in extending the war." Both countries, it added, are loyal to the terms of the Ribbentrop-Molotov nonaggression pact. Therefore the rumors "are without foundation." The movement of German troops to the east, "one must assume," has "no bearing on Soviet-German relations." Equally, any talk about Russian preparations for war were "obviously absurd."

"The Tass communiqué of June 14," the *History of the Great Fatherland War* affirms, "reflected J. V. Stalin's incorrect evaluation of the military-political situation that had developed at the time. The communiqué, published in the days when the war already stood on our threshold, misguided the Soviet people, weakened the vigilance of the Soviet nation and of its armed forces."[4]

[3] Anthony Eden, *The Memoirs of Anthony Eden, Earl of Avon. The Reckoning*, pp. 308-314.

[4] *Istoria Velikoi Otechestvennoi Voiny Sovietskovo Soyuza 1941-1945*. Vol. I, p. 404. This massive six-volume work was prepared by the Soviet Communist Party's Institute of Marxism-Leninism and published by the Ministry of Defense.

The communiqué failed both as an olive branch and as a magic wand that would make the war vanish. It was not published in Germany and elicited no response from the Nazi government. It did indicate to Stalin's subordinates that he had no ear for such "rumors." He continued to believe, Alexander M. Nekrich writes, that "England was only looking for a chance to provoke a Soviet-German conflict."[5]

Stalin saw the entire situation in terms of "provocations." Nekrich quotes Chief Marshal of Artillery, N. N. Voronov, as saying, "J. V. Stalin assumed that 'war between Fascist Germany and the Soviet Union can break out only as a result of a provocation by the Fascist military' and fears those provocations more than anything else."[6]

"Provocation" shifted the blame to others. Stalin's mind rebelled against accepting the dread responsibility for the four-year unexampled calamity about to descend on the nation whose destiny he had held in his hand so long. Nekrich, whose book appeared in Moscow in 1965, attributes Stalin's behavior during this fateful period to "the schematic nature of his understanding of the outside world regarding which he could in fact judge only from the information he received and, for the most part, which he wished to receive. He had never before this time left the Soviet Union. Incidentally, he traveled very little in his country. His statements, speeches and declarations show that in the prewar years he considered England the chief enemy of the Soviet state. In 1941 this feeling must have been intensified because Winston Churchill, the experienced and shrewd politician and old foe of the Soviet government, was Prime Minister of Britain. There is no doubt that the flight to England of Rudolf Hess, Hitler's deputy, reinforced Stalin's suspicion regarding the intrigues of 'perfidious Albion.' "[7]

Stalin did not trust Churchill. He trusted Hitler. When war and bombings came there was not even an air-raid shelter in the Kremlin for the topmost leaders.

Colonel General M. P. Kirponos, commander of the Kiev military district, wrote a letter to Stalin at this juncture referring to the concentration of German troops on the Bug River and urging that, in view of the expected attack, 300,000 civilians be moved out of the area and antitank obstructions be built. In reply Stalin said "such preparations would provoke the Germans and no cause should be given for an attack."[8]

On June 18 a German sergeant major crossed over into the Soviet lines and stated that while drunk he had struck an officer and, since this

[5] *June 22, 1941*, p. 126.
[6] *Ibid.*, p. 127.
[7] *Ibid.*, pp. 131-132.
[8] *Ibid.*, pp. 139-140.

happened at the front, he fled because he expected to be executed. The German invasion, he said, would commence at 4 A.M. on June 22 along the length of the Soviet-German frontier. Men and officers who heard of the deserter's report were disturbed but the first reaction of the commanding general was, "No use beating an alarm."[9]

Stalin's June 14 communiqué had the effect of relaxing tension in forward positions: "Commanders no longer slept in barracks. Soldiers began to undress at night."[10]

For weeks Stalin had striven to drive away reality. The result was a kind of eerie void where fact had no franchise and hundreds who knew the hard, ugly truth wondered how they could penetrate to the brain of the maniacal man on the summit and make him see what persons on the plain had no trouble in discerning. This sense of frustration, accompanied by a powerful impulse to break through to him, seized even the highest German officials in Moscow, notably Gustav Hilger, counselor of embassy, who was born in Moscow, lived there for many years, and married a Russian woman. "Everything indicated," Hilger felt, "that he [Stalin] thought Hitler was preparing a game of extortion in which threatening military moves would be followed by sudden demands for economic or even territorial concessions." Hilger tried to convince his ambassador, Count von der Schulenburg, that they must enlighten the Soviet government "about the seriousness of the situation." Schulenburg protested that he and Hilger would be guilty of treason if they warned the Kremlin of the impending attack. "I argued, however,"

[9] *Ibid.*, pp. 144-145.

[10] *Ibid.*, p. 143. Alexander Moiseyevich Nekrich's book, approved for publication on April 1, 1965, before the post-Khrushchev Brezhnev-Kosygin-Suslov leadership felt secure enough to reverse Khrushchev's anti-Stalin line, aroused a furor in the Soviet Union. Nekrich, a Doctor of Historical Science and candidate for member-correspondent of the Academy of Sciences of the Soviet Union, lost that status, and on July 8, 1967, the London *Times* and the Paris *Le Monde* reported from Moscow that he had been expelled from the Soviet Communist Party. A very lengthy review of *June 22, 1941* by G. A. Deborin and B. S. Telpukhovsky in *Voprosi Istorii KPSS* (Questions of the History of the CPSU) of September, 1967, stated, "It is not surprising that Nekrich's booklet has met with the approval of the most reactionary press of the capitalist countries, which has even published a portrait of the author." Nekrich is accused of a "departure from Marxism . . . Like a true bourgeois historian, the author concentrates attention on personalities, ignoring the social classes which stand behind those personalities . . . From the moment when the Hitlerites seized power in Germany," the two reviewers pretend, "and right up to the end of the world war, the party, the government and the entire Soviet people knew that the chief enemy of the Soviet Union and of all progressive humanity was Hitlerite Germany." They would be hard put to prove this. The Moscow monthly *Novy Mir* gave Nekrich's revealing book a favorable review. Many of Nekrich's sources were Red Army marshals and generals who smarted under the obloquy of their early defeats in the war with the Nazis and wished to show where the blame lay. They were particularly vocal during the "liberal" era of Khrushchev, who also had a score to settle with Stalin. Nekrich, as well as Zhilin, took advantage of this temporary political "thaw" to tell part of the truth about Stalin.

Hilger writes, "that too much was at stake, and that we should not let any concern about our own existence deter us from such a desperate step. I finally allayed his misgivings and obtained his permission to arrange" a secret meeting with Vladimir G. Dekanozov, Soviet Ambassador in Berlin who was visiting Moscow. Dekanozov, accompanied by V. N. Pavlov, Molotov's interpreter, came to lunch at Schulenburg's residence where the Count and Hilger "talked and talked . . . Our efforts proved to be a complete failure." Although the Germans assured their guests that they were acting on their own initiative Dekanozov "kept asking us with maddening stubbornness whether we were speaking at the request of the German government; otherwise, he said, he could not submit our statement to his superiors. . . . Obviously, he could not imagine that we were knowingly and deliberately incurring the greatest danger for the purpose of making a last effort to save the peace. The more we talked to him, the more it became clear that he had no comprehension of the good will that moved us." (Schulenburg, a fervent anti-Nazi, was executed for participating in the July 20, 1944, plot against Hitler.) "Perhaps it was the logical and obvious thing for him to think that we were playing Hitler's game. . . . If I am correct in assuming that Stalin believed Hitler was bluffing, we have a plausible explanation as to why he disregarded the many warnings he was given. The very fact that several sources predicted the German invasion for the same date must have confirmed his suspicion that the story had been planted by the Germans. In any event, Dekanozov acted strictly according to Stalin's directives . . . to act as if nothing was wrong with the German-Soviet relationship."[11] The German-Soviet relationship was Stalin's handiwork; therefore nothing could be wrong with it.

Fixing the responsibility for the disasters that flowed from this miscalculation is not merely a matter of authenticating historical truth. Stalin's rejection of all warning cost many lives. Zhilin, reflecting the bitterness of the military, acknowledges the aggressor's inherent advantage of surprise. But "If," he adds, "the troops in the Soviet frontier regions had been alerted by the supreme military leadership several months or even several weeks earlier about the possibility of a surprise attack by Fascist Germany and if they had been brought up to full combat readiness there can be no doubt that the fighting would have gone differently."[12]

Stalin's morbid complacency engendered by the pact-and-protocol of August 23, 1939, was not the only evil rooted in the arrangements made that day. Zhilin, summarizing Russian expansion initiated by those documents, shows how harmful it was to Soviet interests. "Thus," he writes,

[11] Gustav Hilger and Alfred B. Mever, *The Incompatible Allies*, pp. 330-332.
[12] P. 227.

"the northwestern, western, and southern frontiers of the U.S.S.R. were advanced 150-200 to 300 kilometers during the circumstances attending the beginnings of the second world war. But," he comments, "the existence of the new national boundary did not guarantee a safe defense. It was necessary to strengthen the new frontier, to give it a stable defensive system and modern fortifications equipped with mechanical weapons. This could not be accomplished in one or one and a half years. In the summer of 1941 the new national frontier had only the most primitive field fortifications without sufficient development in depth." To make matters much worse, the 1939 permanent frontier defenses were dismantled. "The defense of the western frontiers of the U.S.S.R. was complicated," Zhilin explains, "by the fact that the old national frontier, backed by powerfully fortified districts, was significantly weakened and lost its stability because the greater part of those fortified districts was disarmed." As a result, he asserts, "there was no sufficiently fortified line" deep in Russia where the defense against the enemy could have been organized in the initial period of the war.[13]

Nekrich, leaning on high military authorities, makes the same point: "A serious error, which had grave consequences in the early stages of the war, was committed as a result of the decision to destroy the old (1939) frontier fortifications in connection with the building of a new defense line. The destruction of the old frontier was carried out speedily, but the construction of the new line moved slowly." Nekrich then cites a report received on April 15, 1941, by Defense Commissar Timoshenko from the general in charge asserting that "the fortified districts being built on our western borders are, for the most part, not combat-ready."[14]

Far, therefore, from adding to the Soviet Union's security the annexations of 1939-1940 actually undermined it. Zhilin found the condition so harrowing that he returned to it again: "This was a period when the old national frontier was dismantled and the new one was being equipped and neither the one nor the other had sufficient mechanical equipment and fire power."[15]

The trouble, Zhilin mourns, was that the plans for the reconstruction of the fortifications did not take into account the sudden intrusion of the enemy. I suggest there were two ways of dealing with such a problem: Stalin might have informed Hitler that the new defenses were not ready or the Kremlin should have remained behind its 1939 boundaries and refrained from annexations. All the foreign territories annexed by the Soviet government with Hitler's permission in 1939 and 1940 were seized by the Nazi Wehrmacht within less than a week of June 22, 1941. The

[13] Zhilin, pp. 211-212.
[14] P. 83. Nekrich's critics do not meet this argument.
[15] P. 226.

Germans, often aided by local inhabitants who hated their recent Red conquerors, captured hordes of prisoners and inflicted hills of casualties in the areas. Russia's war effort would have been furthered if no Soviet boot had ever trod there. Those regions served not as a buffer but as a catapult accelerating the Wehrmacht's progress to the great population centers of Russia.

After four years of some of the bloodiest and most dramatic battles in history, the Nazi invaders were ejected and Russia again advanced beyond her borders. The Soviet-Nazi war, ending in Germany's collapse, saved Europe and spared America. This is one way of judging it. It was not Stalin's duty or intention, however, to save the West. His primary concern should have been the defense of Soviet interests by keeping Russia at peace. Here he foundered. From the point of view of the welfare of the Soviet people the war with Germany was an unmitigated disaster, for apart from the death and devastation, it saddled the Soviet Union with an empire. Therewith began the future—even unto this day.

ACKNOWLEDGMENTS

Many persons helped me gather the material that went into this book; I am grateful to all of them.

I enjoyed the privilege and pleasure of doing research in the archives of the German Foreign Ministry in Bonn, in the British Foreign Office records in London, and in the Quai d'Orsay in Paris. For weeks during the summer of 1966 I spent several hours each working day in the Bonn Ministry where, thanks to Dr. Klaus Weinandy and Dr. Erwin Wickert, heaps of files containing original documents were piled up on a table in an unoccupied office assigned to me. I was free to peruse everything in them and mark the pages that interested me. As soon as I had studied one heap it was removed and another brought in. I found numerous papers not included in the official British and American volumes of captured German Foreign Ministry documents or elsewhere. Those on the secret Soviet-German military collaboration in the 1920's and 30's, on the Soviet-Nazi talks in 1936-37 and the Soviet-Nazi negotiations in the spring and summer of 1939 are particularly revealing. I brought home to Princeton more than two hundred pages of photocopies.

Fortunately, the British Foreign Office had, while I was writing this book, reduced its fifty-year rule to thirty years, making available documents until 1938. Mr. Norman Evans, Mrs. Olive D'Arcy Hart, and Miss Deirdre Randall, my assistant, helped dig out the papers germane to my subject in the Public Record Office. However, the Foreign Office itself had withdrawn some files from the P.R.O. for study by Mr. Rohan Butler, coeditor, with Sir Llewellyn Woodward, of *Documents on British Foreign Policy 1919-1939*. Mr. Peter T. Hayman, Deputy Permanent Under Secretary of the Foreign Office, put me in touch with Mr. Butler who graciously ordered several photostats for me. Miss June Standing of the Foreign Office Library was good enough to send me an enlarged photostat of the original German-language dispatch telegraphed by Count von der Schulenburg on Sir Stafford Cripps' July, 1940 interview with Stalin.

The French Ministry of Foreign Affairs is not distinguished by an eagerness to display its modern treasures before historians. But M. François Puaux, Minister Director for European Affairs, intervened with M. Jean Lalois, keeper of the Ministry's archives, and I was given access to exceedingly interesting files dating back to 1917 and 1918. Mlle. Jacqueline Chartraire volunteered to decipher one long handwritten document.

I have used for this book the copious notes made in the 1920's and 1930's of extended interviews with Soviet Foreign Commissar Chicherin, Maxim M. Litvinov, Soviet Ambassador Rakovsky, Karl Radek, Borodin on his activities in China, and Karakhan, who also handed me a folder of secret letters and the text of a hitherto unpublished resolution whose full significance I did not understand until much later. Rich additional Soviet material was mined in 1965 in the Trotsky Archive of the Harvard University Library where, with the permission of Professor Merle Fainsod and Miss Carolyn E. Jakeman, I obtained several thousand pages of Xeroxed documents.

On annual visits to Rome during the three years and ten months I wrote this book I interviewed Roberto Gaja, Director General for Political Affairs in the Ministry of Foreign Affairs; Pietro Quaroni, former Italian Ambassador to Moscow; Mario Toscano, a senior officer of the Foreign Ministry and author of important volumes on international politics; and had a most rewarding visit with Professor Renzo De Felice, biographer of Mussolini, at which Dr. Piero Melograni assisted Gordon A. Ewing and C. R. Stout, of the U.S. Embassy in Rome, and Paulo Milano, a prominent Italian publicist, made the appointments.

Lord Strang, whom I had known when he served in the British Embassy in Moscow and who was Permanent Under Secretary of the Foreign Office from January, 1949, to December, 1953, received me repeatedly, on my annual sojourns in London, to discuss in detail the knotted international situation that arose in the spring and summer of 1939 when the Soviets negotiated simultaneously with the British and French governments and with the Nazis. Strang participated in those negotiations.

Ambassador Max Jakobson, Finland's Permanent Representative to the United Nations, cooperated fully while I was coping with the problem of Soviet-Finnish relations in 1939-40. He gave me of his time and arranged that I see Ralph Enckell, the Finnish Ambassador in Stockholm. Ambassador Enckell, in turn, arranged a meeting for me in Helsinki with Ambassador Eero Wuori, Chef de Cabinet of President Urho Kekkonen. On that trip to the Finnish capital I had a fruitful off-the-record hour with U.S. Ambassador Tyler Thompson.

Colonel Boguslaw Miedzinski, President of the Senate of pre-1939 Poland, and Jan Weinstein, a scholar writing about prewar Polish politics, spent many hours with me in London sharing their experiences and knowledge. Leopold Labedz, Coeditor of the *Survey* of London, another authority on Poland, whose policies are central to any treatment of the period before and after the second world war, made many contributions to my library on Polish affairs. Mr. Labedz seems to read everything on everything pertaining to the communist world and he is a generous giver.

Foy D. Kohler answered my queries when he was U.S. Ambassador in Moscow and after his promotion to Deputy Under Secretary for Political Affairs in the State Department. The offices of Senator Clifford P. Case and of the late Senator E. L. Bartlett (Miss Mary A. Nordale in particular) responded with alacrity when I asked for data available in Washington.

Occasional research tasks were performed for me in West Germany by Walter Schultz-Dieckmann of Hamburg, Hermann Weber, an author on communist politics in Mannheim, Margarete Buber-Neumann in Frankfurt, and Carola Stern in Cologne; and by Professor Nina N. Berberova of Princeton University, Harry Sigmond of Philadelphia, Pa.; Professor Sidney Ratner of Rutgers University, New Brunswick, N.J.; Mrs. F. A. O. Schwarz, Jr., in Princeton; Miss Deirdre Randall of New York; and by three Princeton University undergraduates, each of whom: Joel Epstein, James Barkás, and David T. Fisher, did my "leg" work and xeroxing in successive years in the Princeton University libraries. The three students needed brains as well as brawn for their work and they were well-furnished with both.

The entire manuscript of this book was read by Don Wolfe, Professor of Creative Writing at Brooklyn College, by Miss Randall, and by Cass Canfield, Jr., all of whom made valuable editorial suggestions. My senior son George read eleven chapters and, as usual, was my severest, yet constructive, critic. Ambassador Jakobson offered comments on the chapter about the 1939-40 Winter War on which he has written an authoritative book. Lord Strang read several chapters and wrote critical remarks. Professor Berberova allowed me to read many chapters to her; I like to try my writing for sound. It is a pleasure to note the meticulous, conscientious copy-editing of the manuscript by Miss Julie Eidesheim.

P.S.

Translations. Except where otherwise stated, all translations from foreign languages are mine.

Italics. I use no italics. Any italics in the text are from the original quotations.

Spelling. In transliterating from the Russian I aim to be phonetic.

Russian names. I have used the Russian spelling of Russian names whenever possible. But it is not always possible. Thus Trotsky's first name in Russian is Lev and so is Karakhan's. But in foreign languages, Trotsky is usually called Leon and Karakhan Leo; Borodin's first name is Mikhail and so is President Kalinin's; but abroad Kalinin is Mikhail and Borodin Michael. I have followed this usage.

Needless to say, the responsibility for this book is mine, not in any degree that of the researchers, authorities interviewed, or of the manuscript readers.

LOUIS FISCHER

BIBLIOGRAPHY

BOOKS

Angress, Werner T. *Stillborn Revolution. The Communist Bid for Power in Germany, 1921-1923*. Princeton, N.J.: Princeton University Press, 1963.

Association for International Understanding, The. *Chronology of Events in China, 1911-1927*. With a Foreword by Sir Frederick Shyte. London: Association for International Understanding, 1927.

Auswaertiges Amt (German Foreign Office). *Dokumente zur Vorgeschichte des Krieges*. Nr. 2. Berlin: Reichsdruckerei, 1939.

Baker, Ray Stannard. *Woodrow Wilson and World Settlement. Written from His Unpublished and Personal Material*. Vols. I and III. Garden City, N.Y.: Doubleday, Page Co., 1922.

Balabanoff, Angelica. *Impressions of Lenin*. Ann Arbor, Mich.: University of Michigan Press, 1964.

Barnett, A. Doak. *China on the Eve of Communist Takeover*. New York: Frederick A. Praeger, Inc., 1963.

———. *Communist China—Continuing Revolution*. New York: Foreign Policy Association, 1962.

Baynes, Norman H. (Ed.). *The Speeches of Adolf Hitler. April 1922-August 1939*. Vols. I and II. Issued under the auspices of the Royal Institute of International Affairs, London. London-New York-Toronto: Oxford University Press, 1942.

Beaufre, André. *Le Drame de 1940 (par) Général Beaufre*. Paris: Plon, 1965.

Belden, Jack. *China Shakes the World*. New York: Harper & Brothers, 1949.

Beloff, Max. *The Foreign Policy of Soviet Russia 1929-1941*. Vols. I and II. New York-London-Toronto: Oxford University Press, 1947.

Bergson, Abram. *The Real National Income of Soviet Russia Since 1928*. Cambridge, Mass.: Harvard University Press, 1961.

Blet, Pierre; Martini, Angelo; and Schneider, Burkhart (Eds.). *Le Saint Siège et la guerre en Europe Mars 1939-Août 1940. Citta del Vaticano* (Rome): Libreria editrice Vaticano, 1965.

Blücher, Wipert von. *Deutschlands Weg Nach Rapallo—Erinnerungen Eines Mannes aus Dem Zweiten Gliede*. Wiesbaden, 1951.

Borkenau, Franz. *The Spanish Cockpit. An Eye-Witness Account of the Political and Social Conflicts of the Spanish Civil War.* Ann Arbor, Mich.: University of Michigan Press, 1963.

———. *World Communism. A History of The Communist International.* New Introduction by Raymond Aron. Ann Arbor, Mich.: University of Michigan Press, 1962.

Bowers, Claude G. *My Mission to Spain. Watching the Rehearsal for World War II.* New York: Simon and Schuster, 1954.

Brandt, Conrad. *Stalin's Failure in China—1924-1927.* Cambridge, Mass.: Harvard University Press, 1958.

Brandt, Conrad; Schwartz, Benjamin; and Fairbank, John K. *A Documentary History of Chinese Communism.* New York: Atheneum, 1952.

British Blue Book. Army. *The Evacuation of Russia, 1919.* Cmd. 818. London: His Majesty's Stationery Office, no date.

———. *Lausanne Conference on Near Eastern Affairs, 1922-1923.* Cmd. 1814. London: His Majesty's Stationery Office, 1923.

———. *Papers Relating to the International Economic Conference, Genoa, April-May, 1922.* Cmd. 1766. London: His Majesty's Stationery Office, 1922.

———. *Communist Papers.* Cmd. 2682. London: His Majesty's Stationery Office, 1926.

———. *A Selection of Papers Dealing with the Relations between His Majesty's Government and the Soviet Government, 1921-7.* Cmd. 2895. London: His Majesty's Stationery Office, 1927.

British White Book. *Correspondence between His Majesty's Government and the Soviet Government respecting relations between the Two Governments.* Cmd. 1869. London: His Majesty's Stationery Office, 1923.

British White Paper. *Russia No. 2. (1927) Documents Illustrating the Hostile Activities of the Soviet Government and the Third International against Great Britain.* Cmd. 2874. London: His Majesty's Stationery Office, 1927.

Budurowycz, Bohdan B. *Polish-Russian Relations 1932-1939.* New York: Columbia University Press, 1963.

Bullock, Alan. *Hitler. A Study in Tyranny.* New York: Torchbooks (Harper & Row), 1962.

Butler, J. R. M. (Ed.). *History Of The Second World War.* Vol. II. *Grand Strategy. September 1939-June 1941.* London: United Kingdom Military Series, His Majesty's Stationery Office, 1957.

Callwell, Major General Sir C. E. *Field-Marshal Sir Henry Wilson, His Life and Diaries.* Vol. II. London: Cassell and Co. Ltd., 1927.

Carr, Edward Hallett. *Conditions of Peace.* New York: The Macmillan Co., 1942.

———. *A History of Soviet Russia.* Vol. III. *The Bolshevik Revolution. 1917-1923.* New York: The Macmillan Co., 1951.

Carsten, Francis L. *Reichswehr und Politik, 1918-1933.* Cologne: Kiepenheuer & Witsch, 1964.

Cheng, Tien-fong. *A History of Sino-Russian Relations.* Introduction by John Leighton Stuart. Washington, D.C.: Public Affairs Press, 1957.

Chiang Chung-cheng (Chiang Kai-shek). *Soviet Russia in China. A Summing Up at Seventy.* New York: Farrar, Straus & Cudahy, 1957.

Churchill, Winston S. *The Second World War. The Gathering Storm.* Boston:

Houghton Mifflin Co., 1948.
———. *The Second World War. The Grand Alliance.* Boston: Houghton Mifflin Co., 1950.
———. *The World Crisis, 1916-1918.* Vol. II. New York: Charles Scribner's Sons, 1927.
Ciano, Count Galeazzo. *The Ciano Diaries 1939-1943.* Hugh Gibson, editor. Introduction by Sumner Welles. Garden City, N.Y.: Doubleday, 1946.
Colvin, Ian. *Vansittart in Office. The Origins of World War II.* London: Victor Gollancz, 1965.
Conquest, Robert. *The Great Terror. Stalin's Purge of the Thirties.* New York: The Macmillan Co., 1968.
Craig, Gordon A. and Gilbert, Felix (Eds.). *The Diplomats, 1919-1939.* Princeton, N.J.: Princeton University Press, 1953.
Curzon, The Hon. George N., M.P. *Persia and the Persian Question.* London: Longmans Green & Co., 1892.
D'Abernon, Lord. *An Ambassador of Peace. Lord D'Abernon's Diary.* With historical notes by Maurice Alfred Gerothwohl. Vol. I. *From Spa (1920) to Rapallo (1922).* Vol. II. *The Years of Crisis. June 1922-December 1923.* London: Hodder & Stoughton Ltd., 1929. Vol. III. *The Years of Recovery. January 1924-October 1926.* London: Hodder & Stoughton Ltd., 1930.
———. *Portraits and Appreciations.* London: Hodder & Stoughton Ltd., 1931.
Dallin, David J. *The New Soviet Empire.* New Haven: Yale University Press, 1951.
———. *The Rise of Russia in Asia.* New Haven: Yale University Press, 1949.
———. *Soviet Russia's Foreign Policy 1939-1942.* Translated by Leon Dennen. New Haven: Yale University Press, 1942.
Davies, Joseph E. *Mission to Moscow.* New York: Simon & Schuster, 1941.
Dedijer, Vladimir. *Tito.* New York: Simon & Schuster, 1953.
Degras, Jane (Compiler). *Calendar of Soviet Documents on Foreign Policy 1917-1941.* London: Royal Institute of International Affairs, 1948.
——— (Ed.). *The Communist International. 1919-1943.* Vol. I. *1919-1922.* Vol. II. *1923-1928.* London-New York-Toronto: Oxford University Press, 1960.
——— (Ed.). *Soviet Documents on Foreign Policy.* Vol. II. *1925-1932.* Vol. III. *1933-1941.* London-New York-Toronto: Oxford University Press, 1953.
Deutscher, Isaac. *The Prophet Unarmed. Trotsky: 1921-1929.* Vol. II. New York: Vintage Books (Random House), 1965.
Dirksen, Herbert von. *Moscow Tokyo London. Twenty Years of German Foreign Policy.* Norman, Okla.: University of Oklahoma Press, 1952.
———. *Moskau, Tokio, London. Erinnerungen und Betrachtungen zu 20 Jahren deutscher Aussenpolitiki 1919-1939.* Stuttgart: W. Kohlhammer, 1949.
Djilas, Milovan. *Conversations with Stalin.* New York: Harcourt, Brace & World, Inc., 1962.
Droz, Jules Humbert. *"L'Oeil de Moscou" à Paris.* Paris: Julliard, 1964.
Dyck, Harvey Leonard. *Weimar Germany and Soviet Russia, 1926-1933. A Study in Diplomatic Instability.* New York: Columbia University Press, 1966.
Ehrenburg, Ilya. *Post-War Years 1945-1954.* Translated by Tatiana Shebnina

in collaboration with Yvonne Kapp. New York: World Publishing Co., 1967.

Erickson, John. *The Soviet High Command. A Military-Political History, 1918-1941.* New York: St. Martin's Press, Inc., 1962.

Eudin, Xenia Joukoff, and Fisher, Harold H., in collaboration with Rosemary Brown Jones. *Soviet Russia and the West. 1920-1927, A Documentary Survey.* Stanford, Calif.: Stanford University Press, 1957.

Fabre-Luce, Alfred. *L'Histoire Demaquillée.* Paris: R. Laffont, 1967.

Fainsod, Merle. *Smolensk under Soviet Rule.* New York: Vintage Books (Random House), 1963.

Farley, James A. *Jim Farley's Story. The Roosevelt Years.* New York: Whittlesey House, 1948.

Farnsworth, Beatrice. *William C. Bullitt and the Soviet Union.* Bloomington, Ind.: Indiana University Press, 1967.

Fischer, Louis. *The Life of Lenin.* New York: Harper & Row, 1964.

———. *Men and Politics. An Autobiography.* New York: Harper & Row, 1966.

———. *The Soviets in World Affairs, a History of the Relations Between the Soviet Union and the Rest of the World, 1917-1929.* New York and London: Jonathan Cape, 1930. Second edition, Princeton, N.J.: Princeton University Press, 1950, and New York: Vintage Books (Random House), 1960.

Fisher, H. H. *America and the New Poland.* New York: The Macmillan Co., 1928.

Fisk, Harvey E. *The Inter-Ally Debts.* New York-Paris: Bankers Trust Co., 1924.

François-Poncet, André. *Souvenirs d'une Ambassade à Berlin.* Paris: Flammarion, 1947.

Frankland, Mark. *Khrushchev.* New York: Stein & Day, 1967.

French Foreign Ministry Ministère des Affaires Étrangères. *Commission de Publication des Documents Relatifs aux Origines de la Guerre 1939-1945. Documents Diplomatiques Français, 1932-1939. Ire* Serie *(1932-1935).* Tome II. *(15 Novembre 1932-17 Mars 1933).* Paris, 1966. Tome III. *(17 Mars 1933-15 Juillet 1933).* Paris, 1967.

French Yellow Book. Diplomatic Documents Concerning the Events and Negotiations Which Preceded the Opening of Hostilities Between Germany on the One Hand and Poland, Great Britain, and France on the Other (1938-1939). London, no date.

Freund, Gerald. *Unholy Alliance. Russian-German Relations from the Treaty of Brest-Litovsk to the Treaty of Berlin.* With an introduction by J. W. Wheeler-Bennett. New York: Harcourt Brace, 1957.

Jackson, Gabriel. *The Spanish Republic and the Civil War. 1931-1939.* Princeton, N.J.: Princeton University Press, 1965.

Gafencu, Grigore. *Last Days of Europe. A Diplomatic Journey in 1939.* New Haven: Yale University Press, 1948.

———. *Prelude to the Russian Campaign. From the Moscow Pact (August 21, 1939) to the Opening of Hostilities in Russia (June 22, 1941).* Translated by Fletcher-Allen. London: Muller, 1945.

Galbraith, John Kenneth. *The Great Crash 1929.* Boston: Houghton Mifflin Co., 1954.

Gantenbein, James W. (Ed.). *Documentary Background of World War II. 1931 to 1941.* New York: Columbia University Press, 1948.

German Information Bureau. *100 Dokumente zur Vorgeschichte des Krieges. Auswahl aus dem Amtlichen Deutschen Weissbuch.* Introduction by Foreign Minister von Ribbentrop dated Dec. 3, 1939. Berlin, no date.

Ginzburg, Eugenia Semyonovna. *Journey into the Whirlwind.* New York: Harcourt, Brace & World, Inc., 1967.

Gorbatov, A. V. *Years Off My Life. The Memoirs of General of the Soviet Army A. V. Gorbatov.* Translated by Gordon Clough and Anthony Cash. London and New York: W.W. Norton, 1965.

Grew, Joseph C. *Ten Years in Japan. A Contemporary Record Drawn from the Diaries and Private and Official Papers of the United States Ambassador to Japan 1932-1942.* New York: Simon & Schuster, 1944.

Habedank, Heinz. *Zur Geschichte des Hamburger Aufstandes, 1923* (On the 1923 Hamburg Uprising). [East] Berlin, 1958.

Hammond, Thomas T. (Compiler and Editor). *Soviet Foreign Relations and World Communism. A Selected, Annotated Bibliography of 7,000 books in 30 Languages.* Princeton, N.J.: Princeton University Press, 1965.

Hard, William. *Raymond Robins' Own Story.* New York and London: Harper & Brothers, 1920.

Higgins, Trumbull. *Hitler and Russia. The Third Reich in a Two-Front War 1937-1943.* New York: The Macmillan Co., 1966.

Hildebrandt, Rainer. *Wir Sind Die Letzten.* Berlin: Michael-Verlag, Neuwied/Berlin. No date.

Hilger, Gustav and Meyer, Alfred G. *The Incompatible Allies. A Memoir-History of German-Russian Relations 1918-1941.* New York: The Macmillan Co., 1953.

Hitler, Adolf. *Mein Kampf.* Translated by Ralph Manheim. Boston: Houghton Mifflin Co., 1943.

Hitler's Secret Book. Introduction by Telford Taylor. Translated by Salvator Attanasio. New York: Grove Press, 1961.

Hitler's Secret Conversations. 1941-1944. With an introductory essay "The Mind of Adolf Hitler" by H.R. Trevor-Roper. New York: Signet Books (New American Library), 1961.

Hyde, H. Montgomery. *Lord Reading. The Life of Rufus Isaacs, First Marquess of Reading.* London: Heinemann, 1967.

Institute of Marxism-Leninism of the Soviet Communist Party. *Istoria Velikoi Otechestvennoi Voiny Sovietskovo Soyuza 1941-1945* (The History of the Great Fatherland War of the Soviet Union 1941–1945). Vol. 1. Moscow, 1960. Vol. 6: *The Results of the Great Fatherland War.* Moscow, 1965.

International Military Tribunal. *Trial of the Major War Criminals.* Vol. XXVI. Nuremberg: 1949.

Isaacs, Harold R. *The Tragedy of the Chinese Revolution.* Stanford, Calif.: Stanford University Press, 1951.

Jakobson, Max. *The Diplomacy of the Winter War. An Account of the Russo-Finnish War, 1939-1940.* Cambridge, Mass.: Harvard University Press, 1961.

Janin, Maurice C. T. Pierre. *Ma Mission en Siberie, 1918-1920.* Paris, 1933.

Kahin, George McTurnan (Ed.). *Major Governments of Asia.* Ithaca, N.Y.: Cornell University Press, 1958.

Kennan, George F. *Memoirs. 1925-1950.* Boston: Atlantic Monthly Press-Little, Brown and Co., 1967.

———. *Russia and the West Under Lenin and Stalin.* Boston-Toronto: Atlantic–Little, Brown and Co., 1960.

———. *Soviet-American Relations, 1917-1920. The Decision to Intervene.* Princeton, N.J.: Princeton University Press, 1958.

Klein, Fritz. *Die diplomatischen Beziehungen Deutschlands zur Sowjetunion 1917-1932.* Berlin: Rütten & Loening, 1953.

Kleist, Peter. *Zwischen Hitler und Stalin 1939-1945.* Bonn: Athenäum-Verlag, 1950.

Kochan, Lionel. *Russia and the Weimar Republic.* Cambridge, England: Bowes & Bowes, 1954.

Korbel, Josef. *Poland Between East and West. Soviet and German Diplomacy Toward Poland, 1919-1933.* Princeton, N.J.: Princeton University Press, 1963.

Kovalyov, A. *Azbuka Diplomatii* (The ABC of Diplomacy). Moscow, 1965.

Krivitsky, Walter G. *I Was Stalin's Agent.* London: Hamish Hamilton, 1939.

Kung-Po, Ch'en. *The Communist Movement in China.* New York: Columbia University East Asian Institute Series Paper No. 7, 1960.

Lansing Papers, 1940. Vol. II. Washington, D.C.: U.S. Government Printing Office, 1940.

League of Nations. *Treaty Series. Publication of Treaties and International Engagements Registered with the Secretariat of the League.* Vol. 19. Lausanne, 1923.

Lenin, V. I. *Leninskii Sbornik* (Lenin Miscellany). Vol. XX. Moscow, 1952. Vol. XXXVI. Moscow, 1959.

———. *Polnoye Sobraniye Sochinenii* (Complete Works). Fifth Edition. Vol. 11. Moscow, 1960. Vol. 21. Moscow, 1961. Vol. 38. Moscow, 1963. Vol. 40. Moscow, 1963. Vol. 41. Moscow, 1963. Vol. 42. Moscow, 1963. Vol. 45. Moscow, 1964.

Librach, Jan. *The Rise of the Soviet Empire—A Study of Soviet Foreign Policy.* New York: Frederick R. Praeger, 1964.

Mackintosh, J. M. *Strategy and Tactics in Soviet Foreign Policy.* London: Oxford University Press, 1962.

Macleod, Iain, *Neville Chamberlain.* New York: Atheneum, 1962.

Macleon, Colonel Roderick, and Kelly, Denis (Eds.). *Time Unguarded. The Ironside Diaries 1937-1940.* New York, 1962.

McLane, Charles B. *Soviet Policy and the Chinese Communists 1931-1946.* New York: Columbia University Press, 1958.

McSherry, James E. *Stalin, Hitler, and Europe.* Vol. I. *The Origins of World War II 1933-1939.* Cleveland and New York: World Publications, 1968.

Maisky, Ivan. *Spanish Notebooks.* Translated from the Russian by Ruth Kisch. London: Hutchinson, 1962. In Russian: *Ispanskie Tetradi.* Moscow, 1962.

———. *Vospominania Sovietskovo Posla. Voina 1939-1943* (Memoirs of a Soviet Ambassador. War 1939-1943.). Moscow: Nauka [Publishers], 1965.

Mantoux, Paul. *Les Délibérations du Conseil de Quatre (24 mars-28 juin 1919). Notes de l' Officier Interprête.* Vol. I. *Jusqu'à la Remise à la Délégation Allemande des Conditions de Paix.* Paris: Centre nationale de la recherche scientifique, 1955. Vol. II. *24 mars-28 juin 1919). Depuis la Remise à la Délégation Allemande des Conditions de Paix Jusqu'à La Signature du Traité de Versailles.* Paris: Centre nationale de la recherche scientifique, 1955.

March, Peyton C. *The Nation at War*. New York: Doubleday, Doran & Co., 1932.

Miksche, F. O. *Blitzkrieg*, with an introduction by Tom Wintringham. London: Faber & Faber Ltd. 1941.

Morley, James William. *The Japanese Thrust into Siberia, 1918*. New York: Columbia University Press, 1957.

Namier, L. B. *Europe in Decay. A Study in Disintegration, 1936-1940*. London: The Macmillan Co., 1950.

———. *Diplomatic Prelude 1938-1939*. London: The Macmillan Co., 1948.

Nekrich, A. M. *June 22, 1941*. Moscow: Nauka [Publishers], 1965.

Neubauer, Helmut. *München und Moskau—1918/1919. Zur Geschichte der Rätebewegung in Bayern*. Munich: Isar Verlag, 1958.

Nicolaevsky, Boris I. *Power and the Soviet Elite. The Letter of an Old Bolshevik and Other Essays*. Edited by Janet D. Zagoria. New York: Published for the Hoover Institution on War, Revolution, and Peace, by Frederick A. Praeger, 1965.

Norden, Albert. *Zwischen Berlin und Moskau—Zur Geschichte der deutsch-sowjetischen Beziehungen*. Berlin: Dietz, 1954.

North, Robert C. *Moscow and Chinese Communists*. Stanford, Calif.: Stanford University Press, 1953.

North, Robert C. and Eudin, Xenia Joukoff. *M. N. Roy's Mission to China. The Communist-Kuomintang Split of 1927*. Berkeley, Calif.: University of California Press, 1963.

Official Reports. Parliamentary Debates. House of Commons. June 25, 1926. Vol. 197. No. 90.

Orwell, George. *Homage to Catalonia*. London: Secker & Warburg, 1938.

Pasvolsky, Leo, and Moulton, Harold G. *Russian Debts and Russian Reconstruction*. New York: McGraw-Hill Book Co., 1924.

Pasvolsky, Leo. *Russia in the Far East*. New York: The Macmillan Co., 1922.

Peking Metropolitan Police. *Soviet Plot in China*. Peking: Metropolitan Police Headquarters, 1928.

Perevertailo, A. S.; Glunin, V. I.; Kukushkin, K. V.; Nikoforov, V. N. (Eds.). *Ocherki Istorii Kitaya v Noveishoye Vremya* (Essays on the History of China in the Modern Era). Moscow: Institute of China Studies of the Academy of Sciences of the U.S.S.R., 1959.

Petrie, Sir Charles. *The Life and Letters of the Right Hon. Sir Austen Chamberlain, K.G., P.C., M.P.* Vol. II. London: Cassell, 1940.

Pilsudski, Joseph. *L'Année 1920. Edition Complète avec le texte de l'Ouvrage de M. Toukhatchevski 'La Marche Au-delà de la Vistule' et les notes critiques du Bureau historique militaire de Varsovie*. Traduit du polonais. Paris: Renaissance du livre, 1929.

Ploss, Sidney. *Conflict and Decision-Making in Soviet Russia. A Case Study of Agricultural Policy, 1953-1963*. Princeton, N.J.: Princeton University Press, 1965.

Ponomaryov, B. N., Gromyko, A. A. Khvostov, V. M. (Eds.). *Istoria Vneshnei Politiki SSSR. 1917-1966. Chast Pervaya 1917-1945* (The History of Soviet Foreign Policy 1917-1966. Part One 1917-1945). Moscow, 1966.

Popov, V. I. *Diplomaticheskiye Otnosheniya Mezhdu SSSR i Angliyei. 1929-1939* (Diplomatic Relations between the U.S.S.R. and England). Moscow, 1965.

Po-ta, Ch'ên. *Stalin and the Chinese Revolution. In Celebration of Stalin's*

Seventieth Birthday. Peking: Foreign Languages Press, 1953.

Rathenau, Walther. *Cannes und Genoa. Vier Reden Zum Reparationsproblem. Mit Einem Anhang*. Berlin: Fischer, 1922.

Rees, J. R. (Ed.). *The Case of Rudolf Hess. A Problem in Diagnosis and Forensic Psychiatry*. London and Toronto: W. Heinemann, 1947.

Ribbentrop, Joachim von. *Zwischen London und Moskau Erinnerungen und letzte Aufzeichnungen*. Leoni am Starnberger See: Druffel, 1954.

Rosenbaum, Kurt. *Community of Fate. German-Soviet Diplomatic Relations, 1922-1928*. Syracuse, N.Y.: Syracuse University Press, 1965.

Rosenfeld, Günter. *Sowjetrussland und Deutschland, 1917-1922*. [East] Berlin: Akademie-Verlag, 1960.

Rossi, A. (Angelo Tasca). *The Russo-German Alliance. August 1939-June 1941*. Translated by John and Micheline Cullen. Boston: Beacon Press, 1951.

———. *Zwei Jahre Deutsch-Sowjetisches Buendnis*. Cologne-Berlin: 1954.

Roy, M. N. *M. N. Roy's Memoirs*. Bombay: Allied Publishers Private Ltd., 1964.

———. *Revolution and Counter-Revolution in China*. Calcutta: Renaissance Publishers, 1946.

Salvemini, Gaetano. *Prelude to World War II*. Garden City, N.Y.: Doubleday, 1954.

Samsonov, A. M.; Karasev, A. V.; Kovalenko, D. A.; Kremer, I. S. (Eds.). *Kratkaya Istoria SSSR* (A Short History of the U.S.S.R.). Vol. 2. Moscow–Leningrad, 1964.

Scheffer, Paul. *Sieben Jahre Sowjetunion*. Leipzig: Bibliographisches institut ag., 1930.

Schmidt, Paul. *Hitler's Interpreter*. Edited by R.H.C. Steed. New York: The Macmillan Co., 1951.

Schwartz, Benjamin I. *Chinese Communism and the Rise of Mao*. Cambridge, Mass.: Harvard University Press, 1951.

Schwartz, Harry. *Tsars, Mandarins, and Commissars. A History of Chinese-Russian Relations*. Philadelphia and New York: Lippincott, 1964.

Scott, William Evans. *Alliance Against Hitler. The Origins of the Franco-Soviet Pact*. Durham, N.C.: Duke University Press, 1962.

Sherwood, Robert E. *Roosevelt and Hopkins. An Intimate History*. New York: Harper & Brothers, 1948.

Shirer, William L. *The Rise and Fall of the Third Reich*. New York: Simon & Schuster, 1960.

Sikorski, Historical Institute, General, *Documents on Polish-Soviet Relations 1939-1945*. Vol. I. *1939-1943*. London: Heinemann, 1961.

Skrzyński, Aleksander Józef. *Poland and Peace by Count Alexander Skrzyński*. London: G. Allen & Unwin, 1923.

Snow, Edgar. *The Battle for Asia*. New York: Random House, 1941.

———. *Red Star Over China*. New York: Grove Press, 1968.

Soviet Communist Party. *XXII Syezd Kommunisticheskoi Partii Sovietskovo Soyuza. October 17-31, 1961* (Twenty-Second Congress of the Communist Party of the Soviet Union. October 17-31, 1961. *Stenographic Record*). Vols. I and II. Moscow, 1962.

Soviet Information Bureau. *Falsifiers of History* (*Historical Survey*). Moscow: Foreign Languages Publishing House, 1948.

Stalin, J. V. *Sochinenia*. Vol. 1 (XIV). Since *The Collected Works of Stalin* published in Russian and English in the Soviet Union ends with Vol. XIII, 1951, which contains his works from July, 1930, to January, 1934, the Hoover Institution on War, Revolution, and Peace of Stanford University published Vol. XIV as its Vol. 1 in 1967, edited by Robert H. McNeal. Vol. 1. *1934-1940*. Stanford, Calif: Stanford University Press, 1967. Vol. 2. *1941-1945*. Stanford: 1967. Vol. 3. *1946-1953*. Stanford University Press, 1967.

(Works.) Vol. 3. Moscow, 1946. Vol. 7. Moscow, 1947. Vol. 9. Moscow, 1948. Vol. 10. Moscow, 1949. Vol. 12. Moscow, 1949. Vol. 13. Moscow, 1951.

———. *Stalin on China. A Collection of Five Writings of Comrade Stalin on the Chinese Question. Written between November, 1926 and August, 1927*. Bombay: People's Pub. House, 1951.

Strang, Lord. *Britain in World Affairs. A Survey of the Fluctuations in British Power and Influence from Henry VIII to Elizabeth II*. London: Faber & Faber, 1961.

Tanin, M. (Maxim M. Litvinov). *Mezhdunarodnaya Politika SSSR. (1917-1924)* (International Policy of the U.S.S.R. 1917-1924). Moscow, 1925.

———. *Dyesat Let Vneshnei Politiki SSSR. (1917-1927)* (Ten years of Soviet Foreign Policy. 1917-1927). Moscow-Leningrad, 1927.

Tanner, Väinö. *The Winter War. Finland Against Russia 1939-1940*. Stanford, Calif.: Stanford University Press, 1957.

Taylor, A. J. P. *The Origins of the Second World War*. Second Edition. *With a Reply to the Critics*. Greenwich, Conn.: Fawcett Publications, 1968.

Thomas, Hugh. *The Spanish Civil War*. London: Eyre & Spottiswoode, 1961.

Thompson, John M. *Russia, Bolshevism, and the Versailles Peace*. Princeton, N.J.: Princeton University Press, 1966.

Toscano, Mario. *Una Mancata Intesa Italo-Sovietica Nel 1940 E 1941*. Florence: C. G. Sansoni, 1955.

Trotsky, Leon. *Collected Works*. Vol. XVII. Part I. *The Soviet Republic and the Capitalist World* (in Russian). Moscow, 1926.

———. *Diary in Exile, 1935*. Translated by Elena Zarudnaya. Cambridge, Mass.: Harvard University Press, 1958.

———. *Lenin*. Authorized translation. Garden City, N.Y.: Garden City Books, 1925.

———. *Literature and Revolution*. New York: Russell, 1957.

———. *My Life. An Attempt at an Autobiography*. New York: Charles Scribner's Sons, 1930.

———. *Problems of the Chinese Revolution*. Translated by Max Shachtman. New York: Pioneer Publishers, 1932.

———. *Stalin. An Appraisal of the Man and His Influence*. Edited and translated by Charles Malamuth. New York and London: Harper & Brothers, 1941.

———. *The Stalin School of Falsification*. Introduction and Explanatory Notes by Max Shachtman. Translated by John G. Wright. New York: Pioneer Publishers, 1937.

Trukhanovsky, V. G. (Ed.). *Istoria Mezhdunarodnikh Otnoshenii i Vneshnei Politiki SSSR 1917-1939* (The History of International Relations and the Foreign Policy of the U.S.S.R. 1917-1939). Vol. I. Moscow, 1961.

Trush, M. K. *Vneshnepoliticheskaya Deyaltelnost V. I. Lenina, 1917-1920* (Lenin's Actions in Foreign Policy Day by Day, 1917-1920). Moscow:

Institute of Marxism-Leninism, 1963.

Ullman, Richard H. *Anglo-Soviet Relations, 1917-1921*. Vol. I. *Intervention and the War*. Princeton, N.J.: Princeton University Press, 1961.

———. *Anglo-Soviet Relations, 1917-1921*. Vol. II. *Britain and the Russian Civil War. November 1918-February 1920*. Princeton, N.J.: Princeton University Press, 1968.

U.S.S.R., Ministry of Foreign Affairs of the. *Dokumenty i Materialy Kanuna Vtoroi Mirovoi Voiny* (Documents and Material on the Eve of the Second World War). Vol. I. *Nov. 1937-1938*. (From the Archive of the Ministry of Foreign Affairs of Germany.) Moscow, 1948. Vol. II. *The Dirksen Archive. 1938-39*. Moscow, 1948.

———. *Dokumenty Vneshnei Politiki SSSR* (Documents on the Foreign Policy of the U.S.S.R.). Vol. I. *November 7, 1917-December 31, 1918*. Moscow: 1959. Vol. V. *January 1, 1922-November 19, 1922*. Moscow, 1961. Vol. VI. *November 20, 1922-December 31, 1923*. Moscow, 1962. Vol. VII. *January 1-December 31, 1924*. Moscow, 1963. Vol. IX. *January 1-December 31, 1926*. Moscow, 1964. Vol. X. *January 1-December 31, 1927*. Moscow, 1965.

U.S.S.R. Central Statistical Directorate of the Council of Ministers. *SSSR v. Tsifrakh v 1960 godu* (The U.S.S.R. in Figures for 1960). Moscow, 1964.

———. *Natzionalnoye Khozaistvo SSSR v 1963 godu* (The National Economy of the U.S.S.R. in 1963). Moscow, 1965.

U.S. Department of State. *Documents on German Foreign Policy, 1918-1945. From the Archives of the German Foreign Office*. Series C. (*1933-1937*) *The Third Reich; First Phase*. Vol. II. *October 14, 1933-June 13, 1944*. Washington, D.C., 1959. Vol. III. *June 14, 1934-March 31, 1935*. Washington, D.C., 1959. Also published by Her Majesty's Stationery Office, London.

Series D. (*1937-1945*). Vol. I. *From Neurath to Ribbentrop. September 1937-September 1938*. Washington, D.C., 1949. Vol. II. *Germany and Czechoslovakia. 1937-1938*. Washington, D.C., 1949. Vol. III. *Germany and the Spanish Civil War. 1936-1939*. Washington, D.C., 1950. Vol. VI. *The Last Months of Peace. March-August 1939*. Washington, D.C., 1956. Vol. VII. *The Last Days of Peace. August 9-September 3, 1939*. Washington, D.C., 1956. Vol. VIII. *The War Years. September 4, 1938-March 18, 1940*. Washington, D.C., 1954. Vol. IX. *The War Years. March 18-June 22, 1940*. Washington, D.C., 1956. Vol. X. *The War Years. June 23-August 31, 1940*. Washington, D.C., 1957. Vol. XI. *The War Years. September 1, 1940-January 31, 1941*. Washington, D.C., 1960. Vol. XII. *The War Years. February 1-June 22, 1941*. Washington, D.C., 1962.

———. *Foreign Relations of the United States. Diplomatic Papers, 1933*. Vol. II. *The British Commonwealth, Europe, Near East and Africa*. Washington, D.C.: U.S. Government Printing Office, 1949.

———. *Foreign Relations of the United States. Diplomatic Papers. 1940*. Vol. I. *General*. Washington, D.C.: U.S. Government Printing Office, 1959. Vol. II. *General and Europe*. Washington, D.C., 1957.

———. *Foreign Relations of the United States. Diplomatic Papers. 1941*. Vol. I. *General. The Soviet Union*. Washington, D.C.: U.S. Government Printing Office, 1958.

———. *Foreign Relations of the United States. Diplomatic Papers. The Soviet Union 1933-1939*. Washington, D.C.: U.S. Government Printing Office, 1952.

———. *Nazi-Soviet Relations 1939-1941. Documents from the Archives of the German Foreign Office*. Edited by Raymond James Sontag and James Stuart Beddie. Washington, D.C.: U.S. Government Printing Office, 1948.

———. *Papers Relating to the Foreign Relations of the United States, 1918. Russia*. Washington, D.C.: U.S. Government Printing Office.

———. *Papers relating to the Foreign Relations of the United States, 1931*. Vol. I. Washington, D.C.: U.S. Government Printing Office, 1956.

———. *Papers Relating to the Foreign Relations of the United States. The Paris Peace Conference. 1919*. Vols. V and VI. Washington, D.C.: U.S. Government Printing Office, 1946.

United States Office of Chief Counsel For Prosecution of Axis Criminality. *Nazi Conspiracy and Aggression*. Vols. I and II. Washington, D.C., 1946.

Unterberger, Betty Miller. *America's Siberian Expedition, 1918-1920*. Durham, N.C.: Duke University Press, 1956.

Vigodsky, S. Y.; Gonionsky, S. A.; Gorokhov, I. M.; Zemskov, I. N.; Zorin, V. A.; Kiktov, S. P.; Kutakov, L. N.; Maiorov, S. M.; Mintz, I. I.; Ostoya-Ovsyany, I. D.; Popov, V. I; Khostov, V. M. *Istoriya Diplomatii*. Vol. III. *Diplomatiya Na Pervom Etape Obshevo Krizisa Kapitalicheskoi Sistemi* (The History of Diplomacy. Vol. III. Diplomacy in the First Stage of the General Crisis of the Capitalist System). Moscow, 1965.

Vishnyakova-Akimova, V. V. *Dva Goda v vosstavshem Kitaaie. 1925-1927. Vospominaniya* (Two Years in Insurgent China. 1925-1927. Reminiscences). Moscow, 1965.

Wales, Nym. *Notes on the Chinese Student Movement, 1935-1936*. Stanford, Calif.: Hoover Institution on War, Revolution, and Peace, Stanford University, 1959.

Weber, Hermann. *Die Kommunistische Internationale eine Dokumentation*. Hannover: Dietz, 1966.

Weinberg, Gerhard L. *Germany and the Soviet Union 1939-1941*. Leiden: E. J. Brill, 1954.

Welles, Sumner. *The Time for Decision*. New York and London: Harper & Brothers, 1944.

Werth, Alexander. *Russia at War, 1941-1945*. New York: Dutton, 1964.

Wheeler-Bennett, John W. *The Nemesis of Power; The German Army in Politics, 1918-1945*. London-New York: The Macmillan Co., 1953.

White, Theodore H. and Jacoby, Annalee. *Thunder out of China*. New York: William Sloane Associates, 1946.

Whiting, Allen S. *Soviet Policies in China, 1917-1924*. New York: 1954.

Whitney, Thomas P. (Ed.). *Khrushchev Speaks*. Ann Arbor, Mich.: 1963.

Wilbur, C. Martin. (Ed.). *Documents on Communism, Nationalism, and Soviet Advisers in China. 1918-1927. Papers Seized in the 1927 Peking Raid*. New York: Columbia University Press, 1956.

Williams, John. *Mutiny 1917*. London and Toronto: 1962.

Woodward, E. L. and Butler, Rohan (Eds.). *Documents on British Foreign Policy. 1919-1939*. Second Series. Vol. II. *1931-2*. London: His

Majesty's Stationery Office, 1948. Third Series, *1938-1939*. Vol. I. *1939*. London, 1949. Vol. III. *1938-9*. London, 1950. Vol. V. *1939*. London, 1952. Vol. VI. *1939*. London, 1953.

Wu, Ai-Chên K. *China and the Soviet Union—A Study of Sino-Soviet Relations*. New York: Day, 1950.

Zetkin, Klara. *Reminiscences of Lenin*. London: 1929.

Zhilin, P. A. *Kak Faschistkaya Germania Gotovila Napadenie Na Sovietskii Soyuz* (How Fascist Germany Prepared the Attack on the Soviet Union). Moscow, 1966.

PAMPHLETS AND ARTICLES

Background of the Manchurian Trouble. New York, no date. 29 pp.

Browder, Earl. *Civil War in Nationalist China*. Chicago: Labor Unity Pub. Association, 1927. 57 pp.

Bukharin, N. I. *Kapitalisticheskaya Stabilizatsia i Proletarskaya Revolutsia. Doklad i Zaklyuchitelnoye Slovo; VII Rashirennomy Plenumy IKKI* (Capitalist Stabilization and the Proletarian Revolution. Report and Concluding Statement at the Seventh Expanded Plenum of the Executive Committee of the Communist International—ECCI). Moscow-Leningrad, 1927. 343 pp.

———. *Problemy Kitaiskoi Revolutsii* (Problems of the Chinese Revolution). Moscow, 1927. 62 pp.

Carsten, Francis L. "The Reichswehr and the Red Army," *Survey*. London, October, 1962.

The China Critic. Japan and the Next World War. Shanghai, 1931. 42 pp.

Friedensberg, Ferdinand. "Die Sowjetischen Kriegslieferungen an das Hitlerreich." *Vierteljahreshaefte zur Wirtschaftsforschung*. Deutsches Institut fuer Wirtschaftsforschung, Berlin and Munich, 4th Quarter, 1962.

Han-Min, Hu. *Government Headquarters Declarations*. Canton, 1925. 49 pp.

Hosoya, Chihiro. "Japanese Documents on the Siberian Intervention, 1917-1922. Part I, November, 1917-January, 1919." *The Hitotsubashi Journal of Law and Politics*. Vol. 1, No. 1 (April, 1960). *Hitotsubashi* University, Tokyo.

———. "Origin of the Siberian Intervention, 1917-1918." *The Annals of the Hitotsubashi Academy*, Vol. IX, No. 1 (October, 1958). Hitotsubashi University, Tokyo.

Khrushchev, Nikita S. *The Crimes of the Stalin Era. Special Report to the 20th Congress of the Communist Party of the Soviet Union*. Annotated by Boris I. Nicolaevsky for an edition of *The New Leader*. New York, 1962.

Linebarger, Paul. *Our Common Cause with China against Imperialism and Communism*. Los Angeles, no date. 30 pp.

The Memorial of Premier Tanaka or A Japanese Secret Design for the Conquest of China as Well as the United States and the Rest of the World. New York, no date. 44 pp.

National Kwangtung University. *Manifesto to the Peoples of the World Re the Deplorable Events Which Took Place in Shanghai, Hankow, and Canton*. Canton, 1925. 10 pp.

Nicolaevsky, Boris I. (Ed.). *Letter Of An Old Bolshevik. The Key To the Moscow Trials*. Rand School Pamphlet, 1937.

The Present Manchurian Tangle. New York, no date. 48 pp.

Radek, Karl. "Stranichka iz Vospominanii" (A Little Page of Reminiscences) *Krasyana Nov*. Moscow, November, 1926.

Sinowjew, G. *Zwoelf Tage in Deutschland* (G. Zinoviev, Twelve Days in Germany). Hamburg, 1921. 88 pp.

Strong, Anna Louise. "The Kuomintang-Communist Crisis in China." New York: *Amerasia* magazine reprint, 1941.

———. "The Thought of Mao Tse-tung." New York: *Amerasia* magazine reprint, 1947.

Survey. "Russia and Germany" issue. London, October, 1962.

Voice of the Chinese People Regarding Sino–Japanese Questions. Shanghai, 1928. 78 pp.

Weigh, Ken Shen. *Russo-Chinese Diplomacy*. Shanghai, 1928.

Wilbur, C. Martin. *Sun Yat-sen and Soviet Russia, 1922-1924*. New York, 1965. Columbia University Seminar on Modern East Asia paper (preliminary). Mimeographed.

Young, Katsu H. "The Nomonhan Incident. Imperial Japan and the Soviet Union." *Monumenta Nipponica. Studies in Japanese Culture*. Vol. XXII, Nos. 1-2. Sophia University, Tokyo.

INDEX

Design by Sidney Feinberg
Set in Linotype Primer
Composed, printed and bound by The Haddon Craftsmen, Inc.
HARPER & ROW, PUBLISHERS, INCORPORATED

69707172738765432 1